The Traffic-Accident Investigation Manual

At-Scene Investigation and Technical Follow-Up

J. STANNARD BAKER

LYNN B. FRICKE

Northwestern University Traffic Institute

Evanston, Illinois 60204

PUBLICATION HISTORY

Beginning with the first edition of this manual, under the same and similar titles, this volume constitutes the ninth edition. The foreword expands upon this history in some detail. In addition, the history of each Topic is listed at the beginning of that Topic.

Ninth Edition, 1986

Copyright 1986 by Northwestern University Traffic Institute

Evanston, Illinois 60204

ISBN 0-912642-06-8

Library of Congress Catalog Number 86-606-16

Printed in the United States of America

ACKNOWLEDGEMENT

The development and publication of this volume has been made possible by grants from:

    The Anheuser-Busch Charitable Trust

    The Kemper Educational and Charitable Fund

    The James S. Kemper Foundation, the Corporate Foundation of the Kemper Group

    Allstate Insurance Companies

Northwestern University Traffic Institute is deeply grateful to these organizations for their generosity and continued support.

Noel C. Bufe

Noel C. Bufe, Ph.D.
Director

Foreword

This book, as its title implies, is a collection of specific instructions for certain of the operations that constitute traffic-accident investigation. It is now the product of numerous individuals who have practiced and taught these functions at Northwestern University Traffic Institute and elsewhere. In one revision after another this manual has been updated in the past, as it will doubtless be in the future.

Looking Back

Before 1925, systematic traffic-accident investigation was practically unknown. The best reports of road accidents were those clipped from local newspapers. The only official record was usually a line on a police station house blotter.

But when traffic deaths produced a conspicuous and worrisome bulge in vital statistics, concerned organizations began vigorously to urge countermeasures. The resulting programs emphasized enforcement, accompanied by accident investigation to obtain convictions in connection with accidents, and also as a basis for targeting safety measures, especially engineering and enforcement.

In 1929, the Evanston, Illinois, Police Department, under Chief Freeman, established an Accident Prevention Bureau led by a young, energetic, and imaginative officer, Franklin M. Kreml. Freeman also sought help from the Political Science department and the Sociology department of Northwestern University in training police for improved law enforcement. To explore this matter more fully, the Police Department and these two University departments sponsored a four-day Midwest Police Conference. One day of this conference was devoted to police traffic work. The interest kindled resulted in a Traffic Officers Training Course held in Room 101 of Harris Hall at Northwestern University in each of the next four years. The course was administered by the Accident Prevention Bureau of the Evanston Police Department. To permit an enrollment fee of two dollars, staff members of the National Safety Council, the American Automobile Association, The National Bureau of Casualty and Surety Underwriters, Northwestern University faculty and other organizations were enlisted as instructors.

Some "accident reconstruction" was taught from the very first, but for years this was limited to simple estimates of slide-to-stop speed from skidmarks.

By 1930, a film strip, *Getting Convictions for Traffic Accidents,* was developed for training and propaganda purposes. In 1933, an exhibit in the Chicago Century of Progress world's fair had a display of traffic law enforcement and accident investigation activities.

To begin with, there were no training materials. Later, a few mimeographed pages were prepared from instructors' lecture notes.

The success of the Evanston and other accident prevention programs was publicized by national organizations in the hope that the results could be duplicated elsewhere.

In 1934, the Evanston police training program was adapted for use in Syracuse, New York, and later in Louisville, Kentucky.

In 1936, the year during which Northwestern University Traffic Institute was established under the then Lieutenant Kreml, police traffic safety training was offered in 40-hour summer courses, first at the University of Alabama and then at the Erskine Bureau for Street Traffic Research at Harvard University and at Rutgers University.

This program was combined with others to form the National Institute for Traffic Safety

Training which met during successive summers at the University of California, the University of Michigan, and the University of Tennessee. These conferences were terminated by World War II.

Up to this time, only a scant outline to guide teaching had been developed in writing. It was not until 1940 that the Northwestern University Traffic Institute published its first book, the original *Accident Investigation Manual*. This was a 6- by 9-inch volume with a dark blue cover. Four people in addition to Lt. Kreml were listed as contributors. The book was put together by the Traffic Institute Publications Division and twice reprinted.

In 1941, in Zurich, Switzerland, the first book on traffic-accident reconstruction was published: *The Mechanics of Motor-vehicle Accidents,* written in German by A. Bruderlein.

In 1946, a second edition of the *Accident Investigation Manual* was published. Five new contributors were listed and three new topics were added. It was reprinted twice.

After World War II, Northwestern University Traffic Institute established a Research and Development Division which was assigned, as one of its jobs, the systematic revision of the "A. I. Manual." In 1953, the fifteen topics completed by that time were published as the third edition of the *Traffic Accident Investigator's Manual*, a light blue paperback. The following year a similar fourth edition containing three additional topics was printed.

The fifth edition, 1957, was the first "complete" one. It had a bright green hard cover with the title *Traffic Accident Investigator's Manual for Police*. The *"for Police"* was added because a separate volume for claim adjusters and other nonpolice investigators was planned. That never happened. The 1957 edition was twice as large as the 1953 one. Only six of the fifteen chapters in that edition were reproduced without substantial revision; the remaining nine were completely rewritten. To these were added fifteen topics first published as articles in the *Traffic Digest & Review*. Twelve names of contributors were listed; only one of these had also been listed as a contributor to the prewar editions. The second printing (1959) was the first in which the publisher included, on the title page, the name of a single "author," J. Stannard Baker.

In 1963, it was time for the book to "appear in a new and more beautiful edition, corrected and amended by the author." This sixth edition had a grey cover and more and better illustrations. It began to be noticed abroad. There were seven reprints, one in Spanish.

The seventh edition was printed in a large format (11- by 8½-inches) better to provide for more and larger pictures. It had a dark orange cover and a glossary; it was reprinted three times, once as a paperback.

That brings you to the eighth edition, which you are now reading. It is the first to be printed in two volumes, and the first to be developed in the Accident Investigation Division of the Northwestern University Traffic Institute.

In the first edition, 1940, topics relating to fact finding and reporting (Levels 2 and 3 of accident investigation) were "covered" in 62 pages with 45 exhibits; this time it has required a 1st volume with 654 exhibits.

Scope

This volume of the *Traffic-accident Investigation Manual* consists of 13 major topics which deal with development of information concerning particular traffic accidents. These topics are closely related to and are used as texts in four of the eight accident investigation courses taught at the Northwestern University Traffic Institute. Each topic consists of a set of detailed instructions for a specific task, such as at-scene photography, that might be the duty of a person especially trained for and assigned to that job, possibly without responsibility for other activities connected with accident investigation. In Volume 2, additional topics relate to accident reconstruction based on whatever information about an accident is available.

Some of the topics are available for use separately. This makes some overlapping of subject matter necessary.

In this volume, seven of the topics are substantial revisions and expansions of topics in the previous edition; two topics are from dividing one of the previous topics; and three were previously published as separate pamphlets. The last three, lamp examination, tire examination, and photogrammetry, were included because they were so often purchased in addition to the manual and were frequently used with the manual as texts in the same classes.

Some subjects in the previous edition have been omitted from this one: enforcement in connection with accidents, handling accident emergencies, civil liability for damages, and giving information in and out of court. These peripheral subjects were omitted because the manual was not bought for them, and was rarely referred to in teaching those subjects.

Organizations other than the Northwestern University Traffic Institute are appropriate sources of information and instruction in some matters connected with traffic-accident investigation. Hence instructions for autopsies, trial strategy, mechanical inspection of vehicles, and some other matters are not needed in this manual. Suitable publications from some of these sources will continue to be used in Traffic Institute instruction.

Arrangement

The manual is divided into two volumes because its present content would make a single book too bulky and expensive for most purposes. Users are generally interested in information collection, which requires almost no mathematics, or in accident reconstruction which involves considerable mathematics, but not both at the same time. That is the basis on which topics are assigned to one volume or the other.

For two reasons, each topic is designed as an independent unit: first, it can be used separately for a class in the specialty of that topic; and second, one topic can be revised without having to repage and rearrange other topics. For instance, by providing suitable examples, self-study questions, and examinations. Topic 828 has already been made the basis of an independent study program for *Measurements at the Scenes of Traffic Accidents.*

To give this flexibility, the pages in each topic are numbered consecutively and separately for that topic. But to facilitate indexing, each page number is preceded by the topic number. For example, the page numbered 25-12 is the twelfth page of Topic 825. This follows the general practice of important reference works such as the *SAE Handbook* and *Marks' Mechanical Engineering Handbook.* It is also a return to the system used in the third through the sixth editions of this manual.

The first digit in all topic numbers in this publication is 8. This follows the general practice at Northwestern University Traffic Institute of starting all publication numbers with a digit representing the division of the Institute responsible for the publication. The number 8 stands for the Accident Investigation Division; 3 refers to the Transportation Engineering Division, and so on. Besides the topics in this manual, there are scores of other pieces of printed matter identified by the number 8. These are used in accident-investigation instruction. To simplify indexing and reference, the repetitive initial number 8 is omitted from individual pages.

There are gaps in the sequence of topic numbers in this manual; the numbers are not consecutive. Gaps permit introducing a new topic in the proper sequence at some future time, without renumbering all of the following topics. For example, there are now topics on lamp examination (823) and tire examination (825). If a topic on brake examination is developed for a possible course on that subject, it could be assigned the number 824 which would place it with other topics relating to vehicle examination. Nonconsecutive numbering is not new. It has been used for years in operating manuals for organizations. It is standard practice in America for house numbers which are assigned in sequence along street segments, usually blocks. There are gaps, however, in the series for vacant property. If a new house is built, it is assigned a number between the numbers of the houses on either side, thereby maintaining a useful sequence.

Topics contain several kinds of illustrative material: photos, tables, maps, charts and so on. Instead of numbering each kind as a separate series, as is often done, all in a topic are numbered consecutively as exhibits. This follows common practice of the legal profession.

Metric System

In these topics it is not necessary to make any special provision for those who use the metric system. The measurements discussed are so straightforward that no one should have difficulty in using either the U.S.A. or the metric system.

Contributors

Instructions for specific tasks usually represent so much common knowledge and the experience of so many people that it is difficult to name an individual "author." Actually, the process of developing guides to specific tasks is more a matter of selecting and fitting together bits of experience and advice than it is of developing original material.

Many ideas in the original *Accident Investigation Manual* are still current in this edition, although none of the contributors to that work have been associated with production of the present edition.

Certainly, since the beginning, the book has been the effort of a number of contributors, mainly people on the staff of the Northwestern University Traffic Institute. To enumerate all whose ideas are represented in these pages would now be impossible and probably to little purpose. Therefore, consider the persons whose names appear on the topics of this volume as those now most familiar with the topic, usually because they have taught it at The Traffic Institute.

Under the heading "Sources," at the end of each topic are listed some of the publications from which ideas have been abstracted. Under the same heading are listed sources of exhibits so far as they are known.

There are also a number of individuals whose contribution to this edition must be gratefully acknowledged: Phyllis Holstead for the index, Nancy Poore for printing production, Bonnie Leoni and Diana Leviton for all graphics and Paul Lane of Photo Source for enhancement of photographic illustrations.

J. Stannard Baker is a traffic engineer specializing in accident investigation. He was Director of Research and Development at The Northwestern University Traffic Institute from 1946 to 1971 and is a guest lecturer for The Traffic Institute.

Lynn B. Fricke is a traffic engineer specializing in traffic-accident investigation. He has been with The Traffic Institute since 1975. In 1981, he became the director of the Institute's Accident Investigation Division.

CONTENTS

Topic 810
TRAFFIC-ACCIDENT INVESTIGATION FUNCTIONS

Topic 812
PREPARATION FOR TRAFFIC-ACCIDENT INVESTIGATION

Topic 815
TRAFFIC-ACCIDENT
INFORMATION FROM AND ABOUT PEOPLE

Topic 817
TRAFFIC-ACCIDENT INFORMATION FROM ROADS

Topic 818
SIMPLE ESTIMATES OF VEHICLE STOPPING DISTANCES AND SPEED FROM SKIDMARKS

Topic 820
TRAFFIC-ACCIDENT INFORMATION FROM VEHICLES

Topic 823
LAMP EXAMINATION FOR ON OR OFF IN TRAFFIC ACCIDENTS

Topic 825
TIRE EXAMINATION FOLLOWING ACCIDENTS

Topic 828
MEASURING AT THE SCENES OF TRAFFIC ACCIDENTS

Topic 830
PHOTOGRAMMETRY FOR
TRAFFIC-ACCIDENT INVESTIGATION

Topic 832
MEASURING THE ROAD FOR
AFTER-ACCIDENT SITUATION MAPS

Topic 834
DRAWING AFTER-ACCIDENT SITUATION MAPS

Topic 836
PHOTOGRAPHY FOR
TRAFFIC-ACCIDENT INVESTIGATION

TRAFFIC-ACCIDENT INVESTIGATION FUNCTIONS

Topic 810 of the *Traffic-Accident Investigation Manual*

by
J. Stannard Baker

NORTHWESTERN UNIVERSITY TRAFFIC INSTITUTE

PUBLICATION HISTORY

1953   *Traffic Accident Investigator's Manual* (Section 12 & 13)

1954   Revised

1957   *Traffic Accident Investigator's Manual for Police* (Sections 12 & 13) Reprinted 1959

1963   Revised
Reprinted 1964, 1965, 1966, 1969, 1970, 1971, 1973

1970   *Manual de Investigacion de Accidentes de Trafico* (Sections 12 & 13)

1975   *Traffic Accident Investigation Manual* (Chapters 1 & 2)
Reprinted 1976, 1979

1985   *Traffic-Accident Investigation Functions*

Copyright 1985 by The Northwestern University Traffic Institute
P.O. Box 1409 Evanston, Illinois 60204

TRAFFIC-ACCIDENT INVESTIGATION FUNCTIONS

This topic relates to the whole business of traffic-accident investigation, its purposes, and the requirements governing it. Investigation procedures are discussed in detail elsewhere. Hence, this topic will have more significance for administrators and supervisors than for those who actually do the investigating.

1. COLLECTING INFORMATION

Traffic-accident investigation — or for that matter, any kind of investigation — is mainly a matter of obtaining, recording, refining, and interpreting information. However, a police investigator also may be required to discharge other responsibilities in connection with the accident. For example, at the scene of an accident, a police traffic-accident investigator may also protect life and property. This is not, strictly speaking, investigation. A person may subsequently become involved in lawsuits, which are also not part of investigation. Hence, the end product of an investigation is a package of information. This information may be only a jumble of disconnected bits and pieces wholly in the mind of the investigator or it may be a carefully sorted bundle of forms, statements, drawings, photographs, and even pieces of vehicles transmitted to someone who has to do something with the data they contain.

The information may have been gathered by one person or many. It may relate to an intricate series of events and circumstances that constitute an accident or only to a minute aspect, such as a tiny lamp filament. The information may be confined to a few bare facts; or it may consist largely of fanciful speculations, unfounded assumptions, or simple guesses. Usually, however, the collected information consists of a mixture of fact and opinion.

Whatever its quantity or quality, the end product of investigation is still a collection of information about the accident.

Uses of Traffic-Accident Information

Mainly, information about traffic accidents is collected with specific uses in mind. Such purposes determine — or should determine — the amount and character of information collected.

At the scene of the accident, the investigator usually does not know exactly what data will eventually be needed. As a result, in gathering information, the investigator must be guided by instructions of some kind or by his own judgment, which may or may not be based realistically on experience. If he obtains too much information, some of it will be wasted; if too little, it may turn out to be inadequate for the purposes. Thus, at the scene of a serious accident, a certain amount of information is collected for possible future use. This is especially important with respect to information which can only be obtained at the time of the accident; or which may be much more difficult to get later. Some data collection, on the other hand, can be deferred until it is clear that it is actually wanted.

Users of traffic-accident information can be divided into two major categories: 1) those who want minimum basic information about all or most accidents; and 2) those who want a lot of information about a single accident.

Statistical Data

Selected information about as many accidents as possible is needed for statistical tabulations, discovery of high-accident locations, and evaluation of the effectiveness of safety efforts.

Statistical tabulations are customarily made to show

- Changes in accident experience from year to year
- Differences in accident experience among cities and states
- Severity of accidents
- Types of accidents
- Types of roads, vehicles, and people involved

• Common circumstances such as day of week and hour of day
• Maneuvers intended.

Accidents are also tabulated as a basis for accident rates, such as fatalities per 100 million miles of driving.

As a basis for designing accident prevention or control programs, data on large numbers of accidents are commonly used in three ways:

1. For selective traffic-law enforcement which considers where and when accidents occur and what kind of enforcement should be intensified to have the greatest effect on accidents
2. To help bring high-risk drivers to the attention of licensing and other authorities so that inadequate drivers may be given appropriate attention
3. In "spot improvement" programs on roads for safety purposes.

Users of mass data are interested mainly in two kinds of information: 1) positive *identification* of time, place, and drivers involved; and 2) *classification* of each accident by severity and other circumstances according to specified uniform categories.

For mass data purposes, accident-report forms are provided to assemble information in the most useful package. There is a place on the form for each piece of information needed. This reminds the investigator of exactly what data are wanted and makes it as easy as possible to record the data. Well-designed accident-report forms also make it easy to use the information because each kind of data is always found in the same place on the form and recorded in the same way.

Mass data on traffic accidents — that which is called for by the report form — are essentially factual: names numbers, descriptions. Attempts have been made to record the cause of each accident on the form for tabulation, but it eventually became clear that the cause of every accident is a complex combination of contributing factors. Exactly what these factors are for a particular accident and how they contribute is always a matter of opinion and often the subject of conjecture. For any accident, opinions about contributing factors can, and usually do, differ, depending on who makes the inferences required to form an opinion and how much and what kind of information the person has for the purpose. Because information on causes is so uncertain, tabulation can be misleading and may do as much harm as good. Today, therefore, most basic accident-report forms, those used for mass data purposes, do not provide for opinions about causes.

The basic report contains all the information that users of mass data need. If additional information were not required for other purposes accident investigation could stop when basic data were recorded. As a matter of fact, for more than half of the known or reported accidents, data recording does, indeed, stop when the accident-report form is completed. For these minor accidents, little or no use would be made of additional information if it were obtained. The process of supplying standard facts to those who want them on a mass basis for all accidents is illustrated diagrammatically in the left column of Exhibit 1.

Interpretive Data

Additional information about the individual accident is nearly always needed if the accident is fatal or has other serious consequences. Some of this information can only be obtained at the scene immediately after the accident, for example, photographs of vehicles where they came to rest. A decision has to be made on the spot by an investigator — usually a police officer — regarding how much of such additional data to collect.

Other data — information on the structural details of vehicles or configuration of the road — can wait days or even weeks.

A decision can be made later about exactly what additional information is needed. Thus, a minimum of effort will be wasted collecting unnecessary information.

Additional data on specific accidents are used for two main purposes: 1) litigation; and 2) research. Litigation, often resulting in trials, decides whether a driver should be found guilty of a law violation in connection with the accident (a criminal case) or who should pay whom how much for injuries and damages received in the accident (a civil suit). Litigation requires more information than is provided by the ordinary accident report. Research related to a particular accident is conducted to determine, from that accident, what might be done to prevent similar accidents in the future. By far the most extensive use of additional data on particular accidents is made in civil law suits; the least extensive use is in research to prevent accidents and reduce their severity. This situation will doubtless continue until bona fide no-fault insurance is broadly adopted in the United States. Then the need for additional investigation for claim-settlement purposes could be expected almost to disappear.

Most lawsuits and research projects require knowledge about events in a traffic accident which were not reliably observed and reported: speed, position on the road, evasive tactics, and who was driving, to mention only some of the more common circumstances. Knowledge about such circumstances must be obtained more or less by inference from the facts available. Therefore, another purpose of investigation is to reach conclusions about circumstances which would otherwise be unknown or imperfectly known, if such conclusions are needed and if adequate data on which to base them are available. The right column of

Exhibit 1 shows the process of adding special information for more serious accidents to the basic data for an accident report.

Special supplementary data collection is another kind of accident investigation. More than simple mass data reporting it is usually a less than detailed study of individual accidents. It has been referred to as "bilevel" reporting, used almost entirely for research purposes. To obtain more complete records of observations relating to some particular circumstances of accidents, a special set of specific data requirements is established to be used for a limited time in a selected area for a particular purpose. The data requirements are usually specified in a special form which is used to supplement the ordinary traffic-accident report form.

The best known program of this kind is that for the study of crash injuries. For designated accidents, police collect more detailed data, including photographs of damage to vehicles and physicians' reports detailing injuries to occupants. Data from both sources are reported on special forms. The data are tabulated and otherwise analyzed to learn how injuries are received in traffic crashes and how effective safety belts and other injury-reducing measures really are.

Another example of collecting supplementary data for accident investigation is a study of tire disablements on high-speed roads. During the course of the year, police investigating accidents involving tire disablements filled out special supplementary forms relating to tire conditions and other relevant circumstances. These reports were studied, tabulated, and compared with other data to determine how many and what kind of accidents may have had tire disablement as a contributing factor.

The advantage of such special temporary investigation programs is that they do not waste effort collecting data on the chance that someone might sometime want it. Data are collected for a specified purpose and when the need is satisfied, data collection ends. Such programs, which focus on very specific problems, are expected to be used increasingly in the future.

Sequence of Information Development

The process of accident investigation can be thought of as a sequence of operations ranging from simple to complex. Some of these operations can take place simultaneously. The process of developing information begins with collecting simple data about the highway transportation components involved: road, vehicle, and people. It continues, if necessary, through inferences or conclusions about the sequence of events that constitutes the accident and the relationship of these components during the events.

A synopsis of these operations summarizes the general process:

- Identify roads, vehicles, and people involved.
- Describe and classify them.
- Observe their condition at the time of the accident.
- Observe the effect of the accident on them: injury and damage.
- Interpret the observations.
- Infer events and circumstances.

Records. Each of these operations requires appropriate records. The simpler operations require only a report of facts or observations; the more complex ones may require a detailed explanation of how a conclusion has been reached from observations. Few accidents go through the whole process; most efforts stop when the need for information has been met.

2. LEVELS OF ACCIDENT INVESTIGATION

Consideration of the uses of traffic-accident information leads to the realization that many kinds of information are required for a great variety of purposes. For most accidents, a few simple facts suffice; but for others, scientific inferences are necessary to develop useful conclusions about the accident. One must also realize the tasks involved in accident investigation vary from simple ones, requiring no special training or experience, to very technical ones that call for scientific knowledge and skills. So, as in other technologies such as medicine and engineering, traffic-accident investigation is practiced at a number of levels. Often the work done at one level prepares the material for work at another. For example, measurements and photographs made by investigators at the scene provide the facts on which an engineer later reaches conclusions about exactly how the accident happened.

Levels of activity in traffic-accident investigation can not be clearly separated; each tends to overlap or merge with previous or subsequent levels.

For many years, only two levels of police traffic-accident data collection were recognized: 1) "reporting," which required obtaining data for the official accident-report form; and 2) "investigation," which involved collecting any additional information. If the only information about the accident was that recorded on the report form, the accident had been reported but not investigated. This simple division of accident-information collection into two categories has disadvantages. For one thing, designating the first category "reporting" rather then "investigating" is contrary to police concepts. Police regard reporting an accident, however simple it may be, as part of investigation. Furthermore, distinguishing only two kinds of investiga-

10-6

tion lumps together all tasks in addition to reporting and so obscures the important differences between recording observations (measurements and photographs) and reaching conclusions about how an accident happened (interpretation and inference).

Five levels of activity in accident investigation can be distinguished:

1. Reporting
2. At-scene investigation
3. Technical follow-up
4. Professional reconstruction
5. Cause analysis

These can be described in several ways but they are most easily understood if explained in terms of the tasks they involve and the kinds of knowledge and skills needed to perform those tasks successfully.

Level 1, Reporting

Definition. Reporting is basic data collection intended to identify and classify a motor-vehicle traffic accident and the persons, property, and planned movements involved. Only strict factual information is required; no opinions.

Information is recorded on a highly organized and largely self-explanatory form. Almost any literate person with little or no special instruction can obtain and record the information required by this form.

Reporting may include not only data required for a standard traffic-accident report but also simple, factual data for supplementary report forms used temporarily for special purposes.

All known accidents, regardless of severity, should be reported at Level 1.

Level 2, At-scene Extra Data Collection

Definition. At-scene extra data collection is examining and making records of the results of the accident and obtaining additional information at the scene which may not be available later and which supplements information on the accident report. Generally, extra data are collected at the scene for fatal and other special accidents.

Only factual information is wanted; no conclusions are required.

Some data may be recorded on supplementary forms, but most will be recorded photographically or as field notes of measurements. Training is required to develop the special skills necessary to perform the following tasks:

- Make preliminary tests for intoxication.
- Find and identify possible witnesses.
- Describe and measure to locate marks on the road and debris.
- Measure to locate final positions of vehicles and bodies of persons killed or incapacitated.
- Photograph marks and debris on the road at the accident scene.
- Photograph external damage to vehicles and to roadside objects.
- Photograph final positions of vehicles.
- Make first attempt to match tires to tiremarks on road.
- Examine condition and functioning of traffic control devices and other road equipment.
- Make preliminary examination of condition of vehicle equipment such as lamps, tires, steering gear.
- Make first attempt to match damage of vehicles to marks on road, and damage on one vehicle to that on another.
- Examine occupant restraints (safety belts, airbags, and child safety seats) for function.

Level 3, Technical Follow-up

Definition. Technical follow-up is collection of additional facts from any source and organization and preliminary study of all available data relating to an accident. Generally, technical follow-up is undertaken only for legal and other specific purposes.

Some observations may be recorded on special-purpose forms but work at this level is largely unsystematized. Training is required to develop skills for tasks listed here:

Additional data collection
- Make measurements to prepare a map of accident site.
- Measure grades, sight distances, view obstructions, falls, and surface friction of road.
- Observe visibility of vehicles, pedestrians, and traffic control under specified conditions.
- Measure speed and acceleration of vehicles and pedestrians under specified conditions.
- Discover and record what participants and other witnesses will say about the accident.
- Examine in detail lamps, tires, and occupant restraints.
- Examine in detail and photograph damage to vehicles.
- Disassemble vehicles to discover possible equipment deficiencies.
- Analyze paint and glass to identify and match specimens.
- Examine injuries to indicate position and movement of bodies during collisions.

Preparation of data
- Draw after-accident situation map.
- Show on a map marks on the road located by a perspective grid.
- Show on a map marks on the road shown in photos but not located by measurements.
- Determine critical and design speed for curves and turns.

- Estimate speed from simple skids, and yaws.
- Match damage areas and thrust directions.
- Determine whether lights were on or off at time of collision.
- Determine whether tires were disabled before first harmful event of the accident.
- Determine how safety equipment functioned.

There are, of course, other functions besides those listed.

Clearly, no one person is able to do all of these things well. Some can be done well only by trained and experienced specialists. For example, autopsies can be done only by pathologists or other medical experts; matching paint samples usually requires special laboratory equipment and skills; examining vehicle damage takes considerable knowledge of vehicles of various kinds.

Technical follow-up, Level 3, is undertaken only with specific needs in mind and only to the extent requested for litigation or research study of the accident.

Level 4, Professional Reconstruction

Definition. Professional reconstruction is the effort to determine, from whatever information is available, *how* the accident happened. Reconstruction was formally referred to as determining "behavioral" or "mediate" causes of an accident.[2]

Reconstruction mainly involves fitting together pieces of information. It is simply thinking about available facts. Some of the facts are based on observations of the results of a particular accident; some are from examination of roads, vehicles, and people involved; and some are from general knowledge of basic sciences.

Reconstruction results in conclusions (opinions, deductions, inferences). These are usually in the form of statements regarding

- Speed
- Positions of vehicles and pedestrians during impact

- How injuries were received
- Which occupant was driving
- How road, driver, and vehicle conditions contributed to a particular accident
- Description of driver tactics and strategy
- How a particular driver or pedestrian might have avoided the accident.

Reconstruction usually does not include evaluation of the adequacy of safety devices, road design, vehicle equipment, or driver training.

Skills must be developed to perform special tasks involved in reconstruction. These include ability to

- Compute energy losses and momentum exchanges in stopping vehicles.
- Make momentum diagrams and calculations.
- Analyze movements of vehicles and bodies in collisions.
- Compare possible and actual driving tactics and strategy.
- Estimate driver or pedestrian perception delays.
- Design experiments in driver or pedestrian behavior.
- Design experiments to determine performance of a vehicle.

Reconstruction skills require a working knowledge of arithmetic and algebra, a good understanding of dynamics, especially as applied to vehicles, a fair idea of reaction time, and familiarity with information gathering processes at Levels 2 and 3 of traffic-accident investigation.

Although reconstruction is mainly a thinking process, the person doing it nearly always finds it necessary to do much of his or her own Level 3 fact-finding. This is so simply because it is cheaper and quicker than arranging for someone else to do it and explaining exactly what is wanted.

The extent to which reconstruction can be carried depends on the quality and quantity of basic data more than on anything else. If enough good data are available, the facts speak for themselves. Then almost anyone can

determine satisfactorily how the accident happened. On the other hand, if information is insufficient and unreliable, no one can be sure of exactly what took place. Information for most accidents is between these extremes. Standing alone, the information fails to tell us all we want to know; but it is adequate as a basis for satisfactory conclusions by people who can add to the information knowledge from experience and science. A highly competent person can form more and better conclusions from the same data than a less experienced and trained investigator.

Professional reconstruction, Level 4 of accident investigation, is undertaken only when there is definite special need.

Level 5, Cause Analysis

Definition. Cause analysis is the effort to determine, from whatever information is available, including results of accident reconstruction, *why* the accident occurred, that is, the complete combination of circumstances that caused the highway transportation system to break down at the time and place of the accident with resultant injury and damage. Cause analysis has been referred to as determining "indirect" or "condition" causes.[2]

Cause analysis is largely unsystematized, without generally accepted methodology or forms for recording results. It is almost entirely inferential and by its very nature involves large elements of speculation.

The investigator who attempts cause analysis should be prepared to try to determine, as objectively as possible, such circumstances as

- Probable contribution of road or vehicle design deficiencies to accident, and to injury, and damage
- Probable contribution of personality peculiarities to accident and injury
- Probable contribution of temporary conditions of the road, vehicle, and weather to accident, injury, and damage

• Probable contribution of temporary driver conditions (such as intoxication) to accident

• Complete combination of probable and possible factors contributing to tactical (evasive action) failures

• Complete combination of probable and possible factors contributing to strategy (precautionary measures) that prevented successful tactics or otherwise influenced the outcome of events.

Cause analysis, Level 5, is undertaken only for research purposes.

Limitations affecting successful cause analysis, like those affecting accident reconstruction, are numerous:

• Completeness and success of accident reconstruction on which cause analysis is based

• Quantity and quality of specific information about conditions at the time and place of the accident

• Knowledge of how vehicles, roads, and drivers function

• Knowledge of how the extent of temporary conditions affected the accident and especially their synergetic effect

• Skill, experience, and imagination of those doing the work

• Expense, which always sets limits on how much can be done for the money available.

The five levels of accident investigation are noted in the middle column of Exhibit 1.

3. QUALITY OF INFORMATION

Evaluating Information

Information obtained in accident investigation is a mixture of observations and opinions. How closely these represent actuality or truth determines the quality of the information and reflects the success of the investigation.

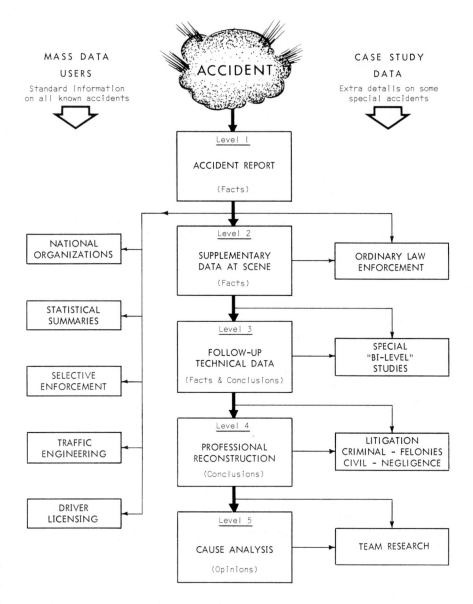

Exhibit 1

PROCESS OF ACCIDENT INVESTIGATION

Hence, an important part of the process of investigation is examining and evaluating bits of information as they are gathered, recorded, and reviewed. With respect to data that are obtained for simple reporting, evaluation is easy; the names, dates, numbers, and descriptions are factual and objective. However, evaluating information about how and why an accident occurred is difficult; statements are likely to be warped and opinions are often largely speculation.

An investigator records the words of a driver. It is true that the driver spoke those words, but it does not follow that the words spoken were truth. If the investigator reports, "Driver said he was going 25 miles per hour," it can usually be accepted as a fact only that the driver said so. If the investigator reports, "Speed of the vehicle was 25 miles per hour," he may be recording an error, perhaps even a lie. An investigator records, "The vehicles collided in the eastbound lane." Unless he actually saw the collision occur, which rarely happens, the information is an opinion of the investigator or of someone else. But how can the user of the information be sure that the opinion is reliable?

Unfortunately, too many investigators at all levels are insufficiently aware of the fine but important distinction between fact and opinion. They slip into the easy error of thinking uncritically that whatever they have come to believe is actually so. From considering a plausible possibility, they move unconsciously into thinking of it as highly probable or even completely certain.

Thus an investigator, in recording and transmitting information, can give it an unwarranted semblance of reliability. Information of questionable quality then passes for accurate data.

An important part of the process of investigation at all levels is to evaluate information obtained for the benefit of users. Evident misinformation is rejected outright. Opinions are "labeled" to indicate the degree of their trustworthiness by answering certain questions:

- Whose opinion is it? Is that person unbiased? Is he competent? Has he access to facts on which to base an opinion?
- On what facts is the opinion based? Are they reliable? Are they adequate?
- How sure is the investigator of this opinion? What words can be used to warn the user of possible inaccuracies, of possibilities, probabilities, and "provabilities"?

To produce information that can be relied on, investigators must develop critical thinking and remain continually alert to detect contaminating misinformation. For many, this is a difficult goal to achieve.

Bias

An insidious obstacle to such critical thinking is starting an investigation with some preconception, even unconsciously. For example, the investigator may believe, to begin with, that there has been a law violation, often a particular law violation. Many investigators carry a built-in bias often stemming from current stereotypes, for example, the feeling that the "young punks" are at fault or "here is another of those sports-car accidents." Sometimes the slightest sign of drinking — a beer can in the car — will trigger the assumption that intoxication was involved. There is a strong tendency to blame vehicle mechanical failure for every out-of-control accident. Few investigators will admit, even to themselves, such bias and, if accused of it, will vigorously deny it. But careful study of results and methods of investigation does reveal this condition.

Even an investigator who starts with an unbiased mind may pick up, early in the investigation, an idea of how the accident happened or who was to blame. This may be the ready and plausible explanation of a driver or the statement of an ill-informed but self-assured witness; it may be suggested by marks on the road or damage to vehicles; or it may be simply a hunch.

Whatever the origin of a preconceived notion, the investigation tends, almost irresistibly, to follow a deceitful course. The investigator seeks, seizes, magnifies every sign that points toward what he already believes, and he overlooks, disregards, and belittles every contrary indication. Then, by the time the investigation is finished, the idea has hardened into a conviction that is nearly impossible to correct.

Do not infer that all investigations which start with some outcome in mind result in misinformation about how the accident happened. That would be committing the error that we have been describing here. When one has jumped to a conclusion, he may well have jumped to the right conclusion. The problem is that we cannot depend on that, and consequently, the reliability of conclusions about the accident suffers; the quality of information resulting from the investigation is questionable.

Lawyers are the most conspicuous examples of investigators who start with desired conclusions and work back. Our system of adversary jurisprudence virtually requires this. Each attorney is obliged to develop and stress whatever testimony or evidence benefits his side of the case and to suppress and discount the contrary. Most attorneys, therefore, try to steer the thinking of police investigators and even reconstruction experts toward the conclusions they favor, and they are often successful in doing so.

All of which makes traffic-accident investigation no simple and easy process.

4. THE POLICE FUNCTION

Traffic accidents are investigated for a number of reasons. For example, attorneys investigate traffic accidents on behalf of clients as they would any other kind of accident. The basis for this investigation is a claim for damages to compensate a victim for losses suffered as a result of the accident.

As a police function, however, traffic-accident investigation has no such singleness of purpose. It provides information for the use of police themselves and for the use of other agencies both public and private. It is an important service to individuals concerned with particular accidents but in no position to make their own inquiries, especially at the scene of an accident.

Police departments are public, governmental agencies. As such they develop programs, including traffic-accident investigation, that serve public purposes. These programs are administered within guidelines of three degrees of authority:

1. Law
2. Standards
3. Administrative arrangements.

Traffic-accident investigation is essentially gathering and packaging information. But in connection with traffic accidents, police perform other functions beside investigation:

1. Protect life and property in the emergency created by an accident on a public way.
2. Manage traffic so that the travelling public will be inconvenienced as little as possible.
3. Enforce traffic laws violated in connection with the accident.

These additional functions are beyond the scope of the present topic.

5. LAWS

Laws relating to traffic-accident investigation are brief and vague. In general, they provide neither guidance nor constraints to the investigator or administrator.

Vehicle Code

State laws are much alike with respect to traffic-accident investigation. Most of them are based more or less on the *Uniform Vehicle Code*[3] in which the only reference to accident investigation is

"10-112 – **Police to report.**

"(a) Every law enforcement officer who investigates a vehicle accident of which a report must be made as required by this chapter, or who otherwise prepares a written report as a result of an investigation either at the time of and at the scene of the accident or thereafter by interviewing the participants or witnesses, shall forward a written report of such accident to the department within 10 days after his investigation of the accident."

"10-113 – **Accident report forms.**

"(b) Every accident report required to be made in writing shall be made on the appropriate form provided by the department and shall contain all of the information required therein unless not available."

"10-116 — **Chemical tests in fatal crashes.**

"(a) When an accident results in the death of any driver or pedestrian within four hours of the accident, the medical examiner (or official performing like functions) shall draw blood or another bodily substance from the deceased driver or pedestrian so that the amount of alcohol in his blood can be determined. When possible, the withdrawal shall occur within eight hours of death."

"(c) The medical examiner (or official performing like functions) or an approved laboratory shall analyze blood or other substance to determine the amount of alcohol in the dead driver's or pedestrian's blood."

"(d) The results of this analysis shall be reported to the department and may be used by state and local officials only for statistical purposes that do not reveal the identity of the deceased person. Nothing in this subsection shall restrict the tests as evidence in criminal or civil proceedings."

Municipal Ordinances

City ordinances relating to traffic accident investigation are based mainly on *Model Traffic Ordinance*[3], a companion piece of the *Uniform Vehicle Code*. The *Model Ordinance* reference to accident investigation is

"2-4 – **Traffic Division to investigate accident.**

"It shall be the duty of the traffic division, assisted by other police officers of the department, to investigate traffic accidents, to arrest and assist in the prosecution of those persons charged with violations of law causing or contributing to such accidents."

Neither the *Uniform Vehicle Code* nor the *Model Traffic Ordinance* specifies what is meant by "investigate." That is presumably left as a matter for standards or administrative arrangements.

Driver Duties

Call police. Motor-vehicle codes in all states provide that police must be notified after all motor-vehicle accidents resulting in more than a specified amount of damage or injury. Most of these laws are patterned after the *Uniform Vehicle Code*.[3] The requirements of the Code in this respect are listed in Exhibit 2. Because laws in individual states may differ, a column in this table is provided for entering the rules in your state. This information can be obtained from state motor-vehicle codes or city traffic ordinances. If your state law is the same as the *Uniform Vehicle Code,* simply write "same" in the blank space. Remember that the *Uniform Vehicle Code* is a standard and not the law of any particular state.

Report to State. In addition to notifying the police, the driver of a vehicle involved in an accident is required by most state motor vehicle codes to make a written report to the state. These generally follow the *Uniform Vehicle Code,* the provisions of which are outlined in Exhibit 3. This table provides a column for recording requirements in your state.

Local authorities also may require a written report of a motor-vehicle accident or a copy of the report made by the driver to the state. But the *Model Ordinance* provides for this only if police are not also at the scene.

6. STANDARDS

Standards are less authoritative than laws. One *must* obey laws, but *may* conform to standards. *The Uniform Vehicle Code* is really a standard for motor-vehicle legislation. So far as it is adopted by a state, it becomes law in that state.

Governmental agencies may make regulations or rules which have the effect of law. They may also publish standards or recommendations to guide rather than control various activities. For example, the official standard for weight adopted for uniformity in a country might be a pound, but that would not bar anyone from using a ton or a kilogram as a measure of weight.

Many standards, including the *Uniform Vehicle Code*, are based on agreement or consensus among members of an independent committee or commission. These members generally represent interested organizations or agencies. Several standards apply to traffic-accident investigation.

Classification

This standard[4] is primarily intended to provide classification of motor-vehicle accidents on the road; but it may also be used to classify other road vehicle accidents on trafficways and any road vehicle accident not on a trafficway. The following classifications are specified:

Persons involved are classified by
• Injury severity: 5 categories.
Road vehicles involved are classified by
• Damage severity: 4 categories.
Accident as a whole is classified by
• Most severe injury to any person involved: same 5 categories as injuries to persons
• Most severe damage to any road vehicle involved. 5 categories
• Number of motor vehicles in transport involved: each number of vehicles involved is a separate category.
• First harmful event (type of accident): 2 categories for noncollision accidents; 8 categories for collision accidents
• Roadway related location: 2 categories (on roadway and off roadway)

• Junction related location: 4 categories
• Class of trafficway: 6 categories
• Access to trafficway: 2 categories: (fully controlled and other)
• Land use: 2 categories (urban and rural)
• Political subdivision: each city,

county, or state is a separate category
• Bikeway relationship: 4 categories
Motor vehicle involved is classified by
• Type: 8 categories.
To make it possible to classify accidents properly according to these categories, the standard defines

Exhibit 2
RULES FOR NOTIFYING POLICE

Questions about Notifying Police	Requirements of Uniform Vehicle Code	Requirements in Our State and City
For how serious an accident must police be called?	Any involving death, personal injury, or vehicle disablement	
By whom?	Driver if he is able	
But if driver is unable?	Any occupant who can	
How soon?	Immediately	
By what means?	Quickest means of communication	
Call which police?	Nearest office of duly authorized police agency.	

Uniform Vehicle Code is not the law in any particular place.

Exhibit 3
DRIVER'S OFFICIAL REPORT TO STATE

Questions about Reporting	Requirements of Uniform Vehicle Code	Requirements in Our State
How serious must an accident be, to be formally reported?	If there is death, injury or $200 or more total damage to all property, unless investigated and reported by police	
By whom?	All drivers if physically able, otherwise owner of vehicle	
How soon?	Within 10 days	
To whom?	State Department of Motor Vehicles	
How?	In writing	
Where can you get forms?	Police, sheriff and other agencies	
Can reported information be used in court?	No - reported information is confidential.	

Uniform Vehicle Code is not the law of any particular state.

precisely a large number of interrelated terms, for example, it makes clear the distinction between *motor vehicle* and *other road vehicle*.

This standard does not preclude classifying people and things involved in traffic in other ways, for example, the standard would not discourage classifying people by age and sex or accidents by hour of day. Nor does the standard presuppose that all traffic accidents will be classified according to all of these classifications.

To conform to this standard on classification, requires two administrative actions: 1) design the accident report form to require the exact information needed; and 2) train investigators and data tabulators to conform exactly to the definitions in reporting and classifying data.

Federal Government

The National Highway Traffic Safety Administration (NHTSA) of the U. S. Department of Transportation has promulgated a series of 18 *Highway Safety Program Standards.* These outline U.S. Government recommendations for state traffic safety programs. Three of these standards relate to accident investigation.

Standard 18, Accident Investigation and Reporting[5], reviews three sources of traffic-accident reporting:

1. *"Owner and Driver Reports.* In accidents involving only property damage, where the vehicle can normally and safely be driven away from the scene, the drivers or owners of vehicles involved shall be required to submit a written report consistent with state reporting requirements, to the responsible state agency. A vehicle shall be considered capable of being normally and safely driven if it does not require towing and can be operated under its own power, in its customary manner, without further damage or hazard to itself, other traffic elements, or the roadway. Each report so submitted shall include, as a minimum, the following information relating to the accident:

   a. Location
   b. Time
   c. Identification of driver(s)
   d. Identification of pedestrian(s), passenger(s), or pedalcyclist(s)
   e. Identification of vehicle(s)
   f. Direction of travel of each unit
   g. Other property involved
   h. Environmental conditions existing at time of accident
   i. A narrative description of the events and circumstances leading up to the time of the impact, and immediately after the impact."

2. *Police investigation.* "In all other accidents, the drivers or owners of motor vehicles involved shall be required to immediately notify the police of the jurisdiction in which the accident occurred. . . . Police investigation shall be conducted for all accidents [of this kind.] Information gathered shall be consistent with the police mission of detecting and apprehending law violators, and shall include as a minimum, the following:

   a. Violations, if any occurred, cited by section and subsection, numbers and titles of the State code, that (1) contributed to the accident where the investigating officer has reason to believe that violations were committed regardless of whether the officer has sufficient evidence to prove the violation(s); and (2) for which the driver was arrested or cited.
   b. Information necessary to prove each of the elements of the offense(s) for which the driver was arrested or cited.
   c. Information, collected in accordance with the program established under Highway Safety Program Standard No. 15, Police Traffic Services[7], . . . relating to human, vehicular and highway factors causing individual accidents, including failure to use safety belts.

3. *"Accident investigation teams* shall be established, representing different interest areas, such as: police, traffic, highway and automotive engineering, medical, behavioral, and social sciences. Data gathered by each member of the investigation team should be consistent with the mission of the member's agency, and should be for the purpose of determining probable causes of accidents, injuries, and deaths. These teams shall conduct investigations of an appropriate sampling of accidents in which there were one or more of the following conditions:

   a. Locations that have a similarity of design, traffic engineering characteristics, or environmental conditions, and that have a significantly large or disproportionate number of accidents.
   b. Motor vehicles or motor vehicle parts that are involved in a significantly large or disproportionate number of accidents or injury-producing accidents.
   c. Drivers, pedestrians, and vehicle occupants of a particular age, sex, or other grouping, who are involved in a significantly large or disproportionate number of motor vehicle traffic accident or injuries.
   d. Accidents in which causation or the resulting injuries and property damage are not readily explainable in terms of conditions or circumstances that prevailed.
   e. Other factors that concern state and national emphasis programs."

Standard 10, Traffic Records,[6] lists the kinds of information to be gathered and says how the data collected shall be made available. This standard provides in some detail for

1. *Identification* of accidents by place and time, identification of vehicles, vehicle owners and drivers.
2. *Description* of accidents by type, description of vehicles by body type, commercial vehicles by gross laden weight, drivers by driving history, roads by environmental condition, personal injury, and property damage.
3. *Conclusions* relating to "cause and contributing factors."

Standard 10 also provides for

1. "Rapid entry of new data into the record system"
2. "Controls to eliminate unnecessary or unreasonable delays in tabulating data"
3. Rapid response to priority inquiries regarding vehicle ownership and driver records
4. "Data availability for statistical compilation as needed by authorized sources"
5. Records available to public except driver identification.

Standard 15, Police Traffic Services,[7] requires procedures for investigating, recording, and reporting accidents pertaining to

1. "Human, vehicular, and highway causative factors in individual accidents"
2. "Human, vehicular, and highway causative factors of injuries and deaths including failure to use safety belts"
3. "The efficiency of post-accident response."

The federal accident investigation standards require minimum data on all traffic accidents, additional routine investigation of the more serious accidents, largely for enforcement purposes, and intensive team investigation of a small number of selected accidents for special purposes.

IACP

The International Association of Chiefs of Police has developed worthwhile guides for the traffic work of police departments. Like the *Uniform Vehicle Code*[3], these models are written so that they can be copied exactly for local use, so far as they are acceptable. In this material, the term *accident investigation* refers to all police activities in connection with traffic accidents, not just investigation in the strict sense of information gathering and interpretation.

The Model Policies[8] includes six relating to police work in connection with traffic accidents:

1. Accident Investigation
2. Accident Reports
3. Accidents on Private Property
4. Employee Accidents
5. Hazardous Material Accidents
6. Accidents – First Officer's Responsibility.

The Model Procedures[9] describes 28 "procedures" for police work in connection with traffic accidents.

Two of these procedures (9 pages) deal with general principles of police activities in connection with traffic accidents.

Eleven of them (28 pages) explain procedures in connection with special kinds of accidents, such as fatal accidents and those involving railway trains.

Five (10 pages) outline information collection in connection with traffic accidents; for example questioning drivers and photographing the scene.

The remaining ten (26 pages) give, with very little explanation, some of the more common equations used in accident reconstruction; for example, "converting miles per hour to feet per second" and "computing speed from skidmarks." Most of these outlines of interpretative "procedures" would have to be supplemented by considerable technical training to be usefully applied.

Accreditation

Standards[10] have been developed for agencies wishing to be accredited by the Commission on Accreditation for Law Enforcement Agencies. One of these standards relates to "Traffic Accident Investigation," which includes all work of police departments in connection with traffic accidents not just the fact-finding part. This standard relates to "written directives" governing

1. *Accident reporting or investigation* to include accidents involving
   - Death or injury
   - Property damage
   - Hit and run
   - Impairment due to alcohol or drugs
   - Hazardous materials
2. *Officer response* to the scene of an accident involving any one of the following:
   - Death or injury
   - Hit and run
   - Impairment of an operator due to alcohol or drugs
   - Damage to public vehicles or property
   - "Major traffic congestion as a result of the accident"
   - "Damage to vehicles to the extent towing is required"
3. *"Accident-scene responsibilities for the first officer* to respond"
4. *"Procedures for determining the officer* or investigator who is *in charge* at the accident scene.
5. *"Procedures for at-scene accident information collection,* to include
   - *Interviewing* principals and witnesses
   - *Examining*/recording vehicle damage
   - *Examining*/recording effects of the accident on the roadway
   - Taking measurements, as appropriate
   - Taking photographs, as ap-

propriate
- Collecting/preserving evidence; and
- Exchanging information among principals"

6. *"Procedures* for accident-investigation *follow-up activities* to include:
   - Collecting off-scene data
   - Obtaining/recording formal statements from witnesses;
   - Reconstructing accidents; and
   - Preparing formal reports to support criminal charges arising from the accident"

7. *"Use of expert and technical assistance* in accident investigations."

8. *"Accident investigation equipment*/emergency medical supplies to be carried in patrol vehicles."

9. *"Guidelines for taking enforcement action* for violations resulting in traffic accidents."

10. *"Reporting* or investigating of traffic accidents occurring *on private property.*"

11. *"Traffic direction and control* at accident scenes."

12. "Accident scene procedures for handling:
   - Injuries
   - Fire hazards
   - Hazardous materials."

13. *"Control of property* belonging to accident victims."

14. *Use of* accident report and supplementary report *forms.*

15. *Conformance* of the agency's classification system with the Manual on Classification of Motor Vehicle Traffic Accidents.[4]

Unlike the *Uniform Vehicle Code*[3] and the *Model Police Traffic Services*,[8] these accreditation standards do not provide models for wording the "written directives" required.

7. ADMINISTRATIVE CONSIDERATIONS

The principal basis for traffic-accident investigation is administrative policy.

Accident investigation is not an end in itself; the information produced presumably serves some useful purpose. Moreover, investigators themselves rarely use the information they obtain; it is collected for others who do intend to use it. Therefore, the traffic-accident-investigation program and the individual investigators working in it must aim to produce only data the users want for the purposes the users have in mind, no more and no less. It behooves whoever is directing the data collection or administering the accident-investigation program — whether it be for statistics, legal processes, safety program supervision, or research — to make clear to investigators exactly what he wants them to find out about traffic accidents and what limitations, such as time to be allocated, are placed on investigations.

Historical Background

For statistical purposes, prior to 1925, traffic-accident data were obtained from two sources: 1) reports by physicians and coroners to bureaus of vital statistics of people killed in traffic accidents; and 2) clippings of newspaper reports of traffic accidents. The vital statistics were reasonably complete and accurate but not very detailed. Newspaper reports were neither complete nor reliable, especially in small towns and rural areas.

For legal purposes — the occasional lawsuit to collect damages for negligence — information on how the accident happened was derived almost entirely from statements of participants and occasionally from witnesses.

Driver licensing and traffic engineering agencies began to seek traffic-accident data as early as 1925. Drivers then began to be required to report accidents to the states. Forms for such reports were provided from the beginning.

Early police records of accidents provided little useful information. Typically such records were a single line on a police blotter, often without useful identification of location or people involved.

Police Activity in Connection with Accidents

Because police patrol streets and highways to protect life and property and to enforce laws, police assumed the task of attending and reporting traffic accidents. For many years before the advent of the motor vehicle, police had directed traffic at congested junctions.

As laws to regulate motor vehicle traffic were enacted, police undertook traffic law enforcement. To facilitate traffic direction, police put up signs and signals; and, to assist in supervising drivers, police were given the job of driver licensing. Police also began to make special reports of accidents they attended. These reports were usually more reliable and detailed than driver or newspaper reports with the result that they were used more and more for statistics, enforcement planning, engineering, driver licensing, and legal purposes.

Police traffic supervision. Today, police have largely been relieved of driver licensing and traffic engineering. The traffic work of police departments, called *traffic supervision,* now has four principal functions:

1. Traffic direction
2. Traffic law enforcement
3. Traffic accident investigation
4. Motorist services.

The extent of police functions connected with accidents varies considerably from one organization to another. Such activity includes duties which are not information collecting and so are not, strictly speaking, investigation:
- Duties connected with the

emergency
- Special motorist services
- Collecting information about circumstances of the accident (accident investigation)
- Enforcing traffic and other laws in connection with accidents
- Maintaining files of accident reports
- Transmitting accident information to other agencies
- Making information obtained available to persons involved and others who may be concerned.

Accident data collection begins when police are informed of an accident by an involved driver or someone else. If it is a minor accident and some time has elapsed, police may do no more than receive the driver's report and file it. However, if the accident has just occurred and appears to be serious, one or more police officers are dispatched to the scene. Here, after attending to urgent matters connected with the emergency, they begin to gather information. How far this information collection is pursued depends on one or more of six circumstances:

1. The form provided for gathering information
2. Instructions relating to gathering information in addition to that needed for the form
3. Equipment provided
4. The interest, experience, and energy of the officer
5. Favorable or unfavorable conditions
6. Time available.

Primary data collection routinely includes data for the basic accident report form (Level 1 of accident investigation). But, because further instructions are generally not specific, the extent of supplementary data collection at the scene (Level 2 of accident investigation), if any, depends mainly on the judgment of the investigator. He will decide, for example, whether to make measurements and take photographs.

Subsequent data collection (follow-up investigation) depends almost entirely on what additional data the investigator's supervisor wants after primary data have been reviewed. If no enforcement action is anticipated, no further data may be collected. If enforcement action appears to be warranted, a decision is made as to whether additional information will be needed and if so what kind. Then the investigation moves into technical preparation of data for further use in connection with that particular accident (Level 3 of accident investigation). The same investigator or other investigators may carry the work forward, depending on the capabilities and availability of investigators.

In important and complicated prosecutions, reckless homicide for example, direction of the investigation usually is assumed by a prosecuting attorney who makes additional arrangements for data collection and interpretation. The kind of information developed at this stage depends on the nature of the charges and peculiar circumstances of the accident.

Police Policy

Policies of one kind or another guide police traffic-accident investigation. Policies may be clearly written guides to action, thoughtfully prepared and conforming to applicable standards as they apply to a specific situation. Standards[4,8,9,10] already reviewed, can serve as useful guides. However, these guides are stronger on describing what general kinds of activity might be undertaken than on how the work should be done; in other words, they are better policy guides than procedure specifications. For example, they provide that measurements shall be made at the scene of an accident, but do not specify in detail what measurements need to be made or how they shall be made. These details can properly be left to training manuals.

The accident investigation program in police departments is too often unplanned. After adopting a report form and issuing it to patrolmen, little else is done. The extent of information obtained in addition to that required for the form (for example, measurements and photos) is left largely to the individual investigator. Yet, decisions are needed about exactly what must be done in the investigation to comply with legal requirements, to meet national standards, and to serve specific needs of various agencies. Decisions must also be made to avoid collecting data that will not be used. In all these decisions, the police effort allocated to accident investigation must be weighed against that needed for other purposes. *All* police responsibilities must be met as well as possible with available resources. Thus, detailed decisions are required concerning how much can actually be done in connection with the many accident investigation activities that must, should, or may be undertaken.

A program for traffic-accident investigation should be largely tailor-made for each department because the needs, resources, and capabilities of police agencies differ significantly. Urban police departments, for example, can train all patrolmen to handle an accident situation immediately after it occurs with the expectation that more highly skilled officers can be dispatched to carry on in more complex cases; but on rural freeways and other remote roads, police patrols must generally be trained and equipped to carry at-scene investigation to completion. Appropriating a program ready-made from some other organization is likely to result in misfit operations.

Matters of policy vary widely according to requirements of departments and the degree to which administrators are concerned with accident investigation. Laws and ordinances may definitely establish some policies. Other policy matters, such as the following, are usually within the purview of an administrator:

- *Degree of specialization* of investigators. Will some investigators be trained and equipped to conduct more complete and technical investigation than others, or will all investigators carry out the same kind of activity? Will there be special accident investigation squads?
- *Classification of accidents for investigation.* Will all accidents receive the same degree of investigation, and, if not, exactly how does the investigator determine the extent of his investigation?
- *Extent of investigation* for each class of accident. Exactly what data are needed in the way of information for each class of accident? What training and equipment will be provided to obtain this information?
- *Use of experts* and technicians. Under what circumstances can an investigator obtain technical assistance from photographers, surveyors, mechanics, physicists, physicians?
- *Arrangements for photographs.* If photographs are required, does the department provide cameras and film, does the department contract with a professional photographer, or does the investigator provide his own camera and film? If photographs are not requried by the department, may the investigator make them with his own equipment, and if so, what arrangements are there for obtaining copies for official use if needed? May the investigator sell his photos to newspapers and attorneys?
- *Availability of information.* How and under what circumstances may various people (reporters, people involved, attorneys) see and obtain copies of the official reports of the accident, and of supplementary data (measurements, photographs, detailed statements)?
- *Filing* reports and other data. How long are accident data kept, by whom, and in what manner? Who has access to such files and under what circumstances can files be removed?
- *Interviews with investigators.* Under what circumstances may investigators be questioned by attorneys, reporters, and others? How is information about specific accidents released and by whom?
- *Training investigators.* How are investigators to be selected and trained? How much training will be provided and how specialized will it be? Will training be conducted within the organization? Will outside instruction be employed, or will investigators be sent outside the department for instructions?
- *Participation in special programs.* Will the department participate in accident data collection for special purposes, for example, supplementary reports on a selected sample of accidents (bilevel investigation) or multidisciplinary team operations? If so, will the department initiate and sponsor such programs, actively participate in them, or only cooperate?

In addition to policies relating to actual investigation (information gathering), additional policies are needed to guide at-scene investigation in associated activities such as giving first aid and relationships to emergency services provided by rescue squads, ambulance operators, tow truck operators, and fire departments. Policies are also needed to guide enforcement in connection with traffic accidents.

Once established, policies are more or less formally reflected in operating guides and, to a degree, in detailed procedure manuals.

Deciding how far to investigate serious and minor accidents is a policy matter which is often neglected by traffic administrators. There are definite advantages in having essentially the same policy apply to accident-investigation programs of various jurisdictions. Hence, the elements of such a policy will be described in some detail here.

Theoretically, specially trained police officers "thoroughly" investigate all traffic accidents or at least all required to be reported by drivers. However, this ideal is not achieved in practice. The time spent on accidents and the information recorded concerning them vary greatly. If "investigate" is defined as having some kind of a record of the accident in file, most accidents known to police are "investigated"; but if "investigate" is defined as determining the cause of the accident, very few are "investigated," because determining the complete combination of contributing factors is so complicated.

In practice, the extent of information gathered by police depends on the seriousness of the accident. Judgments are made as to how much and what kind of information is or may be required. Practices develop, consciously or unconsciously, within a police department that influence these judgments. Individual investigators modify these practices in many ways. This makes it difficult, perhaps impossible, to define exactly what is meant by "investigate" and to determine when an "investigation" is complete. Traffic-accident investigation is not defined — at least not adequately defined — by law, by standards, or by professional associations. As a rule, traffic-accident investigation begins with basic reporting and is carried as far for a particular accident as special interest in that accident demands and available time or resources permit.

Two traditional guides for the police accident investigator are usually provided to indicate the extent of information to be collected: 1) the accident report form for basic data collection (accident investigation Level 1); and 2) prosecutors' requests for special information in connection with case preparation for a particular accident (Level 3).

A third policy guide specifying supplementary data to be collected at the scene (Level 2) is in the IACP *Model Police Traffic Services*[9] procedures. The examples given here conform to that standard in general.

Essentially, this guide classifies accidents in three categories and describes for each the kind of information the investigator is expected to obtain.

The three categories of accidents are as follows:

1. *Class A.* Any accident involving apparently fatal injuries as determined at the scene, or involving a bus, ambulance, school bus, police vehicle, or highway department vehicle with incapacitating injury to any person. An accident causing destructive damage to major structures or equipment such as bridges, buildings, high tension wires, or water hydrants.

2. *Class B.* Incapacitating injury ("Any injury other than a fatal injury which prevents the injured person from walking, driving, or normally continuing the activities he was capable of performing before the injury occurred."[4]) and disabling damage ("Road vehicle damage which precludes departure of the vehicle from the scene of the accident in its usual operating manner by daylight after minor repairs;[4]).

3. *Class C.* All other accidents reported or attended by police. Data collection *at the scene* must, in general, reflect the *probable* need for information concerning the specific class of accident attended. Later, decisions can be made as to what additional data may be needed. Investigators need instructions such as those in the following paragraphs to guide them in initial data collection.

Data collection for Class C accidents is intended only to obtain basic information required for a simplified form. This information is obtained mainly from drivers and others involved. An investigator at the scene obtains and records the information while he is there; if the accident is reported by phone, he gets as much of the information as possible and records it as it is obtained. If a person appears at the station, he is asked to fill out the form which is then reviewed and completed. No special effort such as a letter or phone call is required to complete or verify data. If reports of the same accident are received from two different people at different times, they are fastened together.

Data collection for Class B accidents is intended to get data required by the basic form plus that required by forms for any special data-collection programs being conducted. The investigator is expected to be at the scene of the accident and to record most of the information while there. For a Class B accident, information in addition to that required for the form or forms is obtained for each driver:

- Where the trip began
- Intended trip destination
- Trip purpose
- Where the driver was when he first became aware that he might be involved in an accident
- What called this to his attention

- What the driver did or attempted to do about it.

If a pedestrian is involved, the same information is obtained for him. If a driver cannot be interviewed at the scene, the information is obtained from another occupant of the car if there is one.

The investigator finds out whether any vehicle or body was moved before he arrived at the scene. If it was not moved or if it can be determined where it was before it was moved, this position is located by measurement.

The investigator looks for results of the accident (physical indications) on the road and roadside. He establishes the location by measurement of any which are impermanent (tiremarks, liquid spatter, debris).

Every driver is observed for signs of being under the influence of alcohol or drugs. If there is reason to believe that a driver or pedestrian had been drinking, a chemical test is administered. Each vehicle is examined for signs of drinking in it such as alcoholic beverage containers.

Data collection for Class A accidents is the same as for Class B with some additions.

Photographs are made of final positions of vehicles, damage to vehicles, and physical signs of the accident on the road.

Preliminary field examinations of lamps and tires are made.

Vehicles are examined for signs of road and fixed-object contact such as abrasion, roll-over, and collapse. These are matched with marks on the vehicle if possible. Tiremarks on roads are matched with tires on vehicles that made them if possible.

If the investigator is present when damaged vehicles are removed, this operation is observed and additional tire or other marks made on the road by removal are noted. Which wheels of the vehicles, if any, will not rotate because of damage is also noted.

Divided duties may be useful at the scene of an accident when more than one investigator is available.

The most common arrangement for division of work lets qualified people make needed measurements or photographs. These may be police specialists, professional photographers, or engineers.

Further investigation. Do not infer from the foregoing outline of information gathering at the scene that an investigation goes no further. The investigation can be halted then, perhaps temporarily. But police or others may continue inquiry by additional technical preparation for some kind of litigation.

Program Evaluation

Judging the effectiveness of police traffic-accident investigation is difficult. Measures of accomplishment are still under development, encouraged and financially supported by the National Highway Traffic Safety Administration. These measures must be planned to reflect the degree to which specified goals are approached:

Maximize
- "Officer participation, when needed, in adjudication resulting from traffic enforcement"
- Accuracy and uniformity of definitions so that data can be interpreted and questions answered
- "Extent to which enforcement action is taken whenever adequate evidence is present to support action"
- At-scene investigations made for fatal and personal injury accidents, or where a hit-and-run accident is involved.
- "Feedback and use of information gained regarding accident patterns, contributing factors, and accident-investigation principles and procedures"
- "Identification and apprehension of drivers leaving

the scene without fulfillig their legal responsibilities"
- "Extent to which persons involved in accidents are provided adequate information concerning their rights and responsibilities"
- "Officer participation, when needed, in civil and criminal adjudication resulting from accident investigation"
- "Preservation of human life at accident scenes through immediate emergency care and the provision for speedy transportation to medical trauma centers"

Facilitate
- "Minor accident resolution by insuring that required reports are completed and appropriate information exchanged by parties involved."

Minimize
- "Time required to clear accident scenes and restore them to normal conditions"
- "Potential for further injury or property loss through additional accidents occurring as a result of the primary accident."

Nonpolice Investigations

Claim investigations. Civil law suits are initiated: 1) by reports made by individuals involved to their insurers, who assign the matter to a claim investigator; or 2) by an injured person visiting a plaintiff's attorney who may look into the matter himself or assign it to a technical investigator working for him. Such nonpolice investigation is rarely at the scene because the investigators employed usually do not learn about the accident until after signs of what happened there have been removed or obliterated. Claim investigators attempt to find out how far police have

carried the investigation and then continue the investigation from that point, possibly examining the site and the damaged vehicles, taking statements of informants (participants and witnesses), and ordering whatever measurements and photographs seem desirable. If this subsequent investigation goes far enough, its supervision is eventually assumed by attorneys. Attorneys dealing with specific issues in particular accidents can usually be reasonably definite regarding what they want to know about an accident.

Relation to police. Claim investigators must discover what information police have about the accident for two reasons: 1) police may have the only available information of the situation at the scene after the accident and this information may be critical in determining how the accident occurred; and 2) they want to know, as soon as possible, how their own observations and conclusions compare with those of police investigators, so that unexpected and embarrassing discrepancies will not develop. Claim investigators naturally make use of any police information available to them, therefore, they must be fully prepared either to carry on from where police left off or to start at the beginning if police have no useful information or it is not available to them. In any case, claim investigators gather virtually no information for statistical or accident prevention purposes; their efforts are directed at specific aspects of each individual accident.

Research investigations. Attempts to discover how and why certain kinds of accidents occur and how people are injured in accidents require much more information than is customarily collected. Therefore, special research programs of many kinds have been established. Data collection for these projects may be based on special police reports or on data collected by others, sometimes by "multidisciplinary" teams of investigators. Few of these projects are undertaken solely by police departments.

As early as 1930 some research studies were made. Most of these were for traffic engineering purposes; but at least one team study, which focused on driver problems, was conducted at about that time. A number of "interdisciplinary" team projects were conducted in the U.S. and Europe beginning about 1960. With U. S. Government financing, a considerable number of these projects were under way by 1970, mostly using people connected with university medical and engineering colleges. These independent projects were not sufficiently uniform to permit satisfactory combination of data from them. To remedy this matter, the National Highway Safety Administration started a highly structured National Accident Sampling System (NASS)[11] that features especially trained and supervised units in scientifically selected locations. This sytem was operational by 1979.

8. SOURCES

Contributors

This Topic was developed by the following persons:

J. Stannard Baker, the author, is a traffic engineer specializing in accident investigation. He was Director of Research and Development at the Traffic Institute, Northwestern University from 1946 to 1971 and is a guest lecturer for the Traffic Institute.

Roy Lucke, of the Traffic Institute Research Division, assisted in preparation of material relating to standards.

References

Superscript numbers in the preceding pages refer to the following publications:

1. Baker, J. Stannard and Declan McIlraith. *Tire Disablements Followed by Accidents among Four-tired Vehicles on the Illinois Tollway* (Tire Study 4), 1968, The Northwestern University Traffic Institute, Evanston IL 60204 (74 pages)

2. Baker, J. Stannard. *Traffic Accident Investigation Manual for Police* (Section 54), 1960, The Northwestern University Traffic Institute, Evanston IL 60204

3. *Uniform Vehicle Code and Model Traffic Ordinance.* National Committee on Uniform Traffic Laws and Ordinances, Washington DC (Order from P.O. Box 1409, Evanston IL 60204)

4. *Manual on Classification of Motor Vehicle Traffic Accidents* (ANSI D 16.1 - 1983), National Safety Council, Chicago IL 60611 (43 pages)

5. *Accident Investigation and Reporting* (Highway Safety Program Standard 18), 1978, National Highway Traffic Safety Administration, U.S. Department of Transportation, Washington DC 20590 (4 pages)

6. *Traffic Records* (Highway Safety Program Standard 10), 1972, National Highway Traffic Safety Administration, U.S. Department of Transportation, Washington DC 20590 (2 pages)

7. *Police Traffic Services* (Highway Safety Program Standard 15), 1978, National Highway Traffic Safety Administration, U.S. Department of Transportation, Washington DC 20590 (2 pages)

8. *Model Police Traffic Services* (Policies), 1976, International Association of Chiefs of Police, 13 Firstfield Rd., Gaithersburg MD 20878

9. *Model Police Traffic Services* (Procedures) 1976, International Association of Chiefs of Police, 13 Firstfield Rd., Gaithersburg MD 20878 (297 pages)

10. *Standards for Law Enforcement Agencies* (Chapter 63), 1983, Commission on Accreditation for Law Enforcement Agencies, 4242B Chain Bridge Road, Fairfax VA 22030

11. *The National Accident Sampling System,* Volume 1, (DOT HS 804 027) 1979, National Highway Traffic Administration, Washington DC 20590 (25 pages)

Exhibits

The following are sources of tables and charts used in this publication: Baker, J. Stannard, Glencoe IL
Chart: 1
Tables: 2, 3

PREPARATION FOR TRAFFIC-ACCIDENT INVESTIGATION

Topic 812 of the *Traffic-Accident Investigation Manual*

by
J. Stannard Baker

NORTHWESTERN UNIVERSITY TRAFFIC INSTITUTE

PUBLICATION HISTORY

1940 *Accident Investigation Manual* (Part of Chapter 6)
Reprinted 1941, 1942

1946 Revised (Part of Chapter 7) Reprinted 1947, 1948

1953 *Traffic Accident Investigator's Manual* (Sections 12, 13, 16)

1954 Revised (Sections 12, 13, 15, 16)

1957 *Traffic Accident Investigator's Manual for Police* (Sections 12 through 16)
Reprinted 1959

1963 Revised (Sections 13 through 16)
Reprinted 1964, 1965, 1966, 1969, 1970, 1971, 1973

1970 *Manual de Investigacion de Accidentes de Trafico* (Sections 13 through 16)

1975 *Traffic Accident Investigation Manual* (Chapter 3)
Reprinted 1976, 1979

1985 *Preparation for Traffic-Accident Investigation*

PREPARATION FOR TRAFFIC-ACCIDENT INVESTIGATION

Whoever hopes to succeed in an activity as diverse and complex as traffic-accident investigation must expect to put effort into preparation. The nature of this preparation will depend on who is doing it and for what aspect of investigation. In this topic, preparation will be discussed as it relates to

1. Organizational preparation: what steps the administrator must expect to take to make the accident-investigation program successful
2. Forms and files which must be made ready for data collection
3. Investigator preparation, especially training needed
4. Planning at-scene investigations.

1. ORGANIZATIONAL PREPARATION

Police departments, especially, need to prepare for traffic-accident investigation for three reasons:

1. Many other agencies and individuals depend on police to conduct at least the at-scene investigation.
2. Accident investigation is important to traffic law enforcement, because it can indicate where, when, and what kind of traffic law enforcement will probably be most effective.

3. Inept investigation can seriously impair the value of the effort expended and so squander valuable police resources.

Once policies have been established, especially with respect to exactly what kind of information should be obtained for accidents of various degrees of severity, the program must be put in operation. This involves a number of activities:

- Write a guide for investigators describing what to do and what not to do to conform to policies which apply to them.
- Prepare manuals describing in detail procedures for investigating traffic accidents.
- Delegate responsibility for implementing and evaluating the program.
- Provide necessary equipment, including forms.
- Train and supervise investigators.

The material in this and other topics relating to traffic-accident investigation is designed to be helpful in this organizational preparation.

Some matters requiring special administrative decisions will be mentioned here because they do not fit well with other parts of this topic.

Sometimes several patrol cars are dispatched or otherwise arrive at the scene of a serious accident. These may represent more than one police agency—for example, a state highway patrol and a county sheriff's department. Confusion may result and efforts may be duplicated. For example, a witness may be questioned by more than one investigator or some operations may be neglected, each investigator assuming that someone else is attending to it.

Standards for Law Enforcement Agencies[1] call for "written directives" governing accident-scene responsibilities for the "first officer to respond" and "procedure for determining the officer or investigator who is in charge at the accident scene." Developing such directives may require cooperation among agencies which might be involved.

Photography is another matter which requires special administrative consideration. Specific policies are needed regarding who is responsible for taking pictures, for what kind of accidents, and also who may have copies and under what conditions.

2. PROGRAMS FOR SPECIAL DATA COLLECTION

In addition to collecting standard information about traffic accidents, some investigators may be involved in programs for special data collection. These programs are designed to produce additional data on special aspects of accidents, such as injuries to persons, tire disablements, collapse in collisions, safety belt usage, or single vehicle accidents. The investigator conducting the special study designs forms that he uses himself or has someone else use to obtain data for him. The forms are employed for specific kinds of accidents in a specified area or route for a limited time. The data so obtained are studied in detail. These special programs are varied in nature depending on who wants the information and why it is needed, but most fall into one of three categories:

1. Bilevel reporting in which additional information is obtained on some special aspect of all accidents (or every fifth or tenth accident) investigated by police. The name "bilevel" means that the accident is investigated to the ordinary first (reporting) level in the usual way and then at a second, more intensive level for special purposes. The data required are recorded on a special form which supplements the basic accident report. Such investigations might involve examining a sample of accidents to obtain data on use of occupant restraint systems, trip plan, driver occupation, evasive tactics, or any other items for which more detail might be required.

2. Special circumstance investigation involves more detailed data collection for accidents which involve a particular event or condition. Forms supplementing the basic report specify exactly what additional data are needed. Investigators usually receive appropriate training and sometimes special equipment for the purpose. Such studies involve all or as many as possible of the accidents meeting specified requirements. Studies of this kind have involved forms to collect additional data on

how people receive fatal injuries in traffic accidents, single-vehicle accidents on interstate routes, accidents after which a tire is disabled, and others.

3. "Team" investigations are undertaken by two or more people from different professions such as policemen, physicians, highway engineers, automotive engineers, psychologists, and lawyers. These are sometimes called "multidisciplinary teams." Some of these teams examine only serious accidents, others only certain kinds of accidents. Some teams specialize in one aspect of an accident situation, others do not. All use supplementary forms, selecting the appropriate ones for use in a particular accident. These forms are the basis for data collection. The National Accident Sampling System (NASS)[11] is a U.S. Department of Transportation continuing effort to apply team data collection on a scientific, nationwide basis.

3. FORMS

Traffic-accident report forms are part of an investigator's equipment. Forms should reflect department policies on data collection, not control policy. A basic report form is used for recording routine data. Such data, even in simplified form, are adequate for minor accidents, perhaps eight out of ten accidents; but in the case of fatal and other severe accidents, data on the basic form must be supplemented by additional information such as photographs and measurements.

Purposes

Standard items of information concerning common situations, such as traffic accidents, today are generally first recorded on forms. Later,

the information may be transferred to some kind of data storage and processing equipment or summarized for publication.

Forms are instruments for data collection in accident investigation. As such they have important advantages over other possible data collection methods:

- The form itself specifies the exact data to be recorded.
- A minimum of writing is required to record the information.
- Recorded information is organized in a standardized display so that specific items can be located quickly in the report.
- Information to be classified can be recorded at once by categories, thus simplifying transfer and tabulation of data.
- Storage and retrieval of collected information is simplified.

Specific or individually important items, like time of day or age of driver, are readily recorded on forms. These are generally factual and unqualified statements or observations. Forms are easily designed to accommodate them.

Narrative and argumentative information, on the other hand, is difficult to accommodate on forms because it consists of closely connected and interrelated parts that cannot be readily separated and entered in blank space on a form.

Accident reporting, which collects minimum factual information for statistical tabulation and other mass uses, is easily accommodated by forms. Forms can also be developed to record observations, measurements, and other supplementary data needed at the technical follow-up level of accident investigation. Such forms may require many pages. They may be designed to record data on particular elements involved in the accident, for example, damage to the vehicle, injuries to people, or road conditions.

Accident reconstruction, cause

analysis, and other conclusions, inferences, and opinions, on the other hand, do not lend themselves well to standardized, organized presentation. Therefore, the branch of the accident investigation process which deals with individual accidents in great detail is not readily adaptable to recording data on forms.

Limitations of forms for traffic-accident data collection must not be overlooked. By specifying what information is needed, forms tend, in most investigations, to stifle further inquiry. When the form is filled in, the investigation is finished; there is no more to be done. This may be acceptable insofar as routine mass data collection is concerned, but will not suffice for inquiry into how and why a specific accident occurred.

Consider, for instance, attempts to develop forms for obtaining information from a driver involved in an accident. When such forms list the questions that should be asked and provide a place to record an answer, they are a great help to an untrained and unimaginative investigator. He gets the information required. But no one can anticipate, in designing such a form, all the circumstances of every possible accident.

In questioning a driver, the skillful and imaginative inquirer may have a few routine questions, such as those concerning identification of the road location, vehicles, and people involved; but his really important insights come when one piece of information leads to another, a process which has not yet successfully been reduced to the act of filling out a form.

Highly structured forms, those in which most of the information is recorded by marking listed items, tend to discourage the recording of unusual circumstances and precise descriptions. A largely structured form simplifies the investigator's work and expedites statistical tabulations of the data; but it tends to obscure fine distinctions and unusual circumstances that are not listed on the form. For detailed study of an individual accidents, structured information usually proves to be inadequate.

Basic Form

Standard forms. As of 1984, no national standard accident-reporting form had been developed. None of the standards relating to accident investigation and accident records[2,3,4,5,] provide a model, much less a standard.

The desirability of a standard form is overemphasized. True, a standard form would avoid the need for decisions in form design about what data are needed, how information is to be used and how it is to be recorded. But avoiding the decisions tends toward pointless data collection of which there is probably already too much. Furthermore, encouraging use of a standard form, and especially rewarding agencies for doing so or penalizing them for using other forms, definitely discourages design of forms that

1. Secure data which will certainly be used
2. Avoid collecting data which nobody uses
3. Are well coordinated with other forms and data processing equipment.

Data standards are more important than form standards. They specify performance objectives for information gathering rather than the instrument for data collection. Standards [2,3,4,] specify directly or indirectly what data are needed for coordinated traffic-accident record systems. It is up to the agency using the data to develop the form on which it is recorded.

State laws and federal standards, explicitly or implicitly, now provide that a state department furnish forms for all agencies making initial reports of motor-vehicle trafficway accidents as part of a statewide traffic-records system. Most states supply a form for driver's traffic-accident report. Larger cities often develop a similar form for their own police reports. Such forms must present data in a manner compatible with the state traffic records system.

The basic police traffic-accident report form, typically, is highly structured (organized) for recording identifying and descriptive data; but unstructured spaces are provided for an explanatory diagram and to "describe what happened."

A design for a basic police report form for fatal and other serious accidents is illustrated in Exhibit 1. This design exemplifies a number of considerations in traffic-accident form design. This form

- Identifies and describes the road, the vehicles and the people involved.
- Provides data for tabulations corresponding to the *Manual on Classification of Motor Vehicle Traffic Accidents.*[2]
- Describes damage and injury to the extent that they may be determined at the scene of the accident.
- Calls for enough information on movement of traffic units to permit preparation of collision diagrams of high accident locations.
- Summarizes after-accident operations such as transportation of injured, removal of disabled vehicles, and contemplated enforcement action.

As it should be, this form is limited to a record of strictly factual information. No opinions as to how or why the accident happened or who was at fault are required. Such speculations are matters for other documents. Consequently, there need be no limitations as to who might have access to the report.

For facility in handling and filing, this design calls for only a single, letter-size sheet. For convenient data entry at the scene, it is laid out so that all easily forgotten information, such as names and numbers, are on one side. This achieves a minimum of turning over in use. In practice, the detailed items can be number-coded to assist in transcribing for tabulating.

POLICE TRAFFIC-ACCIDENT REPORT

USE SHORT FORM FOR CLASS C ACCIDENT

☐ CLASS A ACCIDENT
☒ CLASS B ACCIDENT

ACCIDENT NO. S-08 85   Do not write in this space

FIRST HARMFUL EVENT

ROAD OR STREET: **ON CAMPBELL** (W)N S E **AT 15** FT MI (W)N S E OF JUNCTION OR LANDMARK **ELEANOR** OR HOUSE OR MILEPOST NO.

CITY OR COUNTY: **IN LESTER**   STATE **NM**   HOUR OF DAY **22:15**   DAY OF WEEK **WED**   DAY OF MONTH **12**   MONTH **FEB**   **19 85**

☐ AT INTERSECTION ☐ INTERSECTION RELATED ☐ ON ROADWAY ☐ OVERTURNING → ☐ PEDESTRIAN ☐ RR VEHICLE ☐ ANIMAL
☐ DRIVEWAY ACCESS ☐ NONJUNCTION ☐ ON SHOULDER ☐ OTHER NONCOLLISION → ☐ MV IN TRANSPORT ☐ PEDACYCLE ☐ FIXED OBJECT
☐ OFF ROADWAY COLLISION WITH → ☐ PARKED MV ☐ OTHER OBJECT

☐ INTERSTATE ☐ COUNTY ROAD ☐ BICYCLE TRAIL ☐ SHARE ROAD ☒ FATAL INJURY ☐ POSSIBLE ☒ DISABLING DAMAGE ☐ OTHER
☐ U.S. ROUTE ☒ CITY STREET ☐ INCAPACITATING ☐ NONINJURY NONE
☐ STATE ROUTE ☐ ALL OTHER ☐ BICYCLE LANE ☐ NONBIKEWAY ☐ NONINCAPACITATING EVIDENT ☐ FUNCTIONAL DAMAGE ☒

Unit 1	Unit 2	KIND OF ROAD
		1.One lane, alley
X	X	2.Two lanes
		3.Three lanes
		4.Four or more
		5.Divided roadway One-way street
		6.Expressway Toll road
		7.Unpaved, any width

KIND OF LOCATION
1. Apartments Stores, factories
X 2.One-family homes
3.Not built up, rural

Unit 1	Unit 2	ROAD CHARACTER Mark two or three
X	X	1.Level
		2.On grade
		3.On hill crest
		1.Straight road
		2.Curve
		3.Sharp curve
		4.Merging lane
		5.Tunnel or bridge

ACCESS CONTROL
1.Full control
2.Other

WEATHER
X 1.Clear
2.Raining
3.Snowing
4.Fog
5.Other

Unit 1	Unit 2	ROAD SURFACE
X	X	1.Dry
		2.Wet
		3.Snowy or icy
		4.Other

LIGHT
1.Daylight
2.Dawn or dusk
X 3.Darkness

Unit 1	Unit 2	TRAFFIC CONTROL
		1.Stop sign
		2.Stop-and-go signal
		3.Yeild sign
		4.Barrier Line
		5.Officer or watchman
		6.RR gates, signals
		7.Other control
X	X	8.No control

SOURCES OF INFORMATION: **AT-SCENE INVESTIGATION**

PHOTOS MADE BY ——   MEASUREMENTS MADE BY **WILLIAMS**   SUPPLEMENTARY SHEETS **NONE**

ARRESTED OR CITED Name **NONE**   Offense

REPORT BY-Signature **Harald Williams**   Date **13**   Month **FEB 19 85**

BADGE-No. **35**   District or Department **LESTER PD**

TIME NOTIFIED - Hour **12:18**   Date **12**   Month **2-1985**   APPROVED BY **Kelso**

ARRIVED AT SCENE Hour **22:26**   Day **12**   Month **2**   DATE **15 FEB 1985**

DIAGRAM OF ROAD LAYOUT AND FINAL POSITIONS OF TRAFFIC UNITS INVOLVED

SHOW NORTH BY ARROW

SUMMARY OF STATEMENTS AND OTHER COMMENTS

DRIVER: I was turning right from westbound on Eleanor to northbound on Campbell. Pedestrian on corner ran into my trailer and was knocked down

PEDESTRIAN: I was standing on northwest corner about to cross Campbell when car cut corner in right turn and its trailer knocked me down. My head hit the curb.

ti
The Traffic Institute
Northwestern University

Exhibit 1. *Statewide basic traffic-accident report forms provide data for statistical and administrative purposes.*

INJURY CODE: 0 = None; 1 = Possible; 2 = Nonincapacitating; 3 = Incapacitating; 4 = Fatal

TRAFFIC UNIT NO. 1 — Total Persons in Unit: 2

DRIVER-Print or type full name	ADDRESS-Number and Street	City and State		ARREST, CITED	AGE	SEX	INJURY
APPERSON, DONALD, WILLIAM	3725 PARKER ST., TRENTON,	NM					0

OWNER-Print or type full name	ADDRESS-Number and Street	City and State
SAME		

VEHICLE REMOVED BY-Name	TO-Location
DRIVER	HOME

FRONT CENTER-Name	ADDRESS-Number and Street	City and State	AGE	SEX	INJURY

FRONT RIGHT					
APPERSON, EARNEST WILLIAM	805 STEWART AV ELNIGRO	NM	24	M	0

REAR LEFT

REAR CENTER

REAR RIGHT

LICENSE-Type	DRIVER LICENSE -No.	STATE	REGISTRATION-No.	STATE	YEAR	ODOMETER
O P	3 25-84-7281	NM	723051	NM	85	16703

RESTRICTIONS	BIRTH-Date Month Year	VEHICLE IDENTIFICATION NO.	Year model 19

MARK DAMAGE CODE ON EACH DAMAGE AREA — 16 UNDERSIDE

HEADED (N W E S)

- [X] STEADY
- [ ] SPEED UP
- [ ] SLOW DOWN
- [ ] STANDING
- [ ] PARKED
- [ ] BACK UP
- [ ] STRAIGHT
- [ ] L TURN
- [X] R TURN
- [ ] L CURVE
- [ ] R CURVE
- [ ] U TURN
- [X] OVERTAKING
- [ ] OVERTAKEN
- [ ] INTO ROADWAY
- [ ] LEAVING RDWY
- [ ] LOADING
- [ ] OTHER

MAKE	MODEL	SIZE
OLDSMOBILE	88	FULL

- [X] TRAILER
- [ ] NO TRAILER (Details below)
- [ ] Motorcycle
- [X] Automobile
- [ ] Bus
- [ ] Light truck
- [ ] Single unit truck
- [ ] Truck tractor
- [ ] Truck Combination
- [ ] Other motor vehicle

- 3.[ ] DISABLING
- 2.[ ] FUNCTIONAL
- 1.[ ] OTHER
- 0.[X] NONE

TRAFFIC UNIT NO. 2 — Vehicle or Pedestrian — Total Persons in Unit: 2

DRIVER-Print or type full name	ADDRESS-Number and Street	City and State		ARREST, CITED	AGE	SEX	INJURY
[X] PEDESTRIAN PARKER, ROGER MILLS	821 ELEANOR ST, LESTER	NM			73	M	2

OWNER-Print or type full name	ADDRESS-Number and Street	City and State

VEHICLE REMOVED BY-Name	TO-Location

FRONT CENTER-Name	ADDRESS-Number and Street	City and State	AGE	SEX	INJURY

FRONT RIGHT

REAR LEFT

REAR CENTER

REAR RIGHT

LICENSE-Type	DRIVER LICENSE -No.	STATE	REGISTRATION-No.	STATE	YEAR	ODOMETER

RESTRICTIONS	BIRTH-Date Month Year	VEHICLE IDENTIFICATION NO.	Year model 19

MARK DAMAGE CODE ON EACH DAMAGE AREA — 16 UNDERSIDE

HEADED (N W E S)

- [X] STEADY
- [ ] SPEED UP
- [ ] SLOW DOWN
- [ ] STANDING
- [ ] PARKED
- [ ] BACK UP
- [X] STRAIGHT
- [ ] L TURN
- [ ] R TURN
- [ ] L CURVE
- [ ] R CURVE
- [ ] U TURN
- [ ] OVERTAKING
- [ ] OVERTAKEN
- [X] INTO ROADWAY
- [ ] LEAVING RDWY
- [ ] LOADING
- [ ] OTHER

MAKE	MODEL	SIZE

- [ ] TRAILER
- [ ] NO TRAILER (Details below)
- [ ] Motorcycle
- [ ] Automobile
- [ ] Bus
- [ ] Light truck
- [ ] Single unit truck
- [ ] Truck tractor
- [ ] Truck Combination
- [ ] Other motor vehicle

- 3.[ ] DISABLING
- 2.[ ] FUNCTIONAL
- 1.[ ] OTHER
- 0.[ ] NONE

TOTAL UNITS INVOLVED

PROPERTY DAMAGED-Other than vehicles	Nature of Damage	OWNER-Name and address

WITNESSES OTHER THAN OCCUPANTS

NAME	ADDRESS-Number and Street	City and State	SEX	AGE
MASON, CHARLES F	1278 STOWE ST LESTER	NM	M	41

FIRST AID BY-Name	INJURED TAKEN TO
1 RESCUE SQUAD	A CENTRAL HOSPITAL
FIRST AID BY 2	INJURED TAKEN TO B

MOST SERIOUS INJURY
- [ ] NONE
- [ ] POSSIBLE
- [X] NONINCAPACITATING
- [ ] INCAPACITATING
- [ ] FATAL

TRAILER - Registration No.	State	Trailer Make	Size	Body	Use
7325	NM	NON COMMERCIAL	2 WHEEL	½ BOX	PRIVATE

- [X] STAYED HITCHED
- [ ] BROKE LOOSE
- [ ] EMPTY
- [ ] PART LOAD
- [ ] FULL LOAD

Simplified Forms

For perhaps eight out of ten traffic accidents, investigation does not go beyond first-level reporting. Much of this information can be, and in many cases is, reported well enough by drivers, especially if the report is on an easily understood form. Actually, in most such accidents, police reports are based largely on driver information.

For these numerous, minor accidents, only part of the basic report form is needed because 1) the accident does not involve significant injuries, towed vehicles, or witnesses in addition to the people involved; and 2) little or no use is made of part of the information specified on the basic form. To simplify police handling of such accidents, driver reports can be used if police do not attend the accident; if police do attend such a minor accident, data collection can be abbreviated for them without noticeable sacrifice in utility of information.

Abbreviated police data collection for these minor accidents can be accomplished in two ways: 1) by indicating on the basic form, data which are not required for minor accidents, and 2) by using a simplified form. The simplified form must, of course, provide for

1. Most data regularly tabulated
2. Data accumulated for traffic engineering purposes
3. Information entered on driver records.

A design for a simplified form meeting these requirements is illustrated in Exhibit 2. Only data on minor injuries and damage are recorded because incapacitating and fatal injuries require the basic form. Vehicle movements can be described in a specific place on the form so that they do not need to be obtained from a diagram or description. Vehicle identification is omitted because it is not tabulated or otherwise specifically us-

ed. In the rare cases in which vehicle identification is needed, it can be obtained later from the driver, who is identified.

The simplest possible report form and procedure for minor accidents has additional advantages. Confronted by what appears to be an elaborate report for a minor accident, drivers and police both tend to avoid reporting such accidents, especially if they involve only one vehicle. Thus the complexity of the form influences the completeness of reporting. Furthermore, if a large percent of accidents can be handled satisfactorily, more quickly, and with less paperwork, there can be a worthwhile saving of valuable police time and records processing.

Supplementary Forms

Perhaps one in ten accidents is sufficiently serious to warrant extended accident investigation. For such accidents, information collected is more

Exhibit 2. *A simplified form can be used for data on accidents not involving a disabled vehicle or incapacitated person.*

extensive than can be accommodated on the basic form and so supplementary documents are required. Some of these, like photographs, field notes of measurements, and statements of participants and other witnesses, cannot be provided by a structured (organized) form. But some observations, descriptions, and comments beyond the scope of the basic form can be readily collected on supplementary forms.

Descriptive data repeatedly collected represent the kinds of information for which supplementary forms can be provided. But whether it is practical to design and reproduce a form depends on how extensive and complex the data are and how frequently a particular item of information has to be collected.

Published supplementary forms are available for the most common purposes:

- *Statement — Traffic*[6]
- *General Vehicle Examination*[7]
- *Motor-Vehicle Lamp Examination Record*[8]
- *Tire Examination Record*[9]
- *Property Taken Into Custody*[10]
- *Alcoholic Influence Report Form*[14]
- *Vehicle Collision Damage Record*[18]

Data frequently collected. Many investigators prepare forms for their own use if they often have to collect certain kinds of data. The form reminds them of facts they must obtain and makes recording the data easy. The same form may be made available for use by a number of investigators. Here are examples:

- A form or table for recording measurements made at the scene of the accident
- Signal-timing record
- Detailed record of injuries, including a diagram of the body on which injured areas are marked. A simple form of this kind may be used by an attending physician; a more detailed form can be used for autopsies.[12]

Special data collection projects, such as the National Accident Sampl-

Highway Transportation Components	Traffic Accident Phases		
	Precrash	Crash	Postcrash
People Involved	1	2	3
Vehicles Involved	4	5	6
Road Environment	7	8	9

Exhibit 3. *Research investigation is classified in nine categories according to elements of highway transportation involved and the phase of the accident.*

ing System (NASS) and some research projects, aim to collect extensive information on many particular aspects of traffic accidents. Much of the data so obtained are accumulated on many pages of highly specialized forms. This is important if the data are to be statistically analyzed.

Special instructions to investigators may be arranged as a form or list of data to be gathered, such as a number of specific measurements to be made of a road location. Such instructions may be different for each accident, depending on circumstances. The person who requires the information, a prosecuting attorney or a highway engineer, for instance, usually knows exactly what he wants, but the investigator who actually obtains the data has to be told.

Systems for Reporting Conclusions

Forms are easily designed for recording specific factual information. Some of these, like the *Motor-vehicle Lamp Examination Record*[8], provide for recording the *indications* of the recorded observations and certain *conclusions* that might be derived therefrom.

Causes of accidents, on the other hand, involve so many interrelationships among contributing factors that forms to describe and classify them have met with little success. The systems for discovering and describing combinations of contributing factors[15] that constitute causes have not yet been sufficiently tested to make forms practical and reliable.

Highway Safety Matrix, although not really a form, serves some of the

purposes of a form in organizing the information collected. The matrix is a rectangular array or table in which vertical columns cross horizontal columns to form cells.

The National Highway Traffic Safety Administration[16] has used this form to classify its own activities, to describe and collate accident circumstances and causative factors. The horizontal rows of this matrix, illustrated in Exhibit 3, represent the three components of the highway transportation system: people, vehicles, and the road environment. People include drivers, passengers, and pedestrians. Vehicles include pedalcycles. The road environment is the highway layout (geometry), surface conditions, traffic control, traffic, weather, light, and other conditions. The vertical columns of the matrix are three time phases in the series of accident events: precrash, crash and postcrash. These three columns and three lines give nine cells. Observations and conclusions developed in a traffic-accident investigation could be recorded in these cells. For instance, driver's strategy (speed and position on the road) and his evasive tactics with all their ramifications are recorded in the "People-precrash" cell Number 1.

4. FILING

Files must be provided for collected accident report forms and other data. This requires coordinated planning among those who need to use the data. Unfortunately storage of accident records is often poorly planned.

A reference number is generally assigned to each accident. This number is put on every item relating to that accident so that all material relating to the event may be kept together. Otherwise some things, such as photos, become misplaced or can only be located by looking in several places for them. This reference number is usually not known at the scene by those who investigate the accident. It is assigned later.

The accident number may be coded to represent all or part of the date. For example, all numbers for 1986 accidents might begin with 86, followed by numbers in sequence of assignment for that year.

Filing by number makes locating a report difficult; almost no one remembers the number of a particular accident. Therefore, a cross-index file of some kind is necessary.

Filing by date of accident has some of the same difficulties as filing by accident number: the exact date has often been forgotten.

Filing by name of someone involved requires a decision as to which of several names will be used and how to cross index the other names. Such cross indexing may double the bulk of the file without making it any more useful.

Filing by location is generally recommended for three reasons:
1. More people can remember where an accident happened than almost any other fact about it.
2. Location files are the easiest way to accumulate data on high-accident locations for traffic engineering and selective enforcement purposes.
3. Generally, location files require less cross indexing.

Location filing requires a set of rules by which a report may be put into storage and located when needed. Usually a report is filed by the name of the road on which it occurred; but there must be a rule to determine how to file a report of an accident which occurred at the junction of two or more roads and how to locate accidents on a road between junctions.

Supplementary Files

Most accidents are represented by a single sheet in the file; but some serious accidents accumulate a bundle of documents. Two or three supplementary sheets can be attached to the accident report, but more than that tends to be troublesome. This can be solved by putting the accident number on all material relating to the accident and filing all but the official report in a numerical file. There it can be located by the number of the official report in the location file or other cross-reference.

Associated data are often quite varied in size: photos, field notes, special forms, and so on. To keep them from spilling out of a file folder, keep them together in a case envelope[13]. The front of the envelope may be printed with a form in which to list the contents of the envelope and make other notes which will permit rapid review of the case. (Exhibit 4)

Regardless of the filing system used, two thing must be provided for: 1) Who may have access to the files; and 2) How long material will be kept there.

Controlling access to the files is important. Otherwise some documents are sure to disappear. Furthermore, there may be policy decisions as to who may see what is available. Certainly any person involved in a traffic accident should be permitted to see the official report and other *factual* data relating to the accident. If the official report is strictly factual, which it should be, there is no good reason why anybody should not see it.

Never let anybody take any original material related to the accident away for any reason. Arrange to have the material copied for whoever is entitled to it. The separate case envelope[13] for photos and other data makes it easier to control who has access to such material than if it were in the more accessible accident report file.

Clearing the file of obsolete material may be governed by administrative regulation or even by law as to how long it must be kept. The statute of limitations relating to litigation may have to be considered in this connection. It is generally easier to remove obsolete material as the files are being used than to try to do it as a special project from time to time, say once a year. In any case, definite rules must be followed. For example, all accident reports may be kept for three years, but reports of fatal and other specified accidents for perhaps twice that long.

5. EQUIPMENT

What tools are needed for information gathering and recording depends on the extent to which accidents are to be investigated. If the only record of even serious accidents is the official traffic-accident report form, no special equipment is needed. Otherwise equipment requirements depend on two things:
1. The extent to which additional information is to be collected both at the scene and as followup
2. How much of the additional information is gathered by police and how much is obtained by others, for example, commercial photographers and insurance investigators.

Some equipment and supplies are essential for obtaining and especially for recording traffic-accident information. However, excellent data collection is possible with a well-trained investigator who has only pencil and paper for notes. Elaborate equipment is no substitue for investigator competence.

Emergency Equipment

The need for such things as fusees and first aid supplies for emergencies depends on facilities of associated agencies such as fire departments, rescue squads, and towing services. Such equipment is beyond the scope of this topic.

Forms

Forms, of course, are basic equipment, especially the official accident report form. Properly structured, a form can, to a limited extent, guide routine data collection. This is very helpful for inexperienced or ill-trained investigators.

A clipboard or other writing surface is usually provided for making notes in the field.

Interviewing requires only pencil and paper for notes. However, tape recorders for this purpose have much to recommend them. They are inexpensive, easy to carry, and simple to use even in the dark, when it is cold, and otherwise under adverse circumstances. Tapes have the clear advantage of recording exactly what was said at the time by the investigator and others. They are often used to record telephone interviews.

Measuring

Minimum equipment for measurements is a tape, preferably 100 ft. long, at least 5/8 in. wide, and made of reinforced fabric or plastic.

Additional equipment for measuring may include

- *A tape rule,* preferably 25 ft. long
- *A measuring wheel,* preferably one with two small wheels
- *Surveyor's pins* or the equivalent
- *Anchor weights,* for holding the end of a tape when you have no helper
- *Material for marking* spots to be located: lumber crayon or aerosal spray paint, preferably orange or yellow
- *Nails and cards* for marking off-road locations
- *A line level* and chalk ("snap") line for measuring grades and horizontal and vertical distances of falls.

Photography

Although good at-scene investigations can be made without pictures,

---

ACCIDENT NUMBER 5355   **CASE, FILE**   DUNBAR v WELCH TRUCKING

No.	Headed Movmnt	SIZE	BODY	SERVICE	YEAR	MAKE	DRIVEN BY	Age Sex	Inj-ury	OWNED BY
1	W ST	3 AX	TRAC°E	COML	₁₉83	IHC	SELIG, WM. B	31 M	B	WELCH TRUCKING
+		52X4W	BOX	"	19	FRUEHF				" "
2	E ST	FULL	2DR HD	Priv	₁₉84	CHEV	DUNBAR, NORBERT	M	A	SAME
-	E ST	COMP	4DR SD	"	₁₉83	FORD	HEINRICH, PAUL	M	O	SAME

ON Street or road   US 45
AT Intersection, etc.
Distance 220 FT Direction W of Exact place IL 37
IN City or town NR STARK County BARBER State IL
Hour 13:30 Day 15 Month 5 19 8 5

	PHOTOGRAPHS OF	No.	NOTES	
SHOWING FINAL POSITIONS	More than one vehicle	3	5 x 8	DWYER
	Vehicle 1 TRACTOR	3	"	"
	Vehicle TRAILER	1	"	"
	Vehicle 2 CHEV	5	"	"
	Vehicle			
SHOWING DAMAGE	Vehicle 2 CHEV	5	8 x 10	ALLEN, PAUL
	Vehicle			
	Vehicle			
	Vehicle			
	Debris and marks on road	4	5 x 8	DWYER
	Road conditions, traffic control			

DATE OPENED	DATE TRIED	JUDGE	DATE CLOSED
18 MAY 85	19 JUL	WATKINS, JOS	21 JUL 85

NAMES	ADDRESSES
BAHENSKY, GERALD Sheriff	COUNTY BLDG FORBES IL 61896
NELSON, STANLEY Assist. Dist. Atty.	"
RAFT, ADAM Def. Atty	306 S MAIN FORBES IL 61896

DATA	SOURCE	REPORTS	SOURCE
Field notes	DWYER, S.E.	Accident report	STATE POLICE DWYER
Map of location	ATKINS, WALTER	Accident map	
Vehicle damage		Hit-run report	
Photo data	DWYER, S.E.	Deficiency report	
IN-QUEST	PETERS, L.G. CORONER	Case summary	

STATEMENT BY	DATE	KIND	
SELIG DRIVER 1	15 JUN	DEP.	NELSON
DUNBAR DRIVER 2	18 JUN	"	"
PARSONS PASSING DRIVER	15 MAY	SUMMARY	DWYER
HEINRICH, PAUL PASSING DRIVER	20 MAY	DETAILED	BAKER

Physical evidence	Located at

Exhibit 4. *A case envelope holds numerous documents other than the official accident report. It is usually filed by case number which connects it with the accident report file. The contents of the envelope and other data may be summarized on the envelope.*

photography has long been an important adjunct to investigation. Photos are an indisputable, permanent record of observations. They even record details that the investigator failed to note. Nothing is better than a photograph for describing damage to vehicles.

Cameras, even the simplest, can take important pictures. Single lens reflex cameras using 35 mm film are most widely preferred. Within the last decade, models which are highly automatic have been developed. They can use a great variety of films for which processing is readily available. Professional photographers may prefer cameras which use larger film that give somewhat sharper pictures.

Film. Fast film is recommended because lighting at the scene of an accident may be poor. ISO 400 film is, perhaps, the most generally useful. Faster films may be difficult to use in bright sunlight. Color print film is more suitable than color slide film or black and white film.

Lenses. A normal focal length (50 mm for 35 mm film) gives a normal perspective. Longer or shorter focal lengths tend to exaggerate distances. Because light is often unfavorable, a fast lens is desirable, for example f/2.8 or better. For special closeup pictures, such as that of a lamp filament, a macro lens is needed.

Shutters do not need to be fast because in traffic-accident photography nothing important is in motion. 1/125 sec is usually fast enough.

Flash equipment is essential for night photos. Because photos at the scene of a traffic accident may need to picture objects at some distance away, strong flash equipment is needed. Flash bulbs have now generally been superseded by strobe equipment.

Filters are rarely needed in traffic-accident investigation, especially if color film is used.

Tripods would be helpful in obtaining sharp pictures, but few traffic-accident investigators want to be bothered with them.

6. TRAINING

Courses

The effectiveness of an investigator at the various levels of traffic-accident investigation depends on his training and experience. Some activities can be learned well enough with practice; but others, like describing marks left on the road by an accident and measuring to locate the results of an accident, require special training. This need is demonstrated by the fact that investigators who have attended a dozen or more fatal accidents continue to make measurements that really locate little or nothing! Training is especially important when information collection cannot be reduced to filling in blanks on a special form.

Instruction in traffic-accident investigation generally corresponds to the various levels of accident investigation.

Accident reporting is strictly fact finding. Because this work is governed by a very detailed traffic-accident report form, only a few hours of instruction are required. For the most part, this instruction emphasizes matters in which the form is not self-explanatory, such as the description of vehicles and the diagram of the accident situation.

At-scene additional data collection, for fatal and other serious accidents, requires much more teaching since forms to guide it in detail are not available. The most important parts of this training are

1. Observing and describing various results of the accident found at the scene, such as tire marks and debris.
2. Measuring at the scenes of traffic accidents. An excellent independent study (correspondence) course[17] is available for this instruction.
3. Photography for traffic-accident investigation.

At-Scene Accident Investigation is the subject of a two-week course at The Traffic Institute, Northwestern University. About half of this time is devoted to describing and measuring results of the accident found at the scene, including some practice in doing this. There is also a special week-long course in accident investigation photography.

Technical followup of traffic accidents requires additional fact finding, such as more detailed examination of the site of the accident and damage to vehicles including that to tires and lamps. Technical followup also requires training in organizing and to a limited extent interpreting data which have been collected; for example, preparation of after-accident situation maps.

Technical Accident Investigation is also the subject of a two-week course at The Traffic Institute. The course includes an introduction to traffic-accident reconstruction.

Traffic-accident Reconstruction, especially, requires training in relating to each other available bits and pieces of information about an accident and applying some basic science, especially dynamics, to interpreting them. Training needed for this work is comparable to that required for other professions. Some training useful for traffic-accident reconstruction is to be had in engineering, psychology, and other conventional college courses. However such college courses do not focus on the peculiar problems of traffic accidents.

The Traffic Institute offers an intensive one-week course in mathematics and dynamics for those requiring it for traffic-accident reconstruction. The Institute also offers a practical two-week course in Traffic-accident reconstruction. In this course applicable principles are briefly reviewed but most of the time is devoted to practice problems in actual reconstruction.

Cause analysis requires further, usually speculative, interpretation of often inadequate data. Because techniques suitable for cause analysis have never been adequately developed, no training is available for this activity.

Experience

Practice is as necessary for accident investigation as it is for first aid or shooting. Taking successful pictures needs as much "target" practice as handling a firearm. There should be practice test skids to measure the slipperiness of various kinds of surfaces, and practice in measuring and photographing skidmarks.

As practice, an afternoon or two spent in an automobile "graveyard" carefully examining recently damaged vehicles to try to determine from what direction they were struck, the extent of damage to structural parts, and whether any part of the vehicle gouged or scratched the pavement, is time profitably spent. Preparing diagrams of damaged vehicles and taking practice photos adds to the effectiveness of the exercise.

Measurements can be practiced by placing chalk marks on the paving in an intersection to represent tiremarks or vehicle position and then making a field sketch locating them.

All of these exercises take time, of course, but such training can make the difference between a skilled and an amateur investigator.

Habits. This is a good place to mention some important habits to form by practice in preparation for accident investigation. Sometimes even otherwise seasoned investigators overlook these simple rules. You need to learn to

- Be specific. Do not guess or estimate if measurements can be made.
- Evaluate what people say and distinguish fact from opinion. One hard fact is worth a score of theories, conclusions, opinions, and inferences.
- Make personal observations and do not expect to learn all about the accident from what people say.
- Write down information at the time and do not depend on memory.
- Write well enough so there will be no need for copying later.
- Take advantage of opportunities to get facts and avoid thinking, "I'll get that later," because later is often too late.

At every step, think about the data you are collecting; and ask, "Is it reasonable?" Consider how you can verify data, especially if information seems questionable for any reason. Then try to obtain the same information from some other person or in some other manner.

Specific Knowledge

Know the territory. It is important to get to the scene of an accident quickly. Therefore, keep handy, as part of your equipment maps, street guides, and other such directional aids. Still better is firsthand knowledge of the roads in the area.

Various organizations are likely to have specific responsibilities with respect to accidents. Learn what and where they are: the location of hospitals, towing services, and fire departments. A list of these, together with telephone numbers, and the hours of the day in which their services are available is helpful, and it is a good idea to become acquainted with some of the people in these organizations.

Acquaintance with specialists who may be able to help in investigating is also desirable. Photographers, surveyors, stenographers can help with taking statements, and the people in street or highway departments who have plots or maps of the locations in detail can be listed or sought out in case they may be needed. The extent to which you can go in enlisting the aid of such people depends on the policies of the organization.

Department policy. If you are dispatched to investigate an accident, follow policies and rules of your department; your supervisor must explain these to you. Sometimes the guidelines are in written form or made part of investigator training.

7. PLANNING AT-SCENE INVESTIGATION

Principles and Problems

Why planning is needed. Often an investigator wishes that he could go back and investigate an accident all over again. He may have neglected to look into an important matter or forgotten a vital activity. These and other mistakes result from lack of planning.

Planning is laying out a course of action or method of accomplishing objectives. Activities necessary to accomplish the objectives are the various techniques of accident investigation discussed in detail elsewhere. Consequently, in planning, decisions are made about what *must* be done, what *should* be done, and what *might* be done. These decisions establish priorities for activities. Planning also determines the sequence of activities. The most important activity is not always the most urgent. Planning a particular at-scene investigation is always difficult because it must be done on extremely short notice, and usually with very limited knowledge of the situation. Also, planning at-scene investigations must be continually adapted to circumstances as the investigation proceeds. Throughout the investigation, tactics planned must be guided by the objectives of investigation and associated tasks (for example, emergency activities).

Five times during investigation at the scene, the situation can be evaluated well enough to plan what to do next. These stages of planning are

1. On learning of the accident
2. On arrival at the scene of the accident
3. When the emergency is under control
4. When urgent data collection is complete
5. When work at the scene is finished

For each of these five stages, Exhibit 5 lists activities to be considered. Activities are listed more or less in the order in which they might be performed.

Exhibit 5

STAGES OF PLANNING AT-SCENE INVESTIGATION

1.   ON LEARNING OF THE ACCIDENT

Ask first,
  Exactly when and where did the accident happen?
  How bad was the accident and what vehicles were involved?
  Did you see the accident happen and where can you be found?

Decide whether to go to the scene.
  Will the scene have been cleared by time of arrival?
  Is it in the investigator's area?
  Should headquarters be informed or consulted?

Then find out, if necessary,
  Is traffic blocked?
  Has ambulance, wrecker, or fire apparatus been called?

Arrange for any needed help.

Start for the scene. With radio, the two previous things can be done while on the way.

Choose best approach. Consider time, possible traffic jams, possible route of drivers involved, and probable situation at the scene of the accident.

Be alert for vehicles leaving the scene as possibly carrying witnesses or hit-and-run drivers. Record registration numbers of any likely looking vehicles.

Look for conditions confronting a driver approaching scene: low visibility, view obstructions, and traffic controls.

Note hazards to approaching traffic. Place fusees, etc.

2.   ON ARRIVAL AT THE SCENE OF THE ACCIDENT

Select a parking place carefully.
  Is it safe? Will it block traffic?
  Can headlights illuminate scene?

Look over bystanders and others for drivers, possible witnesses and volunteer helpers.

Look for fire and electrical hazards. Get them under control.
  Have spilled gasoline guarded.

Look for traffic hazards.
  Put out flares; ask helper to direct traffic.
  Keep bystanders out of roadway.

Look for physical evidence. Have it guarded until it can be examined, collected, or located by measurements.

Look for congestion. Direct traffic or have it directed.

Care for injured.
  Stop arterial bleeding, help injured from vehicles.

Ask for emergency assistance from bystanders or others.

Locate drivers. Consider the possibility of a hit-and-run accident and need to alert headquarters.

Look for witnesses at scene.
  Arrange to question and get names and addresses.
  Note numbers on vehicles at scene as leads to witnesses.

Arrange for clearing roadway. Delay removal of vehicles, except to aid injured, until positions are marked.

3.   WHEN THE EMERGENCY IS UNDER CONTROL

Preliminary questions of drivers:
  Who was driving each vehicle and what was his travel plan?
  Note unpremeditated statements.
  Look for signs of nervousness, confusion, intoxication.

Gather clues for hit-and-run cases.

Question other witnesses, especially bystanders who may be anxious to leave.
  If important, get signed statements at once from any person who may be difficult to find later.

Examine driver condition.
  Look for signs of intoxication and drugs; question about drinking, get specimen for chemical test.
  Question about trip plan for possible fatigue.

Question drivers more fully:
  Check license and registration; record data from them; verify address and identity.
  Get step-by-step account of what driver saw and did.

Observe vehicle condition.
  Note lights, light switches, gear position, and tires.

Photograph tire marks and location of vehicles.

Measure to locate marks on road and vehicle final positions.

Record place to which injured persons and damaged vehicles were or are to be taken.

Have road cleared if traffic is obstructed.

4.   WHEN URGENT DATA-COLLECTION IS COMPLETE

Decide whether proof of violation is sufficient for arrest.
  If so, make arrest or issue citation.

Tell drivers what reports they must make and dismiss them.

Have involved parties exchange names and insurance data.

Determine exact location of accident and record it.

Make test skids, if needed and not possible later.

Complete examination of vehicles.

Make additional photographs:

  View obstructions, vehicle damage, pavement condition.
  Control devices, general views.

Get additional statements from witnesses remaining at scene.

Measure for map if location will be difficult to revisit.

Clean up location or arrange to have it done.

Report to headquarters.

5.   WHEN WORK AT THE SCENE IS FINISHED

Notify relatives of dead or injured and owner of vehicle.

Inform other agencies of conditions needing attention.

Identify all notes with place and title.

Complete factual data on report if not completed at scene.

Complete report. Submit for approval and file.

Present case summary to prosecutor.

Planning begins on first learning of the accident and continues until at-scene activities are complete. Information on which initial planning is based comes at the time you learn that you will have responsibilities at the scene. At this time, obtain as much data as you can about the accident from informants: where the accident occurred; how long ago; what was involved; extent of injury and damage; obstructions to traffic; whether there is fire; whether ambulance, tow truck, fire equipment and other police or investigators have been summoned; and what assistance may be available if needed. On the basis of this information, plan your route to the scene and consider possible things to be done on arrival. As you approach the scene, begin investigation by watching for vehicles that may have passed the scene. Noting their registration numbers may lead to discovery of a witness who otherwise would have been unknown.

Considerations in Planning

Flexibility is necessary. Trying to follow a fixed step-by-step procedure in investigating at the scene can be as bad as having no plan at all. Plan as far ahead as possible with the information available at the moment. Then adjust and extend the plan as more information becomes available. While each thing is being done, give it careful attention, but at the same time consider the next step.

Urgency is the basis of timing. Decisions based on urgency are intended to accomplish first those things which will be most troublesome if put off. In every accident, for example, the first thing to do on arrival at the scene is to keep the accident from getting worse by preventing fire, attending to the injured, or preventing vehicles from plowing into people or vehicles on the road at the scene. Often several things can be done at the same time. When helping an injured pedestrian for instance, his position and location can be noted and perhaps marked; possibly he may be

questioned. Some activities can be divided and advantageously done at different times during an investigation. For example, necessary photographs of cars in their final positions may be taken soon after arrival at the scene. Then much later, after cars have been moved, other pictures may be made of damage to the vehicles.

It is unnecessary to perform all of the tasks listed in Exhibit 4 in every investigation. Certainly they are not always performed in the same sequence. Accidents are not that much alike.

Severity of the accident will largely determine what must be done first. When you arrive at the scene, you may find urgent matters to be attended to that are not part of actual investigation. Think immediately of what could cause the *worst* additional damage or injury and take care of those things first. Usually three possibilities must be considered:

1. Injured persons must be given what help is possible at the scene, and transportation to hospitals or doctors arranged.

2. Fire must be extinguished as quickly as possible and, if necessary, fire fighting equipment requested. Attention must be given to possible fire and explosion hazards such as spilled fuel or chemicals; the whole area may have to be blocked off to prevent bystanders from contributing to the the hazard. The power company must be called if wires are down.

3. Oncoming vehicles are dangerous, especially at night and at places where visibility is limited by view obstructions: fog, rain, snow, or smoke. Fusees, and later flares, may be placed at intervals along the road. If necessary, someone must be stationed on the road to direct traffic and warn on-

coming drivers of the hazard ahead of them.

Pilferage may be a problem to be considered in conducting activities at the scene of an accident. Valuable property accessible to bystanders may be filched, even from injured persons. A sharp lookout for thieves is the least that can be expected of an investigator; it may be necessary to post someone as a guard or to take custody of valuable belongings.

How and when to get help is essentially a communication problem. Usually it is not known whether help will be needed until an investigation is started. Any of three types of help may be needed:

1. Emergency help, such as ambulance, fire equipment, and help in controlling crowds or traffic

2. Help in investigating, usually in taking statements from witnesses who live far away and will be difficult to talk to later. Much help is also required in hit-and-run investigations.

3. Somebody to take over if you are so occupied that you cannot get to the scene or if you have to leave before investigation is complete.

Calling for help depends on what could cause the worst additional damage or injury. Decide quickly what kind of help is necessary: a doctor, ambulance, fire equipment, rescue squad, tow truck, or additional police. In rural areas, without radio and away from a telephone, somebody may have to be sent to a phone to get help. In requesting help, try to be specific about what kind, how much, where, and how soon. It will often be impossible to provide all of the help needed, especially when conditions such as storms and holidays result in an unusual number of accidents.

Division of work. When there are two or more investigators at the scene of an accident, a logical division of effort may be accomplished by one concentrating on observations and the other on information from people. Observations would include noting marks on the road, final positions of vehicles, and damage to vehicles. This investigator would be responsible for measurements and photographs to record these observations. Information from people would involve inquiries of those involved and other informants as to what they had seen or what they know of the circumstances of the accident.

Planning Hit-and Run Investigations

The first steps in most hit-and-run investigations are the same as those in the investigation of any accident. Get to the scene safely and quickly and handle emergency problems. If you know before reaching the scene that the accident may be a hit-and-run case, watch for vehicles coming from the direction of the accident. Note descriptions and registration numbers if possible. One of these may be the vehicle involved.

At the scene, try to locate the drivers as soon as possible. If a driver cannot quickly be located, consider the possibility of hit-and-run and lose no time in starting a search for the missing driver. This is more urgent than any other step except keeping the accident from getting worse.

Get the best description possible of the missing vehicle and occupants. These may eventually lead to the driver. Remember particularly odd or unusual things such as adornment or marks on the vehicle and deformities or peculiar clothing of occupants.

Communicate available information to a police dispatcher, who can broadcast the description to police in the area. This puts a team to work on the problem. As soon as all available information about the missing driver has been obtained go ahead with other urgent steps of the investigation at the scene.

8. SOURCES

Contributors

This Topic was developed by the following

J. Stannard Baker, principal author, is a traffic engineering consultant specializing in accident investigation. He was Director of Research and Development at the Traffic Institute, from 1946 to 1971 and is a guest lecturer for the Traffic Institute.

References

Superscript numbers in the preceding pages refer to the following publications:

1. *Standards for Law Enforcement Agencies* (Chapter 63), 1983, Commission on Accreditation for Law Enforcement Agencies, 4242B Chain Bridge Road, Fairfax VA 22030

2. *Manual on Classification of Motor Vehicle Traffic Accidents* (ANSI D 16.1-1983), National Safety Council, Chicago IL 60611 (72 pages)

3. *Accident Investigation and Reporting* (Highway Safety Program Standard 18), 1978, National Highway Traffic Safety Administration, U.S. Department of Transportation, Washington DC 20590 (4 pages)

4. *Traffic Records* (Highway Safety Program Standard 10), 1978, National Highway Traffic Safety Administration, U.S. Department of Transportation, Washington DC 20590 (2 pages)

5. *Police Traffic Services* (Highway Safety Program Standard 15), 1978, National Highway Traffic Safety Administration, U.S. Department of Transportation, Washington DC 20590 (2 pages)

6. *Statement — Traffic* (SN 1059), 1975, The Northwestern University Traffic Institute, Evanston IL 60204 (1 page)

7. *General Vehicle Examination,* (SN 8084), 1985, The Northwestern University Traffic Institute, Evanston IL 60204 (2 pages)

8. *Motor-Vehicle Lamp Examination Record* (SN 1122), 1972, The Northwestern University Traffic Institute, Evanston IL 60204 (2 pages)

9. *Tire Examination Record* (SN 8010), The Northwestern University Traffic Institute, Evanston IL 60204 (2 pages)

10. *Property Taken Into Custody* (SN 2042), The Northwestern University Traffic Institute, Evanston IL 60204 (2 pages)

11. *The National Accident Sampling System* Volume 1, (DOT HS 804 027), 1979 , National Highway Traffic Administration, Washington DC 20590 (25 pages)

12. *Medicolegal Autopsy Report* 1968, Registry of Accident Pathology, Armed Forces Institute of Pathology, Washington DC 20305 (32 pages)

13. *Case Envelope* (SN 1064), 1974, The Northwestern University Traffic Institute, Evanston IL 60204

14. *Alcoholic Influence Report Form* (No. 321.99) 1977, National Safety Council, Chicago IL 60611 (2 pages)

15. Baker, J. Stannard and H. Laurence Ross, *Concepts and Classification of Traffic Accident Causes* (SN 1109), 1960, The Northwestern University Traffic Institute, Evanston IL 60204 (119 pages)

16. Fell, James C. and Scott N. Lee, *Program Matrix for Highway Safety Research* (DOT HS 820 094), 1970, National Highway Traffic Safety Administration, U.S. Department of Transportation, Washington DC 20590

17. *Measuring at the Scene of Traffic Accidents — An Independent Study Course* (PN 86) 1984, Traffic Institute, Northwestern University, Evanston IL 60204 (186 pages)

18. *Vehicle Collision Damage Record* (SN 8085), 1985, The Northwestern University Traffic Institute, Evanston IL 60204 (2 pages)

Exhibits

The following are sources of tables, drawings, charts, and photographs used in this publication:

Baker, J. Stannard, Glencoe IL

Forms: 1, 2, 4

Table: 5

Fell, James C., U.S. Department of Transportation, Washington DC

Chart: 3

TRAFFIC-ACCIDENT INFORMATION FROM AND ABOUT PEOPLE

Topic 815 of the *Traffic-Accident Investigation Manual*

by
J. Stannard Baker

NORTHWESTERN UNIVERSITY TRAFFIC INSTITUTE

PUBLICATION HISTORY

1940 *Accident Investigation Manual* (Part of Chapter 6)
Reprinted 1941, 1942

1946 Revised (Part of Chapter 7)
Reprinted 1947, 1948

1953 *Traffic Accident Investigator's Manual* (Section 31)

1954 Revised (Section 31)

1957 *Traffic Accident Investigator's Manual for Police* (Section 31)
Reprinted 1959

1963 Revised (Sections 31, 34, 43, 47)
Reprinted 1964, 1965, 1966, 1969, 1970, 1971, 1973

1970 *Manual de Investigacion de Accidentes de Trafico* (Sections 31, 34, 43, 47)

1975 *Traffic Accident Investigation Manual* (Chapter 4)
Reprinted 1976, 1979

1985 *Traffic-accident Information from and about People*

TRAFFIC-ACCIDENT
INFORMATION FROM AND ABOUT PEOPLE

1. INTRODUCTORY EXPLANATION

Three components of the highway transportation system are involved in every motor-vehicle traffic accident:

1. Roads
2. Vehicles
3. People.

Four kinds of information are obtained in accident investigation for each of these three components:

1. Identification
2. Description
3. Condition prior to the accident
4. Results of the accident on the component. In the case of participants, the results are *injuries* and *memories*.

This topic deals with information from and about people.

In accident investigation, obtaining information from people is more complicated than obtaining data on roads and vehicles. For one thing, numerous people are involved in one way or another with virtually every accident, and it is often difficult to find these people. Furthermore, information is obtained from people not only by observing them, as with roads and vehicles, but, more importantly, by talking to them.

Informants

People connected with the accident. The extent to which a person can contribute to your knowledge about a traffic accident depends, naturally, on his relation to the events of the accident or its aftermath. In this topic, to avoid complicated explanations, the terms used to classify people concerned with the accident will have the following meanings:

1. *Driver:* "Every person who drives or is in actual physical control of a vehicle."[1] Generally this is the operator of a motor vehicle, but it also includes bicyclists. What will be said here about drivers can also be said of people afoot who were involved in the accident.
2. *Passenger:* Any person in or on a vehicle involved in an accident other than the driver. Passengers are usually occupants of vehicles.
3. *Witness:* Any person other than a driver or passenger who was at the scene of an accident while vehicles or people involved were still there. Such a witness may have actually seen some of the events of the accident happen, or he may only have seen some of the re-

sults of the accident. In this respect, police, ambulance drivers, tow truck operators, bystanders, and passers-by are witnesses. This meaning of the term *witness* is quite different than the definition used by lawyers: anybody who gives testimony.

4. *Acquaintance:* Any person other than a driver, passenger, or witness who is acquainted with people or vehicles connected with the accident or knows some of the results or other circumstances of the accident. Acquaintance, as used here, means more than the casual friend of a driver or some other person. It includes such people as physicians who treat the injured, vehicle owners, relatives of people involved, bartenders who saw drivers before the accident, and even highway engineers who might know something about the situation.

If any of these four kinds of people gives information about the accident, he may be spoken of as an *informant.* Do not confuse *informant with informer,* one who reveals a crime committed or names a person who committed a crime. Drivers, pedestrians, and passengers may also be spoken of as *the injured* if they were hurt in the accident.

Levels of Inquiry

The extent to which investigators go in obtaining information from people about a traffic accident depends on circumstances. Ordinarily only a few facts will suffice; but sometimes the fullest possible detail is needed. Thus, there are levels of inquiry that resemble the five levels of accident investigation, but do not exactly correspond to them. These levels may be designated thus:

1. Identification and description only
2. At-scene inquiry
3. Detailed statements
4. Testimony and depositions
5. Interrogation.

This topic applies mainly to serious (Classes A and B) accidents. Minor accidents (Class C) usually present investigators with few problems in obtaining information.

Special questioning in connection with hit-and-run accidents is beyond the scope of this topic.

Place of Inquiry

Questions about a traffic accident are asked of informants at a variety of places:

- *First at the scene.* Information obtained here is most reliable because events are fresh in the minds of persons being questioned.
- *At a hospital* where injured persons have been taken before you have a chance to question them.
- *Later at the site.* Sometimes it is helpful to meet informants at the site some time after the accident when conditions for inquiry are more favorable than they were at the scene.
- *Elsewhere*, depending on the convenience of the investigator and the informant. This may be by telephone.

In theory, you should get all the information possible about the accident while the people involved are still at the scene.

In practice this is impossible for a *number of reasons,* the most obvious of which is that the injured are often in no condition to answer any questions. But even when questioning would be possible, such circumstances as uncomfortable weather, bothersome bystanders, the urgency of restoring normal traffic flow, and the conviction that information can be had later all discourage obtaining detailed written statements. Under these conditions, decisions have to be made in serious accidents about who to question and what questions to ask.

As a rule, it is better to identify as many people as possible who may have information than to try to get detailed statements from one or two.

2. FINDING INFORMANTS AT THE SCENE

There is a revealing first question which you can ask any person who might be an informant: "How did you first know about this accident?" The answer will probably tell you at once whether he has anything significant to say, and it may tell you whether he was involved in any way. Two additional questions (Exhibit 1) will usually tell whether the information he has is worth going after. If you decide he has nothing useful to say, thank him and go on about your business. If the informant does seem to have useful facts, identify him at once by getting his name and address or phone number. Then, if you cannot finish talking to him at the scene, you or someone else can reach him later.

Finding Drivers at the Scene

Locating drivers is the first thing to be done after handling emergencies at the scene. If you cannot find

a driver or account for his whereabouts, start a hit-and-run investigation. In many accidents, finding the driver is not difficult. He may still be sitting at the wheel of his vehicle, or he and another driver may be the only persons at the scene. Sometimes a driver will walk up to you and identify himself right away.

If there are many people at the scene when you arrive, you may not be able to pick out a driver immediately so, as you approach the scene or as you are handling urgent matters, try to locate the driver among the crowd. Look for a person who is doing something or who is a center of attention. For example, two people standing beside a vehicle and engaged in a discussion are likely to be drivers. A person writing something on a piece of paper is apt to be getting information from another driver.

A person inspecting the vehicle for damage, lifting the hood, or picking things up around the vehicle is usually a driver or passenger. You will often have discovered him by the time you are ready to talk to him.

Driver-finding difficulties occur in three different situations:

1. Occupants are dead or too badly injured to say who was driving, and you cannot determine this from the positions of their bodies.
2. The survivor says the dead occupant was driving but you suspect otherwise.
3. Occupants decline to reveal which one of them was driving. Sometimes a passenger in a vehicle will falsely claim to have been driving. This might be done for several reasons. The actual driver may have been intoxicated, under age, or had a bad driving record. Serious violators have gone unpunished because the fact that the offender was driving could not be proved.

Each of these three situations calls for prompt and unusually discreet inquiry and sometimes careful observation.

The natural assumption is that the owner was the driver if he was in the vehicle. Proceeding on this assumption in questionable cases will sometimes bring out acceptable information on who actually was driving. If there is any doubt whatever about who was driving, do not accept such an assumption as fact, but seek additional information that will confirm or contradict the assumption.

Routinely question every witness about who was driving each vehicle involved. If you have an idea that perhaps you are misled, do this in such a way that the witness or others who may overhear may infer that you do know who was driving. For example, ask something like, "Did you help Mr. Poor out of the driver's seat?" or "How fast was Miss Smart driving when she overtook your vehicle?" If the person questioned knows it was not Poor in the driver's seat or Miss Smart driving, he is likely to correct you. If possible, question a vehicle occupant before he has time to think up an explanation that might be to his advantage.

Look for physical signs that might indicate who was driving, especially if there was more than one adult in the vehicle and no one was properly behind the wheel after the crash. Observe or inquire about the final positions of bodies before they are moved and record carefully what you learn about these positions. Look for signs of where bodies struck the inside of the vehicle so they can be matched with injuries, for example, chest injuries inflicted by a steering wheel. Try to get detailed descriptions of injuries from surgeons or coroners for this purpose. Look for telltale clues such as imprints of brake or accelerator pedal on shoe soles or hair in broken windshields (Exhibits 2 and 3).

With such information, it may be possible later to deduce who was driving; but without such informa-

Exhibit 1.

BASIC QUESTIONS TO ASK INFORMANTS AT THE SCENES OF TRAFFIC ACCIDENTS

General First Questions of Anyone at the Scene	
1. How did you first know about this accident?	Reveals relationship to accident. Indicates perception of hazard.
2. Where were you at that time?	Indicates ability to observe.
a. In the vehicle	Helps to identify the driver.
b. Elsewhere	Locates the informant.
3. What were you doing?	Shows opportunity to observe.
a. In the vehicle	Helps to identify the driver.
b. Vehicle movement on road	Describes vehicle movement.
c. As a bystander or passer by	Confirms relation to accident.
4. What is your name?	Identifies informant for future
5. Where do you live?	questioning if necessary.

Any Person in Involved Vehicle	Bystander or Passer By
1. Which direction were you travelling before the accident?	1. Show me where the vehicle (pedestrian) was when first seen by you.
2. Who was driving the car you were in?	2. What was he (it) doing at that time?
3. What was he (you) planning to do?	3. If you saw the actual collision, show me exactly where it occurred.
4. How did he (you) try to avoid the accident?	4. Show me where the vehicle (pedestrian) came to rest.
5. Show me exactly where the collision occurred.	

tion it may be impossible. Occasionally, fingerprints have been taken from the steering wheel or rear view mirror and compared with those of the alleged driver as a check on statements.

It is most embarrassing if the person charged with an offense or with negligence as a driver claims as his defense that someone else was driving and you have no way to prove he is wrong.

Hit-and-run accidents present the ultimate challenge in driver identification. This is usually accomplished by locating the car.

Finding Witnesses and Passengers

Look for witnesses and passengers as soon as possible after getting to the scene. If only a few people are present, witnesses can be located by asking each person if he saw the accident. Often witnesses will be speaking to a driver, talking among themselves, or examining damage to

a vehicle.

Registration numbers. Especially if the accident is severe, it is often useful to write down registration numbers or other identification (such as company names) on vehicles near the accident scene. Do this especially if you have reason to think the accident was hit-and-run. By tracing the numbers or names, you may be able later to locate someone who can give information about the accident. Of course, if you find enough informants at the scene to give the needed information, you need not look for others by this method.

Sometimes you can write identifying information down while approaching the scene. If you are alone, this may be difficult, but if you are with another investigator, one can write while the other drives. Get only numbers of vehicles which would have had to pass the accident scene. There are disadvantages to recording registration numbers in heavily

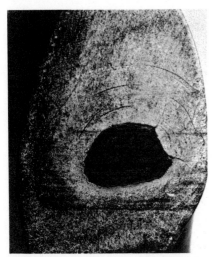

Exhibit 2. *The identity of the driver can sometimes be settled by careful observation such as noting that the sole of a shoe bears a pedal pad imprint.*

travelled urban areas because many of the drivers will not have passed the accident, and chances that you will pick one that can give some information, even if he passed the scene, are small. However, in rural areas or when traffic is light, a driver coming from the scene may have noticed important conditions there. Write down registration numbers of all vehicles parked at the scene when you get there. If you later find that additional witnesses are needed and the vehicles have left, you will be able to trace the owners.

When a crowd has gathered at the scene, locating useful witnesses is often difficult. Because volunteers are rare, you often have to appeal to the crowd. Start, for example, by asking, "Who was here first after the collision?" Later questioning will reveal whether the person actually saw the accident. Sometimes appeals to sympathy are effective. Say, for instance, "Right now, I don't want to question the poor fellow who is hurt. If any of you have information, won't you help him by telling me what you know?"

Another way to locate witnesses is to watch the reactions of people in the crowd to statements made by the driver. For example, suppose a driver tells you that he was going 20 miles per hour. You then repeat this in a clearly audible voice: "You say you were going 20 miles an hour?" This may cause a person in the crowd indignantly to come forward and say, "He was not going 20; it was more like 35." Such a volunteer may be able to give other information.

Occasionally you may find a witness by watching expressions on the faces of people at the scene. People who disagree or are confused may frown, wrinkle their brows, or give some other sign. Ask such a person why he disagrees. If he denies it, say, "I thought you shook your head" or some other appropriate remark.

Useful witnesses are not only those who actually saw the collision, but also people who arrived at the scene before you did, especially the first person there. Such witnesses can tell you whether bodies or vehicles were moved before you came and may report things drivers said to them that drivers would not say later to you.

For minor accidents, it is *necessary* only to identify drivers or whoever, other than a driver, provides the information to the police. Any other people associated with the accident, for example passengers, can be identified afterward by the drivers if identification is necessary.

For more serious accidents, especially if a driver is disabled, try at the scene to record the names and addresses as identification of all

- Pedestrians involved
- Passengers in any vehicle
- Vehicle owners
- Ambulance drivers
- Tow truck drivers
- Police assisting with at-scene investigation or directing traffic at the scene
- Witnesses who say they saw all or some of the events of the accident
- Whoever summoned police
- First persons to arrive at the scene in addition to participants
- Other persons present who might know something about the accident.

It also may help to record the place of business of each possible informant. The object of recording these names and addresses is to get information by which you or someone else could find the person later. It is poor investigation if you do not record the identity of someone at the scene of an accident who gives you information or could probably tell you something about it.

Description of informant. In addition to age, sex, occupation, and relationship of the informant to the accident (driver, passenger, etc.), which have already been mentioned, relationship of the informant to people involved in the accident (friend, relative, employee, etc.) helps evaluate reliability of information. If these descriptive items are not provided for in a printed statement heading, include them in the first part of the statement.

3. INITIAL QUESTIONING AT THE SCENE

The scene of an accident is not the easiest place to ask people what happened in a traffic accident. There is too much going on and many other conditions may be unfavorable. Yet this may be the best and possibly the only opportunity you have to get certain information.

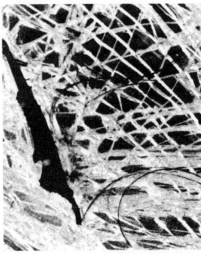

Exhibit 3. *Matching injuries with vehicle damage is a common way of determining who was driving. Hair in a broken windshield can be matched with that of an occupant to establish identity.*

Therefore, try to get *basic* facts from as many informants as you can as quickly as possible and identify each informant so that additional data can be obtained later, either at the scene or elsewhere.

Basic Questions

As mentioned earlier, the first questions of any person at the scene of a traffic accident are intended to find out what he might know and help you decide whether to question him further.

If the answers to these basic questions (Exhibit 1) tell you that the informant may have useful information beyond what he has already told you, identify him at once and continue with other quick questions. These followup questions will be different for a person involved in the accident than for a bystander or passerby.

With the basic data in mind, you can turn to other matters with the understanding, of course, that you or someone else may want more detail later.

Written statements by Informants

Sometimes you can ask the informant to write out at the scene, what he knows about the accident. He may do this either on a blank sheet or some kind of a prepared form. This may be useful if you have to work alone on a complicated accident. However, it really saves little time because you must review carefully what was written to be sure it is legible and sufficient for the purpose. Then you have to ask about basic matters which are not covered.

Additional information sought from people at the scene is essentially that which would be obtained for detailed written statements. In fact, if time and other circumstances permit, the detailed statement can be completed to advantage right at the scene. But if a complete statement is not possible, which is usually the case, people, especially drivers, can be asked a few questions. To some of these questions they might make

less truthful or explicit replies if asked the same questions after they have had an opportunity to think about the matter and to discuss it with others, perhaps attorneys. Informants who have expressed themselves at the scene are more likely to have a better recollection of the events of the accident later than if they had said nothing about it immediately.

4. DETAILED STATEMENTS

Purpose

A detailed statement is taken to obtain a written record of exactly what a certain person says about the accident. It is usually a part of the third level of accident investigation, technical follow up. A detailed statement will not include all a person knows if he is unwilling to tell all he knows. It may include things he has imagined but does not know, and it may include lies. Having his statement recorded is believed to make it less likely that a person will tell a different story later, but it is no guarantee that he will not "remember" more or better at some other time.

Years ago, investigators depended almost entirely on what informants had to say. Such information is rarely completely satisfactory; it is often fragmentary, and may be unreliable. Today, in serious accidents, observations of the results of the accident, such as marks on the road and damage to vehicles, are used much more extensively. These observations, skillfully made and recorded, can supply data not otherwise available and information by which the quality of statements can be judged. But successful techniques for observing and interpreting results of accidents do not lessen the need to find out what people know about an accident.

Circumstances

When. Detailed statements are not required of every person knowing anything about any accident. Except for a few statements ob-

tained when there are favorable opportunities at the scene of an accident, decisions to secure statements are made by prosecuting attorneys or supervisors after the initial report has been evaluated and prosecution or other action is contemplated. Sometimes a statement is postponed for months or even years before the need for it becomes clear.

Try to arrange the statement interview at a time convenient for the informant.

Where. Plan to interview the informant at a place convenient for him. This usually requires making an appointment with him.

If possible, hold the interview where everybody can be seated comfortably and where there are not likely to be interruptions.

It is generally best to have only the investigator and the informant present, but this is not a firm rule. If the informant would be more comfortable with someone else present —a spouse, parent, or friend, for example—by all means so arrange it.

If two or more people have essentially the same facts, one can listen to the other, his own statement being merely what he can add to what has already been said.

Anyone may receive a statement and record it, but statements are usually obtained by professional investigators or attorneys. If you have to get a statement, after you have found the specified person, you must try to do three things:

1. Find out what he will or will not say about the accident.
2. Reduce this to writing.
3. Attempt to get the individual to agree to what has been written about what he knows.

Anyone may give a statement regardless of how much or how little he knows about the accident. Drivers, because they are actually involved, generally provide the most useful information. The best procedure is more or less the same no matter who the informant is, although naturally the questions an individual is asked depend on his connection with the accident.

Who is being questioned? Don't try to ask everybody about everything; that would be impossible. On the other hand, it may be important to ask nearly everybody you talk to about some things on the chance that someone will have the information you want and in the hope that two or more answers to the same question will result in better data than a single reply.

Who is doing the questioning? For example, a person who was not at the scene of an accident will have to ask more about the after-accident situation than one who was there and could see for himself.

Circumstances of questioning. Interviewing at the scene of an accident under unfavorable conditions may have to be limited to a few subjects about which on-the-spot inquiry is the simplest and most reliable. Other subjects may be discussed in greater detail elsewhere, for example, questions about damage to the vehicle may best be asked after owners or repairmen have had a chance to examine it, and questions about injuries may have to be made at a hospital.

Difficult Informants

Worried people.

Keep in mind that your interest in gathering information is quite different from the interest of the person being questioned. A driver, for example, is worried about the damage to his vehicle, what the accident may cost him, what it will mean to his financial condition, even his livelihood. Patience and sympathetic understanding of these concerns may help greatly in obtaining information that you need.

Due to the shocked or dazed condition often experienced by drivers, it may be necessary to question twice, regardless of other conditions at the scene. At the beginning of the investigation, even though very much upset, the driver may give

Exhibit 4. Questioning an informant at the scene should preferably be done away from others and where he can show you what he has observed.

more accurate facts than later on. His memory will be fresh and he will have had little time to rationalize or make up a story. Also, before he has had time to gather his wits, he may give useful information that he ordinarily would not give. This is often true of drivers under the influence of alcohol. A driver may say that he could not see well, that he was lighting a cigarette, trying to read a map, was dizzy, etc. But when calm and collected or sober, he may not make such an admission.

If circumstances are such that a driver must wait to be questioned, try to give him something to do to occupy his time. For example, hand him a sheet of paper and ask him to draw a diagram of the accident, or tell him to copy the data from his driver's license certificate onto the paper. You can even ask him to help with certain phases of the investigation, such as calling a tow truck or an ambulance if necessary. Do not give the impression that he is being passed up and will not have the opportunity to speak. Let him know that his story will be

given consideration equal to its importance.

It is often desirable at first to question drivers individually to avoid conflict between them. However, after each has told his story separately, it may be desirable to bring them together and let them repeat their stories in the presence of each other. If only one driver is present, it may be desirable that two investigators listen to the story. Ordinarily, only one should ask questions, however. Avoid a forbidding, formal atmosphere, which sometimes results from too many persons, official or unofficial, "listening in on" a driver's story. (Exhibit 4)

Injured persons. An injured driver may have been taken to a hospital or to his home. In this case, except for minor information, questioning may have to wait until the person can give a detailed statement. If you request it, a hospital official or attending doctor will probably notify you when a person is well enough to be interviewed.

Conditions at an accident scene may be noisy and confused. Under such circumstances, it is often desirable to get the driver to accompany you away from the scene, where the atmosphere is more likely to produce good results from interviewing. Some drivers, especially if in a hurry, are reluctant to go but they can usually be persuaded if you explain your reasons. Especially in bad weather, your suggestion to "get inside somewhere and talk it over" will be welcome.

Juveniles. You may have to obtain consent of a parent or guardian to obtain a statement from a juvenile. This is especially so if there is a possibility of criminal prosecution. Court approval is sometimes also necessary.

The informant who does not want to talk is a difficult problem. For any such person, you can nearly always establish certain identifying and descriptive data by asking such questions as, "You are James Webster, are you not? Is my information correct that you were at the scene of an accident on April 17th? You were not one of the drivers involved were you? But you did actually see the vehicles collide, didn't you?" If that is as far as he will go, your report on what he will say can be brief. After recording such identifying and descriptive data as you have been able to elicit, conclude your report, in the hearing of the informant, with the comment, "The witness declined to say more."

Informant does not want to be involved. In this case, information can often be obtained by explaining to the witness that he may be subpoenaed to go to court to find out what he knows but that if he answers some questions now it may be unnecessary to go to court.

Drivers instructed not to say anything. Truck and bus drivers are often instructed by employers to say nothing about the accident to anyone except what is required for identification. Then, at the scene, get the identifying and descriptive information and let it go at that. If you want more, seek permission from the employer, the employer's insurance company, or the employer's attorney.

If the driver is a suspect for a law violation, especially a serious violation, and may be charged with an offense, make the usual explanation concerning his right to make no statement.

How to Question

Finding out what a person knows about an accident is more an art than a science. Step-by-step rules are difficult to suggest because a procedure that is effective for an investigator of one temperment may fail for someone with a different personality. For example, one investigator may find a very informal, first-name approach, liberally sprinkled with pleasantries, serves him best whereas another is more successful with brisk, brief, and business-like pursuit of the desired data. True artists in obtaining statements are able to adapt their method to the character and mood of the person being interviewed, but that takes practice. A few suggestions can be made which may prove helpful.

Explain who you are to begin with and what your interest is in the accident. Give your card if you have one. Be candid in this respect and the informant is likely to be the same with you.

Be objective. The biggest obstacle that some investigators have to overcome in interviewing people about accidents is inside themselves. How you *feel* about a person's race or business, your dislike for foreigners or wise guys, your attitude toward women drivers, your interest in certain kinds of accidents, and many other similar personal reactions can get in your own way when you begin to ask questions. These feelings can easily show in the expression on your face and the manner of your speech. The person whom you are addressing, more quickly and surely than you would think possible, senses your feelings and responds accordingly. He resists giving the facts you ask for if you seem hostile; he cooperates if you are friendly. Keep *yourself out of the situation;* don't become involved. That's being objective.

Be positive. The first questions you ask may determine to a large degree how successful you will be in getting information. Make your first questions positive. For example, do not ask, "You don't know anything about this, do you?" Instead say, "How did you first know about this accident?" The latter is more direct, allows less "hedging," and saves time. Never be reluctant to ask many questions, but ask each in a straightforward manner.

Be specific. To get useful answers, be certain that the driver or witness understands your questions. Make them as specific and clear as you would like the answers to be. For example, if you want to know whether the driver was entering the intersection from the north or the east, don't ask, "Where were you going?" He may answer, "I was going home," which is not what you want to know. Better ask, "In which direction were you moving?"

Be sure that you know what the answer really means. Many answers are unclear and indefinite. For example, an informant may say, "He was way back of the intersection and coming fast." To find out what he means by "way back," have him show you where the car was in the road when he saw it, if possible in relation to a fixed object. Ask, "Do you drive an automobile?" If so, he will probably be able to give a much better estimate of the speed of the vehicle he observed than if he can't drive. "Very fast" to some people might mean 70 or 80 miles per hour, while to others it may mean 40 to 50 miles per hour. Much depends on where the car was observed. "Fast" may mean 20 miles per hour at a crowded intersection, but it could mean 70 miles per hour on a rural highway.

Don't argue. Suppress any desire to say such things as, "You are wrong about that" or "I can't believe that you stopped." Remember that your purpose is to find out what the person will say, not to convince him that he is mistaken or to persuade him to your way of thinking. But this does not mean that you should accept what he says as fact. If you doubt a statement, ask about it again later in the interview, preferably in some other way to find out whether he sticks to his story. You can also test a doubtful statement by asking how he knows what he has just said, unless such a question would be ridiculous. For example, you might ask, "Did you actually see the boy run into the street, or did you hear somebody say that is what happened?" or "Do you actually know that the Ford pulled out to overtake, or do you just believe that this is what might have happened?" and if the person says that he knows, ask further, "How do you know?"

Don't suggest answers. Thrusting your own opinions on those you are questioning is akin to arguing. Many people are very susceptible to suggestion, and when you put an idea into a person's mind he is likely to think of it as his own. For example, if you are trying to determine the speed of a vehicle in an accident, do not say to the driver: "You were going about 35 miles per hour, weren't you?" If "35 miles per hour" seems reasonable to the driver, he is likely to agree that he was travelling at that speed. However, if you were to ask, "How fast were you going?" the same driver might think carefully and answer: "I'd say about 20," an answer that might cast an entirely different light on the accident, and represent his own estimate of his speed, not yours.

Be diplomatic and understanding. Your approach depends greatly on whether you are questioning a driver or witness. Drivers of vehicles in accidents are in trouble, often great trouble. They remember vague-

ly that they have certain duties and responsibilities to fulfill in connection with accidents, but few know precisely what they are. Nearly all of them turn to any investigator at the scene for help and advice. They are, with rare exceptions, willing and often eager to tell their stories and answer your questions. This does not mean that you can expect drivers to freely confess their violations or mistakes. Nearly all drivers, consciously or unconsciously, try to avoid blaming themselves. Other informants are different. They are not in trouble, but many think they will be if they say anything about the accident. They dread the possibility of being summoned to testify. They don't want to get mixed up in arguments which don't concern them. They certainly feel no legal obligation to offer information, so try to win their cooperation by arousing interest in the case, for example, by explaining that you are puzzled or confused and need a few more facts to "piece things together." Passengers may behave like either drivers or bystanders when you question them. Getting at what they know will test your resourcefulness as well as your diplomacy.

However, when dealing with informants, you will get better cooperation and better answers to your questions if you are sympathetic, reasonable, understanding, and fair to all. When a person you want to question looks frequently at his watch, and appears to be nervous, tell him, "I know that you are in a hurry. I do not want to hold you here longer than necessary. We'll try to clear this up quickly and let you go as soon as possible."

In many cases, you can get useful information by sympathetically encouraging a person to talk about anything that interests him. Allow a driver who has had his vacation interrupted and his car severely damaged to talk about his problems for a while. If you can do something or make suggestions to help him, he

may reciprocate with information. You probably can do little to help him, but you can listen. Afterwards he may have a much better and more realistic understanding of your problems. He can usually talk and think better about other things.

Be adaptable. In accident investigation, you cannot afford to settle into the routine of asking a set list of questions. If you do, you will run into too many conflicts and miss too many clues. Accident investigation does not have as its object mere collection of information to fill in blanks on a form which can be handled as routine. To be successful at getting the sort of information you need, you must be adaptable enough in interviewing to try to get whatever information the informant is prepared to give. Be willing to shelve the next question you had planned to ask — and return to it later — if a casual remark or a gesture gives you a clue to a more likely line of inquiry. Just as you can spoil skidmarks and scatter debris until they explain nothing, so by plodding blindly through your questioning, you can ruin your chances of getting valuable data from informants.

Subject Matter

Although the form of obtaining information from people about traffic accidents and the extent of the inquiry differ for the five types of information gathering, the subject matter is more or less the same for all.

Information from people is usually fragmentary. Bear in mind that the events of an accident are crowded into two or three seconds. People are not prepared to note exactly what goes on in that brief interval and are often not in a position where they can observe well. Consequently, information from people about the events of an accident must not only be evaluated for reliability, but must also be pieced together, bit by bit, usually with data from several sources to form as complete a picture as possible.

Basic Questions at the scene (Exhibit 1) will yield the most significant information from and about the people involved. For most minor accidents, no other information will be needed. As a rule, however, repeat these questions or their equivalent for any follow up interviews done away from the accident scene at a later time.

Additional detailed follow up facts are generally wanted for serious or complicated accidents. The nature and scope of questions depends on the kind of accident and what lawsuits may arise from it.

Questions about the trip apply not only to drivers and pedestrians involved but to any witness, unless they would be absurd. Knowing something of how an informant came to be at the scene will help to understand and evaluate what he has to say about:

- Time and place trip began
- Intended destination and expected time of arrival
- Time, location, duration, and purpose of stops made before reaching the scene of the accident
- Principal purpose of trip, for example, home from work, shopping, visiting friends
- Intended movement immediately before accident, for example, turning left, merging, overtaking, slowing to park
- Trip vehicle, general description only
- Passengers' names and addresses (if not already known to the investigator), where seated in vehicle, age, sex.

From the trip plan you may be able to determine the direction in which the informant would have to be travelling to get to his stated destination. You may learn whether or not he stopped in a bar or tavern, which may indicate that he had been drinking. You might determine, if you do not know already, whether

the accident happened in daylight or in the dark.

Do not ask questions about the trip plan in a definite sequence. Mingle them with other questions so that you will not let the driver know what you are getting at. Otherwise he may be able to tell you a logical story describing only lawful behavior, but which does not relate the whole truth. If he does not know your intentions, he is more likely to tell the truth.

Results of the Accident

The questions you ask about results of the accident depend on how much you have seen for yourself. If you are at the scene, you only need to ask about circumstances that may have been changed before you arrived. But if you were not there to see for yourself, you may have to ask many people many questions. Then all informants should be routinely asked what they saw and remembered about results of the accident, if anything. If these questions are asked at the scene about conditions that may have changed, positions of vehicles, for example, try to have the locations pointed out rather than have them described, then you can mark them. There may be considerable disagreement among those interviewed about the results of the accident. There may be many "I don't know" answers. The following are typical questions about accident results:

- What was the exact position of each vehicle when it came to rest?
- Where was each involved person after the accident? Especially where were the injured?
- For each person involved in the accident, what injuries did you observe? Was the person unconscious? Was he uninjured?
- For each vehicle involved, what damage did you notice? Was the vehicle drivable? Had there been any fire? If

at night, what lights were on and what ones off? Which tires, if any, were flat? Were any major parts torn loose? Was the car collapsed in more than one area? What were the main damage areas?
- Marks on the road. Were there any signs that fixed objects had been struck or damaged? Did you notice any tire marks on the road or roadside? If so, how did they appear? Was there underbody debris? If so, was it concentrated or scattered? Where was it located? Did you notice any liquid spatters on the roadway? If so, where were they located? Did you notice any gouges or scratches on the roadway? If so, what were they like and where were they located?

Tiremarks. Call these to the attention of the drivers and others at the scene so that you and they both know afterward that marks were observed. If possible, get the driver to agree that his car made, or did not make, certain marks.

Inquiries about vehicle conditions are very useful at the scene. Ask about them in such a way as not to suggest them as possible explanations of the accident. It is better to ask, "Did your vehicle give you any trouble?" or "Was your vehicle in good shape?" than to ask, "Did your brakes fail?" or "Did you have a blowout?"

Inquiries about driver condition are also useful if they are discreet. Before trying to find out whether a driver was under the influence of alcohol, ask about other conditions to which he might later attribute his appearance or behavior, for example, "Have you taken any medicine or drugs in the last few hours?" and "Were you sick or did you feel ill while you were driving?"

Questions about events of the accident are essentially the same at the scene as they would be later for

a recorded statement, but some are more important at the scene than later; for example those about
  • Point of perception
  • Reason for delay in perception
  • Speed and position on the road at that time
  • Intended maneuver
  • Evasive tactics attempted
  • Final position of vehicles.

Other vehicle occupants, in addition to those who are located at once, may be involved. Look in vehicles for signs of them and look about the scene of the accident. Clothing or other items may make it worth while to inquire about who they belong to and why they were in the car. Sometimes an occupant will wander away from the scene and collapse some distance away, and sometimes an occupant will be ejected in such a manner as to be concealed from superficial observation. Occasionally there is an occupant who does not want it known that he or she was in the vehicle and who tries to disappear immediately after the accident.

In obtaining information from people by questioning and listening, an investigator must never forget the important difference between fact and information. The data you want from people are facts; what you get is information. Such information generally does contain some factual truth; but the facts are usually diluted with irrelevant material, mixed with fanciful ideas from fertile imaginations, and sometimes even contaminated with outright lies.

Other people. In addition to inquiries about the people who may have been involved in the accident or may have witnessed the accident or its aftermath, it may be desirable to determine if informants were questioned about the accident by any other person:
  • When you finally talk to a person who was too badly injured to answer questions at the scene of the accident, ask

whom he first saw when he was able to talk and what he said about the accident to that person. This may give you a lead to another informant.
  • Ask any one you talk to, "Have you talked to anyone else about this accident?" If the answer is yes, find out who, when, where, and the general nature of the discussion.
  • "Did you talk to a policeman about this accident?" If so, "What was his name and where did you talk to him?"

5. THE RECORD OF QUESTIONING

A Written Record Is Necessary

Except possibly for a few especially striking details it is impossible to recall later exactly what anybody told you about a traffic accident. You may not even remember whether you talked to a certain person. Thus, to be credible in passing it on, information which you have obtained must be in writing or on tape, preferably made during or immediately after the interview.

On the Accident Report Form

For most minor accidents, the only record of conversations with participants and witnesses appears as very brief comments on the accident report form. These are written down some time after the interview from memory.

Identification of these informants is in spaces on the form for names and addresses of drivers and other witnesses.

Statements they made are much abbreviated under some such heading as "Describe what happened."

In describing what happened, avoid putting down what someone told you as though it were established fact. It is much better to name the person and quote briefly what he had to say, for example, "Driver 1 says

he stopped and looked before entering the intersection but did not see anything coming." That the driver said this to you, you know to be a fact; but that this is actually what happened, you do not know to be a fact because it may or may not be true. (As a witness in court you will ordinarily not be permitted to testify about what someone told you. That is hearsay.)

Records of Detailed Statements

As a rule, the statement of each informant is a separate document.

Identification. For the report of every interview that is more than a brief statement on the official report form, be sure to get information to identify
  1. Who made the statement.
  2. Who the statement was made to.
  3. Time and place of statement.
  4. The accident or event concerning which the statement is made. This must be in terms of where and when the accident occurred and, if it identifies the accident better for the informant, names of people involved, for example, "The accident that occurred on the 22nd of June 1985 on US 35 at the junction of Welch Road in Pratt County, Iowa, the accident in which Walter Williams was injured." Add an accident or case number for filing purposes. That might be enough identification for you, but it means nothing to the person making the statement.

If the statement is recorded by a stenographer or on tape, such identification is made part of the statement itself, usually the first part. But if the form or printed heading used for statements provides for proper identification (Exhibit 5), the identification does not need to be repeated in the statement.

The most common method of

recording brief, informal statements used by a skilled investigator is a simple one. The investigator listens carefully to what is said and writes it down afterwards, perhaps on a sheet prepared for that purpose (Exhibit 5). If well done, such a summary is satisfactory because the statement is brief and well organized. The risk in this method is that some ideas may be omitted or misinterpreted. Therefore, it is important that the person who supplied the information be asked to read it or have it read to him after it has been written. A few pointers in writing such a summary may be helpful:

- Write in the first person as though quoting what the witness said: "I was riding in the right front seat." Do not use third person: "The witness said he was riding in the right front seat."
- Begin a new paragraph wherever the topic changes, but do not put in headings or subheadings.
- Do not write questions and answers. Record the answers, not the questions. But if the answer is simply yes or no, record the question and the answer as a single statement. For example, "Were you on your way home?" answered, "Yes", is rephrased, "I was on my way home."
- Reorganize and rephrase what the informant said but do not change his meaning. It is not necessary to use his exact expressions, especially, slang, colloquial expressions, and bad grammer, unless the meaning would be changed by such omission.
- Omit irrelevant comments and social amenities. They have no bearing on the matter in hand.

Inexperienced or unsure investigators may need to have the questions prepared in advance by someone else, either as a standard list or for the particular informant. Such a list of questions may provide a space after each question for the reply. The informant's replies to each question are written down, omitting only irrelevant material for the sake of brevity. (Exhibit 6).

If the informant has written out his statement, you may wish to ask questions for additional information. Summarize replies to those questions and add the summary to what the informant has written.

If more formal statements are needed later, they are usually made as depositions, in which questions and answers are all recorded exactly as spoken.

Recorded statements can be made by a stenographer or with a tape recorder. In either case, the exact and entire conversation is recorded and may later be transcribed. With modern portable equipment, tape recording is being used more and more extensively. Especially if the conversation is recorded, on tape, be sure that the person giving the information understands that you are recording and agrees to it. Nearly everybody now knows what a tape recorder is. Say something like, "If you don't mind, I want to tape our conversation. In that way, I can be sure that I don't forget some of the important information that you have." Few people are inhibited in what they say by recording it on tape.

Maps and diagrams used in the interview, regardless of who makes them, become part of the report. If they are published material, such as road maps, they can be referred to by name and publisher. Each must be marked in some way to show its connection with the statement.

Page numbering. When the report of the interview is done, number the pages consecutively. Use the form "Page 1 of 4 pages, Page 2 of 4 pages" and so on.

Signature. When the statement is a written summary, ask the person to read it to determine if you have misrepresented him in any way. Corrections can be made on the report. If he signs the report, have him initial each correction and each page. If corrections are numerous or substantial, rewrite the entire page and destroy the uncorrected one. After the informant has read the statement, ask him to sign it: "To show that you have read over what I have written, I would like to have you sign your name at the bottom." If he is willing to do this, write at the bottom, "I have read the above statement and it represents what I have to say about the matter." Then have him sign and date it. If the informant does not agree to sign, draw a line across the page after the last part of the statement and add below the line, "Witness was invited to sign the above statement but declined to do so although he did not object to any part of it that has not been noted as a correction." Then sign this statement yourself.

If the informant will not respond, make the statement read to that effect; for example, "I do not want to talk about the accident. I do not want to get mixed up with it. I have not talked to anybody else about it." Handle his signature on this statement the same as on any other statement. An informant may be willing to sign such a "no-comment" statement when he would not sign a more complete one.

If the statement has been taped or stenographically recorded (shorthand or stenotype), the voice recording speaks for itself and the stenographer will attest to the accuracy of what is said. Therefore, a signature is not needed.

Forms for recording statements are of four general kinds:

1. Blank sheets, letterhead, or memo head
2. Statement sheets with a printed heading for identifying the informant and the circumstances under which the information was given (Exhibit 5)

STATEMENT - TRAFFIC

| NAME SHARP, Walter A. | PHONE NO. 337-2471 | ☒ Accident ☐ Violation | NUMBER 85-183 | CASE OR FILE NUMBER |

| ADDRESS 244 SPRING ST. PALMER   OH |

| AGE 37 | OCCUPATION PIPE FITTER | BUSINESS PHONE NONE |

EVENT

ON Street or road WILSON AV

AT Intersection with or distance from HILL ST

IN City, County PALMER   ROPER   OH

| HOUR 19:25 p m. | DAY 12 | MONTH OCT | 19 85 |

☒ Driver ☐ Passenger | IN WHAT VEHICLE - Make and Year | WHERE SEATED, if passenger

☐ Ped. hit ☒ Witness | LOCATION WHEN EVENT OCCURRED SW Corner Wilson & Hill

CONNECTION WITH DRIVER OR OTHERS INVOLVED None - bystander

STATEMENT

MADE AT SCENE

MADE TO JAMES KOLB   Ptlm. 87

| HOUR 19:35p m. | DAY 12 | MONTH OCT | 1985 |

Statement made by above-named person:

I was going east on Wilson and was about to cross Hill. The light turned to green. I noticed an 84 Chevy 4-door comming South on Hill St going about 40 mph. It looked like he was not going to stop, so I waited to see. Then I noticed the old lady in a black dress was crossing Hill from the NE Corner. Maybe she didn't hear the car so she kept on comming. The car swerved to the left, but the lady did not step back and she got hit. It knocked her about 20 feet. I ran over to help her but she was hurt bad so I went to the house on the corner and asked the lady who came to the door to call the police. The car stopped near the SW corner. The driver was kind of wobbly when he got out I could smell his breath I believe had been drinking.

   I have read the above statement and it is true to the best of my knowledge

                                        Walter A. Sharp

THE NORTHWESTERN UNIVERSITY TRAFFIC INSTITUTE

S.N. 1059

Exhibit 5. The summary of what an informant has said can be put on a form which provides for identification but otherwise permits a simple narrative account. The investigator usually writes the statement; the informant signs it.

TRAFFIC ACCIDENT STATEMENT

ACCIDENT NUMBER **5-3-22**

STATEMENT OF - Last name   First Name   Address   Phone
WEBSTER,   ARNOLD F.   963 WALNUT ST. HARPER MD 21047   623-7706

RELATING TO ACCIDENT - On street or road   At   Date
VALLEY ROAD   PRATT ST.   HARPER   MD   10 OCT. 1984

TAKEN AT - Place   Hour   Date
HARPER MD POLICE DEPT.   16:45   11 OCT. 1984

TAKEN BY - Name   Representing
KENNETH WALCOT   P.D.

OTHERS PRESENT - Names
SHARON WEBSTER (WIFE)

Q Are you (name and address of person giving statement)? What is your age? Are you single or married?
A Yes   27   Married

Q What is your occupation? Where do you work? How long have you worked there?   Phone there?
A Roofer   Wells Construction Co, Harper MD.   3½ yrs.   623-8320

Q What was your connection with the accident that occurred (time and place of accident)?
A Driver of the Oldsmobile

DRIVER OR PEDESTRIAN

Q What road were you on?   Heading or facing in what direction?
A Valley Road   North

Q How fast were you traveling? What had you planned to do? Go straight ahead? Turn? Or other movement?
A 25 mph   Keep on straight ahead

Q Where were you when you first realized you were in danger? What did you try to do?
A Just entering intersection of Pratt St. Tried to stop.

Q Where were you coming from and going to at the time of the accident?
A From work on River Road. Going home.

Q After the accident, where did you finally come to a stop?
A At the curb about a hundred feet beyond the crosswalk.

Q Who else was with you at the time of the accident?
A Nobody

Q Within the last six hours, had you taken any medicine or had alcohol to drink? If so, when and how much?
A No

DRIVER ONLY

Q How long since you learned to drive? How long had you been driving on this trip before the accident?
A About 10 years   Five minutes

Q What vehicle were you driving? Who owns the vehicle?   How much had you driven this vehicle?
A Buick 4 door   I own it   About a year

Q So far as you know, was there anything wrong with the vehicle you were driving? Were the lights on?
A Nothing wrong   No lights

Q What vehicles were on the road at the time and place of this accident?
A My own vehicle, the bicycle ahead and another car going the other way.

Q Was it daylight or dark? What was the weather like? What was the road surface like? Its condition?
A Daylight   Clear   Dry pavement   Good condition

Q Tell me what you saw, especially what you saw happen.
A As I got into the intersection, the boy on the bicycle ahead of me on the right started to turn left in front of me without warning. My left front bumper clipped his rear wheel and sent him sprawling in the intersection. He laid there until I came back. Another man and I helped him to the far left corner. Then the ambulance came.

Continue on back of sheet.

Q Is there anything else you would like to say about this accident?
A It was not my fault

Continue on back of sheet.

Q Now, is everything you have told me the truth? Will you sign this statement?   Date
I HAVE READ THIS STATEMENT AND IT IS TRUE - Signature
Arnold Webster   10/11/84

Exhibit 6. For less experienced investigators, it may be best to have a standard list of questions with places for the informant's replies. Such a form discourages follow-up questions.

3. Topical schedule (Same as Item 2 above but with paragraph or topic headings under which are recorded what the person interviewed had to say about each of the scheduled matters)
4. List of specific questions (The form is printed with a heading like that described in Item 2 above, followed by questions which might be asked and a space for the answer to each, as in Exhibit 6)

The structured set of questions, Item 4, appeals to and is useful for poorly trained and inexperienced investigators because it relieves them of the responsibility of thinking what to ask a witness and reduces the task of obtaining statements to a simple step-by-step operation. The difficulty is that with this structured form the investigator tends to stop inquiry when the listed questions have been asked and so fails to follow up with additional imaginative or probing questioning. Well trained and experienced investigators can do better by following a line of questioning especially adapted to each particular case.

6. FORMAL QUESTIONING OF INFORMANTS

Testimony and Depositions

The fourth level or degree of obtaining information about an accident from a person is testimony or deposition. The former is given in court, the latter is taken elsewhere. Otherwise they are substantially the same. Depositions are sometimes read in court later when the person himself cannot be there. Characteristics of this method of obtaining information from an informant are
1. The person is under oath.
2. A stenographic transcript is made which the person may review for accuracy.
3. Questions are asked by at-

torneys. Ordinarily, attorneys for both prosecution or plaintiff and defendant are present.
4. There can be cross examination.
5. Certain rules of evidence are followed, for example, hearsay is not permitted.

Subject matter of testimony and depositions is, in general, much the same as that for detailed statements.

Interrogation

The fifth and final level of obtaining information about an accident from someone involved is interrogation.[4] Its main purpose is to try to obtain a confession from him if he is guilty of a crime. In connection with traffic accident investigation, the suspected crime is usually serious, like driving under the influence of alcohol, hit-and-run driving, reckless homicide, or possibly auto theft. Interrogation is rarely undertaken in connection with traffic offenses which are misdemeanors.

Interrogation is usually conducted by prosecuting attorneys or police specialists and never at the scene of the accident. Before such an inquiry is undertaken, the suspect must be advised of his right to remain silent, to have his attorney present, and that anything he may say may be used for or against him in a trial.

Interrogation may or may not be recorded stenographically, usually not. Details of methods of interrogation are described in a number of books on police science.[2]

7. IDENTIFICATION OF DRIVERS AND PEDESTRIANS

Up to now, this topic has dealt with obtaining information of various kinds from people. From here on, information about drivers and pedestrians as functional parts of the highway transportation system will be considered. As in the case of roads

and vehicles, the other two parts of the system, investigators obtain and organize four kinds of data about each driver and pedestrian involved:
1. *Identification*
2. *Description*
3. *Condition* before the accident
4. *Result of the accident* (injuries) on the person.

Identification is required mainly for driver records and for criminal and civil litigation.

License certificates nearly always give the data needed on the accident-report form to identify drivers. The most important item is the driver-license number (sometimes the same as the social security number). This number is unique and connects the driver unmistakably with records in the state department of motor vehicles. Theoretically, with his number, all other relevant identifying data could be had from state files; but, in practice, reference to central records is sufficiently uncertain that additional identifying data are required for the accident-report form, namely, the driver's name and address.

If the driver-license certificate is unavailable, for example, because the driver does not have it with him, because he is unlicensed, or because it was lost in the accident, identify him by name and address like any other individual. If you suspect fraud, request other proof of identification.

Follow usual police procedure in accepting driver-license certificates for identification.[3] Be sure that the certificate belongs to the driver and get his current address which may be different from that on the certificate.

Pedestrians, of course, are identified only by name and address on traffic-accident reports.

Traffic-accident report forms all provide spaces for what is supposed to be the most reliable identification of drivers and pedestrians involved in the accident.

8. DESCRIPTIONS OF DRIVERS AND PEDESTRIANS

Accident-report forms require some description of drivers, pedestrians, and injured persons. Any descriptions of other informants should be included with statements made by them.

Classification and Tabulation

Standard descriptions of people for accident statistics are simple.

Age and sex. There is a space on nearly all accident-report forms to record age and sex. These data are customarily tabulated for drivers and persons killed or injured.[4] Age may be recorded directly in years or as a birth date from which, knowing the date of the accident, age may be computed.

Place of residence of driver is usually classified and tablulated in three categories:

1. Local resident
2. Residing elsewhere in state
3. Nonresident of state.

Residence can be determined by comparing the correct address of the driver with location of the accident. Consequently, special provision for such a description is not necessary on an accident-report form.

Height and weight data are sometimes useful in studying pedestrian and cyclist accidents. They are not provided for on traffic-accident report forms. Record them only when you have some special reason for doing so.

Descriptions Suggest Reliability of Information

Whenever a detailed statement is obtained from an informant, a brief description of that person helps to judge the significance and reliability of information obtained from him. For example, the statement of a stranger may be regarded more highly than that of a driver's relative; and that of an adult may be considered more reliable than that of a very young child.

Such a description may be made part of the statement by asking questions the answers to which provide this description, or the descriptive information may be separate, for example, in a memo or report accompanying one or more statements.

9. CONDITION BEFORE ACCIDENT

Driver and Pedestrian will be Considered Together

Most driver conditions that contribute to accidents also contribute to accidents involving pedestrians. Therefore, as indicated earlier, what is said here about drivers applies also to pedestrians. Because more drivers than pedestrians are involved in accidents, only drivers will be mentioned without adding "and pedestrians" even though what is said applies to either.

Determining Driver Condition Before the Accident

After a traffic accident, determining whether unfavorable driver conditions contributed to the event is much more difficult than determining conditions of car and road that may have been contributing factors. For one thing, roads and cars generally remain, for some time after the accident, in about the same condition so that they may be examined carefully and perhaps tested; but people begin to change in important ways soon after the accident so that there is much less opportunity to examine or test them. Also, people cannot be disassembled like cars to find out what was wrong with them. It is always possible, of course, to test for alcohol. Unless the driver is killed or seriously injured, his eyes and his knowledge of road rules can also be tested after an accident; but it is not practical to try to evaluate his driving skills or his attitude, either or both of which can be important accident contributors.

Driver behavior which contrib-uted to an accident must be known before driver conditions leading to that behavior can be appraised. However, discovering, after an accident, exactly what the driver did or did not do is rarely possible. Except as reflected in reported observations of the behavior of the vehicle or in marks left on the road, driver behavior seldom leaves any detectable trace. What drivers themselves can and will say about what they did is generally fragmentary and unreliable. Consequently, inferences about driver conditions that may have been factors in the accident often tend to be speculative. That is to say, such opinions represent possibilities, often a number of alternative possibilities, rather than substantial probabilities or demonstrable certainties.

Driver Condition is Important

Because driver conditions contributing to traffic accidents are so difficult to perceive after an accident, most such conditions go undetected and unrecorded. Consequently, we know very little about driver conditions and tend to overlook their importance.

Driver behavior is a factor, however, in *nearly every traffic accident.* The reason for this is not difficult to understand. The driver makes the decisions and controls the vehicle. The vehicle does not perceive potential or actual hazards; the vehicle does not adjust its speed or position on the road according to existing conditions; the vehicle does not determine what evasive tactics are appropriate; the vehicle does not evaluate the risk of the trip in the first place. In the days when four-legged creatures powered highway transportation, the human driver shared responsibilities for detecting and avoiding hazards with the animal; "horse sense" often literally prevailed over poor judgment on the part of a human driver or rider. But motor vehicles and bicycles provide no such auxiliary controls; the entire responsibility is with the driver.

The best drivers can overcome almost any hazardous situation presented by road and vehicle conditions. The poorest drivers, however, can operate successfully only when road and vehicle conditions are favorable and when traffic presents few problems. Hence we are concerned with what driver conditions make a driver unable, in a specific accident, to solve the problems presented by road conditions, vehicle conditions, and traffic.

Distinguish between driver conditions before and after an accident. The accident often changes the condition of the driver. We are interested primarily in prior conditions as possible factors. Be careful how you judge preaccident conditions by what you see at the scene. You can observe many driver conditions, particularly physical abilities, after the accident; but you must ordinarily use methods other than observation to determine what a driver's attitude or even physical condition was immediately before the accident. It is impossible, after an accident, for example, to determine by observation whether a driver fell asleep before the accident. That condition has to be inferred from circumstances of the accident, from statements of informants, or from the driver's own statement, and such inferences are always of questionable reliability.

Investigation of Driver Condition

At the scene of an accident, an investigator cannot be expected to learn much about unsafe driver condition before the accident. But he should be alert for clues that may point toward the possibility of such conditions. Some of these clues are so obscure that they usually escape attention but others are easily noted for whatever significance they may later turn out to have:

1. Any obvious physical handicap such as crippling; loss, weakness, or stiffness of a limb; deafness; or other infirmity not clearly the result of the accident

2. A statement or suggestion by any informant that a driver was suffering from any permanent or temporary disability, for example, that the driver fell asleep, was under the influence of alcohol, or had some ailment

3. A statement or suggestion by any informant that the driver was doing something or trying to do something that might have interfered with proper driving, for example, eating, drinking, lighting a cigarette, attending to a child, looking at maps, or looking for directional signs

4. Things in the vehicle that suggest driver condition (The most common is an open container of alcoholic beverage. Pills or narcotics on the driver or in the vehicle may also be suggestive. Other things may suggest distractions, for example, partly eaten food; open maps; papers showing directions to locations; or things that may have been spilled or scattered in the car before a crash.)

5. The kind of trip (For example, the place where vehicle occupants came from may suggest intoxication; and how long they had been travelling may suggest fatigue or sleep.)

Follow up any such clues to possible driver condition while you are still at the scene of the accident, so far as you find opportunity to do so, by additional observations and inquiry. Especially, if possible driver conditions are mentioned by an informant, remember to ask the informant what makes him think there was something the matter with the driver. In this manner, you may uncover observations or other facts by which you yourself can judge the significance of the informant's statement. Such further inquiries often reinforce or counteract suspicions of driver condition as a contributing factor in the accident.

Make careful notes of anything you have seen or heard that suggests the possibility of driver disabilities, at least if the accident is serious. Record whatever factual information supports this suggestion, otherwise you may later wonder why you noted the possibility of a driver disability.

Subsequent additional investigation, when required, involves one or more of three kinds of inquiries:

1. Examination of past medical and other records relating to the individual in question to learn what they may indicate, if anything, about his previous condition or capabilities (A driver's family and friends may also provide useful data. Besides medical records, driver-license, welfare, school, employment, and prison records may provide information.)

2. Subsequent physical examination or autopsy

3. Subsequent knowledge and skill tests.

Experts. Most subsequent examination of a driver for conditions which might have predisposed him to accidents will require the help of professionals of one kind or another in determination of facts, in interpreting their significance, or both. Doctors can discover conditions like heart ailments that may have been accident factors. Psychologists can explain personality factors which may be involved. The job of the initial investigator is to make such observations as he can of driver condition and inquire concerning circumstances which might suggest or preclude certain possible conditions; then an expert may be asked for help if it is needed.

It is important that you record

carefully whatever you notice that makes you suspect that one or more driver conditions contributed to the accident. It is not sufficient to write down a condition you believe to have existed; you must also record in detail the factual basis for your conclusions.

Driving Impairment

Five main conditions may temporarily impair ability to drive:
1. Alcohol
2. Drugs and medicines
3. Carbon monoxide
4. Drowsiness and sleep
5. Sudden disablement

Each of these may be manifested by the circumstances of the accident, by observable condition of the driver, or both. Some of the signs of these conditions are the same for more than one of the conditions. Sometimes two or more of these conditions are present at the same time, and one may multiply the effect of the other (the synergetic phenomenon). For example, ingested alcohol may increase the chances that drowsiness leads to sleep.

Alcohol

The first of the five main conditions temporarily modifying driver behavior, alcohol, is probably the most common. In many areas, autopsies of drivers killed in traffic accidents show that about half had enough alcohol in their bodies to be considered under its influence. Persons with less than 0.05 percent of alcohol by weight in the blood, or the equivalent in breath or urine, are legally presumed not under the influence of alcohol; but with 0.10 percent or more of alcohol in the blood, a person is legally presumed to be under its influence.[1] (Some states set somewhat different legal limits.)

Driving behavior that suggests alcohol differs with the individual and with the amount of alcohol the driver has consumed. Moderate amounts of alcohol in the blood, especially in young drivers, seem to reduce caution. Maneuvers become exaggerated; speed goes up, turns are taken faster, overtaking is done at higher speeds and with closer clearances, following distances are shorter and lane changing is more abrupt. There is also often overreaction to hazard such as too sudden braking and disastrous swerves ending in loss of control.

Higher levels of alcohol in bodily fluids, especially in older drivers, tend to result in weaving from side to side or very slow and cautious driving. Sometimes the car is stopped entirely but in an inappropriate place.

These behavioral symptoms of intoxication may be reported by informants or may be suggested by the kind of accident such as sharp swerves off the road, into fixed objects, or toward other vehicles.

If any informant claims or infers that a driver was under the influence of alcohol, or if behavior of the driver or any circumstances of the accident suggest to the investigator that this may have been the case, the investigator should give the matter serious and prompt consideration. Three kinds of inquiry are used to determine the driver's condition with respect to alcohol:
1. Questioning informants
2. Observing the individual
3. Chemical tests.

Because the effect of ingested alcohol wears off, investigation of this aspect of the accident must be commenced as soon as possible, preferably at the scene of the accident.

1. *Questioning drivers,* companions, and others who might know, such as bartenders, is not difficult. Ask whether the driver had been at a tavern or party where he could be expected to have consumed intoxicating liquor. Ask if he had any alcoholic beverage to drink, and if so, how much, what kind, and when. Information obtained thus is often unreliable, but that cannot be helped. Not much is to be gained by asking whether the informant believed the driver to be under the influence. The answers are likely to be evasive. The facts from an informant are more important than his conclusions.

2. *Observing the driver's condition* and behavior. Make a record of your observations for future reference. This can be done by simple notes or on a form for the purpose (Exhibit 7). The form is used for recording facts.[5] From these facts anyone may reach his own conclusion. The form shown in Exhibit 7 indicates what observations you make. Record any observations to make in addition to those suggested by the form.

3. *Chemical tests* of alcohol in blood, breath, and urine represent the most objective and accurate method of gauging the degree to which a driver may be under the influence of alcohol. Interesting data could be developed if every driver involved in a traffic accident could be given such a test. But extensive use of chemical tests for enforcement involving severe penalties and the costs of administering tests has put so many limitations on their use that, for practical purposes, tests are given only under two circumstances: 1) as evidence in enforcement; and 2) in autopsies of drivers killed in traffic accidents.

If chemical tests are made, the results may become part of the investigation record and may be helpful in understanding how and especially why the accident occurred. In this connection it is always important to remember that two difficult conclusions are involved: 1) to what degree does available information indicate that the driver was under the influence of alcohol; and 2) what part, if any, did this degree of intoxication play in the accident.

Drugs and Medicines

The second main condition temporarily affecting driver capabilities

ALCOHOLIC INFLUENCE REPORT FORM

(Check)
- ☒ Driver
- ☐ Pedestrian
- ☐ Passenger

(Check)
- ☒ Accident
- ☐ Violation
- ☐ Other

Date and time of Accident or Violation: 12 OCT 8 19:25 am/pm

Police Dept. PALMER OH
Arrest No. 3781
Accident No. 85-183
Arresting Officer JAMES KOLB
Date and time in custody 12 OCT 85 20:00 am/pm

Name BAXTER, WILLIAM A   Address 878 HILL ST PALMER OH

Age 19   Sex M   Approx. Wt. 165   Operator Lic. No. 345-67-8910   State OH

OBSERVATIONS:

CLOTHES

Describe: (Type & Color)
- Hat or Cap: NONE
- Jacket or Coat: BLACK LEATHER
- Shirt or Dress: YELLOW
- Pants or Skirt: BROW & YELLOW CHECK

Condition: ☐ Disorderly ☐ Disarranged ☐ Soiled ☐ Mussed ☒ Orderly
(Describe)

BREATH — Odor of Alcoholic Beverage: ☐ strong ☒ moderate ☐ faint ☐ none

ATTITUDE
- ☐ Excited ☐ Hilarious ☐ Talkative ☐ Carefree ☐ Sleepy ☐ Profanity
- ☐ Combative ☒ Indifferent ☐ Insulting ☐ Cocky ☐ Cooperative ☒ Polite

UNUSUAL ACTIONS — ☐ Hiccoughing ☐ Belching ☐ Vomiting ☐ Fighting ☐ Crying ☐ Laughing

SPEECH
- ☐ Not Understandable ☒ Mumbled ☐ Slurred ☐ Mush Mouthed ☐ Confused
- ☐ Thick Tongued ☐ Stuttered ☐ Accent ☐ Fair ☐ Good

Indicate other unusual actions or statements, including when first observed: NONE

Signs or complaint of illness or injury: NONE

PERFORMANCE TESTS: (Note—See departmental instructions for conducting these tests)

Check Squares If Not Made | Check appropriate square before word describing condition observed

☐ **BALANCE**	☐ Falling	☐ Needed Support	☐ Wobbling	☐ Swaying	☒ Unsure	☐ Sure
☐ **WALKING**	☐ Falling	☐ Staggering	☐ Stumbling	☐ Swaying	☒ Unsure	☐ Sure
☐ **TURNING**	☐ Falling	☐ Staggering	☒ Hesitant	☐ Swaying	☐ Unsure	☐ Sure

FINGER-TO-NOSE
- Right: ☐ Completely Missed ☒ Hesitant ☐ Sure
- Left: ☒ Completely Missed ☐ Hesitant ☐ Sure

COINS — ☐ Unable ☒ Fumbling ☐ Slow ☐ Sure ☐ (Other)
(Balance during coin test) SUPPORTED SELF WITH HAND ON FLOOR

Ability to understand instructions: ☐ Poor ☒ Fair ☐ Good   Tests performed: Date ___ Time ___ am/pm

OBSERVER'S OPINION:

Effects of alcohol: ☐ extreme ☒ obvious ☐ slight ☐ none   Ability to drive: ☐ unfit ☐ fit

Indicate briefly what first led you to suspect alcoholic influence: STATEMENT OF WITNESS SHARP BREATH ODOR

Observed by: KOLB   Assignment: TRAFFIC
Witnessed by: FOSTER & KING   Date 12 OCT 85   Time 20:30 am/pm

CHEMICAL TEST DATA:

Specimen: ☐ Blood ☒ Breath ☐ Saliva ☐ Urine ☐ None ☐ Refused ☐ Unable

Analysis result: 0.16 %
If Breath, what instrument? Intoximiter

If refused, why?

Exhibit 7. *The alcoholic influence report is a record of observations of a driver's condition.*

INTERVIEW:

Were you operating a vehicle? *Yes* Where were you going? *Home*

What street or highway were you on? *Hill St* Direction of travel? *South*

Where did you start from? *Kilarney Tavern* What time did you start? *18:40*

What time is it now? *9 O'clock* What city (county) are you in now? *Palmer Ohio*

What is the date? *11 Oct* What day of the week is it? *Saturday*

INTERVIEWER TO FILL IN ACTUAL:	*20:30* am/pm	*Saturday*	*12 Oct*	*Kolb*
	Time	Day	Date	Interviewer's Name

When did you last eat? *Noon* What did you eat? *Lunch Hamburgers*

What were you doing during the last three hours? *Visiting with friends*

Have you been drinking? *Yes* What? *Beer* How much? *About 3 glasses*

Where? *Kilarney Tavern* Started? *5* am/pm Stopped? *7* am/pm

Are you under the influence of an alcoholic beverage now? *No*

What is your occupation? *Painter* When did you last work? *Friday*

Do you have any physical defects? *No* If so, what? —

Are you ill? *No* If so, what's wrong? —

Do you limp? *No* Have you been injured lately? *No* If so, what's wrong? —

Did you get a bump on the head? *No* Were you involved in an accident today? *Yes*

Have you had any alcoholic beverage since the accident? *No* If so, what? —

Where? — How much? — When? —

Have you seen a doctor or dentist lately? *No* If so, who? — When? —

What for? — Are you taking tranquilizers, pills or medicines of any kind? *No*

If so, what kind? (Get sample) — Last dose? — am/pm Do you have epilepsy? *No*

Diabetes? *No* Do you take insulin? *No* If so, last dose? — am/pm

Have you had any injections of any other drugs recently? *No* If so, what for? —

What kind of drug? — Last dose? — am/pm When did you last sleep? —

How much sleep did you have? *7 hours* Are you wearing false teeth? *No* Do you have a glass eye? *No*

HANDWRITING SPECIMEN
Signature and/or anything he chooses.

William Baxter Palmer Ohio

REMARKS:

SUPPLEMENTARY DATA:

(Note—Get witnesses, including officers who observed, to prove driving)

WITNESSES			Was Suspect Driving or Operating	What Was His Condition	Where Observed
Name	Address	Tel. No.			
SHARP, Walter	244 Spring	337-2471	Yes	Unsteady	Wilson & Hill

Passengers in Suspect's Vehicle	Name *None*	Address	Condition

National Safety Council 444 North Michigan Avenue • Chicago, Illinois 60611

25M877 Printed in U.S.A. Stock No. 321.99

The back of the alcoholic influence report is a record of questions asked and the suspect's answers.

are ingested drugs and medicines other than alcohol. Some of these produce behavior quite like the effect of alcohol. Others give symptoms something like drowsiness.

Determining whether a driver has been taking certain drugs or medicines by observation of the person or analysis of specimen of blood or other bodily substances is usually not practical for most investigators. If necessary, this may be attempted by specially trained medical or toxicological personnel.

But police investigators at the scene of an accident can make observations of driver behavior and may notice, in the car or among a driver's belongings, pills or drugs in other forms which suggest that his physical or mental condition may have been impaired to some extent by drugs. If you have a suspicion that this may be the case, inquire of the driver and others who might know whether the drugs belong to the driver in question, what kind of drugs they are, and whether and how recently the driver had taken them. What an informant says in reply to this kind of question may or may not be the truth, but his statement becomes a part of the investigation record for whatever it is worth.

If the matter is important, drugs found in the vehicle or on the driver may be referred to a pharmacist, physician, or toxicologist to find out what they are and what effect they may have had on the driver. It may also be desirable to look into the medical history of the driver to determine what drugs he may have been taking and how they may have affected him.

Diabetes is a fairly common disorder which is treated with insulin injections. Without proper treatment, a diabetic person may suffer shock, go into a coma, or both. Most people under treatment for this condition are ordinarily able and willing to explain what has affected them and nearly always their medical histories will reveal this condition.

Carbon Monoxide

Carbon monoxide poisoning is the third of the main temporary conditions which may influence driver performance adversely. Carbon monoxide is an odorless, colorless, gradually poisoning gas present, more or less, in all automobile exhaust fumes. Breathing enough air contaminated by carbon monoxide (CO) is eventually fatal. Most known motor-vehicle deaths from carbon monoxide poisoning are those of people who commit suicide by breathing exhaust fumes in a closed garage or other enclosed space. The number of transport-related motor-vehicle accidents that result from carbon monoxide poisoning is difficult to estimate because most of them probably go undetected.

In autopsies of dead drivers, carbon monoxide is suggested by a cherry-red liver and confirmed by chemical tests of blood.

Drivers not killed in accidents may complain of headache, weakness, dizziness, confusion. These suggest the possibility of carbon monoxide poisoning.

In most cases of carbon monoxide poisoning discovered by police, the driver is found sitting or lying in an undamaged vehicle. These circumstances also suggest intoxication, natural death — for example, from heart disease — foul play, or suicide. If the driver is not clearly dead, get him out of the vehicle and give artificial respiration. If carbon monoxide poison is suspected, examine the vehicle as soon as possible for exhaust leaks. Note whether the engine is running and whether the ignition is on or off. If the engine is not running, note whether fuel tank is empty. Note also the position of heater controls. Later, detailed examination of the vehicle for leaks in the exhaust system should be sought, preferably by mechanics.

Detection of carbon monoxide poison as a contributing preaccident driver condition usually requires collaboration of police, medical authorities (including coroners), and automobile mechanics.

Drowsiness and Sleep

Loss of consciousness due to drowsiness, the fourth main temporary condition affecting driver performance, doubtless contributes to many accidents but it is extremely difficult to substantiate. If the driver is killed, no bodily change occurs which can be detected by autopsy, and if the driver is not killed, no symptoms of drowsiness remain after the accident. Hence this condition must usually be considered a possibility or a probability if no other explanation is satisfactory; sleep is rarely substantiated well enough to be considered a certainty.

Two accident circumstances commonly suggest that the driver fell asleep:

1. The vehicle continues straight ahead off the roadway instead of turning when entering a curve.
2. The vehicle gradually leaves its lane without any sharp swerve. If it leaves to the right, it may hit a fixed object, if to the left, another vehicle or a fixed object. Whatever it hits, it hits head on.

In either case, the driver is more likely to have been asleep if he had been travelling on a straight road for some time.

Drivers are more likely to fall asleep in rural areas than in cities, on straight roads than on curved ones, and where traffic is very light.

Length of trip is not a reliable indicator of the probability of a driver having fallen asleep. For example, drivers often fall asleep during a warm afternoon on a monotonous road after a generous lunch even though they have travelled only a few miles; and drivers who have been 12 hours on the road may seem quite alert. On the other hand, a report of "fighting off drowsiness" or stopping for coffee to wake up suggests that the driver fell asleep.

Fatigue tends to induce drowsiness and sleep. Fatigue without drowsiness is believed to impair driver performance, but the nature of this impairment and its possible extent is not well understood. Fatigue and drowsiness are not so closely related as many believe. It is possible to be extremely fatigued without symptoms of drowsiness. It is also possible to fall asleep when fully rested. Sleep is probably induced as frequently by monotony as by fatigue.

The best confirmation that a driver fell asleep is observation by a fellow passenger who actually saw what happened. The driver's own statement is not so trustworthy because drivers often say they fell asleep when actually some more culpable condition, such as driving under the influence of alcohol, was actually involved.

The best refutation of speculation that a driver fell asleep is some sign on the road or observed vehicle behavior indicating that, before leaving the roadway or striking another vehicle, the driver applied brakes or steered abruptly. One does not do either of these if he is really asleep.

Of course other conditions can produce accidents quite similar to driver-asleep accidents, for example, carbon monoxide poison, diabetic coma, and heart attacks, but probably more common than any of these are prolonged distractions or preoccupations which delay perception of hazard for perhaps five seconds or more.

As in all matters relating to condition of roads, vehicles, and people, it is much more important that an investigator record in detail what information led to the conclusion that a driver may have fallen asleep than to report his own conclusion.

Sudden Disablement

The fifth main condition which can temporarily impair a driver is some kind of sudden and severe dis-

ablement. Unquestionably many ailments diminish the vitality of a driver slightly — like a moderate amount of fatigue or carbon monoxide poison — and so may make the slight difference between having an accident and not having one. But such an effect is not detectable by any available means. Other illnesses set in gradually so that the driver is aware of his condition and either does not attempt to drive, is able to stop before his condition disables him, or can compensate for the condition, thereby avoiding possible accidents. Ailments which can unexpectedly disable a driver are of two kinds:

1. Those which may cause sudden unconsciousness or "blackouts"
2. Those which may cause violent uncontrollable movements or inability to move.

"Blackouts" due to physical or mental disorders result in the same kinds of accidents as falling asleep. Usually they are distinguished from driver-asleep accidents only by an informant's statements or by medical examination of the driver. Either of these may be unavailable or inconclusive, but in many accident investigations it makes little or no difference.

Little is known about what kind of ailments have resulted in sudden loss of consciousness and how frequently this happens. First, this is because such accidents are probably quite rare and, second, it is because when "blackouts" are involved, investigations are not usually sufficiently detailed to reveal and document the circumstance.

Blackouts are commonly ascribed to "heart attacks" but usually more as speculation than as established fact. Strokes, narcolepsy (a disorder causing brief attacks of deep sleep), some forms of epilepsy, diabetes, some circulatory diseases, and some mental diseases, may unexpectedly cause a driver to "pass out". Usually, in such cases, if he survives, the driv-

er does not know what actually happened.

"Seizures" or spasm can result in a great variety of accidents. Some are "no-control" accidents like falling asleep. Others are over-control accidents in which the vehicle swerves violently. Such accidents are very rare and are generally neither fully investigated or adequately documented. Statements of informants or medical examination may yield information suggesting "seizures" but these may be inconclusive.

Sudden and extreme pain is usually associated with seizures. This might come from heart attacks, ulcers, or severe muscular spasms. Digestive disorders causing vomiting or retching, pulmonary diseases causing uncontrolled coughing, and some arthritic conditions can so agitate and distract a driver that he loses control of the car. But seizures are not necessarily accompanied by pain. Some are simply inability to move. Drivers are likely to describe such attacks rather vividly — provided they survive the resulting accident.

The ordinary investigator is not expected to determine whether or how illness or drugs (except alcohol) may have contributed to a particular accident. That is a task for follow-up investigation, usually by professionals. But the ordinary investigator is expected to be alert, especially immediately after the accident, for remarks, complaints, and explanations as well as signs of driver behavior, driver condition, and things in the vehicle which might suggest the possible need for follow-up investigation. The investigator is expected to make notes of such information so that it becomes part of the investigation record rather than to rely on memory which would not make facts available to others working on the case. Such conditions should be reported to the state motor-vehicle administrator so that he can reconsider medical qualifications of the driver.

Permanent Driver Capabilities

Driver conditions, which only change slowly with maturity and experience, are, perhaps, more important than the temporary conditions. These more permanent conditions establish a level of driver capability which may be more or less modified from time to time by temporary conditions such as those which have been described and by others not mentioned. They are more important because they are always present and form the foundation, as it were, of driver performance.

Permanent driver conditions involve many aspects of personality interrelated in complicated ways. These are generally described as

1. Natural abilities
2. Learned capabilities
3. Attitudes.

There are no generally useful methods of determining whether and to what extent any level of any of these three aspects of personality contributed to a particular accident. Still more beyond the reach of present investigators is evaluation of various "mixes" or combination of natural abilities, skills, and attitudes. It does appear, however, that serious physical disabilities, to the hearing for example, or loss of both legs, can be adequately compensated for by special skills and effort which is the product of attitude.

A full description of driver capabilities and their possible effects on accidents would require a large book and, at this stage of our knowledge of these matters, the discussion would tend to be speculative. Nevertheless, some discussion of these might help you understand how certain accidents happened. Therefore, you will find more about driver capabilities in the last section of this topic.

10. INJURIES

Injuries are the principal results of the accident as it affects people at the time of the accident.

Injury Classification

Police officers who investigate accidents at the scene are expected to classify the injuries to all persons involved, that is, every occupant of a vehicle and every pedestrian struck. This classification is to evaluate the severity of the accident.

Observation of persons involved by an attending police officer at the scene of the accident is the basis for classification. Neither medical reports nor special follow up is required for injury classification.

Be careful not to judge a person's injuries by his behavior immediately after a crash. It is better to note his condition as he is leaving the scene of the accident. For a few minutes immediately after an accident, a person may suffer from shock or hysteria which may make him seem more seriously hurt than he is. Also, immediately after an accident, an injured person may not feel or show the effects of his injuries as much as he may a quarter of an hour later.

It is true that some injuries will later turn out to be more serious than they seemed at first, and some less serious than they were judged to be at the scene. But, because it is impractical to keep track of all persons to determine how injuries eventually develop, for sake of uniformity, all injuries are classified according to appearance at the scene of the accident.[6]

Thus, on the basis of his appearance at the scene, the injury to each person involved in a traffic accident is classified in one of five categories.[6]

0. *No injury.* No sign that the person received bodily harm from the accident in which he was involved. This category includes confusion, excitement, anger, and internal injuries unknown to the injured until after leaving the accident scene.

1. *Fatal injury.* "Any injury that results in death within 90 days after the accident." The initial investigator in-

dicates a death on his report if the injured person definitely appears to be dead at the scene of the accident, or the investigator has received reliable information — from a hospital, for example — that the injured person has died before his report is filed.

Corrections in records for later deaths require arrangements that vary according to the relationship of accident investigators to the traffic-records system and the relationship of the traffic-records system to the agency processing vital statistics.

2. *Incapacitating injury.* "Any injury, other than fatal injury, which prevents the injured person from walking, driving, or normally continuing activities which he was capable of performing before the injury occurred." This category includes severe lacerations, broken or distorted limbs, concussions, crushed chest, internal injuries that disable, unconsciousnes when the person was removed from the scene of the accident, or inability to leave the place of the accident without assistance. Momentary unconsciousness is not regarded as an incapacitating injury. Hospitalization is normally required after a disabling injury, but the duration of the disability after injury does not affect the classification.

3. *Nonincapacitating evident injury.* "Any injury, other than a fatal injury, which is evident to observers at the scene of the accident in which the injury occurred." This category includes a lump on the head, abrasions, bruises, minor lacerations and others. It does not include limping (the injury

cannot be seen).

4. *Possible injury.* "Any injury reported or claimed which is not a fatal injury, incapacitating injury, or nonincapacitating evident injury."
This category includes momentary unconsciousness, claim of injuries not evident, limping, complaint of pain, nausea, and hysteria.

The records of injury classifications are provided for on most police traffic-accident report forms. This record requires only marking a box to indicate the appropriate injury category or writing a code number in the appropriate space for the same purpose.

Descriptions of injuries beyond simple classification are rarely expected of police officers because the police investigator has neither the facilities or the opportunity to examine each person sufficiently to make a satisfactory report on injuries.

Technical Injury Descriptions

Examination of injured persons for more complete descriptions of injuries may be required under two circumstances:

1. Special studies made of injuries received in crashes
2. Civil litigation which requires a detailed appraisal of injuries for damage assessment purposes.

In either case, examination is by a physician or, if the person is dead, by a pathologist or medical examiner.

Reports of these special technical examinations are usually made in proper medical phraseology and may either be in the form of a simple memo or on a form used by the doctor or hospital for this purpose. In special studies of crash injuries, a form, usually including a diagram on which injuries are reported, is used for the injury report.[7]

Police or other investigators may have the task of obtaining technical injury descriptions from hospital records or questioning doctors to complete the investigation file.

11. THE DRIVING PROCESS

Driving Strategy and Tactics

To begin with, you must realize that the driving process — the control of the vehicle — operates at two levels: first, driving strategy, and second, driving tactics.

Driving strategy involves the *general* perception of a vehicle-road-traffic situation, an appraisal of *possible* hazards or risks, and adjustments of speed and position on the road to minimize the risk. Stopping at a blind corner before entering the crossroad is an example of strategy: the obstruction to vision is perceived, the possibility that it may obscure a vehicle on the cross street is recognized, and speed is reduced to the point at which, if there was actually a vehicle on the cross street, it could easily be avoided regardless of what the driver of that vehicle might do. Strategy is a driver's reaction to a general situation, the precautions he takes.

Driving tactics are the operations undertaken by a driver to evade or escape from an actual hazard, for example, another vehicle on a collision course. The hazard must be perceived and evaluated, a decision must be made as to what is to be done, and then the decision must be executed. Tactics are the driver's reaction to particular hazards, his evasive action.

If strategy has been faulty, a driver may discover he is confronted by a hazard from which no tactics can effect an escape. He is going too fast to stop in time, is on the wrong side of the road and cannot get back where he belongs soon enough, and so on.

Reactions

Reaction time is the time required from perception to start of vehicle control for tactical or strategic operations. The length of this time depends on the complexity of the decisions to be made and the urgency of the situation. Strategy requires few quick decisions, but some may be

complicated; tactics are more likely to require quick decisions which are usually quite simple. Reaction time includes the time to think and to start to control the vehicle. Time to start to control may include time to move hands or feet to controls, for example, the foot from accelerator to brake pedal in stopping. Quickness of reaction is not so important as appropriateness. There is no advantage in braking suddenly, if it would have been better to swerve.

Reaction time can be measured experimentally. Four different kinds of reaction time are recognized, based on the amount of thinking required for each. The less thinking, the shorter the reaction time.

Reflex reactions are instinctive or mostly so and require the shortest time because they involve no thought. An eye blink is usually a reflex action. Most driving does not involve reflex reaction. In fact, when the stimulus is so sudden and so strong that reflex action results, the act is usually wrong and often disastrous. It is a hysterical or convulsive response that may push the accelerator instead of the brake. Tire blowouts sometimes cause reflex action. Time required may be as little as a tenth of a second.

Simple reactions are the most common kind in driving because the stimulus is expected and the driver has already decided what he will do when the event occurs. Simple reactions are often a matter of habit, for example, putting on brakes when a signal turns yellow. This reaction takes normally about a quarter of a second with another quarter second needed to move the foot to the brake.

Complex reactions call for a choice among several possible responses. The decision has not been made in advance. For example, a pedestrian unexpectedly steps into the roadway ahead and the driver has to decide whether to turn right or left or slow down. Complex reactions are slower than simple reactions. How long a complex reaction takes depends on how complex the stim-

Exhibit 8.

THE DRIVING PROCESS

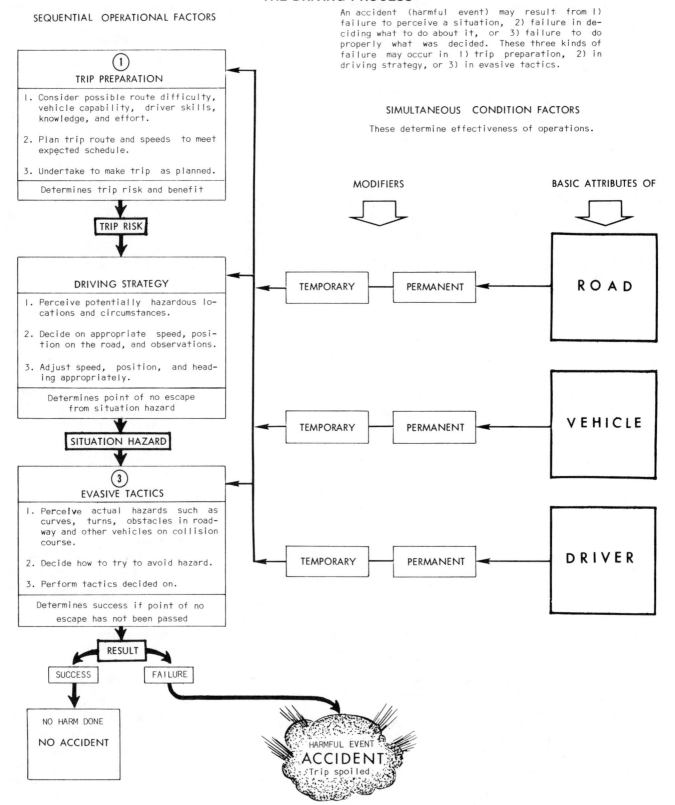

SEQUENTIAL OPERATIONAL FACTORS

An accident (harmful event) may result from 1) failure to perceive a situation, 2) failure in deciding what to do about it, or 3) failure to do properly what was decided. These three kinds of failure may occur in 1) trip preparation, 2) in driving strategy, or 3) in evasive tactics.

① TRIP PREPARATION

1. Consider possible route difficulty, vehicle capability, driver skills, knowledge, and effort.

2. Plan trip route and speeds to meet expected schedule.

3. Undertake to make trip as planned.

Determines trip risk and benefit

TRIP RISK

SIMULTANEOUS CONDITION FACTORS

These determine effectiveness of operations.

MODIFIERS

BASIC ATTRIBUTES OF

DRIVING STRATEGY

1. Perceive potentially hazardous locations and circumstances.

2. Decide on appropriate speed, position on the road, and observations.

3. Adjust speed, position, and heading appropriately.

Determines point of no escape from situation hazard

TEMPORARY   PERMANENT   ROAD

SITUATION HAZARD

③ EVASIVE TACTICS

1. Perceive actual hazards such as curves, turns, obstacles in roadway and other vehicles on collision course.

2. Decide how to try to avoid hazard.

3. Perform tactics decided on.

Determines success if point of no escape has not been passed

TEMPORARY   PERMANENT   VEHICLE

TEMPORARY   PERMANENT   DRIVER

RESULT

SUCCESS   FAILURE

NO HARM DONE
NO ACCIDENT

HARMFUL EVENT
ACCIDENT
Trip spoiled

ulus is, how many choices there are for reaction, and how often the driver has been in a similar situation. Normally, from half a second to two seconds may be required. Much driving is done by habitual complex reactions.

Discriminative reaction occurs when a driver is required to make a choice between two or more actions which are not habitual or practiced, for example, deciding whether to turn to the right or the left of a vehicle which is straddling two lanes. This is the slowest of all the reactions, and may require as much as a minute if the situation is complicated and the urgency slight.

Reaction time is affected by many things such as

- Age (Very young and especially very old people have slow reaction time; the latter often twice normal or average.)
- Strength of stimulus (Somewhat quicker reaction results from stronger stimuli, but the reaction is also somewhat more likely to be the wrong one.)
- Physical condition (Fatigue, sickness, and alcohol or other pcisons usually increase reaction time or decrease the accuracy of reaction.)
- Habits (Well formed habit patterns through training and experience reduce reaction time, especially complex reaction time.)

Perception is the general process of detecting some object or situation and comprehending its significance. Perception must occur before reaction can commence. Perception is affected by sensory conditions such as deficient vision, by ignorance, such as confusion about the meaning of a road marking or sign, and by skill in recognition of shapes and movement.

Perception delay is the interval between the instant when a hazard might have been seen, heard, or felt and when it is actually understood.

Unlike reaction time, perception delay cannot be measured experimentally well enough to give typical values for various circumstances. There are two reasons why perception delay measurements are unsatisfactory: 1) they are affected by such a variety of personal factors that the number of variables involved is large; and 2) more important, perception delay occurs because the driver's attention is often not directed toward the hazard and the time that elapses before he recognizes the hazard is quite indefinite. If an experienced driver is looking at the place where a hazard may appear, he perceives it almost instantly, and there is virtually no delay in perception; but if he is looking in some other direction, he may not perceive the hazard until his attention happens to be directed to it. This may require several seconds. Indeed, he may never perceive the hazard until he is upon it. When a driver falls asleep and runs off the roadway, there is no perception. The perception delay is then indefinite.

The whole driving procedure consists of a continual series of strategic operations by which a driver repeatedly adjusts speed and position on the road to lessen his risk at possibly hazardous locations, and another series of tactical operations to avoid actual hazards such as road curves and other vehicles on a collision course. These operations are summarized in Exhibit 8, a diagram showing how strategic and tactical operations are related. Studying this diagram will help you understand better the complexities of what seems to be the "simple" business of driving.

Natural Abilities

Now we are ready to return to the permanent driver capabilities which were mentioned earlier. It is clear that how well a person performs the operations of driving depends on his natural abilities, more or less modified permanently by knowledge and skill (habits) and possibly tempo-

rarily modified, from time to time, by one or more conditions such as alcohol or illness. These aspects of personality and their relationships are summarized in Exhibit 8.

Natural abilities with which a person is endowed are the foundation on which his driving capabilities rest.

Deficient natural abilities can contribute to accidents in several ways, although they are not actually common contributing factors. We are speaking of relatively permanent conditions, not diseases. Some physical or mental defects are deficiencies with which the person may have been born or which may gradually develop later. These deficiencies are in three areas:

1. *Sensory* conditions, especially seeing and hearing, that keep the driver from becoming aware of road or traffic conditions
2. *Conditions of mind and nerves* that prevent the driver from understanding hazardous conditions and making proper decisions concerning them
3. *Bone and muscle* conditions that prevent the driver from operating the controls of the vehicle properly.

Vision. There are a dozen or more eye conditions that can handicap a driver. Some of the better known ones are mentioned here in approximate order of importance.

Visual acuity or sharpness of seeing at a distance is important mainly in reading signs with specific messages such as "No Left Turn." This deficiency is usually correctable with glasses.

You may suspect that deficient visual acuity contributed to an accident when

- Accident involves movement in violation of a sign, especially a sign with small lettering or which is far away.
- Driver says he did not see or understand such a sign.

Exhibit 9.

PARTS OF DRIVER PERSONALITY

Deficiencies in any part can be made up, to a certain degree, by overplus in one or more other parts

① NATURAL ABILITIES	② LEARNED CAPABILITIES	③ MOTIVES AND ATTITUDES
What the driver has to start with	What he acquires by study and practice	Why the driver behaves the way he does
Good driving requires no exceptional natural abilities. Fairly simple physical and psychological tests can show limitations and need for mechanical aids or better general health and vitality.	Simple tests can show most deficiencies. Improvement fairly easy by education and training. Experience alone is not a good indicator of proficiency.	How the driver thinks and feels about many things, often lead him to drive unsafely even though he can and knows how to drive well. These personality factors are difficult to evaluate even with psychological training.

① NATURAL ABILITIES

SENSES — By which the driver perceives the driving situation.
- Feeling – usually taken for granted
- Seeing – many deficiencies can handicap driver slightly
- Hearing – relatively unimportant
- Smelling – rarely useful in driving

MIND AND NERVES — By which the driver learns, decides, and connects his senses with his muscles.
- Intelligence – high level not necessary or especially helpful
- Judgment of space and motion
- Coordination of bodily movements

BONES AND MUSCLES — By which the driver directs and controls his vehicle and moves his body.
- Stature to fit vehicle and its controls
- Strength to operate controls
- Limbs to connect with and operate regular and special controls
- Body movement – not much needed

② LEARNED CAPABILITIES

KNOWLEDGE OR INFORMATION — Gained by reading, instruction, and observation. Tested by quizzing.
- Of highways – surfaces, alignment, direction signs, route markings
- Of vehicles – care and behavior
- Of sharing the road – road rules, control devices, sight distances, behavior of other street users

SKILL AND HABITS — Gained by practice. Once fixed, habits are not very easily changed. Tests show need for training.
- In making the vehicle behave
- In recognizing road conditions
- In sharing the road – allowing for bad driving by others
- In maintaining attention, resisting distraction

③ MOTIVES AND ATTITUDES

ATTITUDES — Often determine how the driver reacts to the driving situation, how he thinks and feels about the situation. Attitudes may be involved in such behavior as:
- Taking unnecessary chances
- Playing games with moving cars
- Driving while fatigued
- Racing
- Recklessness
- Showing off

MOTIVES — The importance attached to safe driving is what makes a driver try to drive as well as he can and knows how to. Motives may be associated with many different feelings
- Fear of injury and damage
- Pride in perfection of performance
- Social responsibility
- Desire to set an example
- Fear of criticism
- Fear of arrest and punishment

REACTION Using streets and highways with vehicles or afoot involves continuous reactions to road and traffic situations. Reactions usually involve all three parts of personality to some degree. Correctness of reaction depends on the kind of thinking and availability of habitual responses suitable for various situations.

REACTION TIME or quickness of response depends mainly on how much thinking has to be done. Reaction speed is less important than response correctness; snap reactions are often dangerous, especially when there is very little time to correct an error. Well formed habits are the best assurance that reactions will be correct and quick.

REFLEX REACTIONS — Instinctive and unthinking. Usually response to emergency. About a tenth of a second but usually a wrong reaction. May be disastrous.

SIMPLE REACTION — A planned response to one expected situation. About a quarter of a second (plus another quarter second if foot has to be moved to brake).

COMPLEX REACTION — Selection of practiced response suitable to one of several situations. A half second to several seconds depending on complexity and readiness.

DISCRIMINATIVE REACTION — Thinking about what to do when a good habitual response is not ready. May take several seconds or minutes. May involve moral decisions.

CIRCUMSTANCES THAT AFFECT PERSONALITY

Personality can be modified rather quickly and seriously, but often temporarily by numberless circumstances, some of which are brought on by the person himself. These may affect any of the three parts of personality, and therefore driver reactions to traffic situations. People are affected differently by these special circumstances.

POISONS:	DRUGS:	ILLNESSES:	DROWSINESS:
Alcohol Narcotics Carbon monoxide	Insulin Barbiturates Antihistamines	Heart ailments Epilepsy Diabetes	Exhaustion Tension Monotony Fatigue

- Driver is without glasses when license certificate shows such a restriction.
- Confusion arises from failure to read or understand directional or street name signs.

Night blindness is the inability to see objects of low contrast in low illumination — for example, a pedestrian in dark clothing against a dark background 200 feet away from low-beam headlights. Night blindness is most commonly found among older people. It is not helped by glasses. Tinted glasses and tinted windshields intensify night blindness.

Suspect night blindness in accidents outside of cities or in places without street lights, especially with drivers over 50 years old when

- Vehicle runs off pavement on shoulder
- Vehicle strikes a pedestrian in dark clothing, an animal, a pile of dirt, or an unlighted vehicle
- Driver runs into side of freight train
- Driver complains he just did not see object struck.

Glare blindness is slow recovery from viewing dazzling lights at night. It is more common among older people than young. Susceptibility cannot be corrected by glasses. Dark glasses can reduce brilliance of light, but at night they also reduce all visibility, perhaps dangerously. Discomfort from too much brightness by day can be reduced safely by dark glasses.

Suspect glare blindness at night only when the driver has had an accident just after meeting a car with bright headlights or passing low, bright street lights, or other lights, and

- Runs off road
- Runs into pedestrian, fixed object, animal, or slow-moving vehicle
- Complains he was blinded by headlights.

Sometimes susceptibility to glare is due all or in part to looking directly at headlights rather than toward the edge of the road. This is a lack of knowledge and skill rather than an eye defect.

A narrow field of vision is inability to see toward the sides. When the field is very narrow it is called "tunnel vision". It cannot be corrected by glasses. People with sight in only one eye have a narrowed field of vision on the side of the blind eye.

Suspect narrow field of vision in the following kinds of accident situations when there are no view obstructions:

- In right angle collisions, if a car on cross street is moving fast, especially by day
- Driver says he did not see the car or pedestrian on his right or left by day or night
- Driver cuts in after overtaking and passing by day or night.

Color blindness is the inability to distinguish certain shades of red or green. In rare cases the person is completely unable to distinguish any color. Color blindness is probably not very important in accidents. It is not a common condition, and occurs almost entirely in men. Color blindness can be compensated for by *properly using* red or green transparent stripes on top of eyeglasses or windshield, but in practice this rarely is done or needed for driving by color-blind persons, although it is sometimes used by the color-blind whose jobs require them to recognize red or green markings.

Suspect color blindness when a male driver

- Runs a red light and insists he thought it was green
- Describes a red or green object, such as a car, as some other color.

Other eye defects are numerous but rare, difficult to relate specifically to accidents, and difficult to detect without special test equipment. For example, some people have difficulty fusing or combining the images formed by the two eyes. Under certain conditions, especially at night

and when combined with fatigue, difficulty with fusing may lead to confusion and an accident.

Hearing defects rarely contribute to accidents, but you might suspect deficient hearing when

- Someone sounds a horn on overtaking and the driver in question neglects to slow down or give way to right.
- A driver apparently ignores a train whistle.
- A pedestrian fails to heed horn or seems to ignore sounds of traffic.
- A driver has trouble hearing or cannot hear normal conversation.

Not much intelligence is needed to operate a vehicle safely, but if a person drives much, especially in congested areas, extremely low intelligence, such as mental retardation, is usually accompanied by a poor accident record. If a person has passed an examination for a driver's license, he is probably intelligent enough to drive.

Suspect low intelligence as a contributing factor if a person is not injured, ill, shocked, intoxicated, or apparently affected in any other way by the accident and does not seem able to provide sensible or reasonable answers to your questions.

It is quite easy to confuse low intelligence with intoxication or certain forms of mental illness. Rather than attempting to reach conclusions about this, it is better to carefully record the driver's answers to your questions and to note the way he behaves. This information would be helpful to qualified professionals in reaching conclusions about the driver's condition.

Very short drivers and those lacking limbs may have difficulty controlling the vehicle. Such deficiencies contribute to accidents in situations which require high manipulative skill such as turning movements. Modern vehicles have adjustable seats and special equipment for disabled persons is available. Usually, these persons have had special training and being very much aware of their handicaps, can compensate for them.

Suspect such a condition contributed to the accident when you see that the driver or pedestrian has such disabilities, but try to discover how they affected the particular accident, if at all.

Stiff or painful joints can handicap a driver in controlling a vehicle. Some of the special equipment for amputees may be found also on the vehicles of people suffering from chronic stiffness or soreness. Neck and shoulder stiffness may keep a person from looking to one side and therefore contributes to accidents in somewhat the same manner as narrow or tunnel vision. Stiff joints can usually be detected by watching the person walk and drive.

Extreme overweight has some effect on nimbleness of manipulation. It can contribute to accidents in much the same way as stiffness of joints.

Physical weakness of small people, invalids, or the aged, is often associated with stiffness or very small size. It may contribute to such accidents as

- Turning accidents (Driver saves work by cutting corners.)
- Insufficient braking
- Other inadequate evasive action.

Do not jump to the conclusion that because you find some physical impairment, it contributed to the accident. You must also base your conclusion about a possible contribution on other circumstances of the accident, statements of those involved, and your own observations. Some partially disabled persons are *better* than average drivers because they are aware of their deficiency and compensate for it. Therefore, if you see that a disabled person was a driver in an accident, don't *assume* that his disability was or was not a cause.

Learned Capabilities

Natural ability alone is not enough for driving. People in perfect physical and mental condition may have accidents because they have not yet learned to drive, that is, they have not acquired certain additional capabilities in the form of *knowledge* and *skill* (properly formed habits). We might say that such people *can* drive but don't yet *know how* to.

Knowledge by itself is not enough. One might be very well informed about vehicles, roads, and traffic and still be quite unable to drive a car for want of training or practice which develops the necessary habits for skill.

Skill is a combination of proper habits that enables a person to maneuver his vehicle or to detect road conditions. Skill is the result of practice and some natural ability. Sometimes skill is thought of as the entire behavior of a driver reflecting his knowledge, physical and mental capabilities, and attitudes as well as habits; but for purposes of accident analysis it is useful to think of it only as a combination of proper habits.

There are four general kinds of skill that have to be developed in learning to drive well:

1. *Controlling the vehicle* is manipulative skill. It can be tested by subjecting a person to such driving problems as parallel parking, starting on a steep grade without rolling back, and stopping the vehicle by locking all wheels.
2. *Recognizing road conditions* is most easily detected in watching how the driver controls his speed in approaching places where it must be reduced.
3. *Sharing the road* is judging and allowing for possible bad driving by others. It may also be evident in the consistency with which turn signals are given and proper road position is maintained.
4. *Maintaining attention* and

resisting distractions. The importance of this skill is usually underestimated. It is a difficult skill to learn properly and one in which bad habits are easy to develop. Careful investigation will often reveal lack of attention which delays perception.

Lack of skill usually can be considered as a possible cause of an accident under such circumstances as the following:

- Driver unsuccessfully attempts to do something. This may range from bumping a vehicle in parallel parking because he is moving too fast, to trying to get across the tracks before the train gets to the crossing. Lack of this kind of skill is often hard to distinguish from lack of judgment. One way to distinguish between lack of skill and lack of judgment is by what the driver says about what happened. If he says, "I didn't realize how close I was," it is probably lack of judgment. If he says, "I could have made it if I hadn't been so slow in starting," or something like that, it is probably lack of skill, that is, the driver would have been successful if he could have made his plan come out the way he wanted.
- Driver fails to do something that he knows he should do, but does not do habitually. Cutting a corner on a left turn, failure to give turn signals, turning from the wrong lane — all are common errors due to lack of skill, that is, the lack of consistent habits in these routine operations.
- Failure to see or recognize things which were visible usually indicates lack of skill in attention, especially when there is no strong distraction present.
- Improper handling of a side-slip or yaw is almost always lack of skill, especially if the

driver knows what he should have done.

- A gap skid, is evidence of unskillful evasive tactics.
- A new driver with less than six months or 1,000 miles of driving.
- Driver in a strange automobile.
- Driver is out of practice; he has not driven for a year or more.
- Driver in heavy traffic who has not had experience in such traffic becomes confused.

Do not confuse lack of skill with lack of strength, especially in evasive tactics. Failure to avoid an accident after the hazardous situation has developed may be partly to lack of skill and partly to lack of strength. In addition, be certain that the vehicle was capable of doing what the driver wanted it to. For example, if engine stops at a critical time because of some mechanical failure, do not attribute that to lack of skill.

Any kind of accident may be contributed to by lack of knowledge or skill because these abilities are so important in control of the vehicle. This does not mean that *every* accident is contributed to by some shortage of knowledge or skill. A driver may have the needed knowledge or skill but not use it.

Do not confuse lack of knowledge with lack of skillful habits of observation. Suppose a person fails to stop at a flashing red light. If he sees the light but does not know that it means stop, he lacks knowledge. If he knows what it means, but inadvertently failed to notice it when his view was unobstructed, he lacks good habits of attention, that is, of skill. If he sees it and knows what it means but *decides* to continue without stopping anyhow, he has a bad attitude.

Knowledge of evasive tactics. Ignorance of road rules is not the only important lack of knowledge. A driver also needs to know what evasive tactics to take in emer-

gencies. After a person has discovered he is in danger, he can usually save himself by proper evasive tactics if he knows how and discovers the danger in time. Suppose a driver enters a curve or turn at or above the critical speed and begins to slide sidewise. His initial action contributed to his difficulty through lack of knowledge of the dangers of high speed on curves, or by lack of skill in controlling speed in approaching the curve or by lack of skill in attention to road conditions ahead, or some combination of these. Now, suppose he puts on his brakes hard because he finds himself going too fast. He shows lack of knowledge of behavior of the car on the road because he does the wrong thing.

Don't confuse lack of knowledge of evasive tactics with lack of skill in evasive tactics. Either may lead to an accident. One way to try to find out is to ask, "After you found you were in danger what did you do wrong?" You may not get an honest answer to the question because the driver does not want to admit to himself, let alone another, that he did anything wrong. Another way is to ask the question, "After you found yourself in danger, what did you try to do?" If the driver did not know that he did anything wrong or tells you that he tried to do the wrong thing, you can suspect that his trouble is a lack of knowledge. If, on the other hand, the driver seems to know what he should have done but made mistakes in doing it, such as letting the foot slip off the brake onto the accelerator, then it is a lack of skill.

Don't assume that lack of success in evasive tactics means either lack of skill or lack of knowledge. The driver simply may not have had time to avoid the collision. If his previous driving strategy got him into a position from which no driver could escape, he cannot be successful in evasive tactics. If what he does is right and skillful, we cannot say that lack of these abilities contributed to the accident.

Do not include as lack of skill

the confusion of a driver in a strange place except as it may be indicated in such things as sudden stops to read street name signs, unexpected turns at street intersections, and other things that habit as well as knowledge should prevent a person from doing.

Poor judgment of position and speed is another skill deficiency that may contribute to accidents, especially at high speeds.

Suspect poor judgment when a driver

- Misjudges clearances in overtaking
- Tries unsuccessfully to cross in front of a vehicle or train
- Explains that he thought he had time to make a left turn in face of oncoming traffic
- Thought he had time to enter from drive or minor road or after stopping at sign with approaching high-speed traffic
- Apparently picks too small a gap in traffic in which to cross street.

Attitudes and Motivation

Motives and attitudes are necessary to explain personal causes of accidents which cannot be accounted for by the natural and learned abilities. With proper mental and physical abilities, one is able to drive well; with proper training and study, one learns how to drive; but whether a person will drive as well as his abilities and training permit is determined by his attitudes and motives. The fact that some persons do not see fit to drive safely though they have the ability and knowledge is what necessitates traffic law enforcement.

Punishment is one of the methods for getting people to drive safely. Punishment, or the threat of it, has little effect on a person who does not know what is expected of him, or on one who is unable to drive as required. In such cases, the most punishment can do is to stimulate the driver to learn about those things which may subject him to punishment. Punishment is more fruitful with drivers who know what should be done, and yet intentionally do otherwise. In such cases, the effectiveness of punishment derives from the fact that the driver learns that certain behavior on his part leads to unpleasant consequences.

Motive is a psychological concept used to explain "why" behavior occurs. Thus, we often inquire as to the motive for a given act, meaning why the person behaved as he did. Why, for example, did he drink as much as he did, or why did he become angry when he could not pass, or why did he fail to lower his headlight beams. Sometimes this explanation is quite simple and does not involve motivated behavior. A broken beam switch leaves little choice to the driver; but when he does not lower lights because he is angry with other drivers, we speak of his behavior as motivated. But even when we know that the driver is angry, we might want to know why he is angry. The basis for motivation is usually explained by "psychological needs," a concept which is elaborated in psychological texts.

Attitudes may be defined as more or less permanent ways of thinking and feeling about things. Usually attitudes are learned as children from parents and teachers but may change throughout life. Attitudes also are useful in explaining why drivers behave the way they do.

Attitudes may be good or bad for driving depending on whether they promote safe practices. There is some evidence that persons who have attitudes about other areas of life — work, family, and gambling — which tend to get them in trouble also tend to have bad attitudes for driving.

Emotion is one further concept which is useful for understanding driver behavior. Emotion refers to the way a person feels about something. This may be unpleasant or pleasant. Emotion also varies in strength. Sometimes we may be very angry and other times experience only mild displeasure. One important thing to understand about emotion is that expression of it changes with maturity. The child has little control over his emotional expression, but as people mature most of them learn more or less to control emotions or to express them only in appropriate ways. Peaks and valleys of emotion level off as one grows older. However, many drivers show emotional immaturity. They react angrily to the slightest provocation. When driving, this may lead to dangerous behavior.

Emotions, like the other psychological aspects of personality, are often difficult to relate to an accident in a causal way. Nearly all drivers are emotional after an accident. This is only normal, but the inexperienced investigator may take this postaccident emotion as an indication that the driver was emotional prior to the accident. In attempting to investigate the role of emotion in an accident, inquire as to the events leading up to the accident and how the driver felt about them. If some circumstance is suggested that commonly gives rise to strong emotional feeling or the driver admits to this, you may begin to suspect this factor as contributing to the accident. It is usually impossible, however, to prove that an emotional reaction was definitely a factor in an accident.

Undoubtedly many aspects of personality play vital roles in causing accidents. However, personality is one of the most difficult factors to investigate.

12. SOURCES

Author

J. Stannard Baker is a traffic engineer specializing in accident investigation. He was Director of Research and Development at The Northwestern University Traffic Institute, from 1946 to 1971 and is still a guest lecturer at The Traffic Institute.

References

Superscript numbers in the preceding pages refer to the following publications:

1. *Uniform Vehicle Code and Model Traffic Ordinance*, National Committee on Uniform Traffic Laws and Ordinances, Washington DC (Order from P.O.Box 1409, Evanston, IL 60204.)

2. Inbau, Fred E. and John E. Reid, *Criminal Interrogation and Confessions,* 1967, The Williams & Wilkins Co., Baltimore MD

3. Greene, Robert, *Officer-Violator Relationships* (PN550), 1981, The Northwestern University Traffic Institute, Evanston, IL 60204 (6 pages)

4. *Accident Facts*, 1985 National Safety Council, Chicago IL 60611 (98 pages)

5. *Alcoholic Influence Report Form*, (Stock No. 321.99), 1977, National Safety Council, Chicago IL 60611 (2 pages)

6. *Manual on Classification of Motor Vehicle Traffic Accidents* (ANSI D 16.1-1983), National Safety Council, Chicago IL 60611 (34 pages)

7. *Medicolegal Autopsy Report*, 1968, Registry of Accident Pathology, Armed Forces Institute of Pathology, Washington DC 20305 (32 pages)

Exhibits

The following are sources of tables, drawings, charts, and photographs used in this publication:

Baker, J. Stannard, Glencoe IL
  Photo: 3
  Charts: 1, 8, 9
  Form: 6

Indiana State Police
  Photo: 4

National Safety Council, Chicago IL
  Form: 7

Roller, Robert E., Chandler AZ
  Photo: 2

The Northwestern University Traffic Institute, Evanston, IL
  Form: 5

TRAFFIC-ACCIDENT INFORMATION FROM ROADS

Topic 817 of the *Traffic-Accident Investigation Manual*

by
J. Stannard Baker

NORTHWESTERN UNIVERSITY TRAFFIC INSTITUTE

PUBLICATION HISTORY

1953 *Traffic Accident Investigator's Manual* (Sections 32.010 to 32.910)

1954 Revised (Sections 32.010 to 36.850)

1957 *Traffic Accident Investigator's Manual for Police* (Sections 36.010 to 36.850)
Reprinted 1959

1963 Revised (Sections 36.010 to 36.780)
Reprinted 1964, 1965, 1966, 1969, 1970, 1971, 1973

1970 *Manual de Investigacion de Accidentes de Trafico* (Sections 36.010 to 36.780)

1975 *Traffic Accident Investigation Manual* (Chapter 5)
Reprinted 1976, 1979

1985 *Traffic-accident Information from Roads*

TRAFFIC-ACCIDENT INFORMATION FROM ROADS

Purpose

Many accident investigators expect someone to *tell* them what happened; therefore, they neglect to *look* for themselves. In some fatal accidents, nobody is left to tell; then all you know about what took place must be learned from study of the results of the accident. In other cases, drivers or pedestrians really do not know what happened; so what they say is mostly imagination. Sometimes what you are told is actually false.

However, you can often get important and reliable information about a traffic accident by studying the road afterward. Some facts can only be had in that way.

The object of this Topic is to explain what to look for on the road, what it may mean, and how to describe properly what you noticed.

This topic aims to acquaint you with some unusual phenomena which you might not otherwise recognize.

Scope

Special road examination is usually necessary only for fatal and other serious accidents. You can think of studying the road as supplementary data collection at the scene of a traffic accident (second level traffic-accident investigation) and as followup fact finding when required (third level of traffic-accident investigation).

The best time to examine the road is at the scene of the accident or as soon thereafter as possible. But if that is impossible, you may have to do the best you can by studying photographs or even questioning people who saw the road after the accident.

Every motor-vehicle accident leaves some physical sign of what happened. So far as you can discover and *correctly* interpret them, such physical signs cannot be disputed. They can rarely explain all that took place in an accident, but they can often supplement statements by witnesses and people involved, prove or disprove theories of what happened, and guide the direction of further investigation

Some marks left on the road by accidents are so conspicuous that everybody at the scene notices them. Few who have seen them, however, can tell much about them afterwards. A casual glance at marks on the pavement is not enough for an *investigator*. You must look carefully for inconspicuous marks like scuffs, scratches, and spatter that may soon be obliterated. You must examine each carefully to be able to classify it. If the marks are complicated or important, you cannot depend on your memory to describe them later. Record them by photograph, careful measurements, or both.

Keep your record factual. If you get information from photos or other observers, be sure to say so clearly. Avoid reporting as facts hearsay and your own assumptions.

Record information about the road after a traffic accident under the same four general headings that are also used for data about people and vehicles.

1. *Identification* of the accident location
2. *Description* of the road
3. *Condition* of the road at the time of the event
4. *Result* (effect) of the accident on the road.

Arrangement of this Topic

Results of the accident will be discussed first because they tell so much about what happened. They are also what most people want to know about. Later the importance of proper identification, sufficient description, and significant conditions are described.

The effect of the accident on the road is explained under the following headings:

1. *Skidmarks*
2. *Yawmarks*
3. *Acceleration Scuffs*
4. *Flat Tire Scuffs*
5. *Imprints*
6. *Road Scars*
7. *Debris*
8. *Meanings of Marks*
9. *First Contact Point (FCP)*
10. *Off the Ground*
11. *Final Positions*

Relation to Other Topics

Topic 815 tells what can be learned about the accident from people and

Exhibit 1.

CHARACTERISTICS OF TIRE MARKS

	SKIDMARK 1	YAWMARK 2	ACCELERATION SCUFF 3	FLAT TIRE MARK 4	IMPRINT 5
WHEEL MOTION	Slide, no roll	Roll and sideslip	Spin and slip	Roll, no slip	Roll, no slip
OPERATION	Braking	Steering	Speeding up	None	None
NUMBER FROM 4-TIRED VEH	Mostly 4 also 2, 3, 1	Mostly 2 also 1, 3, 4	Usually 1 sometimes 2	Only 1 rarely 2	Mostly 1 also 2, 3, 4
RIGHT AND LEFT TIRES	Equally strong	Outside stronger	Equal if two	Rarely two	Usually equal
FRONT AND REAR TIRES	Front stronger	Usually equal	Only driven wheels		Equally clear
WIDTH	If straight, same as tire	Varies from an inch to a foot	Same as tire	Tire tread edge marks	Same as tire
BEGINNING	Usually abrupt	Always faint	Strong or gradual	Always faint	Always strong
END	Usually abrupt	Strong	Very gradual	Strong	Usually gradual
STRIATIONS	Always parallel to mark	Always oblique or crosswise	Parallel to mark	None	Parallel to mark if any
OTHER DETAILS	Outer edges often stronger	Side rib marks may show	Outer edges often stronger	Outer edges always stronger	Tread design may show. Often broken
LENGTH	1 to 500 feet	10 to 200 feet	0.5 to 50 feet	50 feet to 10 miles	0.5 to 50 feet

Topic 820 describes what vehicle damage shows.

Topics which combine informaton from people, roads, and vehicles are part of traffic-accident reconstruction.

Two topics relate especially to recording what the road shows: 828, *Measuring at the Scenes of Traffic Accidents* and 836, *Photography for Traffic-accident Investigations.*

Simple Estimates of Speed from Skidmarks is the title of Topic 818.

1. SKIDMARKS

Too many people, including some "investigators," pay little attention to differences among tire marks on the road. They are likely to call them all *skidmarks.* That won't do! You must learn to recognize different kinds of marks resulting from accidents on the road, and to use the proper terms to describe them.

Definitions

A tire mark is a mark made on a road or other surface by a tire on a vehicle. You can easily learn to distinguish the difference between the two general classes of tire marks:

1. *A tire friction mark,* is a *a tire mark* made when a slipping or sliding tire rubs the *road* or other surface.
2. An *imprint,* is a mark on a *road* or other surface made without sliding by a rolling tire or a person's foot.

The two main types of *friction marks* are often confused:

1. A *skidmark,* is a *tire friction mark* made by a tire that is sliding without rotation on a road or other surface. Sliding may be due to braking, collison damage or, rarely, to other circumstances.
2. A *scuffmark,* is a *tire friction mark* made by a tire that is both rotating and slipping on a road or other surface.

Characteristics of these and other kinds of tire marks are summarized in Exhibit 1.

Consider skidmarks first. They are common and conspicuous. Most of the ones you see represent successful evasive tactics; the vehicle is braked to a stop before collision.

Some people speak of a skidmark as "burned rubber." This is misleading. The

Exhibit 2. On bleeding bituminous pavement, a skidmark may be very black.

Exhibit 3. A typical skidmark on bituminous pavement is clearly visible.

Exhibit 4. On portland-cement concrete, skidmarks may be nearly invisible.

Exhibit 5. In loose material, a skidmark becomes a shallow furrow. The left wheels are skidding on the pavement.

Exhibit 6. Skidding on turf tends to tear the grass from its roots in the furrow.

Exhibit 7. Skidding furrows in mud or snow tend to be smooth in the bottom. They may be quite deep.

Exhibit 8. Scratches made by loose gravel may be the only sign of skidding, especially when the pavement was wet when the skid occurred. These scratches are a form of striations.

Exhibit 9. When studded tires skid, marks made by the studs are parallel scratches or striations, usually quite even. These are uncommon because studded tires are not much used.

Exhibit 10. Slipping tires on cold bituminous or portland-cement concrete can clean or "erase" making a light rather than a dark mark on the pavement. These are light rather than dark skidmarks.

Exhibit 11. *Skidding tires also squeegee moisture from the surface. Such marks differ little on portland-cement or bituminous concrete. They do not last.*

Exhibit 12. *Sometimes friction heat on a wet pavement is great enough to dry the surface leaving quite distinct skidmarks for a little while.*

black mark on a bituminous concrete pavement is usually bitumen (tar or asphalt) softened by friction-generated heat and smeared on the surface as the tire slides. On Portland-cement concrete paving, where there is no bitumen to smear, friction marks commonly consist of fine particles of material ground from the tire by the abrasive paving surface. Burning or even severe softening rarely occurs with ordinary tires.

Varities of Skidmarks

Skidmarks look different depending on the kind of surface and its condition. For example, on warm, "bleeding" bituninous concrete the skidmarks may be a heavy black smear showing some rib marks (Exhibit 2); whereas on cold, dry, Portland-cement pavement, the mark may be a nearly invisible whitish track (Exhibit 4). A typical mark is shown in Exhibit 3.

In soft material, the skidmark is usually a furrow. The depth of the furrow depends on how soft the material is. The sliding tire pushes loose material ahead of it and to the sides, where

the displaced material forms ridges (Exhibits 5, 6, and 7). The bottom of the furrow is usually roughened, making it quite irregular.

If abrasive material is present between tire and paving, skidding results in surface scratches (Exhibits 8 and 9). This may occur with studded tires or loose gravel on the pavement.

Sometimes skidding results in what amounts to cleaning the pavement by "erasing," removing substances from the surface. These may be dirt, as in Exhibit 10, or water squeegeed from the surface as in Exhibit 11 and 12.

Skidmarks from tires on dual truck wheels are easy to recognize as pairs. (Exhibit 13): For most purposes and especially in measuring, consider the two as a single mark.

Tires may leave a very clear mark on one surface but none at all on the adjacent surface. Reflectorized edge and lane stripes are very likely to show friction marks. The tiny reflector beads in these marks grind off particles of rubber whereas adjacent traffic-polished paving does not (Exhibit 14). Also a

dark tire mark on a white or yellow stripe gives high contrast that makes the tire mark easy to see.

Life of Skidmarks

You may be asked, or you may wonder, how long skidmarks will last. The answer is, of course, "It depends on circumstances." Conditions which may affect skidmark life are

- Kind of mark
- Weather
- Amount of traffic

Exhibit 13. *Dual tires make skidmarks in pairs. If one of the pair makes a lighter mark it may be because it is more worn or has less air pressure in it.*

Exhibit 15. *Most strong skidmarks on paving will be visible for months. The mark shown here is ten days old. Marks may be visible longer than they are noticeable.*

Exhibit 16. *The same mark after 90 days. The life of a skidmark depends largely on the amount of traffic over it. But it also depends on kind of paving.*

- Road repairs or construction
- Sometimes special characteristics of tires.

Squeegee marks on a wet surface (Exhibit 11) may disappear in a minute or less — often before they can be photographed — if rain continues to flood the road surface or if numerous vehicles track over the marks. On the other hand, dark friction marks or deep furrows in roadside gravel or turf may be quite visible for as much as a year after they were made.

Exhibit 14. *A skidding tire may leave a very plain mark on one surface, in this case a beaded pavement stripe, and almost no mark on the surface next to it.*

A typical skidmark on the traffic-polished pavement of a busy street is shown in Exhibit 15 ten days after it was made, and in Exhibit 16 three months later, when it was faint but still visible.

Characteristics of Skidmarks

In an ideal set of braking skidmarks, all four tires begin to skid at the same time. The two rear marks start the length of the vehicle's wheel base behind the front ones. The marks also end at the same time, the rear ones the wheel base length behind the front ones. The marks are straight and parallel. Rear wheel marks are superimposed on the front ones. Exhibit 17 shows a nearly perfect set of four skidmarks.

Such perfect skidmarks are not easy to make experimentally, and you will rarely find them in connection with accidents. Ordinary skidmarks made at the same time vary in length. One or more tires may make no visible mark as illustrated in Exhibits 18 and 19.

Certain characteristics of tire fric-

tion marks help you to recognize braking skidmarks:

- They are relatively straight. They may swerve a little toward the lower edge of the roadway. They rarely turn first one way and then the other.
- They may be any length up to about 300 ft.
- Usually there are four marks from a four-tired vehicle, but there may be only two, three, or one, in that order of frequency.
- Marks made by left and right tires are generally equally dark and equally wide.
- Front tire skidmarks are usually more prominent than rear tire skidmarks.
- Where it begins, a skidmark is the width of the tire tread. Sometimes it is a little wider, but almost never narrower.
- The point at which a skidmark begins can usually be located within a few feet.
- A skidmark nearly always ends abruptly either where the vehicle

Exhibit 17. *A perfect set of four skidmarks, straight, even and clear. Rear wheel and front wheel marks are distinct and begin and end at the same time. Such elegant marks are seldom found.*

Exhibit 18. *Sometimes only a single mark is made. It is important to note carefully how many of the tires made skidmarks.*

stops or where a collision begins.
• Skidmarks often show striations quite clearly. They are always parallel to the mark.
• The outer edges of skidmarks are sometimes more prominent than the middle, but usually both edges are equally distinct.

These characteristics are summarized in the first column of Exhibit 1.

Striations may be rather broad rib marks (Exhibit 3) or narrow scratches from loose gravel (Exhibit 8). They rarely show direction of slippage. As noted above, striations parallel to the friction mark are the best indication that the tire is not rotating and that the mark is a skidmark. Not all friction marks show striations.

Unequal Lengths

At first, when slowing a vehicle, brake pedal pressure is small. There is not much force between brake shoe and drum (or between calipers and disk); so there is slipping between these surfaces but no slipping between tires and road. Yet even without slippage, the tires produce a drag force on the road that slows the vehicle.

As brake pedal pressure increases, force between tires and road becomes greater; the rate of vehicle slowing becomes more rapid. Finally, a point is reached where the grip of the tire on the pavement lets go and tires begin to slip. For an instant, there is slipping both in the brake and between tire and road.

Additional pedal pressure locks the wheel. Then all slipping and friction is at the road surface. Brake slipping stops. Up to this time, the vehicle's rate of slowing (deceleration) increases with greater brake pedal pressure, but once wheels are locked, brakes have done all they can. The slowing force is now only that from road friction; no additional pedal pressure will increase the rate of slowing. The brakes are adequate for prevailing conditions.

Of course, on slippery (low friction) surfaces, brakes lock wheels at much lower pedal pressure than on ordinary road conditions.

Resistance to wheel rotation provided by the brake depends on brake design and pedal pressure. Resistance to wheel rotation by the tire and road depends on the slipperiness (coeffi-

cient of friction) of the tire on the road times the weight (load) on the tire times the distance from the wheel center to the road surface (rolling radius). If the brake resistance to turning is less than the road resistance to wheel rotation, the brake will slip and the tire will not skid; on the other hand, if the road resistance to wheel rotation is less than that of the brake the brake will lock the wheel and the tire will skid.

Brake design is such that pedal pressure produces equal resistance to wheel rotation for corresponding wheels on the right and left sides of a vehicle. Then if loads on right and left tires are equal, if rolling radiuses are equal, and if tires and road surfaces on both sides are alike, increased brake pedal pressure will lock both right and left wheels at the same instant, giving ideal skidmarks.

But the following conditions *increase* resistance to sliding and delay wheel lockup, thus tending to leave relatively shorter skidmarks:

1. *Greater load on the tire* increases the grip of the tire on the road. This may result from
   a. Cargo heavier on that side of

Exhibit 19. Unequal skidmarks may be puzzling but significant. Here only two tires have made skidmarks and these differ greatly in length. They are both skip-skids from over-deflected tires.

the vehicle
  b. Cross slope of the roadway which increases load on the downhill tire.
  c. Steering which increases load on the outside tire in the curve.
2. *Greater coefficient of friction* (less slippery surface), for example, a tire on paving compared to a tire on snow-covered road shoulder.
3. *Less rolling radius* (distance

Exhibit 20. In braking, the pavement exerts a rearward force on the tires, but the upper part of the vehicle tends to keep on going. This increases weight on the front wheels and reduces weight on the rear ones. The front tires are over-deflected by the additional weight and so heat more at the edges than in the middle, making conspicuous edge marks.

Exhibit 21. The weight shift from rear to front in braking makes the vehicle tend to dip down at the front end.

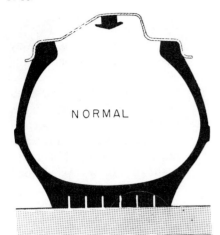

Exhibit 22. *A normally inflated tire with normal weight on it has quite uniform pressure across the tire-road contact area. Tires are designed with thicker tread at the sides to give this uniform weight distribution on the road. It also gives more even wear.*

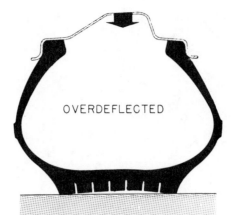

Exhibit 23. *If tire is underinflated, overloaded, or both, it squashes down and most of its weight is carried by the edges of the road-contact area. Thus, it makes flat-tire scuffs and front-wheel skidmarks on road surfaces when sliding.*

from wheel center to road surface).

 a. Less air pressure gives more sidewall deflection; that reduces rolling radius.

 b. Greater load on the tire does the same thing.

 c. Greater tire wear reduces rolling radius.

 d. A thinner tread or shallower tread pattern brings the axle closer to the road, for example, ordinary tires contrasted to snow tires.

 4. *Good brake adjustment* and condition as contrasted to wet or oily brake friction surfaces.

If brakes lock all wheels quickly — perhaps in less than one revolution — delays in starting to slide are insignificant. The vehicle moves only a few feet from where one tire starts to slide to where the opposite tire starts.

But when brake pedal pressure is gradually increased, the vehicle may travel yards from the beginning of one skidmark to the start of the one on the opposite side. Sometimes, brake pedal pressure may be too little to lock one of the wheels. Then the tire on that wheel never does slide and only one skidmark is made by a pair of opposite tires (Exhibit 18).

Front and rear skidmarks differ in length for an additional reason. Vehicles are designed so that front and rear tires carry about the same loads. But when a vehicle is braked, the road applies a slowing force at the pavement surface (Exhibit 20). Inertia, however, develops a force which tends to keep the vehicle moving forward. This pair of equal, offset, parallel, and opposite forces (a *couple*) pitch the vehicle forward (Exhibit 21). This shifts weight from rear to front wheels. If brakes are equally strong, front and rear, the unloaded rear wheels would slide first. This gives an unstable situation and reduces possible brake effectiveness. Therefore cars and some other vehicles have stronger brakes in front than behind. Then, in most cases, front wheels lock and tires start to slide before the rear ones do. That helps to explain differences in lengths of front and rear skidmarks or even the absence of rear tire skidmarks.

So far, we have considered mainly differences in sliding distances. Now, remember that a sliding tire does not always make a skidmark because some surfaces will show clear skidmarks from sliding tires and other surfaces little or none. Then four other factors make a difference in length of skidmarks made at the same time:

 1. *Temperature.* Hot rubber in tires and hot bituminous road material rub off more easily in sliding than when cold. This gives darker marks.

 2. *Weight.* A tire bearing down heavily on the road will have more material ground from its surface than one which is not so heavily loaded, thus producing a darker mark. Furthermore greater load creates more friction heat. That raises the surface temperature with the effect noted in Item 1 above.

 3. *Tire material.* Some tires are softer than others and will, therefore, more easily make skidmarks while sliding. Racing tires designed for high traction generally make conspicuous marks when sliding.

 4. *Tire tread design.* For the same load and air pressure, tires with narrow grooves have more areas on the road surface than snow tires, for example, with wider spaces in the tread pattern. With weight concentrated in a lesser area, friction temperature is greater, resulting in the effects mentioned in Items 1 and 2 above.

Irregularities. In addition to differences in length, you will find many other irregularities in skidmarks. Some of these may be very helpful in understanding how an accident happened.

The more common irregularities are described in the following pages.

Tire Overdeflection

Weight shift in braking has already been explained. As a result of this weight shift, the vehicle tends to nose down. This can be seen plainly if you watch a vehicle sliding to a stop as in Exhibit 21. The front springs compress with the additional weight and the front end dips; the rear springs expand as a result of the reduced load and the rear end rises.

Weight shift to the front in severe braking also overloads the front tires with respect to the air pressure in them. That overdeflects these tires; as illustrated in Exhibit 23. Compare this with a normally loaded and inflated tire in Exhibit 22. When overdeflected, the edges of the tread carry more

Exhibit 24. *A skidmark which is heavy on the edges and light in the middle results from an overdeflected tire. A tire might be overdeflected from underinflation or overload. It may be a front or rear tire.*

weight than the middle; consequently that is where the most friction and heat is developed. The result is that the edges of the tire leave stronger marks than the middle, giving the typical front-wheel skidmarks shown in Exhibits 24, 17, and 19. This effect is less with belted radial tires that have very stiff treads than with bias-ply tires.

The prominent edge marks are a useful means of deciding whether a skidmark is from a front or rear tire, especially at the beginning of a skid. Occasionally rear tires make overdeflected skidmarks. This can occur when rear tires are considerably overloaded, for example when a pickup truck is carrying too much cargo.

Gaps in Skidmarks

Occasionally, you may find an interruption or gap in a set of skidmarks (Exhibit 25). The marks stop and begin again. Gaps occur when a vehicle makes two sets of skidmarks, one after the other. The gap is usually ten feet (3 meters) or more long. To make a gap, pressure on the brake pedal is released and then reapplied. Gaps are most like-

ly to be found in connection with pedestrian accidents. Gaps are made by such actions as

- A reflex reaction of the driver to the sensation of a sudden stopping and the squeal of skidding (The fast stop makes the driver uncomfortable. He reverses the motion that caused him distress and takes pressure off the brake pedal. Then, if the danger is still ahead, he puts the brakes on again. This reflex action is flinching.)
- Brakes are "pumped," or put on and off, with the idea of getting a quicker stop. These gaps are rare.
- The driver's foot slips off the brake pedal and is put back on.
- The hazard apparently disappears and then reappears — for example, as a pedestrian changes his mind and starts to go ahead again after stopping.

Locate the beginning and end of the mark of each wheel before and after the gap. If you measure, record for each tire, the length of the first skid, length of gap, and length of second skid.

Unfinished skids are produced the same way as gap skids except that before brakes are reapplied, the vehicle collides with something. The skidmarks stop short of the collision point. These are rare and may be very puzzling when found unless you know how unseasoned drivers may flinch after sudden brake application.

Skip or Bounce Skidmarks

The tire mark is repeatedly interrupted or narrowed. This results from one of three circumstances:
1. Bouncing during braking.
2. Road bumps or holes
3. Collisions.

The distances between interruptions are usually short, a few feet (a meter) or so.

Unloaded semitrailers with locked wheels can bounce or jump instead of sliding smoothly. See Exhibit 26. Most of these occur in evasive tactics that are successful in avoiding an accident. Drag on the sliding tires makes the

axle twist, thus compressing springs and boosting the semitrailer body. Momentarily this body lift increases load on the tire and road, produces more friction, and makes a dark mark. Upward momentum of the body then carries the spring and wheel upward, relieving the weight on the tire, permitting the spring to expand, letting the axle untwist, reducing friction and making a light mark, if any. Then, as the trailer body begins to fall, locked wheels come down hard on the road again and repeat the process. Long unloaded trailers, especially with single axles, make this phenomenon more likely and more pronounced. If there is much load on the axle, there will be little or no bounce. Usually skip skids occur when trailer brakes alone are applied. This means that the tractor and semitrailer are only partly braked so the skip skids can be very long, often several hundred feet.

Bounce. Examples have been found of what appear to be a special kind of skip skids by passenger cars. The friction marks vary from light to dark and dark to light at regular intervals on a uniform pavement. This indicates varying tire pressure on the road surface. It suggests that the initial forward pitch of the vehicle when brakes were suddenly applied compressed front tires and springs abnormally, leaving a dark skidmark. The rebound from overdeflection reduces pressure on the road leaving a light or narrower mark. Repetition of this sequence gives the effect of bounce skids.

Road bumps can also produce short skip skids. Usually these are not in connection with an accident. A chuckhole, short hump, railroad tracks, or curb can make a tire bounce up and down as it goes over the bump and for a short way afterward, (Exhibit 27). This bouncing varies the pressure on the road and, consequently, the strength of the mark. Such skip skids are most likely to be made by small vehicles. They usually appear from only one wheel and become less and less pronounced the farther away they are from the originating bump. Meas-

Exhibit 25. *A gap skid is really two sets of skidmarks one after the other with brakes released in between. These should be measured as two sets of marks and the gap in each also measured.*

Exhibit 26. *Skip skidmarks are made by sliding tires on a lightly loaded semi-trailer. These are quite common marks. Forget the gaps in measuring.*

ure the mark as though there were no skips in it.

Do not describe skip skid as a road-bump skip skid unless you can clearly identify the surface irregularity that started it. Such a skip skid usually has little significance in connection with the accident because braking was begun before the obstacle was encountered. The bump is unlikely to have an effect on the control of a car that is already skidding.

Collision skip skids occur only in connection with accidents. They are rare but important. They sometimes, but by no means always, result when a sliding vehicle strikes an object such as a pedestrian or pedalcyclist. The vehicle, sliding with weight shifted forward, has a less than normal load on rear tires. Hitting a pedestrian, for example, forces the rear wheels down hard on the road for a fraction of a second. They leave a wider or darker mark when forced down (Exhibit 28). But tires and springs are elastic and rebound as soon as pressure is released. On the rebound, the effect of weight is reduced and so the mark is quite

faint. The bouncing may continue for some distance. Each of the rear wheels usually leaves such a mark.

Collision skip skids are more likely to occur with small, light vehicles than large, heavy ones and would be extremely unlikely with trucks. Be sure that these marks were not started by any paving irregularity.

To measure skip skids, treat them as though there were no skips. Do not try to measure each mark and the gaps between the marks. However, be sure to describe them as skip skids.

Collision Scrubs

These skidmarks are usually not more than 10 ft. (3 meters) long. They start abruptly when damage to the vehicle, rather than braking, locks a wheel. They may be very conspicuous because, during collision the force of the tire on the pavement is greatly increased for an instant. Or they may be inconspicuous if the pavement does not easily show skidmarks (Exhibit 29).

At the end of the impact, the additional downward force of collision is

released from the paving so the mark changes in appearance.

After impact,

- If the wheel is free to rotate, the skidmark stops (Exhibit 30) or changes to a scuffmark.
- If the wheel remains locked by damage, the tire continues to slide but leaves a lighter mark (Exhibit 31).
- If the wheel comes off or is damaged so that it no longer touches the road surface, the scrub mark stops.

Collision scrubs differ greatly in appearance. In same-direction collisions, they tend to be long and straight (Exhibit 31). In opposite-direction collisions they are likely to be short and curved (Exhibit 30). Sometimes, they are the only mark on the road that shows the collision point (Exhibit 29). In any case, they indicate the movement of the tire on the road during engagement (impact) between the vehicle and some other object.

Collision scrubs are true skidmarks; the wheel does not rotate, but they are not braking skidmarks because braking is not what stopped the wheel from rotation.

Exhibit 27. *A tire skidding across an irregular area, such as a pavement patch or chuck hole, may bounce enough to give a skip skid. In this case, both front and rear tires on the right side skipped.*

Exhibit 28. *To avoid a pedestrian, the car is braked to lock all wheels, but only front wheels show skidmarks at A. At B pedestrian hit windshield and forced rear wheels to make bounce skids.*

Broadside Skidmarks

These are also real skidmarks because the wheel is not rotating; but they are not braking skidmarks. A broadside skid occurs when a vehicle is moving sidewise parallel to its axles. The wheel is free to rotate, but when the vehicle is sliding exactly sidewise, the wheels rotate neither backward nor forward.

Such a circumstance occurs momentarily during yaw (rotation about a vertical axis). The yaw or spin has continued far enough so that the vehicle is actually sliding sidewise (Exhibit 32).

Crooks

Crooks in skidmarks are sometimes called bends or offsets.

Skidmarks are normally straight and even. An abrupt change in direction (Exhibit 33), often near the end, means that some external force has deflected the vehicle from its even forward motion. A crook is shorter and sharper than a swerve; a swerve involves no impact force.

A crook, like a collision scrub, marks the postion of a tire at the onset of a collision. It is rarely the actual first contact point (FCP), or "point of impact." Describe or photograph this skidmark abnormality and locate it by measurements. A crook is an excellent clue as to where the first contact occurred.

Do not mark or refer to a crook as the "point of impact." You actually saw the crook but you did not actually see the impact.

Crooks may occur simultaneously in more than one skidmark (Exhibit 33). In an opposite-direction collision, front skidmark crooks may curve in one direction while rear tire crooks turn the other way.

Crooks are often the end of pre-collision skidmarks and the start of after-collision tire marks.

When a tire is skidding, it has "used up" its friction resistance to further motion in any direction. Then efforts of the driver to steer are useless. The front tires slide as easily when turned at a steering angle as when aimed straight ahead. During front-wheel skidding, therefore, steering control is lost.

The same lack of resistance to side forces while skidding forward, makes it possible for a rather small collision to deflect a vehicle perceptibly and cause a minor crook in its skidmarks. Exhibit 34 shows deflected front wheel skidmarks resulting from collision with a bicyclist moving from right to left across the path of a car.

Swerves

A swerve is a slight deviation from a straight-ahead path.

Skidmarks often show deviation from straight paths for reasons other than collisions. As explained in connection with crooks, sidewise movement during skidding (all wheels locked) is relatively easy because skidding absorbs all possible resistance to movement. Then side forces, which would have no effect on a vehicle rolling, normally can produce sidewise motion, swerve, in a skidding vehicle (Exhibits 35 and 36). Do not confuse sideslip skidmarks with yaw marks. Cross winds can produce side slippage

Exhibit 29. *Sometimes a collision scrub skidmark is the only sign of where a collision took place; so it is important.*

Exhibit 30. *Or a collision scrub skidmark may be short and curved, especially in opposite-direction collisions.*

Exhibit 31. *A collision scrub may be long and straight, as at A, especially in same-direction collisions.*

and swerve in a skidding vehicle. Cross slope of the road due to crown or banking can make a skidding vehicle swerve to the downhill side. In these cases, with equal cargo load on right and left sides, the lee or downhill tires will be more heavily loaded and in skidding may make darker skidmarks than tires on the opposite side of the vehicle. If only the front wheels are skidding, only the front end of the vehicle will be affected by the cross wind or cross slope. Then the vehicle will rotate as well as swerve.

Unequal road surfaces can cause swerves while skidding. For example, if the right wheels run off the paving while the vehicle is skidding a sharp swerve may result, as in Exhibit 5. When the coefficient of friction is much less on the gravel shoulder than on the hard paving, the road drag on the left side of the vehicle is much more than on the right. The vehicle will then rotate counterclockwise and swerve left. This swerve may automatically return the vehicle to the roadway, usually very suddenly. Then, without

very skillful driver correction, the vehicle may continue across its half of the roadway into the path of oncoming traffic.

A similar result occurs if a driver runs off the right side of the roadway and locks wheels by braking with the left wheels still on the pavement. Do not assume that the shoulder always has a lower coefficient of friction than the paving. Wet paving and damp, well packed, gravel shoulder may produce nearly equal drag.

Unequal brakes can lock wheels on one side of the vehicle without locking them on the opposite side, thereby producing rotation. Unequal brakes which lock no wheels make the driver feel some "pull" to the right or left. But with additional tire traction available in the absence of skidding, this tendency to swerve can generally be offset by steering.

If brakes lock some wheels but not others, unstable movement may result. Correction by steering then requires great skill and is often unsuccessful. Locking front wheels of a tractor trailer combination is an example. If these wheels skid, no steering can be effective. Then with the semitrailer pushing ahead from behind, jackknifing starts. To prevent such trouble, front axle brakes are designed or ad-

Exhibit 32. *A broadside skid at Y occurred when an out-of-control car slid sidewise. Then, the tire stopped rotating forward and started rotating backward. At H and K the tire mark is a sideslip yaw.*

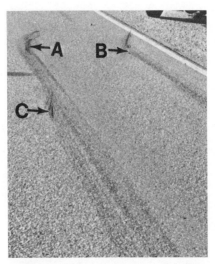

Exhibit 33. *Crooks or offsets in skidmarks, as at A and B, show where a collision changed the direction of the skid. Rear tire skidmarks, as at C, may or may not veer in the same direction as front tire marks.*

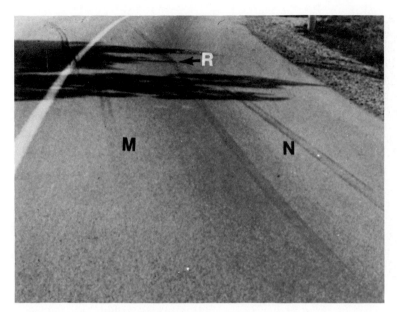

Exhibit 34. *A skidding car can be deflected by even a slight collision. R shows the change of direction of skid by collision with a bicycle. M and N are made by a following vehicle.*

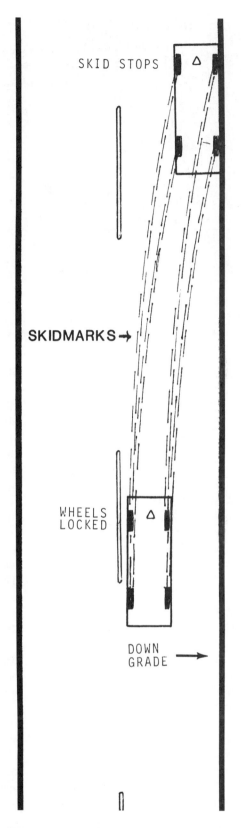

Exhibit 36. *A map of the downhill side slide illustrated in Exhibit 35 shows that the vehicle rotates little as it slides forward on the cross slope of the roadway crown. This movement is not due to steering or unequal braking. It is not the same as swerve due to steering which produces rotation (yaw) as illustrated elsewhere.*

Exhibit 35. *Skidmarks on a cross slope, such as most roadways have, swerve downhill which is usually toward the edge of the road. The downhill tires also usually make darker marks because the additional weight on the downhill side generates more sliding heat.*

Exhibit 37. A tangle of tire marks may be difficult to sort out; some may be skidmarks and some not. Here I and J are before-collision skidmarks made by dual tires. K and L are after-collision skidmarks, continuations of I and J. G and H are acceleration scuffs, not skidmarks; they were on the road before the collision. M is an unidentified dual tire mark.

justed to prevent skidding wheels on tractors; sometimes these brakes are simply omitted or disconnected.

When rear tires skid and front ones do relatively little or no braking, there is serious instability. This was a defect in early motor vehicles which had brakes only on the rear wheels. By very skillful steering, a straight course could be maintained with skidding rear tires. But if a driver attempted to follow a curve, his skidding rear tires had no reserve traction to resist the centrifugal force developed in turning. Then the rear end slid around to the side, while front tires resisted sideslip. The result was a rapid pivoting around the front wheels. The center of the vehicle continued in a fairly straight path, rotating until the vehicle was moving backward. Then the rotation stopped but the vehicle continued to move backward until it came to rest. Modern cars have stronger brakes in front to avoid rear-wheel lockup without front wheel lockup.

Occasionally, wheels on an empty semitrailer lock while the combination is braking on a curve. Then the skidding rear wheels cannot resist the centrifugal force of the turn and the trailer rear end may swing out to the side across the opposite lane, sometimes colliding with an approaching vehicle!

After-collision Skidmarks

As a result of a collision, a motor vehicle's skidmarks usually, but not always, show irregularities: a crook, skip, swerve, or abrupt termination. If the object struck is relatively light, like a pedestrian or pedalcycle, the irregularity may be imperceptible. If the object struck is more massive, after-impact skidmarks are in a new direction (Exhibit 33). A tire which was not skidding before collision may be on a wheel locked by collision damage. Then it may begin to make a skidmark, possibly as a collision scrub (Exhibit 30), or skip skid. A tire that was skidding before impact may leave no skidmark afterward, either because the driver no longer applied brakes or because damage reduced or discontinued contact between tire and road.

Exhibit 37 shows a set of after-impact tire marks. Most of these are skidmarks. At first, a tangle of marks like these may confuse you, but on thoughtful examination, they can reveal much about how and exactly where a collision occurred. They may also be important in estimating after-collision and precollision speeds.

After-collision skidmarks are usually curved because after collision the vehicle is usually rotating (spinning). The marks may vary in width from an

inch to a foot, depending on how the tire is aligned in the slide. There may be gaps in after-collision skidmarks as the wrecked vehicle rotates so as to put more or less weight on that tire. After-collision skidmarks made by a locked wheel may be difficult to distinguish from after-collision scuffmarks made by a rotating wheel. There are two ways to determine this. One way is by careful examination of the mark. If striations (scratches or rib marks) within the mark are parallel to the mark, as at S in Exhibit 38, the wheel is probably locked. If the striations are oblique to the mark, as at Y in Exhibit 38, the wheel is rotating. The other way to determine whether the wheel was sliding or rotating is to examine the vehicle to find out whether the wheel was free to rotate, was locked tight, or could rotate with enough force to drag it on the road.

Never assume that all tiremarks made after collision are skidmarks. If you have a good reason to believe that the tire which made the mark was on a wheel that could not be rotated, you are justified in classifying the mark as

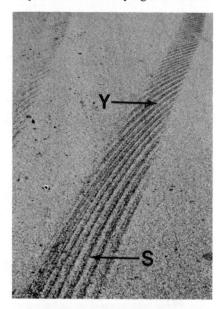

Exhibit 38. Direction of striations, if any, in tire marks help you tell whether the tire that made the marks was skidding or sideslipping. Striations parallel to the marks as at S mean the wheel was not rotating. Crosswise or oblique striations as at Y mean that the wheel was partly slipping and partly rotating. In this illustration, brakes were applied or released where the striations change from parallel to crosswise.

Exhibit 39. *Skidmarks are not always straight. Here B is a skidmark from a flat tire when a disabled vehicle is being towed from the shoulder back on the roadway. There was some question as to whether the movement of the vehicle was on or off the pavement. The furrow on the shoulder at F is not clear enough to settle that. But the small pile of dirt at D clearly shows that the tire pushed dirt ahead of it, against the edge of the paving.*

a skidmark (Exhibit 37). Otherwise, it may be a yawmark, imprint, or even a flat tire scuff.

Do not assume that the lack of a mark in the path followed by a tire after an accident means that the tire was not sliding. If the wheel cannot be rotated after a collision, any movement of the tire in contact with the road is skidding, regardless of whether it makes a skidmark.

These considerations emphasize the importance of examining the vehicle after an accident to determine which wheels could and which ones could not be rotated.

Towing skidmarks. Skidmarks made when a tow truck drags a vehicle with one or more locked wheels (Exhibit 39) are common. Mostly they are short and curved; but sometimes a vehicle may be dragged for a mile or more leaving a very long skidmark. Correct conclusions about how any such marks are made are usually easily reached.

"Impending" Skids

The exact point where skidding begins is difficult to determine for two reasons: 1) tires can slide without leaving a visible mark; and 2) some time is required and some distance is travelled from the instant that brakes start to slow the vehicle until the wheel stops turning. Also after a tire begins to slide, it may go some distance before friction heats the tire enough to begin to make skidmarks. During this slowing period, while brake pedal pressure

is increasing and the wheel is rotating less and less rapidly, the tire may or may not make a visible friction mark. Even after the wheel stops rotating and begins to skid, conditions may be such that the tire may or may not make skidmarks. The length of this transitional period depends mainly on how quickly brakes are being applied.

In examining a road, you can generally tell where there is definitely some sign of friction or slipping and where, before that, there is definitely no such sign. Where you locate these places depends on the amount and direction of light falling on the area, and the distance and angle from which you view it. Unfortunately it sometimes also

depends on the imagination of the observer.

This indefinite area is called by various names: *impending skidmarks, incipient skidmarks, shadow, warmup distance.* These terms are not clearly defined or adequately distinguished.

In discussing this area of uncertainty, perhaps it is useful to consider how the drag of the road on a tire varies from onset to steady skid. This is illustrated in Exhibit 40. Before braking, the wheel has full rotation but where the tire touches the road surface, there is, momentarily, no movement. Compared to the vehicle's speed, the speed of the tire in contact with the road is then 0%. As soon as brakes are applied, a retarding force on the tire is developed by the road. Compared to (divided by) the vehicle's weight, this is the *drag factor.* When this force begins, elastic tire material is pressed into road surface irregularities (asperities). Thus, the drag force stretches the tread rubber for an instant while the body of the tire begins to slow down. At this point, the speed of the tire close to the road surface compared to the vehicle's speed has increased from 0% to something like 1%. The tire tread is moving only about 1% as fast as the vehicle. The drag factor is maximum at this point. When the force

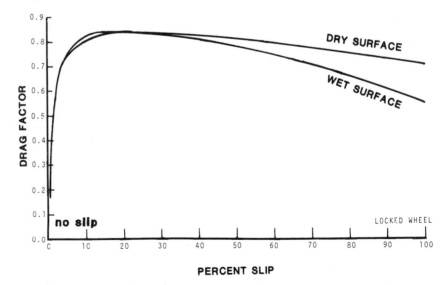

Exhibit 40. *When brakes are first applied, there is zero slip between tire and road. As brakes are applied harder, tires begin to lose their grip and slip more and more until the wheel stops rotating and slipping is 100% complete. During this time, which may be very brief, the drag factor increases rapidly and then drops down to a lower value when wheels are locked. The values here are for a specific tire. Other tires may vary.*

Exhibit 41. *Viewed or photographed looking east, this skidmark is quite visible.*

Exhibit 42. *Looking west, the same skidmark is difficult or impossible to see.*

places:
- The mark begins to be noticeably darker.
- The mark becomes wider because front and rear tires begin to be noticeably offset.
- Heavier edge marks, from an over-deflected tire, begin to appear (Exhibit 17).
- Ribmark patterns change either because front and rear tires have different patterns or because ribs on rear tires begin to cover the groove marks on the front tires.

Description. When you have decided and possibly marked where friction marks begin or end, you are ready to record your observations. If you call a tire mark a skidmark, be sure it has important characteristics of skidmarks. If you have any doubt about it, be on the safe side, simply call it a friction mark or a tire mark. In any event, you must be prepared to describe what it looked like so that others may agree — or disagree — with your classification.

Direction of skid. Someone may want to know in which direction a vehicle was moving that made a skid you have reported. From the skidmark alone it is often impossible to tell (Exhibit 44). Sometimes small spots of bituminous material will be smeared on the pavement so as to indicate direc-

stretching tire material reaches a certain point, the tire loses its grip on the pavement and begins to slip. As slipping increases, the time for the rubber to grip the road surface becomes less and less; the drag force to slow the vehicle drops rapidly until the wheel stops rotating. Then the speed of the tire where it touches the road, compared to the vehicle's speed is 100% of the vehicle speed. The drag of the road on the tire related to the load on the tire is the coefficient of friction which, in this condition is the same as the drag factor. At the instant that the tire material is about to let go of the road surface, the drag from braking is considerably greater than it is later when the wheel is sliding completely. The value of this peak force (drag fractor) depends on the elasticity of the tire material, surface roughness, brake application and other factors.

Thus, slowing due to braking begins before there can be any signs of skidmarks. This tends to make speed estimates from skidmarks lower than they would otherwise be.

Recording Observations

In examining the road at the scene of an accident or at the site later, your job is to describe and record the results of the accident that you found there. To do this for skidmarks, find for each

the place where definite signs of friction start and end. This usually takes close observation.

Viewed from one direction, a mark may be clearly visible, whereas looked at from the opposite direction it may be almost invisible (Exhibits 41 and 42). This is partly because a tire rubbing over a rough surface deposits more black material on the near side of surface irregularities (asperities) than on the far side. Viewed from a lower angle in the direction of the vehicle's travel, these line up and make the mark more visible. From the other direction, one sees mainly the unmarked sides of the little projections in the surface.

It is a good idea to ask someone else, a helper or even a bystander, where he thinks the mark begins. When you have decided on this spot, it is useful to mark it with a crayon or paint (Exhibit 43). That will be helpful in measuring or photographing if the faint friction mark is obliterated by traffic or otherwise.

Where they begin, the first rear skidmarks may be right on top of the front tire skidmarks. That often makes it difficult, to decide which tire made the beginning of the mark and where the single mark separates into distinct front and rear tiremarks. A number of clues will help you determine these

Exhibit 43. *A crayon or other mark at the beginning or end of a faint tire mark will help to locate it for measuring later.*

Exhibit 44. *Usually you cannot tell from the main part of a skidmark the direction in which the tire that made it was moving. In this example, direction of skidding is indeterminate.*

tion (Exhibit 45). A faint beginning and abrupt end may help to determine the direction in which a tire was moving when it made a skidmark.

Identification of the tire which made a skidmark may be necessary. If only one tire on any possible vehicle has the same tread width and rib count or rib spacing, you can be quite sure that the tire made the skidmark. Otherwise, you may only be able to determine what tires could or could not have made the mark. If identification is important, measure and photograph the mark and the tire which you think made the mark.

Measurements of skidmarks are necessary if they are to be the basis of speed estimates. Try to measure the length of each mark separately. If there is a crook in the mark, measure separately the length of the mark to this irregularity and at the length beyond it. Finding the *end* of a skidmark is usually not difficult, especially if it leads right to where the tire that made it is resting. Finding the beginning may be difficult. If you cannot tell whether the beginning of the mark is from a front or rear tire because they appear to be superimposed, measure the distance from where you find the first signs of skidding to where the two marks clearly separate. From that point measure each mark to its end (Exhibit 46). In

recording your measurement, show first which tire made the mark, then record the length of that mark which is clearly separate, and finally the distance of a possible combined mark. Put a question mark after this last figure to show that you do not know how much, if any, of this combined mark belonged to the tire indicated. Thus

$$LR = 32.5 + 37.2?$$

means that the left rear tire clearly skidded 32.5 ft plus possibly 37.2 ft additional as indicated by the combined mark.

If some tire on a vehicle makes a skidmark and one or more others do not, show this in your notes. For example, RR =0.0, with measurements of skidmarks from other tires, would mean, "I looked for skidmarks from the right rear tire and found none."

In many investigations, length of skidmarks is not enough. Their exact position on the road must also be located by measurements. Measurements are explained more fully in Topic 828.

Photographing skidmarks is the best way to record what you see. But photos are not a good substitute for measurements. A picture of the beginning of a mark is especially important. Let it show the road where there is no tire mark (Exhibit 17).

Because photos do not always show as much as you can see, mark the roadway where you think the mark began and ended (Exhibit 43). That will show where you measured from and to.

The effect of road friction on tires, for example in skidding, is usually inconspicuous. It appears as surface abrasion. In most cases, a hundred yards or more of travel will obscure the effect. Certainly, nothing that could easily be recognized as a "flat spot" is produced by even a long skid from a high speed. Tire abrasions are described more fully in Topic 825.

2. YAWMARKS

There are other kinds of tire friction marks besides locked-wheel skidmarks. These are scuffmarks, marks made by a tire which is rotating *and* sliding on a pavement or other surface. There are three kinds of scuffmarks, defined as follows:

1. *Yawmark,* a scuffmark made on a surface by a rotating tire which is slipping more or less parallel to its axis. Sometimes yawmarks are called *centrifugal skidmarks, critical speed scuffmarks,* or *sideslip marks.*
2. *Acceleration scuff,* a scuffmark made when sufficient power is supplied to the driving wheels to make at least one spin or slip on the road surface.

Exhibit 45. *Here is a clue as to the direction of skidding. A little tar spot on the paving is smeared in that direction.*

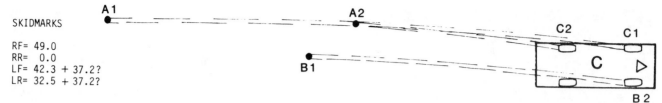

SKIDMARKS
RF = 49.0
RR = 0.0
LF = 42.3 + 37.2?
LR = 32.5 + 37.2?

Exhibit 46. *When skidmarks overlap so exactly that you cannot tell which is which where they begin, let your measurements show separately the parts that you can definitely attribute to each wheel. Then measure and record separately the overlapping parts.*

3. *Flat tire mark,* a scuffmark made by an overdeflected tire, a tire which has too little air pressure in it for the load on it.

Yawmarks are the most important kind of scuffmarks.

Before-collision yawmarks are made by steering as contrasted to before-collision skidmarks, which are made by braking. The difference is naturally important in understanding how an accident happened, and so it is unfortunate that so many accident investigators make no distinction between yaw scuffmarks and braking skidmarks.

The word yaw came originally from sailing. It is also used in aviation. It means that the vehicle, (boat, plane or motor vehicle) is rotating about its vertical axis as it moves along its path. Then the vehicle is not moving in the exact direction in which it is headed. Transportation equipment also experiences two other kinds of angular (rotary) motion: *pitch,* which is up and down motion about a transverse (crosswise) axis; and *roll,* which is side to side angular motion about a longitudinal (lengthwise) axis (Exhibit 47).

In an ordinary turn, the vehicle rotates gradually about its vertical axis so that it is headed in the direction it is moving at each instant. There is no sideslip. Because front rather than rear wheels steer, the rear wheels track inside the front ones in an ordinary turn as shown in Exhibit 48. In an ordinary turn, centrifugal force tending to keep the vehicle moving in a straight line is less than friction force between tires and pavement. The result is that there is no sideslipping and the vehicle follows the curve in which it is steered, as illustrated in Exhibit 48.

In a fast turn, however, the situation is different. Centrifugal force tending to keep the vehicle going straight ahead becomes greater than the friction force between tires and road. So tires slip sidewise. The vehicle no longer follows the path in which it is steered. The yaw situation is illustrated in Exhibits 49 and 50. During a yaw, friction of tires sideslipping on the road slows the vehicle. If the vehicle does not stop or run off the road first, it may veer around enough to slide directly sidewise and then backwards in a yaw.

Varieties of Yaw Marks

Like skidmarks, yawmarks appear differently depending on the road surface material and condition. They may be quite dark on some bituminous concrete paving or they may be barely visible on Portland-cement concrete. Usually yawmarks are lighter than skidmarks because a rotating tire keeps bringing new tread areas in contact with the road and so does not become so hot as a tire sliding continuously on one spot.

Life of Yawmarks

Generally speaking yawmarks do not last nearly as long as skidmarks on the same road surface because they are less dense to begin with. A strong yawmark made on dry paving may remain visible for three months but on a wet surface, a yawmark may disappear in three minutes.

Characteristics of Yawmarks

In Exhibit 1, the second column outlines characteristics of yawmarks. Compare these with characteristics of braking skidmarks in the first column.

Typical yawmarks are illustrated in Exhibits 51 and 52. In Exhibit 53, slippage is evenly balanced between front and rear tires. Although rear tires are tracking outside of the front ones, this divergence is fairly constant. In Exhibits 51 and 52, rear tires are sideslipping more than front ones so that eventually the vehicle goes into a broadside *skid* before it starts to go backward.

Configuration. Yawmarks are always curved because they result from

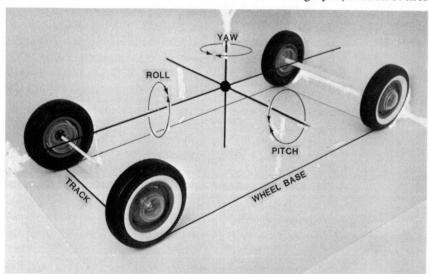

Exhibit 47. *A vehicle experiences three kinds of rotation: pitch (up and down about a crosswise axis), roll (side to side about a lengthwise axis), and yaw (right and left about a vertical axis).*

Exhibit 48. *In normal turning at moderate speeds, the rear wheels track inside of the front ones. The marks left, if any, are prints rather than yawmarks.*

Exhibit 49. *But when a turn is made so fast that traction is lost, the rear wheels track outside of the front ones. Tires sideslip and the mark made is a yawmark.*

steering. Ordinarily there are two marks from wheels on the outside of the curve, but in some material all wheels may show marks (Exhibit 51). On hard, clean surfaces only one may show. Actually, some yaws leave no perceptible mark. If the yaw continues far enough with greater rear-wheel sideslip, as shown in Exhibits 51 and 52, the path of the inside rear wheel crosses the path of the outside front wheel. Of course, if the vehicle stops before this happens, or if either of these tires leaves no mark, no typical crossing will be visible on the road surfaces.

Striations (little stripes or parallel marks) in yawmarks are quite different from those in skidmarks. They are not made by ribs in the tread. They are made either by gritty particles caught in the grooves (Exhibit 54) or by tire sidewall ribs (Exhibit 55). Often neither of these is present and so no striations appear. Any striations that do appear are nearly crosswise of the mark at the beginning (Exhibit 52 and 56), changing to oblique marks (Exhibit 55) as the yaw progresses. If the mark goes far enough, striations become parallel to the mark as shown at crossover in Exhibit 52. At this point the wheel momentarily stops rotating and the tiremark is a skidmark for a short distance.

After-collision yawmarks are very common. They are easily mistaken for after-collision skidmarks. Both are usually curved because of vehicle rotation. If possible, determine whether they are yaw (rotating wheel) or skid (sliding wheel) marks, by observation.

But in any event, record by measurement, photographs, or both, their location and appearance, so that they may be put on an after-accident situation map.

Yawmarks corresponding to collision scrub marks are possible. During impact (engagement), a wheel may be momentarily locked and so make a collision scrub or skid, or it may be momentarily shoved sidewise while still rotating to make a collision scuff. Determining the difference is really not very important, but because both are so useful in determining where the collision took place, locating impact yawmarks and collision scrubs by measurements is important.

Width of yawmark. How narrow the mark can actually be is shown in Exhibit 57, which shows a yawmark on a 3-in. lane-marker stripe. The tiremark is actually only about an inch wide. These narrow marks are always at the beginning of a yaw (Position H in Exhibit 52), before the vehicle has swerved much. After the vehicle has swerved until it is going broadside (Position Y, in Exhibit 52), the mark is as wide as the tire "footprint" on the road is long, as illustrated in Exhibit 58. Actually, when the wheel is sliding exactly sidewise, parallel to its axle, it has stopped rotating. Then, momentarily, the yaw becomes a skid, a side skid, and leaves the kind of mark shown at Y in Exhibit 52.

Variations in widths of yawmarks are easily understood. When a vehicle

Exhibit 50. *This car is in a yaw. It is sideslipping to the right in a left curve with a wet paving. If the driver is skillful he can control the car. Otherwise, the car may spin around and go backward.*

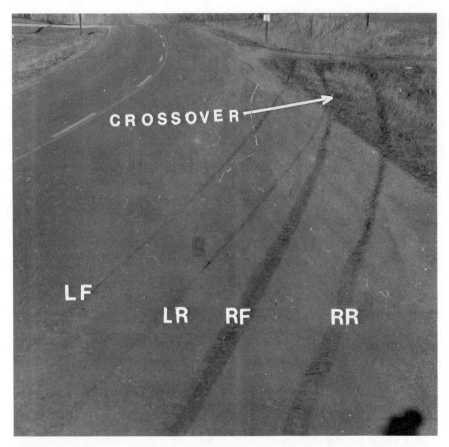

Exhibit 51. *Typical yawmarks are curved. The outside marks are more prominent than the inside ones. Marks begin faint and end strong and abruptly. Marks may vary in width from much less to much more than tire tread width. Striations, if any, vary from crosswise, at the beginning, to parallel where marks are widest.*

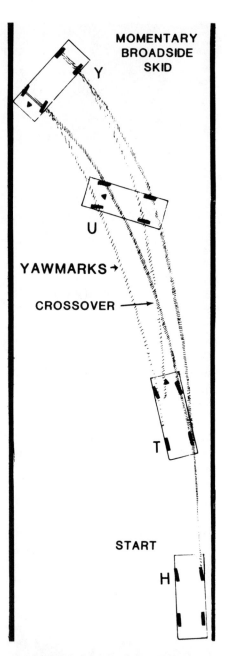

Exhibit 52. *A diagram of the marks shown in Exhibit 51 shows by the position of the vehicle how it rotates from H to Y in a yaw. Direction of sideslip and possible striations is shown for each spiraled tire mark.*

turns sharply, it tends to roll toward the outside of the curve. Then its weight shifts to the outside tires just as the weight shifts from rear to front in braking. The force tending to roll the vehicle over is the centrifugal force of the turn acting at the vehicle's center of mass pushing outward, and the road drag, pushing inward at wheel level as shown in Exhibit 59 (which compares with Exhibit 20 for a braking skid). The effect of these forces can actually be seen in a vehicle on a fast turn as illustrated in Exhibit 60. Additional weight on the tires on the outside of the turn produces more friction heat and makes a stronger mark than the tires on the side of the vehicle toward the inside of the turn. The tire with the greater load is not only over-deflected for that reason, but it is also side deflected so that most of the weight is concentrated on the outside edge of the tire as shown by Exhibit 61. Sometimes the thrust is so great that the side deflec-

tion actually brings the sidewall of the tire in contact with the road as in Exhibit 62. This may wear a hole in the sidewall (Exhibit 63).

Observing and Measuring

Measurements to locate yawmarks are much more complicated than those to locate skidmarks. Simple measurements of the length of the marks are not much use; measurements must be sufficient to plot the marks on a map. That means locating a spot on each mark at 10- or 20-ft (15-meter) intervals as explained in Topic 828.

Direction of striations. When examining yawmarks, look for striations, and if any are visible, note their direction with respect to the mark. Perhaps the best way to do this is to photograph them, but they can also be shown on a field sketch made to record measurements.

On such a field sketch, a single, continuous, curved line can represent the

path of the tire. If striations show along the yawmark, indicate their angle of slippage by little cross marks as in Exhibit 64.

3. ACCELERATION SCUFFS
Definition

An acceleration scuff is a scuffmark made when sufficient power is supplied to the driving wheels to make at least one of them spin on the road surface.

Exhibit 53. *All yaw marks are curved, but not all have the same spiral shape. S and T are an example of yaw marks which are more uniformly curved.*

How Made

Only cars with great power for their weight can generally leave accelerating scuffs on hard, dry paving. Ordinary cars can do it momentarily by "scorching" or engaging the clutch suddenly while the engine is running fast. On gravel or especially in mud and snow, accelerating scuffs often appear at the beginning of tire prints.

Characteristics

On a hard pavement, a few feet of an acceleration scuff looks just like a braking skidmark (M in Exhibit 65). On soft, or loose material, however, you can see a difference. The spinning wheel kicks loose material backwards out of the furrow.

The beginning and end of an acceleration scuff are quite distinctive. If the vehicle is stopped on paving to begin with, the tire spins in one place for a moment before the vehicle begins to move on. That spot becomes very hot and leaves a very dark mark on the road surface. Sometimes, on bituminous concrete paving, the bitumen melts and the spinning tire digs out an actual depression in the surface (S in Exhibit 65). But if the vehicle is moving when the wheel begins to spin, no special starting spot is made.

The end of the acceleration scuff gradually fades out as the vehicle reaches a speed at which the tire is no longer slipping on the road surface (E in Exhibit 65).

Often, as the car accelerates, weight shifts to the rear (as contrasted to the front in braking), tires are overloaded, overdeflect, and leave edge marks. Thus, a section of such a mark would look much like a braking skidmark or perhaps a flat-tire mark.

Two-wheel acceleration scuffs occur when the vehicle has a limited slip ("Positrack") differential that prevents a single wheel from spinning. Sometimes cars without such differentials leave two marks for a short distance when accelerating very rapidly.

Roadway "artwork" is produced, usually by smartaleck drivers, who back up and then shift gears to start forward before they have stopped going backward. That leaves a hook in the scuffmark where the car stopped going back and started going forward. The spinning wheel has lost traction and if both wheels spin, the vehicle can easily slip downhill on a cross slope. Sometimes these loops are repeated to leave an elegant pattern on the road such as shown in Exhibit 66. By this means, the driver tries to impress onlookers or passengers in the vehicle.

Studded tires are intended to give improved traction on slippery surfaces. On a spinning wheel, they can dig into ice and snow to get a better grip on the road. If, while the wheel is spinning, studs strike the pavement, they may leave a special form of scratching which has a "braided" appearance (Exhibit 67). This is not clearly visible while the road is wet or snow-covered, but it is easily seen when the road dries. If a wheel spins for several revolutions on one spot, marks left by studded tires show less clearly the mark of each stud. Studded-tire skidmarks look different; they are straight parallel scratches without the "braiding" effect (Exhibit 9).

Significance in Accidents

Purposely made acceleration scuffs are rarely produced by vehicles involved in accidents. But sometimes at the scene of an accident, especially on rural roads, there may be acceleration scuffs which were there before the accident. These may be confusing (Exhibit 37) if you do not recognize them at once for what they are.

Exhibit 54. *Loose gritty material moved by a sliding tire scratches the surface. This is a sideslip on bituminous concrete, part of a very long yawmark.*

Exhibit 55. *If the striations in a tiremark are oblique to the tiremark, the wheel is rotating. Then the mark is a yawmark and the tire is sideslipping.*

Exhibit 56. *Striations, if any show, at beginning of a yawmark where it is narrow, are crosswise of the yawmark. These are made by shoulder ribs.*

Exhibit 57. *In a yaw, only the outboard edge of the tire may make a mark. That edge is where the load is. Striations are made by shoulder ribs.*

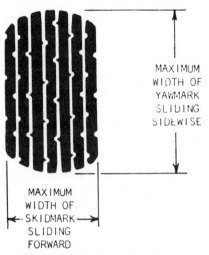

Exhibit 58. *Maximum width of skidmark is width of tire-road contact area. Tread ribs may leave striations in this direction. Maximum width of yawmark is length of tire-road contact area when tire slides sidewise. Striations, if any, are made by shoulder ribs or abrasive material from the road, not by tread ribs.*

Exhibit 59. *Weight-shift on a fast turn makes the vehicle lean or tilt toward the outside of the turn. Compare with Exhibit 20 which shows tilt due to braking.*

It is possible for vehicle accelerators to be stuck wide open and so make acceleration scuffs; but this is less common than acceleration scuffs made when a driver mistakes the accelerator for the brake and floors the gas pedal to try to stop the vehicle. Then you have the often difficult task of trying to determine whether tiremarks on the road were due to acceleration or braking.

Driver skill. Race drivers, trying to make the best possible speed on sharp turns, sometimes steer a car into a yaw on purpose and then accelerate toward the inside of the curve after the car is headed sufficiently in that direction. But most truly skillful drivers do not let themselves get into situa-

tions where quick turning may produce a yaw because that is how a driver starts to lose control. When a yaw begins, steering in the direction of the rear wheel slide to straighten the vehicle out will, if not overdone, correct the situation. But many drivers do not have the experience and skill to know just how much to correct, with the result that they overreact. At slow speeds correction is not difficult, but at high speeds, the road is too narrow and the swerve too quick to correct an overreaction and put the vehicle back on course. Then the vehicle goes off the road, partly sidewise.

Life of Acceleration Scuffs

The main part of an acceleration

scuff has about the same life as a skidmark, because it is made in much the same way.

Where the beginning of an acceleration scuff has dug into the surface of the roadway (S in Exhibit 65), the depression will last for years or until the road is repaved.

Where the end of the scuff tapers off, the mark is light to begin with and so wears away. This makes the mark appear shorter as time passes. Exhibits 68 and 69 show an acceleration scuff soon after it was made and 42 days later.

4. FLAT-TIRE MARKS

Definition

A flat-tire mark is a scuffmark made

Exhibit 60. *When turning sharply or at high speed, a vehicle's weight shifts from the inside to the outside wheels. The vehicle tends to roll to the outside. The outside wheels with greater weight produce more heat and darker marks.*

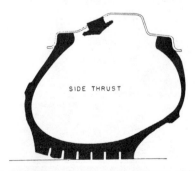

Exhibit 61. *If the tire has a strong side thrust, especially when overloaded or underinflated, the tire deflects to the side. Most of the weight is then on that side. This is the shape of the tire when the vehicle turns a corner fast.*

Exhibit 62. *If the downward and sideward thrust is great enough and the pressure in the tire is low, the tire may flatten. Sidewall wears through quickly if it slides on roadway. Bead may be pulled from rim, releasing air.*

Exhibit 63. At A, tire has worn through sidewall sliding sidewise on pavement. Rim then has contacted pavement at D. Tire rubs fender well at B and C.

by an overdeflected tire; a mark made by a tire which is seriously underinflated or overloaded.

How Made

An overdeflected tire, whether much under inflated or greatly overloaded, gets hot when it is run far or fast. It also rubs the road surface as it rolls. The heat and friction may make marks on dry paving, especially bituminous concrete ("black top") surfaces.

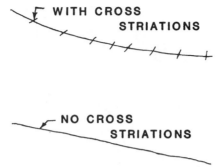

WITH CROSS STRIATIONS

NO CROSS STRIATIONS

Exhibit 64. On your field sketch of yaw-marks, show the angle of striations, if any. A single line for a tire mark indicates that you did not notice any cross striations. Small cross marks on the line show the approximate angle of crosswise striations which you saw.

Characteristics

Column 4 in Exhibit 1 summarizes the characteristics of flat-tire marks.

Such a mark may extend for many miles along a road. You can never find exactly where a flat-tire scuff really began because the beginning is so faint. The flat-tire scuff usually ends where the vehicle was driven on the shoulder to repair the tire. Of course, usually only one tire is flat at a time and so only one mark is made.

Partially flat. If the tire is not entirely flat — perhaps a quarter of normal pressure — it will be definitely overdeflected as illustrated in Exhibit 23. Then it will leave a mark, if any, that is heavy on the edges and light in the middle (Exhibit 70) that looks like a front-wheel skidmark from a tire overdeflected by weight shift in braking.

A driver may be quite unaware of this condition.

Completely flat tires have a somewhat different appearance. The tire bunches up and the sidewalls of the tire also touch the road. Drivers are usually aware of this condition. It jounces the vehicle and makes a noise. The mark made is scalloped and may show sidewall marks as illustrated in Exhibit 71. In this condition tires do not last long, and, if the marks continue for more than a few hundred feet, it is probably because the driver has decided the tire is ruined anyhow and is driving the flat somewhere to get it fixed.

When one of a pair of dual tires on one wheel goes quite flat, the other tire

Exhibit 65. With vehicle standing, an acceleration scuff starts a dark spot at S. The main part, M, looks like a skidmark. The end, E, gradually disappears.

Exhibit 66. Showoff drivers sometimes make roadway "artwork" of acceleration scuffs. An interesting problem is to explain how the marks shown were made.

Exhibit 67. Studded tires leave "braided" aceleration scuffs.

Exhibit 68. An acceleration scuff 6 days after it was made.

Exhibit 69. The same scuff 42 days later, almost invisible.

on that wheel may then be overloaded and overdeflected. Both tires can then make marks on the road as in Exhibit 72.

Accident Significance

Most flat-tire marks are not associated with accidents. But if a clearly

distinguishable flat-tire mark does lead to the point of collision and the car that came from that direction does have a flat tire, you have the best possible evidence that the tire was disabled before the accident. Then it is probable, but not certain, that the tire contributed to the accident.

Drivers are likely to blame "blowouts" for an accident when there is a tire flat afterward. In many of these cases, the blamed tire was disabled during impact or after loss of control rather than before. That makes it important to examine tires and road after an accident to determine exactly how

Exhibit 70. Flat-tire scuffs look like front-tire skids but usually show steering and may be miles long. This tire is not completely flat.

Exhibit 71. When tire loses most of its air pressure, flat-tire marks become very irregular and may show marks from sidewalls of tire as well as tread.

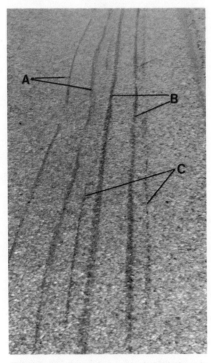

Exhibit 72. One of a pair of dual tires is disabled. A, marks from flat left tire. B edge marks from overloaded right tire. C sidewall marks from much overdeflected tire.

Exhibit 73. *Tire imprints usually show tread pattern. The tire is rolling without slipping*

and when tire disablement occurred.

Many people have come to believe that a "blowout" inevitably results in loss of control. As a matter of fact, a sudden tire disablement usually results in a tendency of the vehicle to "pull" to the right or left; but nearly all able-bodied drivers correct for this almost automatically. It requires only a few pounds of force on the steering wheel to do so. A few drivers are upset by the sensations of sudden disablement and overreact, often with disastrous results. Fewer than one percent of drivers appear to have been unable to cope with a flat tire, even at high speed.[4]

5. IMPRINTS

Definition

An imprint is a mark on a road or other surface made without sliding by a rolling tire or a person's foot. An imprint usually shows the pattern of the tire tread or shoe that made it. Sometimes called print, impression, or deposit.

How Made

Tires rolling along a road as usual make no visible mark on a dry surface. But rolling tires may leave tracks without friction; they may pick up material in one place and deposit in another often showing the tread pattern. They may also press a rut into soft material and the tread pattern may show in this rut.

Characteristics

The last column in Exhibit 1 sum-marizes characteristics of imprints.

Prints on paving are easy to recognize because the tire tread pattern shows plainly as in Exhibit 73. If more than one wheel leaves a tire print, the prints from all wheels are equally strong or prominent. *Wet tires* leave prints on paving. The wetness may come from a puddle through which the tire has just passed, it may be mud from the shoulder, or paint from a fresh paving stripe. At accidents, puddles on the paving from wrecks wet the tires of passing vehicles, after which they leave prints on the paving until the moisture is gone from them. If the puddle that wets the tire is not as wide as the circumference of the tire, only part of the tire is wet and the print is interrupted (Exhibit 74).

An interesting kind of interrupted imprint is sometimes found following a skid (Exhibit 75). The area of the tire touching the road during the skid gets very hot. It may become tacky. Then, when brakes are released and the wheel turns, the tacky spot leaves an imprint every time it touches the pavement. The distance between these imprints is the circumference of the tire. Dual tires on a truck wheel will leave pairs of imprints.

Imprints in soft or loose material made by rolling tires result in ruts or depressions. If the soft material is plastic, such as dirt (Exhibit 76), fine dust (Exhibit 77), or damp snow (Exhibit 78), clear tire prints are left which make it easy to distinguish ruts made by rolling wheels from furrows made by sliding tires.

If loose material is hard, a rolling wheel may make no noticeable rut or print, but a sliding wheel will plow a furrow, disturbing the surface and throwing pebbles to both sides in a skid and to one side in a yaw or sideslip.

Grass and turf complicate the problem of deciding whether the mark was made by a rolling or sliding wheel. With strong, well rooted grass, especially if the vegetation is damp or wet, both rolling and sliding wheels bend the grass forward and push it down. After the tire passes, the grass returns partly to its former upright position. A visible path remains, but whether it was made by a rolling or sliding wheel

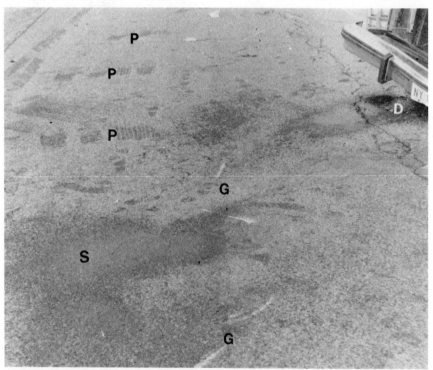

Exhibit 74. *Tires pick up liquid from the wet spatter area at S. Only part of the circumference of the tire is wetted. This wet spot marks the pavement repeatedly as the tire rolls onward at spots marked P. G's are gouges resulting from a collision. D is the puddle where the car came to rest.*

Exhibit 75. *Small imprints at K, L, and M were made by a spot on a tire that became so hot in a skid ending at S that it became gummy and left marks as the tire rolled after brakes were released. This was a dual tire.*

Exhibit 76. *Tire prints in dirt usually show tread pattern in the rut made.*

Exhibit 77. *Rolling wheels in dust or other soft material make shallow ruts.*

Exhibit 78. *Ruts in damp snow may be deep and clearly marked with tire prints.*

Exhibit 79. *In general, grass is packed down in a rut as shown here.*

may be uncertain.

However, if grass is uprooted or torn off in the bottom of the furrow and the surface of the ground disturbed, the wheel was sliding (Exhibit 6). Compare that illustration of a skidmark with Exhibit 79, which shows an imprint rut in turf.

Accident Significance

Tire imprints are much less likely to be important in accidents than braking skidmarks, yawmarks, or scuffmarks. Sometimes prints on the pavement at the scene are confused with skidmarks. But tire prints on the shoulder or roadside can be very useful in showing where the vehicle left the paving and possibly where it came back on again.

6. ROAD SCARS

Definition

A road scar is any sign that the road, roadside, or a fixed object has been damaged or marred by a traffic accident.

How Made

When a moving vehicle is damaged so that metal parts come in contact with the ground, scars are left. Off the pavement, these scars may be furrows, sometimes indistinguishable from furrows made by skidding or scuffing tires. Paving scars take two forms: 1) scratches, which penetrate the surface so little that you cannot feel them, or metal scraped off on the pavement surface; and 2) gouges in which so much material is dug out that the depression can easily be felt with the fingers.

Characteristics

Scratches and scrapes are made with little pressure. They show where sheet metal body parts dragged across the surface or stronger metal parts moved lightly over the area. If the marks are narrow (G in Exhibit 80), they are simple scratches. If they are broad, they represent scraping of an area (H in Exhibit 80). Scratches are most useful to show where a vehicle turned over on the roadway and the path it followed after collision. Scrapes often help in locating the point of maximum engagement.

Towing scratches. Pavements can easily be scratched by metal parts when a damaged vehicle is dragged by a tow truck to a good position for a better towing hookup. An investigator who is there when these marks are made, especially if he notices that the dragging car is marking the roadway, is not likely to confuse them with more significant after-collision scratches; but later, especially if the marks show only in photos, it is easy for someone to suppose that they were made by or right after collision. Sometimes it is necessary to find out how towing operations were conducted to explain such marks on the road surface.

Gouges are places where pavement material has been dug out by strong metal parts such as frames, transmission housing, and control arms which have been forced down on the road. The shape of a gouge may suggest how it was made.

Chips are small deep gouges where chunks of paving have been dug out as might be done with a pick axe (Exhibit 81). They are most likely to occur in bituminous-concrete paving; portland-cement concrete pavements are too hard to chip easily, except at edges and joints.

Except in very soft or loose paving, chips are not made by the weight of the vehicle alone. The metal has struck the road with force greater than the vehicle's weight, a force which can only be produced by the violence of collision. Hence, chips are nearly always made during maximum engagement and mark a spot on the road where the corresponding part of the vehicle was when maximum engagement occurred. Direction of motion of the metal part making a chip is usually difficult and often impossible to determine by examination of the gouge. Small particles and dust may remain on the side of the chip toward which the part moved, but these have usually been displaced or have disappeared by the time the chip is examined.

Exhibit 80. *Scratches, at G and scrapes, at H, are light road scars made by metal not heavy or strong enough to disturb the surface. These show where a car landed after a flip. H is partly paint from the car roof.*

Exhibit 81. *Chips of material gouged from the pavement are very helpful in determining where the forces of maximum engagement made some metal vehicle part dig into the pavement surface.*

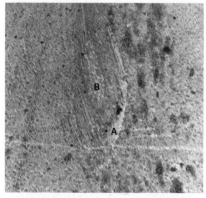

Exhibit 82. *If a broad, strong metal part is forced down on the road during a collision, it chops the roadway surface. Adjacent scrapes show direction of movement of parts during collision.*

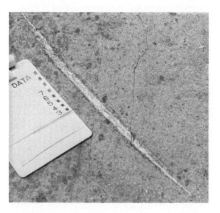

Exhibit 83. *Grooves show paths of strong, projecting parts forced heavily against the road surface. Direction of motion is usually very difficult to determine from groove.*

Exhibit 84. *Curved grooves indicate rotation of vehicle making them. To be useful, position of grooves must be located by measurements.*

Exhibit 85. *Scars on fixed objects such as trees, posts and guard rails are helpful in learning how a vehicle moved when it left the road. They are usually conspicuous and durable.*

Chops are broad, shallow gouges such as might be made by an axe chopped obliquely into the paving. They are made by vehicle frames and sometimes wheel rims (Exhibit 82). A vehicle part that might make a chop in a bituminous-concrete pavement will only scratch the harder portland-cement concrete paving. Chops are likely to occur at maximum engagement.

Generally, chops clearly indicate direction of motion from the deep sharp side to the shallow ragged side (from A to B in Exhibit 82). Chops are likely to be combined with scrapes, as shown in the same exhibit.

Grooves are long narrow gouges. They may be straight (Exhibit 83) or crooked (Exhibit 84). They are made by projecting nuts or studs and sometimes by the drive shaft or some other part dragging on the road. They continue some distance beyond maximum engagement. Examining the shape of the bottom of a groove will help to match the groove with whatever vehicle part made it. Direction of motion of the part making the groove cannot usually be determined from examination, especially after the dust has been swept away, although it is easy for an eager investigator to imagine that he can see signs of motion in one direction or the other.

Grooves made by towing, like scratches made that way, may be confusing at the site of an accident unless the investigator actually sees them made or unless he knows just how towing operations were performed. Towing grooves are uncommon, however, because the weight on the metal part dragging on the road is usually not great enough to do more than scratch the road surface.

Scars on fixed objects are usually, but not always off the road. They may be dents in guardrails, or damage to traffic signs. Perhaps the most familiar are places where an out-of-control vehicle has struck a utility pole or roadside tree (Exhibit 85). All such scars are helpful in determining the path of a vehicle to its final stopping place.

Accident Significance

Chips and chops, like crooks in skidmarks, help to locate the position of a vehicle at maximum engagement. Sometimes, after an accident, they are overlooked because they are covered or filled with water or debris. Scratches and scrapes may indicate where a vehicle rolled over and slid on its top or side. Any of these marks may have to be matched to damage to parts of vehicles in trying to understand how an accident happened.

7. DEBRIS

Definition

Debris is loose material scattered about at the scene as a result of a traffic accident: dirt, liquids, vehicle parts, cargo, personal belongings and other things.

Kinds of Debris

Underbody debris (mud, rust, paint, snow, and sometimes gravel) sticks to the underside of fenders, engine, body, and other parts. In a collision, this comes loose in two ways: 1) the metal to which it is stuck bends or crinkles and debris chips off; and 2) the shock of collision loosens it.

After a collision, underbody debris may be heaped in a pile only about three feet across and several inches deep (Exhibit 86), or it may be scattered thinly over a wide area (Exhibit 87). The distribution of underbody debris is important. In serious accidents, it should be examined, located by measurements, and recorded in photographs.

Accident significance. Remember that, if the vehicle is moving when underbody debris is dislodged, the debris is also moving and so does not drop straight to the ground. It continues to move in the direction the vehicle was moving and at approximately the vehicle's speed until it reaches the ground, unless it first strikes some part of a vehicle moving in another direction because of the collision. Then, the debris is redirected. Because debris scatters so much, it is usually a poor indicator of where collision took place. Look for a better indicator of the collision point.

Vehicle liquids. Coolant, oil, battery acid, fuel, and other fluids may escape from containers in a vehicle during and after collision. Blood and other body liquids may also appear. The importance of such debris and its pattern on the road is often overlooked. Vehicle liquids appear on the road in six ways (Exhibit 88):

1. Spatter
2. Dribble
3. Puddle
4. Run-off
5. Soak-in
6. Tracking.

Do not expect to find liquid debris on wet pavement. Liquid from the car mixes with water on the road and is lost. There are exceptions, some of which will be noted.

Spatter occurs when the container is collapsed by collision with the result that liquid in it squirts out violently and splashes on the road and nearby vehicle parts. For example, the liquid from the radiator in a collision does not drip out and fall to the ground; it is forced out under great and sudden pressure. Such spatter areas are dark, wet spots, irregular in shape, and often composed of or surrounded by many small spots or "freckles" (Exhibit 89). Sometimes copious spatter makes an

Exhibit 86. *Underbody debris is not a very accurate way to locate position of collision point. Lacking tiremarks or metal scars, concentrated debris with vehicles close by may be the best available indication of collision point.*

Exhibit 87. *Widely scattered underbody debris with both cars on the same side may be misleading as to where the vehicles collided. Here, actual collision occurred outside of the scattered debris area shown in the foreground of this picture.*

elongated "splash" pattern (Exhibit 90).

Spatter reaches the road before the damaged vehicle moves very far and it is, therefore, a good indication of where it was when the collision collapsed or broke open the liquid container. Spatter is often accompanied by chips, chops, scrapes, or collision scrubs as in Exhibit 90.

Spatter may be obscured by underbody debris or smeared by road sweeping after the accident. Spatter may dry out or soon be obliterated by passing traffic. Therefore, it may easily escape attention in accident investigation.

Battery acid spatter can penetrate some surface water, snow, and slush. While the road is wet, battery acid does not show, but after it dries, the spot where the acid reacted with limestone in the concrete may show quite plainly as a "bleached" area (Exhibit 91). Acid spatter is rare, of course, but it can be significant information when it is found. Make sure that the mark is from real spatter at a collision point and not a puddle or run-off from dripping where a vehicle came to rest (Exhibit 92).

Dribble is a liquid draining — not squirting — from a ruptured container on a wrecked vehicle. If the vehicle is moving, the dribble marks the path of the leaking part, usually from point of maximum engagement to final position (Exhibits 89, 90, and 93). In general, rapid leakage and slow vehicle

movement gives a conspicuous dribble path, sometimes continuous. But slow leakage and fast vehicle movement give an indistinct dribble path, often just a few scattered drops along the way.

Puddle. As soon as a vehicle that is dripping liquid stops moving, the dribble forms a puddle under the leaking part (Exhibit 94). This puddle shows where that part of the vehicle stopped. This is especially significant when the vehicle has been moved before the investigator gets to the scene.

Run-off occurs when a puddle forms on a sloping pavement. The liquid draining from the vehicle runs downhill in a rivulet (Exhibit 94). This happens even on roads that look quite flat. Acid also may leave run-off bleached areas (Exhibit 92).

Soak-in occurs where liquid is absorbed by soil or pavement cracks, either where run-off reaches the road shoulder (Exhibit 88) or where the puddle forms off the pavement (Exhibit 95). In the latter case, puddling and soak-in occur at the same spot and mark where part of the vehicle stopped.

Tracking of vehicle liquids results when tires roll through puddles, run-off, or spatter and, becoming wet, leave tire prints on the pavement as they roll on (Exhibit 74).

Liquid cargo, usually from tank trucks, becomes debris when it is spilled on the road by a collision. It may gush out and flood the road. Its

position rarely marks any significant point in connection with the accident. If the spilled liquid is flammable, corrosive, or toxic, damage control may be the overriding consideration.

Accident significance. Spatter and dribble help locate collision positions; dribble and puddles indicate where vehicles came to rest. Other kinds of liquid debris do not usually help much in determining how the accident happened.

Sometimes puddles and dribble do not actually signify what they might seem to at first glance. If a wrecker hooks to a damaged vehicle and tows or drags it from where it came to rest, remaining liquids can drain out and form a dribble path (Exhibit 96). If the vehicle is set down temporarily, a puddle is formed. These represent motion and stopped positions connected with towing and so do not have the same

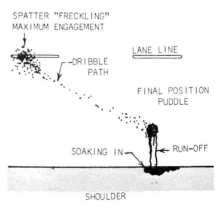

Exhibit 88. *Liquid debris appears on the road in a number of forms illustrated here in this diagram.*

Exhibit 89. *Spatter occurring in a "freckled" pattern shows where fluids were forced violently from crushed containers onto the surface of the road. Spatter may be oil, coolant, or other fluid.*

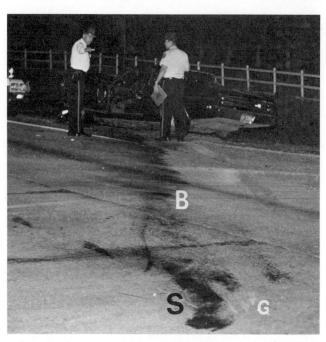

Exhibit 90. *Spatter at S associated with gouges, G, is an excellent indication of maximum engagement area. Here B is a dribble path leading to final position of a vehicle.*

Exhibit 91. *When battery acid spatters, it may leave bleached area on the roadway, even if there is water or slush there. The bleaching is a chemical reaction between acid and road stone.*

Exhibit 92. *However, not all battery acid bleach is where spatter occurred. Here bleaching run-off at R has been imprinted by passing vehicles to S, T, U.*

Exhibit 93. *Pedestrian or animal bodies may also leave dribble paths from collision area to where they come to rest. This may help show where pedestrian was hit.*

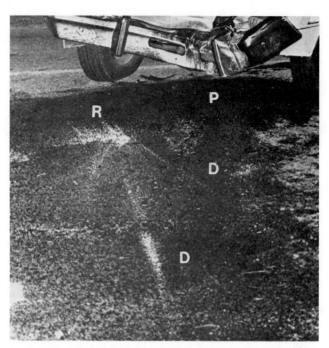

Exhibit 94. *A dribble path at D leads to the final position of the vehicle where a puddle, P, is formed by leaking liquid which runs off at R, down grade.*

Exhibit 95. *Puddles formed off the roadway often soak into the ground forming a stain that marks the point where a vehicle came to rest. It is helpful in locating final position of vehicle.*

Exhibit 96. *Dribble paths made by liquids from a vehicle which is being towed may be confusing. Dribble paths D and E in this picture are unusually conspicuous. W, X, and Y are yawmarks.*

Exhibit 97. *Final position of major vehicle parts such as that at the right are as important to accident investigation as the position of the vehicles; but small pieces of vehicles scattered about have little significance and need not be located accurately; consider them as a kind of debris.*

significance as those left by motion and stopped position after collision.

Vehicle parts. Compared to liquids which have come from vehicles, other vehicle parts are seldom significant as debris. Small parts scatter so widely and irregularly that where they are found cannot mean much. But there are important exceptions, three of which will be noted here:

1. Small parts found at the scene may help identify a vehicle that has left the scene of the accident. They may be useful, therefore, in hit-and-run investigations.
2. Whole sections of the vehicle that have broken loose in collision may be significant because of their final positions (Exhibit 97). This is the case when a vehicle breaks in a collision with

a tree or when the engine is knocked out of a vehicle in a collision with a truck. The positions of these major parts are located by measurements in the same way that final positions of vehicles themselves are located.

3. Tempered glass from rear windows of vehicles may shatter into thousands of pop-corn-sized pieces (Exhibit 98) when the glass is broken in collisions. The glass forms a special pattern on the road, usually some distance from where underbody debris falls (Exhibit 99). When it breaks free, the glass continues to move and so the point at which it lands can be helpful in determining the direction of travel of the vehicle from which the glass came and sometimes the vehicle's speed. Tempered glass debris areas are, therefore, quite worth noting and recording. Windshields which are made of laminated glass, do not shatter and their after-collision positions usually mean little.

Solid cargo from trucks sometimes comes loose in a collision or before a collision (Exhibit 100). Then, the point at which it lands can be important in trying to find out the direction the truck was moving and something about its speed, provided, of course, that somebody has made a record of

where the material or machinery was after the collision.

Personal belongings and other cargo in the vehicle may scatter widely as debris, like vehicle parts, and so rarely signify much about how the accident happened. But they may help understand the nature of the trip and sometimes help in hit-and-run investigation.

Granular cargo heaped above the side boards of an open-topped truck body will keep on moving when the truck is stopped or slowed suddenly in collision. Thus, it may also be helpful in determining direction of travel and estimating speed, provided the pattern of such debris has been recorded. Granular cargo may be such material as gravel, grain, fertilizer, coal, or salt. Sometimes bagged cement, stacked bricks, or baled hay will slide off the top of a pile in collision and the final position may serve the same purpose in accident investigation.

Roadside material scattered on the road after collision will sometimes indicate where a vehicle came back on the road after running off, or how a collision on the shoulder took place (Exhibit 101).

Marked and Damaged Fixed Objects

Bent and broken guardrails, posts, trees, and other fixed objects can give

Exhibit 98. *Tempered glass used in rear and side windows of vehicles shatters into corn-size pieces when it breaks whether as contact or induced damage.*

Exhibit 99. *As debris, broken tempered glass may form patterns which are very significant in accident investigation. If adequately described and located, they may be useful in speed estimates. This pattern has been tracked across by a car leaving yawmarks by a sharp turn to the left to avoid collision with cars on the road after they collided.*

some idea of the speed of the vehicle striking them. Such damage is described best by photographs (Exhibit 85).

But quite inconspicuous scrapes and scratches on roadside objects often reveal much about how an accident happened. Matched with damage or marks on vehicles, they fix the position of the vehicles at a specific point during the series of events that constitute the accident. By this means they also help determine its path. Scrapes and scratches are most commonly found on bridge rails and guardrails. Fresh ones relating to the accident under consideration may have to be distinguished from older ones. These scars are sometimes a long way from other signs of the accident. Therefore, such marks on fixed objects may be quite difficult to discover and classify. They may be easily located by measurement but are best described by photographs. Sometimes particles of paint in the scraped area will help distinguish which of several cars involved came in contact with the object.

8. MEANINGS OF MARKS

Combinations of Marks

In the foregoing descriptions, each kind of mark on the road was described as though it were quite separate and by itself. Generally this is the case, but often marks are made in bewildering combinations.

Now attention will be given to what combinations of marks tell us about events of accidents. Some of these combinations are clear and simple; others are more puzzling.

You will remember that skidmarks show that a tire was not rotating. Where they begin indicates where brakes locked wheels but not necessarily where brakes were first applied; where they end tells where brakes were released or where the vehicle stopped.

Yaw marks before collision indicate where steering started to swerve the vehicle but not exactly where steering began. Other scuff marks show where wheels spun from acceleration or

Exhibit 100. *Cargo, as debris, is usually very conspicuous and scattered. Locate it by measurements. It may be important, especially in roll over accidents.*

where tires had become disabled.

Thus it is the beginning, end, and where changes in marks occur that tell where something unusual happened.

Photo Interpretation

At the actual scene of a traffic accident, you may have some trouble figuring out the exact meaning of some of the signs of the accident that you see there. But you will find it much more difficult to interpret these signs if you only have photos of them which, unfortunately, is often the case. Photo interpretation requires skills that usually develop only with practice and experience. On the following pages are a few examples of photo interpretation to illustrate the observations and reasoning involved. You may find studies of these examples helpful.

Misreading photos is easier than you might think. What was mistaken for a tire mark, for example, turns out to be something entirely different when the site is visited or when additional information is obtained. Three examples, Exhibits 112, 113 and 115 will sufficiently illustrate. Such mistakes as these can usually be avoided by very careful examination of the photos to begin with and, by looking for other photos showing the same area, and by comparing what you think you see in the picture with other information which you have available.

At the scene of an accident it is not important to determine exactly how all

Exhibit 101. *Roadside material sometimes becomes debris when it is disturbed by an accident. It may significantly indicate the motion of a vehicle on the shoulder.*

the marks were made. It *is* important to locate them and describe them well enough so that such a determination may be made afterward at leisure by yourself or someone else. The appearance of such marks can best be recorded by good photographs. If the accident is important, do not spare film for this purpose.

9. FIRST CONTACT POINT

Definition

First contact point (FCP) is the exact spot on a vehicle, pedestrian, or other object touched in a collision or the place on the road or ground closest to the first contact between the colliding objects.

The place on the ground is often spoken of as the *point of impact (POI)* and sometimes the *collision point (CP)*.

First contact point is more specific because impact and collision both suggest a series of events which usually involve motion in an area over a period of time rather than contact at a point.

Carelessly Determined Locations

An important reason for examining after-accident road abnormalities is to establish the positions of vehicles or pedestrians at the start of a collision or impact. Often this is carelessly done by someone who did not actually see the collision and who offers no explanation whatsoever of how he deter-

Exhibit 102. *This is a picture of a mark made by a tire that ran off the roadway on to the shoulder at P, the mark is the print of a rolling tire; at S it is the skidmark of a locked wheel. The arrow shows where brakes locked the wheel but not necessarily where brakes were applied.*

Exhibit 103. *At B, the tire is skidding in dirt. C shows where it stopped, leaving a tread pattern deposit in the furrow, a sidewall imprint at A, and a pile of dirt, D, which the sliding tire pushed ahead of it. E is an imprint in a shallow rut where the tire rolled on after stopping.*

Exhibit 104. *Change from a flat-tire scuff at F to a skidmark at S shows where driver braked hard enough to lock the wheel. Right wheel skidmark shows faintly in gravel at G. U and V are imprints of shoulder dust where a tire went back on the roadway.*

Exhibit 105. *S is the skidmark of a braked pair of dual tires leading to a collision scrub at C and continued to the shoulder at D as an after-collision skidmark. Y is a faint yawmark from a vehicle approaching from the opposite direction. That vehicle made after-collision scratches at K.*

Exhibit 106. *D is a single overdeflected tire mark which may have been miles long. The driver was probably unaware of this condition. The arrow shows where the tire finally blew out and went completely flat as shown by the scallops at L. The blowout did not cause loss of control.*

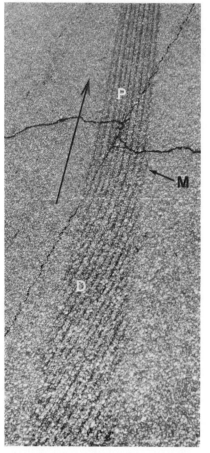

Exhibit 107. *(Above). Typical yawmarks of a car turning suddenly left to avoid a car entering its lane from the right at an intersection. Only the two right wheels made marks, beginning at F1 and R1 and ending at F2 and R2. At M and N, the tires were moving broadside.*

Exhibit 108. *(Left). At M, diagonal striations D, change to parallel striations, P, where the car started to go sidewise. At P, the tire is skidding (not rotating) without being locked by braking. Striations are from shoulder rather than tread ribs.*

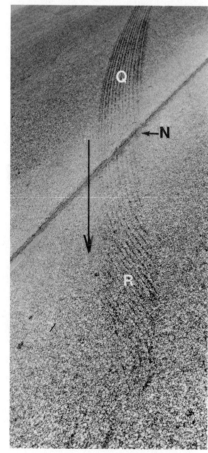

Exhibit 109. *(Right). At F2, the end of the front tire mark, striations change from parallel, Q, which indicates skidding to diagonal, at R where the car stops going sidewise and starts to go backward.*

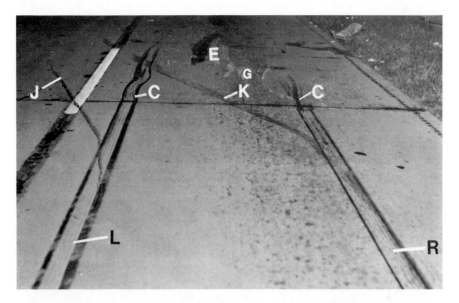

Exhibit 110. *These marks tell the story of a car that struck the rear end of a vehicle ahead. L and R are left and right front tire precollision skidmarks. C is the position of a front tire at first contact. E is a collision scrub of the left rear tire of the vehicle ahead at first contact position. J and K are rear-tire skidmarks as the rear car rotated clockwise during engagement. G is a group of maximum-engagement gouges.*

mined this position. Of course, you can *assume* that there was some kind of sign or mark somewhere on which the opinion about the location was based; but, without an explanation of a factual basis, the opinion must be treated as pure guesswork.

Therefore, you will do well to describe and locate just what you saw — the basic facts — on which you or anyone else can form an opinion about where the first contact occurred.

Method

Where a car hits a fixed object like a tree (Exhibit 85) or a guard rail, the first contact point is easy to find. On a tree, it is a point on the scar the height of the bumper or some other part of the vehicle above the ground. The point can be easily described and located within a few inches.

Two-vehicle collisions are more difficult. Sometimes an irregularity in a skidmark will indicate the position of a *tire* at first contact, but this is not the actual FCP. Exhibit 116, for example, shows skidmarks made by front wheels of a car before and during an angle collision. At first contact, the front wheels were at the ends of the straight part of the skidmarks from Car C (Exhibit 117). At this instant, Car B was starting to apply a force against the left side of Car C. Then the actual FCP is not on the skidmark, but directly below the left front corner of Car C where the front of that car begins to be forced sidewise.

Thus to locate the FCP in this case, you must know three things:
1. Where the curve in the skidmarks start.
2. Dimensions of Car C, particularly the front end overhang.
3. The location of damage on Car C.

Exhibit 118 is a situation with exactly the same skidmarks but a different FCP. These examples show that tire marks alone may not be sufficient to locate FCP accurately.

A more complex example is shown in Exhibit 37. This illustrates how extraneous marks like G and H may be misleading.

In Exhibit 119, the tangle of marks may be confusing at first; but with dimensions of the vehicles and spacing of the centerline stripe, an after-

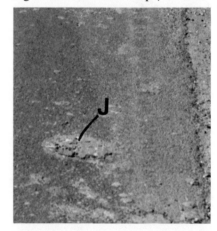

Exhibit 111. *This combination of tire friction marks tells an interesting story. In the foreground are skidmarks of all four tires. At U and V, the front tire marks widen a little because of left steer which has no effect while brakes lock wheels and produce skidding. But when brakes are released, the strong left steer in the front wheels puts the car into a violent yaw with rear tires tracking outside of front at S and T. As yaw progresses, the left rear mark crosses the right front mark at X. Then, at Y, the right front crosses the left front, and at Z, the right rear crosses left rear. This puts the car momentarily in a broadside skid, rotating counterclockwise. Then the car begins to move backward but stops at the end of the marks before it goes fully backward.*

Exhibit 112. *Based only on this photo, an investigator claimed that J was a chip by which maximum engagement could be located. But viewed at the scene or more carefully examined in the photo, it turns out to be a dollop of mud from the roadside. Once you have mistaken something in a photo, you may find it difficult to see it as anything else.*

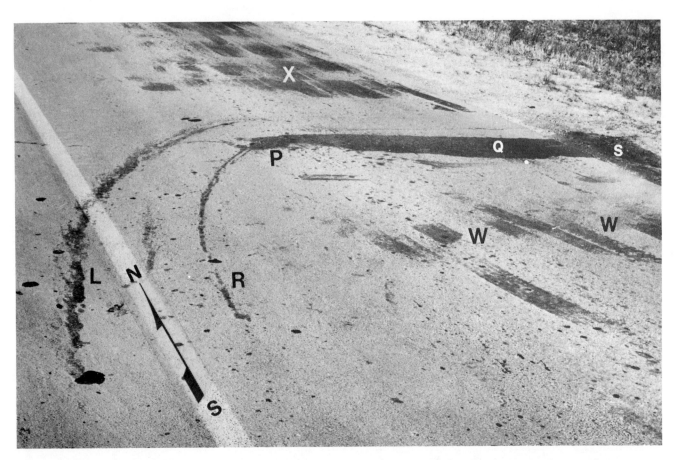

Exhibit 113. This was the site of an opposite-direction collision. Neither vehicle was located by measurements or photographed before being towed away. A Ford was reported to have "stopped with its front end in about the middle of the northbound lane." On the basis of this photo, an investigator said that the Ford had been northbound straddling the center line and turning sharply right just before collision. He pointed to "centrifugal scuffs" as his reason for believing so and noted the "heavier mark on the outside tire and some oblique striations." Do you believe him? Well, R and L are not tire marks but dribble trails made when the Ford was towed away. There are no striations but some spatter marks. The two marks are indeed curved, but not properly related to each other to be yaw marks. P is a puddle where the front of the Ford came to rest. Q is runoff to the edge of the pavement and S is soak in on the shoulder. X is a collection of imprints from northbound tires partially wetted while passing through Q.

Exhibit 114. Here are marks "identified" by an over-eager "expert" as "high speed centrifugal skidmarks." The marks are definitely curved, rather narrow, and the outer one is definitely darker. What else could it be?

Exhibit 115. Here the area shown in Exhibit 114 is outlined in a more comprehensive photo. At the scene or in this picture the marks look the same but they mean something quite different: they are only the shadows of wires strung between utility poles.

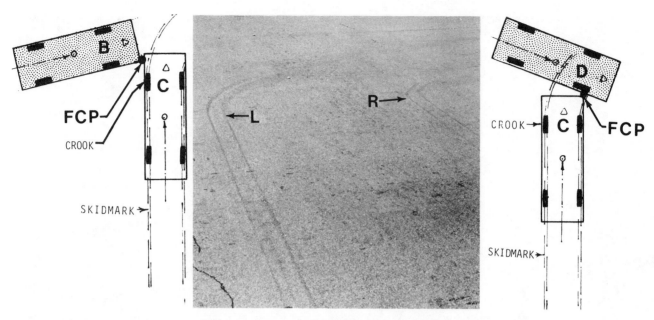

Exhibit 117. *The crook in the skidmarks shown in Exhibit 116 could have been produced by a collision such as that at the left. Then the FCP would be on the left side of C.*

Exhibit 116. *At L and R significant abnormalities appear in the skidmarks. From straight ahead, they swerve sharply to the right. When the front tires were at L and R, something pushed the vehicle to one side. But from these tire marks, it is not possible to say exactly where the force was applied.*

Exhibit 118. *Or, the force that made the crook in the skidmarks could have come from a collision like that illustrated at the right. Then the FCP would be on the other side of Car C.*

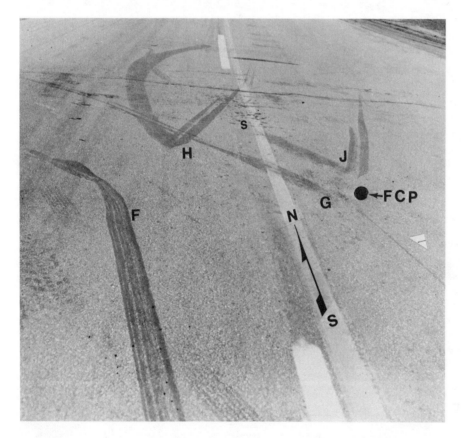

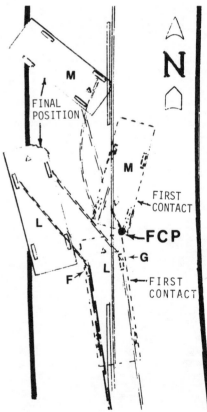

Exhibit 119. *A large car northbound and a medium car southbound left this tangle of tire marks in an opposite-direction collision. The first contact point cannot be determined precisely from this picture alone. The dimensions of the two vehicles must be known. The skidmarks of the northbound car, L, show crooks to the west at F and G. Those of southbound Car M show hooks at H and J. The front tires of the two cars would have been at these spots at first contact. S is a little spatter.*

Exhibit 120. *On an after-accident situation map, you can place the two cars with front wheels where the skidmarks change direction and closely approximate the first contact point both on the vehicles and on the road. Spatter at maximum engagement.*

accident situation map can be drawn (Exhibit 120). On this the first contact position of the colliding cars can be established and then their FCP located.

Spatter on the road is directly below the radiator or other container from which liquid was forcibly ejected by the collision. Spatter is most likely to occur at maximum engagement. Then the ruptured container was over the spatter area at maximum engagement. To locate the FCP from this position may require careful study of the damage to the vehicles and their approach and departure paths. Because spatter may be quite scattered, only an approximation of the FCP can be determined. The FCP is unlikely to be at the center of the spatter area.

Other kinds of vehicle debris are much less satisfactory signs of the FCP. The reason is simple: most other kinds of debris scatter widely. After a crash which dislodges underbody debris, the debris, while falling to the ground, continues to move in the direction of travel of the vehicle and at the vehicle's speed until it strikes the ground, hits some underpart of the vehicle, or is stopped by whatever other object the vehicle struck. After reaching the ground, the debris may slide or roll still farther, in more or less the same direction, before finally coming to rest (Exhibit 121).

If debris is heaped in a limited area (Exhibit 86), and especially if the heap is at the end of skidmarks, first contact was probably about the middle of the debris area, for two reasons: 1) the vehicles were moving so slowly that it could not scatter far after it came

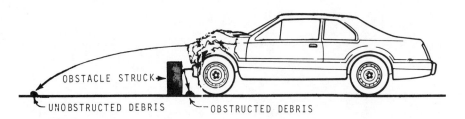

OBSTACLE STRUCK→
└UNOBSTRUCTED DEBRIS   └OBSTRUCTED DEBRIS

Exhibit 121. *When dislodged, underbody debris continues to move in the direction of the vehicle from which it came. If unobstructed, it may come to rest quite a way from where it came loose. If it strikes an obstacle before reaching the ground, it may drop there. So debris is not the most dependable indication of the location of a collision.*

loose; or 2) neither vehicle moved much after collision.

If underbody debris is two feet above the ground when it comes loose, it will take a third of a second to reach the ground. If the vehicle is moving 30 miles per hour (44 feet per second) the debris will land about 15 feet from where it came loose, provided it does not hit something first. Therefore the FCP may be that far from the debris. Same-direction collisions are especially likely to scatter debris widely.

Vehicle parts may scatter even more than underbody debris, and more unpredictably. Hubcaps and wheels may roll, slide, and bounce a hundred feet or more from the collision.

Broken glass, especially tempered glass from rear and side windows, is usually high above the ground when it breaks loose in a collision. Therefore it has far to fall and may land thirty feet or more from the collision area (Exhibit 87).

In pedestrian accidents, the FCP may be very difficult to locate. You are lucky if you can find a significant irregularity in a tire mark to mark the place as in Exhibits 28 and 34. Often there are no tire marks, and when there

are, the marks show no sign of first contact. Sometimes you can find an obscure scuff mark from a shoe or perhaps a little blood or body tissue or a shred of clothing to show where the body began to drag on the roadway. From this it may be possible to make some inferences as to where the collision occurred. Often the best clue to the FCP is the location of some personal debris: a shoe, handbag, cap, or glasses. These will be some distance from the actual FCP in the direction of the vehicle's travel, hence they permit only a rough approximation of that location.

10. OFF THE GROUND

Sometimes a vehicle leaves the ground for a short distance. There are two main ways that this can happen: 1) by a fall, and 2) by a flip. The two are quite different; do not confuse them.

Sometimes, when off the ground, a vehicle is spoken of as being "airborne." This is not actually so. A vehicle is never *borne* (supported) by the air as an airplane or balloon is. Therefore, avoid that expression.

Pedestrians can also leave the

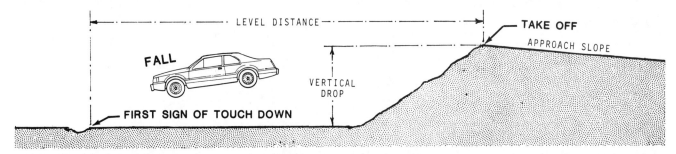

Exhibit 122. *When a vehicle leaves the surface which has supported it, it begins at once to fall under the force of gravity. Note carefully where the vehicle left the ground and the signs of where* *it touched down. Measure the vertical distance of fall from takeoff to landing and the horizontal distance from take off to touch down. If the take off is not level, also measure the slope.*

Exhibit 123. *Be very careful to note exactly where a vehicle touched down after a fall. It may not be tiremarks. In this case, the car took off from the roadway level at the left and struck the bank across the ditch at the right. Then it fell back into the water where it came to rest. Here a cord with a line level is stretched across the ditch to measure vertical distance from take off level.*

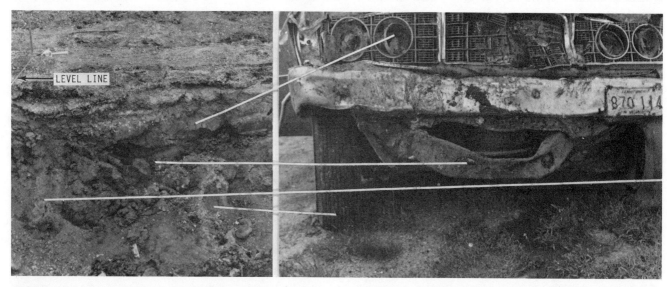

Exhibit 124. *Match parts of the vehicle with imprints on touchdown. Measure the vertical and horizontal distances from takeoff point to the clearest sign of where the vehicle touched down. In these photos, white lines connect recognizable imprints on the bank with the parts of the vehicle which made them. In this case, the imprint of the front cross member of the frame was very clear. Its horizontal and vertical distance from takeoff was carefully measured to permit estimating how far the center of mass of the vehicle travelled horizontally and dropped vertically from takeoff to touch down and from that to estimate speed at takeoff.*

ground, but not in the same ways that vehicles do.

Definition of Fall

A fall is a downward and onward movement in the air under the force of gravity after forward momentum carries an object beyond its supporting surface. Rotation during a fall is gradual and the object usually lands right side up.

Signs of a Fall

In a fall there are no marks between where a vehicle left the surface and where it landed to show that it rolled or slid down the bank. This distance

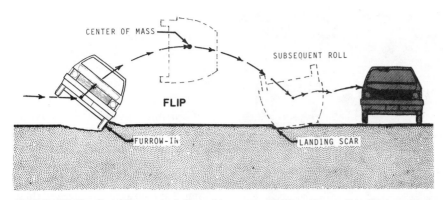

Exhibit 125. *The first flip may be followed by a second flip or by a roll to final position. Only the first flip is significant in speed estimates. Where it begins and ends needs to be located carefully by measurements.*

in the air is the best data for estimating speed when the car left the ground (Exhibit 123).

If the surface from which the vehicle takes off into the air slopes up in the direction of the vehicle's travel, the vehicle will rise above the takeoff at first, but even then it is beginning to fall under the downward force of gravity. *The vehicle nearly always lands right side up* after such a fall. But it may not stop where it landed; it may slide or roll from there some distance. Careful observation of skidmarks, tire prints or other signs of where the vehicle left the bank is important, but still more important is examination of the ground again (Exhibit 122), especially if the vehicle continued beyond that spot. This must be done soon after the accident because the signs may disappear. For example, in Exhibits 123 and 124, the vehicle has struck the far side of an excavation cut across the road for a new culvert. It landed in the creek at the bottom of the ditch. The important point to locate is not where the vehicle stopped, but the scar in the bank made by its front end. More excavation soon may obliterate this scar. Marks in snow where a vehicle landed will disappear when the snow melts. Measurements are needed to locate the mark made by the vehicle and photographs are needed to record exactly what the marks looked like. Later, necessary measurements can be made of the slope at the takeoff and the precise vertical and horizontal distances the vehicle moved through the air, if this becomes necessary.

Definition of Flip

A flip is a sudden upward and onward movement off the ground when an object's horizontal movement is obstructed below its center of mass by an obstacle on the surface supporting the object. Rotation during a flip is rapid and the object usually lands upside down.

Signs of a Flip

As in falls, the absence of any marks between takeoff and landing is the important fact to establish.

The signs of tiremarks at the takeoff point must be carefully located; so must the signs of landing. Landing spots will be indicated by torn up turf or snow, crushed bushes, broken ice, or damaged crops. The scar on the roadside where the vehicle landed is usually irregular and shallow.

Flips follow sideslipping or yaw when the tire hits a curb or furrows as in Exhibit 125 and 126. Flips are much more common than falls or vaults. When a tire slides sidewise, making a furrow in loose material, the furrow deepens and the material piles up until it stops the tire. This is a very distinctive spot and easy to locate (Exhibit 127 and 128). For speed estimation purposes, only the first of a series of flips is important. Try to find signs of the position of the vehicle when it landed. The take-off and landing points have to be identified and located as soon after the accident as possible because they may be obliterated in a short time.

Vaults are endwise flips. They occur only when front wheels, sliding or rolling, are stopped by an obstacle, usually a curb, high enough and vertical so that the wheel does not roll over it. This means three quarters as high as the hub or more. Ordinary curbs are not high enough. The vehicle lands bottom up and unless it lands on a slope, usually

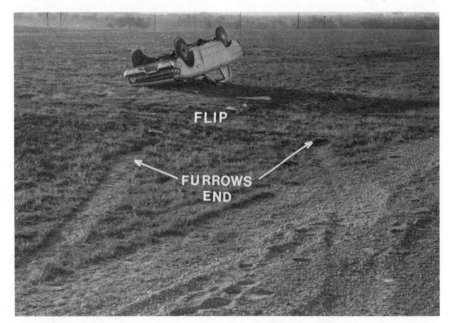

Exhibit 126. *A flip occurs when a vehicle yawing broadside suddenly has its wheels stopped by something on the road or roadside. The obstacle might be a curb, but it is often a pile of dirt at the end of a furrow. Flipped vehicles usually land bottom up.*

Exhibit 127. The hole at the end of a furrow that stops a wheel is not difficult to recognize even days afterward. It is important to locate this furrow-in by measurements if speed estimates are to be made from the flip.

stays right where it lands (Exhibit 129). Obtain data at once on exactly where the vehicle lifted off the ground and where it landed, whether it stopped there or not. Later, more refined measurements can be made if they are needed for speed estimates.

11. FINAL POSITIONS

Definition

Final position is the exact location of a vehicle or body after a traffic accident. It may be controlled or uncontrolled.

Kinds

Uncontrolled final positions are those reached by vehicles or bodies

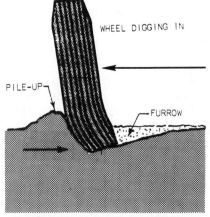

Exhibit 128. The wheel is partly stopped by digging into the ground and partly by the pile of dirt built up ahead of it.

unintentionally after collisions. Locate the vehicle by measurement in any serious accident whether the vehicle is on or off the road. Locate the body of a person by measurement if it is outside of the vehicle.

Controlled final positions are those to which vehicles or bodies are moved on purpose after collision. For example, if a vehicle hits a pedestrian and is then driven to the side of the road some distance away and parked there, its resting place after the accident can indicate less about how the accident happened than if it stopped without being driven. Likewise, if the pedestrian, after being struck, staggers or crawls off the road, where he finally drops, his position means less than if he did not move from where he first stopped. Such controlled or intentional final positions need to be noted but are less significant than uncontrolled final positions.

Locating

Sometimes, when you arrive at the scene of an accident, people who got there before you may have moved vehicles or bodies from where they first stopped to some other place for one reason or another. You can get some idea of whether this has happened by noting blood puddles for bodies and coolant or motor oil puddles for vehicles. If you have any doubt about it, ask people at the scene whether anything has been moved and if so, where it was before it was moved.

If a body or vehicle has to be moved

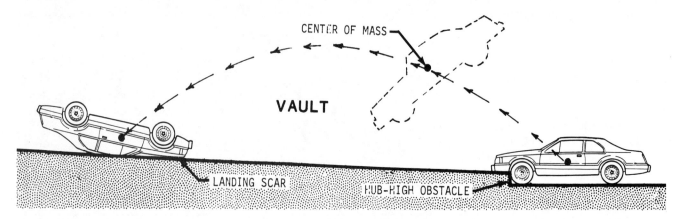

Exhibit 129. A vault is an endwise flip. The object struck must be high enough so that the wheels do not roll over it. Vaults are most unlikely in roadside turf. The object struck is generally a high curb or a deep chuck hole. Vaults are rare.

before it is located by measurements, mark its position before it is moved. An outline of the body on the pavement with chalk or crayon (Exhibit 130) will be sufficient for the purpose. In the case of vehicles, mark the positions of two wheels or two corners.

Topic 828 explains measurements needed to locate final positions of vehicles.

12. IDENTIFYING LOCATIONS

An elementary but essential part of every traffic-accident investigation is identifying precisely where the accident occurred. Such information is used by engineers to determine where inadequacies in the road, traffic-control devices, and the environment may have contributed to the frequency or severity of accidents. If the location is not accurate, the investigation may be useless for that purpose. Accident location identification information is also necessary if other investigators have to conduct additional observations or measurements at the site.

Criteria

Location identification information is satisfactory if: 1) the accident can be easily located on a map or set of plans; and 2) if another person, perhaps as much as a year later, can be sure he is in the right place if he goes to the site. This means locating the first harmful event within a tenth of a mile (about 500 ft. or 150 meters) on a straight, level road between landmarks, usually in rural areas, and within 50 ft. (3 car lengths) at curves, hills, bridges, tunnels, overpasses, intersections, and in urban areas.

If you are at the scene of the accident yourself, you should have little difficulty obtaining information needed to identify the location from road signs or road maps. If you must depend on others, question them carefully so that you can record the location as exactly as their information will permit. Try to record it in such a way that you could go there and find the site yourself.

Exhibit 130. *Outlining a body on the road permits location by measurements after the body has been moved. Vehicle final positions can also be marked before moving.*

Four steps are necessary to identify an accident location:
1. Decide where the accident occured and be as exact as possible.
2. Name the road on which the accident occurred.
3. State at what point on the road the accident occurred.
4. Name the city or county in which the accident occurred.

Report forms. Most accident-report forms have space for road-identifying information required by the last three steps. But some forms do not require sufficient data adequately to locate accidents in divided highways and in complex interchanges, places where accurate location is most important. Even if the form does not require it, record the location in sufficient detail to enable the location to be found again or identified on a map.

First Step: Decide where the Accident Occurred.

This is where the first *harmful* event occurred, that is, where the first damage or injury took place. It is usually the first contact between vehicles. The first harmful event may not be where the most serious damage or injury occurred. It may not be on the road (roadway or shoulder) but on the roadside. Determine this point as exactly as necessary to locate the accident for the accident report, but do not confuse identifying the location of the accident with identifying reference points for measurements to locate results of the accident.

Second Step: Name the Road on which the Accident Occurred.

Generally this presents no special problem; the street or highway has one well-recognized name that appears on signs and on city or state maps. Outside of city limits use a route number wherever there is one. However, some roads are not so easily described. Avoid local names for roads, especially old ones. If you have any doubt about which name to use, show both, for example, "IL 32 = Main." Be especially careful in identifying a road on which no name sign is posted. Local residents may have several different names for it. As a last resort, give the names of the communities connected by the road, for example, "Plainfield-Naperville Road."

Divided highways require specifying on which of a pair of roadways with the same name the accident occurred. Do this by adding the nominal direction of traffic flow to the road name or number. For example, an accident on a section of the Interstate system might be noted as "Interstate 90 west."

Nominal directions. Nearly all highways are considered as running north and south or east and west, although at some places they may actually run in almost any direction.

Diagonal streets in cities generally have house numbers on them corresponding to house numbers on either north-south or east-west streets, depending on whether they are considered as running north and south or east and west.

If you do not know the nominal direction of a divided road, put down the approximate actual direction as N, NE, E, SE, S, SW, W, or NW.

A frontage road (which parallels a limited-access road) may have its own special road or street name. If so, use that name just as though the frontage road were a separate trafficway even if it shares the same right of way as the throughway it serves. If the frontage road does not have a special name, give it the throughway name or number and the nominal direction of traffic on the road the frontage road parallels. Follow this with the word "frontage."

Short connecting roads often have no specific name or number by which to identify them. These may be turning roads (cutoffs) at junctions or ramps at interchanges. For purposes of locating accidents, any road which carries traffic from one named road to another at a junction of highways may be called a connecting road. Then, for purposes of identification

1. State that it is a connecting road (CR).
2. Name the road *from* which traffic in the lane where the accident occurred enters the turning road.
3. Name the road *to* which the turning road carries traffic.

For example, an accident on a ramp connecting two divided roadways might be designated as "ON CR US 41 N to I 94 E." Or a cutoff in a city might be designated as "CR MI 36 to King" (street).

Alleys must be considered roads for purposes of accident reporting. An alley is "a street or highway intended to provide access to the rear or side of lots or buildings in urban districts and not intended for the purpose of through vehicular traffic."[5] If the alley has a posted name or one marked on a map, use that name. Otherwise indicate it as alley and the direction from the next parallel street. For example, an accident might be "ON Alley S of 35th" (St).

Driveways on or leading to private property, for accident location purposes, can be described somewhat like a connector road, for example an accident might have occurred "ON Driveway from IL 35 to Kennedy Farm Orchard."

Accidents at intersections require you to designate one of the intersecting roads as that ON which the accident occurred. If both vehicles were travelling on the same road just before the accident, that is the road ON which the accident occurred. If each of two vehicles was approaching on a different roadway at an intersection, the accident is described as occurring ON the most important roadway according to the following list of priorities:[6]

1. Interstate highway
2. Other U.S. route numbered highway
3. Other state route numbered highway
4. County road
5. City street
6. All others

If two roads are in the same category of importance, locate the accident on the trafficway with the lowest route or number or street name nearest the beginning of the alphabet. Let numbered streets, for example, 31st Street or 5th Avenue, take precedence over named streets.

An accident in a crosswalk is ordinarily not an intersection accident because crosswalks are usually not in intersections.

Third Step: State at what Point on the Road the Accident Occurred.

Having described the accident as

ON a specified road, state AT what place on the road the accident (first harmful event) occurred. If the accident occurred AT an intersection, simply name the intersecting road, for example, "ON B at 25" for on B St. at 25th Av., or "ON WI 36 AT County N."

Between intersections, locate the accident by distance and direction from some permanent recognizable landmark. Use such landmarks as the following:

- Intersection with a nearby crossroad
- Milepost
- Railroad grade crossings
- Underpasses beneath railroads or other highways
- Tunnels
- Bridges over important rivers, railroads, or other highways
- City, county, and state boundary lines, if indicated by signs.

A few examples will illustrate the matter: AT 80 ft N of IL 32, AT 500 ft W of mile 38, AT I98 E of overpass.

If the accident is at one of the definite landmark points along the road, record it as AT that point without distance or direction, for example, "ON Lambert AT C & NW RR."

Less desirable landmarks are those which do not show on maps such as

- Numbered utility or lamp poles
- House numbers
- Driveways
- Buildings, such as stores and churches
- Creeks
- Power line crossings
- Station marks in paving used by highway engineers and contractors
- Towns or villages in general.

Some of these may be useful to describe exact points from which measurements were made to locate results of accidents as explained in Topic 828.

A median opening or crossover which is not a continuation of a cross street of which it may be considered a part is identified like a driveway. Describe the accident as AT *median opening* and locate it with respect to the nearest node or other reference point.

Special systems have been developed in some states to designate points along the roads by which accidents may be located. The best known systems are

- Mileposts mainly for freeways and main rural roads
- Node numbering (A node is usually a junction of two or more roads. An assigned number may be posted at the node point for reference purposes.)
- Structure numbering (Bridges, culvert headwalls, overpasses, lamp posts, traffic signals, even traffic signs may have numbers painted on or placed near them for reference purposes. House numbers in cities may be considered a form of structure numbering.)
- Map coordinates (The distance in miles north or south and east or west from two base or reference lines on maps provided for the purpose.)

Detailed instructions for identifying road locations according to whatever system has been established are generally available.

Measurements. Avoid guessing at distances from landmarks. Measure them in feet if less than 1,000 ft and in miles if more. If no tape is available, step off the shorter distances. Use an automobile odometer for longer distances. It registers to tenths of a mile but you can estimate hundredths of a mile to get more accurate distances.

When measuring distances from crossroads, railroads, and bridges, measure from the near side or near rail rather than the center because edges are more definite than center lines.

Abbreviation. Writing time and space can be saved by abbreviating in identifying locations. If not overdone, abbreviations will not impair accuracy or reading time. The following abbreviations are suggested:

- Omit the words highway and route with numbered routes and abbreviate identifying names: I

90, US 41, IL 63, Lake Co E.
- For state route numbers use standard post office two-letter abbreviations for the state, for example, IL for Illinois.
- Omit words like street, avenue, boulevard, etc, in names of streets in cities when there will be no question about what is meant: S State, W Madison, 22nd, Capital, Fuller. But when the same name is used for a street and an avenue or a place, be sure to specify which, using common abbreviations: Washington St and Washington Av; 22nd St and 22nd Pl.
- Use initials only for the eight principal compass directions; N, NE, E, SE, S, SW, W, NW.
- To indicate direction of movement add N, E, S, or W to the road name: US 41S for US 41 southbound.
- For connecting road use CR.
- Use the word *frontage* alone for frontage road.
- Use *mile* alone for milepost.
- Omit all periods in abbreviations.
- Omit *from* after connecting road but not the *to* between the names of the roads connected.

Fourth Step: Name City or County.

For incorporated places, it is not necessary to name the county; the city alone will do . In counties, it may be useful to add the townships.

13. DESCRIPTION AND CONDITION

The road is described mainly for statistical purposes, but certain aspects of it have a bearing on how an accident may have occurred.

Location Classification Data

Generally, information for classification purposes is recorded on an accident report by indicating which category in each of several classifications best describes the road or roads at the location of the accident.

Administrative class of trafficway, as described by six categories listed earlier in this topic, is usually ade-

quately identified.

Number of lanes for traffic in the road may also be required by the accident-report form.

Land-use character, for statistical classification has only two categories:[6] 1) urban area; and 2) rural area. Proper identification of the location will permit official agencies to determine which category applies to a particular location. Highway departments have maps showing what areas are classified as urban and what are rural. Some accident-report forms require classifying the area in some other way, for example, as "built-up" or "not built up." Even more detail may sometimes be required.

Special Descriptions

Road configuration is sometimes required by a checklist on the accident-report form to indicate curves and grades, but usually this is represented on the form only in a diagram. Part of the supplementary data collected for fatal and other severe accidents, however, should be information on road configuration. At the very least this should be a record of some kind that there is a slope or curve at the site of the accident and a verbal indication of steepness of the slope or sharpness of the curve. Photographs are helpful in describing road configuration, but if numerical values are wanted for speed estimates or sight-distance calculations, actual measurements are necessary unless data from plans are readily available. Measurements may be required of grades, superelevation of curves, width of shoulders, depth of ditches, and radius of curves. For special purposes, additional measurements may be specified. Instructions for mapping ordinary locations are given in Topic 832. It may be necessary, however, to obtain the services of professional surveyors to make some measurements, especially accurate measurements of vertical distances.

Roadway surface material may need to be described in some detail if estimates of speed are to be made from skidmarks or yawmarks. In some cases, measurements of surface friction are desirable.

Traffic-control devices need to be described in detail only if they are relevant to a serious accident. These devices include signs, signals, pavement markings, speed limits, prohibited turns, one-way streets, and others. Sometimes information is required about route markings, bridge clearances, signs, and even roadside-establishment signs. Exactly what descriptive data are required depends on the circumstances of the accident. For example, there are accidents in which the timing of traffic signals is important and must be observed and recorded.

Road accessories such as curbs, guardrails, bridges, culverts, median dividers, islands, tunnels, and toll gates may be mentioned in accident reports if they are involved in any way, but detailed descriptions, measurements, and photographs are only required for extended investigations. Such descriptions are part of technical preparation of accident data for legal or special study purposes.

Condition Classification Data

The road or anything connected with it may be temporarily modified by conditions existing at the time of the accident.

For statistical tabulations, only a few road condition classifications are ordinarily required by the official accident-report form. Some of these do not apply so much to the road itself as to the environment.

Light condition is usually classified according to three categories:
1. Daylight
2. Dawn or dusk
3. Darkness.

This classification appears on most traffic accident report forms.

Road surface condition is classified according to four categories:
1. Dry
2. Wet
3. Snowy or icy
4. Other.

Either road surface or light conditions may have to be described in much greater detail for special purposes. As

a rule, these are described in words rather than by measurements or photographs.

Visibility

Obtaining data for classification of road conditions in accident reporting requires no special skill; but observing unusual road conditions at the scene which may have affected a particular accident is quite another matter. There is no space on the accident-report form to remind the investigator of what information is required; he has to decide by himself what to look for and the circumstances of each accident determine what that is. Permanent road features, like curves and hills, will remain unchanged for a long time and so may be examined later if necessary, but other limitations on visibility may change quickly and so must be noted as soon as possible.

View obstructions are not the same as reduced visibility. In the case of low visibility — usually created by darkness, fog, snow, or other atmospheric conditions — the object gradually becomes visible as it looms up in the distance. When the view is obscured by an obstacle, however, the hazard appears rather suddenly from behind or back of a solid object.

Try to evaluate the seeing problem of the driver or the pedestrian. The best way is to put yourself in his position. For example, the driver has hit a pedestrian in dark clothing in a residential district. The investigator has a pedestrian in similar clothing stand where the victim was struck. Then in a vehicle with headlights similar to those of the vehicle involved, the investigator approaches slowly and notes where he can first clearly see the pedestrian. For example, suppose that he discovers that there is a deep shadow cast by some branches between the pedestrian and the distant light. The pedestrian cannot be seen against the dark background until the vehicle is within, say, about 130 ft (40 meters). At 45 mph the driver would find it difficult to avoid hitting the pedestrian if he stepped in front of the car.

View obstructions on the road are

usually vehicles, either moving or parked. They can prevent drivers from seeing signals, signs at the roadside, other vehicles, or pedestrians. The circumstances described below are rather common:
- Parked vehicles (A view obstruction contributes to nearly every accident in which a pedestrian steps out from behind a parked vehicle. The parked vehicle is a view obstruction to both the driver and the pedestrian.)
- Vehicle slowed at intersection (A vehicle which is stopped or slowed at an intersection obscures possible traffic on the cross street. Buses, because of their size and the frequency of their stops at street corners, are a special hazard of this kind. The vehicle overtaken at the intersection is a view obstruction to both the driver overtaking it and to the driver or pedestrian crossing in front of it.)
- Person hiding tail light (A less common but usually serious view obstruction is a person working or standing on the highway at night and hiding a taillight. Determine whether the taillight was obscured or was not operating. You may have to depend upon the statements of witnesses in this matter.)

Obstacles can keep a driver from seeing another vehicle, a pedestrian, a control device, or some hazard. View obstructions of this sort are, perhaps, the most common traps for unwary drivers. For angle collisions, when a driver claims he did not see the other vehicle until too late, or when other circumstances suggest it, try to determine definitely whether there was a view obstruction. Do not ordinarily accept the statement of just one driver or witness as proof that a view obstruction did or did not contribute to an accident. Make observations to confirm or disprove the statement.

Horizontal view obstructions such as embankments and buildings are permanent and may be examined later; but shrubs, hedges, crops, weeds, piles of snow, and construction materials must be noted at the time of the accident because they may soon change. If it appears to have been a factor in a serious accident, locate a view obstruction by measurements, including its height, and make a picture of it if photos are made at the scene.

Fog and smoke are especially difficult to evaluate because they appear and disappear so quickly. They may be present at the time of the accident but disappear before an investigator arrives at the scene. Be sure to find out, by questioning witnesses, whether the condition was the same as at the time of the accident. Heavy, continuous fog is less a hazard than light pockets or stretches of fog or smoke. Such fog pockets occur in low spots, especially near coasts and at night. Thick smoke sometimes blows across the highway from brush fires or burning grass. A driver running into such a pocket of decreased visibility wisely slows down but often does so suddenly. The following driver may then fail to slow down as quickly and run into him. Then, if traffic is heavy, other cars collide. Multiple accidents, in which large numbers of vehicles are involved, are often caused by fog pockets. More than 50 vehicles have been reported in one multiple accident which was actually a series of collisions.

Falling rain and snow produce the same kind of decreased visibility as darkness and fog, especially if they accumulate on vehicle windows. Study it in the same manner. Of course, it is difficult to obtain a true idea of rain and snow conditions *at the time of the accident.* The thickness of falling snow or rain changes from one minute to the next. Therefore, personal observations of seeing distances which are truly comparable to those at the time of the accident are rarely possible. Information has to come from informants.

All conditions which limit visibility make it difficult to see traffic signs. This fact is particularly true when rain, snow, or fog are *combined* with darkness. Visibility of signs is affected much more than that of signals. The lights of signals penetrate falling rain

or fog. Snow, rain, fog, and smoke all reflect headlights back into drivers' eyes thus further limiting vision. Headlights produce less back-glare in rain, snow, fog, or smoke if they are on the lower beam.

Glare

Glare often goes completely undetected in an accident investigation because it is gone when the investigators get to the scene, and drivers often fail to mention it as a factor. Usually all kinds of glare are hard to evaluate. The best you can do is to determine whether glare is a possibility or probability. A vehicle with glaring headlights is usually not involved in the collision to which it contributes. This is the main reason why it is so difficult to prove glaring headlights as a violation in connection with an accident. Reports of blinding headlights by drivers are as likely to be false as true. Glare is often reported to cover up driver faults.

There are three kinds of glare to look for as contributors to accidents. Two of these, headlight glare and backlighting, occur only at night. The other, sun glare, is most frequent early in the morning and late in the afternoon. Headlight glare is partly a vehicle condition. It is discussed here with road and weather conditions because it is so similar to the two other kinds of glare, backlighting and sun glare.

Headlight glare is most likely to be a factor in rural pedestrian accidents and in running off the road or hitting fixed objects on the right. Consider glare as a possibility in all night accidents of these kinds where there are no street lights, or where such lights are dim. Try to learn from witnesses and a study of the location, whether there was or was not an element of glare in the accident.

Glare from headlights is not likely to be serious if the headlights are on the lower beam, *except* when the lights are out of adjustment or when the vehicle is coming over a hill. In the latter case the glare does not last long, and the position of the collision must be exactly right with respect to the crest of the hill to make it a possibility.

Analyze this by watching vehicles come over the crest of the hill at night. Put your eye in the position of that of the driver who may have been blinded.

Glare from fixed lights or backlighting such as street lights, advertising signs, and flood lights under some conditions can blind drivers just as headlights do. It is a problem worth investigating in many night accidents, particularly in cities. Because such lights are usually not so bright as headlights, the glare is less severe.

Fixed lights are most likely to contribute to accidents by back-light glare when they line up in a driver's field of vision alongside something he should see. In this respect, the result is about the same as a view obstruction. Traffic signals may be very hard to see because of bright back-lighting beyond them.

For example, a driver enters an intersection against the red traffic signal at night in a business district. He claims he did not even know there was a light at that place. You then find that from where the driver approached the intersection, the traffic signal is directly in line with a large, bright, red, flashing neon sign on a store front. You can see the signal when you know where to look for it, but a stranger might very well not notice, especially if his attention was mainly directed to pedestrian and other traffic.

Signs are obscured even more than signals by bright lights in the background beyond them. If the face of the sign is in a very deep shadow, any unreflectorized wording on it is almost impossible to read. This situation is very common where bright street lights are suspended in the center of an intersection, and where signs are mounted on the lamp posts themselves, or are set further from the corner than the lights. The lower the lights are, the worse this condition is. Most stop signs are recognizable by shape, and so can be seen and understood even against very bright back-light. No-left-turn and one-way-street signs are most likely to cause problems because the driver must read the message on them. If a night accident involves a movement prohibited by a sign at the location, try to find out whether back-lighting or fixed-light glare is a possibility.

Street-name signs which are back-lighted likewise can be a contributing factor. Drivers may stop suddenly or even back up for street-name signs which are unreadable because the signs are strongly back-lighted. They also may turn their heads in an intersection to look back at the lighted side of a sign and fail to see a pedestrian on the far crosswalk or may hit some other object because of this distraction.

Sun glare can blind a driver by day as badly as can headlights by night. You will usually learn of it because a driver complains about glare. But if a driver is dead or badly injured, the condition will probably not be revealed. The usual form of sun glare occurs when the sun is low enough to reach the driver's eyes under the edge of the top of the vehicle. This ordinarily means within an hour and a half after the sun rises or before it sets. The sun must be nearly in front of the driver to create such a condition.

Consider the possibility of sun glare in all accidents where the sun is low and in front of the driver, particularly in open, rolling country. To discover this condition you must find out whether the sun was shining at the time of the accident. The danger of sun glare, like that of headlight glare, is multiplied on hill crests and curves. For several seconds a driver may be driving blind, and in those brief moments he can leave the road. Furthermore, when the vehicle is tilted upward climbing a hill, it will be subject to glare from the sun when it is higher in the sky than would be possible if the vehicle were level.

If there is any probability that the sun glare may be a factor, try to study the scene on a sunny day, at the same hour at which the accident occurred, from the position of the driver approaching the scene. Examination of the situation must be made within a few weeks of the accident; otherwise the position of the sun in the sky may change enough with the season to be misleading.

Blinding sun can have the effect of making signs, signals, and pedestrians invisible, as can glaring headlights. It will even obscure an approaching vehicle; it is the only kind of glare which will do this.

Another form of sun glare is dangerous but rare. You learn about it from statements of drivers or passengers. They say they were blinded by the reflection of the sun in a windshield, window, or other shiny surface. This can happen almost anywhere on a sunny day. The reflection usually comes from glass in vehicles, but it can also come from windows in buildings, and even from the surface of water. Reflections from moving vehicles do not often contribute to accidents because they are just short flashes.

Surface Conditions

Almost any surface condition may be blamed for an accident by a driver. Whether a driver says anything about a road condition or not, consider it a possibility in many accidents. If conditions are such as to suggest that some road surface condition might have contributed, make a record of the actual conditions. Do not, at this time, try to decide whether the condition actually did contribute to the accident.

Slipperiness is the most common surface condition contributing to accidents. Whenever there is anything to make the surface more slippery than usual, ask yourself whether the slipperiness either surprised the driver or prevented successful evasive tactics when the driver was confronted by a hazardous situation.

Many conditions make a pavement slippery:

- Moisture makes all hard surfaces more slippery. This is especially true when the surface is dusty (it gives a slick film of mud), or shows an excess of tar or asphalt on the surface (moisture then forms a lubricant), or when there are leaves on the roadway. Moisture is especially likely to make any smooth, hard surface such as steel plates on bridges, worn granite paving blocks, and even wood planks considerably more slippery, although these may not be slippery when dry. A little moisture, such as a mist, heavy dew, or light shower which does not run off is usually worse than heavy rain. The latter washes off the dust and oil film which, with moisture, make a surface more slippery. Moisture makes gravel or cinders *less* slippery because it binds them together slightly so the loose particles of which they are made do not roll so easily.
- Ice and snow make surfaces very slippery. The worst condition is glare ice that is moist from slight melting, or glare ice with a light powdered snow on it. Moist snow which packs may be less slippery, depending on how much it piles up in front of the tire. Often what the driver takes to be moisture turns out to be ice. For example, dew or light frost may be moisture on most of the road but it may freeze on bridges where ground heat does not melt it or in deep shadows where sunlight cannot reach it.
- Loose gravel, stone chips, sand, cinders, or dirt on a hard pavement where traffic does not

Exhibit 131. *Locate and describe a hole in the paving if there is reason to believe it contributed to the accident.*

sweep them away, roll under the tires and give the effect of slipperiness.

- Leaves or grass on hard surfaces, especially when wet or moist.
- Spots of oil or grease on a pavement, especially when wet.
- Asphalt or tar joints or repairs where softened by hot weather, and especially when wet.

More often than not, you will find no tire marks when slippey surfaces do contribute to accidents. Do not let the lack of tire marks deter you from considering slipping a contributing factor. Drivers' statements that the car "skidded" are usually fairly reliable. Witnesses who saw the car slide are still more reliable. Drivers ordinarily do not distinguish between true skidding, due to braking, and sideslip or yaw, due to steering. Pavement slipperiness may contribute to either.

Deep Ruts or wheel tracks in hard material, usually ice, but sometimes dirt contribute to accidents by interfering with normal control. Their effect is much easier to identify than that of slipperiness because ruts remain after the accident. Ruts are much more likely to be a factor at high driving speeds. In general, ruts which run lengthwise in the road are most hazardous. Wheels follow them like rails. The driver tries to steer, but he cannot climb out of the rut until his wheels are at a considerable angle. Then he "jumps" the track, as it were, and leaves the rut suddenly at a sharp angle. Look carefully at the sides of the rut and the tires for signs of scuffing or scraping. You can easily find such evidence in mud ruts whether wet or dry, but it is difficult to find it in snow ruts.

Be sure to consider whether holes or ruts in the roadside or the shoulder were made by the vehicle as a result of the accident, or were there before. This question will usually arise with ruts in soft material, especially where it may have dried hard or frozen afterwards. Sometimes witnesses can tell you whether the ruts were there before or were left by the accident; sometimes you can decide by examining them carefully to see how well they match the tires of a vehicle in the accident.

Overturning. Any rut or furrow more than four inches deep, struck at an angle, especially if a vehicle is sliding sidewise and especially when it is in firm or hard material, may cause a vehicle to turn over. The furrow may be made by the wheel itself. It stops the tire and the rest of the vehicle continues to move. Explore this possibility in all cases in which vehicles roll over unless there is a curb that could make the vehicle overturn.

Holes in the paving have to be a foot or more long and wider than a tire to be hazardous (Exhibit 131). If a driver claims his vehicle was thrown out of control by a small hole, treat this statement with suspicion and look for driver actions which may be contributing factors, such as cutting back into lane after overtaking. Several small holes in a row can give such a rough ride as to make a driver lose control where a single hole would not. The most common case of such a series of depressions is what are called "washboards." "A washboard" is a series of waves or ripples across the road surface. This occurs under two conditions: 1) when high speed traffic travels over roads surfaced with loose gravel; and 2) in asphalt which is pushed into ridges by slowing vehicles, especially buses, when the asphalt is softened in warm weather. When a tire hits a hole hard enough to be dangerous, you will sometime find evidence of the blow on the tire. This may be in the form of cords burst inside the tire. Such marks confirm, rather than prove, a conclusion regarding the hole as contributing to the accident. A vehicle can be turned over by hitting a chuck hole without leaving signs on either the tire or the hole, especially when the edges of the hole are rounded.

Curbs act like ruts. If a tire strikes one at an angle, you may find scuff-marks on the outside of the tire and probably will find them on the curb. Such marks often indicate where the vehicle went off the roadway. It is sometimes important to determine whether the front or rear wheel of the

Exhibit 132. *Look for pavement lip or drop-off if any vehicle left the roadway before going out of control.*

vehicle struck the curb and, if both did so, which one struck first. Examine the curb and tire carefully, and look for other marks of sliding on the road and shoulder to answer this question.

When a vehicle strikes a curb at an angle and then swings toward it so that both front and rear wheels strike, the wheel which strikes first will nearly always leave a much more prominent sign of scuffing, both on the tire and on the curb. This is because the first wheel strikes harder. Striking a curb is also a frequent cause of a vehicle rolling over or running out of control. In most cases of this kind there is also a contributing driver action.

A lip or drop-off at the edge of a rural pavement may be an important factor in an accident. Such an edge lip is illustrated in Exhibit 132. It is often overlooked as a factor when a vehicle runs off the left side of the road or hits a vehicle coming from the opposite direction. Lip drop-off is simply a low shoulder at the edge of a hard pavement. It is important when the shoulder is more than three inches below the pavement, especially on concrete paving with a vertical edge. If the drop-off is four inches or more, an inattentive driver may be startled into a reflex overreaction when the right wheel goes off the paving, especially if the shoulders are soft or rutted. Most accidents involving drop-offs, however, occur when a driver tries to steer back on the paving without slowing enough. The lip acts as a rut or rail, which keeps steering from being effective until the front wheels are turned to a fairly sharp angle. Then, suddenly, the right front wheel climbs the lip. Before the driver can straighten it out, the vehicle runs at an angle to the left across the road. One of several accidents may result:

- Another vehicle on the left side of the road may be hit head-on or sideswiped.
- The vehicle may go into the ditch on the left.
- The driver may overreact again on the road, swing the vehicle sharply back to the right, and ditch it on the right side.

Whenever any of these happen, especially if there is no other adequate explanation, go back and look for a drop-off. This may be more than a hundred feet before the collision point. Often there are matching signs of it on the inside of the front right tire and on the pavement edge. The latter must be fresh to prove it was not left earlier by another vehicle.

Soft shoulders can make a driver lose control. If the vehicle is yawing sidewise, soft shoulders can stop it quickly enough to be dangerous. Usually there is evidence of this at the scene, unless the marks in the shoulder have been obliterated by other vehicles or pedestrians. At low speeds, soft shoulders are not likely to contribute to accidents. The vehicle may bog down in the mud, sand, or snow, but this usually does no damage. It is running on a soft shoulder at high speeds that is dangerous. When an accident has involved running on a soft shoulder, try to find out how the vehicle got there to begin with, and, if possible, what part the driver's actions played. You will usually have to get this information from the driver.

Braking while partly on a shoulder will produce somewhat the same result as a pavement lip, except that braking, rather than steering, precipitates the difficulty. A dirt, gravel, or turf shoulder often has a considerably lower drag factor under most conditions than the adjoining pavement. Therefore, if brakes are applied strongly when right wheels are on such a shoulder, the right wheels will slide much more readily than the left. Hence, the vehicle will have a much greater road drag on the left than on the right and it will rotate counterclockwise with the result that it heads back across the road. One of two things can then happen: 1) the sidewise sliding on the shoulder will cause wheels to dig in and the vehicle will roll over; or 2) especially if brakes are released, the vehicle will suddenly across the road to the left. At speeds of less than about 35 mph (55 km per hr), an alert driver can usually recognize what's happening, steer to the right out of the skid, and recover his position on the pavement. However, at high speeds, he may travel across the road and into trouble in less than his reaction time, that is, before he can decide what action to take. This is disastrous if a vehicle is approaching from the opposite direction.

Control Devices

The condition of traffic control de-

Exhibit 133. *It is important for an investigator to note whether traffic control devices are in effective condition.*

vices must be observed by the investigator, especially if he proposes to initiate enforcement action based on driver failure to respond to them. Traffic lights which are not operating are a conspicuous example of a condition which might have important legal consequences. Failure to note that stop signs, no-left-turn signs, and one-way-street signs were obscured when this condition is relevent is a serious oversight in investigation. Even noting the condition of pavement markings is important for some kinds of accidents. If a deficiency is observed, photographs make a good record of the observation in most instances. Make a report of a traffic-control condition that requires remedying to responsible authorities separately from the accident report. (See Exhibit 133.)

14. SOURCES

Author

J. Stannard Baker is a traffic engineer specializing in traffic-accident investigation. He was director of Research and Development at the Northwestern University Traffic Institute from 1946 to 1971 and afterwards a consultant and guest lecturer at The Traffic Institute.

References

Superscript numbers in the preceding pages refer to the following publications:

1. "Automobile Post Mortem (Demonstration Case B) in *Expert Testimony,* 1966, Institute on Continuing Education of the Illinois Bar, Illinois Bar Center, Springfield, IL (150 pages)
2. Bergman, Walter, "Skid Resistance Properties of Tires and their Influence on Vehicle Control" in *Transportation Research Record* (621), 1977, Transportation Research Board, National Academy of Sciences, Washington DC 20418 (11 pages)
3. Gardner, J. D. and E. A. Moffatt. *Controlled Skid Studies Illustrating Tiremarks Generated by Radial Tires,* The American Society of Mechanical Engineers, New York NY 10017 (53 pages)
4. Baker, J. Stannard and Declan McIlraith, *Tire Disablements Followed by Accidents Among Four-tired Vehicles on the Illinois Tollway.* (Tire Study 4), 1968, The Northwestern University Traffic Institute, Evanston IL 60204 (74 pages)
5. *Uniform Vehicle Code and Model Traffic Ordinance,* National Committee on Uniform Traffic Laws and Ordinances, Washington DC (Order from P.O. Box 1409, Evanston IL 60204)
6. *Manual on Classification of Motor Vehicle Traffic Accidents* (ANSI D 16.1 - 1983), National Safety Council, Chicago IL 60611 (34 pages)

Exhibits

The following are sources of tables, diagrams, and photographs used in this publication:

Alaska State Troopers
Photo: 3.
Baker, J. Stannard, Glencoe IL
Photos: 2, 4, 6, 7, 8, 9, 10, 13, 14, 15, 16, 17, 24, 25, 26, 32, 35, 38, 41, 42, 45, 55, 57, 63, 65, 67, 68, 69, 70, 71, 72, 76, 77, 78, 79, 82, 83, 84, 85, 92, 95, 98, 103, 104, 106, 107, 108, 109, 113, 114, 115, 116, 131, 132, 133.
Diagrams: 20, 22, 23, 36, 46, 47, 52, 58, 59, 61, 62, 64, 88, 117, 118, 120, 121, 122, 125, 128, 129.
Table: 1.
Bergman, Walter, Ford Motor Co., Dearborn MI
Chart: 40.
Brown's Photo Service, Georgetown DL
Photo: 19.
Cooper, Gary W., The Traffic Institute, Evanston IL
Photos: 48, 49, 73, 81, 100.
Cusker, Thomas L., Lake Villa IL
Photos: 5, 33, 86.

Farmer, Tony, Knoxville TN
Photo: 112.
Fleming, Don P., Jr.
Photo: 44.
Fricke, Lynn B., The Traffic Institute, Evanston IL
Photos: 60, 123, 124.
Galloway News & Photo Service, Springfield IL
Photos: 11, 89.
Grall, Frank, Fort Sill OK
Photo: 126.
Green, Ford, San Antonio TX
Photo: 56.
Harrell, B. F., Jr., Atlanta GA
Photo: 29.
Harrison, D., Police Department, Downers Grove IL
Photo: 111.
Kiser Studios, Lawrenceville IL
Photo: 96.
Krapf, Emerson, Waukegan IL
Photo: 74.
Merner, Milton, Deerfield IL
Photo: 90.
Moyer, *Pioneer Press,* Marengo IL
Photo: 119.

Norris, Moyne, Neosho MO
Photo: 37.
Oregon State Police
Photo: 53.
Police Department, Chicago IL
Photo: 27.
Police Department, San Diego CA
Photo: 21.
Potter, Morris F., Cedar Rapids IA
Photos: 87, 99.
Purcell, James A., Police Department, Troy NY
Photo: 130.
Quincey, Sam R., West Palm Beach FL
Photo: 31.
Replogle, E.M., Indiana State Police
Photo: 102.
Roller, Robert, Arizona Highway Patrol
Photo: 66.
Ronnie's Studio, Eldore IA
Photo: 28.
Scheskie, Harold, Lake County Sheriff's Department, Waukegan IL
Photo: 34.
Strappozan, Roy, *Herald News,* Joliet IL
Photo: 97.
Swedenberg, William T., Michigan City IN
Photo: 105.
Tuley, Roy, Chattanooga TN
Photo: 91.
Unknown
Photos: 12, 18, 39, 43, 50, 51, 54, 75, 93, 94, 127.
U.S. Air Force
Photo: 30.
Utah Highway Patrol
Photos: 80, 101.
Waller, Robert, Hattiesburg MS
Photo: 110.

SIMPLE ESTIMATES
OF VEHICLE STOPPING DISTANCES
AND SPEED FROM SKIDMARKS

Topic 818 of the *Traffic-Accident Investigation Manual*

by
J. Stannard Baker

NORTHWESTERN UNIVERSITY TRAFFIC INSTITUTE

PUBLICATION HISTORY

1954   Report of the Traffic Committee in *Police Yearbook*

1956   *Stopping Distance Charts*, Association of Casualty and Surety Underwriters

1957   *Charts and Tables for Stopping Distances of Motor Vehicles*
Reprinted   1960, 1978

1981   *Simple Estimates of Vehicle Stopping Distance and Speed from Skidmarks*

SIMPLE ESTIMATES OF VEHICLE STOPPING DISTANCES AND SPEED FROM SKIDMARKS

The following explanations are intended to help police, attorneys, and other investigators to estimate speeds of vehicles based on skidmarks in simple cases and vehicle stopping distances under certain conditions.

1. SPEED FROM SKIDMARKS

It is well known that when brakes are applied hard (for example, to avoid a hazard), they may lock wheels and keep them from turning. As a result, the vehicle slides. The friction between tires and road usually, but not always, leaves visible skidmarks. The length of these marks is an indication of the speed of the vehicle.

Two factors are important in estimating speed from skidmarks: 1) the distance the vehicle *slid* and 2) the slipperiness (coefficient of friction) or drag factor of the surface on which the sliding took place.

The steps to take in going from observations of marks on the road to calculating the speed of the vehicle which made them are as follows:

1. Make sure that the marks are true skidmarks made by tires on wheels which were not rotating. Friction marks might be scuffs made by steering (yaw marks), acceleration, or overdeflected tires. Any of these other marks are likely to be referred to incorrectly as skidmarks. Usually skidmarks:

- Are nearly straight, or at least do not clearly swerve.
- Are visible for all wheels, or at least one on each side.
- Are nearly equally distinct for left and right tires.
- Begin and end at fairly distinct points rather than gradually appearing and disappearing.
- Are equally distinct for both edges of the tire.
- Have striations or rib marks, if any, parallel to the marks.

2. Decide whether all wheels locked or were nearly locked. This is easy if all wheels make clear marks. If all wheels of a normal passenger vehicle do not make marks, assume that all wheels were braking as though skidding. Consider the vehicle as fully sliding unless:

- There are definite signs that the vehicle was rotating or swerving.
- There is a definite reason to believe that some brakes were not functioning.

Vehicles such as motorcycles, tractors, and trailers may have no brakes on some wheels or may have brakes which are applied separately to some wheels. In stopping these vehicles, therefore, some wheels may contribute little or no drag and so must not be considered as fully sliding unless all wheels leave definite skidmarks.

3. Determine how far the vehicle slid with braking equivalent to that of having all the wheels locked. If you have an opportunity to do so, measure the length of each skidmark separately. If front and rear marks are superimposed so that you do not know whether the first mark was made by a front or rear wheel, consider it to be a rear wheel and assume that the front wheel began to slide a distance from that point equal to the distance between the front and rear wheels of the vehicle. If all wheels make marks, use the length of the longest mark. If it is not known whether each mark was measured separately or measurement was made from the beginning of a rear wheel mark to the end of a front wheel mark, assume that the latter was the case. Then deduct the wheelbase of the vehicle, usually 9 or 10 ft., from this distance to obtain the sliding distance. This will possibly give a shorter sliding distance and so a conservative or minimum speed estimate.

4. Evaluate how much drag the tires and road surface produced to slow the vehicle with all wheels locked. This drag factor is the retarding force compared to (divided by) the vehicle's weight. For example, a drag factor of 0.5 means that the retarding force is

equal to half of the weight of the vehicle. The drag factor is the coefficient of friction between tires and road on a level surface with all wheels sliding. If the surface slopes up or down or if not all wheels lock, the coefficient of friction is not the same as the drag factor.

One way to determine the drag factor is to make a test skid. Duplicate as closely as possible the conditions under which the accident skid was made. It is best to use the same vehicle driven in the same direction at the same location and at approximately the same speed. If the accident vehicle cannot be used, another vehicle, for example, a police car, can be substituted. Usually this has little effect on the results.

To obtain the drag factor from a test skid, on the left scale of the nomograph, locate distance taken to slide to a stop on the test skid. On the middle scale locate the speed at which brakes are applied. Draw a straight line between these two points and across the right scale. The drag factor is read from the right scale where the line crosses it.

Unfortunately, test skids are not as useful as one might think. They are often impractical or dangerous at the specific site of the accident or at the approximate speed of the vehicle that made the accident skids. Moreover, test skids often give too great a drag factor because brakes are not applied quickly enough or strongly enough to lock all wheels instantly. It requires considerable strength, skill and practice to make test skids properly. If wheels are not locked instantly, the test vehicle may lose speed by braking before skidding begins to make tires hot enough to mark the road. Then, if braking distance is obtained by measuring the test skidmarks, the skidding distance is short for

the speed and the drag factor will be high. When applied to accident skids, this high drag factor gives an overestimate of speed, sometimes a considerable overestimate. Accurate speedometer readings for test skids are also difficult to obtain.

Hence if test skid results give drag factors greater than those mentioned hereafter, regard the results of the test with suspicion. The test may have to be repeated by a more experienced investigator.

Lacking proper test skids, approximate drag factors may be used. For hard, dry, clean, level, well travelled paving at essentially urban speeds less than 35 miles per hour, 0.60 to 0.80 will be reasonable. For speeds of more than 40 miles per hour, 0.55 to 0.70 would be appropriate. The lower figure gives more conservative speed estimates; the higher figure gives less conservative estimates. Tests may be needed or data may have to be obtained from other sources for wet roadways (which rarely show skidmarks), slopes great enough so that a car in neutral without brakes will roll on them, gravel, grass, and other unusual surfaces.

5. On the nomograph chart, find the skidding distance on the left scale and the drag factor on the right scale. Draw a straight line between these points. The speed required to slide to a stop is indicated by the point at which this line crosses the middle scale.

6. Remember that the estimate represents the speed to *slide to a stop*. If the slide is not to a stop but ends in a collision, rollover, or fall without ground contact, the starting speed will be higher. How much higher depends on how much speed remained at the end of the skid. *Never add* estimated speed at the end of a skid to the calculated slide-to-stop

speed. These speeds must be combined in another more complicated manner. Thus the speed estimated by Steps 1 through 5 can be considered a minimum, especially if low values are used for drag factor.

There are a number of minor influences on speed required to stop in a specified distance: weight of the vehicle, temperature, tire material and pattern, air pressure in tires, wind velocity, and others. The influence of these conditions is, for general purposes, insignificant and may be ignored.

2. STOPPING DISTANCES

A vehicle is usually stopped in two operations: 1) driver reaction during which the vehicle loses no speed; and 2) vehicle braking which slows the vehicle to a stop.

Consider the second operation first. How far a vehicle goes while braking to a stop depends on how fast it was moving to begin with and how much slowing drag the brakes and road surface can develop. Two rates of slowing can be specified in most cases: 1) maximum slowing and minimum stopping distance determined by the friction of the road (drag factor); and 2) maximum stopping distance permitted by law. In the first case, brake pedal pressure beyond that required to lock wheels produces no shorter stopping distance, assuming that brakes and driver are capable of locking the wheels. Although on slippery surfaces, the vehicle may not in fact stop in the legal maximum distance.

Steps required to estimate braking distances are as follows:

1. Specify the speed from which the stop is to be made. This may be the speed limit, a speed at which a driver stated he was travelling, or some other speed.

2. Determine the drag factor which represents the rate of slowing. For maximum slowing (and min-

18-5

Exhibit 1.

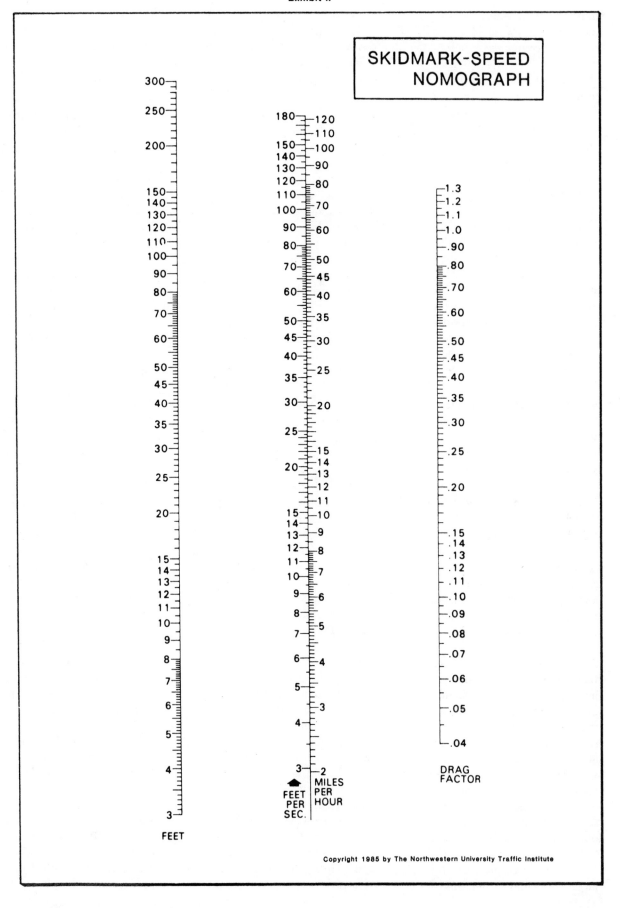

imum braking distance) use values for skidding with all wheels locked in the same way as in estimating speed from skidmarks, either by test skid or by using indicated values. This applies only if the vehicle is capable of locking all wheels on the surfaces involved. If all wheels cannot be locked for any reason, the assumptions required and their effects are too complex to be discussed here.

To obtain the drag factor for legal maximum braking distance, consult the motor vehicle code or whatever regulation applies. Requirements vary from state to state. Standards of the U.S. Department of Transportation may also apply. In laws and regulations, brake performances may be stated in one or more of three ways:

- Braking force as a percentage of gross vehicle weight. Divide this number by 100 to get the drag factor. For example, a braking force of 52.8 percent of the vehicle's weight is a drag factor of 0.528, resulting from 52.8 divided by 100.

- Deceleration in feet per seconds squared (ft/s²). Divide this deceleration by 32.2 ft/s² (the acceleration due to the force of gravity) to get the drag factor. For example, a deceleration of 17 ft/s² is a drag factor of 17 ft/s² $\div$ 32.2 ft/s² = 0.528.

- Stopping distance from a specified speed, usually 20 miles per hour. On the left scale (distance) of the nomograph chart, find the specified distance. Draw a straight line from this point across the middle scale at the specified speed. Read the drag factor for minimum braking where this line crosses the right scale. This is exactly the same as obtaining the drag factor from a test skid

Legal braking distances for large trucks may be in terms of both a distance to stop from 20 miles per hour (or other specified speed) and a sustained rate of slowing. These are too complex to be explained in this publication.

3. On the nomograph (figure 1), locate the desired speed on the middle scale and the selected drag factor on the right scale. Draw a stright line through these points on the two scales and extend it across the left scale. At that point, read the braking distance required to stop under the specified circumstances.

Now consider driver reaction. The time depends on how much thinking is required to decide what to do. When reaction time has been determined, vehicle speed (velocity) will yield distance travelled in reaction time. Reaction distance added to braking distance gives the total stopping distance.

4. Select an appropriate *thinking* reaction time.

- *For a simple reaction,* the driver has decided in advance what to do if something *expected* happens. For example, he has decided to brake if the traffic signal turns yellow or if the brake lights of a car ahead light up. The decision has already been made so time required from perception to action is short: 0.20 to 0.30 seconds for most people. Drivers more than 50 years old generally take a longer time.

- *For complex reaction,* the driver has to evaluate the hazard after he perceives it and then decide which of several possible evasive tactics to employ. The additional thinking takes longer. For example, deciding whether to steer, brake, or accelerate when a child *unexpectedly* runs into the roadway from between parked cars or a car entering the roadway from a driveway *unexpectedly* fails to stop. Depending on how complicated the situation is, complex

reaction may require from 0.3 to 1.3 seconds. Inexperienced and older drivers in more complicated situations take a longer time.

- *For discriminative reaction,* one has to seek additional information to decide what to do. For example, a driver must try to remember which direction to steer if rear wheels sideslip, or watch for other signs when an approaching driver appears to have given the wrong turn signal, or whether the exit he is approaching will or will not take him to his destination. Discriminative reaction may require from a second to a minute or more. Often time is not available to think out what to do so the driver decides on a complex reaction, which may or may not be satisfactory. For example, he may decide to stop to look at a map or examine his tires before going farther. Inexperienced and older drivers are more likely to require discriminative reactions and take longer to complete them.

5. Decide how much time is required for *muscular movement* to begin to actuate vehicle controls. If a driver has decided to steer and hands are already in position, no additional time is required. If he has to move his foot from accelerator to brake pedal, allow 0.2 to 0.3 seconds, depending on distance to be moved, weight of footwear, strength and agility of the driver. Reaching for switches or other controls on the dashboard may require 0.3 to 0.6 seconds.

6. Add thinking reaction time (Step 4) to muscular reaction time (Step 5) to get total estimated reaction time.

7. On the right side of the middle scale of the nomograph, locate the speed (from Step 1). On the left side of the same scale, read the corresponding velocity in feet per second.

8. Multiply the velocity (Step 7) by the total reaction time (Step 6) to get the reaction distance.

9. Add the braking distance (Step 3) to reaction distance (Step 8). This gives the total stopping distance from the specified speed.

3. RELIABILITY

It is clearly impossible to determine precise values for such factors as distance a vehicle has slid, drag factor, and reaction time. Possible high and low values may therefore be used to give a range for each estimate. Sometimes it is possible to make test skids to determine drag factor more precisely. If these are not properly made, they may make the drag factor used less, rather than more, accurate.

If all values are taken to give a low speed or long stopping distance the final estimate will be conservative. On the other hand, values might be chosen to give a high final estimate. In most cases it is desirable to express the esti-mate as a range of values from high one to a low one. The extent of this range depends on the range of values which can be relied on as factors or elements used in making the estimate.

The nomograph used here is not derived from statistics and experiments; it simply represents a graphic method of solving an equation derived from mechanics. The equation for speed is $S = 5.5 \sqrt{df}$; the equation for distance is $d = S^2/30f$. In these equations, S = speed in miles per hour, d = distance in feet, and f = drag factor. The numbers 5.5 and 30 are constants which adjust the equation to the units of measurement used. They would be different if the distance were measured in meters instead of feet. A caculator can be used with these equations to give the same results as the nomograph.

The steps described here outline procedures which will usually result in satisfactory estimates in simple straight-forward cases. But cases involving questionable tire marks; special vehicles such as motorcycles, trail-ers and overloaded trucks; significant slopes; and unusual braking systems require additional information and possibly expert assistance.

4. SOURCES

Author

J. Stannard Baker is a traffic engineer specializing in traffic-accident investigation. He was director of Research and Development at the Northwestern University Traffic Institute from 1946 to 1971 and continued thereafter as a guest lecturer and consultant at The Traffic Institute.

Exhibit

The Skidmark-speed Nomograph was designed by J. Stannard Baker at The Northwestern University Traffic Institute.

Other Material

More detailed information on estimating speeds and stopping distances will be found in a number of other topics in the *Traffic-accident Investigation Manual.*

TRAFFIC-ACCIDENT INFORMATION FROM VEHICLES

Topic 820 of the *Traffic-Accident Investigation Manual*

by
Lynn B. Fricke
and
J. Stannard Baker

NORTHWESTERN UNIVERSITY TRAFFIC INSTITUTE

PUBLICATION HISTORY

1957 *Traffic Accident Investigator's Manual for Police* (Sections 37.010 to 37.910)
Reprinted 1959

1963 Revised (Sections 37.010 to 37.885)
Reprinted 1964, 1965, 1969, 1970, 1971, 1973

1970 *Manual de Investigacion de Accidentes de Trafico* (Sections 3.7-1 to 3.7-68)

1975 *Traffic Accident Investigation Manual* (Chapter 6)
Reprinted 1976, 1979

1985 *Traffic-Accident Information from Vehicles*

TRAFFIC-ACCIDENT INFORMATION FROM VEHICLES

Objective

Examining anything involved in a traffic accident requires obtaining four kinds of factual information about the person, road, or vehicle:

1. Identification
2. Description
3. Condition prior to the accident
4. Effects of the accident.

The object of this topic is to guide you in obtaining such information as it relates to the vehicle.

Arrangement

Identification and description are described first, especially as they relate to applicable standards.

Examination to determine the effect of the accident on the vehicle is divided into two parts: 1) what can and should be done at the scene of the accident; and 2) what is done later as technical follow up for special purposes.

Condition of the vehicle previous to the accident is discussed last. It is considered briefly and generally in terms of deficiencies and deviation from specification, especially as they may be related to vehicle performance.

1. IDENTIFICATION

Uses of Identification Information

Accident records. Identifying the vehicle in traffic accidents is much less important than identifying the driver or road location. This is because driver-license agencies keep track of each driver's accidents, and traffic engineers want accident information about road locations to help them correct hazards, but accident data on individual vehicles are not as systematically accumulated or tabulated. Consequently, little general use is made of vehicle identification data on accident reports. Indeed, if such data were omitted from reports of minor accidents, little or nothing would be lost. Except in rare instances, if the driver is properly identified, he can identify the vehicle whenever that is necessary.

Supplementary accident investigation, especially of serious accidents, often requires identifying vehicles. Especially when a damaged vehicle is to be examined after removal from the scene, identification is useful to prove that the vehicle examined was actually the one involved in the accident.

This information is important as part of the vehicle-examination record rather than as part of the accident report. Proper identification of the vehicle is especially desirable for a person whose only part in the investigation is examination of the vehicle, for example, a mechanic or damage appraiser.

Other purposes of vehicle identification are more important than accident reporting. Investigators may want to know, for example, whether a vehicle involved in an accident was stolen. But this fact becomes part of a criminal investigation and the record becomes part of criminal records, rather than accident investigation and accident records. Current accident-report forms provide no space for indicating whether a car was stolen.

Requirements for Identification in Accident Reporting

Universally, accident-report forms require two methods of vehicle identification: 1) current registration number; and 2) owner's name and address.

Some recent report forms also provide space for the vehicle identification number. Forms now generally reflect current federal standards for identification of vehicles.[1]

Methods of Identification

There are several ways to identify a motor vehicle, that is, to distinguish it from all other vehicles. Identification is not the same as describing a vehicle as belonging to some class of vehicles.

Registration number is assigned by the state department of motor vehicles, displayed on the vehicle by registration plates, and recorded on a registration certificate. In addition to the number, which may consist of numbers and letters, registration identification requires the name (or abbreviation) of the state registering the vehicle and the year, because the same number might be used by several states and might apply to different vehicles in succeeding years. Registration plates are usually removed when the vehicle is wrecked and so are often unavailable as a form of identification if examination is delayed.

Trucks often carry additional registration numbers issued by a state commerce commission, public utility commission, or other regulatory body. Sometimes a truck will carry such numbers from several states. Trucks in interstate commerce are also registered by a federal agency and carry an ICC number in addition to a state number. All these can serve as additional items of identification but they rarely figure in traffic-accident investigation.

Owner's name and address is a kind of identification of the vehicle. It is connected with the registration number by the registration certificate. However, little use is made of this information as identification.

"Vehicle Identification Number (VIN) is the number assigned to the vehicle by the manufacturer primarily for registration and identification purposes."[2] This number is sometimes called the "serial number" or "body number."

The VIN requires 17 digits, divided into three groups:
1. World manufacturer (3 digits)
2. Vehicle descriptor (6 digits)
3. Vehicle identifier[3] (8 digits), which is subdivided into three sections.

Exhibit 1 is an illustration of a vehicle identification number. The coding for model year is illustrated in Exhibit 2.

On all except older vehicles, the number is embossed in part of the vehicle "so that it is readily visible to an observer standing outside of the vehicle without need of access to any compartment of the vehicle."[4]

In most cases, the VIN consists of not more than 17 characters[2] stamped into a metal plate riveted to the deck of the instrument panel at the left side and visible through the windshield. Except for some old vehicles and foreign vehicles, the entire VIN is sufficient because the manufacturer and model year are coded in the VIN (Exhibit 1). Trucks, trailers and motor-

cycles also have VIN's. VIN coding for these vehicles has been recommended by the Society of Automotive Engineers.[5, 6, 7]

Sometimes a vehicle is so badly damaged that the VIN in the usual place cannot be read. If it is important, look for the engine identification number (EIN) or transmission identification number (TIN). These may or may not be the same as the VIN.[8]

Coded descriptions of the vehicle in the form of a series of numbers and letters, sometimes also appear on vehicle name plates. These indicate the color of the vehicle, engine size, axle ratio, and other details. Do not confuse these with the VIN; they are not part of it. If you need to identify a vehicle and are in doubt about what number is the VIN, copy all the numbers shown.

Manufacturer, (coded in the VIN) is "Any person, firm, or corporation engaged in production or assembly of passenger cars,"[9] for example, General Motors, Ford, Chrysler, American Motors, or Volkswagen.

Make (coded in the VIN) is "A distinctive name applied to a group of vehicles from one manufacturer, which may be further subdivided. . ."[9] For example, Lincoln and Mercury are Ford *makes*; Chevrolet, Pontiac, and Buick are General Motors *makes*; and Plymouth and Dodge are Chrysler *makes*. If the *make* is specified, the *manufacturer* does not also need to be specified because no two man-

1P3BM18C6FD385294

VEHICLE DESCRIPTOR

SEQUENTIAL PRODUCTION NUMBER

ASSEMBLY PLANT

MODEL YEAR

WORLD MANUFACTURER IDENTIFICATION

Exhibit 1. *The VIN is coded to indicate manufacturer, vehicle description, model year, and assembly plant.*

YEAR	CODE	YEAR	CODE	YEAR	CODE
1981	B	1991	M	2001	1
1982	C	1992	N	2002	2
1983	D	1993	P	2003	3
1984	E	1994	R	2004	4
1985	F	1995	S	2005	5
1986	G	1996	T	2006	6
1987	H	1997	V	2007	7
1988	J	1998	W	2008	8
1989	K	1999	X	2009	9
1990	L	2000	Y	2010	A

Exhibit 2. *Characters used for coding the model year in the vehicle identification number.*

ufacturers use the same make name. The make rather than the manufacturer is required on accident-report forms.

Model year (coded in the VIN) is "A year designation used by the manufacturer for marketing vehicles (not necessarily the year of manufacture)."[9]

2. DESCRIPTION

Description of the vehicle as it was immediately before the accident serves two main purposes: 1) classification for statistical tabulations; and 2) description of the vehicle and its load, especially descriptions of conditions that may have contributed to the particular accident. Description of the effect of the accident on the vehicle will be treated separately later.

Requirements and Systems

Accident-report forms usually provide space for four or five items identifying the vehicle, but only one in which to describe or classify it. This space is designated "Type" in most forms, although it is sometimes marked "Body Style" or "Model." "Type" of vehicle is not clearly defined, and categories of vehicles are not listed on forms. Most forms do not specifically provide for data on trailers. Consequently, the investigator is left to record whatever he thinks appropriate.

Standards. With respect to descriptions of passenger cars for classification purposes, forms generally follow current federal standards[1] which provide only for "Type of body" without offering any list of categories for the classification. With regard to "commercial vehicles," forms do not usualy conform to the federal standards which require that "registered gross laden weight" be recorded.

Tabulations of "types" of vehicles involved in accidents are based on accident reports. If the accident reports do not systematically and uniformly describe vehicles, the corresponding tabulations cannot be reliable. Data on vehicles with trailers would be especially questionable. Tabulations do not ordinarily attempt to summarize accidents by vehicle size.

Manufacturers' vehicle descriptions are adapted to advertising and marketing rather than accident investigation or traffic records. "Car line" is "A name denoting a family of vehicles with a *make* which has a degree of commonality of construction such as body, chassis etc."[9] The Tempo is a *line* in the Ford *make* of vehicles, and the Cutlass is a *line* in the Oldsmobile *make* of General Motors cars. But these names do not necessarily help one visualize the car. The same line may have different names in one year or appear under a new name after a few years. Two quite similar *lines* in different *makes* will have different names. There are no standard categories for lines, although manufacturers do have some basic guides. In general, car lines tend to represent standard, intermediate, compact, and subcompact cars. *"Series"* is "A specific level of decor, standard equipment, or optional grouping within a car line, usually distinguished by particular marketing characteristics, for example, standard, custom, and deluxe."[9]

"Body type" (body style) is "The general configuration or shape of a vehicle distinguished by characteristics such as number of doors, seats, or windows, roofline, hardtop, convertible, etc." There are no specific descriptions of body types, only general terms. *Model* is "The term applied to a vehicle which, for passenger cars, includes the make, line, series, and body type."[9] This is distinguished for each make by model digits in the VIN (Exhibit 1).

There is still a need for a more practical standard for classification of motor vehicles.

More Useful Descriptions

A problem that often interferes with traffic-accident reconstruction is the lack of useful clues to the size and shape of one or more of the vehicles involved. Typical difficulties are

• *Unknown wheelbase.* For exam-

ple, the vehicle is described only as a "Chevrolet van." Chevrolet vans come in several sizes with different wheelbases. Then there is a question as to which size and which wheelbase applies to this particular vehicle.

• *Indeterminate load.* For some calculations, a truck's gross weight must be known. Then what do you do if there is no information as to whether the vehicle was loaded or empty?

• *Vehicle modifications* may make a difference. For example, a question may arise as to whether the motorcycle had an extended front fork or whether the recreational vehicle had oversize tires.

• *Kind of trailer unknown.* In trying to understand how an accident happened, it is usually not enough to know that there was a trailer; you may also need to know what kind of trailer, how it was hitched, and what it was loaded with.

Criteria. If customary descriptions of vehicles are inadequate for systematic tabulation and for use in investigation, what would constitute a more practical and useful system? Two criteria come to mind at once: 1) the descriptions and classifications should call to mind what the vehicle looks like and what it is used for; and 2) an investigator should be able to classify most vehicles at the scene by observation without reference to voluminous code books or manuals. These criteria imply that the classification must conform largely to ordinary concepts of vehicles, must be easy to remember, and must be a good compromise between too simple to be meaningful and too complex to be practical. These considerations suggest that a single classification is not enough to provide for possible combinations. Three classifications would be better:

1. Size and general structure
2. Body style and appearance
3. User or service.

At the accident scene, you have little time to describe the vehicle. Then a couple of words may have to do. Naming the car manufacturer, Ford for example, is not enough; specifying the make, Ford Escort for example, would be much better. For a truck, describe at least the general type such as pickup or tractor and semi. For trucks, giving the number of tires is easy and helpful. A large tractor and semitrailer is easily recognized as an "18-wheeler." Actually that means that the combination has 18 tires, not wheels, because some of the wheels have two tires. If you describe a truck as having six tires you would be understood to mean a front axle with two tires and a rear axle with four tires.

For technical follow up examination of the vehicle, much additional information can be obtained to describe it. Measurements of wheelbase, track width, and damage can be made. The amount, type, and location of the load can be noted. Technical examination of the vehicle is explained later in this topic.

3. DAMAGE CLASSIFICATION

Methods and Systems

The amount of damage is one measure of the severity of an accident. Therefore, it is considred in accident investigation in three principal ways:

1. It is an element in specifying when a driver shall report an accident.
2. Some record of damage is required in nearly all accident-report forms.
3. At the scene, an investigator considers damage to vehicles, among other things, in deciding how much and what kind of investigation to make.

The standard classification of vehicle damage[10] for accident-severity reporting provides these five categories:

"1. Disabling damage accident
2. Functional damage accident

3. Other motor vehicle damage accident
4. Other property damage accident
5. No damage accident"

Damage-location diagrams provide for a systematic classification of the areas of a vehicle damaged, as in Exhibit 3. The diagram can be marked for damage in more than one area if appropriate. For each area, the extent of damage is indicated by a code for one of three categories:

A. Slight
B. Moderate
C. Severe.

A vehicle damage scale[12] has been developed by the National Safety Council. This scale provides a series of damage pictures in a manual to which actual damage to various parts of a car can be compared. The series for each area of the car ranges from slight to severe. This system gives category code numbers for both the area of vehicle damaged and extent of damage. Until the categories and codes have been memorized, the manual has to be referred to in order to classify damage. Presumably this means that the investigator must carry the manual with him. There is some problem in using this for trailers and large trucks. Comparisons of actual vehicle damage to damage pictures is often a matter of opinion. Even trained observers may differ in their classifications.

The Society of Automotive Engineers has a recommended practice on the coding of the extent of damage.[13] This is one part of a seven character code for collision deformation class-

VEHICLE DAMAGE SEVERITY
A. SLIGHT B. MODERATE C. SEVERE

Exhibit 3. Damage-location diagrams on accident-report forms help to describe the condition of a vehicle after an accident, especially the areas damaged.

ification. The code is not intended for use at the scene of an accident. The code also indicates the direction of principle thrust of force and where damage is located.

Systems for very detailed measurements and descriptions of damage have been developed.[14][15] They are used in studying collapse and distortion of vehicle parts in crashes.

Reporting and Tabulation Requirements

The accident-report forms used provide places to record some facts about vehicle damage:

1. A space, usually one line or less, simply designated "vehicle damage" or something similar, leaving the investigator to enter whatever comes to mind.
2. A check list for the standard classifications
3. A diagram or outline of a vehicle to be marked to show damaged areas
4. A diagram of areas with code numbers to be entered in a coded space (Exhibit 3)
5. Dollar value of damage, which is used mainly for financial responsibility administration and usually requires appalling guesswork on the part of the investigator who is not trained in damage appraisal
6. Coding from a damage scale manual.[12]

For reporting (first level of accident investigation), obtain and record whatever vehicle damage information is required by the traffic-accident report form provided for your use.

Tabulations. Vehicle damage is often tabulated sketchily as part of accident-severity classifications, but usually not otherwise. Additional damage details on the accident report are mainly a record for reference in connection with a particular accident.

4. VEHICLE DATA AT THE SCENE

Minor Accidents

At the scene of a minor accident,

the investigator needs to obtain and record no more information about the vehicle than that required for the accident-report form he uses.

A space for vehicle identification is usually provided on report forms used for both minor and severe accidents; but in fact, so little use is made of identification data in most minor accidents that it is usually unnecessary.

Minimum vehicle descriptions should be included for any accident regardless of severity. The most important information about vehicles in minor accidents is that used by engineers studying high-accident locations. A brief description of the vehicle will do. Usually knowledge of whether the vehicle was a truck or a passenger car is sufficient; but classification by size and general structure, as described earlier, serves all practical purposes.

Damage description, in addition to that used to classify the accident, is unnecessary for the accident report and may be omitted unless otherwise specifically requested.

Severe Accidents

Priorities in data collection are always necessary at the scene of an accident. An investigator, especially a police investigator who has other responsibilities, cannot collect all the information that might be expected of him. He must decide what data will be lost if not collected quickly and what can be postponed. In these decisions, examination of the road is generally much more important than examining vehicles. Signs of the accident on the road, such as tiremarks and final positions of vehicles, soon start to disappear with removal of vehicles, clearing the roadway, restoring traffic flow, and weathering of one kind or another. But signs of the accident on the *vehicle* remain for the most part after it is removed and will be available for examination for days and sometimes months.

Priorities vary greatly with circumstances of the accident so that no definite rules for what to do first and

what next can be established. However, in the following discussion on collecting information to supplement that needed for the standard report, items are arranged in general order of importance. This order will guide judgment in choosing priorities for data gathering.

Final position of the vehicle is usually the most important observation to make in serious accidents. A general idea of the position can be had by a quick glance while doing other things, especially while helping injured people in the vehicle. Later, if someone is to try to determine what happened (accident reconstruction), reliable information about exactly where the vehicle came to rest may be necessary. In Topic 817, final positions of vehicles is considered as one of the signs of the accident visible on the road afterward, so further discussion is unnecessary here. Measurements to locate final positions are explained in detail in Topic 828.

Identification data are the next most important vehicle-information

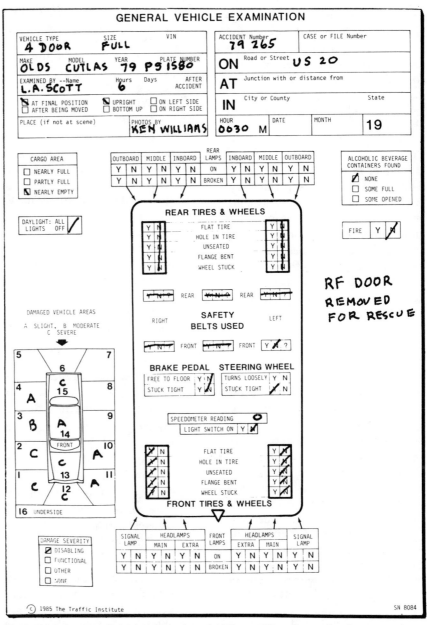

Exhibit 4. *A form is helpful for notes about vehicle condition observed at the scene when time is limited.*

items to collect at the scene of a serious accident. They enable anyone who examines the vehicle later to be sure that he is examining the same vehicle. The registration number is the easiest and most useful identification to get at the scene. But, because registration plates may be removed soon after the vehicle is wrecked, also record at least the make and model year of the car. The vehicle identification number (VIN) is usually not necessary and is sometimes very difficult to read after an accident because of damage to the vehicle, or darkness and weather.

If you can examine the vehicle registration certificate at the scene, that is the easiest source of identification data. Just copy it from there. But first compare it with the vehicle to be sure it applies.

Vehicle description, although available later, can usually be obtained most easily at the same time as identification data.

Damage to vehicle at the scene of a serious accident can be perfunctory. A general survey is usually adequate, because the vehicle may be examined more completely and conveniently if necessary after it has been removed. The main purpose of examination is to be able to judge later whether additional damage was done in removing the vehicle or otherwise. You might have to testify about this.

Good notes on damage are not made quickly or easily. You may not have time for them before the vehicle is moved, or other conditions at the scene may be unfavorable. Therefore, if you are taking pictures, get the four standard damage photos of each vehicle as explained in Topic 836. When the vehicles are in the open at the scene, it is often easier to get good standard damage photos than later when the vehicle is in a crowded salvage yard. Photos generally tell the damage story well enough so no additional notes are needed. In addition to photos, and especially if no photos are taken, try to make notes of these eight kinds of things:

1. *Lamps* after dark. List each external lamp around the car and note its condition when you arrive:
    a. On or off
    b. Broken or unbroken
   Note the position of the headlight switch as *on* or *off*. If off, *never* turn it on to see whether lights work; you may destroy an indication in one of the lamps that it was on or off when the crash occurred.
2. *Major parts detached* (wheels, doors, fenders, engine, hood)
3. *Tire and wheel* condition can be quickly checked. List each tire of the vehicle and note whether it
    a. Is flat
    b. Has a hole in the tire
    c. Tire bead is unseated
    d. Wheel flange is bent
    e. Wheel is stuck and not free to turn.
   Whether a wheel is locked (will not rotate) can often be determined by simple observation, for example if the tire and wheel are locked in the damage. When the vehicle is towed it is easy to tell if a wheel is locked. Watch the wheels on the gound to see whether they turn when the car is towed. If they do turn, find out whether the drive shaft had to be disconnected to permit them to turn. If the vehicle is towed on a dolly, it is probably because wheels would not rotate. Make notes of these observations; you cannot trust to memory regarding such detail.
4. *Steering wheel.* Note whether it is
    a. Locked tight
    b. Spins free
5. *Cargo space.* Inspect it for load. Note whether it is
    a. Nearly full
    b. Partially loaded
    c. Nearly empty.
   Contents of the vehicle must generally be noted at the scene because they may not be available after the vehicle is removed by the wrecker. For passenger vehicles, make a note of what was in the vehicle besides people, for example, animals, trip luggage, sport equipment, food, and particularly alcoholic beverages or their containers. For trucks and trailers, make a note of whether the vehicle was empty, partly loaded, or fully loaded, and the general nature of the cargo. Great detail is not necessary unless the cargo is either very valuable or very dangerous; then get a little more information about it.
6. *Alcoholic beverage containers.* Locations, if any.
7. *Speedometer reading.*
8. *Safety belts used.*

A form is available for indicating damage and condition of vehicles at the scene.[16] A completed example is shown in Exhibit 4. One advantage of the form is that it lists specific data that are often available only at the scene. You can then quickly complete the form and move on to other things. Some parts of the form can be filled out later, particulary the information needed to identify the location of the accident.

Matching. Except under unfavorable conditions, the best time and place to match contact damage on vehicles to marks on the road and roadside is at the scene. If there are gouges or scrapes on the paving, there are nearly always corresponding wear, abrasion, or breakage of vehicle parts. Some of these may be easy to see, for example, broken door handles, scraped fenders, or dented roof if the vehicle has rolled over. Damage to the underside of a vehicle is usually more significant and is often entirely overlooked. The easiest time to look for signs of road contact on the vehicle is when it is lifted for towing (Exhibit 5). Brief notes on the vehicle inspection form or any available paper will suffice. List the areas on the underside of the car where there are signs of road contact and describe what each looked like. Here are examples:

• Rear drive shaft universal joint:

broken, severely abraded

- Right, rear, outboard rim: scratched, grass and twigs between rim and tire
- Transmission case: broken open, oil out, part broken away and missing
- Frame, left side under front door: bent down, heavily scratched obliquely.

If any such signs on the vehicle appear to you to be the right size, shape, and kind to have made marks, note your *opinion* as to which damage to the vehicle matched which sign on the road. But be prepared to justify this opinion with your observations and reasoning. Photographs of both the mark on the road and the corresponding mark on the car are useful.

5. TECHNICAL FOLLOW-UP EXAMINATION OF VEHICLES

Nature of Technical Examination

At the scene of a severe accident, the vehicle is given a more or less general inspection to note conditions and results of the accident about which someone may possibly raise questions later. You can record results of this brief but important examination on a simple form like that in Exhibit 4.

In a follow-up vehicle examination, however, you usually concentrate on some particular matter, such as measuring deformation or examining lamps. But because you may be asked later what you noticed about other conditions, make it a habit in follow-up examinations to systematically note general as well as specific observations.

If you filled out a form such as Exhibit 4, or if you have similar data obtained by someone else, that will serve the purpose. Otherwise, get and record the general data. Do not try to make this represent the condition of the vehicle at the scene; let it represent the vehicle as you found it. For example, you might note that the lights on the vehicle were off when you examined it although you had reason to believe that they were on at the scene after the accident.

Because technical follow-up vehicle examinations are nearly always made with specific questions in mind, these examinations can vary from a quick look at a tire to determine whether it is flat, all the way to disassembling the vehicle by a team of engineers to try to discover some malfunction. Preliminary or provisional vehicle examination is usually done at the scene but may be done elsewhere if there is no opportunity to do so at the scene. Part or all of a technical examination may be conducted at the scene if you have the opportunity and know what to look for. Ordinarily, technical examination is made after the vehicle has been removed, often a long time after.

Scope. Many aspects of vehicle examination involve high levels of engineering and scientific skill and much knowledge of vehicle design and construction. The details of such examination are beyond the scope of this topic. Consequently, vehicle examination, as described here, is that which a specially trained police officer or other technical investigator

might reasonably be asked to do. This information is expected to help form conclusions about how the accident happened rather than why.

Instructions for inspecting the vehicle for mechanical defects are also not within the scope of this Topic. Such an inspection requires special tools to take the vehicle apart. If this seems to be necessary, expert help will be required unless you have special training and experience in the mechanics of motor vehicles.

Authority to Examine

At the scene of an accident, anyone can look at the damage or, for that matter, photograph it, provided this does not interfere with police investigation. But moving the vehicle, entering it, or taking parts can only be done with permission of the owner or his representative. However, anyone at the scene of an accident may enter a vehicle to save life or property. The only requirements are that there be an emergency and that the person use ordinary care. A police investigator, in

Exhibit 5. *The easiest time to look for road abrasions and other damage on the underside of the vehicle is when it is lifted for towing. Note in this case the turf on the muffler and left rear wheel.*

the course of his duties at the scene of an accident, may enter a vehicle for normal inspection. *Normal* inspection implies gathering information on the make, model, age, and ownership of the vehicle and inspecting damage, sources of injury to occupants or pedestrians, and vehicle condition. If the vehicle has been taken off the street or highway to a garage, storage lot, or home, you must get permission from both the owner of the vehicle and the owner of the place where it is located, or the owner's agent, to examine the vehicle.

Records and Reports

Records vary greatly. Because complete technical examination is not feasible even in very severe accidents, except on rare occasions, the examination should be undertaken with a clear notion of what questions need to be answered. That means that the record of observations made will depend on the purpose of the examination. The record may consist of notes on observations and tests, or sometimes photographs.

Forms can be used for some common kinds of vehicle examinations. The form shown in Exhibit 4[16] is suitable for the initial examination of a vehicle, especially at the scene, or in connection with detailed examination of particular parts of the vehicle. Special forms are also available for examination of lamps[19] (Exhibit 47), tires[18] (Exhibit 46), and details of damage to body and chassis[17] (Exhibit 6).

Forms serve to remind the investigator of the observations that he should make and record. In this respect they are very helpful, especially to an inexperienced investigator. But forms have a corresponding disadvantage. The investigator tends to look for *only* the kind of damage specified by the form and may overlook important facts; this also is especially the case with inexperienced investigators.

Photographs are necessary to record many aspects of vehicle damage and condition. Written descriptions cannot begin to capture the necessary detail with the required reliability. Photographs are quickly made and are less expensive than any practical alternative. Suggestions on making photographs of vehicle damage are given in Topic 836. In addition to high credibility, photographs have the advantage of recording detail that the investigator did not notice at the time of examination.

Parts of vehicles — sometimes even all that remains of a vehicle — may be retained as part of the record. This is most common with lamps and tires.

Identification and description of the vehicle must be a part of every examination report. The VIN is the most positive and satisfactory identification. Registration number, state, and year should also be included if plates are on the vehicle when it is examined. Name of owner or driver is usually unimportant at this stage of the investigation and, indeed, may not be known to whoever is assigned to examine the vehicle.

Time and place of examination is an important and sometimes overlooked part of the record.

The name of the investigator who made the examination and report is also needed to authenticate it. If there were others present, their names should be noted whether they assisted in the examination or not. The name of whoever took photographs is also necessary because additional copies of the pictures may be required later and he may have to authenticate his work.

Contact and Induced Damage

Contact damage is damage to any part of a motor vehicle by direct contact with some object which is not part of the vehicle. The other object is usually external: another motor vehicle, a pedestrian, a fixed object, or even the road surface. But the object may also be internal: usually it is an occupant of the vehicle but sometimes it may be something carried in the vehicle. External contact damage is shown by rub-off of paint, tire rubber, road material, bark, and even pedestrian's clothing or body tissue. It is also indicated by imprints of headlamp housings, wheel rims, bumpers, door handles, poles, and other fixed objects. Mainly, however, contact damage is indicated by closely compacted, crumpled vehicle body parts with fine hard scratches (striations) in the surface of metal; smearing of paint due to heat of friction; ragged tears in sheet metal; and punctures (Exhibits 7 and 8).

Induced damage is damage to any part of a motor vehicle caused by some other part of the same vehicle or by the shock of collision. In a front-engine, rear-drive car, for example, damage to the differential is usually induced because differentials are not often broken by contact with other vehicles. Instead, the front end of the vehicle is pushed back in an opposite-direction collision with contact damage to grill, radiator, fenders, bumper, and headlamps. This forces engine and transmission back, causing induced damage to them. Transmission displacement then forces the drive shaft back and induces the damage in universal joints or differential.

In a collision, deceleration or acceleration of the vehicle may be so sudden that the tendency of parts, seats, and headlamps, for example, to keep moving, develops sufficient force to tear them from their fastenings. That would also be induced damage. Shock of collision may damage headlamps that are not actually hit by anything. The most conspicuous induced damage is usually that which occurs to vehicle body parts. A vehicle hit squarely on the right side, for example, may have the front seat pushed a foot or more to the left by collapse of the right door. The seat bursts open the left door, thereby producing conspicuous induced damage. Induced damage of body parts is generally indicated by displacement and by folds, bends, creases, and wrinkles rather than by scratches and crumpling (Exhibits 9 and 10).

Distinguishing between induced

20-11

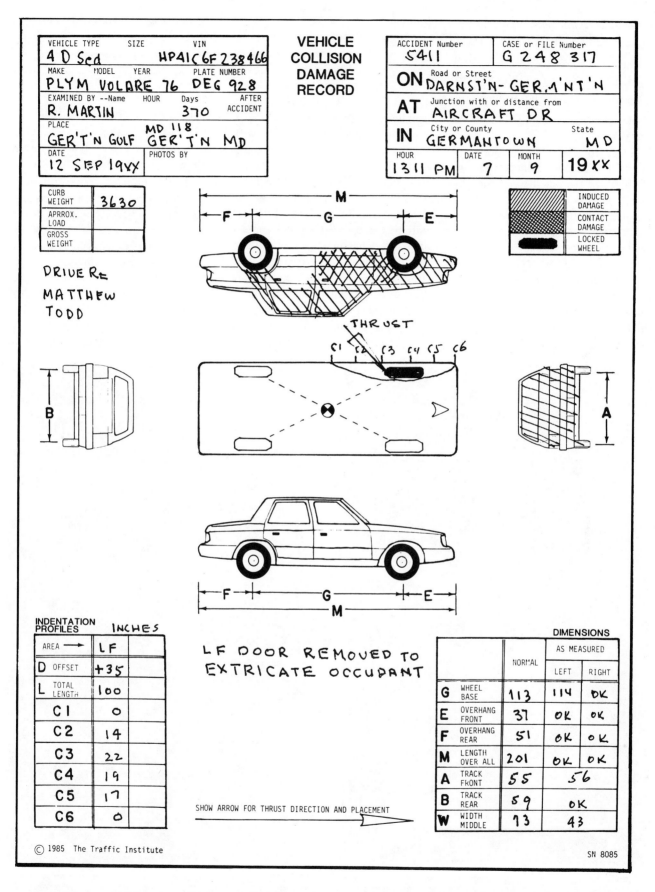

Exhibit 6. *A special form is useful for recording observations made after the vehicle has been removed from the scene.*

and contact damage is important because it helps to determine the exact position of the vehicles with relation to each other during collision and to determine whether the accident involved more than one collision, as many do.

Tempered glass. Distinction between contact and induced damage of shattered tempered glass, such as that ordinarily used in rear windows of cars, is almost impossible. It gives no indication of whether it was damaged by contact with some object or by distortion of the frame (Exhibit 11). In either case the stress set up in the glass by the hardening process causes it to disintegrate into thousands of corn-size pieces (Exhibit 12). Tempered glass is used in rear and side windows.

Laminated safety glass, on the other hand, holds together and by fracture lines shows rather clearly whether the damage was by contact or induced. Parallel fracture lines usually result from induced damage. There may be two sets of these with the fracture lines crossing at an angle. Distortion of the frame bends the glass and it breaks in the general manner shown in Exhibit 13. Contact damage usually produces fractures radiating and encircling the contact area somewhat in a spiderweb fashion. Cracks are closer together near the center of the contact area. There may be an actual hole in the glass (Exhibit 14).

Multiple contact damage areas. In a single accident, one vehicle may ex-perience several collisions. Ordinari-ly there is a separate contact-damage area for each collision. Contact-damage areas indicating more than one collision in an accident are usually separated by undamaged areas showing only induced damage.

The most common double contact damage occurs in evenly matched angle collisions as indicated by Exhibit 15. Here the front ends of the vehicles collide heavily, resulting in rapid rotation of both cars in opposite directions. The vehicles separate momentarily as they become parallel to each other and then their rear ends collide. An example of such damage is shown in Exhibits 16 and 17.

Sometimes, especially when a vehicle rolls over, there may be three or

Exhibit 7. *Contact damage from other vehicles usually appears as scraping, tearing, and crumpling with paint or rubber rub-off, especially on body parts.*

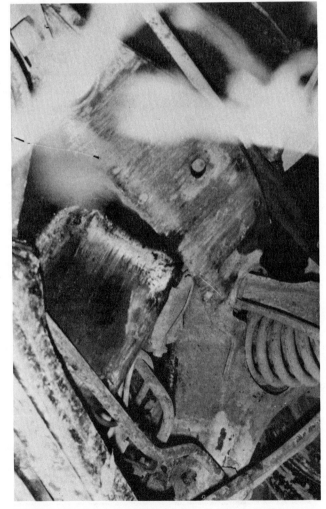

Exhibit 8. *Contact with pavement usually appears as abrasion striations; contact with the roadside results in dirt or grass in the contact-damage area.*

Exhibit 9. *Induced damage appears usually as crumpling without abrasion.*

Exhibit 10. *Induced damage is often found on the roof or body areas.*

more contact-damage areas, perhaps with another vehicle or with fixed objects. Exhibits 18, 19, and 20 show a vehicle with four separate contact-damage areas, each representing a separate collision. Sometimes a vehicle has two or more contact-damage areas from separate accidents, the accident situation having stabilized after the first and before the second.

Superimposed contact-damage areas occur when two or more separate collisions involve the same area on the same vehicle. These are very difficult to detect. Two kinds of paint rub-off in the same area may suggest more than one collision. Sharp abrasion from contact with a concrete surface combined with crumpling from contact with another vehicle may also suggest this.

Diagramming contact damage is the best way to make a record of it. On an outline of the vehicle draw a small arrowhead pointing to each end of the area and connect these with a loop. See the diagram in Exhibit 6. Ground contact by the underside of the vehicle or the roof in a roll-over are not readily indicated that way. Encircle them and mark the circle CD for contact damage.

Imprints and Rub-off

General contact damage often fails to indicate the exact position of a vehicle with respect to the object with which it collided. You must, therefore, seek specific signs, especially when the vehicle experienced several collisions in the same accident and when more than two vehicles are involved in the accident. The most useful signs are imprints of the object struck and rub-off surface material.

Imprints are dents pressed into body parts by some stronger object and clearly show its shape; for example, the pole imprint in Exhibit 21. Headlamps, bumpers, and wheels are most likely to make characteristic imprints. Exhibits 22 and 23, for instance, show quite distinctive markings from a headlamp and a bumper in a right-angle collision.

Door handles and radiator ornaments leave punctures or small deep dents. Strong truck bumpers leave broad, flat, usually clear imprints. Automobile bumpers, on the other hand, are not very strong; therefore, the irregular imprints they leave are indistinct (Exhibit 24). Imprints are usually made on areas which are damaged or collapsed and so may be difficult to recognize. Even an imprint as that shown in Exhibit 23 may be overlooked, especially if you do not suspect what may have made it.

Imprints definitely fix the position of one vehicle with respect to another during collision.

Obscure imprints, may easily go unnoticed. For example, in a four-car accident, it was impossible to decide the sequence of collision until the imprint in Exhibit 25 made on the door of a car by the tire of a truck was found. The imprinted serial number positively identifies the tire that left the mark. Registration plates sometimes leave similar tell-tale imprints. Sometimes imprints are very useful in identifying vehicles in hit-and-run accidents.

Measure imprints and the parts assumed to have made them to confirm any conclusion that they match. For example, the wheel imprint in Exhibit 26 is exactly the same diameter as the rim on the wheel that made it.

Comparing distances from the ground to the imprint and from the ground to the object assumed to have made it, may help to match the imprint with the object which made it. It may also yield interesting information about the manner of collision.

Rub-off also shows surface contact between vehicles. It is usually paint but may also be rubber from tires,

Exhibit 11. *Shattered tempered glass, used in rear windows, gives no indication of contact or induced damage.*

Exhibit 12. *Tempered safety glass either shows no breakage or it breaks into thousands of small pieces.*

Exhibit 13. *Parallel or checkerboard fracture lines in laminated windshield glass indicate induced damage.*

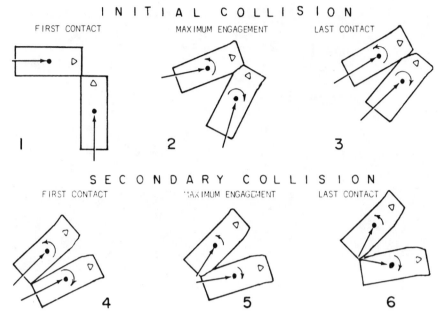

Exhibit 15. *Angle collisions often result in two collisions between the vehicles involved, a severe one at the front ends and a moderate one at the rear ends.*

fabric from pedestrian's clothes, pedestrian's skin, hair, blood, tree bark, road dust, mud, or other things. Rub-off includes, in fact, all parts of one object that are deposited on another. In collisions between vehicles, this may be bits of glass and part of ornamental trim. Information about rub-off is valuable in studying collisions between three or more vehicles. It helps determine which vehicles collided and where. Inspection of color is usually sufficient for the purpose. Sometimes rubbing or chipping of paint removes the finish and exposes undercoating of a different color. This is often mistaken for rub-off from another object. If you have any doubt, scrape, file, or sandpaper the surface to see what the undercoat looks like.

Whenever rub-off may be impor-tant in determining how the collision occurred or in identifying possible hit-and-run vehicles, collect samples of it and preserve them. When collecting samples of paint try to get chips rather than smears. These can often be found in crumpled body parts. Edges of chips can be examined with a microscope to match the layers of paint used in finishing the surface (Exhibit 27). Scrapings of one kind or paint rubbed off on another generally are unsatisfactory. It is nearly impossible to scrape off the deposited paint without getting some of the paint on which it was deposited and that so contaminates the sample that chemical or spectroscopic analysis is

Exhibit 14. *Spider-web fractures in laminated glass indicates contact damage, usually from inside the vehicle.*

Exhibit 16. *Damage at both front and rear on the same side resulting from an angle collision. Front damage is more than rear damage.*

Exhibit 17. *Double contact-damage areas in angle collisions result from rapid rotation. Not all angle collisions result in double damage areas.*

Exhibit 19. *Along the left side of the same car (at B) the car has struck a guardrail. On top of the car (at A), abrasions show signs of rollover.*

usually indeterminate or questionable. If the paint rub-off is on chrome it may be removed without contamination, but the sample is usually so minute that it is better to preserve the whole bumper, or whatever the chrome part is, than to try to scrape off and save a microscopic sample.

Rubber rub-off from tires may be difficult to recognize because it often looks so much like ordinary dirt.

However, when it can be found and identified, it is very useful for suggesting how the accident occurred. For example, by observing the rubber rub-off shown in Exhibit 28, you could tell that a particular tire from the other vehicle had contact with this vehicle.

Sometimes measuring and counting tire tread or side rib marks in rub-off may help identify the tire which made the mark and therefore the relationship of the vehicles in collision.

By verifying the freshness of imprints, paint rub-offs, and abrasions, you can often establish that they occurred as a result of the accident rather than in earlier collisions. The amount of rust is almost always an indication of how long ago the part was damaged and, hence, whether damage was from a previous accident. A damaged part with an area that has a bright metallic sheen was probably struck very recently by another vehicle or fixed object.

Motion during contact is often indicated by imprints and rub-off. Clear, unsmeared imprints (Exhibits 25 and 26) are only made when the surfaces are pressing together with virtually no sliding between them. Therefore, when the imprints were made, the parts were stationary with respect to each other; that is, those parts in contact were moving for an instant, at least, at exactly the same speed. This indicates what is called a

Exhibit 18. *Multiple contact damage areas mean multiple collisions. The front of this car hit the side of a bridge.*

Exhibit 20. *The rear of the car shows damage caused by another vehicle when the car was at rest.*

full impact. Smeared imprints (Exhibit 29, shows the opposite; the parts in contact were not standing still with respect to each other but were moving at different speeds. That would indicate a partial impact. What is often spoken of as a "sideswipe" is a partial impact. Sometimes careful observation is needed to determine whether the impact is full or partial because the surfaces in contact slide past each other leaving slippage marks until they reach a position, usually at maximum engagement, when the motion between them has stopped. The distinction between full and partial impact is often useful in determining how an accident occurred.

Collapse and Thrust

Use of vehicle damage for determining how an accident occurred is an important part of technical accident investigation and professional traffic-accident reconstruction. One aspect of the use of such data is determining where the principal force (thrust) was applied during collision and from which direction it came. This is usually the key to determining how the vehicles were related to each other at maximum engagement when the forces between the vehicles were greatest. At this instant, as at all times during collision, the force against one vehicle is exactly opposite in direction to that against the other. Therefore, if we know the direction of the thrust against each vehicle, we can determine the angle of the vehicles to each other.

Thrust of a vehicle against another object or thrust of another object

Exhibit 22. *In a collision, each vehicle may leave its "trade mark" on the other. The rectangular headlamp, H, made the imprint, H, shown in Exhibit 23.*

Exhibit 23. *The dent at B corresponds to the end of the bumper at B in Exhibit 22. Such matching of vehicle damage is often very important in accident reconstruction.*

against the vehicle are indicated by contact damage. This thrust shows the direction of the force between the vehicle and the other object, whatever it may be. Collapse resulting from contact damage also helps to judge where this force, which may have been applied over a considerable area, is centered. It is easy to make mistakes in judging the direction of thrust from studying damage to vehicles. You are still more likely to be misled if you have only photographs

of the damage, especially if the photographs are not taken as described in Topic 836. It is commonly believed that the thrust or force was directed toward the collapsed area. For example, if the left front corner of a car is crushed in after collision, it may be inferred that the force came from the left front. That may or may not be true. Determination of thrust direction is not that simple.

Thrust direction is determined by the direction in which specific parts

Exhibit 21. *The shape of collapse in contact-damage areas helps determine what the contact was with. In this case, a pole has been hit.*

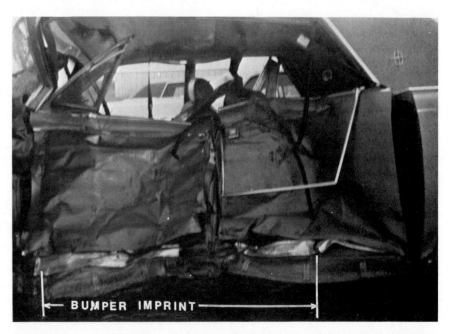

Exhibit 24. *Car-bumper imprints are usually difficult to distinguish because car bumpers are irregular in shape and not especially strong.*

Exhibit 25. *Obscure imprints, like this tire serial number on the door of a car, are often important in determining the manner in which a collision occurred.*

Exhibit 26. *The wheel of another vehicle has clearly made this imprint. The imprint shows no slippage during impact. That indicates a complete impact.*

are moved during impact. This is sometimes difficult to judge. You will understand better by comparing three examples (Exhibits 30, 31, and 32). In all three, contact damage is to the front end and in the first two more from the driver's left than from his right. An inexperienced investigator would be likely to conclude that the thrust was toward the left front corner in two of these cases and toward the right front in the other. But more careful consideration of Exhibit 30 shows major thrust straight back at the left front corner; Exhibit 31 shows the thrust force toward the rear and right but centered; and Exhibit 32 shows the thrust also centered but toward the rear and left.

Thus thrust direction is best determined by the direction sheet metal and other parts are deformed or moved during impact, but there are other ways to get at thrust direction.

If a vehicle hits a standing object, a tree for example, or a stationary vehicle, thrust direction is opposite to the vehicle's direction of movement.

This may not be the direction in which the vehicle is headed because the vehicle could be moving backwards or sidewise.

If both vehicles are moving, the forces against them are always opposite in direction, but these directions depend on the relative weights, speeds, and direction of travel of the vehicles involved. The direction will be influenced more by heavier and faster vehicles.

Sometimes, thrust direction can be judged by how vehicle occupants move during collision. The direction of thrust against the vehicle is generally opposite to the direction of movement of occupants during impact. So if you know where an occupant was seated and where he hit the inside of the vehicle, you can figure about where the force against the vehicle came from. Such a conclusion is not dependable, however, if the vehicle rotates rapidly during collision.

Thrust (principal force) may be applied to any part of a vehicle. Generally you can consider it be concentrated at the point of maximum penetration. This occurs at maximum engagement.

A vehicle can be in two or more collisions. The deformation produced by each indicates the direction and point of concentration of a separate thrust. Sometimes two collisions produce damage in the same area. That makes it difficult to sort out the separate thrust directions and points of application.

Diagramming thrust is done by drawing an arrow to show the direction of thrust. Put the tip or arrowhead at the point of maximum penetration and the shaft of the arrow in the direction from which the thrust force came (Exhibits 30, 31, and 32). A refinement of this scheme is to show the arrrowhead only as an angle. The spread of this angle shows your opinion of the possible range of directions from which the force may have come. You can also suggest the amount of force by the length of the arrow.

Describing thrust direction can be done in two ways:

1. Clockwise degrees from the lengthwise axis of the vehicle. Thus a force straight toward the right side is 90° and toward the left side would be 270°.
2. Hour numbers from the clock face with 12 o'clock representing a force from straight ahead. A force straight toward the right side would be 3 (for three o'clock).

Variations in thrust are usual. During most impacts, the angle between

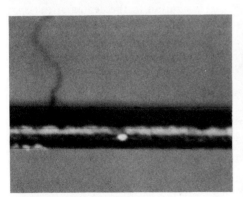

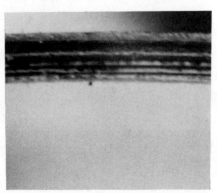

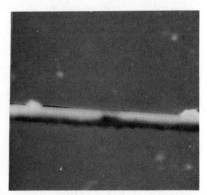

Exhibit 27. *Paint chips left on one car by another are better for matching than paint scrapings. Under magnification, the edges of the chips are clearly distinctive.*

Exhibit 28. *Tire rubber rub-off left on one car will suggest the relative positions of the two cars during a collision.*

Vehicle Damage Measurements

Good photographs are usually a sufficient record of vehicle damage. (Vehicle damage photography is discussed in Topic 836.) But when damage is to be the basis of speed estimates, detailed measurements can importantly increase the accuracy of the estimates.

Damage measurements are also helpful in determining direction of thrust. For example, if a collision moves a headlamp rearward 1.9 ft. and 1.2 ft. to the right, the direction of thrust at maximum engagement can be determined as illustrated in Exhibit 34. Movement of wheels, bumpers, and even door handles and tail lamps can serve the same purpose.

It is rarely necessary to measure vehicle damage at the scene of the accident. A follow-up examination of the vehicle affords the time and convenience for better measuring.

A computer program, CRASH3,[15] is available to make speed estimates from damage measurements. A detailed explanation of this program is beyond the scope of this topic, but a general outline of the measurements required may be helpful here. A more complete explanation is available elsewhere.[14] [22]

Three kinds of vehicle measurements are needed for the CRASH3 program:

1. Length of indentation
2. Depth of profile (penetration) at various points
3. Transverse or longitudinal distance from center line of indentation to the center of mass of the vehicle.

the vehicles changes and the force goes from zero at first contact to the greatest force at maximum engagement and then back to zero force when the vehicles disengage. Thus, both direction and amount of force change. Your diagram only shows your *opinion* of the thrust at maximum engagement. When the contact between vehicles is not momentarily fixed during engagement (full impact), the vehicles slide by each other during impact. The most common indication of this is a much longer contact-damage area on one vehicle than on the other (Exhibit 33). In that case, thrust varies not only in amount and direction but also in the point of application. Further consideration of these matters is part of accident reconstruction, rather than collection of information from the vehicle.

These measurements and their symbols are shown in Exhibit 35.

The total length of indentation (L in Exhibit 35) includes both induced and contact-damage. Exhibit 36 is an example. But if induced damage is far from the contact-damage area, do not include it. For example, if there is contact with the front of a vehicle and induced damage on the rear, do not include the induced damage with the contact damage.

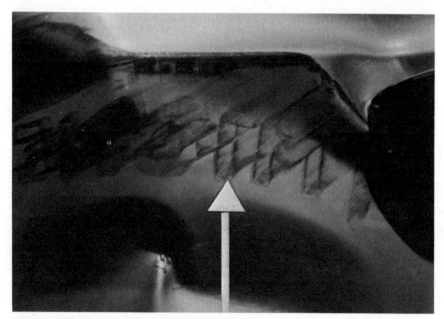

Exhibit 29. *Smeared imprints or rub-offs indicate that the surfaces in contact were moving with respect to each other during contact.*

Exhibit 30. *Note that the major deformation is at the left where the front wheel has been forced straight back toward the left edge of the windshield. Contact damage extends across the front two thirds of the way from the left side.*

Exhibit 31. *Note that the whole front end has been moved a foot to the right but also pushed back a little more on the left than on the right. Contact damage is across three quarters of the front from the left side.*

The depth profile, labeled C1, C2, C3, etc. in Exhibit 37, represents the extent of damage. Measuring this profile is not so simple as it might seem to be. If the whole front end of the car, for example, is damaged, you have no reference line for the original front of the vehicle. Often, however, the profile can be established by measuring from some other undam-aged part, for example the rear bumper or axle (Exhibit 38). Then measure the distance from this artificial reference on an identical but undamaged vehicle. From this subtract each of the C measurements in turn to obtain the corrected indentation at that point as illustrated in Exhibit 38. A possible problem in this method is finding a comparable undamaged vehicle.

Sometimes, published vehicle dimensions can be used.

To get a good indentation profile, six equally spaced measurements along the indentation length, L, are recommended. For the width of each of the six spaces, divide the indentation length by five. Fewer C measurements are satisfactory when the crush distance is essentially the same along the whole damage area.

Try to adjust the number of uniform spaces so that one of the C measurements is at the greatest indentation. Exhibit 39 shows how this may be done. With six C measurements, none is at the greatest indentation; but with four measurements, one of them is.

You will sometimes find contact damage around the corner of a vehicle. There will be deformation of indentation on both one end and adjacent side. Then you must decide whether to measure for the profile from the end or the side. Do this by considering thrust direction. If thrust direction is more from the front than the side, make C measurements from the front; if the thrust direction is more from the side, make penetration measurements from the side. For damage illustrated in Exhibit 34, make C measurements rewarded from the front bumper line because the thrust is clearly more from the front than the side.

The last measurement that CRASH3 needs is D, the distance of the center line of damage from the center of mass of the vehicle. For this dimension it is suggested[14] that the center of mass be taken as at the middle of the wheelbase length and track width of the vehicle. Exhibit 35 shows how this is measured for both side damage and end damage. Be sure to note whether D is in front or behind the center of mass for side damage and to the left or right in end damage cases.

Other measurements that may be useful in later analysis are the wheelbase and track width of the vehicle. Take measurements (Exhibit 40) so that change, if any, in wheelbase and

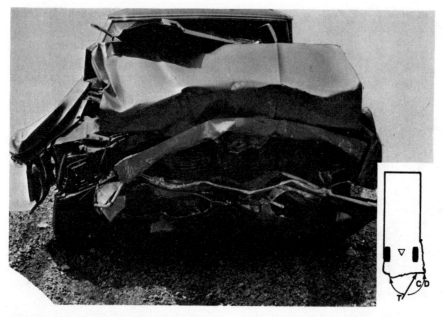

Exhibit 32. *Here the whole front end has clearly been moved a foot to the left and about the same distance back clear across the front. Contact damage extends across the entire front, from one side to the other.*

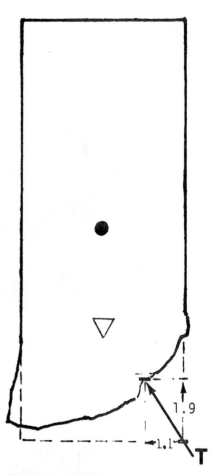

Exhibit 34. *The movement of vehicle parts in a collision indicate the direction of force placed on the vehicle during a collision. For example, a headlight has been moved 1.9 feet rearward and 1.1 feet inboard. This clearly indicates direction of thrust.*

track width can be determined. Do not become so involved in measuring the L, C, and D values that observations and measurements of movement of other vehicle parts are overlooked. Do not forget to note the movement of key parts (bumpers, wheels, lamps etc.) of the vehicle which are helpful in determining direction of thrust (principal force).

Signs of Ground Contact

If there are roadway scars, grooves, scratches, etc., in the roadway, be sure to look carefully on the vehicles for the parts that made them. Have the vehicle hoisted for this purpose (Exhibit 5) or if a very detailed examination is required, have it turned upon its side (Exhibit 41). Otherwise you

may have to lift it with a jack or get down and look underneath it. Parts that leave gouges are usually severely abraded or ground off and may be bent over if they protrude, like the ends of bolts. If the vehicle is examined immediately after the accident, these surfaces will be bright, as in Exhibit 42. Sometimes, until they begin to rust, they may show slight blue or straw color from the heat produced in them by friction. Later they will be rusted over. When the road surface contains tar or asphalt, especially in warm weather when it is soft, there may be some of this road material still clinging to the parts that dug into the roadway. When you find the part that made the mark, measure to compare its dimenstions with those of the gouge or mark in the road. When such measurements are possible, they

Exhibit 33. *The contact damage on this vehicle essentially extends from the rear to front along its right side. Such a long area generally means a partial impact, during which thrust varies in direction, quantity and point of application.*

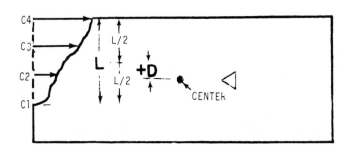 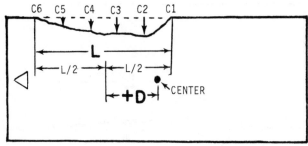

Exhibit 35. *These are coordinate systems and damage measurements as defined by the CRASH3 program. L is the length of indentation; C values are for the crush profile; D is the distance from the center of damage to the center of mass.*

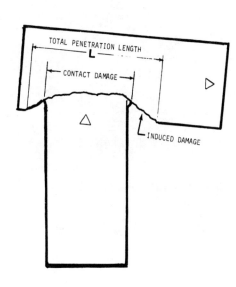

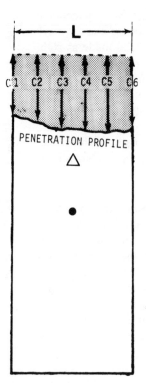

Exhibit 36. *The total length of indentation, L, is established as shown above. For this situation, induced damage can be considered as part of indentation.*

Exhibit 37. *Depth of crush profile is shown. The C values indicate the amount of crush at six evenly spaced stations along the indentation, L. Fewer than six C values can be used.*

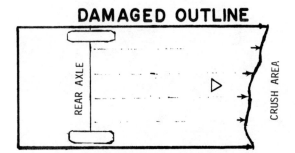

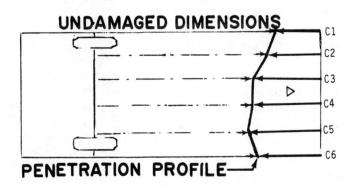

Exhibit 38. *By taking measurements shown in the two diagrams, the depth profile can be determined by subtracting the measurements in the left sketch from those in the right sketch. If the rear axle has been moved, consider measuring from the rear bumper.*

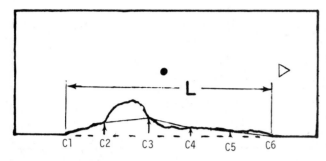
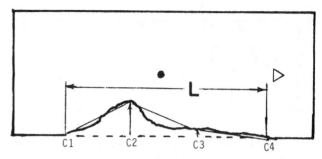

Exhibit 39. *Set up stations so that maximum crush is measured. By adjusting the spacing and using four measurements for depth of crush profile the maximum crush is measured in (b) where it would be missed in (a).*

are very convincing. Measurements of both the part of the car and the mark on the road must be made at right angles to abrasion striations; otherwise the connection between the two may be obscured or misinterpreted (Exhibit 43). If litigation is likely to arise from the accident, try to save these parts as possible evidence in court or at least have them photographed.

An important circumstance to be determined is whether a vehicle turned over. You may need proof of the fact that the vehicle *did* roll over to justify your reconstruction. A vehicle that has rolled over nearly always shows evidence of such a roll, even if it is resting on its wheels after the accident. Look for dirt and abrasion marks along the rain gutter or curved edge of the roof and hood as in Exhibit 44. Identifying each set of marks will help you to trace the exact movement of the vehicle from initial point to the final position. From this it is often possible to verify estimates about speed and direction prior to the collision.

Downward or sideward collapse of roof, windshield frame, and trunk lid may indicate roll-over. When a vehicle rolls over, it usually also slides, and the road surface scratches the top and sides, especially at corners as in Exhibit 44. The vehicle may also be rotating end for end while it rolls. If so, the direction of scratches in the sides and top may be at various angles. These signs can be very helpful in deciding how the vehicle moved. A vehicle which has rolled may not show ground scratches on all sides. Some

Exhibit 40. *Measurement of front wheel displacement by collision may be useful in reconstruction. Accurate damage measurement is difficult.*

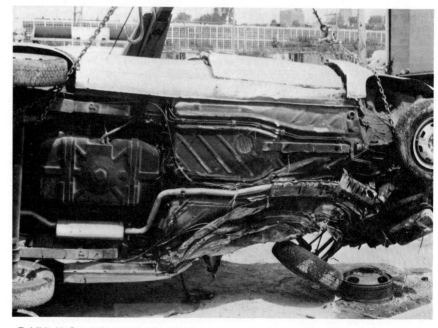

Exhibit 41. *Sometimes it is necessary to turn the vehicle on its side properly to examine damage underneath.*

Exhibit 42. *Recent road abrasion leaves metal vehicle parts bright and clean. Heavy rust suggests that the surface was abraded earlier.*

Exhibit 43. *Measurements of abraded parts must be made at right angles to striations if they are to be compared with dimensions of gouges or scrapes on the road surface.*

vehicles, especially broad cars with a low center of mass, flip if they hit a road-level obstacle while skidding sidewise and land on their tops or even on the opposite side without ground contact with areas in between. Wild guesses are often made as to how many times a vehicle rolled over. Unless the vehicle is rolling down a steep bank, it seldom turns over more than once. That would bring it to rest on its wheels. If it is of any significance, examination of the roadside may show how many times the vehicle revolved in rolling over, but it is usually very difficult to determine this from damage alone. Statements of occupants and witnesses are usually unreliable because they tend to exaggerate.

Grass pinched between the tire and rim as shown in Exhibit 45 indicates that the wheel moved violently sidewise on the shoulder — violently enough to pull the tire away from the rim momentarily. There is generally a broad furrow in the turf where this happened. It enables you to locate one position of the vehicle between collision or running off the road and the vehicle's final position. Tubeless tires may pull away from the rim enough to pinch and hold grass without losing air. Sometimes small pebbles may also be pinched between tire and rim.

Effect of Accident on Tires

The ways in which tires mark the road are explained in Topic 817. The effect of accidents on tires is also of some interest. We can learn from them something about how the acci-

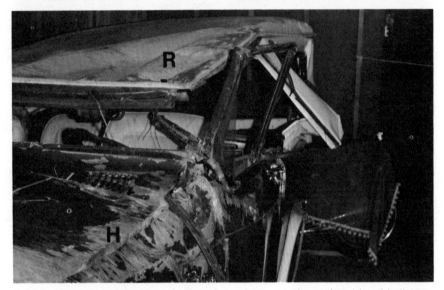

Exhibit 44. *Contact damage — dents and scrapes — on the roof and hood indicate ground contact, hence, rollover.*

dent happened. Accidents do surprisingly little harm to tires, because tires are tough and resilient. Some collisions which dent the rims and collapse body parts surrounding tires leave the tires themselves almost unmarked.

In some cases involving tiremarks, there may be a question about possible friction marks on the tires. Another question is whether a tire became disabled before the driver had difficulty, during loss of control, during impact, or after collision. If there is any question concerning whether a tire disablement contributed to an accident, obtain, mark for identification, and preserve the

tire. Then a more detailed examination is required.

At the scene of a traffic accident, note, if you can, whether any tire is disabled (flat). If so, record whether there is a visible hole in the tire and whether it is unseated from the rim. There is a place for such data on the *General Vehicle Examination form* (Exhibit 4).[16] Topic 825 describes *Tire Examinations Following Traffic Accidents*. Exhibit 46 shows one side of a form designed to record detailed observations of tire and rim damage: *Tire Examination Record*.[18]

Effect of Accident on Lamps

Routine data collection on lamps

20-24

is usually important only for night accidents or when there is some special question as to whether a lamp, such as a turn or brake signal, was operating. Observations and records then indicate only whether the lamp was actually lighted and if not, whether the glass was broken. These data can be recorded quickly at the scene on the *General Vehicle Examination* form (Exhibit 4).

Special studies of lamps can often reveal whether the lamp was on or off at the time of the crash. They require examination of the filaments to determine what effect the collision had on them. This can be done any time after the accident. If there seems likely to be a question of whether any lamp or set of lamps was lighted, get the lamps before they are lost. Remove them carefully, identify them completely, and store them securely, being sure not to break the glass and especially careful not to break the filament if the glass is already broken.

Topic 823 tells how to remove and package lamps for possible future study. It also explains how to examine lamps for ON or OFF at the time of the accident. A special form is available (Exhibit 47)[19] for recording details of a follow-up lamp examination after an accident.

Sources of Injury to Occupants

Who was driving may be an issue after a traffic accident, especially when an occupant is found outside after a collision. There are two approaches to this problem:

1. Consider what injuries you would expect each occupant to

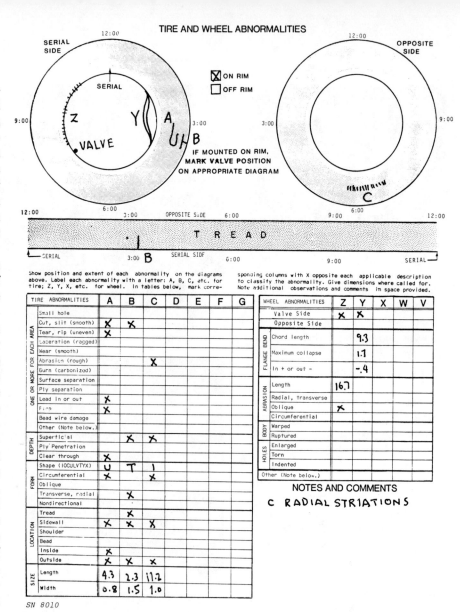

Show position and extent of each abnormality on the diagrams above. Label each abnormality with a letter: A, B, C, etc. for tire; Z, Y, X, etc. for wheel. In tables below, mark corresponding columns with X opposite each applicable description to classify the abnormality. Give dimensions where called for. Note additional observations and comments in space provided.

TIRE ABNORMALITIES		A	B	C	D	E	F	G
ONE OR MORE FOR EACH AREA	Small hole							
	Cut, slit (smooth)	X	X					
	Tear, rip (uneven)	X						
	Laceration (ragged)							
	Wear (smooth)							
	Abrasion (rough)			X				
	Burn (carbonized)							
	Surface separation							
	Ply separation							
	Lead in or out	X						
	Flap	X						
	Bead wire damage							
	Other (Note below.)							
DEPTH	Superficial		X	X				
	Ply Penetration							
	Clear through	X						
FORM	Shape (IOCULVTYX)	U	T	)				
	Circumferential	X		X				
	Oblique							
	Transverse, radial		X					
	Nondirectional							
LOCATION	Tread		X					
	Sidewall	X	X	X				
	Shoulder							
	Bead							
	Inside	X						
	Outside	X	X	X				
SIZE	Length	4.3	2.3	11.2				
	Width	0.8	1.5	1.0				

WHEEL ABNORMALITIES		Z	Y	X	W	V
	Valve Side	X	X			
	Opposite Side					
FLANGE BEND	Chord length		9.3			
	Maximum collapse		1.7			
	In + or out –		-.4			
ABRASION	Length	16.7				
	Radial, transverse					
	Oblique	X				
	Circumferential					
BODY	Warped					
	Ruptured					
HOLES	Enlarged					
	Torn					
	Indented					
	Other (Note below.)					

NOTES AND COMMENTS

C RADIAL STRIATIONS

SN 8010

Exhibit 46. *Report of examination of a tire after an accident to determine time and kind of disablement.*

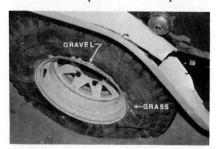

Exhibit 45. *Gravel and grass between the rim and tire indicate vehicle slid sidewise. If tire digs in deep enough, the vehicle may roll or flip.*

receive while being knocked about inside the vehicle during collision or by further movement to a final position afterward (qualitative dynamics). Then try to match these with actual injuries reported by whoever examined the injured occupant or the body afterward.

2. Examine the vehicle minutely — windshield, dashboard, roof, doors — for blood, hair, body tissue, bits of clothing, and any other signs of bodily injury. Then consider which occupants would have been positioned before collision so as to receive such injuries. For example, Exhibit 48 shows the lower rim of the steering wheel bent up and

backwards. This indicates the movement of the driver after first contact. This damage corresponded to injury to an occupant's pelvic area indicating that the person was in the driver's seat when the collision occurred.

In such an inquiry, do not forget that some injuries may have been received outside of the vehicle. Look for signs of injury there.

If both of the two approaches lead to similar inferences about who was driving, your conclusions are greatly strengthened.

If your observations and reasoning lead to satisfactory conclusions about who was driving, be sure to photograph signs of body contact in order

MOTOR-VEHICLE LAMP EXAMINATION RECORD

Show on diagram location of lamp, contact damage area, and direction of thrust

FORD   FRONT

ACCIDENT OR CASE No. **Q 8024**   LAMP NO. **2**

ON **IA 311** (Street or road)

AT **ALBION RD** (Intersection with or distance from)

IN (City) **MADISON** (County) (State) **IA**

HOUR of event **21:40**   DATE **5**   MONTH **9**   **1980**

IDENTIFICATION

OBTAINED FROM **L.A. BOYLE (IN PERSON)**   AT Place **TRAFFIC INST 405 CHURCH, EVANSTON**   BY Person **J.S. BAKER**

USED FOR **RIGHT HEADLIGHT**   DAMAGE IN HANDLING **NONE KNOWN**   DATE **13**   MONTH **3**   **1981**

EXAMINED By Person **J.S. BAKER**   AT Organization, City **TRAFFIC INST 405 CHURCH, EVANSTON IL**   DATE **20**   MONTH **3**   **1981**

☒ Lamp photo ☒ WHERE STORED **LAMP CABINET NO.2**   DATE **20**   MONTH **3**   **1981**
☐ Veh. photo ☐ HOW DISPOSED **433 WOODLAWN, GLENCOE, IL**

DESCRIPTION — See back of sheet for designations

TRADE NUMBER **6012 S**   MANUFACTURER **TUNG-SOL**

BASE **3-LUG**   BULB **PAR**   FILAMENTS **C6/C6**   VOLTS **12**   ☒ WATTS **50** / ☐ OHMS **40**

For each abnormality observed, mark the appropriate column X opposite the applicable description. Record estimated percentages where required. Notes may be added below.

Mark indications, if any, for each filament thus: X for definite, / for possible.

ABNORMALITIES OF SUPPORTS, GLASS, AND BASE	Single Small Low beam	Other, if not single		ABNORMALITIES OF FILAMENTS	Single Small Low beam	Other, if not single		INDICATIONS AND OPINIONS	Single Small Low beam	Other, if not single
Broken	A			Broken	X	X		Incandescent		X
Bent	X	X		$ missing or detached	⊙	⊙		Hot	X	
Rusted				Loose in bulb				Cold		
Pitted				End melted or tapered		X		Aged		
White deposit				End fractured	X			Burned out		X
Dirt or other deposit				Blackened		X		Impact shock	X	X
$ missing	90			Tinted or light colored	X					
Loose in base				White deposit						
Darkened				Moderately elongated						
White deposit				Stretched out, uncoiled	X	X				
Dirt or other deposit	C			Fused glass		X				
Damaged				Pitted				Off	✓✓	
Pitted				Other, show in note below	B	B		On		✓✓
Dirt or corrosion		X						Indeterminate		

For definite opinion, put two marks, ✓✓, on the applicable line in the column for the filament. If an opinion is not definite but only probable, put one mark, ✓, in the applicable line for the filament. If which one of two filaments was on is indeterminate, put one mark, ✓, in both the on line and the indeterminate line for each of the pair of filaments.

Additional descriptions and sketch of abnormalities may be put on the back of this sheet

Ⓐ **SHIELD DETACHED** Ⓑ **TANGLED TOGETHER**
Ⓒ **REFLECTOR PAINTED WHITE FOR PHOTO**
SEE OTHER SIDE FOR SKETCH

© TRAFFIC INSTITUTE, NORTHWESTERN UNIVERSITY   870:776 RV   STOCK NO. 1122

Exhibit 47. Report of examination of a lamp after an accident to determine whether it was off or on at the time of the collision.

to have a trustworthy record of exactly what you saw.

Signs of Pedestrian Injuries

Pedestrian injuries occur as a result of contact with the vehicle or some object such as a curb, another vehicle, or post. Get the exact point of contact by looking for dents, broken parts, scratches in paint, bits of

Exhibit 48. Note the position of the steering wheel. The bottom is bent up which indicates an upward force.

clothing, bloodstains, and such marks on the vehicle. For collisions that are

- *Head-on:* look for headlight and grill breakage, and check for slight impact dent in hood with signs of scraping or wiping (Exhibit 49).
- *Sideswipe:* look for brushmarks from button and clothes.
- *Backed into:* look for blood, torn clothing caught on bumper, trunk, lights, and number plate; usually low speed and faint marks.
- *Run-over:* bloodstains, bits of clothing, swipe marks on underside of running gear, motor, frame, and wheel.

These observations are especially important with respect to a vehicle suspected of having been in a hit-and-run accident.

There are also vehicle parts which are especially dangerous because of their design or location. Examine outside mirrors and door handles, especially in a sideswipe, because they project and may thus cause injury. Radiator ornaments, bumper brackets, and headlight frames of sharp or piercing design usually clearly show the effects of contact with pedestrians.

Additional Observations of Vehicle

In the preceding pages, vehicle damage and other after-accident conditions which are most useful in traffic-accident reconstruction have been described and how some of these may be interpreted has been explained. The significance of tire and lamp conditions is treated in separate special Topics. This leaves some vehicle matters of occasional or marginal interest — brakes for example, of which you might be expected to be aware.

When such particular conditions are the object of special follow-up study, you should have no difficulty in obtaining and recording desired information. But ordinarily you would not notice such things at the scene of an accident, and if you did happen to, you could not be expected to remember them in detail months or years afterward.

There are two things you can do to be better prepared to answer common questions about what you might have seen:

1. Take standard and other photographs of vehicle damage. These

Exhibit 49. Note the damage to the grill and headlight area at G and the damage to the hood at H caused by a collision with a pedestrian. Two contact damage areas in a car-pedestrian accident often occur.

Exhibit 50. *Damage to the interior of a vehicle can be useful in determining how bodies moved in the collision. Here dashboard has suffered.*

will often show details you never noticed when you were actually examining the vehicle. They can also describe conditions such as interior damage (Exhibit 50) far better than you could possibly do it with words.

2. Make the same routine observations and brief notes that you might make for a general vehicle examination at the scene of a serious traffic accident. These observations have already been described elsewhere.

As in many kinds of investigations, a form for such more or less routine observations is helpful. A simple one designed for this purpose has been mentioned in connection with tire and lamp examinations. It is illustrated in Exhibit 4.

The additional recommended routine observations relate to the following matters:

1. *Light switch,* whether on or off

at the time observed

2. *Speedometer reading,* Exhibit 51
3. *Brake pedal,* whether stuck tight or free to floor
4. *Steering wheel,* turning loosely or stuck tight
5. *Safety belt* for each occupant, in use, not in use, or indeterminate from your observations
6. *Load* in addition to occupants, cargo space nearly full, partly full, or nearly empty
7. *Fire,* none noted, causing damage, contributing to injury
8. *Alcoholic beverage containers,* none noted, some full, some opened.

Do not hesitate to add comments to your notes of any of the conditions that you find especially interesting or that you believe may be significant. These may include conditions not routinely looked for, for example, you might add a comment that some of

the damage to a door was from force used in opening it to get an occupant out.

Remember that a record of your observations does not imply any inference on your part as to how the conditions noted may have affected the events of the accident.

Vehicle Deficiences

One purpose of vehicle examination is to evaluate the condition of the vehicle before the accident.

At-scene investigation, brief and superficial as it usually must be, sometimes reveals vehicle deficiencies which were clearly not the result of the accident. These are conditions which a prudent vehicle owner would have remedied. Perhaps the most conspicuous example is tire wear to the bottom of the tread grooves. Other precollision deficiencies, such as loss of brake fluid, failure of electric power, or exhaustion of fuel supply may be discovered by an investigator at the scene as a result of a driver or someone else complaining of a vehicle malfunction.

Note your observations and any circumstances that led you to make them, but at this stage, and in the standard, official report, assiduously avoid expressing an opinion as the relationship of the condition to the accident. That can come later after more careful consideration and possibly further investigation.

Subsequent technical examination of the vehicle for preaccident deficiencies is almost always undertaken with specific questions in mind. It may require disassembly of the vehicle and making tests. Engineers and other specialists may have to be employed for the purpose.

The general procedure in postaccident investigations undertaken to evaluate preaccident vehicle conditions usually involves several of the following five steps but not necessarily all of them:

1. Statement of the problem (What information leads to the supposition that there was a

Exhibit 51. *Speedometer reading after an accident may or may not be significant. Usually it is zero. Take care in removing the speedometer from the vehicle for further inspection.*

Exhibit 52. *It is possible after an accident for a speedometer to read higher than the car's actual speed.*

vehicle deficiency? What part or parts of the vehicle are consequently suspect?)

2. Examination of parts in question and comparison with normal parts to determine exactly in what respects, if any, the questionable parts are abnormal at the time of examination

3. Statement of reasons for believing or not believing that any difference between the vehicle component involved, and a normal corresponding part, was the result of wear, corrosion, abuse (for example, overload), neglect (for example, of maintenance), heat, deviation from manufac-turing standards, road hazards, collision forces, or a combination of these

4. Determination of whether the deficient condition as found after the accident was clearly a result of the accident rather than a condition that existed prior to it

5. If the condition was not the result of the accident, consideration of whether the abnormal condition would produce the kind of vehicle behavior involved in the accident by itself in spite of what a driver might do.

Operating the vehicle or a similar vehicle with the deficient part or with a substitute part with like or greater deficiency may help to determine the effect of the deficient part on vehicle behavior and driver responses. Such tests may be difficult and may involve hazards. A sufficient solution to the problem is usually achieved without taking all these steps. Often the cost of going the whole route does not warrant the expense, and the task is abandoned as not worth the effort.

Deficient vehicle design is a still more complex matter involving, as it does, consideration of social responsibilities and economic realities quite beyond the scope of traffic-accident investigation.

6.SOURCES

Contributors

This topic was developed by the following persons:

J. Stannard Baker is a traffic engineer specializing in accident investigation. He was Director of Research and Development at The Northwestern University Traffic Institute from 1946 to 1971 and is a guest lecturer for The Traffic Institute.

Lynn B. Fricke is a traffic engineer specializing in traffic-accident investigation. He has been with The Traffic Institute since 1975. In 1981, he became the director of the Institute's Accident Investigation Division.

References

Superscript numbers in the preceding pages refer to the following publications:

1. *Traffic Records* (Highway Safety Program Standard 10), 1976, National Highway Traffic Safety Administration, U.S. Department of Transportation, Washington DC 20590 (2 pages)

2. *Vehicle Identification Number Systems* (SAE J272 Dec81), 1983, Society of Automotive Engineers, Warrendale PA 15096 (one page)

3. *Passenger Car Vehicle Identification Number System* (SAE J273 Dec81), 1983, Society of Automotive Engineers, Warrendale PA 15096 (one page)

4. *Vehicle Identification Numbers* (SAE J853 Dec81), 1983, Society of Automotive Engineers, Warrendale PA, 15096 (one page)

5. *Vehicle Identification Numbers-Motorcycles* (SAE J364a, 1983), Society of Automotive Engineers, Warrendale PA 15096 (one page)

6. *Truck Identification Terminology* (SAE J1229 Dec81), 1983, Society of Automotive Engineers, Warrendale PA 15096 (one page)

7. *Truck Vehicle Identification Numbers* (SAE J187), 1983, Society of Automotive Engineers, Warrendale PA 15096 (one page)

8. *Engine and Transmission Identification Numbers* (SAE J129 Dec81), 1983, Society of Automotive Engineers, Warrendale PA 15096 (one page)

9. *Passenger Car Identification Terminology* (SAE J218 Dec81), 1983, Society of Automotive Engineers, Warrendale PA 15096 (one page)

10. *Manual on Classification of Motor Vehicle Traffic Accidents* (ANSI D 16.1-1983), National Safety Council, Chicago IL 60611 (34 pages)

11. *Traffic Records*, (Vol. 10, Highway Safety Program Manual), 1972, National Highway Traffic Safety Administration, U.S. Department of Transportation, Washington D.C. 20590

12. *Vehicle Damage Scale for Traffic Accident Investigators*, 1984, National Safety Council, Chicago IL 60611 (29 pages)

13. *Collision Deformation Classification* (SAE J224 Mar80), 1983, Society of Automotive Engineers, Warrendale PA 15096 (11 pages)

14. *Advanced Training in Collision Reconstruction for the National Accident Sampling System* (Vol. 1 Reference Manual), 1983, Calspan Field Services, Buffalo NY 14225 (132 pages)

15. *CRASH3 User's Guide and Technical Manual*, National Highway Traffic Safety Administration, U.S. Department of Transportation, Washington, DC 29590 (219 pages)

16. *General Vehicle Examination* (SN 8084), 1985, Northwestern University Traffic Institute, Evanston IL 60204 (2 pages)

17. *Vehicle Damage Record* (SN 8085), 1985, Northwestern University Traffic Institute, Evanston IL 60604 (2 pages)

18. *Tire Examination Record* (SN 8010), 1973, Northwestern University Traffic Institute, Evanston IL 60204 (2 pages)

19. *Motor Vehicle-Lamp Examination Record* (SN 1122), 1972, Northwestern University Traffic Institute, Evanston IL 60204 (2 pages)

20. Bruderlein, Ad., *Die Mechanik des Verkehrsunfalls bei Kraftfahrzeugen*, 1941, (Translated by Haim Reizes as *The Mechanics of Vehicle Collisions*), 1973, Charles C. Thomas, Springfield IL 139 pages)

21. *Crash Measurements* (Vol. IV), Allen Corporation of America, Alexandria, VA 22314 (140 pages)

22. *Collision Deformation Classification*, 1981, Calspan Field Services, Buffalo, NY 14225 (269 pages)

Exhibits

The following are the sources of photographs, diagrams, charts, tables, and forms that are used in this topic as exhibits:

Ayock, Thad, Traffic Institute, Evanston IL
Photo: 21

Baker, J. Stannard, Glencoe IL
Photos: 7, 12, 14, 25, 27, 29, 42, 43
Diagrams: 15, 34
Forms: 4, 6, 46, 47

Bartley, Ronald, Police Department, Lake County IN
Photos: 16, 17

Carp's Studio, Billings MT
Photo: 8

Cooper, Gary W., Traffic Institute, Evanston IL
Photos: 5, 10, 11, 22, 23, 28, 40

Cusker, Thomas L., Villa Park IL
Photo: 33

Eaves, James B., Arizona Highway Patrol, Phoenix AZ
Photo: 24

Fricke, Lynn B., Traffic Institute, Evanston IL
Photos: 8, 9, 13, 18, 19, 20, 30, 31, 32, 41, 44, 45, 50, 51, 52
Form: 6

National Highway Traffic Safety Administration, Washington, D.C.
Diagrams: 35, 36, 37, 38, 39

Sheriff's Department, Cook County IL
Photo: 49

Society of Automotive Engineers, Warrendale PA
Chart: 1
Table: 2

Unknown
Photos: 26, 48
Diagram: 3

LAMP EXAMINATION FOR ON OR OFF IN TRAFFIC ACCIDENTS

Topic 823 of the *Traffic-Accident Investigation Manual*

by
J. Stannard Baker,
Thad L. Aycock
and
Thomas Lindquist

NORTHWESTERN UNIVERSITY TRAFFIC INSTITUTE

PUBLICATION HISTORY

1964 *Examination of Automobile Lamps for Traffic-accident Investigation*
(Unpublished research report)

1972 *Lamp Examination for ON or OFF in Traffic Accidents* (PN 802)
Reprinted 1973, 1974, 1975, 1976

1977 Revised. Reprinted 1978, 1979, 1980

1981 Revised. Reprinted 1982

1985 Revised

LAMP EXAMINATION FOR ON OR OFF IN TRAFFIC ACCIDENTS

1. CIRCUMSTANCES WARRANTING LAMP EXAMINATION

The most common circumstance calling for examination of lamps to determine, if possible, whether they were on or off at the time of motor vehicle crash occurs when a participant or some other witness says that one of the vehicles lacked lights. The statement may refer to headlights at night or signal lights by day or night. Sometimes such a statement is quite true; sometimes the person making the statement is lying for one reason or another. But usually, whoever makes the statement does not remember having seen lights, either because he took no note at the time or because he was looking elsewhere. So he *infers* that the lights in question were off. In any event, such a statement about lamps warrants checking by examination of the lamps.

Even when no statements are made with respect to whether lamps are operating, numerous occasions arise where lamp examination might develop useful information.

Opposite-direction collision at night — or whenever headlights might be helpful — sometimes involve situations that suggest examination to determine whether lamps were on or off. Three examples will illustrate this.

First, a fatal, opposite-direction collision occurred when one of the two cars involved was overtaking and passing a third. Why did the approaching car not slow down to let the overtaking car complete its pass? Examination showed the headlamps of the overtaking car were not on. The approaching driver did not see the dark overtaking car while facing lights of the overtaken car.

Second, two cars approaching from opposite directions disastrously collided, with slight overlap, on a straight, narrow road, Examination showed the left headlamp of one had burned out. The driver was probably unaware that it was out; certainly an unlighted left headlamp would make it difficult for an on-coming driver to judge close clearance accurately.

Third, at a road junction or access driveway, a left-turning car collided with an opposite-direction, straight-through car. Was the driver of the left-turning car signalling the turn as he is supposed to? Examination of the turn signal lamp showed it was broken while the flashing lamp was on.

In a surprising number of night collisions between motorcycles and automobiles, especially automobiles turning left into driveways, automobile occupants claim that the motorcycle showed no headlight. In such cases, enough of the headlamp is usually available to show, by the effect of the collision on the lamp, whether it was actually on or off at the time.

Same-direction accidents also often present circumstances in which lamp examination may help explain what happened. In such collisions, tail lights present problems in a variety of situations.

One common situation is a nighttime, rear-end collision on a high-speed road. Then two questions may arise: 1) did the overtaken, slower vehicle have lighted tail lights, and 2) was the overtaken vehicle being slowed unexpectedly by braking. In either case, examining damaged lamps may provide the answer.

Another situation occurred when the car ahead slowed for a turn at a road junction or access driveway. Then the question is whether a left turn was properly signalled. This is a difficult and often indeterminate problem in lamp examination because the same filament in a lamp usually indicates both braking (steady light) or turning (flashing light).

A parked or stopped car involved in a night-time collision immediately raises the question as to what, if any, lights were on. Especially in collisions on freeways, one wants to know whether emergency, flashing, position (corner) lights were operating.

Angle collisions (right-of-way) at night are most likely to produce statements by participants and other witnesses that lights were off. But even if no statement is made, circumstances often warrant lamp examination. The usual junction collision, especially where there are traffic signals or other control devices, is unlikely to be a situation where an unlighted lamp was a factor; but some other special angle-collisions are.

Sometimes the question rises as to whether side-marker and other lights on a trailer were functioning. The tractor had passed the intersection, and the driver of the other vehicle did not realize that the tractor was followed by a long trailer. If trailer lamps are damaged by collision it may be possible to tell whether they were on or off.

A much more common night-time angle collision warranting lamp examination occurs when a vehicle enters a road from an access driveway (private drive, or especially, a service station). Drivers who have started from a lighted area sometimes fail to switch on lights until they are in traffic on the roadway entered. It is useful to learn whether lights were on or off from examination of lamps of the vehicle involved.

Lone-vehicle accidents sometimes give rise to driver claims about lights which can be confirmed or denied by lamp examination. For example, a driver claimed he ran off the road because his headlamps suddenly failed. Or he may claim to have been blinded by the lights on an oncoming car.

Then, if his own damaged lamps prove that he had high beams operating, the inference is warranted that he was probably not meeting another vehicle.

Hit-and-run investigations may make use of lamp examinations. For example, a driver suspected in a night-time, hit-and-run collision claims the damage to his car was done in a previous day-time accident. Examination of damaged lamps show that they were on at the time of collision. The conclusion is that the damage was done in a night-time, hit-and-run accident, not an earlier day-light crash. Or, if the hit-and-run accident occurs by day, but is claimed to have occurred at night, the claim can be discounted if the damaged lamp is found not to have been on.

Fleeing pursuit. A suspected driver in a night-time accident may claim that he was not fleeing from the scene of a crime or attempting to escape police pursuit. If lamp examination shows that lights were off, his statement that he was not fleeing becomes most unconvincing.

In other circumstances than those suggested here, it may be useful or helpful to examine motor vehicle lamps or lamps on other vehicles, such as bicycles and farm machinery, involved in collisions.

But do not suppose that a positive determination of whether the lamp was on or off can always be made. Like many other kinds of investigation, lamp examination may often be fruitless, but when it is successful, the results can be so rewarding that all the unsuccessful attempts are more than paid for.

There is a report[3] that traffic signals damaged in accidents have been examined to determine, by looking at lamp filaments, which street had the green light and which the red. This is a possibility to keep in mind when appropriate circumstances arise.

2. THE NORMAL LAMP

If a lamp is normal after an accident, it shows no signs of having been lighted or unlighted at the time of the

crash. Whether it was on or off is then indeterminate from examining the lamp alone.

Determination of Normal Appearance

Exhibit 1 summarizes the normal appearance of lamps.

To facilitate the reader's ability to conduct lamp examination and determine whether the bulb is normal or not, a detailed description of appearance and operation follow.

Lamp Descriptions

Lamps for motor vehicles are described by four classifications:
1. Filament configuration, Exhibit 103
2. Base arrangement, Exhibit 104
3. Bulb shape and diameter, Exhibit 105
4. Volts and watts or amperes

Lamps bearing the same "trade number" made by different manufacturers are interchangeable, although not necessarily identical. Lamps are nearly always marked with the trade number and a name, abbreviation, or symbol to identify the manufacturer. Foreign lamps usually do not carry American trade numbers. Locations of trade numbers on lamps are shown in Exhibits 2, 6, and 99. Trade numbers and corresponding descriptions of lamps commonly used in motor vehicles are listed in Exhibit 102.

Filaments are made from tungsten wire which is usually formed into a uniform coil similar to a tiny coil spring (Exhibit 3). A filament is smooth, regular, and has a silver luster. The filament may show fine straight lengthwise scratches or "draw" lines (Exhibit 4). The ends of the filament are clamped or crimped to a much larger wire, the filament support, made of steel.

In most lamps, the filament coil goes straight across from one support to the other, but in small lamps it may be arched or looped, sometimes with a steel wire support in the middle to keep a thin filament in place (Exhibit 103). Arched filaments sometimes look like filaments distorted by impact shock. The difference is described in Exhibits 54 and 59.

Two-filament lamps are used on most motor vehicles. The double filament makes the lamp serve two purposes, most commonly a tail light and a brake or turn signal light.

Headlamps usually have one filament for high beam and one for low beam. When the lamp is positioned as in the vehicle, the upper filament projects the lower beam and the lower filament projects the upper beam (Exhibit 6). Both filaments are nearly the same size and shape: they are about equally bright when lighted. In most vehicles only one filament is in use at any time.

In front of the upper (low beam) filament is a metal hood (shade or shield) which keeps upward light from the low beam from reaching the lens (Exhibits 6 and 8). This hood reduces "back-dazzle" reflected from moisture droplets in the air ahead of the vehicle and so makes the low beam more useful in fog, rain, or snow.

Exhibit 107 shows which terminal lug (contact) connects to the low beam and which to the high beam filament.

Another type of headlamp is in general use in many parts of the world. It is not a sealed beam lamp in which the reflector and lens form a large bulb in which the filaments are located. In these "bilux" or "duplo" lamps there is a separate bulb which can be removed from the reflector and lens for replacement. These lamps also differ in the arrangement of the filaments: the low beam filament is ahead of the high beam filament rather than above it and instead of a shield above and ahead of the low beam filament, there is a reflecting cup below the low beam filament. This arrangement is shown by a diagram in Exhibit 7 and is pictured in Exhibit 9. The same principles apply in examining the fore-and-aft filaments of headlamps as apply in examining filaments in sealed beam lamps. The big exposed bulbs of sealed beam lamps are more likely to be broken in

Exhibit 1.

CHARACTERISTICS OF NORMAL LAMPS

NEW	Bright luster of filament Evenly spaced coils Longitudinal draw lines Undarkened glass Bright base	**Exhibits** **3, 4, 12**
AGED	Bright luster of filament Evenly spaced coils Rough, pitted filament Possible downward sag Possible darkened glass Possible dirty base	**Exhibits** **5, 12, 56**
BURNED OUT	Bright luster of filament Parted filament Open circuit Rounded or ball ends Possible darkened glass	**Exhibits** **5, 12, 13**

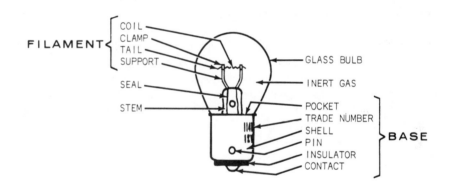

Exhibit 2. *Typical small lamp and its parts (Trade No. 1141, Bulb S8, Filament C6, Base SC Bay, Volts 12).*

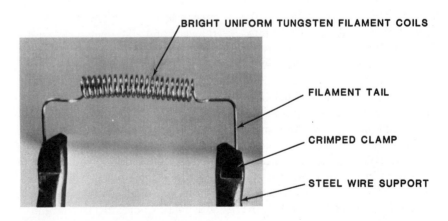

Exhibit 3. *Normal, new, lamp filament.*

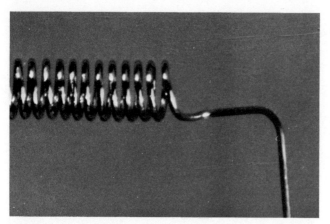

Exhibit 4. New filament is bright and may show longitudinal striations or "draw" lines.

Exhibit 5. After burning 1500 hours a filament looked like this, bright but showing surface pitting.

crashes than the smaller protected bulbs of European design. Hence the sealed beam lamps are more likely to show significant abnormalities resulting from collisions.

Dual purpose lamps also have two filaments in the same bulb. They are principally used in two places: 1) in front, where one filament is for a parking light or to delineate position and the other is for turn signal indication or emergency flasher; and 2) in the rear where one filament is the tail light and the other a brake signal, turn indicator and emergency flasher.

The smaller filament, usually farther from the base, is for the rear or parking light. The larger filament is for the signal light. Exhibit 106 shows which filament is connected to which terminal in the base.

Halogen lamps are sometimes called quartz-iodide lamps, halogen regenerative cycle lamps, or halide lamps. They became available for motor vehicle headlamp use in the United States in 1978 after the maximum permissable candela was increased. Halogen lamps have several advantages: they require only about half the power for the same light output; they are considerably smaller and lighter; and they maintain their original brightness much longer. For headlamp use, the small halogen capsule is enclosed in a sealed reflector and lens combination in either round or rectangular form (Exhibit 10). These are interchangeable with convention-

al sealed beam headlamps, especially with the four-lamp system. A halogen lamp is shown separate from reflector and lens in Exhibit 11.

Principle of Operation

Nearly all automobile lamps are incandescent electric lamps. When examining them, it is helpful to understand how they work.

A wire carrying an electric current produces heat. If the current is great enough for the size of the wire (filament), the heat will raise the wire's temperature to incandescence or white heat. The wire then produces light. Many metals lose strength and some melt before they are hot enough to produce light. So, incandescent filaments are made of metal which holds its shape at incandescent temperatures. Tungsten is the metal used.

At moderate temperatures, tungsten and most other metals do not combine (react) with oxygen in the air; but tungsten and other metals do oxidize rapidly in air at incandescent temperatures. To prevent such oxidation the filament is enclosed in a glass bulb (globe or envelope) and the air is removed and replaced with nitrogen or another inert gas that will not oxidize the filament. In ordinary lamps, the pressure of this gas is slightly less than that of the atmosphere (a partial vacuum); in halogen lamps, the pressure is 4 to 8 times that of the atmosphere.[7]

Wires to support the filament and carry electricity to it are sealed where they go through the glass to prevent gas leakage. They are attached to contacts at the lamp base to connect with a source of electricity to heat the filament and light the lamp (Exhibit 2).

When heated to incandescence, tungsten gradually evaporates or "boils off" weakening the filament. In ordinary lamps, this vaporized metal is deposited on the glass bulb. The deposit darkens the glass as the lamp ages, especially in small lamps. The darkened glass severely limits the light output.

Halogen lamps prevent virtually all glass blackening. A small amount of a halogen, usually iodine, but sometimes bromine or chlorine, is added to the gas in the lamp. In the cooler part of the lamp, near the glass, the tungsten particles which boil off from the incandescent filament combine chemically with the halogen vapor instead of depositing on the glass. Circulation of the gas in the lamp brings the tungsten-halogen compound to the filament where the much greater heat breaks the compound into atoms. The tungsten is then redeposited on the filament and the halogen is carried back to the bulb wall where it again combines with evaporated tungsten. Thus the tungsten is continually and automatically recycled.

To make the halogen cycle work, the temperature at the glass must be more than 250° C. This means two things: 1) the glass must be close to the filament, requiring a small bulb; and 2) the glass must not soften at temperatures which may exceed 500° C. Consequently, halogen lamps must be made of quartz or heat resistant glass. Furthermore, because the gas is pressurized, halogen lamps tend to explode when they are broken or even cracked or scratched.

If the glass breaks, air quickly reaches the filament and if hot, the filament begins to oxidize. White tungsten oxide escaping from the hot filament may be deposited on other nearby filaments, supports, and glass. The incandescent filament quickly develops a hot spot where oxidation has weakened it most, melts there, forms an arc, and burns out, turning black in the process.

Sealed beam lamps. In headlamps, it is important that the light be projected ahead in the most useful pattern for road illumination. The rearward light from the filament is therefore reflected forward by a curved mirror, the silvered rear part of the lamp. Further modification of the light distribution is obtained by a specially designed lens. Unless the silvered surface is carefully protected, it becomes dull in use. To prevent this, reflector and lens are hermetically sealed together for the life of the lamp; hence the name "sealed beam." In ordinary sealed beam headlamps, the glass lens and reflector combination actually forms the envelope of the lamp. In halogen sealed beam lamps, and others with smaller inner bulbs, the sealing of reflector and lens serves only to protect the silvered surface which, in these lamps, may be made of metal. In halogen lamps, there is a separate small bulb inside the lamp.

Aged Lamps

As explained earlier, lamps normally change appearance a little as they grow old with use.

Bulb. The first sign of age is usually darkening of the bulb by metal from the filament (Exhibit 12). This is most conspicuous in very small bulbs and imperceptible in large bulbs

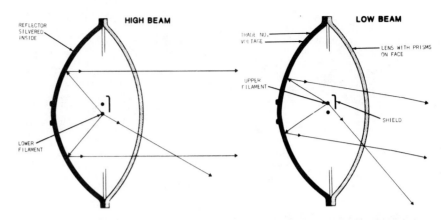

Exhibit 6. *Sealed beam headlamps are arranged so that light from the centered lower filament gives the high beam and that from the off-center upper filament gives the low beam. Part of the light from both filaments goes directly through the lens and part is reflected from the parabolic mirror. A shield or hood intercepts upward "stray" light from the low beam filament. This reduces "back dazzle" reflected from moisture droplets and so makes it easier to see ahead in fog, rain, and snow.*

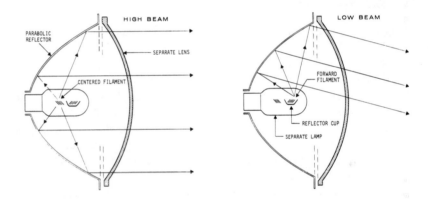

Exhibit 7. *Some foreign headlamps are arranged so that light from the centered rear filament gives the high beam and that from the off-center forward filament gives the low beam. Most of the light from both filaments is reflected through the lens by the parabolic mirror. A small cup or reflector under the forward low beam filament redirects some light upward to reduce "back dazzle" in fog. Bulb may be separate from reflector and lens. The reflector is usually metal.*

such as sealed beam headlamps.

The filament begins to show age by roughening and pitting, which can be seen with a magnifier (Exhibit 5).

Age sag sometimes apears in long, thin filaments used horizontally for low-intensity lamps. The filament gradually sags downward and stretches out uniformly a little (Exhibit 56). Age sag is intensified in filaments subject to jolting in normal use. Not all filaments sag before they burn out.

Lamp Failure

Eventually every lamp fails to func-

tion. Not counting accidental bulb breakage, filament failure occurs in one of two ways: 1) burnout or 2) brittle breakage.

Burnout occurs when tungsten leaving the filament by evaporation produces pitting to such an extent that the filament is thinner and weaker at certain places. These narrower spots have greater electrical resistance and current through the filament makes them hotter. The increased heat accentuates the loss of material and still further increases heating at these weakened points. When the filament temperature at the narrowest point

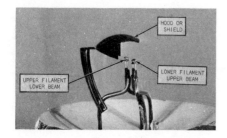

Exhibit 8. *Arrangement of filaments and supports in a sealed beam headlamp. Shield reduces "back dazzle" in fog, rain and snow.*

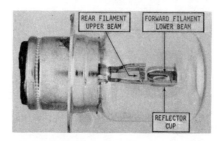

Exhibit 9. *A European headlamp which is separate from the lens and reflector. A cup under forward filament reflects low beam into parabolic reflector.*

Other Notes

Some normal features of lamps may puzzle investigators who examine them for abnormalities resulting from accidents.

A third filament in a headlamp will sometimes be found. It is a thin filament connected across two filament supports near the base. It is to give a glow in the lamp if the main filament burns out. It remains lighted whenever the lamp is turned on, but has a longer life than the large filaments. It is called a safety filament. See Exhibit 17.

Exhibit 10. *Small single-filament halogen lamp capsule inside a reflector and lens.*

Exhibit 11. *Halogen lamp capsule may be separate and removable from reflector*

Many small lamps, such as those used for tail and signal lights, have a daub of white or drab substance on a filament support or stem (Exhibit 18). This is getter, a chemical that gets rid of oxygen remaining in the bulb. Do not mistake this for tungsten oxide from a filament incandescent after glass is broken. Its purpose is to suppress filament oxidation in a new lamp.

Sometimes a sealed beam lamp will show a faint white clouding at the top of the lens and reflector. This is tungsten oxide resulting from manufacturing processes and not due to air reaching an incandescent filament when the glass is broken.

Heavy duty lamps are made to last longer and resist vibration better. They are commonly used on trucks. For the most part they do not look any different than ordinary lamps designed for the same service. Some sealed beam heavy duty lamps have a ceramic reinforcement on the lamp

reaches the melting point of tungsten, the filament parts at that point. An electric arc forms across the gap further increasing the heat and loss of material on either side of the gap. The arc flares up brightly for an instant until the gap widens enough to interrupt the current flow. Then the lamp has burned out.

Where the filament separates, the ends of the filament may be tapered or necked as in Exhibit 13. Sometimes little balls or beads of melted tungsten form on the ends of the filament as in Exhibit 13.

Brittle fracture occurs with vibration or impact in a cold filament. When it heats to incandescence, a filament gradually regains a crystalline structure which was modified to permit drawing the tungsten into fine wire for the filament. Such recrystallization makes the filament brittle when it is cold, especially in parts of the filament which are hottest in use. Vibration or impact may stress the filament where it has recrystalized the most, where the filament has been weakened by loss of metal, and where the vibration or impact forces are

greatest. If sufficient, this stress will break a cold filament. The break often occurs in the first turn or two of the filament coil. Lamps on trucks and motorcycles are unusually subject to vibration and so are likely to fail by fracture.

Because fracture occurs mainly when the lamp is off, no arc is formed and no melting occurs. The ends of the filament break off square, or with sharp projections as in Exhibit 14.

The filament may break in two places so that part of it is loose in the bulb. Knocking about in the lamp may break it into more pieces as illustrated in Exhibit 15. Sometimes there may be many pieces, some of which may be less than a single coil (Exhibit 16).

Sometimes, free ends of a filament move about enough with jolting to make contact again or even make contact with an adjacent filament. If the lamp switch is on when this occurs, electricity flows and an arc may be formed. Sometimes the filament melts and fuses together where contact occurs, thereby permitting the filament to become incandescent for a while.

Exhibit 12. *Lamp with glass darkened by aging, left, compared to new lamp, right. Small lamps show much more age darkening than large ones.*

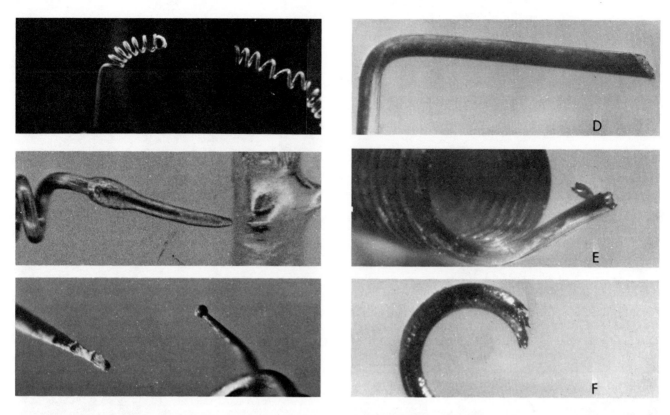

Exhibit 13. *Three examples of burned out filaments. Arc formed when filament separates produces intense heat which melts filament. If glass is unbroken, filament remains bright and full. If glass breaks, filament wastes away by oxidizing. Separated ends may be tapered.*

Exhibit 14. *Three examples of fractured filament broken by shock or vibration, especially when repeated heating has recrystalized the tungsten. Fracture indicates filament was cold at this point. Fractured filament nearly always means that the lamp was off when the filament broke.*

supports to dampen vibration (Exhibit 19).

In some lamps, especially those used for such purposes as instrument illumination, there may be noticeable variation in filament configuration among new lamps of the same trade number. Be careful not to confuse such variation with accident-induced deformation.

Some foreign lamps are interchangeable with U.S.A. lamps but do not have the same trade numbers.

If there is any question about what the lamp would look like if it had not been in an accident, examine a new lamp of the same kind. For very small lamps, look at several new ones because small lamps may vary in manufacture.

Indexing is required for double filament lamps to be sure that each filament is connected to the proper circuit. Indexing is accomplished by arranging the base so that the lamp can be inserted in its socket or con-

nector in only the correct way. Exhibit 107 shows the arrangement of connector lugs on a 2-filament sealed beam lamp and the high and low pins which keep 2-filament indicator and signal lamps from being put in the socket in the wrong way.

3. LAMP MARKINGS

Nearly all electric lamps are marked in one way or another to indicate how they may be used.

Trade Number

The most common marking on an automobile lamp is the trade number. Lamps with the same trade number are interchangeable, even if made by different manufacturers. Thus, the trade number represents the size, shape, contact arrangement, voltage, wattage, filament configuration and other characteristics. You buy a new lamp with the same trade number as

the one being replaced.

Most of the digits in the trade number have no special meaning. You have to look up the trade number in a catalog to learn what the lamp is like. For example, the most common trade number for automobile lamps is probably 1157. It is a 6-volt, 2-filament lamp with indexed bayonet base. It is used for rear tail and signal lamps and for front parking and turn signal lights.

A prefix H for a headlamp denotes a halogen-cycle lamp. A suffix A stands for amber and IF for inside frosted. Trade numbers are usually printed on the base of small lamps (Exhibit 2) and on the back of a headlamp reflector (Exhibit 6).

Not all lamps show trade numbers. Foreign lamps may not have the same trade numbers as U.S. lamps

Exhibit 102 is a list of common motor-vehicle lamps arranged by trade number.

Exhibit 15. *Recrystalization may make filament so brittle that it breaks into pieces which may be loose in the bulb. These show filament was cold when filament broke from impact or vibration.*

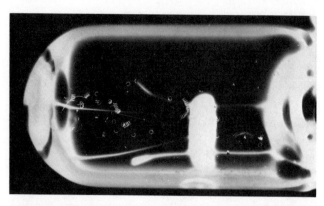

Exhibit 16. *Shadowgraph of filament broken into many little pieces even after it had come loose from supports. If glass breaks, these pieces are usually lost.*

Exhibit 17. *A small third filament, indicated by arrows, is sometimes found in headlamps. It is a safety feature which continues to glow after the main filament burns out.*

Exhibit 18. *A daub of material on filament supports or stem is normal for small lamps. It absorbs oxygen in the lamp. If it is white, it is sometimes mistaken for burnout oxide.*

Lens Markings

Regular sealed beam headlight lenses have the following designations embossed on the front:[1]

1. The words "SEALED BEAM"
2. Manufacturer's name or trademark
3. A designator number.

The designator is at the top of the lens (Exhibit 20). The first digit, a number, designates the type:

1. High beam filament only and two contact lugs.
2. High and low beam filaments and three contact lugs.

The following digits, A and B, denote rectangular lamps.

There may be other small numbers on the lens. They are significant only to the manufacturer.

Separate lenses for auxiliary front and rear lamps are usually plastic and colored red or yellow. They may cover more than one lamp.

Such lenses usually have small letters visible from outside embossed on them.[2] These are manufacturer's identification markings:

1. SAE (Society of Automotive Engineers) specification
2. One or more letters indicating the functions of the light according to SAE specifications
3. Last two digits of the year in which the specification was established
4. Name of manufacturer
5. Manufacturer's model number.

For example, the identification might be

SAE AIST 75
SPARKLE 205

The first line means that the lens and fixtures meet SAE lighting specifications A, I, S, and T which were promulagated in 1975. The second line means that the device was Model 205 of the Sparkle Corporation. Here A is the specification for reflex reflectors, I is for turn signal lamps, S is for stop lamps, and T is for tail lamps.

Voltage Markings

Most lamps are marked for voltage. This is printed on the back of the reflector of headlamps and on the base of many other lamps. Some very small lamps show voltage by color of a small bead on the filament supports, white for 12 volts.

The trade number also represents voltage, although voltage is not coded as part of the number.

Nearly all motor-vehicles now have 12-volt lamps, but there are a few 6-volt and 24-volt systems.

Power

Sometimes the amperage of the lamp or the wattage is also marked on the lamp. Volts times amperes gives watts, which is the power rating of the lamp.

The trade number also represents power requirements.

Identification

Markings on a lamp do not identify it the way a vehicle identification number (VIN) identifies a motor vehicle or a license number identifies a driver.

Whoever handles a lamp from a vehicle involved in an accident must, therefore, identify it in his own way as described later in this topic.

4. AT-SCENE OBSERVATIONS

Circumstances

Limited time, facilities, and other circumstances make it impractical to examine motor-vehicle lamps properly at the scene of an accident. But a record of lamp observations at the scene is important when

1. Anyone at the scene says or even suggests that a vehicle lacked a required light. This is common when a left turning vehicle is struck by an oncomming motorcycle.
2. A signal should have been given for slowing or turning.
3. There is a question as to whether

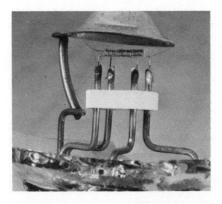

Exhibit 19. A ceramic collar around filament supports on heavy-duty headlamps prevents vibration which might cause brittle filament to fracture.

a vehicle was braking when struck in the rear by a following vehicle in traffic.
4. Other circumstances involving lights occur to the investigator.

Leave Lamps Alone

Never switch on lamps at the scene of an accident to see if they work! If any lamp has been broken at the scene of an accident, switching it on may burn it out and so destroy signs of whether the lamp was on or off.

Avoid removing lamps at the scene. Later removal is better because questions of whether it is legally permissible can be settled first and because, with proper tools, removal can be accomplished with less chance of losing or damaging important evidence.

Observations

At the scene of a serious accident, a number of simple observations can be quickly made. They may result in valuable information:

- Note which lamps were on
- Note which lamps were broken
- Observe whether the lamp switch was on or off
- Locate the contact damage areas on the vehicle so that possible impact shock to lamps may be evaluated.

Of course these observations represent what you see when you examine the vehicle. Do not try to report what circumstances might have been when the accident situation stabilized.

Exhibit 20. A marking on the lens of a sealed beam lamp indicates the top of the lamp and whether the lamp has one or two filaments.

Records

Except in unusual circumstances, you cannot be expected to remember, after a few days, exactly the condition of each lamp when you looked at it. Therefore, your observations will not be worth much unless you make a record of them at the time you make them.

Your notes can be on a form for general vehicle examination at the scene (Exhibit 21). The form provides for most of the information as simple check marks.

Lacking a form, a little list of the principal lamps on the vehicle will do. Indicate whether each lamp was on or broken (Exhibit 22).

Any record must be identified with the vehicle and the accident. Also record who made the inspection and how long after the accident it was done.

It is often possible to determine, right at the scene of an accident, whether a lamp was on or off at the time of the crash; but it is best not to record this opinion on your notes of observations. If the record is kept strictly factual, it will not have to be modified if subsequent more technical examination changes your opinion.

5. LAMP ABNORMALITIES RESULTING FROM ACCIDENTS

An automobile collision may have no effect on a lamp or the lamp may

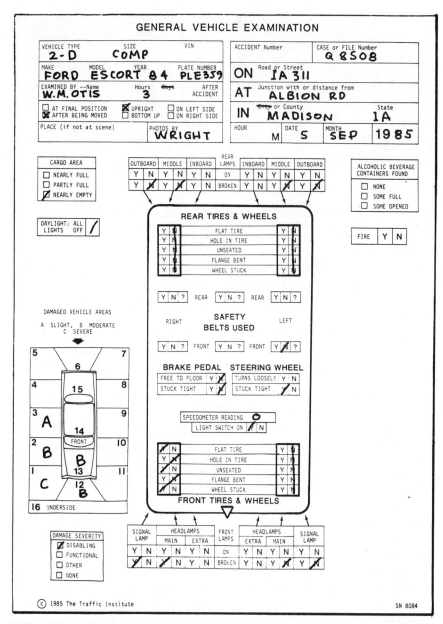

Exhibit 21. *Notes of lamp examination at the scene are easily made on a form for General Vehicle examination. The form includes identification of the accident, the vehicle, and the observer.*

be destroyed so that significant parts of it cannot be found. In either case, whether the lamp was on or off cannot be determined by lamp examination.

But between these two extremes, the crash may affect the lamp in such a way as to indicate whether a filament was incandescent. That can lead to a conclusion as to whether the lamp was on or off.

Procedures for determining whether a halogen lamp was on or off after a crash are essentially the same as for other tungsten-filament incandescent lamps. Being small and strong, halogen lamps are less likely to be broken in collisions and so are less likely to indicate on or off. If a halogen lamp is unbroken, use great care in removing it. Halogen lamps are pressurized and may shatter if scratched. When handling the lamps, use protective eye glasses and gloves.

Principles Involved

The effect of a crash on a filament is quite different when the filament is incandescent and when it is cold. That fact gives two bases for judging whether the lamp was on or off. First, if the glass breaks and air replaces nitrogen surrounding the filament, oxygen in the air has no effect on a cold filament but speedily blackens an incandescent one. Second, collision shock may sharply fracture a cold, brittle filament but stretch out and uncoil an incandescent filament which is quite ductile.

In addition to these two main effects there are a number of other phenomena which also indicate the condition of a filament at the time of a crash and so help to determine whether the light was on or off.

However, to detect these varied effects of a crash, especially when they are marginal or fragmentary, is sometimes difficult and uncertain.

Exhibit 23 summarizes the abnormalities which may indicate whether a filament was incandescent at the time of a collision. These abnormalities will now be described in some detail.

Filament Oxidation

Oxidation occurs only when glass is broken to let air reach the filament. If the bulb is broken wide open, air rushes in and oxidation occurs very rapidly. If the glass is only cracked, air may enter very slowly and oxidation may be gradual and the filament may cool before oxidation has proceeded far. Filament oxidation is sometimes called "hot break."

Blackened filament, heavy oxidation, indicates that filament was incandescent after the glass broke. See Exhibit 24. The filament itself may be intact or broken and it may or may not be deformed.

If the electric circuit is opened by the crash or otherwise (for example, by flashing operation) the filament cools gradually. Then, if the glass is broken within a fraction of a second after current stops flowing, oxidation will still take place. A large filament naturally stays hot longer than a small

LAMPS AT SCENE   5 SEP. 1985
IA 311 @ ALBION RD. MADISON CO. FORD
1. RF Signal, CD Area, All gone
2. RF Head, CD Area, Broken, Fil broken, tangled
3. RF Side, CD Area, OFF, Lens OK
4. LF Head, CD Area, OFF, Unbroken
5. LF Signal, CD Area, OFF, Lens broken, Lamp OK
6. LF Side. OFF, Lens OK
SWITCH ON   W.M. Otis

Exhibit 22. *Example of notes made for at-scene vehicle lamp examination.*

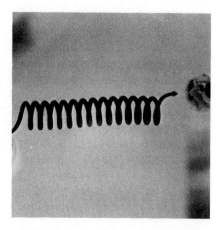

Exhibit 24. *Blackening indicates that filament was incandescent after glass was broken.*

Exhibit 23.

LAMP EXAMINATION AFTER COLLISION

		INDICATIONS → ABNORMALITIES OBSERVED ↓	FILAMENT INCANDESCENT	OTHER FILAMENT INCANDESCENT	FILAMENT HOT BUT NOT INCANDESCENT	AT LEAST ONE FILAMENT INCANDESCENT	FILAMENT COLD	FILAMENT BURNED OUT	LAMP ENERGIZED POWER ON
GLASS BROKEN	FILAMENT COLOR	BLACKENED (Exhibits 24,87)	X			X			X
		TINTED (Exhibit 25)		/	X	X			X
		BRIGHT (Exhibits 3,4,7,11,26)					X		
	WHITE OXIDE	ON GLASS, SUPPORTS, STEM (Exhibits 27,28,29)				X			X
		ON FILAMENT ITSELF (Exhibit 30)		X		X			X
		FUSED GLASS ON FILAMENT (Exhibits 34,35)	X			X			X
		SUPPORT OR BASE BURNED, MELTED, PITTED (Exhibits 32,49,51)				/			X
GLASS BROKEN OR UNBROKEN	FILAMENT BROKEN OR UNBROKEN	GLASS ETCHED (Exhibit 37)				X			X
		STRETCHED OUT, UNCOILED (Exhibits 3-38,39,41,42,44)	X		X	/			X
		MODERATELY ELONGATED (Exhibits 25,62,47,86)	/	/	/	/			/
	FILAMENT BROKEN	ENDS FRACTURED, ANGULAR (Exhibits 14,15,48)					X		
		ENDS MELTED, TAPERED, ROUND (Exhibit 13)	/					X	/

[X] DEFINITE INDICATION OF CONDITION   [/] POSSIBLE INDICATION OF CONDITION

*Incandescent generally means that the filament was lighted and **cold** means that it was not lighted. However, determination of whether light was on or off may require consideration of other circumstances than indications of abnormalities.*

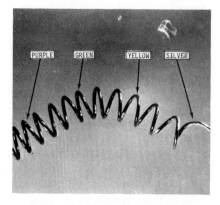

Exhibit 25. *Tinted filament, varying from bright to purple or brown, indicates that filament was hot but not incandescent after glass was broken. Colors are light where filament is coolest.*

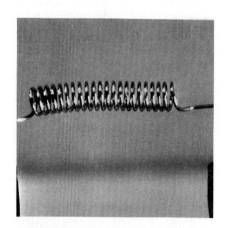

Exhibit 26. *Bright, shiny filament indicates that filament was cold when glass was broken.*

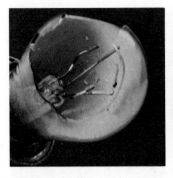

Exhibit 27. *White oxide on inside of cracked bulb indicates lamp was on after glass broke.*

Exhibit 28. *White oxide on filament supports also indicates lamp on after glass broke.*

Exhibit 29. *White oxide on stem. Filament is entirely gone, but on indication remains clear.*

Exhibit 30. *White oxide on one filament indicates other (missing) was on after glass broke.*

one.

Very dark color, such as brown, purple, or green, is the usual indication of oxidation. It may be produced, however, by applying power to an unbroken filament after the glass is broken.

Discoloration usually extends on filament tails almost to filament supports although sometimes the ends of the coil and tails are not so dark as the middle of the coil. (Exhibit 25)

Bright filament (unoxidized) definitely indicates that the filament was cold when the glass broke. See Exhibit 26. This is sometimes referred to as "cold break." The filament may be intact or broken but is is rarely much deformed or stretched out.

A tinted filament, Exhibit 25, occurs with broken glass. The filament is lightly oxidized. It may be pale yellow, light brown, green and purple. The filament may be broken or intact and it may or may not be deformed or stretched out. To be oxidized at all, a filament must have been hot; to be heavily oxidized (blackened) it must have been incandescent.

A tinted filament is usually found in a two-filament lamp with the other filament heavily oxidized. The blackened filament was incandescent, lighted; the tinted one was heated by the nearby incandescent filament but only enough to oxidize lightly. It was not incandescent and therefore not lighted.

If one of two filaments in a broken lamp is gone, and the remaining one is lightly oxidized, the missing filament was incandescent.

Occasionally a broken single-filament lamp will be found with a tinted filament. This could not have been due to heat from an adjacent incandescent filament. This tinted filament was hot because it had been incandescent an instant before but the circuit was broken before the glass broke permitting the filament to cool before air found its way to the filament. That permits light oxidation but prevents heavy oxidation. In this case glass may not be broken wide open but only cracked or slightly broken so that air reaches the filament slowly.

Usually tinted filaments are bright or lightly tinted near the supports, which draw off heat from the filament, and darker farther from the supports where they are hotter as illustrated in Exhibit 25. Tinting is actually a very thin surface layer of oxide, thicker where it is darker.

Oxide "smoke." When a filament exposed to air is incandescent because of electric current flowing through it, the filament continues to oxidize rapidly. The oxide rises from the filament in the form of smoke consisting of oxides of tungsten. The principal oxide is actually yellow but the smoke looks whitish. This whitish dust is deposited on nearby surfaces, leaving telltale signs that there was an incandescent filament in the lamp after the glass broke, even if the filament itself is completely gone. The oxide may appear on the glass (Exhibit 27), on the filament supports (Exhibit 28), or on the stem (Exhibit 29), or on an adjacent filament (Exhibit 30).

While the filament is oxidizing, the tungsten in the filament wastes rapidly away. At a spot where the filament is thin, the filament becomes hotter and oxidizes faster creating a thinner spot, more heat, and faster oxidiation. Finally the temperature at that point exceeds the melting point (3370°C = 6100°F) of tungsten, the metal liquifies and forms a gap or opening in the filament. For an instant, a bright electric arc forms between the parted filament ends with still greater heat. When this gap widens, with additional melting, to the point where available voltage can no longer maintain the arc, the current ceases in the broken circuit. The filament has then "burned out." This burn-out is the same thing that occurs during normal aging but the filament wastes away in seconds rather than days. Moreover, in old-age burn-out, metallic tungsten vaporized from the filament is deposited on the glass and darkens it; there is no oxidation.

Small filaments burn out more rapidly in air than large ones; 12-volt filaments more rapidly that 6-volt filaments; and old filaments more quickly than new ones. For example, times for new 12-volt burnout with bulb wide open are approximately as follows:

Headlamp filament
7 to 10 seconds
Signal filament
3 to 5 seconds
Tail light filament
2 to 4 seconds

Exhibit 31. *Without bulb breakage, direct contact with collapse, as at A and B, produces extreme incandescent filament stretch-* *ing and tangling; it may produce cold fracture and possibly elongation of filaments, and multiple fracture of old brittle filaments.*

Exhibit 32. *Collapse near the lamp without lamp breakage, as at C and D, will produce substantial stretching of incandescent fila-* *ment and it may produce brittle fracture of old filaments. These comments apply to both head and tail lamps.*

Exhibit 33. *Contact damage and collapse some distance from the lamp, as at headlight in E and taillight in F, is unlikely to produce* *significant deformation or fracture in new filaments, but may produce brittle fracture in old filaments.*

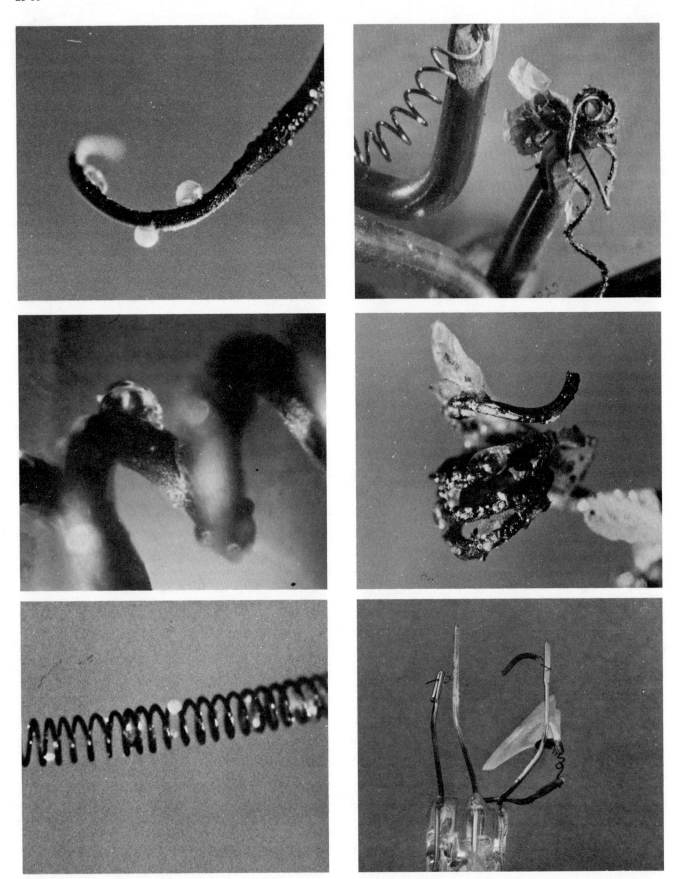

Exhibit 34. *Three examples of droplets formed when flying glass particles are stopped and melted by hot filament.*

Exhibit 35. *Three examples of chunks of glass fused to an incandescent filament when bulb was broken with lamp on.*

Dash light filament
0.1 to 0.5 seconds

If the electric circuit by which the lamp is energized is broken before burnout is complete, the filament cools and oxidation stops. The filament may have produced almost no white oxide and will not, of course, burn out. But the filament does blacken.

Oxide coating one of two filaments (Exhibit 30) means that the other filament, which is blackened, was incandescent. Then the filament with oxide on it was not incandescent. The oxide is thrown off by the incandescent filament and deposited on cooler surfaces nearby.

Time of oxidation is important. Filament oxidation in a broken lamp can occur in two ways:

1. The filament was incandescent when the glass broke or had been incandescent an instant before.

2. The glass broke when the filament was cold (off) and the filament was energized afterward.

Both of these indicate that the filament was incandescent after, but not necessarily when the lamp glass was broken. Therefore inferences as to whether the lamp was on or off when the glass was broken in a crash must be guarded.

There are two ways that a filament can be cold when glass breaks and then later oxidizes when current is switched on:

1. Glass broke in an earlier accident which went unnoticed. Then current is switched on in normal operation. The filament oxidizes and burns out. In a subsequent crash, the glass is broken again and the indication is mistakenly read for lamp on at the second crash whereas in fact, the lamp was burned out and off.

2. Glass broke when the filament was cold and then, before filament was examined, current is switched on for some reason. After that, examination may

lead to a false inference that the lamp was on at the time the glass broke.

The second of these circumstances usually occurs when, after an accident and before the lamp is examined, someone carelessly turns on a switch to see whether the lamps work and immediately burns out any in which glass has been broken. Then the lamp gives a false indication.

There are some circumstances which help determine whether such false indications are present. If there is no deformation of a heavily oxidized filament in a broken lamp, one can infer that the shock that broke the glass did not affect the filament. This might be because the filament was actually cold when the glass was broken. Such an inference should also involve consideration of damage to the vehicle in the vicinity of the lamp and whether the vehicle was moving or standing (Exhibits 31, 32, and 33.)

Fused glass particles definitely indicate that filament was incandescent when the glass broke. Flying particles of broken glass stopped by an incandescent filament will be fused by the filament's heat and may adhere to it. Sometimes these melt to the point of forming droplets (Exhibit 34); sometimes they retain most of their original shape (Exhibit 35); and sometimes they are partly melted. Glass particles are more likely to adhere to large filaments than to small ones because there is more heat in the large filament to fuse to the glass. Rarely, a very small glass particle will stick to a hot but not incandescent filament in a two-filament lamp. That could indicate that one of the two filaments in the lamp was incandescent but might not alone show which one.

Glass dust sometimes adheres to incandescent filaments and appears under magnification as tiny whiskers or fuzz.

The absence of fused glass fragments does *not* mean that the lamp was not lighted; glass may break without scattering fragments on the filament.

Other things may sometimes be mistaken for fused glass fragments, for example, particles of road rock or unfused glass lodged in filament coils and heavy dust settling on the filament. (Exhibit 36) These may be distinguished by microscopic examination and may usually be brushed off with a fine brush.

Etched glass may be considered a form of glass fusing by an incandescent filament. It is not common. The filament comes in contact with glass usually by stretching due to shock. Where it touches the glass, the glass is slightly etched or roughened. There is some softening of the glass surface and there may or may not be filament adhesion. The glass bulb is ordinarily not broken but if broken most of it remains in place. Sometimes the filament blackens the glass in the area touched as in Exhibit 37.

Filament Deformation

A hot filament is ductile and will stretch out, uncoil, or even tangle without breaking or before breaking (Exhibits 37 and 38). Inertia of the filament during collision impact often makes this happen. Hence the resulting deformation is often called "hot impact" or "hot shock." Stretching of the filament may also occur when the glass breaks and some foreign object snags the filament or bends the filament supports (Exhibit 39).

The glass bulb may or may not be broken. But, because hot shock is the only indication that the light was on if the glass bulb is unbroken, hot shock is most significant when the bulb remains intact (Exhibit 40).

The filament must be hot but need not be incandescent. With the same impact, the hotter of two filaments in a lamp will usually deform more than the cooler. Hence, if one filament in a two-filament lamp is deformed much more than the other, the one with greatest deformation was incandescent and the other was hot because near the incandescent filament (Exhibit 41). If both filaments were more or less equally deformed both are indicated as incandescent (Exhibit

42). If one filament is heavier than the other, the lighter filament usually stretches somewhat more (Exhibit 42).

Longitudinal deformation (Exhibit 43) tends to compress the filament at one end and stretch it at the other.

Direction of distortion is not a reliable indication of force direction (Exhibit 44).

Halogen lamps are incandescent tungsten lamps and so behave in impact like other tungsten lamps (Exhibit 45). But the filament in a halogen lamp is more compact than that in the conventional headlamp; Therefore it deforms somewhat less under the same impact. This is illustrated in Exhibit 45 where the two kinds of lamps are compared.

Absence of hot shock does not mean that the lamp was off; the shock may not have been great enough to stretch the filament.

A substantial bump or jolt is needed to give hot impact deformation; much less, however, than that required for cold impact elongation or fracture. How much a filament is distorted in impact while hot depends on four factors: 1) most importantly the severity of the impact, that is, the rate at which the lamp is accelerated or decelerated during the crash; 2) filament age; 3) size of the filament; and 4) temperature of the filament.

Severity of impact (sudden change in motion) that a lamp receives in a collision depends not only on the speed at which the vehicle is moving when the crash occurs but also how close the lamp is to the contact damage area (Exhibits 31, 32, and 33). Lamps in a substantially collapsed area will nearly always show hot impact distortion if they are on at the time of the crash. If they are near the collapsed area they may show impact distorton; but if a lamp is more than a few feet from contact damage, it is unlikely to show distortion even if it is incandescent.

Be very careful, therefore, about inferring that a lamp from a severely damaged vehicle was off because it shows no sign of impact deformation

Exhibit 36. *Other things may be mistaken for fused glass particles.* **A** *is road mud stuck on coil.* **B** *is dust deposited on coil. These will brush or wash off; fused particles will not.*

which would indicate that it was on. The conclusion is only warranted if the lamp was actually struck hard or was in the contact damage area. If it is only a few feet from contact damage, the vehicle structure may so attenuate (weaken) the impact that the lamp suffers no significant deformation. Consider Exhibit 46. The vehicle was clearly in a violent collision subjecting it to great impact forces. The headlamp in the right front contact damage area shows extreme filament deformation indicating that it was definitely on at the time of the crash. But the similar left front headlamp, only about three feet from the contact damage area, shows no deformation although it was also on at the same time. Concluding that the left lamp was off because it shows no deformation by the impact would be a great mistake.

A hot filament can be stretched to the breaking point. When it cools after hot stretch, the filament remains deformed.

Broken Filament

Filaments may be parted in a collision in essentially the same two ways that they can fail in normal use as described earlier: 1) burnout, and 2) cold or brittle fracture.

Fractures are produced by impact of collision. A fracture definitely indicates that the filament was not incandescent when impact occurred either because the filament had previously failed due to brittle fracture, in which case it would have been off at the time of the crash, or because the light was off and the filament was cold when impact broke the

Exhibit 37. *Filament stretched by hot shock until it strikes inside of bulb where it darkens glass.*

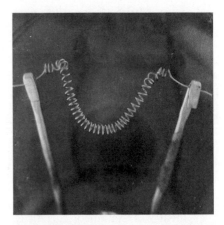

Exhibit 38. *Stretching of an incandescent filament with moderate shock. Deformation is less at ends where filament is cooler.*

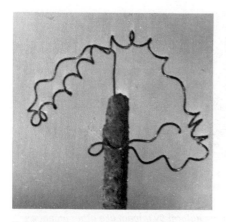

Exhibit 39. *Stretching and uncoiling of incandescent filament snagged by an external object which broke the glass of the lamp.*

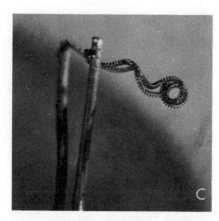

Exhibit 40. *Extreme deformation and tangling of incandescent filament with great shock. Bulb glass remained unbroken.*

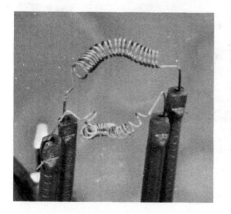

Exhibit 41. *If one of two similar filaments is hotter than the other, the hotter one will stretch most with shock.*

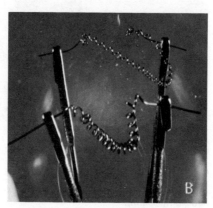

Exhibit 42. *Two filaments about equally deformed by shock indicate both as incandescent. Smaller deforms most.*

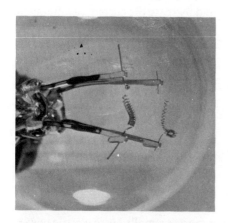

Exhibit 43. *Lengthwise filament impact produces longitudinal deformation; the filament is compressed at one end and stretched at the other. In this case, filament coils shorted at the compressed ends.*

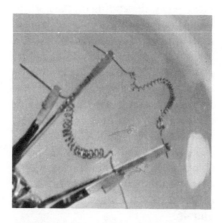

Exhibit 44. *The same impact on two filaments may deform one in one direction and the other in another direction. Hence, direction of deformation is not a reliable indicator of the direction of impact force.*

filament.

The glass bulb may or may not also be broken. But because cold shock is the only indication that the light was *off* if the glass bulb is unbroken, cold shock is most significant when the bulb remains intact.

The absence of brittle fracture does *not* mean that the light was on. The impact may not have been great enough to break the filament.

The appearance of fractured filaments is described in the discussion of normal filament failure and illustrated in Exhibit 14.

Silver luster remains. There is no sign of oxidation whether glass is broken or not. There may be roughness or pitting depending on how much the filament has been used.

A filament with a single break may remain attached to supports but is usually somewhat elongated (Exhibit 47). If the filament breaks in more than one place it may be loose in the bulb (Exhibits 15, 16, and 48), unless the glass is also broken and the loose filament is lost. Such slight cold stretching is easily distinguished from the much greater uncoiling when the filament is hot.

Sometimes impact forces which do not fracture a filament are enough to bend filament supports, damage the base shell, or crack the insulator in the base (Exhibit 49).

Impact must be very great to produce cold shock (much greater than for hot shock). Hence the lamp must be in or very near contact damage from a collision. If a lamp is more than a foot or so away from a contact damage area, the filament is unlikely to suffer from cold impact (Exhibit 46).

Old filaments which have become crystalized and weakened in spots by pitting may fracture with very little impact, much less than for filaments in new lamps.

With filaments having about the same amount of aging, heavy filaments such as those used in headlamps are less subject to cold break than fine filaments, such as used in tail lamps.

A peculiar circumstance may make a fractured filament indeterminate if the bulb is broken open in the crash and both ends of the filament are broken off right at the filament supports. This can happen with the filament incandescent. Whatever breaks the glass continues on and tears the filament from both supports, and the filament is lost. Close to the support, the filament is cold enough to fracture. Oxidation is minimum there, and not enough filament is left to show what little there might be. Thus, without reliable indications of filament temperature, whether the filament was incandescent or not is, in this case, indeterminate.

Filament burnout in an accident is quite different from that described under normal lamp failure. It does not occur unless the bulb is broken because even great filament deformation does not hasten burn out. But if the bulb breaks and lets air in, the filament quickly oxidizes and wastes away leaving a whitish residue as already explained. The effects on the ends of the filament are illustrated in Exhibit 13.

If a lamp was already burned out when a crash occurred, it would not be incandescent, that is, it would be off. Then if shock further breaks the filament in a crash, the fracture, without elongation, would give the nonincandescent indication. If the glass broke in a lamp in which the filament had already burned out, there would be no oxidation and the bright filament would give the correct nonincandescent indication even though the melted filament end indicated that the filament was incandescent when it burned out.

Force of Impact

Like others, you may want to know how strong an impact is required to produce a significant abnormality in a filament. Only a general idea is available; conditions vary greatly. As an approximation, stopping a lamp going 20 miles per hour in a quarter of an inch will usually do the trick.

The acceleration or deceleration of

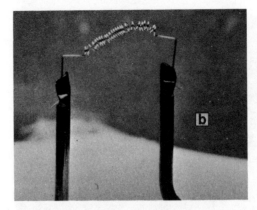

Exhibit 45. *Incandescent halogen lamp filaments deform by impact like other incandescent filaments. Halogen lamp filaments, **A**, require more impact to deform than ordinary lamps, **B**, both headlamps shown here were given the same impact. The standard sealed beam on the left deformed more than the halogen lamp on the right.*

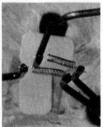

Exhibit 46. *The filaments shown are from headlamps of this vehicle. The low beam of each lamp was incandescent. The lamp in the contact damage area shows extreme deformation of both filaments. The lamp a few feet away from the contact damage area shows no deformation of either filament. It would be unwise to infer that the unaffected lamp was off when the collision occurred because it showed no sign of being on. Then, if the right headlamp were missing, it would be foolish to conclude further that the car had no headlamp on.*

the filament during impact is a better measure of the inertial force required. During impact, this force increases in milliseconds from zero to a peak and decreases to zero. The increase and decrease are not steady but definitely jerky, depending on the natural vibration frequencies of the filament and supporting structures. In tests on aircraft lamps[4] the peak acceleration producing deformation was found to be in a range between 400 and 900 times the acceleration due to gravity (400 to 900 g's) a drag factor, if you please, of 400.0 to 900.0

The irregularities in this acceleration are probably what leaves two filaments in the same bulb deformed in different directions as in Exhibits 44 and 46.

Short Circuits

Another peculiar circumstance can produce filament burnout in a crash without glass breakage. This can happen if there is a short circuit between two filaments or if part of one filament is shorted out. That can reduce the electrical resistance of the circuit and increase the current in a filament to the extent that it overheats and will soon burn out, not by oxidation but by evaporation of tungsten, provided power continues to be supplied to the lamp. Such a circumstance is illustrated in Exhibit 50.

Sometimes a lamp is so smashed that an energized filament support touches a grounded one (Exhibit 51), or the edge of the base (Exhibit 52). The short circuit often results in an abnormality which indicates that the lamp was supplied with electric power, a circumstance that may be especially significant if no filament remains for examination.

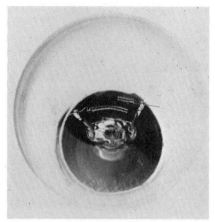

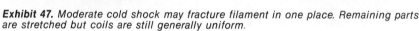

Exhibit 47. *Moderate cold shock may fracture filament in one place. Remaining parts are stretched but coils are still generally uniform.*

Exhibit 48. *Extreme cold impact may fracture filaments at both ends*

If power is on when such a short occurs, one or more of the following effects result:

- The fuse protecting the circuit burns out.
- The support and whatever it touches melt at the point of contact and may weld together. The weld is usually weak and the parts are easily separated.
- At the point of contact or weld, the parts may be pitted or "burned."
- The filament support melts and burns out between the point of contact and the stem.
- Wire connecting the base contact and the filament support melts and burns out.

Careful examination, usually with magnification, may be required to detect these abnormalities.

Abnormalities produced by short circuit indicate only that there was power on the lamp when the lamp was smashed. This leads to the further inference that the filament was incandescent *unless* it had already burned out. Thus signs of short circuit in the lamp strongly suggest but do not necessarily prove that the lamp was on.

A burned out fuse indicates that there was a short somewhere in the circuit but, because a fuse may serve several lamps, a burned out fuse does not necessarily mean that a particular short-circuited lamp had power on it. The short circuit may have been some-

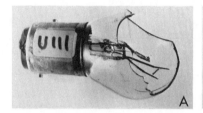

Exhibit 49. *Impact great enough to damage other parts of the lamp, such as filament supports and glass (A), base (B), and contacts (C) may have no significant effect on cold filaments.*

where else.

Temperatures Affecting Lamp Filaments

Data on temperatures related to lamp filaments will assist in understanding what can happen in a lamp during a vehicle collision (Exhibit 53.) Glass particles will not stick to filaments unless the filament temperature is above the melting temperature of glass.

Colors. As the heated filament is exposed to air, it first turns pale yellow. It soon turns darker and becomes greenish and then purple if is hot enough. These light colors are "interference" colors and represent very thin layers of oxide. In lamps that have been broken open while hot, these light colors appear on the filament which is not itself heated by electric current, but is near to one that is incandescent. At these temperatures, the filament gives off little light, only

a dull red glow. If the filament is hotter, however, it turns black with oxide. In broken lamps, this filament has been very hot. The black surface oxide turns to a yellow coating which rarely appears in lamps broken in accidents because at incandescent temperatures, yellow oxide turns to a white oxide which blows away from the filament like a puff of smoke and coats surrounding surfaces. This rapid oxidation continues until the filament cools down. Cooling occurs after the tungsten has been eaten away by oxidation until the filament parts at some point and interrupts the flow of current that kept it hot.

6. INDEFINITE INDICATIONS

In any inquiry, you may run into situations in which the signs of what happened are unclear.

Between strong on-or-off indication in lamps on one hand and no indication whatever on the other hand, there may be weak, questionable, or confusing signs that something happened to lamp filaments but exactly what is obscure. It is better to consider these confusing indications as indeterminate than to take sides.

Discoloration

A bit of filament may be neither clearly bright or definitely black. Viewed in one way, it looks oxidized; in another light it does not.

Record the fact that it does not look normal but you are unsure what the condition means, and let it go at that. Do not be persuaded to say that it looks one way more than the other.

Glass Particles

There may appear to be minute particles stuck to the filament. These do not look like the ordinary bits of fused glass. You have never seen anything just like it before. It is impossible to say exactly what they are and difficult to explain what they might mean. Then leave the matter open, perhaps recommending a more minute examination by someone with the experience and scientific equipment to iden-

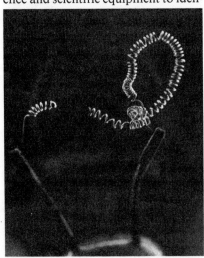

Exhibit 50. *With glass unbroken, this lamp suggests two indications: 1) a tangled filament suggesting incandescent at impact; and 2) burnout without oxidation suggesting lamp was off. Note that filament deformation has created a loop which short-circuits most of the filament. The remaining shorter part, with lower resistance, draws more current, overheats and soon burns out. Lamp was definitely on at and after impact.*

Exhibit 51. *Short circuit when "hot" filament support touches a grounded one. Pitting or welding may occur at the point of contact.*

Exhibit 52. *Short circuit when "hot" filament support touches edge of base. This may cause burnout of support or pitting of base.*

tify the particles.

Deformation

The most common difficulty is in judging filament deformation. If the filament is clearly uncoiled or stretched out, as in Exhibits 38 and 42, there is no question that it was hot, if not incandescent, at impact. On the other hand, if it is so straight that you can see through the coil, you can be sure that there was no deformation remaining after impact. It is the slight curve or abnormality that is questionable.

There are at least six possible explanations of a modest elongation or slight bend in a filament. Some of these indicate that it was hot and others that it was cold.

1. *Normal curve in* the filament (Exhibit 54, Type C2R) can be determined by comparing the lamp with a new lamp of the same trade number or by finding the filament configura-

tion for the trade number in Exhibit 103. Exhibit 54 is an example of normally bowed or arched filaments used in automotive lamps. In these curves, filament coils are evenly spaced and the bow or curve is even from one filament support to the other.

2. *Manufacturing irregularities* may produce a slight curve in a filament which is supposed to be straight. This condition is not common. As in the case of normally curved filaments, the coils are evenly spaced and the curve is even from one support to the other. The bowing is most likely to be up when the lamp base is down (Exhibit 55).

3. *Age sag* sometimes develops in filaments which have been in use a long time (Exhibit 56). It affects only very small filaments such as tail light filaments; it will not be found in headlamps. The sag is downward when the lamp is in the position in which it was in use in the vehicle. Filament coils

Exhibit 53.

TEMPERATURES RELATED TO LAMPS IN ACCIDENTS

Occurrence	Centigrade	Fahrenheit
Light oxidation begins	600	1100
Red glow, dark oxidation	675	1250
Black oxidation, glass of small lamps fuses	710	1310
Yellow oxide forms, sealed-beam glass fuses, orange glow	750	1380
Incandescent light, white oxide	2200	4000
Tungsten melts	3370	6100

Exhibit 54. *This arched filament is not deformed; it is designed to be like that.*

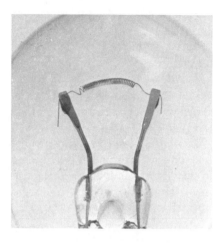

Exhibit 55. *Some filaments, like this one, are curved by manufacturing irregularities.*

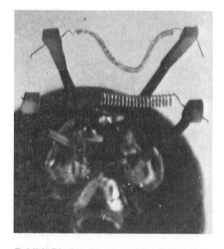

Exhibit 56. *Age sag sometimes looks like hot shock. Age sag is always downward. Shock deformation may be in any direction.*

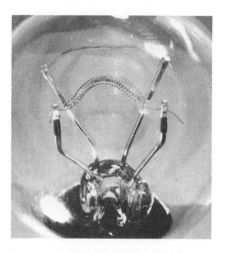

Exhibit 57. *Mild hot shock deformation usually shows more stretching in the middle where it is hottest than at cooler ends.*

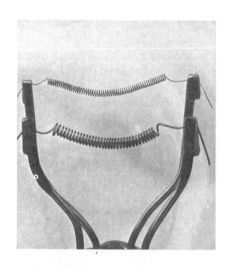

Exhibit 58. *Mild cold shock can arch the filament without breaking it. Coils and curves are generally uniform.*

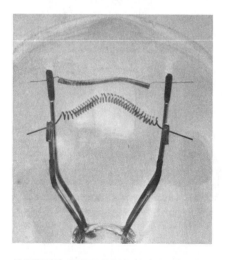

Exhibit 59. *Repeated sharp jolts can produce significant deformation in an incandescent filament*

may show slight irregularities. The downward curve is much more pronounced in the middle than at the ends. Other signs of age are nearly always present: bulb darkening (Exhibit 12), which is easy to see; and filament roughening (Exhibit 5), which is difficult to detect in small filaments which show age sag.

The three foregoing lamp conditions are all natural and not the effect of accidents. The two following, which are quite similar, are the effect of accidents. If they are sufficiently pronounced to be clearly distinguishable, they can indicate whether the lamp was lighted or not. Only conspicuous deviations from normal shape can be attributed to collision forces.

4. *Mild hot deformation* (Exhibit 57) usually shows noticeable irregularities in spacing of filament coils which are stretched out more toward the ends than in the middle. The curve is usually in a direction opposite to that of the force that produced deformation. The curve or sag is likely to be more pronounced in the middle than at the ends with the result that the curve is not regular throughout.

5. *Slight cold stretch* without breaking filament (Exhibit 58) may be virtually indistinguishable from a manufacturing irregularity. It is usually in a direction opposite to that of the force that produced the deformation; for example, if the tail lamp is base forward and the car is struck from the rear the filament is bowed away from the base in the same direction as is likely in a manufacturing irregularity. In the slight cold shock, the tails of the filament are likely not to be quite in line with the filament coil.

6. *Repeated small bumps* or jolts will gradually deform a filament. These are most likely to appear on trucks and motorcycles which may subject lamps to jolts. Exhibit 59 shows a lamp which has been tapped briskly on a table about 20 times while one filament was incandescent. The filament illustrated could be mistaken for hot shock in a single impact. That

Exhibit 60. Bullet or road stone may have put hole in bulb causing lamp to burn out before accident.

much deformation from bumps is very rare. There is no record of it in passenger cars. You would have to judge its significance by the amount of deformation and the kind of treatment it may have experienced in operation.

In this connection, remember that lack of deformation is not always proof that a lamp was off during impact. Some lamp filaments resist, to a surprising degree, deformation even while incandescent.

7. PECULIAR CIRCUMSTANCES

Indeterminate

Determination of whether a lamp was on or off is often impossible. In that case, do not hesitate to say so. There are several clear indications of an indeterminate situation:

Lamp destroyed or missing. Not enough is left of filament or filament supports to show signs of light being on or off.

Lamp appears normal in all respects. Glass is unbroken and impact shock was not great enough to affect the filament.

Lamp has been removed by someone for some reason and is no longer available for examination. A replacement lamp will, of course, appear normal.

Questionable

In some lamps, indications of on or off are not clear. Then, the best the investigator can do is to express possibilities, as opposed to probabilities or certainties. There may be several possibilities.

It may be that other circumstances of the accident such as statements by reliable witnesses, well established switch positions, or condition of other lamps operating from the same switch will assist in a determination in questionable cases.

If there are several weak indications that point toward the lamp having been on and none that suggest it was off, it is reasonable to conclude that it was, indeed, on. Likewise, several indications that a light was off and none that it was on warrant the opinion that it was actually off. But when some conditions indicate a light was on and others that it was off, any conclusion is questionable.

Most of Filament Missing

An indeterminate condition may occur in broken lamps when the filament available for examiantion is only a few millimeters of the tail attached to the filament support. The filament is broken near the first coil or, more likely, at a sharp bend in the tail. Nothing remains to show possible filament deformation. The filament is broken off where brittle fracture is most likely to occur without any sign of melting.

Then, lacking whitish oxide deposits elsewhere, discoloration of this bit of filament is the only possible sign of on or off.

If the filament still attached to the support is definitely blackened or at least clearly tinted, there is indication of heat when air reached the tungsten. Then that filament or possibly another filament in the lamp was definitely incandescent.

But no discoloration does not mean that the filament was off when the glass broke. That is because so close to the cold support, the filament may not have been hot enough to oxidize. In the tail, the temperature of the filament varies from incandescence at the first coil to much below that required for oxidation at the support. Discoloration on exposure to air varies with this temperature. Even with an incandescent coil, the tail may not be hot enough where it connects with the support to change color. Then, if it breaks in the cooler part, as it may well do, there will be no sign of heat. Consequently, a fragment of bright filament next to the support gives no

Exhibit 61.

FILAMENT ABNORMALITIES WITH CURRENT OFF JUST BEFORE IMPACT

Power off before impact seconds	Oxidation		Deformation		
	Tail Light	Turn Signal	Tail Light	Turn Signal	Head Light
4.0	None	None	Slight	Medium	None
1.3	None	None	Medium	Large	Medium
1.0	None	None	Medium	Large	Large
0.5	None	Light	Medium	Large	Large
0.2	Light	Heavy	Large	Large	Large
0.0	Heavy	Heavy	Large	Large	Large

indication of heat; on or off is indeterminate.

On-or-Off Indications Other than Lamps

Sometimes when examination of the lamp gives no clue or only an uncertain clue as to whether the lamp

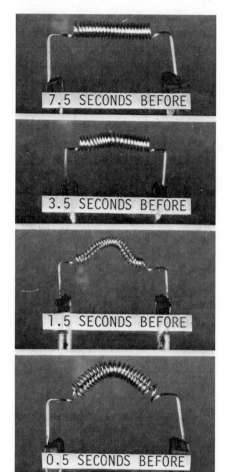

Exhibit 62. A headlamp filament can show definite signs of deformation from a severe impact if current remains on to within two or three seconds of impact.

was on or off, other circumstances may help in the determination.

Position of the light switch may be an indication under certain circumstances. This is discussed elsewhere.

A lamp in a heavily damaged area, where it would be clearly have been subject to great shock, appears normal. That condition strongly suggests that it was off rather than on. The impact was not enough to result in cold shock to prove it was off, but it was enough to result in hot impact if the lamp was on.

Adjacent lamps which would have been lighted at the same time both receive approximately the same impact. One clearly shows hot impact. The other is indeterminate. It is reasonable to conclude that the latter was off or it would presumably also have shown some hot impact.

Lamp Affected by Previous Accident

It is possible that the effect of a previous accident will remain in a lamp and be mistaken for the effects of a subsequent accident. This is a rare occurrence. Unless the fact of a previous accident with contact damage collapse in the area of the lamp or other significant indication of lamp damage has been well established, do not presume or surmise that a previous event rather than the one under consideration produced the observed condition of the lamp.

Hot impact deformation may occur without glass breakage if the lamp is in a contact damage area on a vehicle. Then, if the filament is unbroken, which is usually the case, the lamp will still light and will, indeed, appear to be still serviceable. If put back into use, in a second collision, with the light off and the glass unbroken, the lamp still exhibits hot impact deformation, giving a false indication that the light was on when the second collision occurred. This can also happen when a repairman replaces a broken lamp in a damaged vehicle with an unbroken one from another vehicle which has been cannibalized after a

crash. In these circumstances, other information is requird to determine in which collision the filament was deformed. For example, the proposition that the lamp filament was deformed by a previous impact must be ruled out by proper inquiry concerning the history of the vehicle.

Hot break. A lamp may also show hot break from a previous accident. The most common occurrence of this kind is when a road stone puts a small hole in headlamp lens (Exhibit 60). If the lamp is on, or as soon as it is turned on afterwards, the filament oxidizes and burns out. If another accident breaks the lamp more before the driver notices the broken lamp and has it replaced, it will appear to have been on, even though it was off. Signs of the earlier break may be obliterated by the later one.

Tampering

Sometimes, after a collision, a driver switches on lights which should have been on before, or he may be accused by someone of doing so. If there is hot-impact filament deformation, the light was on during the collision and not switched on afterward. If there is brittle fracture of a filament, the light was off at impact, either because the cold filament was fractured by the impact or because the lamp had failed by brittle fracture some time before.

Oxidation of a filament in a broken lamp is indeterminate as to whether the lamp was on at the time of impact or was turned on afterward. In either case, the filament oxidizes and blackens in air at once. But glass particles fused to a filament indicate that it was incandescent when the glass broke and glass particles were flying about.

After the vehicle comes to rest, there is no loose glass to stick to the filament.

If filaments are gone from a lamp that broke open in a collision, deposits of whitish tungsten oxide may remain to help decide whether the lamp was switched on after impact. If the filament is on when the glass breaks, the oxide smoke will swirl about and deposit thinly and irregularly because of the motion of the vehicle; but if the vehicle is standing and the lamp is switched on, the smoke will rise up and deposit evenly on surfaces above the filament.

If a driver claims that the other car's lights must have been switched on after collision, the idea is preposterous if the driver of the other car was killed or too badly injured to turn on the lights. However, the impact may, under certain circumstances, switch a car's lights on or off without any person operating the switch. How this may occur is explained in the next section of this topic.

Current On or Off Just Before or After Crash

What happens to the filament if current is turned on or off just before or after the lamp is involved in a crash? That must be considred when someone claims that the lights were switched just before or after a collision; but it is most important in connection with flashing signal lights.

Time required to light-up. Lights appear very quickly after current in filaments is switched on. A cold filament has a much lower electric resistance than a hot one, consequently there is a great inrush of current to heat the filament after voltage is first applied. Filaments reach normal current or incandescent operating temperatures, in 0.03 to 0.08 seconds.[7] Therefore, the filament would show hot shock or oxidation if the crash occurred more than about a tenth of a second after lights were switched on.

Time to cool off is much greater than time to light-up. Exhibit 61 shows the results of tests in which current was shut off just before an ordinary two-filament tail-signal lamp (Trade No. 1157) impacted a fixed object at 24 miles per hour. If glass is broken, oxidation shows in the flasher filament if impact occurs within half a second after current shutoff and in the small filament within a quarter of a second. But hot shock distortion appears in the flasher filament as much as four seconds after crash and in the small filament for more than a second. The larger, flasher filament continues to show effects of having been lighted longer after current shutoff than the smaller one.

Exhibit 62 shows what happens when current is shut off in a head-lamp at various intervals before impact at about 25 miles per hour. With current off seven seconds or more before impact, there is no visible permanent deformation. If power is stopped three to four seconds before the impact the filament shows some deformation, but not really enough to be sure about. But if current is on until a second or two before impact, there is definite deformation.

Flasher operation. Turn signal and emergency flashing lights go on and off between one and two times per second.[8] Current is flowing in the filament about half that time, more or less depending on frequency of flashing; a signal could have as much as 0.6 sec. cool-off between flashes. Then a question could be raised as to the significance of an indication that the flasher was on or off.

Filaments can oxidize more than half a second after current is off, and hot deformation can occur several seconds afterward (Exhibit 61). Then for more than 0.6 sec. after current stops, the maximum time that current is off in the flasher operation, the filament will continue to show the effect of having been incandescent. Therefore, while flashing, lamps can only show an on indication regardless of whether the crash occurred in the light or dark phase of the flashing.

Combined signals. In rear lamps the turn flasher and brake (steady) signals are usually in the same filament. Then, if the indication is that the lamp was on, it would be impossible, from the lamp alone, to determine whether the brake signal, the turn signal, or both were operating. If the indication is that the lamp was off, neither would have been operating. In front signal lights, where brake signals do not show, any indication refers only to the turn signal.

Short Circuits

Short or crossed circuits sometimes occur in a two-filament lamp when

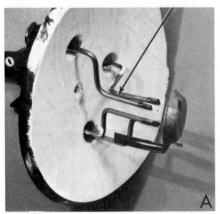 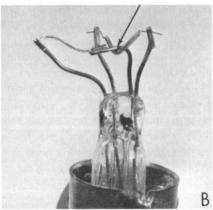 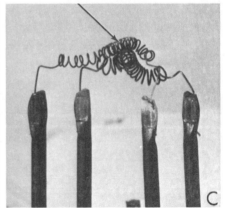

Exhibit 63. *Short circuit in a damaged 2-filament lamp may affect the on-or-off indication of some other lamp. Short circuit may be between supports,* **A,** *between a support and a filament,* **B,** *or between the two filaments,* **C.**

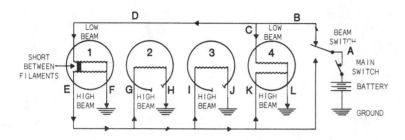

Exhibit 64. *In a 4-headlamp system, a short circuit between filaments in one of the 2-filament lamps may make broken high- beam lamps appear to have been on. This is illustrated here. Beam switch is on low beam. Current from battery goes through connections **A**, **B**, and **D** to low beam filament in Lamp 1. There the short circuit takes it to high beam and it follows connection **E**, **G**, **I** and **K** to high beam filaments and ground through Lamps 2, 3, and 4. If any of these break they will then burn out as though they had been on instead of off.*

one broken or stretched filament touches or tangles with another or a filament support, (Exhibit 63) or when two filament supports are forced together by whatever broke the lamp.

Then current flowing in one filament can reach ground through that filament as usual or through the other filament. Filaments often fuse together where they make contact.

Short circuits most commonly occur when filaments are stretched by hot shock or when objects which break the bulb also bend filament supports or stretch filaments out of shape.

Which filament was lighted? With a short circuit, there is no special problem in deciding whether some filament or no filament was lighted. But there may be a problem of deciding which of two filaments was lighted. Then complicating factors must be considered.[9] But this problem occurs so seldom that detailed discussion of the complicating factors is not warranted.

Four-headlamp problem. In a 4-headlamp system, one lamp on each side has only a high beam; the other has both high and low beams but only one filament at a time in each is in use. Under these circumstances, a short circuit in a damaged double-beam lamp while low beam is on may make all damaged headlamps on the same vehicle give a high beam indication. Exhibit 64 shows how that can be. So

it is sometimes not enough to get an indication from a single lamp; the situation of all lamps on the same circuit may have to be considered.

Direction of Impact

There has been theorizing that the direction in which a filament is stretched in hot shock will indicate

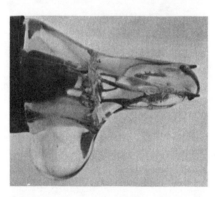

Exhibit 65. *Extreme external heat may melt glass into a lump, imbedding the filament.*

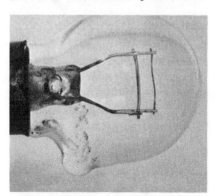

Exhibit 67. *If glass is intact, external heat expands the gas inside the bulb. The resulting pressure causes ballooning or stretching where the glass is hottest. Indications as to on or off are normal so long as bulb remains closed.*

the direction of collapse of the parts holding the light fixture containing the lamp, or the direction of motion of the vehicle in which the lamp was damaged.

Experiments with lamps teach that little confidence can be placed in such a conclusion, except for mild hot impact. During impact, the attitude of the lamp and direction of forces can change so quickly and so much that they cannot properly be represented by the direction of stretch of the filament in a lamp. But, perhaps more important, during impact, because of the elasticity of supporting structures, a lamp may jerk first one way and then another while the filament is still hot. This often produces the tangling effect (Exhibit 39).

The foregoing is not to be construed as meaning that hot shock will look the same regardless of the direction of the force producing the distortion.

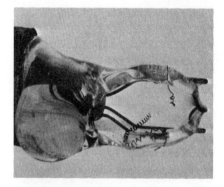

Exhibit 66. *Imbedded filament may still show on or off by deformation.*

Exhibit 68. *Where it balloons with external heat, glass eventually blows out at the weakest spot leaving a vent that relieves internal pressure. That lets air in. Filament distortion still indicates on or off but any oxidation may be due to external heat.*

Rollover

Examination of lamps in cars after rollover shows they are not ordinarily affected by the jolting produced in that manner. Therefore, whether lights were on or off before the rollover is usually indeterminate from examination of the lamps alone.

The exception to this rule occurs when the lamp is in an area where car structural collapse was considerable, for example when that part of the vehicle strikes something very solid such as a guardrail, tree, post, or bridge.

Lamps in Fires

If a fire starts after a collision, especially a fire from spilled fuel, lamps may be affected, especially rear lamps. Whether the lamp was on or off is usually indeterminate either because the lamp shows no abnormalities other than a smoke-blackened exterior or because the lamp is so badly damaged that no filament remains to be examined.

External heat may affect the lamp in different ways depending on the kind of lamp, how it is mounted, what part of the lamp is exposed to heat, and the length of time external heat is present. Fire may melt solder holding contact lugs to a sealed beam lamp or the solder in the contacts of smaller lamps. It may disintegrate the cement holding the glass to the base. It may also soften the glass. In extreme cases, the glass is more or less melted into a lump (Exhibits 65 and 66); on the other hand, the glass may be softened just enough so that the bulb is a little off center.

Glass usually softens first or most in a limited area of the bulb. The heat expands the gas within the bulb putting it under pressure. If the bulb is unbroken, the softened area stretches or "balloons" as in Exhibit 67. Where it stretches, the glass becomes thin and may blow out. The hole opened may be very small (Exhibit 68). When the hole opens, pressure is relieved and no further "ballooning" occurs, although the soft glass may continue to sag or droop. Where glass has thinned

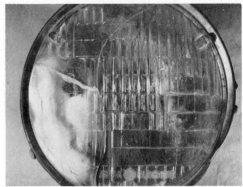

Exhibit 69. If lamp is broken in the crash, fire does not increase pressure inside. Glass may sag, but there is no ballooning. It is important to note signs that the glass was broken before the fire started.

Exhibit 70. If a sealed beam lamp is unbroken in a crash, it may balloon in a hot fire. The stretched glass is very thin and breaks easily. It is important to know whether the glass broke during the fire or by handling after it has cooled. All edges melted and smooth indicate bursting during the fire. Sharp broken edges, as in this picture, are indeterminate. There may or may not have been an opening in the glass before breakage in handling occurred. Filament oxidation is then inconclusive, but filament impact deformation remains significant.

out, it breaks easily when it cools (Exhibits 69 and 70). It is important to note whether glass is broken before attempting to remove the lamp for examination. If glass is broken before the fire, as sometimes happens, the expanding gas in the lamp escapes at once without pressure buildup and there is no ballooning but perhaps some melting or softening.

If glass is intact after a fire, indications of on or off are the same as for any unbroken lamp, regardless of how the bulb may be deformed. But make sure that there is no tiny hole in a ballooned bulb which permitted air to enter.

If the bulb is open after a fire, filament deformation indicates hot impact and glass particles fused to the filament indicate incandescence because these two conditions occur only

during impact and are not significantly affected by fire which occurs later. In fact, melted glass may imbed the filament in its deformed condition and so still show that the lamp was on during impact (Exhibit 66).

Filament oxidation in a lamp which is open after exposure to fire is another matter. External fire can oxidize a filament exposed to air. Thus if, in an open bulb which could have been affected by fire, both filaments are blackened or if there is only one filament and it is blackened, on or off may be indeterminate because there is no way to know whether discoloration was due to oxidation of an incandescent filament when the glass broke or to external fire after air reached the filament.

If one of two filaments is blackened and the other is still bright or only tinted after exposure to some heat from a fire, the blackened filament would have been incandescent and the other off because the filaments are so close together that fire would discolor both if it discolored either.

There is another circumstance which may help to decide whether the filament was discolored because it or an adjacent filament was incandescent when the bulb broke. If a filament is discolored from heat within the lamp itself, especially if it is only tinted by light oxidation, it is much more discolored in the middle where it is hottest and discolored little if any next to filament supports where it is coolest, as illustrated in Exhibit 25. However, if external heat from a fire reaches a filament which is exposed to air, the temperature is about the same throughout the filament and the discoloration is the same from one end of the filament to the other. Even filament tails beyond the supports usually show the same discoloration. Such uniform discoloration could occur by fire whether the lamp was on or off. Hence the matter is indeterminate.

A lamp ballooned by external fire, whether a sealed beam or small lamp,

may be open to the atmosphere or still airtight when the fire is out and the lamp cools. Whether it is open makes a difference as to the significance of filament oxidation. Glass stretched out by ballooning is very thin and fragile. It breaks easily in handling, and if so broken makes it nearly impossible to determine whether, after the fire, the bulb was open or intact. Consequently, lamp examination and handling after a fire must be done with great care.

Lamps Under Water

Sometimes lamps on motor vehicles or motor boats are submerged after an accident. How does this affect the lamps and what they indicate as to on or off?

Lamp damage before submersion is affected little by water. Deformation, discoloration, and glass particle stuck to filament remain the same. An exposed filament which has started to burn out in the air completes burnout under water. Tungsten oxide deposits on stem, supports, inner bulb surfaces and adjacent cooler filaments are not formed or may be washed away. Therefore indications are about the same as they would be

without submersion.

With damaging impact under water, filament deformation is almost unaffected. If filament is exposed by glass breakage under water, oxidation and possible burnout occur as in the air but with less oxidation. Filament discoloration does not appear. Adherance of glass particles to incandescent filament is unlikely. No tungsten oxide is deposited on adjacent surfaces. Hence principle indicators are the same as they would be if the glass broke in air.

If an intact filament in a broken lamp is switched on under water, it does not oxidize or burn out soon. Water keeps the filament from heating up to incandescence.

Variable Voltage Lamps

Most motor-vehicle lamps operate at a fairly constant voltage which depends on the battery. But bicycles and some other small vehicles supply current to lamps from a magneto or generator without any battery or voltage regulator. Then the light is off when the vehicle is standing and becomes brighter the faster it goes.

Sometimes, in a misguided attempt to increase the light, original bulbs are replaced by bulbs of lesser voltage.

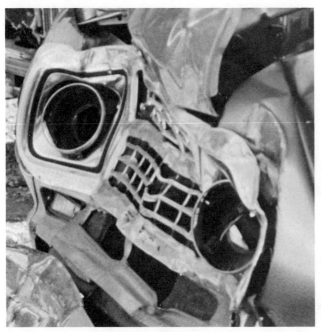

Exhibit 71. *The contact damage area from which the left front headlamp was removed for examination.*

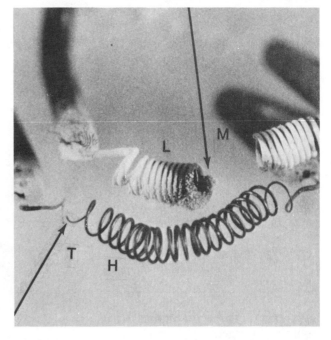

Exhibit 72. *Abnormal filaments in the lamp examined. Why were both burned out when only one at a time is supposed to be on?*

ABNORMALITIES OF FILAMENTS	Single / Small / Low beam	Other, if not single
Broken	✗	✗
% missing or detached	⊙	⊙
Loose in bulb		
End melted or tapered	✗	✗
End fractured		
Blackened		✗
Tinted or light colored		
White deposit	✗	
Moderately elongated	✗	
Stretched out, uncoiled		✗
Fused glass		
Pitted		
Other, show in note below		

Exhibit 73. *Observed abnormalities are recorded on special form in lamp examination report.*

That would work on a constant-voltage system but with the limited output of a variable voltage system, it only makes matters worse.[5]

However, when broken, such a lamp may still show particles of glass fused to the filament, an indication that it was "on." With the voltage available, the filament can be hot enough to make glass chips stick to it but not hot enough to produce more than a faint light, so the current can be "on" but the light "off." (Exhibit 53)

Exposure to Weather

What effect does exposure have on filaments in broken lamps that stand outdoors for months before they are examined? Such weathering has no effect on signs as to whether the lamp was on or off when damaged. Broken lamps with heavily oxidized, lightly oxidized and unoxidized filaments were left exposed to rain and snow for a year with no effect on oxidation.

However rain and weather may wash white tungsten oxide deposits from some surfaces.

Filaments may collect some dust and dirt which can usually be brushed off with a small artist's paint brush (Exhibit 36). Steel filament supports usually rust to a brown color on exposure. Sometimes traces of this rust creep over filament tails near where they are clamped in the supports.

Partly broken headlamps left outdoors will often accumulate water or ice inside even though the lamp is not wide open. Water mottles the silver on the headlamp reflector but has little other effect.

In a headlamp with a hole in it, signs of weathering inside, such as a mottled reflector, dirt, or collected water, noted immediately after a crash, indicate that the lamp was already open from previous impact and therefore was definitely off at the later accident, because if it had been turned on after the first damage, it would have burned out at once.

Statement of Conclusions

Do not offer a conclusion as to whether a lamp was on or off unless you are prepared to explain in detail two things: 1) exactly what abnormalities were observed in the lamp examined; and 2) what these abnormalities indicate or signify with respect to the temperature of the filament at the time of the accident. Any report relating to conclusions, such as that illustrated in Exhibit 84, should include such reasoning from observations to conclusions.

It is worth repeating here that when a conclusion that a lamp was on is based on oxidation in a broken lamp, one should be careful to say that the lamp was on when the glass broke *or* was turned on after the lamp was broken. From the lamp itself, no distinction can be made. Then other information may be necessary to determine which of these alternatives is acceptable.

Logical Reasoning

It may not be enough to conclude from a filament's deformation that it was on at impact. You must be able to explain peculiarities of abnormalities.

For example, the left front headlamp shown in Exhibit 71 was clearly broken by heavy contact damage. Examination of the lamp (Exhibit 72) results in noting the abnormalities summarized in Exhibit 73 (part of the form for *Motor-vehicle Lamp Examination Record*).

Both filaments are deformed. The low filament (high beam), H, significantly more than the upper filament (low beam), L.

Both filaments are parted, the high beam by tapered burnout at T in Exhibit 72 and the low beam by heavy melting at M.

The same number of coils remain in each filament; hence, there is virtually no loss of filament in either.

The high-beam filament, H, is blackened by oxidation. The low beam filament, L, is covered by whitish oxide from one end to the other, mainly on the lower side closest to the high-beam filament.

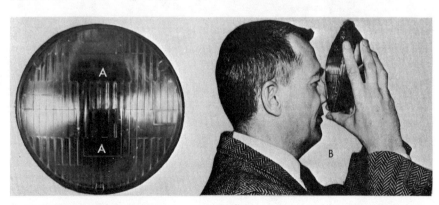

Exhibit 74. *Sealed beam filaments can be examined without opening bulb by looking directly into clear areas shown at **A** toward the reflector as shown at **B**. Filaments are seen magnified in the reflector.*

Both filaments indicate by elongation that they were hot at impact. The absence of brittle fracture in both indicates that they burned out after glass broke and let air in. But that implies that both filaments were on when glass broke, that is at the same time, which is not supposed to happen. Several circumstances indicate that both filaments were not on at the same time:

1. To have both on would require unusual lamp wiring. A test of the lamp socket and switch would show whether both could be on at once.
2. Both oxidation and stretch indicate that the high beam was incandescent. The lesser deformation of the upper filament shows that it was hot from being near and above the incadescent one but that it was not itself incandescent.
3. The whitish oxide from the lower filament was deposited on the under side of the upper filament by heated air rising from the incandescent filament.

If the low beam filament was not on when the lower one burned out, how did it get switched on and burned out later? There are two possibilities:

1. The lamp was broken in a previous accident and, perhaps because the break was not noticed, it was not repaired. Then, when the low beam was switched on later, the broken lamp promptly burned out the second filament. This is very unlikely. It can usually be ruled out if nobody remembers an appropriate previous accident.
2. After the collision, in which the high beam filament burned out, someone, inadvertently or to "test" the lights, switched on the low beam which then immediately burned out.

This hypothesis would be supported if the light switch was found in the low-beam positon after the accident.

8. EXAMINING LAMPS AND TESTING CIRCUITS

Caution

Do not look directly at lighted lamps, especially headlamps, with the naked eye. The intense light may injure eyes. Lights may be viewed directly through welder's goggles or an overexposed photographic film. Ordinary sunglasses are not dark enough.

Do not apply full voltage to a lamp which has broken or cracked glass. Circuits can be tested at three volts without harm.

Be very careful in handling halogen lamps. When lighted, the glass is almost red hot. Careless handling may cause the lamps to explode.

Permission to Remove and Examine

Do not remove or work on lamps after an accident without the owner's permission or other proper legal authorization. To do so may make your examination worthless as evidence in court. This usually limits preliminary examination to observation of the lamp in the vehicle. For legal authorization to remove the lamps, consult the attorney handling the case for a civil action, or the prosecutor in a criminal case.

Off-Vehicle Examination

After lamps have been removed — with permission — they can be examined more carefully in a convenient place.

Lamps with broken bulbs and exposed filaments are easily exmained with the unaided eye, with a magnifier, or if necessary, with a microscope. It may be helpful to bend aside the shade (hood) in a headlamp to look at filaments; but if you do so, make a written note of it so that it will not appear to have happened in the accident.

Lamps with bulbs intact rarely need to be broken open for examination. Filaments of miniature lamps are usually sufficiently visible through the glass of the bulb. Filaments of sealed beam lamps can be viewed by looking straight into the lamp through one or another of several spots in lens where the glass is unshaped. (Exhibit 74) The eye must be held very close to the lens surface (Exhbiit 74). The filaments are seen mirrored and magnified in the silvered rear surface of the bulb.

If you are not sure by visual examination whether the filament is intact, test the filament circuit to determine whether the filament will conduct electricity. Use low voltage to prevent damage. (Exhibit 85).

To examine broken or parted ends of filaments with a microscope or high-powered magnifier, one must place the lens very close to the filament. Then the glass bulb may have to be opened.

Opening Motor-Vehicle Lamps

Avoiding opening if you possibly can.

All but a few filaments in unbroken bulbs can be examined adequately without recourse to destructive measures. Exceptions are

1. Very small lamps so blackened by age deposits that the filament is invisible from outside.
2. Headlamps which have such bumpy lenses that the filaments are not clearly visible. There are not many such lamps.
3. Microscropic examination of filaments is *necessary*. This does not happen often.

Some laboratories routinely open all unbroken lamps examined. They seem to have no good reason for this usually needless operation.

An opened lamp is always more difficult to handle and store without further damage. In many cases opening the lamp leads to loss or breakage of parts which show signs of on or off.

Sometimes, especially with headlamps, it is desirable to open bulbs to photograph the filaments. Courtroom explanation of abnormalities may make photographic enlargements desirable. That may be sufficient reason to open a lamp.

Exhibit 75. *After a round sealed beam lamp is set to spinning on a smooth, level surface, a pencil-point propane torch flame can heat a circular strip on the reflector around the contact lugs.*

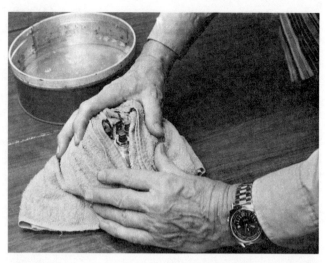

Exhibit 76. *After about half a minute of heating, the lamp reflector is suddenly cooled by covering with a wet towel. Normally, a crack forms in the reflector along the heated strip, thus opening the lamp.*

Exhibit 77. *If different kinds and sizes of sealed beam lamps are to be opened, rig up a turntable to rotate them. The one shown here is a cut-down can held to a baseboard by a nail through a hole in the center of the bottom.*

Exhibit 78. *Covers are made to hold lamps of different kinds on the turntable. In this case, the lamp is rotated by pulling one end and then the other of a cord wrapped around the can. The torch can be held in a rack.*

Halogen headlamps are special. The lamp itself is a thumbsized capsule of very strong quartz or glass. It is mounted in and protected by a reflector behind and a lens in front like those of a conventional headlamp. Advice against opening goes double for the little halogen capsule. It is difficult and dangerous to open and quite easy to look into. But the surrounding lens and reflector have to be opened, as a rule, to examine the filament. However, this does not expose or endanger the filament in the capsule.

Miniature bulbs are easily opened. One way is to cover the bulb with a plastic bag and squeeze it in a vise un-

til it breaks. The plastic bag catches the glass and loose bits of filament.

Another way is to score the bulb around the neck where the glass joins the base. Do this with a small triangular file. Then hold the base firmly and tap the bulb briskly with a pair of pliers or small hammer. Often the bulb will come loose where it has been scored and can be lifted neatly off. If this does not happen try squeezing it in a vise.

Note condition of filament before and after breaking open the bulb so that you know whether the filament was damaged in breaking the glass.

Instrument panel lights are usually little bulbs without metal bases, some-

time called "wedgies." If you have to open one of these, with a small triangular file, score around the bulb opposite the bead on the filament supports. Before you have scored well all the way around, the bulb may break off or break apart. If it does not do so, tap it briskly with pliers. On such a small bulb, there is danger of damaging the tiny filament when the glass breaks. Watch out for this.

Opening headlamps is difficult because lenses and most reflectors are made of very strong glass and are fused or cemented together.

The easiest to open are lamps in which an inner bulb can be removed from the rear of the reflector for

Exhibit 79. *Lacking other facilities, a slot can be cut in the reflector with tungsten carbide hacksaw blade.*

Exhibit 80. *Put the tip of a screwdriver in the slot and twist. This is at best a makeshift method.*

Exhibit 81. *The least damaging way to open a sealed beam lamp makes use of a can fitted with a block to go over the contact lugs of the lamp.*

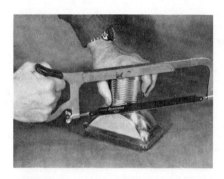

Exhibit 82. *With the can held down on the contact lugs as a guide, make a circular score in the reflector with a tungsten carbide hacksaw blade.*

Exhibit 83. *Heat the scored circle with an electric starter for a charcoal grill until the reflector cracks. Lift off the separated part.*

A *sealed beam lamp* can be broken open by smashing in the lens with a hammer. This destructive operation may easily do more harm than good. Do it only when you cannot possibly postpone opening until a better method can be used. If smashing is necessary, tape the lens to prevent glass shards from damaging the filament, and put the lamp in bag to catch the pieces, especially loose bits of filament.
replacement. These are usually manufactured outside of the U.S.A. They are not sealed. Exhibit 9 shows a removable inner lamp. The removed

bulb can then be opened, if necessary, like a miniature lamp.

Round sealed beam lamps can be opened easily if a propane torch with a pencil-point burner is available. Place the lamp, lens down, on a hard, smooth, level surface such as a plate of glass a foot or more square. By twisting the contact lugs, gently but firmly set the lamp spinning. Too much force will make it wobble. It may take a little practice to get the knack of it. Properly started, the lamp will spin for about a minute. Immediately after the lamp has been set spinning, direct the tip of the torch flame at the back of the reflector about halfway between the lugs and the rim, as in Exhibit 75. Hold it there half a minute or until the lamp has nearly stopped turning. If the reflector has not cracked by the this time, cover the lamp with a very wet towel which has been readied for this purpose (Exhibit 76). The reflector should crack with a click. If it does not, repeat the heating and chilling. Chilling can also be done by lifting the heated lamp by

one lug stem with a pair of pliers and plunging the lamp in a pan of water. When the reflector is cracked, grasp one of the lugs with pliers and lift. If the base does not come off after it is cracked, tap the reflector gently with a light hammer to extend the crack. When the base with filaments comes loose, set it aside carefully to cool. Be careful with the torch so as not to melt the solder holding the lugs in place. This method will not work with rectangular sealed beam lamps; they will not spin.

If you have to open rectangular sealed beam lamps, which cannot be spun around, or if you may have to open a number of lamps, rig up some kind of a turnable to rotate the lamp. A simple one made from a cut down steel can pivoted on a nail through a hole in the center of the bottom is illustrated in Exhibit 77. Wooden covers are cut to fit various round and rectangular lamps. A cord is wrapped twice around the can and rotation is accomplished by pulling alternately on the ends of the cord (Exhibit 78). Heat is applied to the rotating lamp and the lamp is suddenly chilled as already described.

Tungsten carbide hacksaw blades will cut glass. One way to open a sealed beam lamp is to saw through the reflector with such a blade at a point an inch or so from one of the terminal lugs (Exhibit 79). This is a tedious job. A power-driven abrasive disk can also be used to produce the opening. Then put the tip of a screwdriver through the slot so formed and twist (Exhibit 80). Do not pry. Breakage by this method is likely to be irregular.

The least damaging method of opening sealed beam lamps makes use of a tungsten carbide hacksaw blade and an electric starter for barbecue charcoal. A tin can with the same diameter as the loop in the starter is fitted with a block in which a T slot has been cut out to fit the lugs on the back of the lamp (Exhibit 81). Place the can over the lugs and hold it down firmly on the lamp. Then with the hacksaw, score the reflector around the edge of

MOTOR-VEHICLE LAMP EXAMINATION RECORD

Show on diagram location of lamp, contact damage area, and direction of thrust

FORD

FRONT

IDENTIFICATION

ACCIDENT OR CASE No. **Q 8024**		LAMP NO. **2**
ON street or road **IA 311**		
AT Intersection with or distance from **ALBION RD**		
IN City	County **MADISON**	State **IA**
HOUR of event **21:40**	DATE **5**	MONTH **9** · **1985**

OBTAINED FROM **L.A. BOYLE (IN PERSON)**	AT Place **TRAFFIC INST 405 CHURCH, EVANSTON**	BY Person **J.S. BAKER**		
USED FOR **RIGHT HEADLIGHT**	DAMAGE IN HANDLING **NONE KNOWN**	DATE **13**	MONTH **9**	**1985**
EXAMINED By Person **J.S. BAKER**	AT Organization, City **TRAFFIC INST 405 CHURCH, EVANSTON IL**	DATE **20**	MONTH **9**	**1985**
☒ Lamp photo ☐ Veh. photo	☒ WHERE STORED **LAMP CABINET NO. 2** ☐ HOW DISPOSED **433 WOODLAWN, GLENCOE, IL**	DATE **20**	MONTH **9**	**1985**

DESCRIPTION	See back of sheet for designations	TRADE NUMBER **6012 S**	MANUFACTURER **TUNG-SOL**

BASE **3-LUG**	BULB **PAR**	FILAMENTS **C6/C6**	VOLTS **12**	☒ WATTS **50** ☐ OHMS **40**

For each abnormality observed, mark the appropriate column X opposite the applicable description. Record estimated percentages where required. Notes may be added below.

Mark indications, if any, for each filament thus: X for definite, / for possible.

ABNORMALITIES OF SUPPORTS, GLASS, AND BASE		Single Small Low beam ☒	Other, if not single
FILAMENT SUPPORTS	Broken	A	
	Bent	X	X
	Rusted		
	Pitted		
	White deposit		
	Dirt or other deposit		
GLASS	% missing	90	
	Loose in base		
	Darkened		
	White deposit		
	Dirt or other deposit	C	
BASE	Damaged		
	Pitted		
	Dirt or corrosion	X	

ABNORMALITIES OF FILAMENTS	Single Small Low beam ☒	Other, if not single
Broken	X	X
% missing or detached	0	0
Loose in bulb		
End melted or tapered		X
End fractured	X	
Blackened		X
Tinted or light colored	X	
White deposit		
Moderately elongated		
Stretched out, uncoiled	X	X
Fused glass		X
Pitted		
Other, show in note below	B	B

INDICATIONS AND OPINIONS		Single Small Low beam ☒	Other, if not single
INDICATIONS	Incandescent		X
	Hot	X	
	Cold		
	Aged		
	Burned out		X
	Impact shock	X	X

For definite opinion, put two marks, √√, on the applicable line in the column for the filament. If an opinion is not definite but only probable, put one mark, √, in the applicable line for the filament. If which one of two filaments was on is indeterminate, put one mark, √, in both the on line and the indeterminate line for each of the pair of filaments.

OPINION	Off	√√	
	On		√√
	Indeterminate		

Additional descriptions and sketch of abnormalities may be put on the back of this sheet

Ⓐ SHIELD DETACHED   Ⓑ TANGLED TOGETHER
Ⓒ REFLECTOR PAINTED WHITE FOR PHOTO

SEE OTHER SIDE FOR SKETCH

© TRAFFIC INSTITUTE, NORTHWESTERN UNIVERSITY   870:776 RV   STOCK NO. 1122

Exhibit 84. Form for recording observations and conclusions resulting from lamp examination. A form is used for each lamp.

the can as in Exhibit 82. The scoring can also be done with a diamond glass cutter, but glass cutters with wheels are unsuitable. They require far too much pressure. Remove the can and hold the red hot charcoal starter loop on the scored circle, rotating the lamp slowly (Exhibit 83). In a few minutes, the reflector should crack along the scored line with a distinct click. Remove the heat. If the crack does not go completely around the reflector, tap the reflector on the scored line with a small hammer or pliers to extend the crack. Grasp a lug with pliers and lift off the part of the reflector attached to the filaments. Another tap or two may be needed to separate the parts. Before discarding the lens and remainder of the reflector, recover any fragments of filaments in them.

Headlamps with metal reflectors and inner bulbs which are soldered in place are sometimes found on motorcycles. The lens is attached to the reflector with an elastic sealant. The rim of the reflector may be crimped down over the edge of the lens. To open, pry the edge of the reflector from the lens with a screwdriver and pliers. Then loosen and remove the sealant around the entire circumference to separate the lens from the reflector.

After opening, the part of a sealed beam lamp with the filaments must be properly labeled for identification. Tape the sharp glass edges with masking tape to avoid cut fingers in handling. The silvered reflector can be painted or sprayed to reduce the reflection in examining the lamp, and especially for photographing the filament.

Lamp Examination Report

Any laboratory examination of a motor vehicle lamp to determine whether it was off or on at the time of a collision should result in a report covering a number of relevant topics:

Identification. Unlike motor vehicles, lamps do not carry identification numbers. Therefore label each lamp examined with a number to identify it as described in Section 9. Put this number on the lamp examination re-

port and also record, if known, the vehicle on which the lamp was used and its position and function on the vehicle. If the assigned identification number also connects the lamp with a particular accident, no further identification of the accident is necessary. But if the lamp number does not also identify the accident, add to the report the time and place of the accident so far as it is known.

Operations involving the lamp should be noted on the lamp examination report. Record when, where, and from whom or how the lamp was obtained; when, where, and by whom it was examined; and what was done with it afterward. This information is important in establishing continuity of possession of the lamp.

Description of the lamp is needed. If the trade number of the lamp (Exhibit 102) is known, that is adequate. Otherwise type of filament, base, and bulb are required in addition to the lamp voltage. These descriptions may be coded. (Exhibits 103, 104, and 105).

Abnormalities observed in the lamp must be recorded in detail on the lamp examination report. Drawings of the filament configuration may be useful for this purpose. If photos have been made, note that fact on the report; also note who made the photos.

Indications. Record opinion as to what each observed abnormality signifies. This is an important step in reaching a final conclusion. Indicate the degree of certainty of the indication.

Conclusions as to on or off for each filament in the lamp are the final items on the lamp examination report. The conclusion may be that the matter is indeterminate. A degree of certainty of conclusions may be noted: possible, probable, certain. Conclusions may be and often are based in part on other things besides the examination of the lamp, for example, damage to the vehicle, condition of wiring, switches, and fuses, and examination of other lamps and filaments associated with the specimen under consideration.

A lamp examination report form,

such as that illustrated in Exhibit 84, provides a very convenient way to record identification, operations, description, observations, indications and conclusions as to whether the lamp was on or off at the time of the crash. If you expect to examine lamps technically from time to time, it is worthwhile to obtain and use such forms. The form is designed primarily for reports of laboratory examinations, but it may also be used for in-vehicle examination, especially if you are not permitted to take the lamp from the vehicle for examination. Use a separate form for each lamp examined. There is a disadvantage in the use of a form: it discourages recording unusual or puzzling observations, drawings or sketches of conditions observed, and writing notes or comments relating to reasoning leading from observations to conclusions.

Light Switch Position

Position of a light switch noted after a crash may suggest whether the controlled lights were on or off but is usually not, by itself, conclusive.

In minor accidents, a same-direction collison with a parked car for example, the driver, realizing that lights should have been on when they were actually off, may switch them on after the crash, as described earlier.

It is possible that in removing injured or examining the interior of the vehicle after a crash, light switches

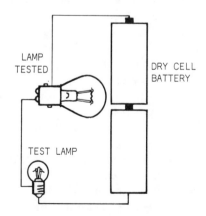

Exhibit 85. *Simple circuit tester made from flashlight batteries and lamp. It will not burnout automobile lamp filaments.*

may inadvertently be turned on or off. Because plunger switches are off when pushed in, lights are more likely to be turned off than on inadvertently.

Severe crashes may open or close a plunger switch. If the vehicle is suddenly slowed (decelerated) by crashing into an object ahead, inertia of the plunger which keeps it moving forward when the car crashes may force the switch into closed position. In the same way, a car suddenly accelerated by being hit in the rear may tend to snap the switch from off to on position. Sidewise crashes would not affect the position of the switch. Turn signal levers may also be repositioned by a crash, but rocker and tumbler switches are not likely to be affected.

A light switch turned off during or after crash will have no effect on what the filaments show about whether lamps were on or off. But examination of filaments will sometimes indicate whether the light switch was turned on during or after the crash.

Circuit Testing

Circuit testing serves two purposes: 1) to determine whether the filament in the lamp is intact (neither broken nor parted), 2) to determine whether wires and other parts of an electric circuit to a light on a vehicle are functional. The former is easy; the latter more difficult.

Test equipment. Simple suitable test equipment can be contrived from a two-cell flashlight and its lamp. This gives a 3-volt circuit which will not heat lamps enough to burn them out if they are broken (Exhibit 85). A volt-ohmmeter can also be used to measure resistance of the circuit.

Do not use full 6- or 12-volt power sources for testing circuits. That much voltage can burn out or oxidize filaments in broken lamps.

Lamp filaments are tested after the lamp has been removed from the vehicle. Connect the dry cell (flashlight) battery, the test lamp and the auto lamp in series. (Exhibit 85). If the test lamp lights the circuit is intact; if it does not, the filament is broken or

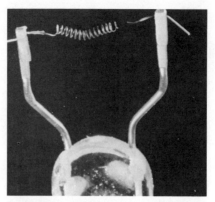

Exhibit 86. *Conditions under which a filament is observed may be deceptive. This filament, with front light and dark background, seems to have no discoloration.*

burned out. With a volt-ohmmeter, a very high ohm reading means that the circuit is open and the filament is not intact; otherwise it is intact.

Vehicle circuits can be tested if you cannot determine from the lamps whether the light in question was on or off. If the circuit is broken somewhere (defective switch, broken wires, burned-out fuse, loose connection, for example) the light would presumably have been off at the time of the crash; and it would have been on if the circuit is unbroken. To test the circuit, remove the lamp if it has not already been removed. Disconnect the terminals. Connect the 3-volt battery between the battery terminals. Connect wires from the test-lamp to the socket to be tested. Be sure connections are good. Turn on the light switch. If the test light lights, the circuit is good, if not it is open. To use a volt-ohmmeter,

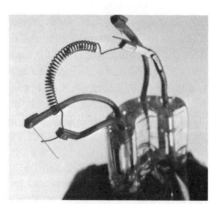

Exhibit 88. *This filament certainly looks deeply discolored with light background and side lighting. It could easily be mistaken for a heavily oxidized lamp filament.*

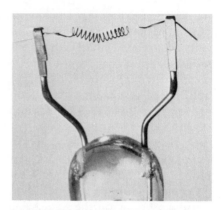

Exhibit 87. *The same filament, with diffuse light and light background, shows its true colors: black from heavy oxidation. Note that the filament is burned out.*

connect the battery terminals together and close the switch. Connect the meter terminals to the lamp socket. Very high ohm readings show an open circuit; otherwise it is normal.

If the circuit is open, one must also know that is was not broken in the crash to conclude that the light was off at the time of the accident. You may have to trace out individual wires to determine whether wiring was damaged or a fuse blown because of a short circuit caused by the crash. If the circuit is complete, one must also know that the lamp was not burned out and that the switch was on to be confident that the lamp was burning.

Circuits can also be tested with the car battery. But first be sure to remove all lamps with broken glass and all with known broken filaments. A properly charged battery must be in place. Turn on the switch for the lights

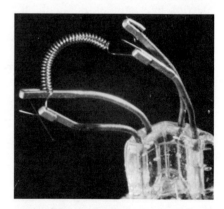

Exhibit 89. *But under different light and background, the filament shows no discoloration whatsoever. One must be very careful, about how filaments are observed.*

in question. If they light, the circuit is operational. If the lamp has been removed replace it for testing with another of the same trade number.

If the lamp does not light normally when switched on, check wiring to determine whether a short circuit to the ground caused by the crash made a fuse blow when power was switched on.

Lighting May Affect Lamp Examination

The light by which a lamp is examined may make accurate observations difficult. This is especially so in viewing filaments through sealed beam lenses, in examinations with a magnifier, and when observing small pieces of filament still attached to supports.

With strong front lighting, a heavily oxidized filament may look light, especially with a dark background (Exhibit 86). Also with weak front light, a bright filament may appear dark or discolored, especially with a light background (Exhibit 87). To avoid such misleading difficulties, examine the filament under different lighting arrangements. Exhibits 88 and 89 show how an oxidized filament looks under different lighting.

Comparison Lamps and Experiments

Sometimes it is useful to have an undamaged lamp to show the difference between it and a lamp from the accident. The comparison lamp should carry the same trade number (Exhibit 102) as the lamp in the accident and should be made by the same manufacturer. If the trade number has been obliterated on the lamp, it can usually be determined from a description of the lamp.

Sometimes tests of similar bulbs can demonstrate results of collisions on lamps. Experiments can also be conducted to try to reproduce observed conditions in lamps or to test assumptions about the results of certain treatment of lamps.

Exact experimental duplication of abnormalities, especially filament deformation is, of course, impossible. There are too many variables. Experiments can, however, be highly instructive to the investigator seeking to learn how abnormalities come about. If you do make experiments, be sure to keep a detailed record of what you did and the results obtained. Keep the experimental lamps for future reference.

9. HANDLING AND STORING LAMPS

Equipment

Whoever has to remove lamps from vehicles to examine them will be well advised to have at hand certain equipment.

Phillips and ordinary screwdrivers, large and small, will be needed to get lamp housings free. A short pry bar is helpful in removing fixtures jammed in wreckage. Slim nosed and slip-joint pliers can be used to take broken lamps from sockets. Diagonal cutting pliers are indispensable for cutting off wires to headlamps and lamp fixtures. Avoid hammers; they may do as much harm as good.

A roll of ¾-in. masking tape and a dozen styrofoam (not paper) drinking cups will help in temporary labelling and packing.

Removing Lamps from Vehicle

The purpose of removing a lamp from a vehicle in traffic-accident investigation is to examine it more closely than is possible on the vehicle or to keep it as evidence after the vehicle has been sold, destroyed, or repaired.

Unbroken lamps require little special care in removal or subsequent handling. They are strong. Small ones may be carried loose in a car. Any box for shipping will do if the lamp does not rattle about in it. No ordinary handling is likely to further damage the filaments although a sharp bump may break loose a crystalized filament which is already detached at one end or break a loose filament into smaller parts.

Sometimes bases and sockets of small lamps are so corroded that the lamps cannot easily be loosened. Do not try to force them. The glass bulb may break or it may come loose from the base. It is better to remove as much of the light fixture as is necessary to get the lamp without risk of breaking. (Exhibit 90). Tail lights can often be removed from the inside of the trunk.

Broken lamps require great care in removal and handling. Permit nothing to touch exposed filaments. If pieces of filament are missing, search for them in the lamp housing. It may be possible to recover them.

Sealed beam lamps. In removing broken sealed beam lamps, do not try to pull terminal lugs from the connector, especially if glass between the lugs is cracked; cut the wires off beyond the connector. (Exhibit 91).

Broken sealed beam lamps can sometimes be removed with the mounting ring and retaining ring attached to hold the lamp together (Exhibit 92).

Put masking or other adhesive tape across cracks; if possible do it before removing the lamp (Exhibit 93).

If lamp has an opening in the glass but the filament is not exposed, tape over the opening to protect the filament (Exhibit 94).

If lens is all or nearly all gone, cover it with a paper cup taped or tied firmly in place to protect the filament supports. Do not try to straighten filament supports (Exhibit 95A).

Broken small lamps are usually best handled by removing the entire light fixture or at least the part supporting the lamp base (Exhibit 90).

If the lamp base and filament supports are removed but a filament is exposed, stick the lamp base in a hole punched in the bottom of a styrofoam hot drink cup. Put another cup with the bottom torn off over this as a spacer and put a third with the bottom in as a cover. Tape the cups together (Exhibit 95B). The open ends of the cups can be trimmed off to reduce space requirements. Identifying information can be written easily on the cups with a ballpoint pen.

Pieces of broken filament may have dropped into the broken bulb or lamp

Exhibit 90. *When removing broken lamps, remove the entire lamp housing if possible.*

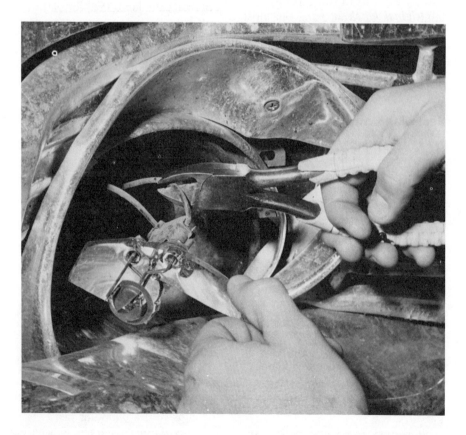

Exhibit 91. *If a sealed beam lamp is broken between lugs; leave connector, cut wires.*

housing. Look carefully for these. After removing a broken lamp, tip it over and empty it out on a piece of white paper to recover any bits of loose filament. The paper may be folded over or put in an envelope temporarily to contain the loose material. As soon as practical, however, spread the loose material out and scoop up bits of filament with a narrow strip of thin strong paper folded length-wise as in Exhibit 96. Do not try to pick them up with a moistened fingertip. Avoid tweezers, which may break a fragile bit of filament into smaller pieces.

Loose bits of filament are easy to lose. Package them carefully. One way is to put them in small acetate envelopes such as stamp collectors use (Exhibit 97). Use an adhesive label to seal the envelope and identify its contents.

Another good way to package loose bits of filament is to put them in square cardboard folders such as coin collectors use. Each side of the hinged folder has an opening covered with a transparent film. Fold two halves together with the specimen between and then staple the halves together. Write identifying data on the folder (Exhibit 98). Both of these methods permit examination of the filament without removal from the holder and easy storage.

Photographing

For record or exhibit purposes, damaged lamps may have to be photographed. Sealed beam lamps must be opened for this purpose. A macro lens is required for close up pictures of filaments either while the lamp is still on the vehicle or after it has been removed.

To avoid bothersome reflections coat headlamp reflectors, with flat water based paint or cover them with masking tape.

Photograph filaments against a medum gray background with very diffuse lightning. That gets rid of contrasts which might be misleading as to the degree of discoloration of the filament.

Exhibit 92. *With broken headlamp, try to remove entire housing to prevent further damage.*

Identification

Label every lamp removed from a vehicle at the time of removal. Do not depend on memory to identify where a particular lamp came from on a particular vehicle. Do not depend on a label on an envelope or other container; it is too easy for lamps to be switched in containers. The label should identify the accident (number or time and place), the vehicle (registration number or brief description), and the location on the vehicle (part of the vehicle and function of lamp).

Original label. Perhaps the most satisfactory way to label lamps when they are taken from the vehicle is to write the data on ¾-inch masking tape which is then stuck to the lamp. (Exhibit 99). There is usually room enough for this on the lens or reflector of a sealed beam lamp, but if most of these surfaces are gone or if the lamp is a small one, the masking tape can be folded back on itself to cover the adhesive back of the inscribed area and then the other end wrapped around the base of the lamp. The label may be larger than the lamp (Exhibit 99).

Final labels generally replace original ones when the lamp has been examined and a report is prepared. This can be a small adhesive label with the accident number and a lamp number on it; details are on a corresponding report. Covering the label with transparent Mystic tape will help hold the label in place and protect it (Exhibit 49).

Personal identification. As with such objects as weapons and burglary tools collected for possible use as evidence, whoever examines a lamp may want to mark it with some personal positive identification for future reference. Tags, labels, and crayon markings on glass are unsuitable; they are too easily removed. A notch filed in a contact or base or something like that is more suitable, as illustrated in Exhibit 100. If such a mark is put on a specimen, note that fact on the lamp examination report; otherwise you may forget about it later.

Storage After Examination

Unbroken sealed beam lamps can be kept indefinitely on a shelf or in a box without special packing.

Opened sealed beam lamps and smaller lamps can be conveniently stored in square, pint-size, polyethylene freezer containers. A slab of 1-inch styrofoam cut to fit snuggly in the bottom of the container will hold the lamp in place. The lamp may be tied or wired to it or pushed into the holes cut in it. The styrofoam base can be removed for lamp inspection without disturbing the lamps. Edges of broken sealed beam reflectors may have to be nipped down with pliers to fit in these containers or else larger similar containers may be used (Exhibit 101).

Accidents in Handling

Broken lamps are easily damaged further in handling. Perhaps the most common accident is breaking an ex-

Exhibit 93. *If cracked lens has loose pieces, put tape over cracks before removing.*

Exhibit 94. *To protect filaments when a piece is broken out of headlamp, tape paper over the opening.*

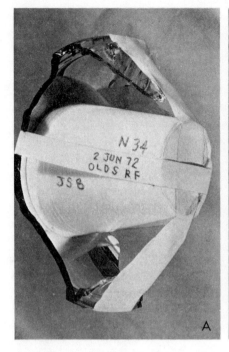

Exhibit 96. Bits of filament can be scooped up from among bits of glass with a narrow paper trough.

Exhibit 95. Styrofoam cups are useful in protecting filaments of broken lamps. Right, three cups used to support and protect a small lamp. Left, cup taped over sealed beam filaments to protect them.

posed filament.

This can happen in removing the lamp from the vehicle. In a small lamp, the filament can be snapped by a tool or by a finger. In headlamps, a cracked reflector can separate between filament supports and stretch or break a filament.

Harm can also occur in packing. The most common damage comes from well-intended but misguided efforts to protect the filament by packing it in crumpled paper, tissues, or cotton. Any of these can snag and break a filament and some leave fibers on a filament that can be disconcerting in examining.

If a filament is broken in removing the lamp, (or if it has been broken in the accident) try to find loose parts and preserve them.

Do not Scotch tape a filament to a card. The filament is difficult to see under the tape, it may break when the tape is removed, and adhesive from the tape leaves the filament surface gummy.

Damage by dropping. The most common accident in handling is dropping a lamp. Experiments were made

to discover what harm that might do. Cold lamps were dropped from four feet first on commercial carpet, then on wood or asphalt tile, and finally on portland-cement concrete.

A new, 12-volt, single-filament headlamp was dropped repeatedly face down. No significant effect was noted until it fell on concrete. Then lens and reflector shattered. The reflector cracked between filament supports and the filament fractured.

But in our test on an aged 12-volt two-filament headlamp, both filaments of which had been lit until the low beam burned out, the burned-out filament broke off on the first drop on carpet and the other one on the first drop on asphalt tile floor.

A new, 12-volt, 2-filament tail-signal lamp showed no effect when dropped base down on concrete, but when dropped bulb down, the glass broke, supports bent and filament stretched but did not break.

A similar, 6-volt bulb was dropped with essentially the same result.

An old, 12-volt tail-signal lamp showed no effect except a cracked insulator after base-down drops on concrete. Dropped sidewise, glass broke

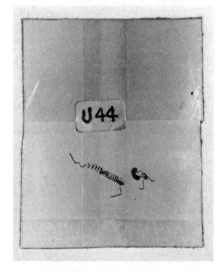

Exhibit 97. A plastic envelope is useful as a place to store loose bits of filaments.

and filament supports bent a little sidewise.

Thus, except for lamps with filaments burned out or weakened by long use, accidental dropping is unlikely to have any noticeable effect on filament. If the effect of the handling accident is known and reported, dropping a lamp would ordinarily not interfere with determining whether the lamp was on or off when the collision occurred.

Continuity of Possession

When you examine a lamp after an

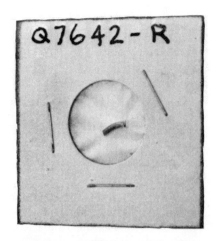

Exhibit 98. *Folders with transparent opening used by coin collectors will protect bits of filament.*

Exhibit 99. *Label every lamp as soon as it is removed. Masking tape is suitable for this purpose. Later it can be replaced with more permanent identification.*

automobile accident you can report your observations of the condition of the lamp *when you examined it* and your conclusions relating to whether it was on or off based on its condition *when you examined it.*

If you examined the lamp in the vehicle immediately after the accident, your conclusions as to whether the lamp was on or off then naturally also apply before the accident. But if you examined the lamp later, especially if you received it from someone else, you must be very careful about what you say or imply with respect to its operating condition before the crash. Something may have happened to change its condition between the collision and the time you examined it. For example, an unbroken headlamp in a damaged car can be easily broken in towing the car from the scene of the accident. It is useful in this connection to have detailed photos of the lamp in the car at the scene.

Then it may be up to others to show what, if anything, happened to affect the lamp from the time of the accident until you received it. In other words "continuity of possession" must be established from the scene of the accident to your examination.

For any lamp you examine, the main thing to be sure of is that the lamp is the same one that was in a particular position in a particular vehicle in a particular accident.

If filaments of an unbroken lamp

are intact, you can be confident that its condition has not been accidentally changed by handling. But of course someone, on purpose, could have produced hot impact shock that was not present after the accident.

Damage after accident. If filaments in unbroken lamp bulbs are not intact, make sure of two things: 1) nobody burned it out by "testing" it with over voltage, for example connecting a 6-volt lamp to a 12-volt power source; or 2) it was not dropped on a hard floor which might produce cold shock. Lamps packed in boxes are unlikely to be damaged by dropping.

If the lamp bulb is broken, it is important to establish whether breakage occurred in removing the lamp or handling it after removal. It is also important to know whether filaments were damaged in removing, packing, or handling the lamp.

The importance of establishing who kept or handled the lamp and what may have happened to it between accident and examination is one reason for a record of preliminary, in-vehicle examination (Exhibit 21 and 22) and for records of who had the lamp at any time before examination.

Testifying in Court

In many cases the examination of lamps will result in testimony in court either in a civil negligence case, or a criminal prosecution, or possibly both. Either the prosecutor or attor-

ney handling the case has the responsibility of placing you on the witness stand and laying the foundations for your testimony. Important rules of evidence apply in this connection.[10] Also, in criminal cases, the legal authority to seize and examine lamps is governed by search and seizure law.

10. LAMPS COMMONLY USED ON MOTOR VEHICLES

Lamp Descriptions

Lamps for motor vehicles are described by four classifications:
1. Filament configuration, Exhibit 103.
2. Base arrangements, Exhibit 104.
3. Bulb shape and diameter, Exhibit 105.

Exhibit 100. *If lamp cannot be kept, a special mark may be useful to identify it later. In this case, it is a small notch filed in a contact.*

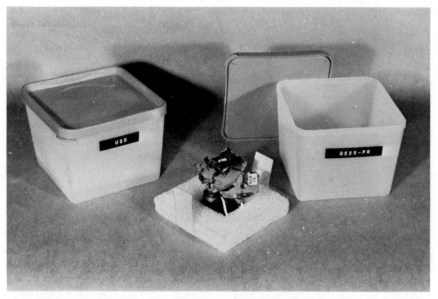

Exhibit 101. *Plastic freezer boxes fitted with styrofoam blocks make an excellent permanent storage for broken lamps. Be sure to label each properly.*

Exhibit 102.

LAMPS COMMONLY USED IN MOTOR VEHICLES

Trade Numbers	Uses	Filaments	Bases	Bulb Shapes, Sizes	
		6-Volt Service			
6006	Headlamp	C6/C6	3-lug	PAR	179 dia.
4020	Cycle headlamp	C6/C6	3-lug	PAR	146 dia.
1154	Tail, stop, turn, park	C6/C6	DC Index	S	25 dia.
1158	Stop, tail, signal	C6/C6	DC Index	S	25 dia.
1133	Back up	C2R	SC Bay.	RP	35 dia.
1128	Interior, turn, stop	C6	SC Bay.	S	25 dia.
		12-volt Service			
H6054	Low-beam, halogen	C6/C6	3-lug	PAR	142 x 200
6052	Low-beam	C6/C6	3-lug	PAR	142 x 200
H6052	Low-beam halogen	C6/C6	3-lug	PAR	142 x 200
H6024	Headlamp halogen	C6/C6	3-lug	PAR	179 dia.
6017	Headlamp	C6/C6	3-lug	PAR	179 dia.
6016	Headlamp	C6/C6	3-lug	PAR	146 dia.
6014, 6015	Headlamp	C6/C6	3-lug	PAR	179 dia.
H6014	Headlamp halogen	C6/C6	3-lug	PAR	179 dia.
6012, 6013	Headlamp	C6/C6	3-lug	PAR	179 dia.
H5006	Low-beam halogen	C6/C6	3-lug	PAR	146 dia.
H5001	High-beam halogen	C6	2-lug	PAR	146 dia.
H4656	Low-beam	C6/C6	3-lug	PAR	100 x 165
4652	Low-beam	C6/C6	3-lug	PAR	100 x 165
4652	Low-beam	C6/C6	3-lug	PAR	100 x 165
4651	High-beam	C6	2-lug	PAR	100 x 165
H4651	High-beam halogen	C6	2-lug	PAR	100 x 165
4420	Cycle headlamp	C6/C6	3-lug	PAR	146 dia.
4002, 4005	Low-beam	C6/C6	3-lug	PAR	146 dia.
4001, 4006	High-beam	C6	2-lug	PAR	146 dia.
4001	High-beam	C6	2-lug	PAR	146 dia.
4000	Low-beam	C6	2-lug	PAR	146 dia.
1895	Indicator, marker	C2R	Min. Bay.	G	11 dia.
1178	Auto heavy duty	C2V	DC Bay.	G	19 dia.
1176, 1376	Tail,park, turn, stop	C6/C6	DC Bay.	S	25 dia.
1141, 1159	Turn, stop, back	C6	SC Bay.	S	25 dia.
1073, 1156	Back, turn, stop	C6	SC Bay.	S	25 dia.
1034, 1157	Tail, park, stop, turn	C6/C6	DC Index	S	25 dia.
1004	Interior	C6	DC Bay.	B	19 dia.
1003	Interior	C6	SC Bay.	B	19 dia.
631	Instrument, tail,	2C/2V	SC Bay.	G	19 dia.
194	Indicator, marker	C2F	Wedge	T	10 dia.
67	Instrument, registr.	C2R	SC Bay.	G	10 dia.

4. Volts and watts.

The categories in each of the first three classifications have been assigned standard abbreviations and code numbers by the American National Standards Institute[6] (Exhibits 103, 104, and 105).

Trade numbers and corresponding descriptions of lamps commonly used in motor vehicles are listed in Exhibit 102.

Filament configurations commonly found are illustrated and identified by their code numbers in Exhibit 103. In these codes, C means coiled. Most automobile lamps have coiled filaments that go straight across from one support to the other, code C6. When there are two filaments in the same lamp the two designations are separated by a virgule (slant). Thus a two-beam headlamp has C6/C6 filaments.

Bases of motor-vehicle lamps are rarely of the screw-in type, such as are found in house lamps, because screw-in lamps would come loose too easily by vehicle vibration.

There are three main kinds of bases: 1) lug connectors for sealed beam lamps usually used for headlights, 2) bayonet bases (designated by Bay) which are pushed straight into the socket against a spring and given a slight clockwise twist to hold them in place, and 3) wedge bases used in the small lamps for instruments.

Base arrangements are illustrated and identified in Exhibit 104. In these codes, SC means single contact and DC means double contact. Two filament lamps have DC bases. PAR means parabolic reflector.

Lamps with two filaments are usually "indexed". That means they can be put into their sockets in only one way so as to connect each filament contact with the proper circuit for its function (Exhibits 106 and 107). These are the most commonly used two filament lamps. Knowing these connections is useful in testing circuits and examining lamps.

Headlamps usually have lug terminals or prefocused bases; instrument

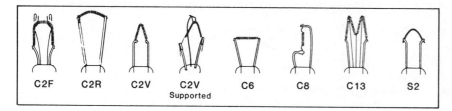

Exhibit 103. Filament arrangements in automobile lamps.

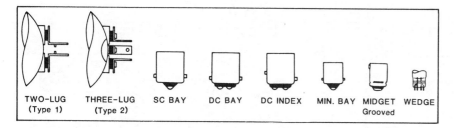

Exhibit 104. Bases used in automotive lamps.

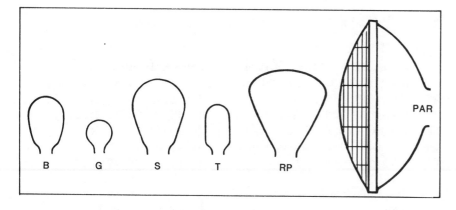

Exhibit 105. Bulb shapes of automotive lamps.

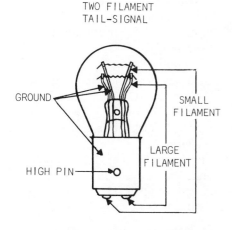

Exhibit 106. Terminal connections for two-filament small lamps.

On small lamps, the voltage is sometimes indicated by the color of a glass bead on the filament supports. White beads are for 12 volts. It is very important to have voltage of the lamp the same as the voltage of the electric power supply. Otherwise the light output of the lamp and its life will be seriously affected.

Sometimes the current (amperes) resulting from operating the lamp at the rated voltage is also shown on the lamp or on descriptive material relating to it, for example 6 A for 6 amperes. The current rating times the voltage rating gives the wattage or power requirement of the lamp.

Wattage is rarely shown on motor vehicle lamps. It is usually stated in descriptive material relating to the lamp, for example 35 W. Wattage is approximately proportional to light output or "strength" of the lamp.

11. SOURCES

Contributors

This topic was developed by the following persons:

J. Stannard Baker principal author of this publication, is a consultant in traffic accident investigation. He was director of Research and Development at the Northwestern University Traffic Institute from 1946 to 1971.

Thad L. Aycock has been on The Traffic Institute staff since 1967 and in the Accident Investigation Division since 1981. Formerly a member of the Georgia Highway Patrol, he was graduated from Piedmont College, Georgia, in Business Adminstration. Aycock has been an instructor in the Institute's Lamp examination course since it was started.

Thomas D. Lindquist is a Captain in the Colorado State Patrol. Capt. Lindquist has been with the patrol since 1955 and has also served as an administrative staff member and instructor at the Colorado Law Enforcement Training Academy. He is a graduate of The Traffic Institute's Police Administration Training Program.

lamps may have wedge or midget grooved bases; other lamps usually have bayonet bases. Some other bases than those shown are used in motor vehicles.

Bulb shapes are illustrated and designated in Exhibit 105. The abbreviation PAR is the familiar sealed beam lamp bulb. Other bulb shapes than those shown are sometimes used in motor vehicles.

Lamp Power

Voltage is nearly always marked on the lamp as in the 12 V in Exhibit 99.

CONNECTIONS IN 2-FILAMENT SEALED BEAM HEADLAMPS
114,146, and 178 mm DIAMETER

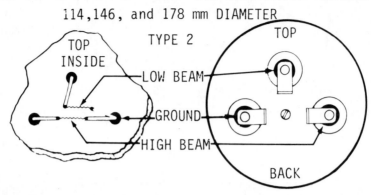

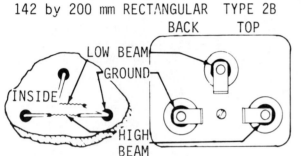

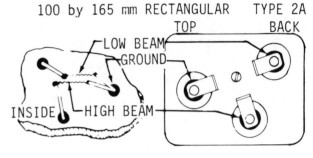

Exhibit 107. *Terminal connections for sealed beam lamps and similar halogen lamps.*

References

Superscript numbers in the preceding pages refer to the following publications:

1. *Dimensional Specifications for Sealed Beam Headlamp Units* (SAE J751); Feb 1981, Society of Automotive Engineers, Warrendale PA.

2. *Lighting Identification Code* (SAE J759), May 1983, Society of Automotive Engineers, Warrendale PA 15096 (1 page)

3. Bleyel, Robert L., "Who Had the Green Signal?" in *Journal of Police Science and Administration,* International Association of Chiefs of Police, Gaithersburg MD

4. Heaslip, T. W., M. Vermij, and M. R. Poole, "Advances in the Analysis of Aircraft Crash Impacted Light Bulbs" in *ISASI Forum,* International Society of Air Safety Investigators, Washington DC (12 pages)

5. Zyss, Victor, *Problems in Investigation of Vehicle Accidents at Night,* (unpublished report to Israeli police) 1971

6. *Miniature Incandescent Lamps* (ANSI C78.390 — 1964) American National Standards Institute, New York NY 10018

7. *Miniature, Sub-miniature and Sealed Beam Lamps* (Specification Guide S-604), 1972, Westinghouse Electric Corp., Specialty Lamp Div. Bloomfield NJ

8. *Turn Signal Flashers* (SAE Standard J590e), 1977, Society of Automotive Engineers, Warrendale PA 15096

9. Kremmling, G. and A. Schontage, "Zur Systematik Unterschung von Fahrzeuglampen nach Verkehrsunfallen" in *Archiv fur Kriminologie* (Vol. 28), 1961, Schmidt-Romhild, Lubek, Germany

10. LaFave, Wayne R., *Search and Seizure, A Treatise on the Fourth Amendment,* (Sec.7.3(a), 1978, West Publishing Co., St. Paul MN

Exhibits

The following are sources of tables, drawings, charts and photographs used in this topic:

Aycock, Thad L., Traffic Institute, Evanston, IL

Photos: 45, 46, 62, 71,72

Baker, J. Stannard, Glencoe, IL

Photos: 3, 4, 8, 9, 10, 11, 12, 14, 17, 18, 19, 20, 24, 25, 26, 27, 28, 29, 30, 32D, 35A, 36, 37, 38, 39, 41, 42, 43, 44, 47, 48, 49, 51, 54, 55, 56, 57, 58, 59, 60, 63, 65, 66, 67, 68, 69, 70, 74, 77, 80, 81, 82, 83, 86, 87, 88, 89, 90, 91, 92, 93, 94, 95, 96, 97, 98, 99, 100, 101

Diagrams: 2, 6, 7, 85, 106, 107

Chart: 23

Tables: 61, 73, 102

Forms: 21, 22, 84

Fricke, Lynn B., Traffic Institute, Evanston, IL

Photos: 75, 76, 78, 79

Galloway News and Photo Service, Springfield, IL

Photo: 33F

Herald Leader, Lexington KY

Photo: 31A

Lindquist, Thomas, L., Colorado State Patrol

Photos: 5, 13, 15, 16, 34A, 35B, 50, 52, 58

Diagrams: 1, 64

Table: 53

Sundeen, Gene L.
Reese Airforce Base TX
Photo: 40
Ross, Terry, Mishawaka IN
Photo: 32C
Unknown
Photos: 33E
Diagrams: 103, 104, 105
Zehring & Ross, Mishawaka IN
Photos: 31B
Zyss, Victor, Tel Aviv, Israel
Photo: 34B

Other Material

Technical articles on examining lamps after motor-vehicle accidents have been appearing from time to time since 1950. They originate mainly from crime laboratories.

Additional reading related to this topic may be found in the following publications:

• Dolan, D. N. 1971. "Vehicle Lights and Their Use as Evidence," in *Journal of the Forensic Science Society,* Vol. 11 No. 2. London.

• Haas, M. A., M. J. Camp, and R. F. Dragen. 1974. "A Comparative Study of the Applicability of the Scanning Electron Microscope and the Light Microscope in the Examination of Vehicle Light Filaments." *Journal of Forensic Sciences.*

• Mather, J., 1975, "Evidence Obtained from the Examination of Incandescent Electric Lamps, Particularly Lamps of Vehicles Involved in Road Accidents" in *International Criminal Police Review* (No. 284), Paris, France.

• Powell, G. L. F. 1977. "Interpretation of Vehicle Globe Failures: The Unit Condition." *Journal of Forensic Sciences.*

• *SAE Ground Vehicle Lighting Manual* (HS-34). 1985, Society of Automotive Engineers, Warren PA 15096 (256 Pages)

• Schaudinishchky, H. L. 1964. "Hat die Kraftfahrzeug-Schlussleuchte vor einem nachtlichen Auffahrnufall noch Gabrannt?" in *Zeitschrift fur Verkehrssicherheit,* 10 Jahrgang, 1964, IV Quartal, Heft 4, P. 253. Dr. Arthur Tetzlaff, publisher. Frankfort am Main, Germany.

• Severy, D. M. "Headlight-Taillight Analysis for Collision Research" 1967. Society of Automotive Engineers Paper 660786 in *10th Stapp Car Crash Conference*

• Thiele, Roland. 1958. "Examination of Car Lights after a Road Accident" in *International Criminal Police Review,* No. 116. Paris, France.

• Thompson, J. W. 1971. "Switched On?" in *Journal of the Forensic Science Society,* Vol. 11, No. 3. London.

• Thornton, J. I., G. Mitosinka, and T. L. Hayes. "Comparison of Tungsten Filament by Means of the Scanning Electron Microscope" in *Journal of the Forensic Science Society,* Vol. 11, No. 3. London.

• Woods, Joseph D. 1977. "Headlights Are Tools in Traffic Accident Investigation" in *Law & Order,* June 1977, p. 60.

TIRE EXAMINATION FOLLOWING ACCIDENTS

Topic 825 of the *Traffic-Accident Investigation Manual*

by
James D. Gardner
and
J. Stannard Baker

NORTHWESTERN UNIVERSITY TRAFFIC INSTITUTE

PUBLICATION HISTORY
Topic 825

1968 *Tire Disablements and Accidents on a High Speed Road*

1972 *Examination of Tires after a Traffic Accident* (SN 8040)

1977 *Tire Examination Following Accidents* (PN 83)
Reprinted 1978, 1979
1981 Revised (PN 803)
1985 Revised

TIRE EXAMINATION FOLLOWING ACCIDENTS

During a traffic-accident investigation, there may be a question as to whether a tire contributed to the accident. To answer this question properly takes thoughtful investigation. Unquestionably tire disablement can be a factor in an accident, but experience shows that it is nearly always in combination with deficiencies in other parts of the vehicle, with irregularities in the road, or probably most commonly in connection with driver ineptitude. For example, it is not uncommon for air loss in a front tire of a tractor hauling a trailer over the road to cause a pull toward that tire. Ordinarily a driver would have no trouble correcting for that drift. When a particular driver could not do so, a careful investigation revealed a worn out steering gear as an important contributing factor. A study of tire disablements on a high-speed road[1] indicates that only about one tire disablement in 4000 was followed by an accident. It seems, therefore, that a small number of drivers are unable successfully to handle a flat tire. Other studies have shown that power or center point steering would have made the difference between an accident and no accident following a tire disablement.

Systematic tire examination and careful consideration of all related aspects of the accident can usually show well enough whether disablement led to the accident or the accident resulted in tire disablement.

A tire is a much more complicated structure than it appears to be. Therefore, to determine whether tire failure was due to abuse, misapplication or defect takes special skills, equipment, and experience which are not commonly available.

This topic deals with highway accidents, therefore, the discussion is limited to automobile and truck tires.

Under some circumstances tires may contribute to accidents in the following ways:

1. Tread characteristics such as the amount of wear may affect the performance of the vehicle, particularly on wet surfaces.
2. Rapid loss of air.
3. Intermix of non-compatible tires, such as radial and bias, on the same vehicle.
4. Improper tire selection affecting vehicle control and stability.

1. TYPES OF AUTOMOBILE AND TRUCK TIRES

There are three basic types of tires used on highways today: radial tires, bias belted tires and bias tires. These constructions are used to make automobile tires, light truck tires, and heavy truck tires.

The *radial* tire has grown in popularity in recent years because of its inherent advantage of increased wear and reduced fuel consumption. It derives its name from the direction of its body plies. The body ply cords in a radial tire run radially straight across under the tread plies from bead to bead. Radial tires also have belts or tread plies that run around the circumference of the tire in the tread or road contact area of the tire. Exhibit 1 shows the components of a typical

Exhibit 1. *Radial belted tire construction.*

Exhibit 3. *Belted bias tire construction.*

Exhibit 2. *Bias truck tire construction.*

radial passenger tire.

The *bias* tire has served the motoring public and commercial carrier for decades and continues to be in widespread usage. In the bias tire, the body plies run from bead to bead in a bias or somewhat diagonal direction. The plies generally alternate in direction. In some instances, particularly in truck tires, narrower plies called breakers are used in the tread region. Breaker plies generally run at the same angle as body plies. Exhibit 2 shows the components of a typical bias truck tire.

The *belted bias* tire has body plies like those in a bias tire. Like the radial tire, it has belts that run circumferentially around the tread region of the tire. The belts are stiffer and generally run at a more circumferential direction than the body plies. Exhibit 3 shows a typical belted bias passenger tire.

2. TIRE LABELLING

Labelling is molded in the sidewall of each tire. This describes the tire and identifies the maker.

Copy pertinent parts of this information on your notes of the tire examination. If you do not know what information is important copy all of it.

Exhibits 4 and 5 are the sidewalls of a tire showing the information molded there.

Serial Number

The most important number appearing on the tire is the serial number which starts with the letters DOT indicating that the tire meets Department of Transportation (DOT) requirements. DOT is usually followed by ten letters and numbers in four groups, as follows:

DOT HYV3T1J444

- YEAR
- WEEK OF MANUFACTURE
- MAKER'S CODE
- SIZE CODE
- MANUFACTURING PLANT
- DEPARTMENT OF TRANSPORTATION

After the DOT, the next two characters are a code for the manufacturing plant where the tire was made. This is followed by two characters that are a code for the size of the tire.

The next three characters are optional and are used by tire manufacturers for coding. The last three characters are numbers and indicate the date of manufacture. The first two show the week of manufacture (01-52) and the last is the year of manufacture (0-9).

For example, in Exhibit 4, the serial DOT HYV3T1J444 shows that the tire was manufactured at Oklahoma City, Oklahoma in the 44th week of 1984. It is size L78-15.

One side of the tire is identified by the serial number. This is better identification than referring to the "white sidewall side," because, in some cases, neither side has a white sidewall. It also avoids the confusion of *inboard* and *outboard* side which cannot be determined if the tire is off the vehicle.

Tire and Maker Names

The name of the tire and the manufacturer name are generally found

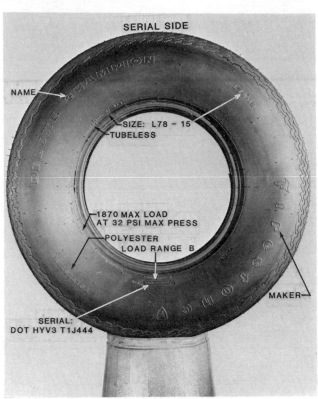

Exhibit 4. Serial side of typical passenger car tire.

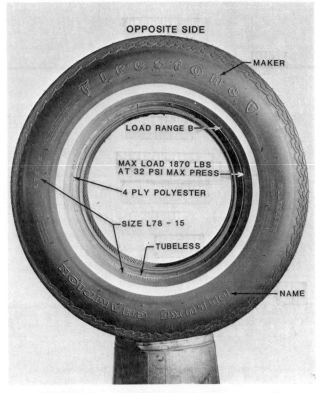

Exhibit 5. Opposite serial side of passenger car tire.

Exhibit 6.

"P" METRIC SYSTEM

P165/80R13

Nominal rim diameter, inches

Construction: B = belted bias, D = bias. If preceded by a letter to indicate speed rating, S = 180 km/h, H = 210 km/h, V = more than 210 km/h.

Cross section height divided by width

Section width, millimeters

Service: P = passenger car, LT = light truck, T = temporary use. Prefix is omitted on commercial tires.

Exhibit 7.

ALPHA NUMERIC SYSTEM

G R 70-15

Nominal rim diameter, inches

Cross section height divided by width

Construction: R= radial (omitted if not radial).

Load-size relationship. For a given letter, there is a maximum load specified for each operating pressure.

Exhibit 8.

METRIC SYSTEM

195 R14

Nominal rim diameter, inches

Construction: R = radial. If preceded by a letter, S = 180 km/h, H = 210 km/h, V = more than 210 km/h.

Section width, millimeters

Exhibit 9.

NUMERIC SYSTEM

10.00 R20

Nominal rim diameter, inches

Construction: R = radial, — = non radial

Section width, inches

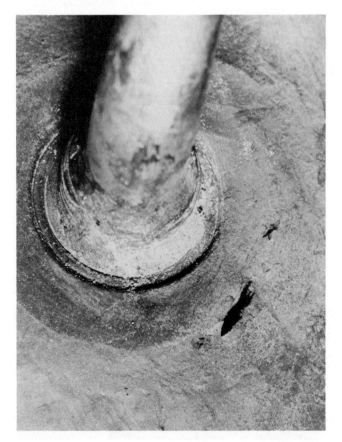

Exhibit 10. Leak in tube near valve which had been improperly installed on rim.

Exhibit 11. After tire lost air through tire crack speed resulted in this damage to tire.

on the tire. For example, in Exhibit 5 the names "Firestone" and "Deluxe Champion" are molded on the tire sidewall.

Size

Size is also on the tire sidewall. Depending on when the tire was manufactured, one of four size designations is used:

1. "P" Metric System (Exhibit 6)
2. Alpha Numeric System (Exhibit 7)
3. Metric System (Exhibit 8)
4. Numeric System (Exhibit 9).

Sometimes, a suffix is used with the numeric systems to designate a type of service: LT (Light Truck), TR (Nominal rim diameter + .156″ or .250″), ML (Mining and Logging), MH (Mobile Home), NHS (Not for Highway Service) and ST (Trailer in Highway Service).

Load Rating

The load range of the tire is molded on the sidewall. The load range determines the upper limit of the operating pressure of the tire and replaces the previous systems of ply rating.

Two systems are used:

1. A single letter such as B, C, D, E, F, etc. For example the letter B indicates the maximum operation pressure (cold) is 32 psi. B is commonly found on passenger tires.
2. P-Metric passenger tires use a system of designating a standard load or extra load. The maximum operating pressure (cold) for a standard load tire is 35 psi (240kPa) and for an extra load tire is 41 psi (280kPa). The maximum load at the maximum cold inflation pressure is molded on the tire.

The tire shown in Exhibit 5 has a maximum load of 1870 lbs. at a maximum pressure of 32 psi. Truck tires show this information for single as well as dual use.

The construction of the tire is also molded on the tire. It is shown for both the tread and the sidewall The tire shown in Exhibits 4 and 5 consists

Exhibit 12. *Overheated brakes led to this tire failure in the bead area, suddenly disabling the tire.*

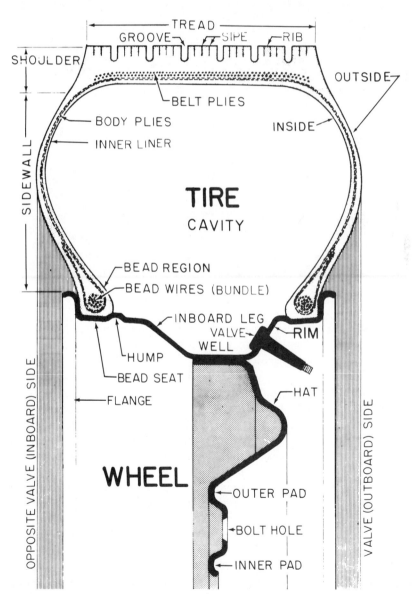

Exhibit 13. *Names for parts of a wheel and tire. Use these names when describing locations of abnormalities found in tire examination.*

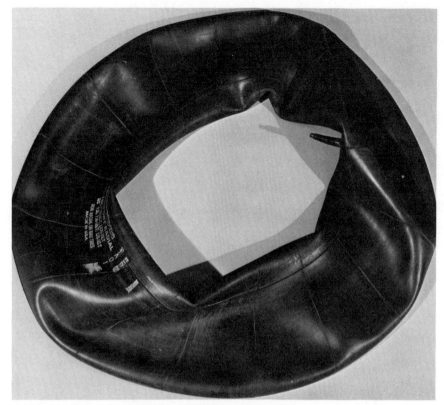

Exhibit 14. Inner tube and valve, part of a wheel-tire assembly.

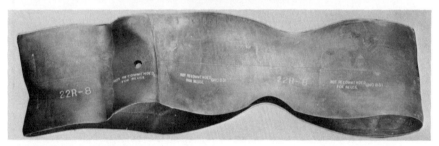

Exhibit 15. Flap which fits between the tube and the rim of the wheel.

of four plies of polyester in the sidewall and four plies of polyester in the crown or road-engaging region of the tire.

There are often mold and equipment numbers molded on the tire. There are sometimes quality grades for temperature, tread wear and traction as well as safety warnings. Truck tires that have operating speed restricted below 55 mph will be molded accordingly.

Beyond information molded on the new tire, information is sometimes branded on the tire after manufacture, or molded on the retread or tire during the retreading process. Information molded on tires during the retread process shows the time and

place of retreading as well as other information.

3. TIRE AND WHEEL ASSEMBLY

The rubber tire and metal wheel must be considered together when investigating a traffic accident.

The tire is the only part of the vehicle that normally touches the road surface; hence all the forces between the vehicle and roadway are transferred through the tire. However, the tire does not act alone. It is part of an assembly that is fastened to the vehicle. The valve is part of the assembly. So are the tube and flap for a tire with a tube.

The rim is part of the steel wheel

that supports the tire and tube assembly. Consider the assembly as a whole, especially when air loss is involved. The rim, valve, and tube are often the keys to where and how leakage started. For example, Exhibit 10 shows a crack near a valve. The crack resulted from improper installation of the tube in the rim. Exhibit 11 shows the resulting tire disablement that occurred after the tire lost air through the crack while the tire operated at highway speed.

The tire and wheel assembly is part of the the vehicle suspension system which also includes brakes, linkages, springs, spindles and so on. A tire failure may well have resulted from a malfunction of one of these other components. Tire failures have resulted from overheated brakes and bent tie rods. Exhibit 12 shows a failure in the bead area of a tire. It was caused by overheated brakes. Thus, to determine why a tire failed or what part a tire played in an accident, you often have to look beyond the tire and wheel to other parts of the vehicle.

Terminology

Use the correct words and phrases to describe wheel and tire assemblies and in reporting observations and conclusions. Some significant terms are defined here. More complete lists are published elsewhere:[2, 3] Names of major parts of a wheel and tire are shown in Exhibit 13.

Wheel is the part of a vehicle which connects the tire to the hub or brake drum.

Rim is the part of the wheel which supports the tire or tire and tube assembly.

Tube or *Inner Tube* is the continuous rubber element that fits inside a tire and holds the internal air pressure (Exhibit 14).

Flap is a continuous extruded rubber material that fits between the tube and the rim (Exhibit 15).

Certain parts of wheels and tires have specific names. Most of the important names are shown in Exhibit 13.

Valve or *outboard side* of the wheel

is the side that contains the hole for the valve.

Opposite valve or *inboard side* is the side of the wheel opposite the valve.

Serial Side is the side of the tire bearing the DOT serial number.

Opposite-Serial Side is the side of the tire opposite the side bearing the DOT serial number.

Outside is the surface of the tire which is visible when mounted on a wheel. It is exposed to outside air.

Inside is the surface of the tire which cannot be seen when the tire is mounted on the wheel. It is exposed to inside air under pressure.

4. AT-SCENE TIRE INVESTIGATION

At-scene examination of tire disablements is important in fatal accidents because all tires and wheels are generally in their after-accident positions and condition until the vehicle is moved. At the scene debris trails can be discovered, measurements made, and necessary photos taken. Decide what can be done later and what must be done at the scene. Of course emergency operations, such as looking after injured persons, take priority.

During at-scene investigation there is little opportunity to examine tires in detail because other duties are usually more urgent. Often, conditions such as light and weather are unfavorable. However, if one or more special investigators are dispatched to work on serious accidents, more attention can be given to tires. Such technicians have been very successful in obtaining tire data at the scene.

Routine Inspection

Initial at-scene general vehicle examination calls for minimum data on tires. You will have to keep notes on what you see, because, later you cannot be expected to remember exactly how it was. The one-page general vehicle examination report (Exhibit 16) provides for a record of preliminary tire observations.

With or without a form, make at-

scene notes for each tire to include:
1. Its position on the vehicle
2. Whether it was flat
3. Whether there was a visible hole in it
4. Whether either bead was unseated from the rim
5. Whether a rim was visibly bent
6. Whether the wheel could be rotated or was firmly stuck in place.

If all tires are normally inflated after the accident, as is often the case, no further examination is ordinarily required.

Further Investigation

Some circumstances suggest need for additional at-scene inquiry related to tires:

1. A wheel is detached from the vehicle.
2. Pieces of a tire or wheel have come off.
3. The driver or anyone else blames a tire for loss of control.
4. Signs of vehicle behavior make you think that there might have been some tire problem.

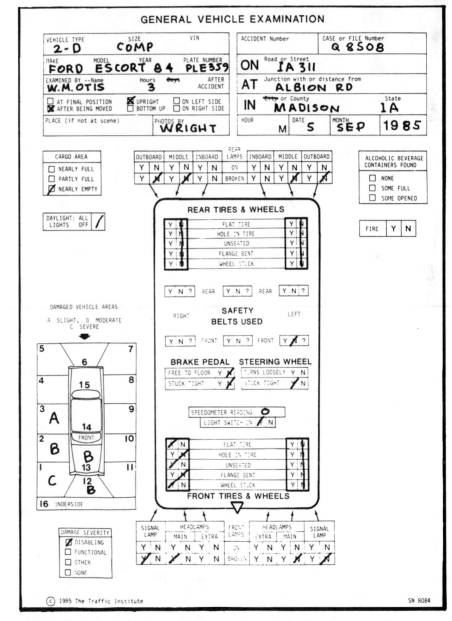

Exhibit 16. General vehicle examination report for recording observations of the vehicle at the scene of a traffic accident. It includes basic data on tires.

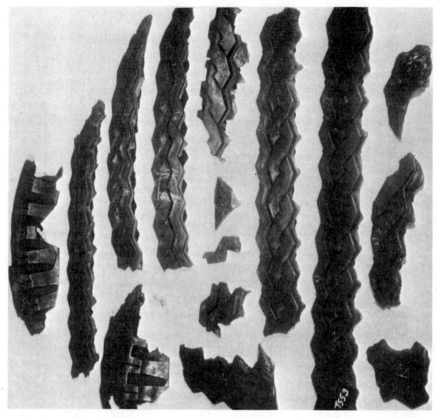

Exhibit 17. *Pieces of tire picked up on a debris trail leading to the final position of a vehicle after a traffic accident. Matching these to the tire may help in understanding how the tire failed.*

and hard angular objects such as concrete blocks which might account for tire rupture or other damage. Look for places where the tire may have left or returned to the roadway, especially where the shoulder is lower than the paving. Look for tire scrubs which occur during collision and may explain tire and rim abrasion or tire rupture.

Measurements to locate what you find may be made by whoever is making measurements for other purposes. You may have to suggest or request that this be done. Otherwise, you may have to make the special measurements yourself.

Removal of Tire and Wheel

If, at the scene, a tire seems to be especially interesting or significant, plan on further examination later and elsewhere.

When a tire is to be examined later, ask the tow-truck operator to remove the tire and wheel assembly from the vehicle before towing the vehicle. This is especially important if the tire was burned or a bead unseated during the accident. Towing can further damage a tire.

If you believe that further examination of the tire or wheel will be needed, collect pieces picked up at

Under any of these circumstances look for additional signs of what happened.

Debris Trail

Especially when tires or wheels have come apart, go back along the path followed by the vehicle to its final position. Look for detached pieces of tires or wheels. If you find any, locate the position of each by measurements and collect the parts. Exhibit 17 shows typical pieces picked up at an accident scene.

Before you leave the scene, mark each piece for identification, describe its location when found, and note whether you have any reason to believe that someone had moved it from where it first came to rest, for instance, to get it off the roadway. Parts of tires are most likely to be pieces of tread. Going back along the pre-accident path of the vehicle may yield other useful information. Look for overdeflected and flat tiremarks as

described in Topic 817 and illustrated in Exhibit 18. These marks may explain where and possibly why a tire was disabled. Look for chuck holes

Exhibit 18. *Heavy edge marks of an overdeflected (under inflated) tire. There is still some pressure in the tire.*

Exhibit 19. *Marks of a tire that is completely deflated. Operation in this condition will quickly damage the tire severely.*

Exhibit 20. *Offset in a curb. Even at less than ten miles per hour, this corner tore a hole in the sidewall of a tire similar to that in Exhibit 33. This instantly disabled the tire.*

the scene and store them for future attention.

Keep records of the chain of possession of the tire. Consider ownership rights of custody based on laws in your jurisdiction. Do no destructive testing or experiments, and keep components in as close as possible to their condition at removal as you can.

Photography

If you or someone else is prepared to take photos at the scene, consider making pictures of possibly significant things that you saw on the debris trail. These may substantiate and enhance other records of your observations. Also, think about making photos of damaged tires and wheels still in position on the wrecked vehicle, especially if you may not have access to the tire after it leaves the scene.

5. DETAILED EXAMINATION

You can rarely remove a tire from its wheel or the wheel from the vehicle at the scene of an accident. For this and other reasons, at-scene tire examination is, at best, preliminary. But that does not mean that it is unimportant.

Regardless of whether there has been an at-scene tire examination, you may have to examine the tire and wheel abnormalities in detail as a basis for evaluating their possible contribution to the accident. Almost always, you will have to do this after the vehicle has been removed from the scene. This is a disadvantage because the tire may have been damaged further in removal, especially if the vehicle is dragged with a locked wheel. On the other hand, it is better to ex-

amine the tire and wheel where it can be done carefully and conveniently, without hurry. This is another way of saying that it is best to examine a tire as soon after the accident as you can do it well.

To begin with, be sure that you have any necessary permission to study the tire and wheel. Also have at hand proper equipment: forms or paper for records; measuring devices such as pocket tape, pressure gage, tread depth gage; and photographic equipment.

When you first see it, the tire and wheel may still be on the vehicle. That gives you a chance to make sure that the tire and wheel are removed with as little additional damage as possible.

Do not try to examine a tire in detail while it is still on the vehicle; you may miss something important.

Photographs. Before removing a tire from a vehicle, especially if you think that the tire may not be available later, you may want to photograph it. Unfortunately, this photography is often poorly done. Because tires are mostly black and are located under the vehicle, there is usually much less light on the tire than there is on the rest of the scene. If an overall scene exposure is used, the tire may not show adequate detail. Good pho-

Exhibit 21. *Photo exposed for a general view of the car. Details of the tire are in deep shadow and largely invisible.*

Exhibit 22. *Photo exposed to show detail in a disabled tire. Exposure meter readings close to the tire were made.*

tographs can be had if the light reflected from the tire is metered directly and the exposure set accordingly. Practice in taking tire photos is desirable. Exhibit 21 shows a tire photo exposed as part of an over-all scene while Exhibit 22 shows a tire photo properly exposed. If you can read the tire markings for size, type, etc. in your photo, the exposure was satisfactory.

Try to have tire pressure measured as soon after the accident as possible. This may be an assignment of whoever first inspects the tire after removal from the scene.

Allow sufficient time for the examination. Sometimes it is necessary to interrupt the examination and return to it later when more information or additional time is available.

Identification

When you first get a tire for examination, with or without the wheel, label it for identification if that has not been already done. Otherwise it may not be possible to locate it with certainty after it has been stored, perhaps for months or even years. Label both tire and wheel in case they have to be separated.

For a wheel with a tire, a good place for the label is on a shipping tag tied through one of the wheel bolt holes. Without a tire, the best place for a label is on adhesive plaster or strong masking tape stuck on the rim in the well.

For a tire, with a wheel, a good label location is on adhesive plaster or masking tape stuck on the sidewall. Place the label next to the valve hole in the rim. That will show how the tire was mounted if the tire and wheel are separated. With an unmounted tire, put the label on an inside sidewall.

Before applying any label, clean and dry the surface. Use pressure sensitive labels, not lick-and-stick ones.

If you are examining more than one tire from a vehicle, treat each one entirely separately; do not try to handle them as a group.

Information on each label must include at least three items:
1. Accident or case number (If these are not known, the date and exact location of the accident)
2. Vehicle distinguishing description (make, model, year; type, such as truck, car, van; owner or driver)
3. Location of the tire or wheel on the vehicle.

Identification on the tire or wheel label is copied on notes of the examination for each specimen. Keep separate notes for each tire-wheel combination.

Delayed Examination

Tire examination is warranted only under special circumstances, usually when a tire condition may be an issue in litigation. Once the tire has been obtained, the expense of detailed examination may be postponed until need for it has been definitely established.

The tire is then stored in a safe place until needed. Its condition will not significantly deteriorate while kept as possible evidence.

It may be that one person may obtain and identify the tire in anticipation of possible later examination by another more expert individual.

Description

The actual examination begins with a written description of the tire. Some of the description is molded into the outside surface of the tire:
1. Make and name
2. Serial (DOT) number
3. Size
4. Load rating
5. Special features such as inner tube, recap, snow tread.

Condition of Parts

Record inflation pressure measured as soon as possible after the accident. If possible, pressure should be measured with a gage calibrated for accu-

Exhibit 23. Disabled tire with the bead still seated on the rim.

Exhibit 24. Disabled tire with the bead unseated from the rim.

Exhibit 25. Measuring tire groove depth with instrument reading in 32nds of an inch.

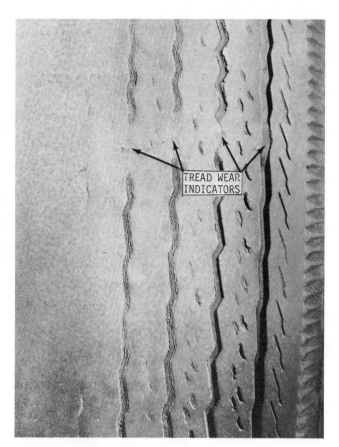

Exhibit 26. Do not measure groove depth where there is a tread wear indicator between ribs.

racy. Note whether a valve cap, valve extension, or wheel cover was removed to measure inflation pressure. Replace these parts to prevent their loss.

If the valve is not properly aligned with the valve hole in the wheel cover, record that fact and photograph the misalignment.

If a tubeless tire is flat, note whether both beads are seated on the rim flange. Exhibit 23 shows a tire with the bead still seated; Exhibit 24 shows tire with the bead unseated.

If a tube tire is found flat, pick up the tube, flap, and any loose parts of the wheel. Note where such loose parts were found.

Measure tread depth as shown in Exhibit 25. Avoid measuring the groove where there is a tread indicator (Exhibit 26); measure the full groove depth. Knowing the original groove depth and the worn groove depth, you can calculate the percentage of the tire's life that has been used or that remains.

When there seems to be significant variations among groove depth measurements, make a chart to show the wear pattern across the tread and in four places on its circumference. Exhibit 27 is an example of a tread wear chart.

Tire Abnormalities

Abnormality is a condition that is unusual or unexpected; something remarkable. Significant damage is an abnormality. So is irregular or extreme wear, but normal wear or other signs of aging, such as minute cracks in the tire surface, are not abnormal.

Searching for abnormalities and recording a description of each one discovered is essentially the fact-finding part of tire examination in traffic-accident investigation.

Form no opinions and reach no conclusions during this part of the tire investigation. Stick strictly to fact finding until all the data are at hand.

Avoid recording unimportant information. A description of every scratch on the tire is not necessary or productive. As you obtain skill through experience, you will develop a better understanding of what things are important enough to record.

If the tire appears to be quite normal with respect to conditon and wear, your examination record can be marked "Condition unremarkable". The same goes for the wheel. Then, with nothing noteworthy to report, detailed examination is ended. Keep the report as a record of the effort

Exhibit 27.

GROOVE DEPTH IN 1/32 INCH

		CLOCKWISE FROM SERIAL			
		12:00	3:00	6:00	9:00
NUMBER FROM SERIAL SIDE	1	7.5	8	8	8
	2	7	7	7	7
	3	5	5	4	5
	4	3	4	3.5	4
	5	4	6	4	5
	6	5	7	5	6

Exhibit 28. *Tire cut by a sharp object. This is a radial cut.*

Exhibit 30. *Impact break caused when an angular object forces the tread down to the flanges and possibly into the rim well.*

Exhibit 29. *Cuts in tires have clean edges without loose cords.*

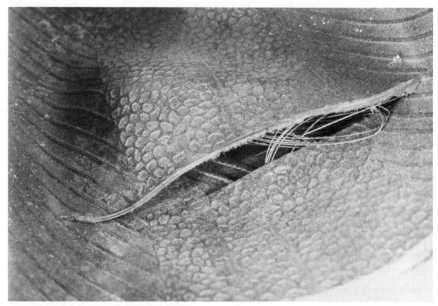

Exhibit 31. *An impact break usually shows in the inside of the tire as a tearing or slit in the liner parallel to the cords.*

that is available after the tire and wheel are gone.

A tire may have several abnormalities. Designate each by a letter: A, B, C, etc. Then describe each abnormality in some detail especially if the tire cannot be kept for future reference. Some of the more common abnormalities are described below.

Small hole. An opening less than 3/8 in. (1 cm) across. It may be any shape. This category includes punctures by nails or similar sharp metal pieces and small cuts. Many small nicks in the tire tread may be disregarded as too insignificant to be noted except possibly for identifying a particular tire as having made an impression in soft material. Any hole that penetrates into the tire body can be significant and should be noted.

Cut. An opening generally having smooth and even edges and little or no fraying of cord ends. Cuts are often made by a sharp edge of metal or other subjects such as glass. Commonly they show a lead-in or flap.

They may be any direction and long or short. Exhibits 28 and 29 shows cuts. Keep in mind that all cuts do not look like these exhibits.

Impact break. A rupture or fracture of cords or rubber components or combinations of these (Exhibits 30 and 31). They are sometimes more prominent inside than outside. Indeed, it may be a contusion showing only on the inside. It results from sudden, severe, inward bending of tread or sidewall by localized external pressure. It shows a lead-in or surface damage only when a rough, sharp object was the cause. If the object was smooth, there may be no external damage.

Tear or rip. An opening with irregular edges. Often has frayed or unraveled cord ends showing. Uneven surfaces are without striations. They usually have an irregular shape and may be accompanied by separations of laminater. Exhibits 32 and 33 show an example of a tear. Not all tears look like these illustrations.

Laceration. A very ragged opening or area with extensive and often severe shredding or tearing often accompanied by severe abrasion. There are usually frayed and loose cords and some surface or ply separation (Exhibits 11 and 12).

Wear. Loss of surface material over a broad area without striations or abrasions. Surface is smooth. There is usually little fraying of exposed cord ends or loose cords. This occurs mostly on tire tread. Worn areas may be cupped or scalloped with no loose material. Exhibit 34 shows an example of wear. Wear does not always look like Exhibit 34.

Abrasion. Surface areas with striations or other signs of friction or rubbing. Abrasions may be very rough or only scratched and may be inside or outside surface. Exhibit 35 shows an example of an abrasion on the tread surface of two tires. Not all abrasion looks like Exhibit 35.

Heat Deterioration. Burning or charring of materials. This results in hardening or stiffening of cord ends

Exhibit 32. *A tear is irregular and generally in side wall. This is paralleled by deformation of the flange.*

Exhibit 33. *This tear is flanked by radial friction marks indicating direction of movement of object striking the tire.*

of thermoplastic materials such as nylon or polyester and charring of non-thermoplastic materials such as rayon. Heat deterioration may be considered in four general categories.

1. *Heavy burn* in which tire material has actually been consumed by fire. In extreme cases, virtually the only remaining part of the tire is wire from the bead area in the tire. The tire itself has been on fire. Exhibit 36 shows a tire with a heavy burn. All heavy burns do not look like Exhibit 36.
2. *Scorching* or blistering, usually superficial, in which the tire surface has been affected by adjacent heat or flame.
3. *Heat generation* due to overdeflection causes separation and/or breakdown of tire components. In severe cases there is rubber reversion (softening) and cord degradation. The flexed broken cord endings become hard and brittle. The rubber sometimes becomes tacky and plastic (Exhibit 12).
4. *Tread friction* heating in which sliding of tire generates heat so rapidly as to raise temperature to the point where rubber changes character without actually being

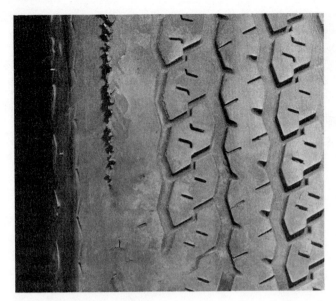

Exhibit 34. Abnormal wear is irregular on the tread. It does not actually disable the tire until it penetrates the cords and they give way to let air escape.

Exhibit 35. Abrasion on the surfaces of dual tires. The striations, parallel to the tread, indicate that the tire was sliding due to braking. Heat in sliding heavily loaded tires damage, the surface.

set on fire (Exhibit 35).

Separation. A condition where one or more of the laminate components (layers) of the tire has come apart. The separation can be between any of the components. Separations often exhibit one or more of the following characteristics:

1. *Fresh tear* appearance showing clear, crisp impressions of the pre-separated components (Exhibit 37).
2. Polished surfaces that have worn smooth by rubbing against each other (Exhibit 38).
3. Multiplane surfaces that go from one laminate surface to another as the separation propagates.
4. Single plane surfaces that follow a single plane or laminate.

Lead in or out. A sign that some object pressed against the surface while moving toward, or sometimes away from, a main abnormality. May be a gradually increasing depth of cut or only surface abrasion, striations, scratches, or dirt smudges. It is not the end of a long tear. The tear shown in Exhibit 33 has a lead-in.

Bead break. A sign that one or more bead wires are broken. The wires may or may not be exposed to view but the bead has a significant discon-

tinuity. Exhibit 39 shows a tire with a broken bead. Broken beads do not necessarily look like Exhibit 39.

Other abnormalities may not fit the foregoing categories. In that case, describe each separately. For example, damage to inner tubes; imbedded bits of glass, metal, or other material (but not pebbles caught in tread grooves);

patches and repairs.

Distinction between categories of abnormalities is not always clear. Thus, classification may be questionable. For example, it may be difficult to decide between tear and laceration or between laceration and abrasion. In such cases, two or more categories can each be indicated.

Exhibit 36. Tire damaged by external fire which has exposed the radial sidewall plies.

Exhibit 37. *Ply separation which developed suddenly as shown by cords and imprints of cords without signs of rubbing. No tread came off, no air was lost and so tire was not disabled.*

Exhibit 38. *Ply separation which developed gradually as shown by smooth surfaces produced by rubbing between the layers. Some tread came off but the tire was not disabled.*

Combinations of abnormalities are not unusual. For example, tears and separations are often found together or are accompanied by abrasions. Therefore, an abnormality is not always adequately described by a single classification, and the abnormality may be described by two or more categories.

Location of Abnormalities

On a report, there are two ways to describe the location of an abnormality: 1) position on the tire with respect to a reference point; and 2) mark the abnormality on a diagram of the tire. In either case, a reference point on the tire is necessary. The position of the DOT serial number is convenient for this purpose.

Looking at the side of the tire with the serial number at the top, the abnormality, designated by a letter, can be located by how far around the tire it is clockwise with twelve o'clock at the serial number. An abnormality at six o'clock would be diametrically across the tire from the serial number.

To avoid confusion, give locations on the non-serial side of the tire the same position numbers as on the serial side, hence, locations on the non-serial side numbers run counter clockwise from the DOT serial position.

With a diagram, the abnormality can be sketched in proper relation to the serial number and identified by the assigned letter. In any case, the abnormality must also be located with respect to serial or opposite serial side or tread of the tire and whether it is inside the tire, outside, or both.

Depth of the abnormality can be described by one of three categories:

1. *Superficial* or surface. No plies or bead wires are exposed. May be quite deep where tread rubber is thick or very shallow on sidewall where rubber is thin.
2. *Penetration,* which exposes plies or bead wires.
3. *Through,* which extends from outside to inside. If not clearly visible, an opening completely through may be discovered by inserting a probe such as a paper-clip wire. Sometimes external and internal openings are connected, but far enough apart so that a probe will not go through but the tire will leak air.

Alignment of abnormality may be described by one of four categories which are illustrated in Exhibit 40.

1. *Circumferential* or longitudinal. The long dimension of the abnormality is generally parallel to the bead or edge of the tread. The angle of the long dimension to the edge of the tread is less than 20°
2. *Transverse* or radial. The long

dimension of the abnormality is generally across the tread or sidewall. The angle of the long dimension to the edge of the tread is more than 70°
3. *Oblique.* The long dimension is neither circumferential nor transverse.
4. *Nondirectional.* The length and width of the abnormality are about the same.

Shape of abnormality can be described by capital letters which suggest the configuration. Some exam-

Exhibit 39. *Bead wires are sometimes broken in mounting a tire. The added stress on the remaining wires in the bead bundle may break them suddenly. Then the tire tears apart at that point.*

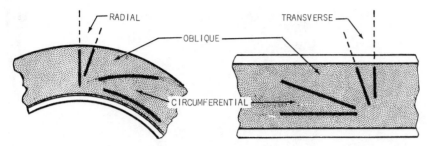

Exhibit 40. Terms used to describe the alignment of abnormalities on a tire.

ples are shown below:

O Round or irregular in shape without branches and clearly nondirectional.

I Long and narrow without branches and clearly directional.

L Two branches with an obtuse angle (greater than a right angle) between them.

V Two branches with an acute angle (less than a right angle) between them.

T Three branches, one at right angles to the other two.

Y Three branches with approximately equal angles between them.

X Four branches.

U Curved break in the shape of a U.

C Curved break in the shape of a C.

Few abnormalities correspond neatly with the letter shape available to describe them. Hence, the letter description is an approximation. Sometimes U or V could equally well describe the same two-branch tear. It is often helpful to sketch the shape of the abnormality as in Exhibit 49 or describe it with words.

Location of abnormality on the tire may be specified as tread, sidewall, bead, or shoulder. If the abnormality is in more than one of these parts of the tire, note each part in which it is located. Indicate inside or outside. If an abnormality goes through, record it as both inside and outside.

Size of the abnormality is given as length and width in inches or centimeters. Length is the longest distance from one point to another. Length

may be a circumferential measurement around the curve of the tire. It may be the distance from one branch of the abnormality to another or it may be the distance between the ends of a curved abnormality. If the abnormality runs completely around the tire, it actually has no beginning and end; then note its length as "All." Width is the distance across the abnormality, generally at right angles to its measured length. A long cut or tear may vary in width. If so, measure its widest part. If a slit or cut is so narrow that the edges fit closely together, the width is zero.

Repaired punctures are abnormalities. There is a question then as to whether the repair was made properly or leaked air and so led to disablement. It may be possible to remount the tire or use special devices to find out whether the repair leaks. If this is not possible, be cautious about inferring the significance of the repair.

Wheel Abnormalities

Note whether the rim is deformed on the valve side or opposite valve side and then use three measurements to describe the extent of deformation.

Chord length. The straight-line distance across the rim from where the flange bend begins to where it ends. See Exhibit 41.

Maximum radial collapse. The greatest radial displacement of any point on the flange from its original position to its deformed position. The distance that the flange is pushed in toward the center of rotation of the wheel. See Exhibit 41.

Axial collapse is the greatest displacement of the flange parallel to

the axle and at right angles to the plane of the wheel. It is the amount that the flange is pushed toward or away from the opposite side of the wheel.

If the deformation is *toward* the wheel or axle, as is usually the case, the distance is marked "+" or left unmarked; if pushed *away* from the wheel or axle, as sometimes happens, the distance is always marked "−". This distance can be measured from a straight edge placed across the flange from one undamaged point to another. In Exhibit 41, the flange is pushed in and the distance would be marked "+".

Note abrasion, scratching, or roughness on the flange of the rim and record the direction of striations, if any. Also note whether the striations are found around the entire circumference or in localized areas. Exhibit 42 shows flange abrasion on a rim flange that was running on a paved road surface after a tire lost its air but before the vehicle came to rest.

Length is the extent of abrasion around the flange. If the flange is abraded all around, mark the length as "All."

Radial or transverse striations are at an angle of more than 70° to the flange.

Oblique striations are between 20° and 70° to the flange.

Other Wheel Abnormalities

If the wheel is bent so that it would wobble if turned on its axle, note it as warped. This may occur with or without the rim being bent.

Bolt holes may be damaged. Call them ruptured if the hole is broken out to the nearest edge. Note a hole as enlarged if it is elongated or deformed so as to increase its size. If the inside of the hole shows little dents or groves made by the threads of a bolt, note the condition as dented.

Some wheel damage may not fit well in the foregoing categories. If so, describe such abnormalities separately. Examples include rivets loose or broken, valve missing or damaged,

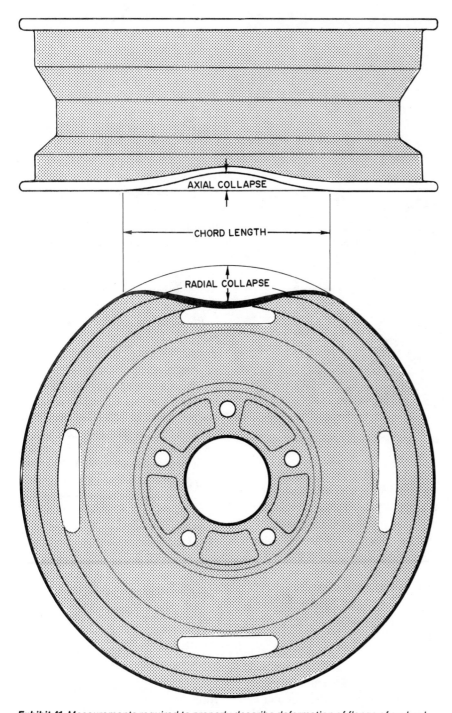

Exhibit 41. *Measurements required to properly describe deformation of flange of a wheel.*

tact does, in fact, have an imperceptible leak. To resolve this question, inflate the tire, submerge it in water, and look for tell-tale bubbles. If you do not have the wheel or if the rim is much deformed you may have to mount the tire on a new rim for this test.

Destructive testing, which requires cutting or tearing the tire, must not be done except by specific agreement of all interested parties or when ordered by a court or some other proper authority.

6. WHAT ABNORMALITIES INDICATE

Abnormalities immediately suggest related circumstances. An abnormality may indicate more than one circumstance. Most indications are more or less logical inferences from the character of the abnormality. That is why it is so important to study each abnormality carefully.

Discovering and describing abnormalities is a fact-finding effort of careful observation and classification. Deciding what the abnormalities indicate requires more thought and a better understanding of tire behavior and vehicle operation. Circumstances other than the abnormalities themselves must usually be considered. For example, consider the events of an accident, the surface on which the tire was run, and how the tire may have been handled before it was examined. It goes without saying that inferring indications is more likely to result in error than observation of the abnormalities.

Sometimes an indication is clear and definite. Sometimes it is only a possibility, or perhaps one of two possibilities. It is useful, therefore, to designate an indication as definite or as possible.

A number of inferences or indications of tire-wheel abnormalities are basic and are outlined here. It is not practical to list all possible indications of all possible abnormalities and all combinations of abnormalities.

dents or holes in rim flange or well, spokes broken, bead seat roughness or corrosion, surface scorched or melted.

Experiments

While examining abnormalities, it may be useful to make some harmless experiments.

At the scene it is usually difficult to determine whether a piece of tire or wheel picked up along the debris trail belongs to a tire or wheel in the accident. If these pieces have been collected and labelled, you can try to fit them to the tire being examined. This may help you to determine the nature of an abnormality.

There may be a question whether a tire or tube which appears to be in-

Exhibit 42. *Flange abrasion from contact with pavement after tire was disabled. Oblique striations show that wheel was sliding parallel to its axis and extent of abrasion on rim indicates that the wheel was also rotating.*

General Indications

A number of general terms are used, often carelessly, to describe tire and wheel condition as indicated by abnormalities. Try to use these words exactly so that your meaning will be as specific as possible.

Unremarkable has already been mentioned as meaning that there is nothing the matter with the tire or wheel.

Overdeflected is a condition of a tire when it has too little air pressure in it for the load on it. Overdeflection, therefore, may result from either overloading or underinflation. Overdeflection results in more tire tread wear at the edges and in heat which may damage the tire, especially at high speeds. Overdeflection may produce edge heavy skidmarks or soft-tire marks on the roadway. (See Exhibit 18.)

Disabled means that the tire and wheel combination will not function properly. The vehicle can be driven

with difficulty, if at all. A tire which has lost its pressure is disabled. A tire may have conspicuous abnormalities such as surface separation or superficial cuts without being disabled. A wheel-tire combination may be disabled without abnormalities, for example, when a tire is forced from the rim in a yaw (sideslip) without damage to either tire or rim.

A thorough knowledge of tire components, as well as user and field maintenance, is important in analyzing tire disablements. It is not unusual for some of the tire-wheel components to be lost or mutilated during an accident. Hence, the tire examiner must understand what components and pieces should be there and how they fit together.

Damaged means that the tire is not in its original condition for reasons other than normal wear. Extreme wear damages a tire. A tire may be damaged, even badly damaged, without being disabled, for example when

some tread comes off (Exhibit 38).

Defect generally refers to an imperfection in tire or wheel before it is put into use. The word *defect* takes on significantly different meanings by different people. For example, manufacturers think of a defect as a manufacturing error while an installer thinks in terms of installation damage. Lawyers attach a legal meaning to the word. Take care when using this word so there is not any confusion as to what you mean. A defect may or may not be visible. A defect does not necessarily immediately disable the tire or wheel; otherwise, the tire and wheel would not have been put into use. Many defects affect only a tire's appearance, not its performance.

Blowout is a sudden loss of pressure. A blowout may occur before, during, or after collision impact. It may also occur when a tire bead is forced from the bead seat while the vehicle is moving sideways. To many people, blowout suggests only disablement before the driver experiences any difficulty; hence, the use of this term is discouraged.

Failure occurs when an abnormality, not always visible, results in disablement of a wheel, tire, or valve. Failure does not imply any defect; it may be due to abuse, such as running flat, or damage such as puncture.

Specific Indications

Other indications from tire abnormalities suggest circumstances of an accident, especially how a disablement occurred.

Rate of Onset

Some tire abnormalities develop rapidly, others slowly. The character of the abnormality usually indicates the rate of onset. There are five general categories:

1. *Gradual* abnormalities develop in days, weeks, or even months. The tire may have run many miles during development. An example is extreme or uneven tread wear. Another is an internal separation which comes on

as a blister in which the separated surfaces, when finally exposed, are smooth from rubbing against each other (Exhibit 38).

2. *Slow* abnormalities develop in hours. Ply separation or rim chaffing when a tire is run seriously overdeflected may take a number of miles of fast driving.

3. *Quick* abnormalities develop in minutes. A burn from external fire may require a minute or two to produce the resulting abnormality (Exhibit 36).

4. *Sudden* abnormalities develop in seconds, for example, rim or tire abrasion from road friction (Exhibit 42). In some punctures penetration appears to have been progressive due to a sharp object imbedded in the tire working its way during a number of wheel revolutions into the tire.

5. *Instantaneous* abnormalities develop in a fraction of a second. Most punctures, tears, cuts, and rim bends are instantaneous.

Of course, it is often difficult or even impossible to definitely determine from an abnormality which of these five categories applies. Consequently, two of the categories may have to be marked as possibilities.

The rate of onset or development of an abnormality must not be confused with the rate of air loss or disablement of the wheel. For example, a small puncture may develop instantly, but the air loss through it might require a matter of hours before noticeable disablement took place. On the other hand, a weakening of a tire due to travel in an overdeflected condition might go on for days, but when the tire finally gives way, loss of air could be explosive.

Rate of Air Loss

The rate at which air is lost, that is, the time required for the tire to become disabled, depends on the size of the opening through which the air escapes, and the time during which the opening persists. Most tire open-

ings remain the same size or increase in size as air is lost; but sometimes a tire will be pulled from the rim for only an instant and reseat before much of the air pressure is gone. The rate at which air is lost may be described by four categories:

1. *None.* There is no indication of any air loss. Most superficial abnormalities are in this category.

2. *Slow* leaks result from small holes that go clear through, malfunctioning valves, or an improperly seated bead. Air escapes without noise. Reinflation of the tire will usually permit continued use on a temporary basis.

3. *Rapid* loss of air occurs usually with hissing through a hole a quarter of an inch or more across. Such holes may result from large punctures, small tears or cuts, or a tire momentarily forced away from a rim.

4. *Explosive* air loss occurs with a loud report when a hole, usually large enough to put fingers through, is instantaneously produced in a tire or between the tire and rim. Cuts, tears, or bursts may make such large holes. Explosive air loss is often spoken of as a blowout especially when it is not connected with a collison. Often explosive loss of air occurs from tire damage in a collision which does so much other harm and makes so much other noise that the tire disablement is disregarded at least until the vehicle has to be moved. Often a slow leak will progress to rapid and sometimes explosive air loss because pressure loss in a tire during the vehicle operation can produce abnormalities such as ply and tread separation or even bead abrasion.

Contact

The nature of an abnormality may indicate what unusual contact the tire or rim may have had with external

surfaces or objects. Contact damage may occur to a tire from three main sources:

1. *Road surface* causes smooth wear, either excessive wear that penetrates to or through plies or irregular wear. Very abrasive road surfaces can score or scrape the tread if the tire slides. Ordinary road surfaces can heat the tread of a sliding tire to the point where scorching occurs. Pavements can grind off the surface of a tire if it is dragged 50 feet or more without rotating. When sidewalls slide under heavy pressure on a pavement, the tire may wear completely through suddenly.

2. *Other parts of the vehicle* can cut, puncture, tear, and even burst a tire in a collison. Sometimes vehicle parts produce abrasions. Sometimes careful examination of the vehicle will reveal exactly what part damaged the tire. These parts are usually inside of fender wells and not easily seen. Abrasions inside of fender wells are the easiest to find.

3. *External objects* of many kinds, including parts of other vehicles, can leave their marks on a tire in a collision. Such marks are usually on the outboard side of the tire. A common external object which damages a tire is a rough curb that abrades or scrapes the tire sidewall and may also bend the rim, sometimes sufficiently to produce a slow leak. Nails, bolts, broken glass, sharp stones, and similar objects can cut, puncture and bruise tires while the wheel is rotating (Exhibit 43). The abnormality resulting from such objects is usually small and localized on the tread. When a tire strikes a strong, hard, edge or corner, for example, the edge of a chuck hole, a curb, (Exhibit 20) railroad rail, or parts of another vehicle, the tire may be bent in-

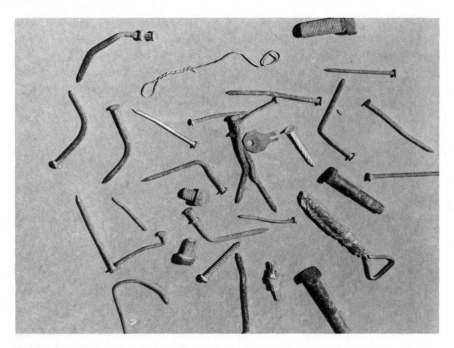

Exhibit 43. *External objects which can puncture tires. Sometimes such objects do not reach the tire cavity until they have been imbedded in the tread for a long time. That delays disablement.*

ward so far and so severely that it bursts or fractures. This results in slits or very clean-edged tears of cords in one direction but not in the other. The rupture is generally completely through but may appear only on the inside. The shape is usually I or X. Damage is much more extensive inside than outside. It may run entirely across the tire to sidewalls on both sides. Outside, a tear may appear in tread and sidewall, but not in the thicker shoulder. Ply separation often accompanies such a burst or rupture. A good indication of force and damage from an external object, and sometimes from part of the vehicle on which the tire was used, is abrasion leading a major part of an abnormality.

Determining what external object was responsible for a particular tire abnormality usually requires knowledge of what objects were present. Often a particular object may be found which, in character and shape, matches exactly the damage to the tire.

Wheel Motion

Abnormalities may indicate what the wheel was doing when the wheel or tire condition was produced:

1. A stopped wheel can be indicated by localized flange abrasion or striations parallel to direction of tire movement (Exhibit 35).
2. Rotating wheels are indicated by smooth wear and abrasions extending around the flange. Punctures or cuts from objects on the road and bursts from holes or bumps on the road indicate rotating wheels.
3. Sideslipping wheels are indicated by transverse striations on sidewalls and sometimes on treads. Heavy sidewall abrasions and transverse or oblique rim edge abrasions usually indicate sideslipping because a tire cannot be deflected so much as to contact the road without a sideslip. Sideslip can occur with wheels locked or rotating. Hence, a sideslipping indication may be accompanied by an indication of a stopped or rotating wheel. Exhibit 44 shows road

abrasion to the edge rib of the tread only. This indicates sideslip with a rotating tire.

Damage which indicates whether a wheel was stopped or rotating may be useful in concluding whether the vehicle was standing or moving at the time of the collision. But such a conclusion must be approached with great caution and all imaginable implications should be carefully considered. A tire on a moving vehicle, for example, may be stopped by collision and thereafter damaged in such a way as to suggest it was not rotating when the collision occurred.

Other Indications

Just as there are other abnormalities than those listed, there are also other indications. Remember that possibilities have not been exhausted when the items in the lists of abnormalities and indications have been considered. Any other indications must be separately described.

Be very cautious in interpreting tire abnormalities beyond the basic indications described above. Remember that if an abnormality suggests only the possibility of a circumstance, the circumstance is a matter of conjecture until the indication is confirmed or supported by other observations and reasoning leading to the same conclusion.

For a particular abnormality, be careful to mark only indications suggested by that abnormality. Thus, if it is known from other sources that a vehicle was standing at that time of collision and therefore that the wheel was not rotating, do not mark as an indication of a tire abnormality that the wheel was not rotating unless the abnormality itself was of such a character as to indicate that the wheel was not rotating.

7. CONCLUSIONS

The main purpose in studying a tire and wheel after an accident is to form an opinion as to how, if at all, an observed abnormality affected the occurences that constitute the accident.

Exhibit 44. *Abrasion on only the rib at the edge of the tread indicates that the tire was deflected sidewise. That the tire was rotating, is indicated by the fact that the abrasion is circumferential.*

In most cases, this is a matter of trying to discover whether a tire or wheel condition was a factor in causing the accident or the accident was a factor in causing the wheel or tire condition.

Reaching a conclusion for this purpose is essentially a problem of deciding whether the observed abnormalities disabled the wheel, and if so, at what time in the events of the accident the wheel became disabled.

Clearly, if an abnormality did not disable a wheel, that is, if it did not impair its function, it would not have *directly* influenced the behavior of the vehicle. A normally inflated tire, although badly worn or severely damaged, can do what it is supposed to; that is, it supports the load on the wheel and affords traction necessary for steering and braking.

If, after an accident, the tire has lost most or all of its air pressure, the wheel is functionally impaired, that is, it is disabled. Then there is the task of attempting to find out when the tire became disabled.

Other information, such as witness statements, auxiliary tests, examination of other vehicle parts, and so on, wheel component examination, etc. is often necessary to form meaningful conclusions. In any event, it is almost always better to wait until all information is known before forming a conclusion.

Time of Disablement

Essentially one of six conclusions concerning the time of disablement can be reached as a result of studying a tire and wheel after an accident:

1. *No disablement* actually occurred. There was damage such as tread separation, but the tire was nevertheless functional. Contribution to the behavior of the vehicle is then *indirect,* if indeed there was a contribution. The indirect contribution results from the effect the occurrence had on the driver. A tread separation is often accompanied by a great noise and more or less severe vibration which certainly distracts the driver momentarily. It may result in reflex actions, such as over-correction, with disastrous results. The effect on the driver depends largely on his skill and experience.

2. *Before difficulty* relates to a wheel disablement that occurs during vehicle operation before the driver realizes that he may be in trouble and before any evasive

tactics. For example, when a tire wears through the cords and suddenly becomes disabled by loss of air pressure, disablement occurs before any difficulty in controlling the vehicle is experienced or anticipated by the driver.

3. *During control loss* relates to disablement during steering or braking, but before collision or rollover, for example, a wheel disabled by road friction in a yaw or braking at very high speed. Indications on which this opinion is partly based are stopped wheels (except on a standing vehicle), sideslipping wheels, sudden onset, and road contact.

4. *During collision impact* or start of rollover is the most common time for wheel disablement in connection with an accident. A tire burst or tear while striking a curb or hole in the paving is during collision. Cuts and tears inflicted by other parts of the vehicle are generally during collision. Indications on which this opinion may be based are stopped wheels, instant onset, explosive air loss, contact with other parts of the vehicle, and contact with external objects, including other vehicles. Substantial rim collapse is usually during collision of one kind or another.

5. *After collision* disablement may result from the tire being pulled away from the rim while sliding sidewise or digging in when it flips or rolls. Most fire damage is done after collision or other first harmful event. The opinion that disablement occurred after the first harmful event is often based on indications of road surface contact, quick or slow onset, rapid air loss, and stopped or sideslipping wheels. An important and sometimes confusing kind of after-collision disablement is that caused by towing operations. Often the damaged vehicle is dragged by a powerful tow truck, sometimes

for long distances. This can produce severe tire abnormalities, sometimes cuts in tires which are jammed into wreckage, and sometimes extensive abrasion on a tire dragged down the roadway.

6. *Indeterminate.* Occasionally information available is inadequate for more than speculation as to the time of tire disablement. In such cases, there are usually several possibilities with no means of clearly confirming one. Then any opinion is essentially a matter of guesswork and it is best to consider the matter indeterminate. It may be possible to obtain additional data to settle the question. One may, of course, enumerate the speculative possibilities so long as he clearly explains that they are indeed speculation.

It is proper to suggest the degree of confidence one has in an opinion. If the opinion is largely speculative without much foundation in observations and indications, it is best to let the matter rest as indeterminate. On the other hand, if indications are clear, the opinion can be expressed as certainty. In between one should be guarded and claim only that the events probably occurred as explained.

Relationship to Other Circumstances

Usually, when an investigator examines a tire, he has some notion to begin with about the accident or other event that affected the tire. But sometimes the tire is received for examination unmounted and without any such supplementary information. Without any background data, the investigator can properly make and record his observations and he can even suggest what they indicate, but he must be very cautious about venturing opinions relating to exactly how and when the observed tire conditions developed.

It is a good idea therefore to with-hold final opinion on the ultimate issue until sources of information in addition to the tire itself have been explored. These other kinds of data may be numerous and highly significant. Some warrant mention here.

Road. Tire and rim marks on the road may clearly indicate whether a tire was overdeflected or entirely flat (Exhibit 18) before the vehicle swerved or collided. Such marks may be more significant than damage to the tire. But remember that overdeflected and fully disabled tires often leave no mark at all on the roadway. Nevertheless, the lack of a mark does not necessarily indicate that the tire was disabled.

People involved in the accident and other witnesses may report observations or other sensations which assist in choosing among general possibilities indicated by tire abnormalities. However, regard conclusions or opinions of such people with great skepticism for they are likely to be imaginative, speculative, or biased.

Tow-truck operators can sometimes contribute useful bits of information. They may remember whether the tire had to be replaced for towing, whether it was inflated or deflated, when they first saw it, and whether the beads on one or both sides were unseated from the rim. They may be able to say whether the tire rolled freely or was dragged in towing, which could explain certain observed abnormalities as having developed during towing operations.

Examining the vehicle may show exactly what it was that cut, burst, or punctured a tire during impact. It may also show whether the tire was kept from rotating by collapsed vehicle parts so that movement after collision would produce road abrasion on the tire.

Information from other souces than the tire and wheel which were studied must be carefully documented if they are used in forming opinions relating to when the disablement occurred. Otherwise conclusions appear to be speculation. It is not sufficent

to assume or suppose that certain other conditions existed. It is not wise to put much credence in statements of people, especially interested participants in the accident. Preferably, statements are referred to with qualifying introductions such as "If it is true, as driver A says,..."

Double disablements are always disconcerting. Two sets of indications lead to the conclusion that there were two disablements. If there is reason to believe that the two disabling indications developed simultaneously, the time of disablement of one is the same as that for the other. For example, if there is a cut through the tire which appears to have been produced by impact and also rim and sidewall abrasion which appears to have been from pavement friction in a sideslip the question is whether the abrasion occurred during control loss or after collison. It may be possible to resolve this question by considering how far and in what manner the vehicle moved after collision and whether this would have been sufficient to produce the observed abnormaility. Other information may also help resolve this question. If there is no way to come to a credible conclusion, the matter may have to be left as indeterminate.

Tire Failure Analysis

It is often clear that disablement was due to tire failure rather than damage in an accident. Explaining the tire failure may be difficult, even impossible. Tires are complex structures with invisible parts, and conditions of use afford a host of means for injuring tires.

Therefore analysis of tire failure is where lack of knowledge and skill, usually due to inexperience, can easily lead to very wrong conclusions.

Tire examinations for failure analysis must be done in a properly equipped facility with enough time for the task. It may involve destructive testing which must be done with agreement among all interested parties. Perhaps most important, failure analysis must carefully consider pos-

Exhibit 45. An obvious puncture. No one would fail to recognize that a metal strip made the two holes in the tire.

sibly contributing road, vehicle, and even driver factors.

Within the scope of this topic, it is impossible to describe in detail even the principal strategies that might be involved in failure analysis. In fact, situations are continually developing for which new methods of analysis must be devised.

Some aspects of failure analysis have already been suggested in the preceding pages. Some additional comments may be helpful.

Take the matter of tire punctures. Often, as in Exhibit 45, puncture, as

a reason for disablement, is so evident that there can be no doubt about it in anyone's mind. There is little damage to the tire other than that resulting from penetration by a sharp object.

But Exhibit 46 is quite another matter. Few people would call this sidewall damage the result of a puncture; they would be more likely to blame it on a tire defect. In fact it resulted from a small puncture in the tread that did not penetrate as far as the tire cavity. The tire ran for less than 50 miles while losing air pressure. Air got between the sidewall surface and cords. The resulting flexing and friction developed heat which resulted in sidewall failure.

Exhibit 47 shows the result of another puncture. A nail punctured the tire which ran for a long time before enough air escaping from the tire had caused tread separation and heat generation in the crown region that finally resulted in complete disablement.

Mixed Tires

One tire condition contributing to an indeterminate number of traffic accidents involves no tire disablement and therefore could not be determined by after-accident tire examination. This condition is a bad combination of tires, tire mismatch, which affects the handling characteristics of the vehicle.

The effect of mismatch is insignificant at moderate speeds with ordinary maneuvers; but at speeds, let us say, greater than 50 miles per hour and with quick turns, proper control may be troublesome. The driver may describe the vehicle behavior as "mushy", "wobbly", or "fishtailing".

Consequently, if control is lost at high speed and the driver is vague about what happened, take the trouble to note the kind of tires on each wheel. This may rule out mismatch as a factor contributing to the accident.

The proper tire mix for a vehicle can be found in the owners manual or on RMA (Rubber Manufacturer Association) mixing charts. When one of the following conditions is found

there is a need for further study by someone with expertise in this subject.

Passenger Cars and Light Trucks
a. Radial tires on the front axle with any non-radial tire on the rear axle.
b. 50 series or 60 series radials on the front axle of the car with any other kind of tire on the rear axle.
c. Belted Bias 70 series on the front axle with Bias Metric or Bias 80, 78 or 75 series on the rear axle.
d. Belted Bias 60 or 50 series on the front axle with any other series of tire on the rear axle.
e. Bias 70 series on the front axle with bias or Belted Bias metric or 80 series on the rear axle.
f. Bias 50 or 60 series on the front axle with any other series tire on the rear axle.
g. Different tire construction or size on the same axle.

Trucks With Two Axles
a. Different tire constructions or sizes on the same axle.
b. Radial tire on the front axle with non-radial on the rear axle unless the rear axle uses duals.

Trucks With More Than Two Axles
a. Different tire constructions or sizes on the same axle.
b. Different tire constructions on drive axles.

Whether a given combination of tire mixing will adversely affect handling may be dependent on conditions other than mixing. For example at 10 mph it is unlikely that any mix will cause an accident. Hence a complete investigation is necessary when an improper mix is found.

Other Inferences

Many other inferences beside the basic ones described above may be made from observing tire abnormalities. For example, some tire damage such as extensive abrasion indicates that the tire slid in contact with the

Exhibit 46. *It takes an expert to discover that this extensive damage and disablement started from a small puncture. Running flat did the great damage.*

Exhibit 47. *Starting with a puncture, it took a long time for leaking air to separate plys and lead to this damage and disablement.*

road surface for a considerable distance. That in turn suggests that the vehicle had substantial speed either from its own motion or imparted by another vehicle in collision. Inferences may also sometimes be made about overdeflection of the tire which, in turn, suggests operating for some distance while overloaded or underinflated.

Accident Causation

Be circumspect about inferring how tire abnormalities contribute to accidents. It is easy to go astray by jumping to conclusions in this respect. The most common mistake of this kind is to find a deflated tire with a hole in it after an accident and conclude that a "blowout" caused the vehicle to go out of control. Although this may be the firm belief of the driver and other vehicle occupants, a reasonably careful examination of the tire usually indicates loss of pressure as a result of the collision rather than a factor in its cause.

Driver response to a disablement is usually the determining factor in whether a tire disablement results in an accident. Serious tire disablements often occur. That is why a spare tire is part of the equipment of nearly every vehicle. Yet it is only a very small proportion of the disablements, even the most sudden and severe ones, that are followed by accidents. In other words, all but a few drivers cope successfully with their flat tires. There are some cases in which a tire would cause driver difficulty. For example, if the tread separates completely from the bead, as it may do if the vehicle is driven fast and far with a seriously overdeflected tire, the tread may wad into the fender well and suddenly stop that wheel from rotation. Even then, a surprising number of drivers manage to keep the vehicle under control.

In some cases it is not so much the forces developed by the tire trouble as how the driver responds to the unexpected situation. Suppose, for instance, that a piece of tire tread comes off at very high speed. By itself this will not "throw" the vehicle out of control except in most unusual circumstances because there is generally no loss of air. Trouble follows when the driver, disturbed by noise, vibration, and possibly a slight tendency to move gradually to one side, is momentarily distracted and fails to correct an off-roadway movement or over-reacts to put the vehicle in a yaw from which there is no escape. The loss of tread was not so much the problem as the driver's response.

Tread loss was not the sole cause of the accident. It was indeed a factor in the accident, because without it there would have been no accident, but tread loss was only one in a combination of factors that caused the accident. Another factor was the driver's lack of skill and experience in coping with a manageable contingency. Indeed, the driver's prolonged excessive speed may well have been why the piece of tread separated in the first place.

Skills Required

How far you can safely go with an analysis depends on your skill and experience. Some of the issues may be indeterminate. You cannot resolve them with the data you have; perhaps nobody can.

Be especially careful when thinking about tire defects. Discovering significant defects may require partially dismantling and testing the tire with special equipment and procedures. Unless you are a seasoned specialist, you may have to seek help in this matter.

8. RECORDS AND REPORTS

General Vehicle Examination

If you make a routine inspection of

the vehicle at the scene of an accident, whatever you note about tire conditions is a natural part of your record of that inspection. This record may be only what you happen to remember; or it may be what you wrote down at the time, possibly on a general vehicle examination form such as that illustrated in Exhibit 16.

Special Tire Inspection

If you are specially assigned to examine a tire after an accident, find out from whoever wants the tire examined exactly what kind of a record or report is expected. Maybe only a brief verbal report, perhaps by phone, is necessary with nothing in writing required. Then the only record you need is what you remember.

However, if you are asked to examine a tire after an accident professionally, you are usually expected to try to find out how the tire may have contributed to the accident. You must then be prepared to describe your observations and conclusions in detail, possibly in court and perhaps years later.

In that case, you will need a permanent record of your observations and conclusions such as most professionals make for their work. Notes made by a doctor or dentist of the examination of a patient and the treatment prescribed are examples.

Professionals make their records in several different ways:

1. Simple written notes on plain paper
2. Entries on a form with additional separate comments on plain paper
3. Dictated to stenographer
4. Recorded on tape as observations are made.

These records are kept until there is no longer possible need for them.

Photographs

It is always a good idea to photograph anything that will be changed in an examination prior to making that change. For example, if you take a tire from a wheel, photograph it before it is removed.

Supplementary records of abnormalities can be made photographically. Photos are rarely needed if the tire itself can be retained for future reference. However, do not depend on photographs as a substitute for careful examination. An exception to this is when photos are made of a tire by someone who does not know what to look for, so that another person, more qualified, may examine the photos. Of course, this is unnecessary if the tire itself is available.

If you can keep the tire and wheel indefinitely, your record may be much simplified. You will not need to record details of observations that you can easily repeat later. A summary of conclusions may be sufficient for the time being.

If tests are performed on the tire or if it is manipulated in any way, such as removing it from the rim, inflating it, or removing specimens of the material, make separate specific notes of what you do so that there will be no misunderstandings about it later. It is also a good practice to mark the location of the tire on the wheel before removing the tire. This can easily be done by marking the location of the valve on the tire.

Contents

The record of a tire examination, like the systematic record of the examination of anything else after an accident, consists of a number of items:

1. *Identification* of
   a. The tire (Usually a special label or marking applied by the investigator or someone else)
   b. The event (Accident number or time and place)
   c. Person doing the investigating (Name and address)
   d. Place and time of examination
   e. Source of tire (How the investigator got it)
   f. Disposal (What became of the tire after it was examined)

2. *Description of*
   a. Tire (Data molded in tire surface)
   b. Event (Type and severity of accident)
   c. Special characteristics (Tread type, tube, recap, etc.)
3. *Condition as received*
   a. On or off wheel
   b. Bead seating
   c. Air pressure
   d. Tread wear (Groove depth)
4. *Significant abnormalities*
   a. Shape and size of each
   b. Location on tire
   c. Depth
5. *Significant wheel abnormalities*
   a. Size
   b. Location
   c. Characteristics
6. *Indications of abnormalities*
7. *Operations* (Taking tire from wheel, inflation, etc)
8. *Conclusions* (Opinions and inferences)
9. *Comments*

Form

When one expects to examine tires from time to time, a form may be useful for recording routine data and conventional observations. Such a form is illustrated in Exhibits 48 and 49.

A form speeds up recording of description, identification, and simple observations. Because similar data are always in the same location, it makes finding particular information easy. The form also reminds one of data needed.

A form discourages observations which are not specifically provided for and tends to encourage guesswork to fill in spaces for which relevant facts are lacking.

No form can be designed for all of the data which might come to light in some tire examination. The form is, therefore, nearly always supplemented by additional special written material or photographs. Sometimes it is only a small part of a much more elaborate and definitive report.

TIRE EXAMINATION RECORD

SOURCE OF TIRE	VEHICLE TBF678 IL	Position on Vehicle LF	ACCIDENT OR CASE No. 513H

OBTAINED FROM FORD WAGON | Street or road ON PARKER RD

BY – Person J.S. BAKER | Intersection with or distance from AT 750 FT N OF IL 57

AT – Place FERRYDALE JOE'S AUTO PARTS | DATE 29 | MONTH DEC | 19XX | IN | City NR FERRYDALE | County IL | State

PHOTOS BY J.S. BAKER | HOUR of event 01:50 | DATE 17 | MONTH DEC | 19XX

☐ WHERE STORED
☒ HOW DISPOSED LEFT WITH VEHICLE AT JOE'S AUTO PARTS | DATE 29 | MONTH DEC | 19XX

DESCRIPTION	MAKE GOODYEAR2	NAME SUPER	SIZE C7814	☐ RECAP ☐ TUBE ☐ STUDDED ☐ SNOW

SERIAL DOT LEV263427 | MAXIMUM PRESSURE 32 | MAXIMUM LOAD 1300 | OTHER DATA | VALVE CAP ON ☐ YES ☒ NO

GROOVE DEPTHS (Serial to Opposite) | Each groove at serial in 1/32's: 7 | 8 | 8 | 8 | 7 | | | Each groove opposite serial in 1/32's: 7 | 8 | 8 | 7 | 7 | | |

☐ OFF RIM ☒ ON RIM | SERIAL BEAD ☒ TIGHT ☐ LOOSE | OPPOSITE BEAD ☒ TIGHT ☐ LOOSE | REMARKS

EXAMINED BY – Person J.S. BAKER | AT – Organization or place JOE'S AUTO PARTS FERRYDALE IL | DATE 29 | MONTH DEC | 19XX

WHAT THE ABNORMALITIES INDICATE

Mark one or more indications for each abnormality as follows: X for definite; / for possible.

TIRE INDICATIONS		A	B	C	D	E	F	G
RATE OF ONSET	Gradual, days							
	Slow, hours							
	Quick, minutes							
	Sudden, seconds			X				
	Instantaneous	X	X					
AIR LOSS	None		X	X				
	Slow							
	Rapid							
	Explosive	X						
CONTACT	Road surface			X				
	Flange							
	Other part of veh.	/	/					
	External object	/	/					
WHEEL	Not rotating	/	/					
	Rotating	/	/					
	Sideslipping			X				
Other								

WHEEL INDICATIONS		Z	Y	X	W	V
RATE OF ONSET	Gradual, days					
	Slow, hours					
	Quick, minutes					
	Sudden, seconds	X				
	Instantaneous		X			
AIR LOSS	None	X				
	Slow					
	Rapid					
	Explosive		X			
CONTACT	Road surface	X				
	Tire only					
	Other part of veh.					
	External object		X			
WHEEL	Not rotating		X			
	Rotating	X				
	Sideslipping					
Other						

OPINION CONCERNING TIME OF DISABLEMENT

For the first disablement, and on the basis of information available, mark x the applicable item in the list below. If undecided, leave the schedule blank.

At disablement, tire remained inflated	While swerving or skidding before first harmful event	After collision or other first harmful event.
Before driver difficulty, before swerve or skid	During collision impact or start of rollover X	Indeterminate with information available

Copyright 1986 – Northwestern University Traffic Institute   1270:186RV   SN 8010

Exhibit 48. *Front of form for recording identifying and descriptive data and summarizing indications of abnormalities.*

TIRE AND WHEEL ABNORMALITIES

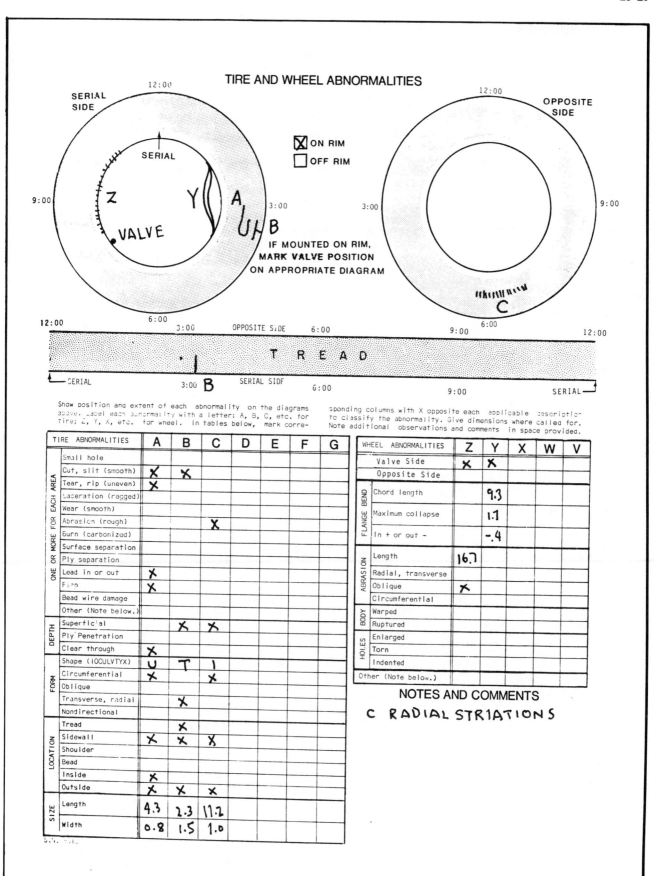

☒ ON RIM
☐ OFF RIM

IF MOUNTED ON RIM,
MARK VALVE POSITION
ON APPROPRIATE DIAGRAM

Show position and extent of each abnormality on the diagrams above. Label each abnormality with a letter: A, B, C, etc. for Tire; Z, Y, X, etc. for wheel. In tables below, mark corresponding columns with X opposite each applicable description to classify the abnormality. Give dimensions where called for. Note additional observations and comments in space provided.

TIRE ABNORMALITIES		A	B	C	D	E	F	G
ONE OR MORE FOR EACH AREA	Small hole							
	Cut, slit (smooth)	X	X					
	Tear, rip (uneven)	X						
	Laceration (ragged)							
	Wear (smooth)							
	Abrasion (rough)			X				
	Burn (carbonized)							
	Surface separation							
	Ply separation							
	Lead in or out	X						
	Flap	X						
	Bead wire damage							
	Other (Note below.)							
DEPTH	Superficial		X	X				
	Ply Penetration							
	Clear through	X						
FORM	Shape (IOCULVTYX)	U	T	I				
	Circumferential	X		X				
	Oblique							
	Transverse, radial		X					
	Nondirectional							
LOCATION	Tread		X					
	Sidewall	X	X	X				
	Shoulder							
	Bead							
	Inside	X						
	Outside	X	X	X				
SIZE	Length	4.3	2.3	11.2				
	Width	0.8	1.5	1.0				

WHEEL ABNORMALITIES		Z	Y	X	W	V
	Valve Side	X	X			
	Opposite Side					
FLANGE BEND	Chord length		9.3			
	Maximum collapse		1.1			
	In + or out –		–.4			
ABRASION	Length	16.7				
	Radial, transverse					
	Oblique	X				
	Circumferential					
BODY	Warped					
	Ruptured					
HOLES	Enlarged					
	Torn					
	Indented					
	Other (Note below.)					

NOTES AND COMMENTS

C RADIAL STRIATIONS

Exhibit 49. *Back of form describes abnormalities observed in tire and wheel examinations.*

25-30

9. SOURCES

Contributors

This topic was developed by the following persons

James D. Gardner, a mechanical engineer and Manager of Product Analysis, Firestone Tire and Rubber Co., Akron OH

J. Stannard Baker, a traffic Engineer specializing in accident investigation. He was Director of Research and Development at the Northwestern University Traffic Institute from 1946 to 1971 and is still a consultant and guest lecturer at the Traffic Institute.

References

Superscript numbers in the preceeding pages of this topic refer to the following publications:
1. Baker, J. Stannard and McIlraith, G. Declan, "Tire Disablements and Accidents on High Speed Roads" in *Highway Research Record* (No 272), 1969, Highway Research Board, Washington DC (14 pages)
2. *Truck Wheels and Rims — Nomenclature* (SAE J393), 1969, Society of Automotive Engineeers, Warrendale PA 15096 (4 Pages)
3. *Passenger Car Wheels — Performance Requirements and Test Procedures* (SAE J328a), 1970, Society of Automotive Engineers, Warrendale PA 15096 (2 pages)

Exhibits

The following are sources of photos, diagrams, forms, and tables in this Topic:
Baker, J. Stannard, Glencoe IL
   Photos: 18, 25, 28, 29, 30, 31, 37, 38
   Diagrams: 13, 40, 41
   Forms: 16, 48
Baker, Warren S.
   Photo: 70
Gardner,
   Photos: 1, 2, 3, 4, 5, 10, 11, 12, 14, 15, 17, 19, 21, 22, 23, 24, 26, 32, 33, 34, 35, 36, 39, 42, 43, 44, 45, 46, 47
   Diagrams: 6, 7, 8, 9
   Table: 27

MEASURING AT THE SCENES OF TRAFFIC ACCIDENTS

Topic 828 of the *Traffic-Accident Investigation Manual*

by
J. Stannard Baker
and
Lynn Fricke

NORTHWESTERN UNIVERSITY TRAFFIC INSTITUTE

PUBLICATION HISTORY

1940   *Accident Investigation Manual* (Part of Chapter 4)
Reprinted 1941, 1942

1946 Revised (Part of Chapter 5)
Reprinted 1947, 1948

1953   *Traffic Accident Investigator's Manual* (Sections 41 & 42)
1954 Revised (Sections 41 & 42)

1957   *Traffic Accident Investigator's Manual for Police* (Sections 41 & 42)
Reprinted 1959

1963 Revised (Sections 41 & 42)
Reprinted 1964, 1965, 1966, 1969, 1970, 1971, 1973

1970   *Manual de Investigacion de Accidentes de Trafico* (Sections 41 & 42)

1975   *Traffic Accident Investigation Manual* (Part of Chapter 7)
Reprinted 1976, 1979

1983   *Measuring at the Scenes of Traffic Accidents* (Independent study course)
1984 Revised

1985 *Measuring at the Scenes of Traffic Accidents*

MEASURING AT THE SCENES OF TRAFFIC ACCIDENTS

One thing is clear from examination of data collected for hundreds of fatal traffic accidents: measurements locating results of the accidents, such as final positions of vehicles, are unsatisfactory in nine out of ten reports. Yet these measurements are the very foundation for speed estimates and other conculsions as to how the accidents happened.

For the most part, deficiencies in measurements do not appear to be due to stupidity or laziness on the part of investigators. They seem to be bungling as the result of no clear notion as exactly how to go about this important part of investigating a fatal accident. This conclusion strongly suggests inadequate training of most at-scene traffic-accident investigators.

For serious traffic accidents, two kinds of measurements may be made:

1. *At the scene measurements* are made to locate marks on the road and final positions of vehicles. These measurements result in a simple field sketch.
2. *At the site* of the accident, measurements of the road layout are made later and only if required. These result in another kind of field sketch.

If required, the two kinds of measurements are combined later in an after-accident situation map, which is drawn to scale.

The present topic explains how to make the at-scene measurements. How to measure the site and prepare the after-accident situation map is another topic.

Whoever makes at-scene measurements should know exactly what results of the accident to look for and how to describe them. While there is a brief resume in this topic of what results of the accident need to be located, this matter is much more fully discussed in a separate topic. If you are importantly involved in at-scene traffic-accident investigation, and especially if you have to make measurements at the scene, you would do well to carefully study the topic relating to obtaining information about the accident from observing the road afterward.

For developing skills in measuring at the scenes of accidents, the Traffic Institute includes this subject in courses on the Institute campus and elsewhere. The Traffic Institute also offers a well tested independent study (correspondence) course for this activity.

Policy on measurements. Whether an accident is serious enough to warrant measurements at the scene depends on policies of those administering accident investigation. This subject is discussed elsewhere. For the following explanation of meas-

urements, it is assumed that a map of the situation after the accident is required and that measurements for it are to be made.

Methods described here are not the only ones that can be used. Some investigators and engineers may have learned or developed other methods. If your way of measuring produces satisfactory maps of the location, including the results of the accident, there is no reason to abandon or change it. The methods discussed here have produced excellent results with simple equipment and without wasting time, interfering with traffic, or causing unnecessary hazard to the investigator.

1. WHAT TO LOCATE—SPOTS TO WHICH YOU MEASURE

Before you start to measure anything at the scene of a serious traffic accident, decide exactly what you must locate. You will save yourself much trouble and avoid mistakes if you do this! Look carefully for results of the accident. Although circumstances may vary, these observations are not difficult. Just keep in mind all the different kinds of things that someone may later want to locate exactly on a map or diagram of the road at the site of the accident.

The final product of your efforts to locate things has two parts:

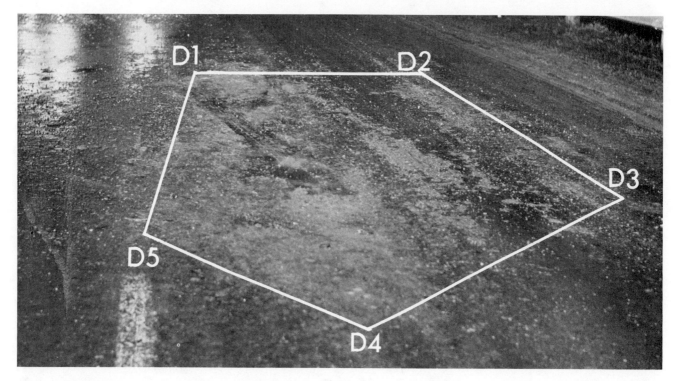

Exhibit 1. *Three or more spots are needed to locate a debris area or any other area on the road, if the area is more than about three feet long. The number of spots depends on the extent and shape of the area. Sometimes there are two rather distinct solid areas.*

1. A FREE HAND (without ruler) field sketch showing the general configuration (layout) of the roadways and the results of the accident (spots) you have located.

2. *A list or other record* of the measurements which you have made to locate these spots.

What Signs of the Accident to Look for

Look for eight kinds of results of the accident on the road and roadside:

1. *Positions of vehicles* where they came to rest after collision. For this purpose, trailers are considered separate vehicles regardless of whether they remain attached to the towing vehicle. Also, bicycles and motorcycles are classified as vehicles.

2. *Places where dead or injured persons lie* after the accident, if they are not in vehicles.

3. *Gouges* (chips, chops, and grooves) are made by strong sharp, metal objects which displace pavement material. You can see and feel gouges.

4. *Scratches and scrapes* are made by weak or rounded metal objects which do not displace pavement material. You can see scrapes, but you cannot feel them.

5. *Tiremarks* on the paving or elsewhere unless it is quite clear that they are not relevant.

6. *Scars* on the roadside. These may be ruts or furrows in surface material beyond the shoulder.

7. *Debris* of various kinds: underbody dirt or snow (Exhibit 1), loose vehicle parts such as hood or wheels; pedestrian's belongings such as shoes, handbags, glasses; vehicle liquids such as spatter (Exhibit 2), dribble path (Exhibit 3), runoff rivulets (Exhibit 4), and puddles (Exhibit

5) which may be related as in Exhibit 6. Blood and body tissue from victims of the accident are forms of liquid debris.

8. *Objects on or near the road* which were broken or marked as a result of the accident.

To locate results of the accident by measuring, you do not need to know their significance. That can be worked out later, if necessary. A general indication of their character, such as the descriptions in the previous paragraph, is all that is necessary.

In addition to results of the accident, it may be useful to locate some other things which seem to be significant. These may include:

1. *Parked or disabled vehicles* which may have been view obstructions or traffic obstacles not involved in the collision.

2. *Places where witnesses were* when the accident happened.

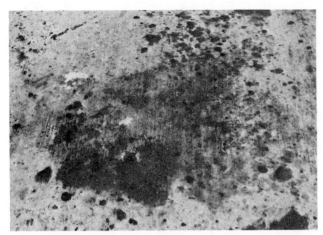

Exhibit 2. *Spatter occurring in a "freckled" pattern shows where fluids were forced violently from containers onto the road.*

Exhibit 3. *Dribble may form a path from a spatter area to vehicle final position, light to begin and heavy later.*

Exhibit 4. *Runoff rivulets run downgrade from puddle toward edge of paving. Not the same as dribble path. Begins where vehicle came to rest.*

Exhibit 5. *Puddle on paving or roadside where vehicle liquids have come to rest and formed a pool. Often shows final position of vehicle.*

3. *Ice patches,* puddles, snow heaps, barricades, and excavations which may have had some effect on events of the accident and which may soon be gone.

At first, it is not necessary to measure the width of the road, locations of signs, or other things which are permanent and may be located later.

Spots To Be Located

After deciding what it is you want to locate by measurements, decide how many spots on each mark or object must be located. For cars or long tiremarks, one spot is not enough. For example, if you locate only the left front corner of a vehicle, as in Exhibit 7, the left rear corner of the vehicle could be north,

south, east, west, or any other direction from the left front corner. With only one spot, therefore, you can locate only one part of a vehicle.

One spot will adequately locate relatively small things such as:

1. *A human body* (Locate only the middle of the waist unless there is some reason to do otherwise; for example, if the body is in two parts, locate each part.)
2. *Gouges* or groups of gouges in an area less than three feet across (Locate the middle of that group, possibly sketching or photographing a group of gouges to give details.)
3. *Grooves,* collision scrubs, and tiremarks, less than 3 ft. long (Locate the middle of the mark.)

4. *Small scrapes* or dents in guardrails; damage to posts and trees.
5. *Spatter areas* and puddles less than 3 ft. across.
6. *Small debris* areas.
7. *Vehicle parts,* such as wheels, that have become detached.

Two spots are needed to locate such things as

1. *Vehicles.* Ordinarily, locate undamaged corners on the same side of the vehicle. Avoid using corners on the same end, especially if one is damaged, because they are too close together to locate the vehicle well. If the vehicle is at the end of tiremarks, locate wheels rather than corners. This will serve to locate the end of the tire-

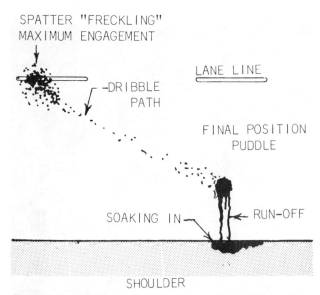

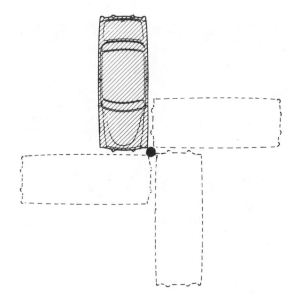

Exhibit 6. *Liquid debris is found on the road in a number of forms illustrated in this diagram. Spatter and final position puddle are especially important to locate by measurements. Do not overlook these signs of what happened.*

Exhibit 7. *One spot on something large, like a vehicle locates only one part of it. The rest might be in any direction from that one spot. At least two spots are needed to locate vehicles, preferably one at each end.*

marks.

2. *Straight tiremarks.* Locate both ends of each mark.
3. *Curved tiremarks more than three, but less than eight feet long.* Locate the ends.
4. *Straight grooves* more than 3 ft. long. Locate both ends of each.
5. *Long sections of railings* or fences scraped or damaged.
6. *Dribble paths.*

Three or more spots are required to locate adequately such things as:

1. *Curved tiremarks* more than eight feet long, especially YAW (centrifugal, sideslip) scuffs. Locate each end and spots where the tiremark crosses a roadway edge, lane line, or center line. If this leaves a long stretch of curved tiremarks without a spot, add spots at intervals of about 10 ft. If the mark is more than 30 ft. long, locate spots at 10- or 20-ft. intervals (stations) as will be explained later. (Exhibit 8)
2. *Straight marks with angles,* crooks, gaps, or other irregularities in them. Locate both ends of each mark and

the angle or other irregularity.

3. *Large debris areas.* Locate three to six spots on the perimeter of the area. Include only substantial deposits of debris and not all widely scattered debris, as in Exhibit 1.

When a tiremark on a roadway or pavement continues as a furrow off the pavement, consider it as a single mark. Locate a spot at each end and one where it leaves the pavement.

A very useful spot to locate is where a tiremark, especially a curved one, starts at or crosses

1. Another tiremark
2. The edge of the roadway
3. A center line or lane divider line
4. A railroad track.

Note that it is not necessary to locate a spot where a vehicle lies across the edge of the roadway, a center line, or a lane line. Two spots for the vehicle are sufficient.

Identifying Spots

Assign an identifying letter to each item to be located. For example, suppose there are three tiremarks, simply designate one A, another B, and

the remaining one C.

You will find it useful to identify an object to be located by a letter which reminds you of what that thing is. For example, a truck might be labeled T and a car in the same accident C. If two cars are involved, F might represent a Ford and C a Chevrolet. Debris can be labeled D, a gouge, G, and a body B or F for female and M for male. Of course, it is not necessary to use associative initials. If no associative letter comes to mind, or if it has already been used, any letter will do. It is generally better not to use numbers (Vehicle 1, Vehicle 2, etc.) by which vehicles are identified on an accident report because

1. Vehicle numbers in accident reports are usually not assigned when measurements are made.
2. Numbers are not initials which remind you of what they represent.
3. Accident report numbers do not identify trailers separately.

If more than one spot is needed to locate something to which you have assigned a letter, call these spots 1, 2, 3, and so on. For example, if a debris area is marked D, the five spots on its

Exhibit 8. *Three or more spots may be required to locate a long curved mark on the road. One spot is needed for each end, one or more in between to show the curve, and other spots where it crosses roadway edge or lane lines.*

Exhibit 9. *If a skidmark or yawmark on the roadway continues on the roadside as a furrow, label it as a single mark with spots at the beginning, end, and where it crosses the roadway edge line. Here eight tiremarks continue on the roadside. Only two are labelled.*

perimeter would be called D1, D2, D3, D4 and D5 (Exhibit 1). However, if you have a curved tiremark more than 30 ft. long on paving, you can mark spots on it or do it another way which will be explained later.

A locked wheel may produce a skidmark on the paving but in soft or loose material on the shoulder or roadside, it may continue as a furrow in which dirt is pushed ahead of the tire and plowed off to either side. Also a tire which is slipping and rotating may leave a yaw mark on the paving but a furrow on the roadside in loose material. When a skidmark or yawmark thus changes to a furrow, consider and label it as a single mark. For example, consider tire mark A in Exhibit 9. It is labelled

    A1 where it begins (outside of the picture)
    A2 where it crosses the edge line
    A3 where it ends.

Using numbers for spots after a letter identifying what is to be located tells you at once how many spots you have to locate for that particular thing.

Mark Spots on the Road

If there are more spots than you can keep in mind — usually six or more — mark their identifying letters and numbers on the road.

Marking can be done with bright aerosol spray paint, by heavy lumber-marking crayon, or, off the pavement, by small cards held down by nails stuck through them and into the ground as in Exhibit 10.

2. COORDINATE METHOD OF LOCATING THINGS

Having decided what spots you must locate — spots *to* which you will measure — the next step is to decide *from* what to measure. This is where many investigators fail. Actually it is easy if you understand a few basic ideas.

In the after-accident situation mapped in Exhibit 11, you need to locate three spots: C1 and C2 where the car came to rest and B where the pedestrian's body lay. Now some people would give only the shortest distance between car and body, 10.0 ft. But that locates neither the vehicle nor the pedestrian. They could be anywhere on the map so long as they were 10.0 ft (to scale) apart. But if you say that Spot B is 13.0 ft north of the south curb of Oak St. and 46.0 ft east of the nearest crosswalk, there is only one place where the pedestrian's body could have been. You can testify to *that* with confidence.

Two Measurements Per Spot

Thus, to locate any spot, you must make at least TWO measurements, one from each of two permanent, recognizable landmarks. These two measurements, in the coordinate system, are the COORDINATES of the spot. Select the two landmarks and have them clearly in mind *before* you start to measure. With such landmarks, you or any one else can return to the site of the accident later and locate exactly from what you measured to locate spots at the scene.

The coordinate system is generally the most useful and easiest to use. With this method, one landmark is a REFERENCE LINE (RL) and the other is a REFERENCE POINT (RP) on the RL. The reference point is sometimes called the "zero" point or "Starting" point. In Exhibit 11, the RL is the south (S) edge of Oak St. or possibly an IMAGINARY EXTENSION of this edge. The RP on this RL is where an imaginary extension of the east (E) edge of the east sidewalk of Elm St. crosses the RL.

You must always state the DIRECTION of the spot being located from the RL, N, S, E, or W, and the direction *along* the RL from the RP to the place on the RL nearest the spot being located. The measurements *and* directions are coordinates of the spot.

Exhibit 10. *A card pinned to the ground marks a location on the roadside where crayons are useless and spray paint is not much good. A reference number can be marked on the card.*

Describe Your References Accurately

For future reference always describe the RL and RP on your field sketch. Make this description as simple and brief as possible
    1. To save time in writing at the scene.
    2. To take up less space on the field sketch.

Use abbreviations and omit all unnecessary words. The description for the example in Exhibit 11 is

    RL = S edge Oak

    RP @ E edge E sidewalk Elm.

In such a description *is* may be abbreviated by = and *at* may be abbreviated by the sign @. In descriptions, *always* name the RL first and then the RP. Then you will avoid later confusion.

Thus, the two coordinates to locate a spot are:
    1. The direction and distance along the RL from the RP to the place on the RL nearest the spot to be located.
    2. The direction and shortest distance from the RL to the spot to be located.

Note that these two coordinate measurements are at right angles (90°) to each other, if the RL is straight as in Exhibit 11.

The coordinate system applies to any map location. For example, if you live in Indianapolis, Indianapolis is probably your reference point for locating other places in the United States. Then if someone tells you that Detroit is 250 miles from Indianapolis, you cannot, from that information, locate Detroit. It might be somewhere south in Tennessee (about where Nashville is), or, perhaps, west in Missouri (about where St. Louis is). But, if you are given coordinates for Detroit from Indianapolis, 190 miles north and 160 east, you can place Detroit exactly, it can be nowhere else.

With *coordinates,* remember five things:

1. *Two measurements* are necessary to locate a spot from a reference point.
2. One measurement is the *shortest distance from the spot to be located to a reference line.*
3. *The other measurement is the distance from that place on the reference line to the reference point* which is also on the reference line.
4. These two measurements are usually at *right angles* (90°) to each other.
5. In addition to giving the

distance of each measurement, its *direction* must be specified.

It is easy to see how this works by looking again at Exhibit 11. The reference line chosen here is the south roadway edge of Oak St. The RP (reference point) is where the east edge of the east crosswalk of Elm St. crosses the reference line. In this case, because the crosswalk is not marked and the curb is curved, the reference point is the intersection of two imaginary extensions of two real edge lines: one, the south edge of Oak St., and the other, the east edge of the east crosswalk of Elm St. The two coordinates would then be referred to as east 46.0 and north 13.0 ft. For recording, these are abbreviated to E46.0 and N13.0.

The reference line does not have to be straight. It can be a curved roadway edge as in Exhibit 12. In that case, measure straight across from the RP to the place on the RL nearest to the spot to be located, and from that place directly to the spot to be located. This is illustrated in Exhibit 12. The coordinates of the Spot A1 are S46.0 and E13.0.

The direction of the measurement does not have to be an exact compass

direction, north, south, east, or west. It may be a *nominal* compass direction. A nominal direction is that which you choose for the general direction of the roadway when

1. The roadway curves at the scene of the accident.
2. The roadway runs more or less between compass directions, for example northwest and southeast.
3. You do not know the exact compass direction at the scene of the accident.

Thus, in Exhibit 12, the curved road runs approximately northwest and southeast. For reference purposes you can call it either a north-south road or an east-west road. You arbitrarily choose the former, and it becomes, nominally, for your purposes, a north-south road. Later, if necessary, someone can establish the true compass directions for other uses. In Exhibit 12, the RL has been chosen as the East edge of OH 28 and the RP has been selected as a point on the RL opposite (op) the south end of the culvert headwall. These references are described as

RL = E edge OH 28

RP op S end culvert headwall.

There is an important advantage

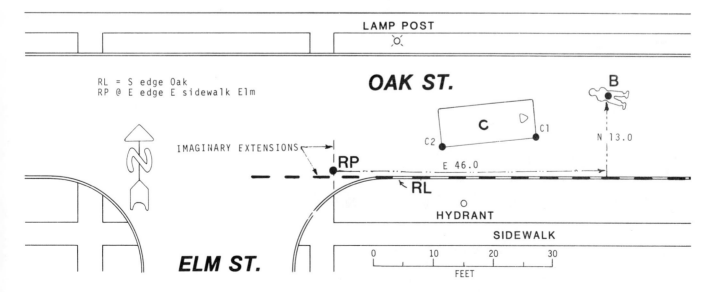

Exhibit 11. *The distance between Spots C1 and B does not locate either spot on the roadway mapped here. But the spots can be located exactly by coordinates from an RP (reference point). For spot B, coordinates are E46.0 and N13.0.*

of coordinate measurements at the scene of an accident. All measurements along the edge of the roadway can be made on the shoulder or roadside without getting on the roadway itself where there is traffic interference. Many measurements to spots from the edge of the roadway can also be made with minimum exposure to traffic.

3. TRIANGULATION TO LOCATE THINGS

Coordinates are not the only way to locate spots. There are a number of others, some of which require surveying instruments. But all methods require *two* measurements for each spot; one measurement from each of *two* landmarks of one kind or another. You should know about one of these other methods, TRIANGULATION, for two reasons:

1. Occasionally triangulation is better and easier to use than coordinates.
2. You may see triangulation used by investigators and others who have not learned to use coordinates.

When To Use Triangulation

There are only a few circumstances in which triangulation is better than coordinates. These are generally where no good reference line, such as a clear roadway edge, is available. Here are some examples of such circumstances:

1. Edges of roadway are difficult to find or are indistinct, as on gravel or dirt roads or when road is covered with snow. See Exhibit 13.
2. Spots to be located are more than about 30 ft. off the roadway. See Exhibit 14.
3. Roadway edges are very irregular as in traffic circles, and some complicated junctions, especially in cities. See Exhibit 15.
4. Spots are off the road in swamps or woods. See Exhibit 16.
5. Some obstacle, such as a pond, bank, building, or trees prevents making shortest distance measurements from a spot to a reference line. See Exhibit 17.

6. There are no clear roadway edges for reference lines as in construction sites, gravel pits, large parking lots, and open fields. See Exhibit 18.

Principles of Triangulation

The idea of triangulation is simple: the distance of the spot to be located is measured directly from each of *two* RP's (reference points). Exhibit 19 is an example of triangulation. This is the same after-accident situation that was used in to illustrate the use of coordinates (Exhibit 11). You have to locate Spot B, the body of a pedestrian. There are two landmarks to serve as reference points: a hydrant, RP1, and a lamp post, RP2, on opposite sides of Oak St. The distances from these two will locate Spot B. These distances are 29.6 ft. from RP1 and 36.3 ft. from RP2. A triangle is formed by Spot B and reference points RP1 and RP2. That is why this method is called triangulation. Triangulation reference points must also be described. The

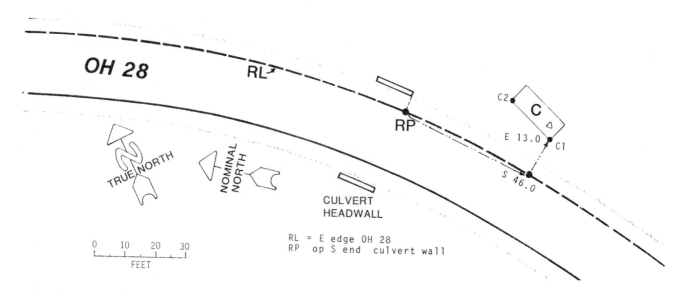

Exhibit 12. *The edge of the roadway does not have to be straight or run true north-south or east-west to be used as a reference line. A convenient nominal compass direction can be used. Exact compass direction can be determined later.*

Exhibit 13. *When roadway edges are obscure, triangulation may be better than coordinates for locating spots.*

Exhibit 14. *Spots more than about 30 ft. off the roadway are often better located by triangulation than coordinates.*

Exhibit 15. *Curved and irregular roadway edges may make triangulation preferable to coordinates for at-scene measurements.*

Exhibit 16. *Spots on vehicles coming to rest in swamps or woods may make triangulation easier than coordinates.*

Exhibit 17. *Some obstacles, such as woods, buildings, or water, make the shortest-distance measurements for coordinates difficult.*

Exhibit 18. *Triangulation may be best where there are no roadway edges or other natural reference lines.*

two in Exhibit 19 can be described thus:

RP1 = Hydrant S of Oak

RP2 = Lamp post N of Oak 28.2 ft from RP1.

As pointed out above, Exhibit 11 shows for coordinates the same after-accident situation that Exhibit 19 shows for triangulation. Thus, in this case and also in most other cases, either coordinates or triangulation can be used for after-accident measurements. Therefore, you must choose either coordinates or triangulation whichever is better under the particular circumstances. In Exhibit 19, triangulation looks simple enough.

Difference Between Triangulation and Coordinates

But consider how triangulation differs from coordinates: in this example, the two coordinate measurements in Exhibit 11 tie measurements directly to the roadway; but the two triangulation measurements in Exhibit 19 do not. To tie triangulation reference points to the roadway in Exhibit 19 (and also in other cases), three addi-

tional measurements are *necessary:*

1. The shortest distance from RP 1 to a roadway edge.
2. The shortest distance from RP 2 to the *same* roadway edge.
3. The distance from RP 1 and RP 2.

These additional measurements which must be made are shown by dotted lines in Exhibit 19.

Triangulation is like coordinates in that it takes *two* measurements to locate each spot. In fact, any method of measuring requires at least two measurements to locate a spot. Triangulation differs from coordinates in three ways:

1. No reference line is used (unless you consider a line between the two reference points a reference line).
2. The two measurements are not necessarily at right angles to each other.
3. There is no need to specify directions of measurements.

RP's for triangulation do not have to be posts or trees and do not have to be on the same side of the roadway. If only one natural landmark is convenient for a triangulation RP, you can always locate a second with ref-

erence to it as illustrated in Exhibit 20, which is the same situation illustrated in Exhibit 12. You would describe the RP's in Exhibit 20 as follows:

RP 1 = SW corner E curlvert wall

RP 2 = E edge OH 28 50.0 S of RP 1.

Why Coordinates Are Usually Better

In most situations, triangulation is not as satisfactory as coordinates

1. Because suitable landmark RP's for triangulation may be far from the roadway. Thus, measurements are generally longer with triangulation than with coordinates.
2. For the same reason, triangulation measurements are likely to be over ditches, banks, or rough ground and so more difficult than measurements along the edges of roadways and across paved surfaces.
3. When drawing maps of accident situations, spots are easier to place when located by coordinates than by tri-

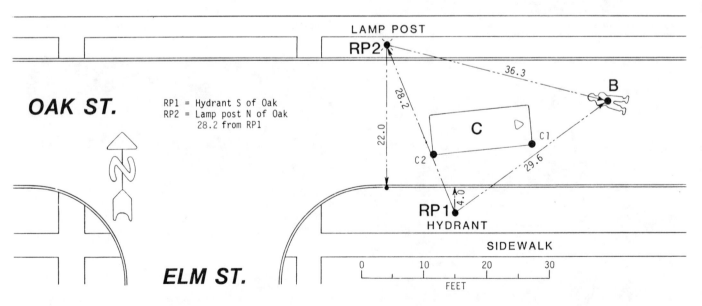

Exhibit 19. *Location by triangulation involves measuring the distance of the spot to be located from two reference points, RP1 and RP2. To relate these points to the roadway, three additional measurements are needed: The distance between the two RP's and the shortest distance from each to the same roadway edge. RP's do not have to be opposite sides of the roadway.*

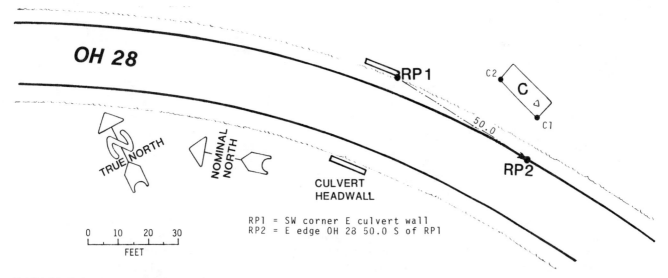

Exhibit 20. *Reference points for triangulation can be wherever most convenient. In the situation illustrated here, both are on the same side of the roadway. Only one good natural RP is available, a corner of the culvert wall. The other can be located from it.*

angulation. To place a spot on a map by coordinates, you only have to scale one distance along a reference line and another at right angles to it. But with triangulation, you have to draw an arc with a compass from each RP as the center. The spot is where the two arcs intersect.

4. If triangulation measurements are made without relating the reference points to the roadway, someone has to go back to the site of the accident and make those measurements before the data can be used in mapping.

5. Triangulation gives a false as well as a true location of a spot. For example, in Exhibit 21, Spot S is 19.0 ft. to scale from RP 1 and 31.0 ft. from RP 2. But a false Spot S is also the same distance from the two RP's but on the opposite side of an imaginary line connecting the two RP's. So, when locating spots on a map of the accident situation, it may be difficult to tell, from the meas-

urements, which is the true and which is the false location.

6. When the angle between measurements to a spot is very small or very large, that is, extremely acute or extremely obtuse, as in Exhibit 22, the measurements must be very exact to locate the spot accurately. In practice, it is quite difficult to make such accurate measurements at the scene of an accident.

You can avoid many of these difficulties with triangulation

1. By using coordinates

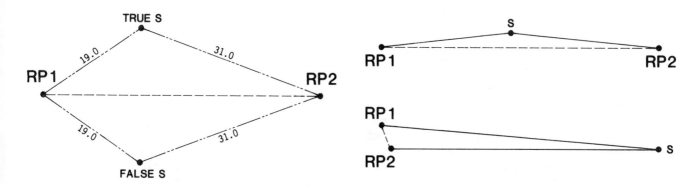

Exhibit 21. *Distance from two reference points in triangulation will give the locations of **two** spots as shown in this diagram, one on either side of the straight line between the two reference points. One of these is the location of the **true** spot and one is a **false** location. Sometimes this gives trouble.*

Exhibit 22. *In triangulation, avoid arrangements in which the angle formed by measurements to the spot located are either very large or very small as in this illustration. Such angles require more accurate measurements to locate the spot than are ordinarily possible at the scenes of traffic accidents. Select RP's with this in mind.*

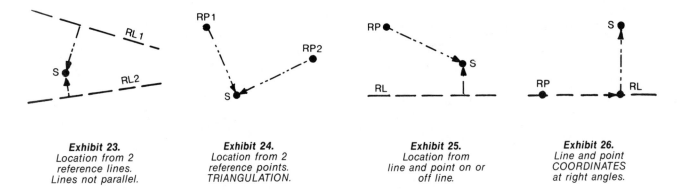

Exhibit 23.
Location from 2 reference lines. Lines not parallel.

Exhibit 24.
Location from 2 reference points. TRIANGULATION.

Exhibit 25.
Location from line and point on or off line.

Exhibit 26.
Line and point COORDINATES at right angles.

2. By careful selection of reference points
3. By especially accurate measurements
4. By written notes accompanying the measurements.

4. REFERENCE LINES AND POINTS

Other Measuring Methods

You should know something about systems of measuring other than the two described so far. Understanding them will help you avoid using them when you do not intend to; that would be misleading. Some of these systems, commonly used by engineers, involve measuring angles. That requires surveying instruments. Because you may have only a tape for measuring, methods requiring angle measurements will not be described.

You now know that to locate a spot on the ground you must make two measurements, one from each of two different references. In addition to triangulation and coordinates, which have already been explained, there are two other systems, making four methods in all. These four require measuring the shortest distances from

1. *Each of two reference lines.* See Exhibit 23. This will not work if the two lines are parallel.
2. *Each of two reference points.* See Exhibit 24. This is triangulation.

3. *A line and a point.* See Exhibit 25. The point may or may not be on the line.
4. *A point to a line and* then the shortest distance along the line from that place to a reference point on the line. (See Exhibit 26.) These distances are coordinates.

In any of these methods, the relationship of the two references to each other must eventually be established. If the two reference lines in Method 1 are at right angles (90°) to each other, the measurements are the same as for Method 4, coordinates. Thus, if you are using Method 1 for the situation illustrated in Exhibit 27, the two reference lines would be RL1 = E edge First and RL2 = N edge King. The measurements to spot B2 would be N 6.5 from RL2 and E 12.0 from RL1 which would be the same coordinates as with the RP at the intersection of these two RL's and either as the reference line. But this is *not* so if the roadway edges do not make a right angle.

Coordinates at Angle Junctions

Therefore, if the RP you use for coordinates is at the intersection of two roadway edges *not* at right angles, you can use either edge as a reference line, but *not* both. Make all measurements along the chosen reference line and at *right angles* to it. *Never* make some measurements from one line and some from the other. Now look at Exhibits 28 and 29 which show the same 3-legged oblique junction and the same RP

for coordinates, the intersection of E edge Will with S edge Watts. Note what a difference the choice of a reference line makes in the coordinates for Point C2. In Exhibit 28,
RL = E edge Will
RP @ S edge Watts
Coordinates of C2 are N 39.0, W 12.0
But in Exhibit 29,
RL = S edge Watts
RP @ E edge Will
Coordinates of C2 are N 20.0 W 35.5
Be very careful not to describe one RL and RP combination and then use another. In describing, *always* specify the reference line FIRST, and then the reference point on that line.

Reference lines must be very specific so that you or any one else can go to the site of the accident and locate their exact positions.

ROADWAY EDGES AS REFERENCE LINES

Roadway edges, as *landmarks,* are NATURAL reference lines from which you can measure to spots you wish to locate. But be sure you know exactly what is meant by "roadway edge." The *roadway* is the part of the road intended for vehicle travel. It does not include paved or otherwise improved shoulders or what is sometimes called a "berm" or "breakdown lane."

1. Preferably the center of a painted white or yellow edge line or stripe separating roadway from shoulder. See Exhibit 30.

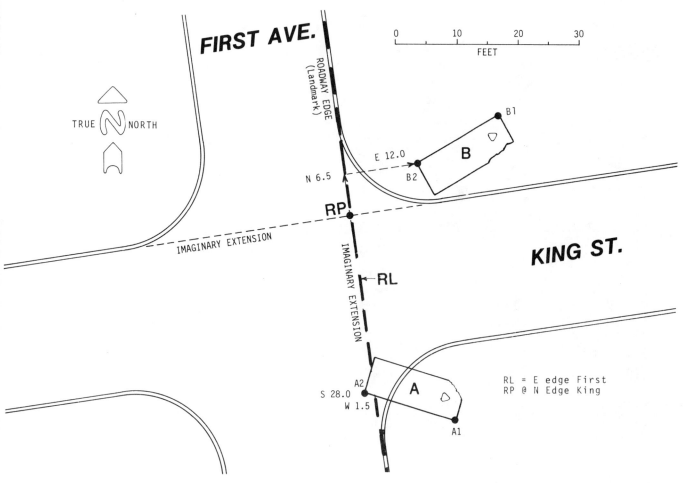

Exhibit 27. *The edge of the roadway is usually the best reference line. Choose the edge that is closest to the spots to be located. An imaginary extension of the actual edge may be necessary as a reference line in intersections.*

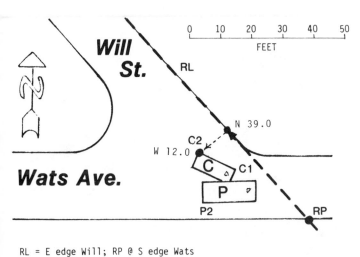

RL = E edge Will; RP @ S edge Wats
Spot C2: N39.0, W12.0

Exhibit 28. *E edge Will is a good RL for this situation. It is close to the vehicles to be located. Then the best RP is @ S edge Wats. With this RL, you must measure all distances along and at right angles to the E edge of Will. Do not measure any distances from the S edge of Wats, except those along the east edge of Will.*

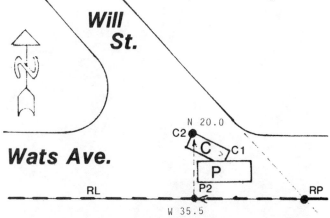

RL = S edge Wats; RP @ E edge Will
Spot C2: N20.0, W35.5

Exhibit 29. *S edge Wats is equally good RL. Then the appropriate RP is @ E edge Will. In these two examples, the RP's are the same, but the RL's are different. With the RL shown here, do not measure any distances from E edge of Will, except along S edge of Wats. With an oblique angle, coordinates must match the RL chosen.*

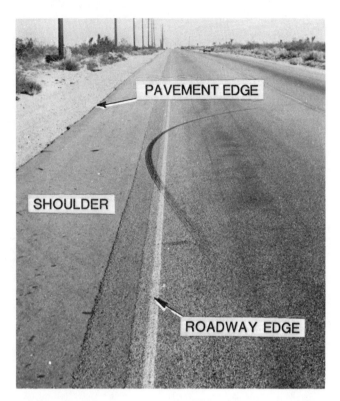

Exhibit 30. *Edge of roadway as a reference line is the center of the painted stripe or line separating the roadway proper from the shoulder or "break-down lane". Where there is such a stripe, the edge of the roadway is not the edge of the paving.*

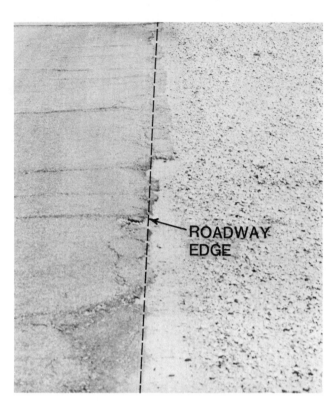

Exhibit 31. *If no painted stripe marks the edge of the roadway, use the edge of the pavement as a reference line. If this edge is irregular, use what seems to be the average edge. If necessary, remove dirt or snow to uncover the edge.*

Exhibit 32. *On gravel or dirt roads, locate the edge of the travelled roadway as well as possible by difference in character or slope of the surface. Try to use an average edge line.*

Exhibit 33. *If roadway is edged by a vertical (unmountable) curb measure from the middle of the upright face of the curb unless there is a painted roadway marker stripe.*

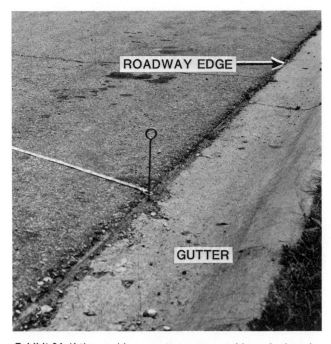

Exhibit 34. *If the road has a gutter or mountable curb, the edge of the roadway is where the curb joins the paving, unless there is also a painted roadway edge marker stripe.*

Exhibit 35. *To measure from an imaginary extension of roadway as a reference line, sight along the edge of the actual roadway. It is not necessary to mark this imaginary line on the roadway.*

2. Edge of paving if there is no painted edge line or stripe. If the edge of the paving is irregular, measure from what seems to be the average edge line. See Exhibit 31.

3. On unpaved roadways, gravel or dirt, the edge of the travelled part is indicated by wheel tracks, beginning of a slope toward the ditch, limit of maintenance grading, or beginning of grass or other vegetation. See Exhibit 32.

4. If there is an *unmountable* curb (one which you would not ordinarily drive over), the roadway edge is the middle of the most nearly vertical slope of the curb, provided there is no edge line or stripe. See Exhibit 33.

5. For a *mountable* curb or paved gutter, the edge of the roadway is where the pavement joins the curb unless there is a painted roadway edge line elsewhere. See Exhibit 34.

Every roadway has two edges. Use whichever is most convenient as a reference line. But do *not* try to use both edges in one set of measurements. That will be confusing when you refer to your measurements later.

Center and Lane Lines Are Undesirable References

Civil engineers designing roads and some accident investigators use the center line of the roadway as a reference line. Reasons for not using center lines as reference lines are

- Center lines are often not marked, and on dirt and gravel roads cannot be precisely determined.

- Measuring from a center line, especially where there is considerable traffic, is slow and risky.

- In intersections, turn lanes, merging areas, and three-lane roads, the center line is difficult to locate.

Lane marking lines have many of the same disadvantages as center lines for reference purposes. Therefore use center lines and lane lines as reference lines only when you can find nothing better.

Other Reference Lines

Although roadway edges are usually the best reference lines, other reference lines may be better:

- The *imaginary extension* of the roadway edge may be a very useful part of a reference line as already pointed out. For example, in Exhibit 27, there is no natural reference line across the intersection, so you will have to sight along the roadway edge to find places on the extension from which to measure as illustrated in Exhibit 35.

- *Guard rails and bridge rails* make good reference lines. They are easily recognized and are especially useful when roadway edges are buried in snow. But imaginary extensions of bridge and guard rails generally do not make good reference lines. The imaginary extensions are likely to be off the road in ditches or bushes.

- *Railroad rails* are excellent natural reference lines when the results of an accident are scattered along the tracks.

Choosing Reference Lines

You can save time and effort in measuring by selecting your reference line carefully. Choose the one which has most of these advantages;

- Easily recognized and described.
- Close to the greatest number of spots to be located.
- Requires minimum measuring in and across traffic lanes.
- Handy to a suitable landmark for locating an RP on the RL

For example, in Exhibit 27, there are four possible natural reference lines using roadway edges and their extensions:

1. RL = W edge First
2. RL = E edge First
3. RL = H edge King.
4. RL = S edge King.

You can quickly rule out the first, RL = W edge First, because it is too far from all spots to be located, and all eight of the measurements required to locate the four spots would be across traffic lanes. The N edge of King is close to Car B but far from Car A. The S edge of King is just the opposite. One is as good as the other. But the E edge of First is close to both cars and in this respect would be better than any of the other three. All of the last three would require two of the eight measurements to be across two traffic lanes. Hence the E edge of First is the best RL for this situation.

While you are considering what spots to locate and preparing your field sketch, think about what would make the best reference line. In some cases either of two lines would be equally good; then it makes no difference which one you use.

Avoid a sharply curved roadway edge as a reference line. It is easy to make mistakes in measuring along these curves from an RP and measuring the shortest distance from the curve to spots being located (Exhibit 36). With sharp curves consider using long imaginary extensions of straight roadway edges as reference lines. Short sighting distances, such as those commonly used at intersections, are very useful; but long ones at curves are likely to be inaccurate. Try not to use imaginary extensions more than 50 ft. long (Exhibit 37).

Locating a Reference Point on the Reference Line

Having selected a suitable road edge for a reference line, select a suitable reference point on that line. The reference point must be related to a definite landmark. A *landmark,* for this purpose, is something which you, or someone else can easily find and clearly identify in the general area months later. The landmark for an RP may be on the RL or fairly close to it. Examples of suitable landmarks are

- *An intersecting roadway edge,* as already mentioned. It is usually an imaginary extension of a roadway edge as illustrated in Exhibit 27. Locate it by sighting along two roadway edges as shown

in Exhibit 38. One roadway edge may be that of a private driveway if one is handy.

- A pole or tree if it is near the reference line (Exhibit 39)
- Traffic signs or signals
- Mail boxes, fire hydrants
- The end of a bridge rail, guard rail, or culvert headwall as illustrated in Exhibits 12 and 40
- The *corner* of a building or fence close to the reference line
- The end of a traffic island, divider, or gore (where roadways seperate)
- A railroad rail where it intersects the reference line
- The beginning or end of a specified curve. In remote areas, this may be the best available. See Exhibits 42 and 43.
- Station marks on paving as illustrated in Exhibit 41.

If the landmark is not on the reference line, as in Exhibit 12, the reference point is at the closest point on the reference line to the landmark.

Curves as RP Landmarks

When you use the end of a curve to establish a reference point, be sure to specify which end, thus

RL = E edge MI 61
RP @ N end of curve

The particular curve must also be clearly identified. To do this, show the distance to a crossroad or other good landmark as measured to a tenth of a mile on a vehicle odometer. Show this

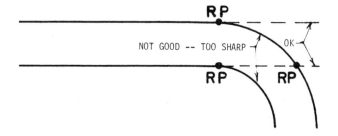

Exhibit 36. *Short imaginary extensions make good reference lines, but sharp curves as reference lines make measuring difficult.*

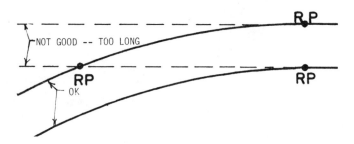

Exhibit 37. *Long imaginary extensions as reference lines may be inaccurate. Long curves are usually much better.*

Exhibit 38. *When your RP is where two imaginary extensions of roadway edge cross, mark that point on the roadway before beginning to measure. If the RP for coordinates is on the roadway edge, it is useful to mark that place also.*

distance on your field sketch next to a small arrow pointing in the direction of the landmark (Exhibit 53). You can note how many R or L curves this is from the landmark, for example, "Second R curve E of Parker River Bridge," as in Exhibit 78.

At the beginning or end of a curve, there are a number of possible RL's and RP's. You could use either edge of the roadway where it stops being straight and begins to turn. Or, if it is more convenient, you can disregard the curved part and use the straight part and its imaginary extension. These possibilities are illustrated in Exhibits 36 and 37. Whichever of these reference lines you choose, you have three possible RP's from which to pick. As you can see from Exhibits 36 and 37, you can have one on each edge of the roadway where the curve begins and the tangent (straight edge)

ends. The third RP is where the outer curved edge crosses the imaginary extension of the opposite straight edge.

You can locate this point quite well by sighting along the straight edge. In this situation, there are four possible RL's: each of the two roadway edges may be treated as entirely straight or as partly straight and partly curved. How do you choose between these posssiblities? Of course that depends partly on which is closest to the spots to be located and which will give the least amount of traffic interference.

Note that in Exhibit 43, the end of the curve has been chosen as the landmark for the RP. Either of the two poles in this situation could be used, but they are too far from the reference line. The East edge of the roadway was chosen as the RL because it is closer to the spots to be located. Exhibit 43 is also an exam-

ple of a reference line which is neither straight nor in a true compass direction.

Unsuitable Landmarks

Some things are usually not good as reference-point landmarks. Try to avoid using the following:

- *A remote, indefinite point,* for example 10.2 miles south of Woodville Road. That is fine for locating the general area, but does not permit pinpointing the RP at the site of an accident.
- *The name or number of a house* or other building. If the building is a good landmark designate a specific corner or other part of the structure.
- *Advertising signs* which may

Exhibit 39. *A reference point can be on the roadway edge opposite a numbered utility pole, if one is convenient.*

Exhibit 40. *Any identifiable structure, such as a culvert, will serve as a reference point, if properly identified.*

Exhibit 41. *Station marks stamped in the roadway surface are satisfactory reference points on portland-cement paving.*

Exhibit 42. *If the best available RP is the beginning or end of a curve, mark that point on the roadway before beginning to measure.*

be gone when you come back.

- *Manhole covers* and drains which may be covered with snow or something else later.
- *Shrubs, ponds,* river banks, and crop areas which are indefinite and may change almost from day to day.

A common blunder among police traffic-accident investigators is to locate such things as final positions of cars by measuring from the POI (point of impact). *Never* do that. The POI is *not* a landmark. It is someone's opinion about where something happened, and is almost impossible for someone else to locate later.

RP Landmarks away from Reference Line

When a landmark for a reference point for coordinate measurements is away from the reference line, it is *not* necessary to measure the distance from the pole or other land-

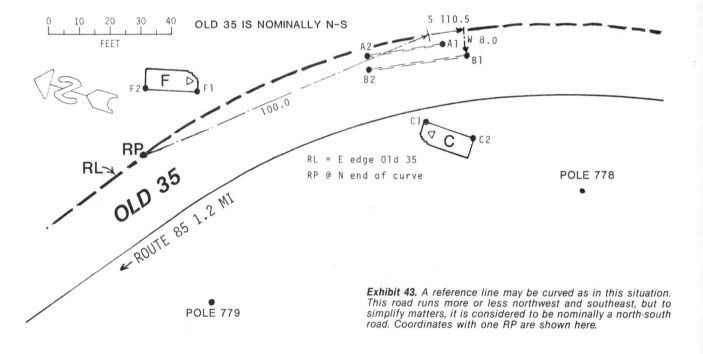

Exhibit 43. *A reference line may be curved as in this situation. This road runs more or less northwest and southeast, but to simplify matters, it is considered to be nominally a north-south road. Coordinates with one RP are shown here.*

mark to the reference line. It is always the *shortest* distance, and that will enable you to locate the RP accurately later if necessary. Then the RP is opposite (op) the landmark.

If you have a choice as to which of two landmarks off the reference line is to be used to locate the RP, the one nearest the RL is preferable. That is because in locating the place on the RL closest to the landmark, a short distance is always more accurate and easier than a longer distance.

For example, if an easily identified pole is 30 ft. beyond the far edge of the roadway (50 ft. from the RL), as in Exhibit 43, it would be difficult to fix the RP on the RL within 10 ft.

But if a well identified mailbox post is within seven feet of the roadway edge, the closest point can easily be located within a foot.

Identifying Reference Points

Once you have decided on a reference point, it is a good idea to mark the RP right on the reference line with aerosol spray paint, heavy crayon or otherwise as illustrated in Exhibit 42.

Before doing any actual measuring, write down, near where you are going to record your measurements, the briefest possible description of the reference line and point. Abbreviate nominal directions, north, south, east, and west as N, S, E, and W. Use @ to abbreviate "at". The RP in Exhibit 27 would be described as follows:

RL = E edge First
RP @ N edge King.

Note that the first line defines the reference line and the last line the reference point on the reference line. Another example is the logical reference line and point for the situation in Exhibit 43:

RL = E edge Old 35
RP @ N end of curve.

Triangulation Reference Points

If you have to use triangulation for any reason, two or more triangulation reference points must be described with reference to appropriate landmarks. Actually, the reference points for triangulation are usually landmarks themselves, such as trees or poles. For example, in Exhibit 44, imagine that the roadway edges are not suitable as reference lines, perhaps because they are buried in snow. The skidmarks would then probably not be visible, but you would have to locate the final positions of the vehicles. The two poles, identified as No. 778 and No. 779 are the logical reference points for triangulation. Let No. 778 be RP1 and No. 779 be RP2. Then the description of these two is as follows:

RP 1 = Pole 778 W of Old 35
RP 2 = Pole 779 W of Old 35 & 161.5 ft. from RP 1.

The distance from RP 1 to RP 2 is not necessary, but desirable. If someone must make an after-accident situation map, it will save him the trouble of returning to the site of the accident to measure the distance. With these two reference points, the location of Spot F2, the right rear corner of Car F, is as follows:

RP 1 = 146.5
RP 2 =   70.0

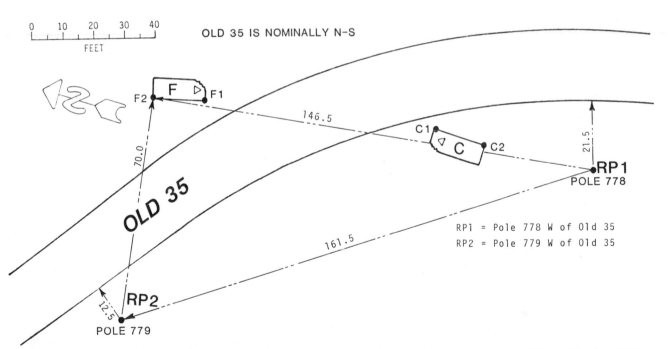

Exhibit 44. *The same situation as in Exhibit 43 could be measured by triangulation with two power poles as RP1 and RP2. Triangulation would require more and more difficult measuring than coordinates.*

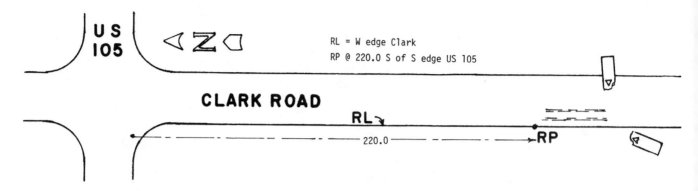

Exhibit 45. *When spots to be located are all more than 100 ft. from a suitable reference point landmark, the reference point can be located a measured distance closer to the results of the accident to be located in this example, 220 ft. closer.*

Exhibit 44 also illustrates some of the advantages of coordinates compared to triangulation. If you are locating Spot F2 by coordinates, (Exhibit 43), you measure 12.0 ft. from the RP along the roadway where the walking is easy. Then you measure 16.5 ft. from the reference line (roadway edge) to Spot F2. That is a total of 28.5 ft. In this case, with triangulation, (Exhibit 44) you measure 146.5 ft. from Pole 778 across a ditch and the roadway to Spot F2; then you measure 70.0 ft. from Pole 779, again across the roadway, to Spot F2. The two triangulation measurements total 153.5 ft. as compared to 28.5 for coordinates.

Moreover, to do the job right, you have to make three more measurements: Pole 778 to the nearest roadway edge, 21.5 ft.; Pole 779 to the same roadway edge, 12.5 ft.; and RP1 to RP2, 161.5 ft. That is a total of 195.5 ft. more of measuring.

Difficult Locations

Sometimes the place on the RL nearest to a suitable landmark for locating the RP is a hundred or more feet from the nearest spot to be located. Then many long measurements would be required from that as a reference point. In such a case, locate the RP on the RL at a specified distance closer to the spots to be located, (Exhibit 45). Here are additional descriptions of such relocated RP's:

RP @ 100.0 E of E end of Welch River bridge rail

RP @ 350.0 N of point op N side of Smith barn.

A roadway edge is almost always available as a curved or straight reference line; and in built-up areas, there are always handy landmarks near or across the road by which to establish your RP. But sometimes, in deserts, mountains, or forests, finding a good landmark may be very difficult. Within miles, there is no identifiable crossroad or driveway, no numbered power poles, bridges or culverts worth noting, no recognizable buildings, and no milepost. In the desert, there may be no curves, and in the mountains so many curves that you cannot tell one from the other.

This challenges you to describe a point on the roadway so well that several years later, a total stranger, with your field sketch, can locate that RP within two feet. A car odometer reading from a distant landmark will not do. It indicates only to tenths of a mile and even guessing at tenths of tenths will not locate a point to within 100 ft. Sometimes you can count unnumbered utility poles or right or left turns from a distant crossroad or other landmark and then tape measure from there to an exact reference point. Sometimes there is a peculiar rock formation or tree of some kind (Exhibit 78) close to the road that you can describe so well

that it can be easily recognized. From there, measurements can be taped to the exact point.

Once a reference point has been located, a knowledgeable investigator may mark it for easy future idenitification. Marks on the roadway are likely to disappear, but spray paint on a guard rail or on a conspicuous tree trunk or rock formation will be noticeable for years. It is also possible to pile up stones in some particular way in some place where they will not be disturbed. Such a "monument" will help you or someone else spot the place later. With such an initital landmark, a specific point on the road can be established. Then it is easy to measure off an appropriate distance up to about 500 ft. for the most convenient exact RP.

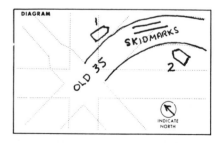

Exhibit 46. *The space for diagrams on official traffic-accident reports is generally too small for more than a very few measurements. The example here is the exact size of one such diagram.*

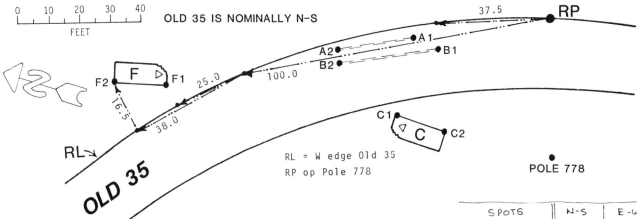

0 10 20 30 40
FEET

OLD 35 IS NOMINALLY N-S

37.5 RP

A1
A2 B1
B2

F2 F F1
25.0   100.0

16.5
38.0

RL

OLD 35

C1
C C2

RL = W edge Old 35
RP op Pole 778

POLE 778

Exhibit 47. *Coordinate measurements are made from a single reference point on a reference line (roadway edge). Measurements for the situation shown here are recorded in table, exhibit 5-3.*

SPOTS		N-S	E-W
CHEV	RF C1 RR C2		
FORD	RF F1 RR F2	N 125.0 N 138.0	E 16.5
SKID MARKS	A1 A2 B1 B2	N 37.5	W 6.5

RL = E edge Old 35
RP op Pole 778

Exhibit 48. *A table for recording two coordinate measurements to each of eight spots requiring location.*

5. RECORDING MEASUREMENTS

It goes without saying that you must write down each measurement immediately after you make it. You cannot expect to remember a measurement for more than few minutes after you make it, or to remember more measurements for half that long. Distances will be described as measured in feet and tenths. Other units of measurement will be discussed later.

List Measurements in a Table

What is the best place to record measurements? The little diagram on an official traffic-accident report (Exhibit 46) is good for only one or two measurements, far too few for most serious accidents. The field sketch is suitable if there is room on it. But do not crowd the field sketch with measurements! If you do, you will probably discover, some time later, that you cannot make out what distances some of the numbers represent. Therefore, in most cases, and certainly when half a dozen or more spots have to be located, put the measurements on a separate sheet. That will give you all the room you need to write clearly.

Be systematic. Before you actually begin to measure, prepare for record-ing measurements as soon as you make them. A table or chart is best for this purpose. Suppose, for example, that you are about to record coordinate measurements to the eight spots to be located for the situation illustrated in Exhibit 47. Begin by preparing a table as shown in Exhibit 48. The table has three vertical columns. The left column is a list of spots to be located, so make the heading of this column "SPOTS". Head the second column "N-S" for nominal north and south coordinates measured to locate the listed spots. Head the third column "E-W" for measurements of east and west coordinates. Then in the first column, list the spots to be located. For the example in Exhibit 47, there are eight spots. This requires eight crosswise lines in the table. The first vertical column is also used for a word or two to tell what each of the set of spots locates. Thus Spots C1 and C2 locate a Chevrolet, and F1 and F2 locate a Ford.

Lined paper helps in preparing neat tables. Tables with column headings can be prepared in anticipation of having to record measurements. This saves time at the scene, but is not essential.

Enter measurements in the table as soon as you make them. They do not have to be in the order in which they are listed in the table. A step-by-step examination of how you go about this uses Exhibit 47 as an example. After the table is ready, start measuring by having your helper hold the zero end of the tape at RP, the reference point on the reference line. Then measure across the curve to a place directly opposite the nearest spot, B1. There the tape reads 37.5 ft. You are nominally north of the RP, so you enter N37.5 in the N-S vertical column on the B1 line as in Exhibit 48. Next, while your helper remains at the RP, you move a little way along the reference line until you are opposite the next spot, C2. There you again pull the tape taut and read the distance, marking it down in the N-S column on C2 line. You repeat this process for the next spots in order, A1, C1, A2 and B2. Your 100-ft. tape will not reach to a place opposite the next spot in order, F1. Therefore, you mark a spot on the reference line exactly 100 ft. from the RP straight across the curve rather than along the arc. Your helper comes up to the 100-ft. mark and holds the zero end of the tape there while you go on to a place opposite

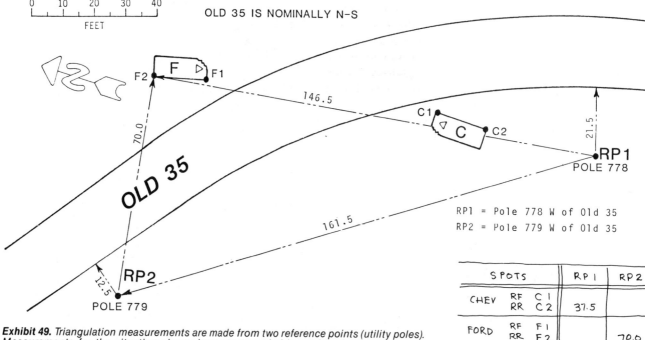

0 10 20 30 40
FEET

OLD 35 IS NOMINALLY N-S

146.5

21.5

RP 1
POLE 778

RP1 = Pole 778 W of Old 35
RP2 = Pole 779 W of Old 35

161.5

70.0

OLD 35

12.5

RP2
POLE 779

Exhibit 49. *Triangulation measurements are made from two reference points (utility poles). Measurements for the situation shown here are recorded in a table, Exhibit 50.*

SPOTS			RP 1	RP 2
CHEV	RF	C 1	37.5	
	RR	C 2		
FORD	RF	F 1		70.0
	RR	F 2		
	RP 1		0	161.5
Wedge	Old 35		21.5	12.5

RP1 = Pole 778 W of Old 35
RP2 = Pole 779 W of Old 35
         & 161.5 from RP1

Exhibit 50. *A table for recording triangulation measurements including three to relate RP's to the road layout.*

Spot F1. There you read the additional distance, 25.0 ft., which makes a total distance, as measured, of 125.00 ft. Then you enter N125.0 in the N-S column on the F1 line, as in Exhibit 48. You continue on to a place opposite Spot F2, read the distance, 38.0 ft., add 100 ft., and enter the total, N138.0 in the table as shown in Exhibit 48. This last distance is less than 100 ft. from where your helper holds the zero end of the tape, so your helper does not have to move again. The N-S column in the table is now complete.

Now you roll up the tape and start back, measuring the nominal east and west coordinates from the reference line (Exhibit 47). First is the shortest distance from the reference line to Spot F2, 16.5 ft. Although the measurement is nearly due northeast at this point on the curve, you remember that the road is *nominally* north-south and distances *along* the reference line were all recorded as nominally north, so you call this measurement E16.5 and enter it in the E-W column on the F2 line as in Exhibit 48. You measure for Spot F1 in the same way and enter the measurement in the proper box in the table. The next spot is B2. It meas-

ures 6.5 ft from the reference line, but is nominally west, so you enter W6.5 in the E-W column on the B2 line as in Exhibit 48. And so on until the E-W column and the table is completed by the E-W entry for Spot B1. You are pleased by how neatly this works out.

There is an advantage in preparing a table in which to record measurements. By noting boxes in the table which contain no entries, you can quickly see which measurements have been missed. Then you can make the missing measurements before leaving the scene.

Table for Triangulation

For triangulation, a table is made in the same way as for coordinates except that the last two vertical columns are headed RP1 and RP2 instead of N-S and E-W. If you have to make triangulation measurements for the situation shown in Exhibit 49, prepare a table as shown in Exhibit 50 before you start to measure.

Remember that with triangulation, the two RP's must be linked, if possible, to the roadway with additional measurements. (That has already been explained.) The distance

between the two RP's which is *most* important, can be included in the measurement tables quite easily. Simply add RP1 in the left column which lists spots to be located. Then in the RP1 column, the distance from RP1 will always be zero; they are the same point (Exhibit 50). In the RP2 column, however, the distance figure will be for the distance between RP1 and RP2. In Exhibit 49, it is 161.5 ft. That is how it is shown in Exhibit 50. Handle the distances of the two RP's from the roadway edge in the same way: at the bottom of the column for spots, enter the roadway edge designation. In Exhibit 49, this is the west edge of Old 35. With this entry, your table (Exhibit 50) is ready for measurements. Note that if either RP1 or RP2 are actually on the nearest roadway edge, as they sometimes are, the distance to this line is zero. That would give one or two more zeros in the table, a possible total of three.

Order of Listing

The order of listing spots in a table for recording measurements is not significant. But it is important that all spots to be located are listed. Therefore it is useful to follow some pattern in listing. It will help you avoid overlooking something. The following is a helpful sequence for listing spots in measurement tables:

1. Four-tired vehicles (cars and light trucks)
2. Two-tired vehicles (bicycles and motorcycles)
3. Vehicles with six or more tires (large trucks, busses, tractors)
4. Bodies outside of vehicles, including animals
5. Gouges and scratches
6. Roadside scars
7. Tire marks
8. Debris areas.

Trailers and large parts broken from vehicles come right after the vehicles to which they had been attached. Alphabetical listing by the identifying letter-number combinations assigned to the spot is usually more trouble than it is worth.

Enter measurements in the table as they are made. For the case illustrated in Exhibit 49, start by having your helper hold the zero end of the tape at Pole 778, which is RP1. For tie-in, measure the shortest distance to the nearest edge of Old 35, 21.5 ft. Enter 21.5 in the table on the Old 35 line in the RP1 column (Exhibit 50). Then, with your helper still holding the zero end of the tape at RP1 (Pole 778), measure the distance to Spot C2 (right rear of Chevrolet), 37.5 ft. Enter that distance in the RP1 column on the C2 line as in Exhibit 50. Continue with Spots C1, F1, and F2 in that order. The last two spots are more than 100 ft. from RP1 and so, for each, you have to hold a place 100 ft. from RP1 and in line with the spot to be located, then have your helper move to the 100-ft. mark and you shift the tape for the remainder of the measurement. The last measurement from RP1 is the important distance to RP2, 161.5 ft. Write 161.5 in

the RP2 column on the RP1 line as in Exhibit 50.

Now shift your helper to Pole 779, which is RP2. Start from here by measuring the shortest distance to the west edge of Old 35, 12.5 ft. This number goes in the RP2 column on the Old 35 line. Next, measure from RP2 (Pole 779) to F2 (right rear of Ford), 70.0 ft. Enter in the RP2 column on the F2 line (Exhibit 50). Continue until all measurements have been completed. Many investigators using triangulation fail to make the three tie-in measurements. Be careful not to forget them.

Identification

If your table is separate from your field sketch, you must complete it by identifying the accident on it. Otherwise someone, perhaps yourself, will see the table of figures some months or years later and wonder what the numbers are all about. The following four items are needed to identify the accident:

1. ON — Name the principal road.
2. AT — If at an intersection, name the cross road; if not, give the distance in feet or miles and tenths to a landmark shown on road maps, for example, a cross road, railroad, bridge, city limit, or milepost.
3. IN — Name the city or county and state.
4. TIME — Give hour, day, month, and year of the accident.

Examples of such identification appear in some of the exhibits. If you have an accident number that will refer to a report which gives such identifying data, this number may be used instead of the detailed identification data.

As further identification, put on the measurement sheet

1. Your name as responsible for the measurements and, if you like, the name of a helper.
2. The day on which measure-

ments were made if not the day of the accident.
3. A description of the reference lines and points used.

6. FIELD SKETCHES

A field sketch is an important part of the record of your measurements at the scene of a serious traffic accident. The field sketch serves two purposes:

1. It describes and defines the spots to be located and the reference points used to locate them.
2. It gives a quick general picture of the after-accident situation.

Simplified Road Layout

Start the field sketch at the scene of the accident. Draw it *free hand* (without a ruler) and not to scale; but show the general layout of the road and the results of the accident to be located, such as final positions of vehicles and tire marks on roadways. You generally begin the field sketch as you are deciding what spots require locating. You complete it after you leave the scene. A field sketch is usually made on a letter-size sheet (11-in. by 8½-in. — the size of this page) held on a clipboard. However, field sketches can be made in notebooks or elsewhere.

Do not crowd a field sketch on a sheet. If necessary, extend the sketch on an additional sheet or even two additional sheets. If there is room, the table of measurements may be put on the field sketch.

Typical Example

An example will help you understand how to go about making a field sketch. Get a sheet of paper and a pencil, and, as this example is explained, make a field sketch exactly as described. Imagine that you are at the scene of the accident shown in Exhibit

Exhibit 51. *Looking north at the scene of accident on IA 21 in Pike County IA at 3 pm 12 Mar 1984.*

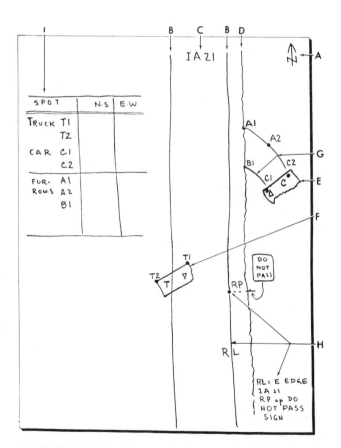

Exhibit 52. *Field sketches made at scene of accident shown in Exhibit 51 ready for recording measurements required.*

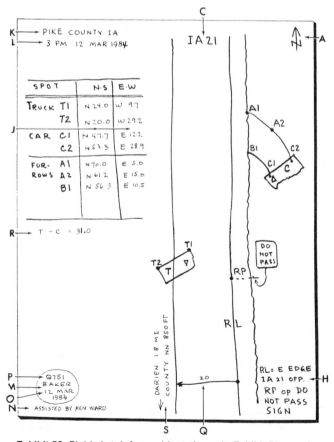

Exhibit 53. *Field sketch for accident shown in Exhibit 51 complete with measurements and identifying data fully recorded.*

51. When you are ready with a sheet of paper on a clipboard and a pencil in your hand:

1. *Decide what spots you need* to locate: two for the pick-up truck, one at either end; two more for the car in the ditch. (Remember to use spots on undamaged corners or wheels of vehicles.) Although you cannot see them from where you stand, two tire furrows in the snow lead from the road to the right wheels on the car as in Exhibit 52. The nearer furrow is short and slightly curved. One end of it is at the right front wheel location and the other at the edge of the shoulder. The farther mark is longer and curved. One end of it is at the right rear wheel location. For this furrow, two additional spots are needed, one at the edge of the shoulder and the other in the middle of the mark.

2. *Start your diagram by drawing a small nominal* (approximate) *north arrow* in a corner of your field-notes sheet where it will be out of the way as at A in Exhibit 52. The north arrow helps keep directions straight from the beginning. You are looking north in Exhibit 51.

3. *Draw roadway edges* from the top to the bottom of the sheet as shown at B in Exhibit 52.

4. *Before you forget it, put the name of the road,* IA 21, at the top edge of the sheet as at C.

5. *Add road shoulders,* lane lines and center lines, if they are present and significant. In the picture, Exhibit 51, no pavement markings are visible and only the shoulder on the east where the car went in the ditch is important. So draw only the east shoulder edge as a slightly wavy line to show that it is a little irregular as at D.

6. *Draw the final positions of the vehicles.* Show the direction each was headed by a small arrowhead pointed forward. If the collapse or distortion of a vehicle is considerable, show it in the outline you draw. If the vehicle is not right side up, note this on the diagram or show wheels if the vehicle is bottom side up. In this example, Exhibit 51, the vehicles are both right side up. Label the vehicles, in this example, T for Truck and C for Car. Mark the spots to be located on each vehicle, in this car, C1 for the right front wheel and C2 for the right rear wheel. Wheels are used in this case instead of the corner of the vehicle because the wheel is also the location of the end of tire furrow leading from the edge of the shoulder. To show that the wheel rather than the corner of the vehicle is to be located, place the spot *inside* the vehicle outline, as at E in Exhibit 52. With no tire marks leading to the truck, put the spots to locate it at the corners as at F in Exhibit 52.

7. *Draw tire furrows* from the edge of the shoulder to the respective wheels on the outline of the car. Call the farther one A. Because it is longer and curved, two spots are needed for it, Spot A1 at the shoulder edge, spot A2 half way between the shoulder and the wheel. The mark ends at the right rear wheel which is spot C2. The nearer furrow needs only one additonal mark, B1, where the mark starts at the edge of the shoulder. (G in Exhibit 52). The other end is at the right front wheel of the car, Spot C1.

8. *Decide whether to use triangulation* or coordinates. The east edge of the roadway, although somewhat covered by snow, is quite distinct and very convenient. It makes an excellent reference line so you should choose to use coordinates for measurements. Mark this RL at any convenient place along the east edge of the roadway, as indicated by H in Exhibit 52.

9. *How about a reference point* on the reference line? What could be better than the DO NOT PASS sign as a landmark? Then the RP will be the place on the roadway edge closest to this sign post. Mark it, RP, on the field sketch, Exhibit 52. Also, while you are about it, describe the RP in a corner of the sheet (H in Exhibit 52.)

10. *Now you are ready for the table* in which to record measurements. There is plenty of space on the field sketch, so prepare a table for measurements. Near the left margin of the sheet, list the seven spots to be located and then make two columns, one for N-S measurements and the other for E-W measurements (I in Exhibit 52).

Identification

The field sketch described so far, for example Exhibit 52, is not quite finished. At some time, before or after the measurements have been entered in the table, as at J in Exhibit 53, you must add important identifying data. Too many investigators forget to do this with the result that someone examining the field sketch

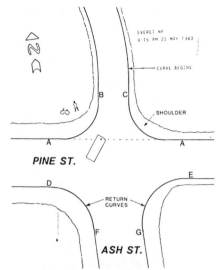

Exhibit 54. *An irregular road layout, such as that shown here, makes field sketches a bit more difficult, but no great problem if simplified and drawn a step at a time.*

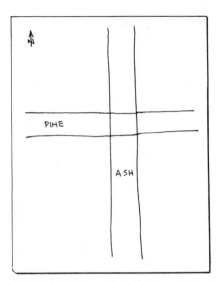

Exhibit 55. *The simplest form of field sketch "skeleton" for the road layout shown to scale in Exhibit 54. Curves, angles, returns, and offsets are disregarded.*

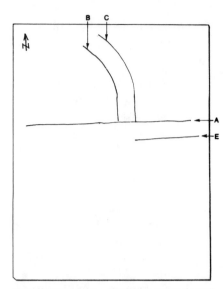

Exhibit 56. *A better field sketch "skeleton" for the same intersection is begun by drawing an edge line that is aligned on both sides of the intersection.*

later wonders what it is all about. The identifying data do not have to be put on the sketch while you are at the scene of the accident; but be sure to add them before the sketch is filed away. You have already entered some identifying data as shown in Exhibit 52: the nominal north direction at A, and a description of the reference point at H. Now add identification of the *accident,* as previously described.

1. If you have not already done so, label the road ON which the accident happened.

2. The general place AT which the accident occurred. If a crossroad, railroad, or other landmark is shown and labeled in the field sketch, that will do. If not, show direction and approximate distance to some easily recognizable landmark such as a crossroad, railroad, river, or county line as at S in Exhibit 53.

3. Note the city or county and the state IN which the accident occurred in any convenient remaining space on the field sketch, as at K in Exhibit 53.

4. Near the geographical location on the field sketch write the TIME of the accident: hour, day, month, and year. Thus the accident is completely identified (L in Exhibit 53).

And, finally,

1. Indicate who made the measurements and the field sketch. If you did it, put your name on it. If you have done a good job, you should be proud to sign your work (M in Exhibit 53). You may want to add the name of anybody who helped you make the measurements (N in Exhibit 53).

2. Near your name, put the date on which the sketch and measurements were made (O in Exhibit 53). Usually, the date will be the same as the date of the accident, but sometimes measurements are made later.

3. If the accident is assigned a number for reference and filing purposes, that number can be added to the field sketch when it becomes known, (P in Exhibit 53).

The Skeleton

Edges of roadways are "skeletons" of field sketches. Those shown in the example just described (Exhibits 51 and 52) are the simplest possible — just two straight parallel lines running north and south on your sketch. Most accident locations are a bit more complicated but are still not difficult to sketch well if you go about it right. To begin with, get down to the bare bones of your sketch skeleton (using Exhibit 54 as an example). Disregard:

1. *Shoulders,* such as those shown in Exhibit 54.

2. *Returns* (curves which connect roadway edges at intersections) such as those in Exhibit 54.

3. *Angles* between intersecting edges that are only a little more or less than right angles (90°).

4. *Small difference in roadway widths.*

5. *Moderate curves.*

This will reduce an interesection to its simplest form. The road layout in Exhibit 54 can be represented by a pair of parallel lines running north and south crossed by another pair running east and west as illustrated in Exhibit 55. This simplification will serve most purposes. On this skeleton

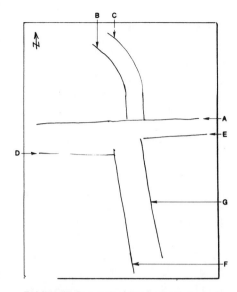

Exhibit 57. *The better field sketch is continued by adding other road edges, paying attention to angles, widths, and offsets. Curved edge returns are not needed unless especially significant.*

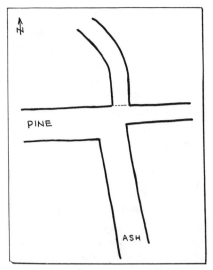

Exhibit 58. *The completed "skeleton" field sketch showing essential peculiarities of the intersection. Dotted line indicates that north edge of Pine east of Ash is aligned with north edge west of Ash.*

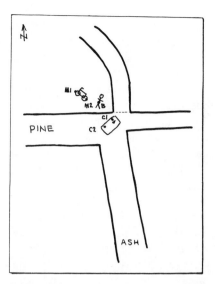

Exhibit 59. *After the roadways are outlined in a field sketch, add the things to be located: final positions of vehicles, marks on the road, etc. Mark the spots to be located on these things and label the spots to identify them.*

framework, you can show results of the accident, such as marks on the road and final positions of vehicles. For these results of the accident you can show spots required to locate them; and you can show reference point for these spots. Of course, even this simple sketch needs an arrow to show nominal north, and the roads must be named.

Significant Details

The simple field sketch in Exhibit 55 does not give much of an idea of the layout in Exhibit 54 which it is supposed to represent. Shoulders may be added where they have significance, as they had in Exhibit 51. Return curves between roadway edges at intersections can also be shown if needed, for example to show tire marks of vehicles turning from one roadway to another. For a more professional job, a more representative field sketch can be made with very little additional time or effort. For this purpose, look for the following before beginning to draw:

- Curves in roadways which are not the edge return curves at intersections (Ash north of Pine in Exhibit 54).
- Edges of roadways that are aligned on both sides of an intersection (north edge of Pine in Exhibit 54).
- Angles between roadway edges that are not right angles. (Angle between Ash and Pine south of the intersection).
- What roadway edges are offset at an intersection so as to make the roadway a different width on one side of the intersection than it is on the other. For example, the south edge of Pine east of Ash does not line up with south edge of Pine west of Ash, so Pine is wider west than east.

With these observations in mind, start your field sketch. As an example, prepare a better sketch of the intersection shown in Exhibit 54. Begin by drawing lightly on your sheet a line that represents an edge that is aligned on both sides of the intersection. This is A in Exhibit 54, the north edge of Pine. Draw it as an east-west line across the sketch sheet as A in Exhibit 56. Next draw an edge that is at right angles to this, C in Exhibit 56, showing it as straight north for a short distance from A and then curving toward the west (C in Exhibit 56). Then draw B parallel to C, re-

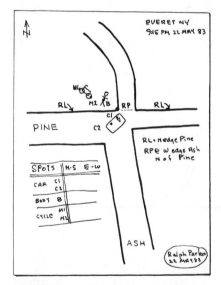

Exhibit 60. *Finally, select a reference line and a reference point. Label and describe them on the field sketch. Add a table for recording measurements, if there is room for it, and complete your sketch by identifying the accident.*

membering that is a narrow roadway. Now draw E parallel to A. It is about the same distance from A as B is from C, because both are narrow roadways.

Next, as shown in Exhibit 57 draw G (east edge of Ash south of Pine), noting that it is not square with Pine and does not align exactly with C (east edge of Ash north of Pine) but is a little to the west of it. Now draw F parallel to G, but note that it is a wide street so F should be farther from G than B is from C, as shown in Exhibit 57. The remaining edge is D (south edge of Pine west of Ash). It is parallel to A but farther from it than E is because Pine is wider west of Ash than east of it. You now have the skeleton layout. Having drawn all of these lines lightly, darken the main edges and erase any unnecessary extensions of the edge lines in the intersection (Exhibit 58). To show that the north edge of Pine on the west aligns with the north edge on the east, draw a dotted line across Ash to connect these two edges (Exhibit 58). Add the names of the roads, and you have a very credible representation of the layout of the roads. As mentioned earlier, you may add curve returns at the corners, shoulders and other things such as guard rails or roadside objects if they mean anything in connection with the particular accident. Also add dotted lines to show *all* roadway edges which are aligned on opposite sides of an intersection, except where the roadway edges are sharply curved. Only one aligned edge is shown in Exhibit 58 because the other three are all offset rather than aligned.

The principles illustrated by the foregoing example can be applied to almost any arrangement of roadways. Straight sections of roads, such as in Exhibit 51, present no difficulties in drawing a field sketch. An ordinary curve is no problem either. The usual right-angle intersection is easily represented in a field sketch. But other than these, you look for pecularities such as:

- *Curves*, especially where the roadway changes from straight to curved as in Ash north of Pine in Exhibit 54.
- *Angles* between roadways such as the angle between Ash and Pine south of Pine in Exhibit 54.
- *Changes in width* of roadways, either between junctions or at an intersection as Pine east and west of Ash in Exhibit 54.

- *Offsets* in roadway edges on opposite sides of an intersection, sometimes accompanied by a change in roadway width as Pine in Exhibit 54.

Always start drawing the field sketch skeleton with the most regular edges and angles, the straight through edges and the right angles.

Results of Accident

Now draw in the results of the accident: in Exhibit 54, the positions of the car, body, and motorcycle.

A simple rectangle will outline the vehicle. Add a little arrowhead to show which way it was headed.

Draw the body as a "stick figure" with single lines for arms, legs and torso. A little circle will show where the head was. Because only one spot is used to locate the body, show it headed in the direction in which it came to rest, as nearly as you can from the information you have.

The motorcycle is also drawn as a "skeleton," with two circles for wheels and a rectangle for a frame. A little hooked line will represent handlebars and indicate the position of the machine, as in Exhibit 59. This exhibit also illustrates another useful technique. The car was blocking the roadway and had to be moved before measurements could be made. Therefore the positions of the left front and left rear wheels were marked on the paving with spray paint before the vehicle was moved, as illustrated in Exhibit 59. Consequently, measurements had to be made to wheel positions rather than corners of the car. To make this distinction clear, the spots for the car in Exhibit 59 are shown *inside* the car outline rather than at the corners as for the truck in Exhibit 52.

Your representation of the situation is now complete and you are ready to prepare for measurements. Mark the spots to be located: two for the motorcycle, one at each end; one for the body, in the middle; and two for the car, at opposite ends on the undamaged side. Label the spots to identify them, as in Exhibit 59.

Reference Point

The location of this accident (Exhibit 54) has good roadway edges and the spots to be located are close to them. Therefore, use coordinates to locate the spots. The north edge of Pine is closest to the spots to be located and is aligned on both sides of the intersection. It is the logical reference line. Mark it on your diagram as in Exhibit 60. Next, choose your reference point on the reference line. The obvious one is where the imaginary extension of the west edge of Ash crosses the reference line. But be careful, now! The west edge of Ash is not aligned north and south of Pine. Their imaginary extensions will not intersect the RL at the same place. You must be sure to specify which of these two intersecting places you are using as your RP. The more convenient edge is the one north of Pine. Then you describe the reference point as "Rl = N edge of Pine, RP @ W edge of Ash N of Pine."

Table for Measurements

Now you are ready for a table in which to record measurements. This is a small table and there is room on your field sketch for it. Draw your table and list the spots to be located in it. (Exhibit 60). Do not forget to describe your RL and RP on the field sketch. Measurements can be started now.

Before or after the measurements are entered, complete your field sketch in two ways: 1) identify the accident (ON, AT, IN, TIME) and 2) add your name and the date of the measurements. This finishes the field sketch and the accompanying table for measurements. (Exhibit 60).

There is no reason why additional factual data cannot be put on the field sketch if there is room, and especially if they do not appear elsewhere, for example:

- The kind of paving or road surface
- The condition of road surface at the time, wet, dry, icy, etc.

- The name of someone who took photos
- Positions of parked cars or vegetation, especially if they might have been a view obstruction
- Supplementary measurements, such as that for the width of the roadway (Q in Exhibit 53), and distances between final positions of vehicles (R in Exhibit 53).

What to Omit From Field Sketch

There are some things which you should *not* put on a field sketch. Remember that your field sketch is a strictly *factual* record of your personal, first-hand observations. It is not the place to record opinions or conclusions of any kind. Thus, *do not show*:

1. *Point of impact* (POI) or collision point. If you did not actually see the impact, its location is your opinion, and has no business on your factual field sketch. But if there are signs on the road on which you base an opinion as to the point of impact (such as debris, gouges, pecularities of tire marks) show them in detail; they are important *facts* to be recorded.
2. *Paths of vehicles* to the collision point or from there to final positions. These are matters of opinion, not observed facts.

Putting opinions and conclusions on field sketches may ruin their effectiveness as evidence, no matter how right the conclusions are.

Copying Field Sketch

If you were reasonably neat in making your field sketch and recorded your measurements, you should not have to copy them to make them look neater. Copies may be inadmissible as evidence. It can be argued that they were not made at the scene and may contain mistakes. Preserve your original notes carefully.

Corrections

Before you leave the scene, review your notes for missing measurements. Unfilled spaces in the measurement table may call your attention to the most important of these. Others may be supplementary measurements that someone might find useful. And before you finish your measurement record, review it for lacking general data such as identification of the accident. At this time, also look for weak or illegible lines, numbers, or words and clarify them.

Erasing for correcting your own mistakes is generally not objectionable.

In statements prepared by someone else for your signature, errors are crossed out and corrections added. Then you initial each change to show that you approved it. Such technical precautions are much less important in your corrections of your own measurements. Erasures to correct obvious errors, such as the direction of north or the name of a road, need no explanation. If you feel you need to be very careful, avoid other erasures by crossing out errors and writing in corrections with each change initialed. If these corrections are numerous, they may be confusing on a field sketch.

Keep Field Sketch Simple

Keep your field sketch simple. The purpose of a field sketch is to identify measurements made. Anything else tends to clutter the sketch and may be confusing. Here are suggestions for simplification.

- Show in your field sketch only *significant* road elements, just a bare skeleton. Unless they are involved or used for reference purposes, you can omit or simplify shoulders, edge returns at intersections, sidewalks, buildings, most curves, hill crests, guard rails, street lights, traffic signs, and signals. Information on all of these can be had later if needed.
- Describe vehicles and pedestrians only enough to distinguish between them and connect them with information recorded elsewhere, for example on the accident report. The outline on the field sketch will sufficiently describe a single vehicle or body on the ground. It will distinguish between a car and a motorcycle. To distinguish between two or more vehicles with similar outlines, add a single letter to each outline; that will indicate whether the outline is a truck (T), or car (C), whether it is a Ford (F) or a Buick (B). Two bodies are distinguished in the same way, for example, M for male and F for female.
- It is unnecessary to include the names of drivers or owners of vehicles, the registration numbers of vehicles, or numbers assigned to them on the accident report. These are often not known when measurements are made.
- You may omit information about kind of paving, weather, light, amount of traffic, or other matters which would ordinarily be remembered or written down elsewhere.
- Definitely, do not include anything about paths of vehicles approaching the accident or location of a point of impact. For whoever makes the measurements, these are matters of hearsay or mere speculation.
- You do not need to note that the field sketch is "not to

scale." That is obvious. Likewise it is not necessary to indicate that compass directions shown are approximate or nominal.

- Do not overdo supplementary measurements, such as widths of streets. Limit these to what you think someone would be pretty sure to ask about and which might not be easily judged from the routine measurements which you have made.

7. EQUIPMENT AND ITS USE

Consider, now, what equipment is readily available to make at-scene traffic-accident measurements and how to use it under various conditions.

Equipment will be discussed here in order of its importance, the most needed first. If you plan to equip yourself, you can start with some remarkably simple items. Bear in mind that very useful measurements can be made with very little equipment if you know what you are doing.

The Bare Necessities

The necessary equipment is what you need to make a field sketch and record the measurements, that is pencil and paper. Up to this point, it has been assumed that you also have a 100-ft. tape, but even without that, it is possible to step off distances sufficiently well for most traffic-accident investigation purposes.

Letter-size paper (8-1/2 by 11-in.) is usually most convenient. Strong paper with a hard surface will give less trouble from wind than light paper. It will not become spongy if it gets wet while being used. *Graph paper*, with light lines printed lengthwise and crosswise at intervals of 1/10 in. or 1/4 in., is best in preparing field sketches and tables for measurements.

A No. 2 black lead pencil will do very well for writing and sketching. Pens can be used, but pencils are usually handier because mistakes can be erased for correction.

Additional Items

Additional equipment for sketching and writing is very useful and may be had readily:

1. *An eraser,* preferably on the pencil, is useful to correct mistakes and clean up field sketches.
2. *A light-weight clipboard* suitable for the paper size used makes writing easier.
3. *A rubber band* or a pair of small clips will hold the bottom edge of the sheets on the clipboard and keep the sheets in place if there is a strong wind.

Measuring Devices

A tape is the principal device for measuring. There are many kinds available, any of which will serve the purpose. If you can choose, some tapes are better than others. One hundred feet is the best length. Large plain numbers are very desirable, especially at night; this means a tape at least 5/8 in. wide. A fabric or plastic tape with wire or fiberglass reinforcing (sometimes called a "metallic" tape) is much better than a steel tape (Exhibit 61). It can be stepped on or even run over by a tire without damage. A reinforced fabric tape is much easier to whip out of the way when used where traffic is heavy. Any tape should be in a wind-up case or reel. An engineer's tape, marked in feet and tenths, is better than a builder's tape marked in feet and inches, but either is acceptable.

A spring steel pocket tape-rule, preferably 12-ft. or more long and 3/4-in. wide is very useful for shorter measurements. One with a white surface and big numbers is best. These can be had in feet and tenths, but are usually more available in feet and inches (Exhibit 61). A belt clip on the

case helps in handling.

Measuring wheels have many advantages in accident-investigation work (Exhibit 62). They are especially useful:

1. *In heavy traffic,* because measurements on smooth surfaces can be made so much faster with a wheel than with a tape.
2. *When you have to work alone,* because no one is required to hold the other end of a tape.
3. *For long distances,* because they measure a thousand feet without stopping.
4. *In strong winds.*

A wheel only supplements a tape; it is not a substitute for one. It is useless for measuring across ditches or irregular ground. It is unsatisfactory for any but clean, paved sur-

Exhibit 61. *The most useful measuring equipment for accident investigation is a 100-ft. tape (left), preferably made of reinforced fabric. A tape rule, 12 or more feet long (right), is better for short distances.*

Exhibit 62. *The measuring wheel is ideal for measurements along smooth surfaces. It is very quick, especially for distances greater than tape length, and can be used without a helper; but it is no substitute for a tape.*

Exhibit 63. *A little line level is often useful in making vertical measurements.*

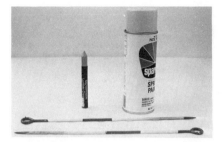

Exhibit 64. *Aerosol spray paint is best to mark the road for measuring. Lumber marking crayons will also do very well. Off the road, a surveyor's pin may be more convenient.*

faces in fairly good condition. Wet surfaces do not affect a wheel, but snow and ice make a wheel useless. Short distances, like the widths of tiremarks, are not well measured by wheels, especially the larger wheels.

A line level and strong cord in connection with measuring tapes is the simplest device for measuring how far a car dropped in a fall from one level to another, as will be described later. One is pictured in Exhibit 63. Line levels are not often needed. If necessary, one may be obtained inexpensively in most hardware stores.

In some cases, it may be more convenient and in some cases necessary to use regular surveying instruments for measuring slopes and vertical distances.

Marking Supplies

To mark RP's and other places on the roadway any of several things can be used:

1. *Crayons* are most commonly used. Big lumber crayons in bright yellow are best (Exhibit 64). Smaller ones break easily and wear down quickly on rough surfaces. Go over the mark several times, especially if you want it to show in photographs.
2. *Chalk* will do if crayons are not available, but chalk breaks apart easily and does not mark well on wet surfaces.
3. *Spray paint* in aerosol cans is very effective. Use a bright orange color. It will put a mark on wet surfaces, snow, gravel and grass where crayons would be useless. (Exhibit 64).
4. *Surveyor's pins or* metal

skewers are useful in marking points at the edge of the road, for example at tape ends in measuring. (Exhibits 69 and 34).

5. *Common nails 3-1/2 in. long* are useful on gravel roads, where there is snow, in turf, and in some other circumstances where the surface cannot be marked. Nails, if used by themselves, cannot easily be seen, so pin them through 3- by 5-in. cards or paper as in Exhibit 10. For hard ground, you will need a hammer or something like that with which to drive nails.

Where Marks Are Needed

Marking the pavement in preparation for measuring has already been mentioned briefly. It is done with crayon or, preferably, with spray paint. Mark

1. *RP's for coordinate measurements.* Such a mark on

the edge of the roadway is always useful but it is especially important when the RP is where the imaginary extensions of two roadway edges cross, as in Exhibit 38, or where the RP is at the beginning or end of a curve, as in Exhibit 42.

2. *The place where the end of your tape* (usualy 100-ft.) *reaches* when you are measuring distances greater than tape length. Beside this mark put the total distance to that place from the reference point, 100, 200, etc. or with a 50-ft. tape, 50, 100, 150, etc.

3. *Around the final position of a body* before the body is moved so that you can locate it later (Exhibit 65).

4. *The ends of tire marks* or spots on the perimeter of debris areas which are indistinct and might be difficult to see when measuring later (Exhibit 66).

5. *The position of two preferably undamaged wheels* of a vehicle on the roadway if the vehicle will be moved before actual measurements can be made (Exhibit 67). Ordinarily undamaged corners of the vehicle are the spots to measure to, but it is easier to mark the positions of wheels than corners. If you do mark a wheel position as a spot to which a measurement is

Exhibit 65. *Outline a body on the road before it is moved so that it can be located later.*

Exhibit 66. *It may be helpful in measuring and photography to mark the faint beginning or end of tire marks.*

Exhibit 67. *If a vehicle has to be moved before measurements can be made to locate it, mark on the roadway the positions of two tires.*

made, indicate this by a clear dot at the wheel position just inside the outline of the vehicle on your field sketch, as in Exhibit 59.

6. *Spots to be located for tire and other marks* on the road. When there are more spots than you can easily remember, mark at least some of them with the identifying number-letter combinations which you have assigned them. This helps you to be sure that the two locating measurements are actually made to the same spot.

7. *Stations* along the edge of the roadway (reference line) at 10- or 20-ft. intervals where these would be useful in locating spots on long curved tire marks. Next to each of these, mark the distance using only the number of 10-ft. intervals. For example the mark at 120 ft. from the RP would be simply 12 as in Exhibit 68.

Stepping off Distances

A few words about stepping off distances may be helpful at this point. If the situation calls for measuring, and you have no tape, makeshift measurements are possible by stepping off the distances. Simply walk the distance and count your steps. If there is less than a step at the end, estimate a quarter, half, or

three quarters of a step. Do *not* try to take three-foot steps. Walk naturally and take even steps. Stepping up and down slopes is especially inaccurate, but do the best you can. Stepping off distances is always better than guessing them.

Record the number of steps; do *not* try to change steps to feet at the scene, for example, multiplying by three. To do so suggests that the distances were actually measured with a tape or some other device; it gives a false or spurious impression of accuracy.

Later, if you want to change the steps to feet, step off that number of steps again from a fixed starting point when you do have a tape, and measure the distance stepped off. Then you can say, for example, "I stepped off the distance from the car to the body. It was seven and a half steps. Later, I stepped off seven and a half steps again and measured that distance with a tape, it was 23.5 ft." Because such a statement is honest and straightforward, it is highly believable.

Avoid the word "pace" because it does not mean the same thing to everybody. The military *pace* is 2.5 ft. for quick time and 3 ft. for double time. A "geometrical" or "great" pace, sometimes used by engineers and farmers, is usually considered to be 5 ft. and represents the distance from where either foot is taken up in walking to where the same foot is put down again. That is two steps.

Footing can be used for distances

of a few feet, but is not much better than simple estimation by observation. Put down one foot after the other with heel touching toe. Count the number of "shoes" and record them as such, not as feet which suggests that the distance was actually measured with a tape or other scale. You can later change "shoes" to feet the same way that you might change steps to feet.

Using Tapes

Measure distances less than 12 ft. with pocket tape rule. You can use a tape rule without help and in many cases with one hand, because you do not have to unroll part of a long tape. The pocket tape rule is handier and quicker for measurements for such things as

1. *Wheel-base lengths,* and track widths of vehicles
2. *Heights and sizes* of traffic signs
3. *Heights of curbs* and view obstructions
4. *Widths of sidewalks*
5. *Distances of tiremarks* and debris from edges of roadways
6. *Lengths and widths of scratches* and gouges.

For simple measurements from 10 ft to tape length, get a helper. If he is inexperienced, have him hold the

Exhibit 68. *Sometimes marking the reference line along the edge of a roadway at 10- or 20-ft. intervals will help in measuring. This mark represents 120 ft.*

end of the tape at the point you show him and do everything else yourself. Any bystander can hold the end of the tape for you. If your helper is experienced, he should also record the distances as you read them from the tape. Eight steps are usually required:

1. Have your helper hold the end of the tape at the reference point or line while you walk toward the spot to be located and unroll tape as you go.
2. When you reach the spot, lower tape so it rests on the ground, grasp it about 6 in. beyond the spot, draw it taut and call out, "Ready."
3. Your helper holds the tape-end exactly on his point and calls, "Read."
4. Read the distance which is in line with the second point while the tape is tight.
5. Relax your pull and call out the distance to your helper. Then, before you let go of the tape, look again to see whether the reading is right.
6. Whoever is doing the recording writes the number *clearly* and carefully in the place *previously* provided for it. He then calls out the number.
7. The other answers "Check," if he agrees with it.
8. Rewind the tape completely unless you have another measurement to make at once.

Measurements longer than tape on paved surfaces. If the distance is along the pavement, curb, or other firm surface, here is how you measure, also eight steps:

1. Start out with a helper as in shorter measurements.
2. When you come to the end of the tape, slow down, lower the tape and have your helper motion you to right or left until the tape lines up

the distant spot to which you are measuring.
3. Draw the tape taut and call out, "Ready."
4. The helper holds the end exactly on his mark and calls, "Mark."
5. Make a 3-in. crayon mark at right angles to the tape on the pavement opposite your highest-numbered foot mark, or if off the paving, put a pin in the ground at that point. Relax the tape and write the number of feet on the pavement beside the crayon mark.
6. Both you and your helper walk toward the distant point holding the tape taut off the ground. When he nears the mark on the pavement, he calls, "Stop."
7. Repeat lining up and marking. Write the total distance from the original starting point along side of each mark put on the roadway.
8. When you reach the distant point, roll up the tape until your helper reaches the last numbered crayon mark and use the method already given in the previous section, except that you call out the *total* distance.

A helper may do other things besides hold the end of a tape. He may, if qualified, mark spots on the roadway or record data as it is obtained. The helper can assist you in any way you direct.

If you have to work alone you will need something to anchor one end of the tape which a helper would normally hold. Where the surface is not too hard, a surveyor's pin or skewer, mentioned as a marker, can be used. Where the surface is too hard for a pin, a weight with a hook or ring attached may be used. Preferably the weight should be five pounds or more and flat rather than tall.

Measuring Methods

Measuring along a curved roadway edge from an RP on that edge to a place opposite to the spot to be located, as in Exhibit 47, presents some practical problems in handling a measuring tape. You cannot very well lay the tape along the curved edge. It will not stay put. The best way to measure is to pull the tape taut and measure the *chord* (straight line between two points on a circle) instead of trying to measure the *arc* along the curve. The chord measurement will give the exact place along the curve. If the distance along the reference line is more than the length of the tape (usually 100 ft.), measure that distance straight across to the roadway edge used as a reference line and mark the 100-ft place on the reference line, just as you would have to do on a straight roadway edge. Then begin again with the zero on the tape at that place. Thus, the north coordinate for B1 in Exhibit 47 is 100 + 38.0 = 138.0 ft. This method gives accurate results, but you may have to explain exactly how the measurements were made.

Measure to the center of the poles, posts, trees, hydrants, and round or rectangular objects on the road surface such as manhole covers and drains. This is customary engineering practice and will be assumed by others unless you specify something else. There is no special difficulty in judging the center of something on the road surface, like a manhole cover, with sufficient accuracy for accident-investigation purposes. But you cannot get at the center of large poles and trees. Therefore, measure to the side of the pole or tree opposite the center as illustrated in Exhibit 69.

Measure to the center of tire marks as a regular thing (Exhibit 70).

If you do not measure to the center, for any reason, be sure to note on your field sketch exactly to what it was that you measured.

One coordinate is always the *shortest distance* from a reference line to a spot to be located. This is so

Exhibit 69. *Measure to or from the center of poles and trees. This usually means measuring to a point on the side opposite the center.*

Exhibit 70. *Measure to the center of tire marks. This is a skidmark because striations are parallel to the mark.*

whether the reference line is straight or curved. You may also need to measure the *shortest distance* from a triangulation RP to the edge of a roadway. Ordinarily you can locate the place on the RL closest to the spot to be located well enough just by looking. When the RL is straight, the shortest distance measurement is at right angles (90 degrees) to the reference line. This fact helps you decide where the closest place is.

You can make a more exact determination, when necessary, by having the zero end of the tape held at the spot to be located. Then swing the tape back and forth along the line to find the shortest distance, as in Exhibit 71. Finding the shortest distance is more difficult when the RL is far from the spot than when it is close. That is why it is so important to select a reference line that is close to most of the spots to be located.

Reading Tapes and Recording Distances

Tapes and measuring wheels used in the United States come with either of two different scales: feet and tenths and feet and inches (twelfths). Some tapes have both scales. These two scales are illustrated for the first foot of a tape in Exhibit 72. Measurements in feet and tenths are generally used by engineers and are preferable in accident investigation work. Measurements in feet and in-

ches are used by architects and builders. Examine the equipment you use to know which scale it has.

If you misread tenths of a foot for inches, no great harm is done because measurements at the scene of a traffic accident are usually accurate enough if they are measured to the nearest half foot. Reading 0.9 feet as 9 inches would give the greatest error from misreading scales. That is an error of 0.15 ft. or 1.8 in., not enough to worry about. However, misreading scales will bother some people and tends to undermine the credibility of your work.

If your tape is marked in *feet* and *tenths* of a foot, record what you read with a decimal point to separate feet and tenths. For example, record six and a half feet as 6.5 ft. But if your tape reads feet and inches, six and a half feet will be six feet six inches. *Underline* the inches and write six feet six inches as 6⁶. If your pocket tape reads only in inches, as some do, six and a half feet is 78 in. Write it⁷⁸. Do *not* use prime (′) to represent feet and double prime (″) to indicate inches, as is often done. Primes are sometimes mistaken for l's. In accident investigation routinely record measurements to the nearest inch or tenth of a foot, even if the roadway edges and other things you measure from and to cannot be located that accurately. The refined measurement suggests that you have been careful in your work, and

avoids unnecessary discussion. If the measurement comes out an even number of feet, show a zero in the tenths or inches position. Thus thirty feet exactly is written as 30.0 or 30⁰. That will make all your distance notations uniform. Most tapes have graduations at intervals of less than an inch or a tenth of a foot. In Exhibit 72, for example, each tenth of a foot is subdivided into ten intervals of a hundredth of a foot. In that exhibit the inch has 16 subdivisions. You can disregard these smaller subdivisions; measurements to less than an inch or a tenth of a foot are rarely possible or necessary.

In most countries, measurements are not made in feet but in meters. Tapes and scales marked in meters and centimeters are used. But the principles and procedures of measuring at the scene of traffic accidents are exactly the same whether the U.S.A. system or the metric system is used.

Safety

Be careful in measuring on roads, especially with tapes, to protect both yourself from traffic and your tape from being run over or stepped on. Plan measuring with this in mind. To keep off the road as much as possible, first decide exactly what you want to measure *from* and *to* and prepare a place to record your mea-

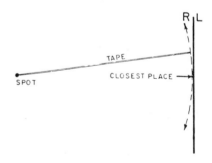

Exhibit 71. *To find the shortest distance from a spot to a reference line, hold the zero end of the tape on the spot and move the other end of the tape along the reference line to where the distance measured is least.*

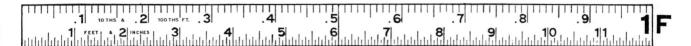

Exhibit 72. *The two common scales for measuring tapes are feet and inches (lower scale), and feet and tenths (upper scale). When you record measurements be sure to indicate inches by underlining and tenths of a foot by a decimal point. Disregard fractions.*

surements. Thus, you will not have to stop out in the roadway to decide what to do next. Using coordinates, mainly with short measurements in from the edge of the roadway, is better than using triangulation with long measurements across the roadway. Avoid measuring from the center line. That keeps you out in the roadway too much.

Measurements in heavy traffic may be dangerous and are always tedious. Avoid them if possible. If you can, postpone measurements until traffic is light. If necessary, have traffic warned by flagging. Take special precautions at night. Put out flares or fusees and turn headlights on the spot where measurements are being made. If you have to measure across the road where gaps in traffic are short, have your helper hold the zero end of the tape firmly at one edge of the roadway. Unroll the tape while you walk briskly across the road. As you approach the other side of the roadway, hold the tape case in your left hand and play out the tape between your right thumb and finger. When you reach the spot to be located, lower the tape, pull it taut, grasp the tape firmly, directly over the spot to be located, and shout, "Let go." Now, holding the tape firmly, *run* in the same direction you were walking, and whip the tape out of the roadway. The zero tape end quickly clears the road without rewinding. When the tape has cleared the roadway, read the distance where your right hand still holds it. Record it and rewind the tape.

Do not leave your tape on the ground any more than necessary. If you do, sooner or later someone will damage it when he steps on it or runs a car over it, especially if it is a steel tape. Do not roll up a wet or dirty tape; wipe it off. If it is a steel tape

without enamel, wiping with an oily rag helps keep it in good condition.

When you wind up a fabric tape, let the tape feed into the case between two fingers, as illustrated in Exhibit 73. By this means you can detect kinks and can prevent them from winding into the case, which will jam the tape inside.

Accuracy

Measuring at the scene of a traffic accident must be accurate but rarely has to be very precise. Your notes on what landmarks you measure from and what spots you measure to must be specific and reliable; your records of distance and direction of measurements should be free from error; and your identification (ON, AT, IN, TIME) must be correct. Otherwise you and others will have trouble using the results of your efforts later. But highly precise measurements are rarely possible at accident scenes and rarely needed. The landmarks you measure from and the spots you measure to are not sharp lines or points; they are irregular objects and areas. The beginning of a tire mark, for example, cannot possibly be determined to within an eighth of an inch; within a foot would be more like it. The corner of a vehicle is an indefinite rounded area; the edge of a roadway is often very irregular. Thus, at the scene, pin-point precision of measurements is neither expected nor required. Routinely recording distances as feet and tenths with a decimal (or feet and inches) indicates what kind of measuring equipment you are using without implying that all measurements are precise to within a tenth of a foot or an inch.

Mistakes in measuring. It is easy to measure distances quickly and correctly, but do not let carelessness cause you to make errors. There are

seven kinds of errors you must guard against:

1. Reading numbers upside down, for example, a 9 for a 6
2. Reading wrong footmark, for example, 18.7 as 17.7 or 19.7
3. Getting the zero-point of your tape measure confused (Most tapes begin calibrations with the end of the ring as zero. *Know* how *your* tape is made.)
4. Losing count of the number of complete tape-lengths measured (Use the methods described to avoid this error.)
5. Forgetting to reset a measuring wheel before making measurements
6. Attempting to remember distances rather than recording them immediately
7. Adding separate measurements mentally (Record each and add them later.)

After you form proper habits, you will automatically make more correct measurements.

Exhibit 73. *Hold tape between two fingers when rolling it up. That keeps the tape cleaner and prevents fabric tapes from kinking and jamming in the case.*

If you think you may have to testify, you can guard against your measurements being discredited by having your helper check them when they are made. Here is how:

1. Stretch the tape as usual for a measurement and then let it lie in that position on the ground.
2. Read and record the measurement.
3. Change ends with your helper.
4. Note that the end of the tape is at the beginning point.
5. Have your helper read distance at other end of tape and record the length.

Now, both you and your helper "know of your own knowledge" that the reading was correct. A measurement made by two different persons is not easy to discredit in court. However, such elaborate precautions are seldom necessary.

Spurious accuracy means reporting figures which suggest much greater accuracy than was possible or than was actually employed. This is a common mistake in reporting distances stepped off. Measurements to a tenth of a foot (3 cm) to a pedestrian's final position are false accuracy; reporting the location to within the nearest half (0.5) foot (15 cm) would be more appropriate.

Testimony in court. If your equipment is good and you have used the methods described, you will ordinarily have no difficulty testifying to your measurements. However, you can rarely do this from memory. Keep your field sketch and all other original notes to refresh your memory in court. You may be asked to verify, from original notes, the dimensions on a map drawn by yourself or someone else.

The most precise measurements are made with a calibrated steel tape pulled with a spring scale to a specified tension and corrected for temperature. To expect such precision at the scene of an accident would be ridiculous. Sufficient precison is available with an ordianry commer-

Exhibit 74

ACCURACY OF VARIOUS MEASURING DEVICES

METHOD OF MEASURING	CONDITIONS	SPEED	ERROR Ft per 100 ft
Steel tape, standard	5-lb pull		- 0.005
	10-lb "		0.000
	15-lb "		+ 0.010
Metallic (wire fabric)	5-lb pull		+ 0.065
	10-lb "		+ 0.120
	15-lb "		+ 0.165
Fabric tape, good, new	5-lb pull		- 0.23
	10-lb "		- 0.06
	15-lb "		+ 0.10
Cloth tape, cheap, old	5-lb pull		- 0.31
	10-lb "		+ 0.08
2-ft single wheel	Dry pavement	3 ft per sec	+ 1.3
	"	7 "	+ 3.9
	Dry gravel	3 "	- 4.5
	"	7 "	- 6.2
	Dry grass	3 "	- 4.2
	"	7 "	- 1.3
1-ft single wheel	Dry pavement	3 ft per sec	- 1.0
	"	7 "	- 2.6
	Dry gravel	3 "	- 5.9
	"	7 "	- 5.8
	Dry grass	3 "	- 6.3
	"	7 "	- 6.7
1-ft double wheel	Dry pavement	3 ft per sec	- 0.1
	"	7 "	+ 0.1
	Wet pavement	3 "	- 0.1
	Dry gravel	3 "	- 4.4
	"	7 "	- 7.2
	Wet gravel	3 "	- 2.8
	Dry grass	3 "	- 2.0
	"	7 "	- 1.5
	Wet grass	3 "	- 1.0
Optical range finder			± 5.0
Stepping			± 5.0

The error in feet per 100 ft is the same as the percent error. The errors indicated are the average for several measurements with typical equipment. These error figures should not be used to adjust or correct actual measurements.

cial tape. On regular road surfaces, a measuring wheel is quite precise enough for practical purposes. Sometimes a pernickety lawyer will question the precision of your equipment. You can respond with some such statement as, "I am confident that my equipment was sufficiently precise for the kind of measurements I was making."

Accuracy of measuring instruments. Also, in a sharply contested case, an attorney may ask, "How do you know your tape was accurate?" Do not claim your tape was accurate. Actually, very few tapes are exactly their graduated length. Temperature makes a tape change length. This change is not much. A 100-ft steel

tape will lengthen only about three quarters of an inch, or this much _____ when temperature goes from 0° to 100° F ($-22°$ to $+42°C$).

Different amounts of pull also cause slight changes in length. A pull of 10 lbs too much would stretch a 100-ft steel tape only about a quarter of an inch. A steel tape made by a reputable manufacturer is usually very nearly accurate — within an inch of its total graduated length in 100 ft.

If you expect the accuracy of your tape to be challenged, compare it with the tape of a licensed surveyor and be able to state in inches how much difference there is. The accuracy of a measuring wheel or roller is more apt to be questioned. Compare it in the same way with a surveyor's tape so that you can say just how much difference there is. The best answer to a question about the accuracy of your measuring instrument is, "I compared the length of the tape I used with that of a tape used by a registered surveyor and it differed only one-half inch in 100 feet," or whatever the amount is. Another reply which is usually satisfactory is, "The department supplied the tape I used. The name on it was that of a well-known manufacturer. I have no reason to question its accuracy."

Accuracy of your measurements with a tape can be increased thus:

1. Always hold the tape taut to get correct distances. When using *steel tapes* pull from 7 to 10 lbs. and a metallic *woven* tape from 2 to 3 lbs.
2. If possible, have your tape supported over the entire distance measured. When you hold it off the ground it sags and gives you a distance which is slightly long.
3. Hold the tape level when measuring.

If you do not make mistakes in reading or counting, your measurement of 100 ft. will almost always be within the distance shown in Exhibit 74 for various measuring methods.

8. SPECIAL SITUATIONS IN MEASURING

Some accident situations present special problems in measuring, but there are ways to deal with them. Some of these methods are in general use and you may be able to work out suitable solutions to many unusual problems.

Measurements across puddles, ditches and other obstacles are no great problem if you can stretch a tape across them. But if an obstacle is wider than your tape is long, or if you cannot stretch a tape straight through it, you have to work out a way to get around the obstacle.

Thus some measurements longer than tape length over water, mud, ravines, embankments or buildings cannot be made by the usual straightforward methods. Holding the zero end of the tape on the reference line for coordinates and the 100-ft. end in line with the spot to be located is difficult, if not impossible. For example, in Exhibit 75, the shortest distance from the reference line to Spot S lands you in the pond at the end of a 100-ft. tape. This does not happen often, but when it does, there are ways you can get around the difficulty.

One method is to supplement coordinates with triangulation as illustrated by Exhibit 75. The two reference points for triangulation are points on the reference line measured from RP. The first, RP1, is 35.0 ft. west of RP and so would be designated RP1 = W 35.0. Then, in the same way, RP2 = W 215.0. From each of these, there is a clear line to the spot to be located, S. Starting at RP2, a distance of 100 ft. is measured off toward S. The 100-ft. place is marked and the tape is shifted to put the zero end where the 100 ft. measurement ended. Then a second measurement of 72 ft. takes you to spot S. The total distance, 100 + 72 = 172.0 ft. is recorded. The distance from RP1 is a little more complicated because the pond is an obstacle. A first measurement of 100 ft. would land you in the pond. So make the first measurement to the edge of the pond, 78 ft. The second measurement across the water takes you an additional 87 ft. to Spot S. The total distance is then 78 + 87 = 165.0 ft. Thus, for situations which appear difficult with regular coordinates, you may be able to work out a plan to get around the difficulty without calling on a professional surveyor to do it for you. For Exhibit 75, describe RP1 in your notes as RP1 = N 0, W 35.0. Of course the N-S coordinates of RP1 is 0 because it is right on the reference line, the edge of the roadway. Then the other triangulation reference point is RP2 = N 0, W 215. In the table of coordinates, enter

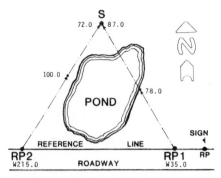

Exhibit 75. *If some obstacle, such as a pond, prevents direct measurement from RP to spot, it is often possible to measure around it from two points on the reference line, thus supplementing coordinates with triangulation.*

SPOT	RP1	RP2
	N 0.0, W 35.0	N 0.0, W 215.0
S	165.0	172.0

Exhibit 76. *If triangulation is used with coordinates to get around obstacles, as in Exhibit 75, prepare a separate little table for the triangulation measurements.*

RP1 and RP2 as spots to be located. Then make a second triangulation table with columns for RP1 and RP2 as in Exhibit 76. It is a very brief table in this example, because there is only one spot to be located, Spot S.

There is another possible way to get around an obstacle as shown in Exhibit 77, an offset method. Measure the shortest distance from the reference line to a place directly off to one side of the spot. In this example that represents the N-S coordinate, N144.0. Of course the E-W coordinate will be the place on the reference line actually closest to Spot

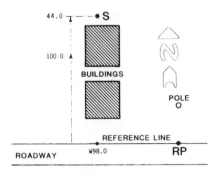

Exhibit 77. *When an obstacle prevents direct measurement, a parallel measurement of the same length can usually be substituted without great loss of accuracy.*

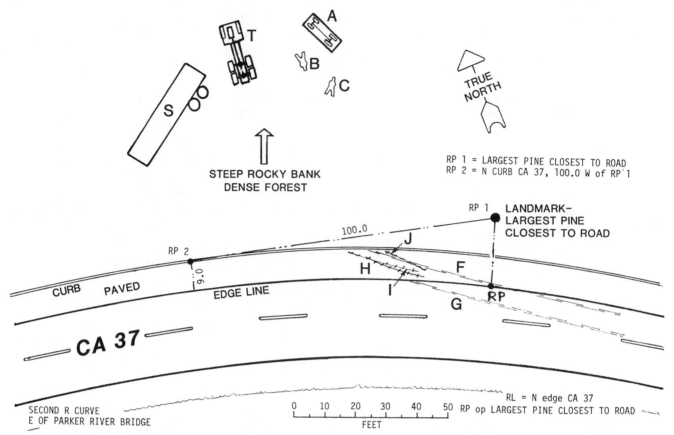

RP 1 = LARGEST PINE CLOSEST TO ROAD
RP 2 = N CURB CA 37, 100.0 W of RP 1

Exhibit 78. *Although it is rarely necessary, coordinates and triangulation can be combined. In this example, one group of spots is off the road and can best be located by triangulation whereas* *another group is on the road and can best be located by coordinates. The two sets of measurements must be tied together by locating the triangulation RP's by coordinate measurements.*

S, in this example W98.0. The triangulation method is very accurate if done carefully. The offset method is naturally less accurate because of the sighting that has to be done. It is especially inaccurate if there is not a clear line of sight from the nearest point on the reference line to the point to be located as would be the case if there were a building instead of a pond obstructing direct measurement.

Sometimes there is an advantage in combining triangulation with coordinates. This is generally when one group of spots can be located better by coordinates and another group better by triangulation. An example of such a situation is illustrated in Exhibit 78. In this case, a car, a tractor, a separate trailer, and two bodies, (marked A, B, C, S, and T) are far off the road down a steep and densely wooded bank. They are best located by triangulation. But five tire marks on the road (F, G, H, I, and J) are better located by coordinates.

The best landmark in the area is the largest pine tree that is closest to the roadway on the north side. A point on the edge of the roadway closest to this pine is used as the RP for coordinates to locate the spots on the road. The same pine is used as RP 1 for triangulation. The second reference point for triangulation, RP 2, is located on the ede of the curb 100 measured feet west of the pine, RP 1. In this way the two systems are tied together. Combined coordinates and triangulation is rarely necessary. You might investigate accidents for many years without having to use a combination.

The description of the coordinate reference point is as follows:

RL = N edge CA 37

RP op Largest pine closest to road

The description of the triangulation reference points is as follows:

RP 1 = Largest pine closest to road

RP 2 = N curb CA 37 100 ft W of RP 1.

N and W are, of course, nominal directions in this example. Two separate tables for measurements are required, one for coordinates and the other for triangulation. The two systems are connected by including RP1 and RP 2 in the table for coordinates. Including RP for coordinates in the table for triangulation would not be satisfactory; it would not establish the *angle* of the RL to the triangulation measurements. In this particular example, Exhibit 78, however, the customary procedure for relating two triangulation RP's to the nearest roadway edge would serve the purpose of relating the two systems of measurement.

The advantage, that has just been described, of using triangulation for one group of spots and coordinates for another is not the only reason for using two separate sets of measurements for the same accident. Sometimes spots to be located are in two distinct groups so far (more than 100 ft) apart that long measurements

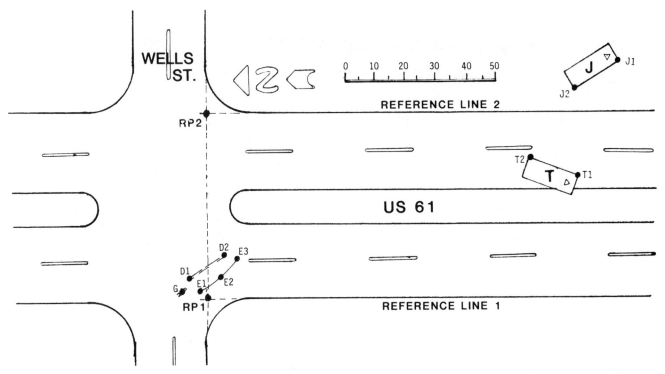

Exhibit 79. *If there are widely separated groups of spots to be located as in this example, each group can be treated separately,* *each with its own reference point and reference line. The two groups must be tied together.*

S P O T S		N-S	E-W
TIRE MARKS	D1 D2		
	E1 E2 E3		
GOUGE	G		

RL1 = W edge US 61 Southbound
RP1 @ S edge Wells

S P O T S		N-S	E-W
JEEP	RF = J1 RR = J2		
TOYOTA	LF = T1 LR = T2		
RP1		0.0	

RL2 = E edge US 61 Northbound
RP2 @ S edge Wells

Exhibit 80. *If groups of spots to be located are handled separately, each must have its own table for recording measurements. Listing the RP for one set of measurements in the table for the* *other set will tie the two systems together. In this example, both systems are coordinates.*

would be required, possibly across heavy traffic as illustrated in Exhibit 79. In that case, you may be able to save yourself trouble by treating the spots as separate groups, almost as though there were no connection between them. Thus, in Exhibit 79 locate the tire marks on the road from RP1, and locate the final positions of the vehicles from RP2. Treat these as separate systems of coordinates with separate tables for recording measured distances as in Exhibit 80. This will avoid having to measure long distances across busy

roadways, for example, to locate Car J from RP1. Note that in this case, RP1 and RP2 refer to reference points in two separate coordinate systems; they are not two RP's for triangulation. If the two RP's are both located with reference to good landmarks, there is no real need to locate the two coordinate systems with respect to each other; that can be done later if necessary. However, the systems may usually be connected easily by listing RP1 as a spot in the coordinate system for RP2 along with the spots on things to be

located. Thus, in Exhibit 80, the table for RP2 is prepared in the usual way, but then another item, RP1, is added to the spots column. In this particular example, the RP1 line would show N 0 (N zero) in the N-S column. The E-W column is for the distance between the two RP's. Of course the two RP's do not have to be on the same N-S or E-W line, as they happen to be in this example.

Sometimes you need to locate a number of spots along a tire mark to establish its *curvature*. Establishing curvature of a yaw (sideslip side-

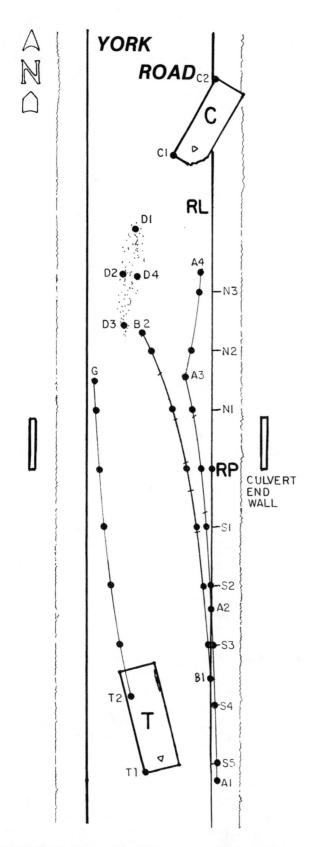

Exhibit 81. *When spots are needed in a long tire mark to show its curvature, stations from which to measure may be marked along the reference line at 10- or 20-ft. intervals from the reference point.*

RL = E EDGE YORK
RP op S END CULVERT END WALL

SPOTS		N-S	E-W
CAR	RF = C1 RR = C2		
TRUCK	RF = T1 RR = T2		
DEBRIS	D1 D2 D3 D4		
TIRE MARKS	BEGIN A1 A2 A3 END A4	S 51.7 S 23.5 N 15.5	E 1.0 E 0.0 W 5.0
	BEGIN B1 END B2		
	BEGIN G1		

Exhibit 82. *When stations are marked along a reference line for measurements to long curved tire marks, two tables are needed. One is the ordinary kind which includes the beginning and end of each curved mark and, of course, spots for vehicles and other objects.*

RL = E EDGE YORK
RP op S END CULVERT END WALL

STATIONS	A	B	G
N 30	W 2.4	—	—
N 20	W 4.0	W 10.8	—
N 10	W 3.7	W 7.0	W 19.6
RP 0	W 1.9		
S 10	W 1.0		
S 20	W 0.3		
S 30	E 0.4	W 0.5	W 15.4
S 40	E 0.8	—	—
S 50	E 0.9	—	—

Exhibit 83. *The other table is for distances from the RL to a spot on each mark opposite each station. The left column, lists the stations distance and direction on either side of the RP. Then there is a column for each curved mark to be located.*

scuff, critical speed, centrifugal) mark is essential for estimating the speed of the vehicle which made the mark. In the usual manner locate *natural* spots on the tiremark, such as the beginning and end. If three or more additional spots are needed at intervals along a curved tiremark, mark *stations* along the reference line at intervals of 10 or 20 ft. Then you can easily measure distances from the reference line at each of these stations.

Now consider an example of this technique, Exhibit 81. You locate spots in the usual way as follows:

Car, final position:
1) RF Corner,
2) RR corner 2
Truck, final position:
1) RF Corner,
2) RR tire at end of tire mark 2
Debris area: perimeter 4
Yawmark A:
1) start, 2) crosses roadway edge, 3) crook, 4) end 4
Yawmark B: 1) start, 2) end 2
Tiremark G: start
(ends at truck tire) 1
Total spots 15

The natural reference line for these spots is "E edge York." It is close to most of the spots. The best landmark to locate an RP on the RL is the culvert end wall. Either end of the wall will do. Suppose the south end is selected. Then you have "RP op S end culvert end wall." You do not have to specify the east or west wall, because the RP would be the same with either. All three tire marks are long and curved so you need to locate spots to establish curvature. You could pick out additional spots along the curves and locate them as usual, but there is a better way.

Mark *stations* along the RL at intervals of 10 ft. north and south from the RP. Number them 1, 2, 3, etc. for 10, 20, 30 ft. You could label them 10, 20, 30, etc., but the shorter form requires less marking and will sufficiently specify the distance. Next you can measure the distance of each tire mark from the RL at each station. For example, at Station 1, 10 ft.

north of RP, Mark A is 3.7 west of the RL, B is 7.0 west, and G is 19.6 west. They are measured at the same time, one after the other.

You could list all these station measurements in your usual measurement table, but you will find it simpler to prepare a separate table for the station measurements. Exhibit 82 is the table for regular measurements. You are familiar with such a table by now. The table for station measurements (Exhibit 83) is a little different. Instead of listing spots in the first (left) column, list the stations in sequence from one end of the field sketch to the other. Do not forget to include the RP as Station 0. It is neither north nor south in the example and so has a distance of 0.0 Then provide a column for each tire mark. In the example there are three columns for the three marks. Label the columns at the top, in this example, A, B, and G. The table for this example is shown in Exhibit 83. Note that nominal directions, N, S, E, or W are recorded for each measurement as in the ordinary table of coordinates. If all measurements in a column are the same direction from the RP, you can put that direction in the column heading and omit the direction with the distance number. This cannot be done in the example, however. A tire mark may not extend far enough to be opposite some of the stations. For example Mark G does not go as far as station S5. Do not leave the box in Column G for Station S5 blank; that would suggest that you forgot to make the measurement. Do not put 0.0 in that space; that would mean that the tire mark crossed the roadway edge reference line at that station. Simply drawn a line across the box as in Exhibit 83; that means that the space is not applicable.

If the curved tire marks are less than 30 ft. long, station marks are not required. A midpoint on the curve located by the usual coordinates will suffice. If the tire marks are very long, say more than 100 ft., stations every 20 ft. instead of 10 ft.

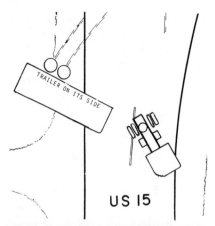

US 15

Exhibit 84. *If vehicles in accidents come to rest across lines which require measuring, it is best to mark the spots to be located and do the measuring after the vehicles have been removed.*

will do very well. Label them 2, 4, 6, etc. to indicate distance of each from the RP. Straight tire marks, usually skidmarks, do not require station marks. Simply locate each end, crooks in them, and where they cross roadway edges and center or lane lines. Sometimes one curved tire mark will cross another. This crossing is a good spot to locate in the usual way. Using stations to measure long curved tire marks is not suitable for triangulation.

When a vehicle in an accident comes to rest across the edge of a roadway which is used as a reference line, you may have trouble measuring past the vehicle (Exhibit 84). This situation can be handled quite simply in one of four ways:

1. Choose a reference line which will avoid such obstacles.
2. Mark on the ground spots to be located and measure to them after the vehicle has been moved.
3. Work around it by measuring a parallel distance off to one side.
4. If the vehicle is small enough, measure over it, being careful to keep the tape level. This is a kind of offset measuring.

Remember, always, that good measurements to locate results of traffic accidents require planning. Do not unroll your tape and start measuring until you have planned what spots need to be located and what reference points are to be used in locating these spots. Prepare the field sketch and table for recording measurements in advance. While preparing to locate results of the accident, do not worry about measurements of the road layout needed to draw a scale map of the after-accident situation. Such a scale map may never be needed, and if it is, whoever needs it can return to the site and take the necessary additional measurements.

9. ADDITIONAL AND SPECIAL MEASUREMENTS

There are a number of reasons for making certain measurements at the scene of a traffic accident in addition to those for locating spots by coordinates or triangulation:

- As a check in case measurements have errors. For example, the distance between two vehicles is a check on measurements locating the positions of these vehicles.

- To permit at least a preliminary after-accident-situation map to be made without returning to the site. For example, if someone needs a map of the situation quickly, you can make the layout at once if you have already made measurements of the width of roadways. Then, nobody has to return to the site to obtain this simple information.

- To be able to answer directly, without plotting the coordinate or triangulation data, common questions about distances such as length of skidmarks.

- To obtain detailed data about the size of gouges and scrapes on the road and roadside.

- To record significant vertical distances.

- To record observations of striations in tire marks.

Some additional measurements will serve more than one of these purposes, for example, the direct distance between two vehicles will be a check (verification) of your basic measurements when they are plotted on a map and they will also answer directly questions asked as to how far apart the vehicles were.

How far you go with additional measurements at the scene depends on a number of circumstances:

- How much time it takes to make the measurements compared to how much spare time you have at the scene. Measuring the distance between two vehicles where they come to rest ordinarily takes about half a minute. That much time is usually available.

- How long after the accident the things to be measured will remain unchanged. For example, the height of crops obscuring the view of a driver must be measured at the time of the accident (or very soon after) because the height may be quite different in a week. On the other hand, collision with a bridge rail may leave scars that will be visible for years and the height can be measured later by whoever wants the information.

- How likely it is that the information will be needed and whether it is cheaper to get it at the time of the accident, or later. For example, width of the roadway will remain the same

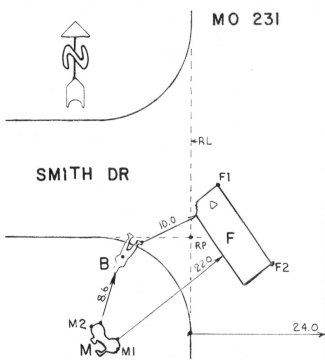

MO 231

SMITH DR

RL = Wedge   MO 231

RP @ S edge Smith Dr

SPOTS		N-S		E·W	
FORD	RF = F1	N	8.0	E	4.3
	RR = F2	S	4.8	E	14.0
M'CYCLE	F = M1	S	17.0	W	12.0
	R = M2	S	9.0	W	16.2
BODY	B	S	2.7	W	10.9

B to F = 10.0
B to M = 8.6
F to M = 22.0

Exhibit 85. *It is generally helpful to measure the shortest distance between vehicles or between a vehicle and a body in addition to the coordinate or triangulation measurements made to locate these objects. Record these distances separately from the table for basic measurements from reference points. In this case, the additional measurements are below the table.*

for a long time, but someone is quite likely to ask about it and it takes only a moment to measure the width at the scene compared to the time it would take to return later for the measurement.

- How professional you want your work to be. A truly professional job would include these additional observations and measurements, at least those which could not readily be obtained later.

Widths of Roadways

The width of each roadway is easily measured from the edge on one side to the edge on the other side. This can usually be recorded most conveniently on the field sketch. From a dot on one edge line, draw a line across the roadway to an arrowhead at the other edge. Beside this arrow write the distance in feet. The dimension line does not have to be exactly where the measurement was made as long as the roadway is the same width at both places. If this notation clutters the field sketch, put a note in any convenient spot, even on a separate sheet used for the table of coordinates, for example, "IA 21 is 20.0 wide." You may have noticed an example of across-the-road roadway dimension at Q in Exhibit 53.

Distances Between Objects

The distance between two vehicles in their final positions helps to verify measurements made to locate them, but it is not necessary for their location. The distance between the vehicles is always the *shortest* distance between the closest parts of the ve-

hicles, damaged or undamaged, as illustrated in Exhibit 85, unless, for some reason, you specify otherwise. In Exhibit 85, the shortest distance between the car and the body is not the distance (15.5 ft) between the closest spots used to locate them. It is much less, 10.0 ft. Of course, the shortest distance might just happen to be that between spots located. Recording these special measurements is easy; simply indicate which objects the measurement was made between, for example "F to B = 10.0". If the distance is measured to a spot or between spots which are also used for coordinate or triangulation measurements, indicate the particular spots. Do not try to fit these measurements into a table for coordinates; simply list them on the same sheet, preferably below the table as in Exhibit 85. If the vehicles are in contact when they come to rest, enter the distance between them as 0.0. If your after-accident *location* of vehicles and bodies is good, you could plot their positions on a map of the location and so determine how far apart they were. Therefore you need to make special measurements between things only when you think someone might ask about them in particular. If vehicles are clearly 25 feet or more apart (Exhibit 43) it is unlikely that anyone will want to know exactly how far apart they were. But if it is a matter of whether they were actually in contact (Exhibit 28) or almost touching, someone is quite likely to ask and so special measurement is warranted. Someone may want to know how far the pedestrian's body was from the car that struck him, when both came to rest, unless the distance was more than 100 ft. If there are three final posi-

tions, three measurements are needed for all of the distance between them (Exhibit 85). This is a reasonable number to measure. But if there are four final positions, six measurements are required. You cannot be expected to make that many especially when they can be obtained, if required, from your systematic location measurements at the scene.

Another common question is, "When it came to rest, how far was the car from the guard rail (or tree or other fixed object nearby)?" Again measure the shortest distance. Record it as a simple note like "Car to bridge rail = 0.6." If the car is touching the fixed object, do as you would for two cars in contact and record the distance as 0.0.

Length of Skidmarks

After accidents, perhaps the most common question about measurements is this: "How long were the skidmarks?" When spots locating the beginning and end of tiremarks have been plotted to scale, the length of the marks can be scaled from the map. With additional direct measurements, however, the question of tire mark length can be answered at once. The usual skidmark length measurement, from the first beginning of any mark to the farthest end of any mark is unsatisfactory. It does not tell whether only one tire left a mark or all four did. It does not make clear whether the measurement was from the beginning of a rear tire mark to the end of a front one or something else. To do it right, measure each mark separately. What is wanted from your observations and measurements is the distance that *each* wheel left a visible mark on the road. For a vehicle with four

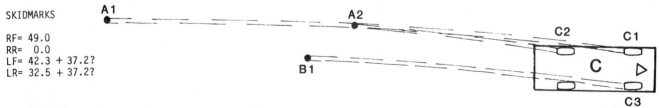

SKIDMARKS

RF= 49.0
RR= 0.0
LF= 42.3 + 37.2?
LR= 32.5 + 37.2?

Exhibit 86. Lengths of skidmarks also deserve additional measurements recorded in a separate list. Account for the mark of each wheel. If a wheel leaves no mark, record its length as 0.0.

Exhibit 87. (left) If a skidmark has an irregularity (peculiarity), such as a gap or crook, measure and record separately the length of mark before and after the peculiarity. Marks R and S have offsets to the right at the far end. Mark G is offset to the left. F has no offset.

SKIDMARKS
R1-R2 = 12.0; R2-R3 = 1.5
F1-F2 = 38.7
S1-S2 = 30.0, S2-S3 = 1.7
G1-G2 = 42.2, G2-G3 = 2.1

Exhibit 88. In your record, identify the mark by the same letter used to identify the mark on the field sketch. Measure separately lengths both before and after any peculiarity. Generally, spots to be located on a tire mark are numbered with number 1 at the beginning of the mark.

skidmarks, this is four distances. If some tire makes no mark, consider the length of that mark to be zero. Exhibit 86 is an example of skidmarks of different lengths made by tires on the same vehicle. A single tire mark definitely leads to the right front tire only. It measures 49.0 ft. Record this as "RF = 49.0". No mark leads to the right rear tire. Apparently it did not slide. With no visible mark, record the slide distance of the right rear tire as "RR = 0.0".

Thus, there is no problem with measurements for the right tires. The left tires, however, present a common difficulty. Separate marks lead to front and rear tires. It is clear that both wheels slid, but you cannot tell where either front or rear tire began to slide because there is only a single mark for both tires to begin with; the front and rear marks are exactly superimposed. By careful inspection, you must determine where the two marks definitely separate. Look for signs such as slight widening of the mark or definitely lighter marks at the edges. This is Spot A2 in Exhibit 86. You should have located this spot by coordinates or triangulation. Without any indication as to whether

the mark from Spot A1 to Spot A2 was from the front tire or the rear tire or both, the length measurement can be handled in several different ways. Only one way will be described here. Measure separately the distinct marks from Spot A2, where they separate, to the tires that made them. In Exhibit 86, this is 42.3 certain for the left front tiremark and 32.5 certain for the left rear. Then measure the distance from Spot A1 to Spot A2, where it is not possible to tell which tire made the mark. In Exhibit 86 this amounts to 37.2 ft. Show this extra distance as a possible but questionable addition to both front and rear definite tire marks. The notation then reads like this: "LF = 42.3 + 37.2?", and "LR = 32.5 + 37.2?". The question mark shows that you were not able to tell which tire made this mark. Remember that, at this stage, you are recording exactly what you see, tire marks. You do not need to determine whether they are skidmarks; you do not have to say whether the right rear wheel in this example did or did not do any braking.

Treat dual tires on a single bus or truck wheel as one. If one tire on the

wheel skids, the other also skids whether it leaves a mark or not. A big tractor with a semitrailer may have five axles and ten wheels (eight wheels with dual tires). Then you have to account for ten tire marks, one for each wheel. Several of these wheels may make no mark and so would measure 0.0. The 0.0 figure is your way of saying, "I looked for marks from all wheels, and on some I found nothing to measure." Somewhere on your field sketch or on your separate measurement sheet, record the tire mark measurements for each wheel as at the left in Exhibit 86.

It is important in examining and measuring tire marks to note peculiarities such as crooks (offsets) and gaps. *Gaps* are where a skidmark stops and begins again ten feet or more farther on. Do not mistake skips for gaps. *Skips* are brief light and dark stretches in skidmarks. You might note that there are skips, but you are not expected to measure and record the spacing of these light and dark areas. Genuine peculiarities, however, are spots to be located by coordinates or triangulation. In measuring length, treat skidmarks before and after peculiarities as

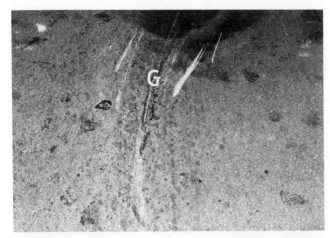

Exhibit 89. *A cluster of small scars on the roadway is measured to the middle of the group. These may then be described and measured separately.*

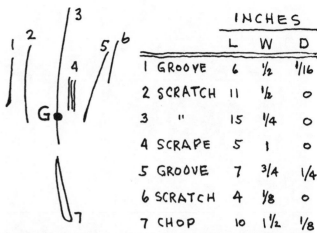

	INCHES		
	L	W	D
1 GROOVE	6	1/2	1/16
2 SCRATCH	11	1/2	0
3 "	15	1/4	0
4 SCRAPE	5	1	0
5 GROOVE	7	3/4	1/4
6 SCRATCH	4	1/8	0
7 CHOP	10	1 1/2	1/8

Exhibit 90. *A small sketch and separate listing of length, width and depth will give the desired information about the group of scars.*

separate marks. For example, Exhibit 87 is a picture of a tire mark with definite irregularities, (crooks). A listing of these marks before and after the crooks is needed. Such a listing in preparation for the measurements is shown in Exhibit 88. From this example, it is clear enough that the crooks are the position of tires when a collision took place. This means that skidmarks before and after collision are measured separately. In pedestrian accidents, there may be no visible irregularity in skidmarks at the collision point; separate before and after measurements are therefore impossible. The only tiremarks you need to measure the *length* of separately are locked-wheel *skidmarks*. These are usually quite straight before collision but have a crook or other irregularity at the collision point (Exhibit 87) and may continue thereafter as irregular curved tire marks. Measure separately the length of marks before and after the irregularity, although they are all parts of one friction mark. If these leave the pavement, measure separately the length before and after the edge of the pavement. Tire marks beginning at collision may be skidmarks (locked wheel) or scuffs (rotating wheel). The length of marks that begin at a collision area do not have to be specially measured, but where they begin, end, and cross, roadway edges etc. must be located.

If a long tiremark definitely curves more sharply as it progresses, if the mark is narrow to begin with and gets wider as it goes on, and if the marks from tires on the same side of the vehicle DIVERGE (get farther apart), the mark is probably not a skidmark, but a *yaw* mark. If it is not a skidmark, you do not need to measure its length. You should locate spots along the mark to show its curvature. The *length* of skidmarks and the *curvature* of yaw (sideslip or centrifugal) marks are needed for speed estimates.

Size of Scars

Locating the ends of long narrow scars (grooves, scratches, and scrapes) is sufficient to indicate their dimensions; but where a group of smaller scars has been located by a spot in the middle of the group, a professional investigator would make some record of the size and character of the scars in the group. This is easily done by a little sketch, usually somewhere on the field sketch sheet. An example will illustrate this. Exhibit 89 is a picture of a group of scars on the roadway and Exhibit 90 is a corresponding detailed record of measurements. Identify the group of marks by the letter assigned to it in the field sketch and the table of measurements. In the general table, the small scar or cluster of small scars is represented by a single

letter identifying the spot to be measured to, the center of the cluster or group. Then in the detailed sketch of this group, each individual mark, if more than one, is identified by a number: 1, 2, 3, etc. Then, in a little table like Exhibit 90, give length, width, and depth in that order. For scrapes and scratches, the depth is written as zero because the scratch does not go below the surface.

Sometimes, where a collision took place, there is a hodge-podge of marks on the road as in Exhibit 91. To locate all of these by measurements would usually take more time and perhaps more patience than you have available. Do not let such a situation dismay you. If there is, in this area, a clear gouge which shows where some strong metal vehicle part dug into the surface, locate each such spot as usual. Do the same for a group of gouges and scrapes such as those illustrated in Exhibit 89. If a tire mark continues into or starts from such an area, locate as much of it as you can in the usual way. If you see a clear short skidmark (collision scrub) locate that. Do not try to locate spots for many small smears, crisscross tire marks, miscellaneous small vehicle parts, or spatter areas and dribble paths which have been nearly obliterated by footprints or tire tracks. Such confused signs of what happened can ordinarily be handled better and always more

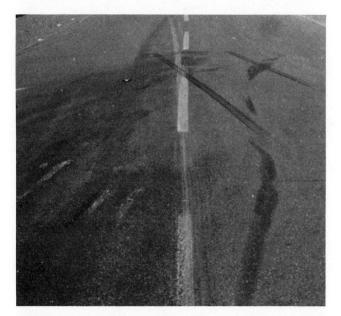

Exhibit 91. *It is almost impossible to sort out and locate all the details in a confusion or hodgepodge of marks on the roadway. Try to locate long marks which enter or leave this area. Photographs of such areas are very helpful.*

Exhibit 92. *Scars on poles, trees, bridge rails, etc. usually require two vertical measurements, one to the lower and one to the upper edge of the scar. This is especially important when the scars show that the vehicle making them had probably left the ground.*

quickly by photography than by the many measurements necessary.

Vertical Measurements

Vertical measurements are also sometimes needed at the scene of a serious traffic accident. If whatever needs measuring, for example a scar on a bridge rail, will remain as it is indefinitely, there is no special need to measure its height at the scene; someone can do that later if the information is needed. But if the situation will change soon, for example by repair of the bridge rail, do not delay in making the vertical measurements. Vertical measurements are of several kinds:

- Height above the roadway or ground of collision scars on poles, trees, guard rails, bridge rails, overpass pillars, and buildings
- Height of temporary view obstructions
- Temporary overhead clearance such as sagging wires, scaffolding, and construction cables
- Branches which obscure view of signals or traffic signs when the branches are soaked by rain or loaded with snow

- Distance a vehicle drops (or rises) without touching the ground when it takes off into the air
- Pavement edge drop-off or lip

Temporary View Obstructions

Permanent view obstructions, such as hill crests, embankments, buildings, and walls, do not need to be located at the time of the accident; they will remain long after the accident and can be measured later if necessary. But the height of temporary view obstructions must be measured soon after the accident because they may change. Temporary view obstructions are such things as parked vehicles, hedges, crops or other vegetation, and construction material or equipment. You need be concerned only with questionable obstacles to view. If the obstacle is only two or three feet above the roadway it would clearly not interfere with seeing, so no measurements are required. On the other hand, if the temporary object is so high that it would obviously interfere with seeing, locate one or more spots for the obstacle by the usual methods. Then measure its

height above the roadway. Record your height measurement on your field sketch near the spots locating the view obstruction. You do not have to decide at the time of the accident to what extent the view was actually obscured. With proper measurements, that can be done later for anyone who wants to have it done. You can make most of these measurements quickly and you can record them by a little note on the field sketch.

Heights of collision scars ordinarily call for two measurements: the distance from the ground to the lowest part of the scar and the distance to the highest part. That enables the height of the scar to be matched with bumpers, wheels, and other parts of vehicles. Height of scars are especially important when they are high enough to suggest that the vehicle left the ground before hitting the pole, tree, or other object as in Exhibit 92.

Dropoff

If you have any reason to believe that one or more wheels left the edge of the pavement, mark the pavement where each tire left the pavement and

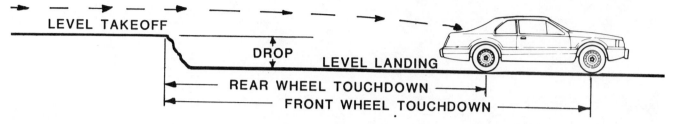

Exhibit 93. *If a vehicle goes off a level surface and drops only a short distance to another level surface, measuring the vertical fall is not difficult.*

where it returned as well as you can tell from careful observation. These are spots to which you measure by coordinates or triangulation. In addition, if the shoulder (berm) was not flush (level or even) with the pavement, measure the vertical drop (lip) if it is more than an inch as illustrated in Exhibit 94. The measurement is not difficult with a tape-rule. Record it as, for example, "Drop 6" on the field sketch near the spots where the tire left or returned to the paving. If the drop varies along the pavement edge, as it often does, measure it at several points. In connection with your measurements of dropoff, do *not* record any opinion that you or anyone else may have formed as to what effect this dropoff had on the vehicle leaving or returning to the paving. Such an opinion may be recorded or expressed elsewhere, but it has no place in the record of your observations and measurements.

Falls

Measuring the distance a vehicle falls when it takes off into the air may be quite simple or a bit complicated. An example of a simple situation is the fall when a vehicle takes off where a slab of pavement under construction ends and the vehicle drops to the unpaved subgrade. The spot where the vehicle took off is located by coordinates or triangulation. So is the mark made where it landed. The vertical distance is from the surface of the paving to the surface of the subgrade at the place of takeoff. Record it on the field sketch with a note, such as "Drop 16" (Exhibit 93). Measuring the vertical fall is more difficult

when the vehicle goes off the top of a bank into a deep ditch. You will usually have little difficulty determining where the takeoff was. Landing is not so simple. It is usually marked by scars in the bank or ground or tire marks on hard surfaces. In the case of tire marks, try to determine where front and rear wheels touched down and include these among spots to be located by the usual methods. If the landing scars or marks extend over some distance, as they often do, measure the vertical drop from takeoff separately to the beginning and end of the scars. Of course, the vehicle may not stop where it lands; it may slide, flip, or roll farther. Vertical measurements are needed only to the landing place. Some special equipment is needed to measure accurately a large or long vertical drop. A surveyor, who has special equipment, may have to help in some cases. The simplest equipment, which you can use yourself, is a chalk line and a line level (Exhibit 63) which are obtainable at most hardware stores. Stretch the line from takeoff to landing, holding the line on the ground at whichever end is higher. Hang the level on the line at about the midpoint from takeoff to landing. Stretch the line tight. Raise the other end of the line until the bubble is centered in the level and measure the distance from the line to the ground at the low end. Record this as the drop, usually on the field sketch. Exhibit 95 is a picture of where a car hit the far bank of a ditch after taking off into the air. Exhibit 96 is a pair of pictures of the same situation. They show how scars in the bank are

matched with vehicle damage to show just where the vehicle landed. If the fall is into water, and there are no scars, measure the drop to the water level.

Striations

Striations in tire marks are noted by skillful investigators and their angle to the mark is recorded if the striations are crosswise. Striations are parallel stripes or streaks. They may be as wide as tread ribs or as narrow as pebble scratches. Look at Exhibits 97 and 98. Striations show the direction of slippage of the tire on the pavement. Striations parallel to the mark, usually tire rib stripes show no side slipping. The mark is, therefore, a skidmark (Exhibit 97) or an acceleration scuff. Crosswise or oblique striations generally indicate yaw (sideslip) marks (Exhibit 98). Not all tire friction marks show striations; some are just smudges. If striations show sideslip, it is well to note your observations as to angle of stri-

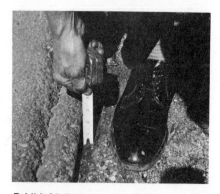

Exhibit 94. *If you have any reason to believe that any tire left the paving, look for dropoff (lip) at the place where the tire went off and where it came back on. If the difference in level is more than an inch, measure it and record the measurement in your field sketch.*

Exhibit 95. Be very careful to note exactly where a vehicle touched down after a fall. It may not be tiremarks. In this case, the car took off from the roadway level at the left and struck the bank across the ditch at the right. Then it fell back into the water where it came to rest. Here a cord with a line level is stretched across the ditch to measure vertical distance from takeoff level.

Exhibit 96. Match parts of the vehicle with imprints on touchdown. Measure the vertical and horizontal distances from takeoff point to the clearest sign of where the vehicle touched down. In these photos, white lines connect recognizable imprints on the bank with the parts of the vehicle which made them. In this case, the imprint of the front cross member of the frame was very clear. Its horizontal and vertical distance from takeoff was carefully measured to permit estimating how far the center of mass of the vehicle travelled horizontally and dropped vertically from takeoff to touch down and from that to estimate speed at takeoff.

Exhibit 97. *Striations may be as wide as tire ribs. Note whether striations are parallel to the tiremark as here or at an angle as in Exhibit* **98.**

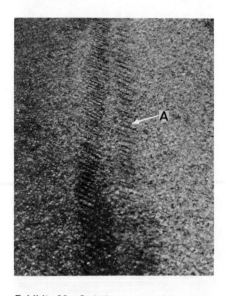

Exhibit 98. *Striations may be narrow scratches. If striations are not parallel to the tire mark, the wheel is rotating and the mark is, not a skidmark.*

ations on your field sketch to refresh your memory in case you should be questioned about this matter, or asked whether the mark was a skid-mark or a yaw mark. You can show striations on your field sketch by cross marks along the tire mark as in Exhibit 99. The angle of the cross marks shows approximately the angle of the striations to the path of the tire. If no striations are visible or if they are parallel to the path of the tire, show the marks by a simple line as skidmarks. The exact angle of striations to the tire path could be measured by a protractor or by other means, but such refinement is not expected in connection with measurements at the scene of an accident.

Photographs

Photography is very useful in connection with measurements. Photography at accident scenes is a whole special subject; it can only be mentioned here briefly to show how photography relates to measurements. Photographs are useful additions to measurements in a number of ways:

- They show shape and character of marks on the road better than you or anyone else can describe them in words.
- Photographs confirm your descriptions and observations.
- Photographs refresh your memory later about what you saw.
- It is often quicker and usually more accurate than sketching things you measure.

Do not get in the habit of taking pictures to avoid making measurements. You will have great difficulty trying to estimate distances from pictures only.

If someone is taking pictures at the scene of the accident, you may be able to suggest some which will be especially useful in connection with your measurements:

- Beginning, end, any peculiarities in tire marks.
- Groups or clusters of road surface scars.
- Where vertical measurements are made.
- Striations in yaw marks.
- Final positions of vehicles and bodies.
- The troublesome hodge-podges of marks mentioned earlier (Exhibit 91).

It is best to take photos of scars on the road and striations in tire marks straight down on them just as you would draw them. This shows dimensions and angles without distortion. You may have difficulty remembering exactly where a straight down picture was taken unless you do one or more of three things:

1. Put a mark on the surface that will show in the photo and tie the picture into the other measurements. This may be the same mark that you make to indicate a spot to be located by coordinates (Exhibit 101)
2. Make detailed notes which identify the picture and connect it with the place it was taken.
3. Take a second photo, not straight down, which shows the same area as the straight down picture, but also in-

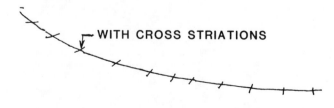

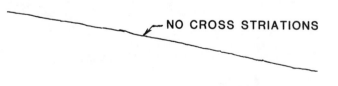

Exhibit 99. *On your field sketch, show the angle of striations, if any. A single line for a tire mark indicates that you did not notice any crosswise striations. Small cross marks on the line indicate the approximate angle of crosswise striations which you observed.*

Exhibit 100. *When a close-up photo is made to show details of a group of gouges or a tire scrub, as on the right, include this mark in another photo, as at the left, which shows distant objects to identify the location of the close-up view.*

cludes other things which will show what the picture represents and where it was taken (Exhibit 100)

Photos and measurements can be coordinated in a number of ways. One method is to mark on the road for each picture the position of the camera and the direction in which it was aimed. These camera positions are then located as spots in your measurements, numbering each one for reference purposes. This pro-

cedure slows up both measuring and photographing. It is usually done for special purposes. A much easier and still very useful plan is to arrange marks put on the pavement for measurements so that they will also help to identify and orient the photos in which they appear. This means that lettering on the paving must be bold and large. Letters and numbers need to be about five inches high. Spray-paint is much the best for this purpose. If you have only crayon, go

over each mark four or five times to make it really stand out. This is especially important where the pavement has a very rough surface. Another helpful refinement is to align all lettering on the pavement in the same compass direction so that all lettering that shows in photos will indicate directions in the pictures. For example, some investigators arrange to have all letters and numbers right side up when viewed from the nominal south direction.

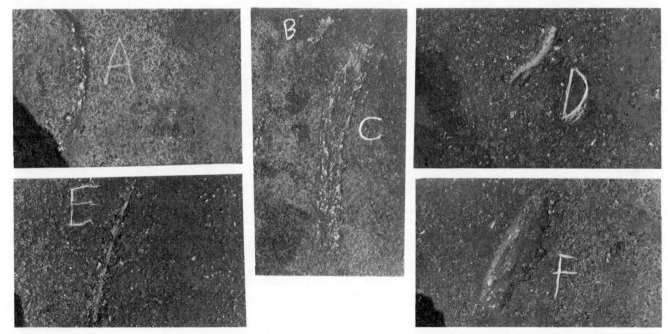

Exhibit 101. *Take photos straight down toward pavement marks to show details. Label each mark to correspond with your measurements to locate it. It is helpful to have the tops of all identifying letters in the same direction, for example, north.*

10. SOURCES

Contributors

This Topic was developed by the following persons:

J. Stannard Baker, a traffic engineering consultant specializing in accident investigation. He was Director of Research and Development at the Traffic Institute, Northwestern University from 1946 to 1971 and is a guest lecturer for the Traffic Institute.

Lynn B. Fricke, a traffic engineer specializing in accident investigation. He joined the Traffic Institute, Northwestern University in 1975 and became Director of the Accident Investigation Division in 1981.

Exhibits

Here is a list of individuals and organizations whose drawings, photographs, and other works appear as exhibits in Topic 828.

Baker, J. Stannard, Glencoe IL
Photos: 2, 8, 10, 13, 15, 31, 33, 34, 38, 39, 40, 41, 42, 61, 63, 64, 67, 68, 73, 91, 94, 100, 101
Diagrams: 6, 7, 11, 12, 19, 20, 21, 23, 24, 25, 26, 27, 28, 29, 36, 37, 43, 44, 45, 46, 47, 49, 52, 53, 54, 55, 56, 57, 58, 59, 60, 71, 72, 75, 77, 78, 79
Chart: 102
Tables: 48, 50, 74, 76, 80, 82, 83, 88, 90

Baker, Warren S., Corvallis OR
Photos: 35, 69, 70

Cusker, Thomas L., Lake Villa IL
Photo: 14

Fricke, Lynn B., Traffic Institute, Northwestern University, Evanston IL
Photos: 18, 95, 96

Keneipp, J.M., Barton-Aschman Associates, Evanston IL
Diagram: 22

Lawyer's Photo Service, St. Louis MO
Photo: 32

Merner, Milton, Deerfield IL
Photo: 3

Potter, Morris, Cedar Rapids IA
Photo: 1

Seyfried, Robert K. Traffic Institute, Evanston IL
Photo: 9

Shaffer, James L., Dubuque IA
Photos: 62, 92

Unknown
Photos: 5, 16, 17, 22, 51, 65, 66, 87, 89, 97, 98

York, Richard W., Hackettstown NJ
Photo: 4

PHOTOGRAMMETRY FOR TRAFFIC-ACCIDENT INVESTIGATION

Topic 830 of the *Traffic-Accident Investigation Manual*

by
J. Stannard Baker

NORTHWESTERN UNIVERSITY TRAFFIC INSTITUTE

PUBLICATION HISTORY
Topic 830

1964 *Simplified Photogrammetry for Traffic-Accident Investigation*
(Unpublished research report)

1972 *Perspective Template for Mapping Photographic Evidence*
Reprinted 1975

1977 *Perspective Grid for Photographic Mapping of Evidence* (PN 801)
Reprinted 1978, 1979, 1983

1985 *Photogrammetry for Traffic-Accident Investigation*

PHOTOGRAMMETRY FOR TRAFFIC-ACCIDENT INVESTIGATION

1. AFTER-ACCIDENT SITUATION MAPS

Use

Perhaps nothing can contribute more to an understanding of *how* a traffic accident occurred than an after-accident situation map. It is the foundation for most traffic-accident reconstruction because it brings together many essential facts in an easily understood display.

The map represents, to scale, things at the scene when the accident situation has settled down. Unimportant details are omitted.

Sources of Data

Information for the map usually comes from a number of sources:

- Verbal reports of police or other investigators about the accident location, road layout, marks on the road, and final positions of vehicles or pedestrians involved
- Field notes of measurements made to show where things were located at the scene
- Field notes of measurements of the road layout made at the site, usually some time after the accident
- Street and highway construction plans
- Published or measured dimensions of vehicles
- Photographs of the scene and the site.

Quality and Quantity of Data

Ideally, whoever draws the after-accident situation map has complete and accurate measurements at hand to begin with. Unfortunately this desirable arrangement is rarely realized. Sometimes no measurements whatever were made at the scene; often measurements which were made fail to locate important results of accidents. Such unfortunate deficiencies usually occur because investigators lacked knowledge, skill, equipment, time, or motivation.

Whatever the cause, shortage of original data handicaps the map maker. At best he can go to the site or some other source and get at least some of the needed data; at worst, he is obliged to estimate or guess.

In this effort to produce an evidence map, photographs are a valuable source of reliable data. They even record information not noticed by whoever made the photos or had them made. Sometimes photos are the only source of data for an after-accident situation map.

Purpose of this Topic

This topic is intended to explain how photographs can be used to make up for lack of suitable measurements at traffic accident scenes, to supplement inadequate measurements, and in some cases, substitute for measurements.

2. PHOTOGRAMMETRY

Definition

Photogrammetry is the use of photographs in making maps.[3]

It is employed in a variety of ways. On one hand it may simply supplement measurements, for example in drawing the outline of a building; on the other hand, photogrammetry may be the only source of data, for example in mapping the surface of the moon.

Principles

The common idea of photogrammetry is aerial mapping. A photo is taken straight down from an aircraft. The resulting orthogonal (perpendicular) view is essentially a map (Exhibit 1). It can be reduced to an ordinary map by tracing significant details, such as edges of roadways, fences, fields, and building outlines, and then adding identifying names of landscape features such as roads and rivers.

To use a ground-level (low angle) photo for mapping[4] requires adjustment for the direction of view (camera aim). The ordinary photo taken at eye height shows perspective: a man near the camera stands much taller in the picture than a man 200 ft. away. At a mile away, the man is just a dot. In a map, the view is straight down at right angles to the mapped surface; it shows all parts to the same horizontal scale. In perspective, near objects are represented at a different scale than far objects.

To use an ordinary photo for mapping requires changing a perspective view to an orthogonal view. This is not difficult if precision is unimportant. For greatest accuracy, very refined methods are needed. The translation can be made graphically by drawing or mathematically by calculation. Either method depends on the detail and sharpness of the photos used.

Accuracy

In making photos intended for photogrammetry, give special attention to picture quality viewpoint and camera aim. That will make their use simpler and results more precise. But if ordinary snapshots must be used because proper measurements are lacking, photogrammetry may be troublesome.

3. SIMPLE DRAWINGS

Perhaps the most common form of making traffic-accident maps from photos is simple drawing. Even without an understanding of the principles of perspective you can examine a photo and draw a map that "looks about right," just as you might make a field sketch if you were actually at the scene. (Topic 828) Architects and artists, by training and experience, find drawing maps from photos easier than policemen and attorneys do.

Whoever does such primitive photogrammetry must have a good notion to begin with of the actual dimensions of things shown in the picture. Commonly the width of roadways and dimensions of vehicles have been measured or otherwise may be known, at least approximately. It is naturally desirable, and usually possible to map the roadways from measurements actually made at the site. Then only things like positions of vehicles and marks on the road have to be added from photographs.

Without specifics of road configurations, perspective in ground-level photographs may be misleading. Photos commonly make curves appear sharper than a map does. Angles are especially difficult to judge in perspective. Consider, for example, the angle between Grove St. and Lake St. in Exhibit 2. From the photo, what would you estimate the angle between Grove and Lake to be? How does your estimate compare with the angle

Exhibit 1. A vertical aerial photo is a map of the area but it rarely depicts an after-accident situation.

Exhibit 2. *In low level pictures, it is difficult to judge distances and angles, for example, the angle between the two roadways being measured here.*

in a map of the same location drawn from actual measurements (Exhibit 3).

Fortunately, one is usually able to measure the actual road layout at the site, sometimes years later. Then the main problem is locating such things as vehicle positions and marks on the road which have long since disappeared. If these things show in photos made at the time, you may be able to locate them on a map of the location which you drew from measurements made long after the accident. In doing this you will find it useful to show in your location map, things like pavement joints and cracks, lane stripes, drain inlets and manhole covers, that show in available at-scene photos.

Details

On the location map, however produced, you must fill in details. You may find it helpful to cut from stiff paper patterns of vehicles to the map scale. Modify the outlines of these patterns to represent crash damage and add wheel positions.

Move the pattern about on the map so that positions correspond to what the photos show. Bodies of injured can be located in the same way. If there are some actual measurements, for example the distance between final positions of two cars, you must adjust your map to correspond to these.

In this procedure make sure that the map looks right when compared to the photograph. If it does not, correct it.

A good way to make this comparison is to set your map on a table near the edge with the nearest things shown in the picture closest to you. Then view your map from about the same low angle that the camera height produced when the picture was taken. If you notice differences, move things around to get greater similarity.

If you have two or more photos of the same things from different directions, compare your map with each of these. If necessary, make adjustments in the map.

Labelling

Before putting the map aside, be sure to add usual identifying data:
1. Names of roadways
2. City or county in which the mapped area is located
3. Date and time of the situation represented
4. Nominal (approximate) direction of north
5. Scale used in drawing things actually measured
6. Distinguishing description of each vehicle or body located
7. Accident number, if known
8. Your name as the map maker
9. Date on which you completed the map.

If all or part of the map has been drawn from photos, it is a good idea to explain this in a note on the map.

Topics 832 and 834 give more suggestions for measuring and map drawing.

Exhibits 4 and 5 are photos from which a map was drawn. Exhibit 6 is a map drawn without measurements from these photos. Light dashed lines on the map show the edges of what was actually visible in the two pictures. These lines are for comparison purposes and should not appear on the finished map.

4. NATURAL PERSPECTIVE GRIDS

There is another, more accurate, method which can be used under

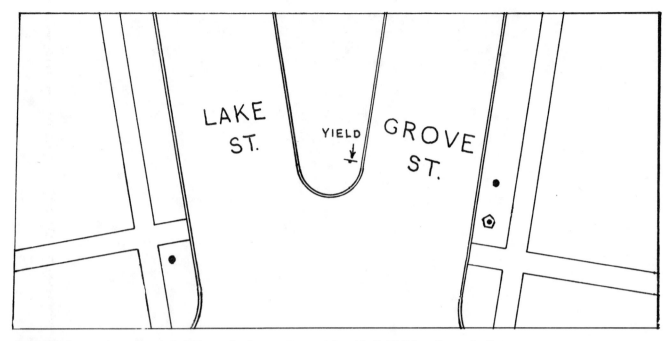

Exhibit 3. *A map shows the angle between the two roadways pictured in Exhibit 2 as they actually are.*

some circumstances when photos must make up for inadequate measurements. It makes use of any natural perspective grid.

A perspective grid is a system of crisscross straight lines which can be drawn in perspective on a photograph and without perspective in a corresponding map area. The grid location of a point in the picture permits the point to be located in the corresponding map grid position.

To use this method, three requirements must be met:

1. The photo must picture an area of roadway which can be represented on the map as a parallelogram (four-sided plane figure with opposite sides parallel).
2. The lengths of adjacent sides of the parallelograms must be known, usually by actual measurement at the site. One angle or diagonal of the parallelogram must also be known.

3. The surface represented by the parallelogram must be reasonably flat but not necessarily level.

In traffic-accident work, the roadway areas selected are nearly always defined by traffic lanes, pavement joints, and the beginning and end of interrupted lane stripes. These must be in essentially straight sections of road and the pictures must have been taken looking nearly parallel to the roadway, as recommended in Topic

Exhibit 4. *One of several photos of an accident scene for which no measurements were made.*

Exhibit 5. *Another of the photos of the same scene. From these pictures a map of the scene had to be drawn.*

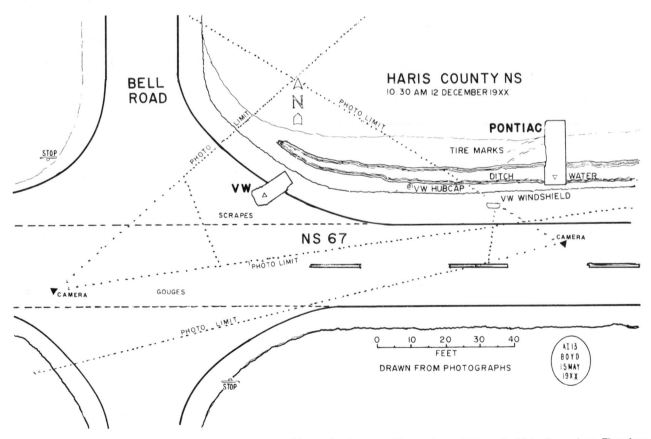

Exhibit 6. *The dimensions for the resulting map were reasonably good estimates of the roadway widths and vehicle dimensions. Therefore, the map is only approximately to scale.*

836. Preferably dimensions of selected areas have been or can be actually measured at the site of the accident. Otherwise you can assume representative values: standard lane widths are 12 ft on main rural roads and standard center lines have 10-ft stripes with 30-ft gaps between them.

Principle

The idea back of perspective grids is simple. A point, for example the beginning of a skidmark, shown in the photo is to be located on the map. It is identified by the grid area in which it is located in the picture. Then it is put in the corresponding grid location on the map. Grids in the photo are in perspective. The grid areas on the map are parallelograms.

A line on the photo is represented on the map by a number of points along that line. If the line is straight, only the ends need to be located because a straight line in photo perspective is always a straight line on the map.

Establishing Grids

An example will show how the photo grid and the map grid are laid out and how points are located on the map.

Exhibit 7 is part of a photo showing four tire marks made on a bridge by a motor vehicle. The marks end where a crash took place. Only the length of the marks was measured: 106.4 ft. To estimate speed, the path of the vehicle making the marks must be carefully plotted. Parts of these tire marks were also shown in two additional photos.

Width of roadway (24 ft) and spacing of pavement joints (30 ft) were obtained from a local investigator by telephone. Grid boundaries for both photo and map are the two edges of the roadway and three pavement joints. In the map, roadway edges and pavement joints are parallel; in the photo, roadway edges definitely converge; pavement joints are almost parallel.

A transparent sheet over an en-

largement of the required part of the photo lets you draw the photo grid without harm to the picture (Exhibit 7).

Pavement joints and tire marks are faint in the photo. Therefore some of them have been enhanced (accentuated) on the transparent overlay. On both photo grid (Exhibit 7) and map grid (Exhibit 8) corresponding points are identified by letters A, B, C, etc. Lines are designated by points they connect, AB, CD, etc. Areas are identified by letters at their corners, ABCD, EFGH, etc.

Sides of the map grid are curbs extending from A to C and from B to D in Exhibits 7 and 8. The ends are the pavement joints AB and CD also in Exhibit 7. This area is divided into two equal rectangles by another pavement joint, EF.

The perspective grid in the photo is identified by the same letters where pavement joints meet curbs. Any straight line in the photo appears as a straight line on the map. But in the

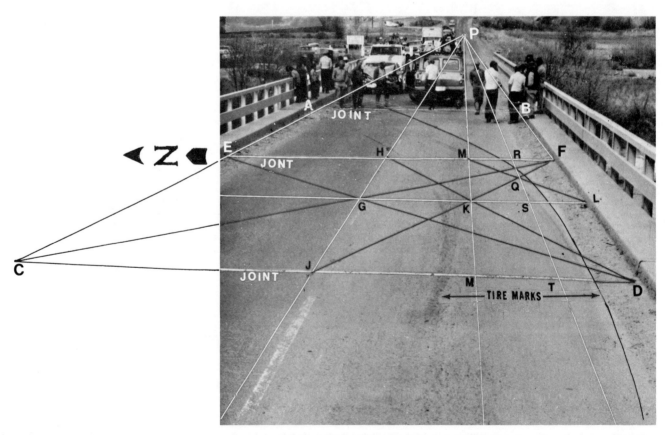

Exhibit 7. A photo with an excellent natural perspective grid: roadway width and pavement joint spacing. Construction of grid is shown here.

photo, due to perspective, sides of the grid area are not parallel as in the map. The area in the photo is a trapezoid rather than a parallelogram.

To form corresponding grids in the photo and map, the grid areas are subdivided into smaller areas. By drawing diagonals CF and DE on both map and photo, corresponding areas in each grid are divided into four triangular areas. Where these lines cross at G is the center of the grid area.

To establish the center line of the road on the map (Exhibit 8) is easy: draw a line through G parallel to the curb lines CE and DF.

Establishing the center line in the photo is different. Extend the curb lines CA and DB to where they meet. This is the vanishing point, P. A straight line from P through the midpoint G, (Exhibit 7) represents the center line of the road in the photo. (The painted center line is not in the exact middle of the roadway.) The center line crosses pavement joint EF at H and Joint CD at J.

To further subdivide grid areas draw, on both photo and map, diagonals FJ and HD. These cross at K. On the photo, draw a line through the vanishing point, P and the crossing at K. It crosses joint EF at M and joint CD at N. On the map, draw a line through the crossing K and parallel to the curb DF. It also crosses joint EF at M and joint CD at N.

Extend GK to the curb DF in both map and photo. Identify the place where GK extended meets the curb, DF, by the letter L. Identify the crossing of ML and KF by Q. For still smaller grid areas draw a line on the photo through vanishing point P and the crossing Q. On the map draw a line through Q parallel to the curb DF.

In both grids, identify the places where the new line, PQ, crosses old ones as follows: R for the crossing of joint EF; S where it crosses GL and T for the crossing with CD.

This series of steps can be repeated to obtain smaller and smaller grid divisions. For present purposes, to plot part of the south tire mark in Exhibit 7, the subdivision of the CEFD grid area is enough.

Plotting Points

Now proceed to plot points on the southern tire mark in the MFND area in the map grid. Start with the point where the south tire mark crosses pavement joint EF.

Note that in the photo, this tire mark crosses the joint about a third of the way from R to M. On the map

mark a spot on joint EF about a third of the way from R toward M.

Next the tire mark crosses GF and RS just about where they cross. Mark that spot on the map.

The mark crosses KF and ML a little south of Q. Mark those points on the map. The mark crosses GL a bit more than a third of the way from S to L. The tire mark crosses the middle of TD. That is as close as it gets to the south edge of the roadway, FD.

You now have six points on the southern tire mark located. Draw a smooth curve through these six points and you have part of the southern tire mark on your map.

Follow the same procedure in other grid areas through which this and other tire marks pass. The resulting four tire marks are shown in exhibit 9. Other photographs in addition to Exhibit 7 are used to establish the exact final position of vehicles involved.

The process described may be a bit tedious but it is not really difficult. The results are often gratifying.

Checking and Finishing

Be sure that the plotted tire marks correspond in detail to the photograph. For example, note that near joint CD, the two right tire marks are superimposed and are closest to the curb there. Before that they are slightly farther from the curb. Let your map drawing reflect this. It means that the vehicle was headed slightly toward the curb up to joint CD but then steered away from it.

To the scale of the map from the beginning of the tire marks to where they end in the photo west of CD, measures about 71 feet. But remember that investigators reported the length of the marks as 106.4 ft. Therefore, their beginning does not show in the photo. That would not be surprising. To show this on the map, the clear marks, the overlapping south ones, can be extended backward to the 106-ft distance, gradually angling away from the curb. Show this extension as a light dashed line to

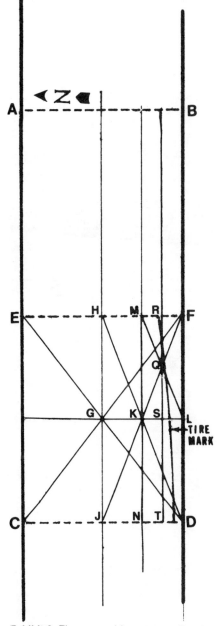

Exhibit 8. The map grid corresponding to the photo grid in Exhibit 7.

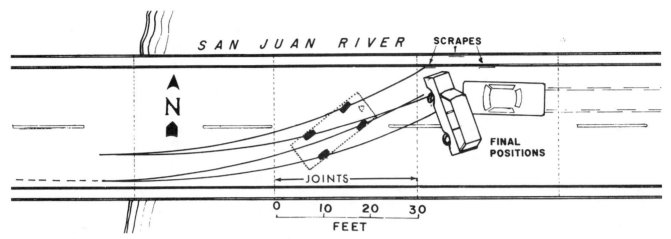

Exhibit 9. *Part of the completed after-accident situation map drawn without at-scene measurements by taking advantage of a natural perspective grid.*

Exhibit 10. *Another natural perspective grid used where no at-scene measurements were made for a fatal accident. The grid was established by measuring lane widths and lane line spacing. In this case the grid units were parallelograms.*

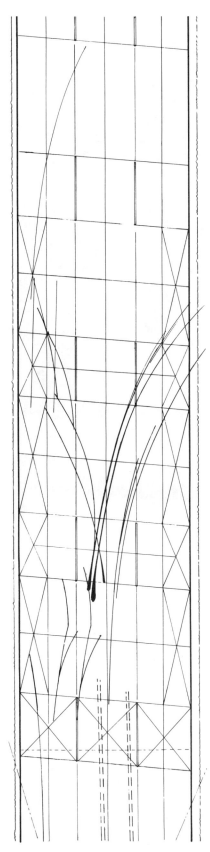

Exhibit 11. *The fully developed map grid corresponding to the photo grid in Exhibit 10. No daylight photos showed final positions of vehicles.*

indicate that it is less well founded (Exhibit 9).

Another verification is possible. On a clear acetate sheet, or on very transparent tracing paper, draw to your map scale a rectangle representing the wheel base of the vehicle making the tire marks. The width of the rectangle corresponds to the vehicle's track (distance between right and left wheels); the length of the rectangle corresponds to the vehicle wheelbase (distance between front and rear axles). Place this on your map with a corner, representing a wheel position, on each tire mark. At any place, the wheel corners should fall on the corresponding marks. If not, make adjustments in your map. Such an outline is shown in Exhibit 9.

Exhibit 10 is an example of a photograph of a more extensive and complicated set of tire marks at the site of an accident. A perspective grid has been drawn on it to produce the map shown in Exhibit 11. No measurements of the tire marks were made at the scene. Measurements of lane width and striping were made later.

5. SQUARE PORTABLE GRID

There are three circumstances un-der which details of results of an accident are unlikely to be located by measurement:

1. Marks on the road are so intricate that locating them would require an inordinate number of measurements. (Exhibit 12)
2. Traffic is so fast and heavy or view is so obscured that proper measuring would be risky.
3. The investigator must work alone without proper equipment.

Investigators who anticipate such difficulties are grateful if a location affords a natural perspective grid, so that distances can be derived from their photographs. But because good natural grids are so seldom available when needed, some investigators and photographers carry a portable perspective grid with them to use when circumstances make at-scene measuring difficult.

The portable grid is simply a heavy cardboard rectangle which can be placed on the road or other flat surface and included (Exhibit 13) in the foreground of certain pictures.

With this, no time is wasted making measurements which will probably never be required. If the measurements are ever needed they can be had from a photo with the grid in it.

Exhibit 12. *A cluster of tire marks which would take many measurements to measure properly for a map. This is a situation where a portable perspective grid would be useful.*

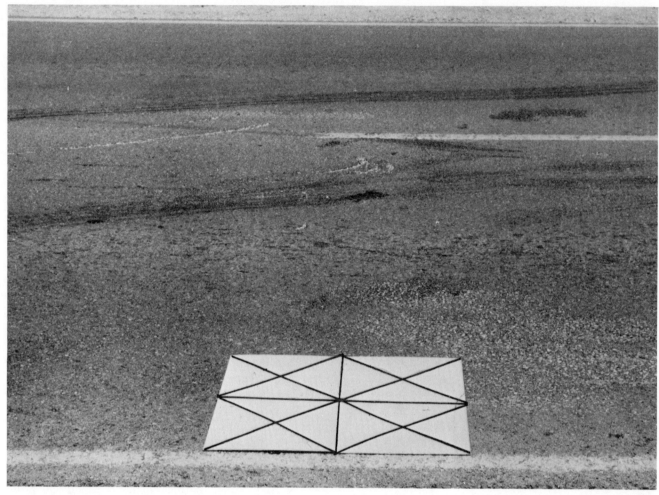

Exhibit 13. *A perspective grid placed so that it is square with the roadway edge and centered in the photo. It is at the edge of the roadway where traffic interference is minimum.*

Construction

The rectangle on the surface can be almost any sheet of paper or cardboard, letter size or larger. But this kind of photo mapping will be easier and more accurate if the perspective grid is prepared in advance. Making one is not difficult.

A *two-foot square* is the most useful size and shape (Exhibit 13). For outside uses, it must be heavy enough not to blow away. For convenience in carrying and storing, it can be made to fold into a one-foot square as in Exhibit 14. Exhibit 15 is a drawing of a perspective grid made from four white one-foot squares of artists (Crescent) illustration board, 1/8 in. thick. It is hinged with white, self-sticking, cloth tape (Mystic) across two inline joints on the front and

one other on the back so as to fold with the face in to keep it clean. Diagonals and edges are marked with a waterproof felt-tip marker (Sanfords). To protect them, edges can be bound with plastic electrician's tape. Cost for materials is less than two dollars.

You can put the perspective grid anywhere on the surface in the picture. But drawing the map is easier if one edge of it is parallel to and near the lower edge of the picture as in Exhibit 13. It is also helpful if some edge of the grid is parallel to a line on the surface such as a road edge or lane line.

Drawing the Map

The procedure for making a map

from a portable perspective grid photo is not difficult:

1. With the grid rectangle as a base, draw fine lines on the photo to represent one- or two-foot squares.
2. Prepare a sheet for the map. On it draw squares to the proper scale, one square representing the grid.
3. One grid square at a time, draw, in each square on the map, what appears in the corresponding "square" in the photo.

Locate vanishing points. Start with an enlargement of the photo. Make it 8- by 10-in. or larger. Fasten it down on a much larger sheet of paper so that lines can be drawn which run off the photo. The rectangle in Exhibit 16 represents such a photo. In it corners

Exhibit 14. A two-foot square grid can be cut and hinged for easy carrying.

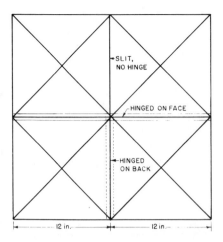

Exhibit 15. Design for a perspective grid.

of the perspective grid are marked **A**, **B**, **C**, and **D**. In the diagram, two marks on the surface to be mapped are numbered. No. 1 might be a lane-line stripe and No. 2 a curved tire mark on the roadway left by an accident.

In the photo, the right and left edges of the perspective grid slant toward each other as shown in Exhibit 16. These are represented by edges **AC** and **BD** in the diagram. Draw extensions of these until they meet, which will usually be off the photo as is the case in Exhibit 16. Point **X**, where the extended sides of the grid meet, is the vanishing point of the perspective. If the surface and camera are level,

Point **X** will be at the horizon in the picture. Extend diagonals of the perspective grid in both directions in the same way. They meet at two points, **Y** and **Z** in Exhibit 16.

Vanishing points **X**, **Y** and **Z** should be in a straight line, the vanishing line. If not, locate them again more carefully. If necessary, adjust them — as little as possible — so that they are in a straight line.

Line **XC** and **XD** are the right and left edges of a series of "squares" on the surface shown in the picture. They extend from the grid toward the vanishing point.

Draw perspective grid on photo.
Extend the near and far edges of the

grid in the picture to and beyond the left and right edges of the photo like the line drawn through **AB** and the one through **CD** in Exhibit 17. These lines will be the near and far edges of a row of 2-ft "squares" on the surface in the picture with the grid in the middle.

Next draw a straight line from **Y** through **B** and extend it until it crosses the line through **CD** at **F**. Do the same from **Z** through **A** to **E**. Then draw **XE** and **XF** to give the edges of two more rows of "squares" extending toward the vanishing line. You now have three 2-ft. "squares", including the grid, shown on the photo surface.

From **G** (where **YA** crosses **XE**), draw a straight line clear across the picture through **H** (where **ZB** crosses **XF**). You now have outlines of six 2-ft "squares," including the grid, on the surface in the picture.

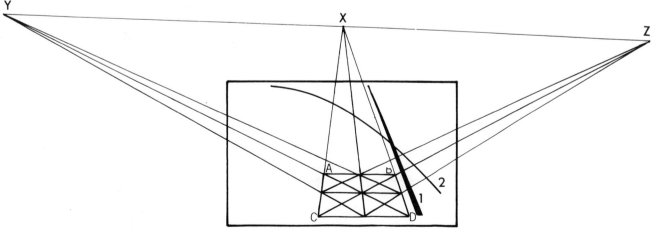

Exhibit 16. Perspective grid (A, B, C, and D) in a picture of two lines (1 and 2). Vanishing points (X, Y, and Z) are located.

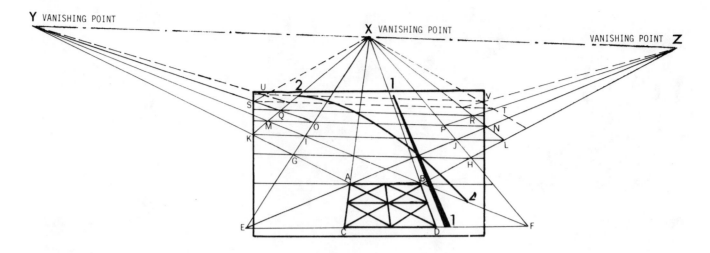

Exhibit 17. *Perspective grid construction for "squares" on the photo with the grid (A, B, C, D).*

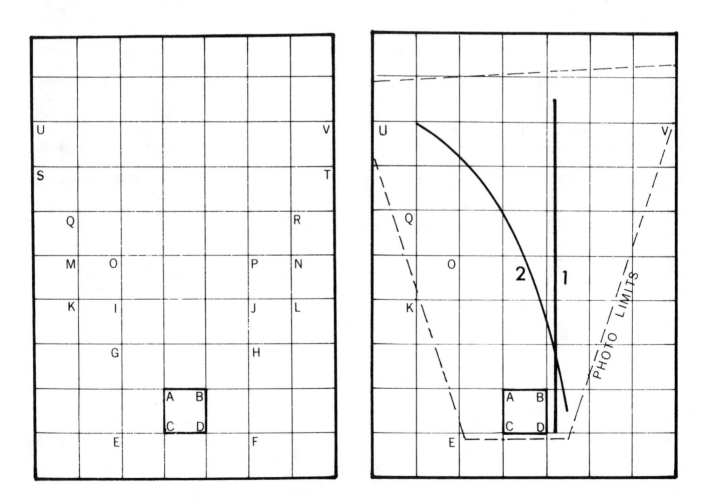

Exhibit 18. *Orthogonal grid to scale prepared for drawing map. Letters correspond to those identifying points in Exhibit 17.*

Exhibit 19. *Marks transferred from perspective grid on photo to orthogonal grid on map.*

Exhibit 20. A legal-size (8½- by 13-in.) pad photographed on the roadway as a substitute for a square perspective grid.

To draw in more distant "squares", continue the process. Draw a line from **I** (where **YB** crosses **XE**) across the picture through **J** (where **ZA** crosses **XF**). This results in outlines for three more "squares". Then draw a line from **X** to **K** (where **YA** crosses **IJ**) and another from **X** to **L** (where **ZB** crosses **IJ**). Then draw across the photo through **M** (where **YB** crosses **XK**) and **N** (where **ZA** crosses **XL**) to add another row of "squares".

To outline the next row of "squares", draw a line from **Y** to **O** (where **XE** crosses **MN**) and a similar line on the opposite side from **Z** to **P** (where **XF** crosses **MN**). Then draw another straight line clear across the photo through **Q** (where **YO** crosses **XK**) and through **R** (where **ZP** crosses

XN). Repeat this process until "squares" on the surface shown in the picture cover all of the marks which you wish to show on the map. In Exhibit 17, these additional needed lines are shown dashed.

Prepare orthogonal (right angle) map grid. To transfer the location of objects on the surface in the photo to the map, draw 2-ft. squares lightly on the map paper to map scale to represent those on the photo. Mark one of these squares to represent the grid as in Exhibit 18. You may want to number the "squares" or lines on the photo and put the same numbers on corresponding squares on the map so as to locate corresponding positions quickly. You are now ready to transfer locations.

Transfer points. In Exhibit 17 locate the far end of curved Line 2. It is where line **UV** crosses **KQX**. Then on the map grid as in Exhibit 18, mark the corresponding spot as in Exhibit 19 and mark that point on the map (Exhibit 19). Then find where Line 2 crosses **EOX** in Exhibit 19. The next line that line 2 crosses is **ST** between **EOX** and **CAX**. Mark this place. Continue marking all lines where line 2 crosses them. If greater accuracy is needed, draw diagonals in squares and from the center where they cross draw lines to divide the square into four smaller squares. After enough points on the line have been located, connect the points with a smooth curve to show the line on the map. Any straight line on the

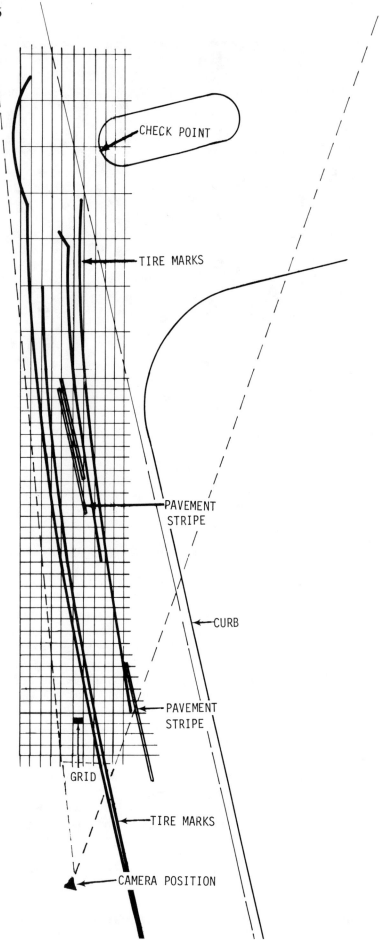

CHECK POINT

TIRE MARKS

PAVEMENT
STRIPE

CURB

PAVEMENT
STRIPE

GRID

TIRE MARKS

CAMERA POSITION

photo will be a straight line on the map. Therefore, only the two ends of a straight line need to be located. Connect them on the map. This is illustrated by straight Line 1 in Exhibits 16 and 19. When finished, erase the light square construction lines on the map or trace the map on tracing paper.

Picture limits on map. Sometimes it is useful to indicate on the map limits of the area shown in the photo. Locate the edges of the photo on the map like any other straight lines as in Exhibit 19.

Substitutes for Square Perspective Grid

Any rectangular sheet will do if a special grid is not available. Exhibit 20 shows a picture made by a photographer who tossed a legal size pad of paper on the pavement to show scale. From this 8½-by 13-in. area, a perspective grid was drawn on an acetate sheet over the photo. From that the map in Exhibit 21 was derived. Accuracy was proved by comparing distances between tire marks on the map with known distances between wheels on the car. Speed to yaw was calculated from the radius of the car's path worked out from the mapped tire marks. Of course the rectangles composing the perspective grid on the map are not "squares" in this case, but oblongs. The unusually great distance to which the tire marks extended made extremely careful drawing important.

Special Problems

Composites. If a single photo will not cover all of the area to be mapped, two or more overlapping photos can be made. Each photo must cover some of the surface area shown in one of the other photos including at least two identifiable points by which to match the pair. The perspective grid is relocated for each photo made. The map is made to the same scale for each photo, preferably on tracing paper to make matching pairs easier. Then the maps are combined by superimposing points that are common to each pair. Three pictures for such a composite or mosaic procedure are illustrated for a crime scene in Exhibits 22, 24, and 26 . The three partial maps drawn from these photos with perspective grids are Exhibits 23, 25, and 27. Exhibit 28 is the completed map without the grid showing.

Protecting the photo. Sometimes it is not desirable or may not be permissible to draw lines on a photo for mapping purposes. Then one of two things can be done.

The photo can be covered by an acetate sheet or slipped into a transparent sheath or envelope and the perspective grid drawn on that. Be sure to fasten the photo and the transparent sheet together so that they will not change positions. As a precaution, mark the corners of the photo on the transparent sheet so that exact registration can easily be reestablished. Exhibit 20 was made with a transparent sheet to avoid any markings on the only available photo.

The other method uses narrow (1/64-in.) drafting tapes with pressure sensitive adhesive for the lines. These can be removed and repositioned easily. They can also be stripped from the photo completely leaving it unmarked. Exhibit 22 shows perspective grid lines made with tapes.

Accuracy

If carefully done, maps made from perspective grid photos are adequate for all ordinary purposes. You can test this if you like. When the photo is made, actually measure the distance between two points. Then scale the distance between the corresponding points on the map and compare the actual with the scaled measurements. For example, if the length of Line 1 in Exhibit 16 measured at the scene was 15 feet. Scaled from the drawing it comes out 15.3 ft. This is a differ-

ence of 0.3 ft in 15. The error is then 0.3/15 or 0.02, that is, 2 percent. If a perspective grid map is to be used for court work, it is a good idea to take at least one actual measurement to test accuracy.

Generally anything 10 squares away from the grid location is difficult to locate precisely. The "squares" on the photo are very small at that point.

Beware of uneven surfaces. If the surface is not flat, errors will be introduced. Most floors and road surfaces are flat enough. The surfaces may slant up, down or sidewise and still be flat. Avoid large areas on roads with high crowns and curves with high superelevation. On these, a 10-foot square area may be flat enough, but not 30-foot square. Of course objects down in ditches or up on banks or even sidewalks cannot be mapped with a perspective grid.

If the surface is not quite flat errors can be reduced by making the picture from as high as possible looking down on the grid and the surface it is on.

Kind of camera unimportant. The perspective grid map is not noticeably affected by the kind of camera, or focal length of lens. This is easily demonstrated by using two or more kinds of equipment to take perspective grid pictures of the same scene and comparing maps made by each. Many lenses reproduce straight lines near edges of the picture as slightly bowed. In these lenses straightness is sacrificed for lens speed. Theoretically they introduce some distortion in the resulting map, but in practice it is so small that you cannot detect it in the finished map.

6. GRID REFINEMENTS

Greater Precision

The portable grid process is difficult when spots to be located are remote, the grid is small or the photograph is not sharp enough. Exhibit 21 is about as far as one can go even by checking with measured curbs or road

markings and comparing with wheel base dimensions of vehicles which made tire marks.

To increase precision, a number of things can be done:
1. Use a bigger grid, for example, a four-foot grid rather than a two-foot one.
2. Use a larger photo negative, for example 4- by 5-in. rather than ordinary 35-mm film.
3. Use a tripod.
4. Take the picture from higher up, for example straight down from a helicopter overhead rather than from ground eye level.
5. Position the grid and camera more precisely.
6. Make the photo grid on a greater enlargement, for example 16- by 20-in. rather than 8- by 10-in.

All of these take more time and care and more elaborate equipment.

Short Method

Positioning the grid and camera more accurately is the easiest way to get a little more refined results. Mark a line straight across the roadway to show in the photo as a base for the grid. Place the near edge of the grid precisely on this base line. Aim the camera so that the lower edge of the picture is close to and exactly parallel to this base line. In the picture have the grid centered exactly between the right and left edges of the camera finder (Exhibit 13). Such care warrants the use of a tripod.

These precautions make laying out the photo grid easier and quicker.

A single vanishing point, **X** in Exhibits 22 and 29 is used. It is located where extensions of the sides of the grid, **AC** and **BD**, intersect.

Extend the near edge of the grid, **CD**, to the left a distance, **CE**, equal to **CD**. Also extend **CD** to the right the same distance to locate the point **F**.

Connect **E** and **F** to the vanishing point, **X**. Extend the far edge of the grid right and left as far as necessary. You now have a row of three perspec-

Exhibit 22. *A single photo will often include only part of the area to be covered.*

Exhibit 24. *A second photo will include another area but must also cover some included in the first.*

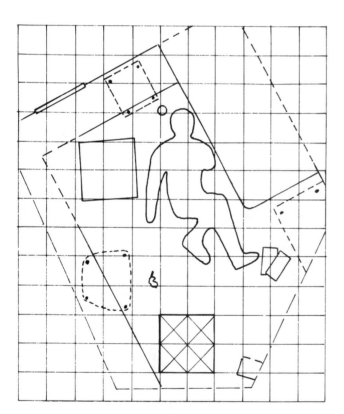

Exhibit 23. *A square perspective grid in the photo permits mapping the area shown on the flat surface pictured.*

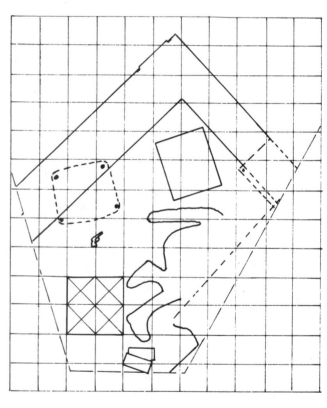

Exhibit 25. *The second photo also includes a square perspective grid but not in the same position.*

tive "squares" across the bottom of the photograph.

Draw a straight line from **D** through **A** to its intersection with line **EX** at **G**. Locate **H** on the line **FX** in the same way. Connect **G** and **H** with a straight line. You now have two rows of three perspective "squares."

Draw a straight line from **E** through **A** to where it intersects **FX** at **J**. This line should pass through the intersection of **DX** and **GH**. Locate **I** on the line **EX** in the same way. Connect **I** and **J** with a straight line. You now have three rows of three perspective "squares."

From the point where **AB** intersects **FX** draw a straight line through the point where **IJ** intersects **CX**. This line intersects **EX** at **O**. Locate **P** on line **FX** in the same way. Connect **O** and **P** with a straight line. You now have four rows of three perspective "squares."

Exhibit 26. A third and even more photos may be needed to cover the whole scene. Each includes the grid.

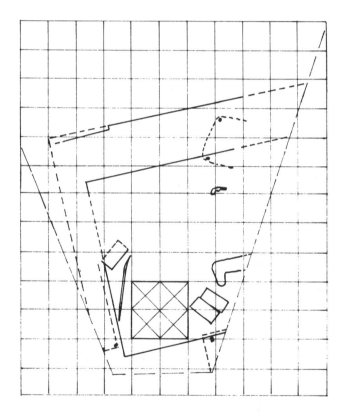

Exhibit 27. The body location is shown outlined with chalk, the body itself having been removed before the photograph was made.

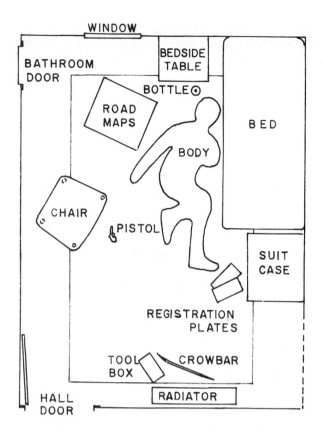

Exhibit 28. Make the final map by superimposing the overlapping areas of several maps drawn from perspective grids. Do not superimpose the grids in the partial maps; they have been moved for each picture. Align the separate maps by superimposing points which appear in two or more of the partial maps.

OVERLAPPING GRIDS

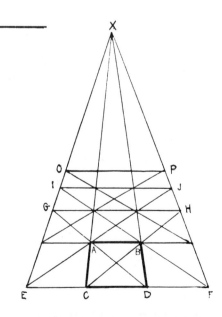

Exhibit 29. Simplified perspective grid extensions using a single vanishing point.

The same process may be continued until all points in the photograph which are to be located on the map are included in grid "squares" in the photograph.

Circular Disks

Instead of one square grid[7] to show scale, three circular disks can be used. Mark the center of each to show in the photo. The diameters of the disks is equal to a side of a square grid, usually 2 ft (50 cm).

No special care is needed in placing the three disks, but, of course, they must all be on the same *flat* surface. One is placed in the foreground of the picture, as a square grid would be. The other two are placed some distance, possibly 10 ft (3 m) beyond the first (Exhibit 30). No measurements are required to locate any of the disks. All three must appear in the photo, but precise camera location and aim is not necessary.

To locate other spots shown on the flat surface in the photo, proceed as follows:

1. Draw a line tangent to (touching) the left sides of the near disk and the more distant disk on the left.
2. Draw another line tangent to the right sides of the same disks. Where these two lines cross is a point on the vanishing line (Exhibit 30).
3. Draw two more lines tangent to the right and left sides of the near disk and the far disk to the right. These two lines also cross at a point on the vanishing line.
4. Draw a straight line connecting the two points that have been located on the vanishing line. This line is the vanishing line for the flat surface in the photo.
5. Draw a straight line through the center of the near disk and at right angles to the vanishing line. Where this line crosses the vanishing line is the vanishing point, P, in Exhibits 30 and 31.

This establishes the foundation and scale for a square grid which is completed as follows:

1. From the vanishing point, draw two straight lines each tangent to one side of the near (larger) disk (Exhibit 31).
2. Parallel to the vanishing line, draw two lines, one tangent to the near side and one tangent to the far side of the elliptical picture of the large disk in the photo.
3. Label the points in the photo where these four line cross each other A, B, C, and D as in Exhibit 31.
4. Extend the nearer parallel line to the left of C and to the right of D a distance equal to CD to locate points E and F on the base line of the square grid.
5. Draw straight lines from E and F to the vanishing point.

You now have a grid system exactly like that of a portable grid with a single vanishing point in Exhibit 29. You can go on from there to locate corresponding spots on the map as already explained for the square grid.

There are a number of advantages of the circular disk scales in a perspective grid system:

1. Reduced error in locating the vanishing line. That results in greater precision in establishing grid lines.

2. Reduced error in locating the grid lines, especially those at great distances from the grid.
3. Neither measurements nor special care are needed in placing the disks.

There are disadvantages:

1. There are three devices to carry and place instead of one.
2. They require greater free road space.
3. They are more subject to interference from traffic flow because some of the disks must be placed well into the traffic lane.
4. Three disks are more trouble in strong wind and in wet weather.

7. MATHEMATICAL METHODS

For those who are handier or more comfortable with measuring scales and a computer than with technical drawing, there are numerical methods of transferring perspective locations on a photo of a *flat* surface to an orthogonal map. The idea is to relate the cartesian coordinates (*x* and *y* axes at right angles) of any spot on a flat surface shown in the photo to corresponding cartesian coordinates on the map. This relationship is established by equations.

With Square Grid or Circular Disk Shown in the Photo[6]

Coordinates in the photo may be

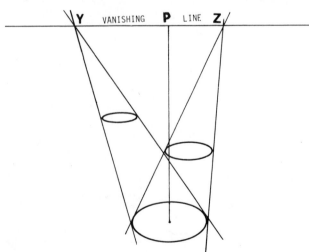

Exhibit 30. *Three identical circular disks can be used instead of a square grid. Spaced some distance apart, they assist in locating the vanishing point more precisely.*

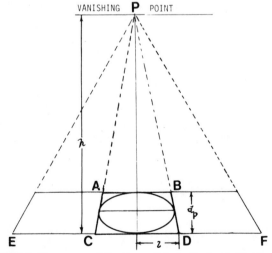

Exhibit 31. *The nearer of the three disks is the basis for drawing a square perspective grid which can be treated like any square perspective grid.*

designated x_p and y_p, while the map coordinates are designated as x_m and y_m.

Photo units of measurement may be any for which you have a suitable scale available. Ordinarily, this would be millimeters but it might be fiftieths of an inch on a U.S.A. engineering scale.

Map units of measurements are whatever your drawing calls for, feet or meters to scale.

The x_p axis in the photo is usually the base line of the square grid. The origin (starting place for measuring, $x_p = 0$) is the left edge of the square grid on the base line (C in Exhibit 31). Any x_p coordinate measured to the left from this line is negative. Put a minus sign, $-$, in front of it.

The y_p axis in the photo starts at the same origin (C in Exhibit 31). It is at right angles to the x_p axis and not parallel to the left margin of the grid in the photo.

To begin with, draw the x_m axis and the y_m axis for the map without attempting to locate them exactly on the map of the road layout drawn from measurements of the site. You can fit them into your map later.

The two grid equations relating photo coordinates to corresponding map coordinates are

$$x_m = \frac{d_m x_p}{l}\left[\frac{h}{h - y_p}\right]$$

and

$$y_m = c\left[\frac{h}{h - y_p} - 1\right]$$

In these two equations,

$$c = d_m\left[\frac{h}{d_p} - 1\right]$$

This is actually the horizontal map distance between the base line of the square grid and the position of the camera lens when the picture was taken.

d_m = diameter of the circular scale disk or edge length of the square scale grid in map units, usually feet or meters.

d_p = minor (shorter) axis of the elliptical image of the disk in the photo or the distance be-

tween parallel sides of the trapezoidal image of the square grid in the photo, d_p in Exhibit 31, measured in photo units.

h = distance in photo units between the vanishing point and the base line of the grid (x_p axis) in the photo (h in Exhibit 31).

l = half the side of the square grid measured in photo units along the base line in the photo (l in Exhibit 31).

All of these five quantities are constant for any particular combination of photo and map.

In practice, you will find it handy to have a transparent sheet with cross section lines on it in millimeters or other suitable photo units. Align this sheet with the x_p and y_p axes on the photo. With this you can easily obtain values for coordinates of spots in the photo.

Use these values in the equations to compute map coordinates for the corresponding photo spots. Repeat this for all spots, such as ends of tire marks, that you want to locate on your after-accident situation map.

Without Disk or Grid Showing in the Photo

Even if no natural or portable perspective grid is included in a photograph, it may still be possible to locate on a map some things shown in the picture.

Requirements. This photogrammetry is possible under the following conditions:[1]

1. The spots to be located must be on a flat surface, the map plane.
2. Four or more calibrating spots which can be located on the map by measurements must clearly show in the photo.
3. No more than two calibrating spots may be in the same straight line.

The exact location of each of the four calibration spots in the photo and on the map must be systematically described. This is done by meas-

uring the two coordinates of each spot in the photo and the two coordinates of the same spot on the map.

The coordinates of a point on a flat surface (plane) are its distances, x and y, from two lines which cross at right angles. The place where the lines cross is the origin of the coordinates. The the distance east, so to speak, is designated as the x coordinate; then the distance north is the y coordinate. On the photo, the coordinates of a spot are designated as x_p and y_p; on the map the coordinates of the same spot are x_m and y_m. An example will illustrate how the coordinates are measured. Exhibit 32 is a photo of an accident scene. No measurements were made to locate the two tire marks and final positions of two vehicles, but they do show in this picture. Four calibration points are selected. These are spots that can be located at the site after all signs of the accident are gone. For instance, the point marked B in the photo is on the paving at the beginning of a curve in the curb. The other three control points are labelled A, C, and D.

The lower edge of the photo is chosen as the reference line, the x_p axis. The left edge of the photo is chosen as the y_p axis. The origin or starting point for measurements is where these two axes cross. Other pairs of axes could be used. For example, the x_p axis could be a line through C and D. Then the y_p axis, at right angles to the x_p axis, could pass through point A. That would simplify some of the calculation. From the scales along these axes, the coordinates of calibration point B in the photo are: $x_p = + 106$ and $y_p = + 107$ mm.

Coordinates of the other three calibration points, A, C, and D are measured in the same way.

Exhibit 33 is a map of the accident location to a scale of 1 in. = 10 ft. The four calibration points are shown on it. Their positions have been located at the site by careful measurements. On this map, for computation purposes, the x_m axis has been drawn 10 ft away from and par-

Exhibit 32. With no natural or portable grid available, positions in a photo may be transferred to a map mathematically. The spots must be on a flat surface in the photo. They are located by coordinates. The measured position of at least four spots (A, B, C, and D) on this surface must be visible in the photo and no more than two of them may be in the same straight line.

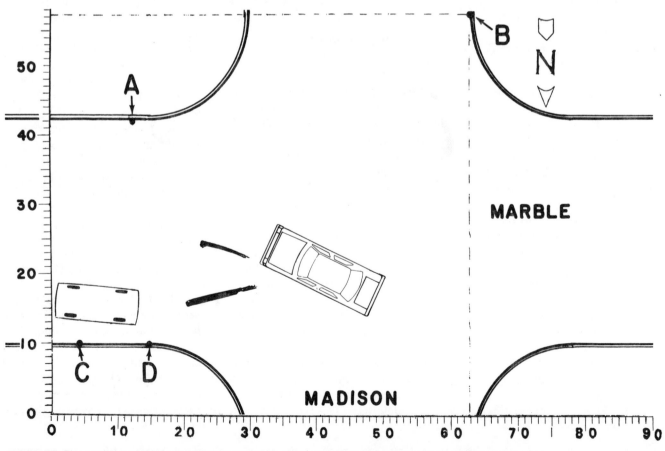

Exhibit 33. The position of the four calibrating spots (A, B, C, and D) must be located by coordinates on the map.

allel to the north edge of Marble Street. The y_m axis, at right angles to the x_m axis, is 30 ft to scale east of the east edge of Madison Street.

Coordinates of any point on the map are described in the same way as those on the photo. For example, the coordinates of calibration point B on the map are $x_m = 63.0$ and $y_m = 57.3$ ft to scale.

To relate calibration points on the photo to corresponding points on the map, two photo measurements and two map measurements for each point are required, four measurements per point. To describe all four points, a total of sixteen measurements are required.

Coordinates for Exhibit 32, the photo and for Exhibit 33, the map, are shown in Exhibit 34 as an illustration.

Calibration constants. Two equations, one for each map coordinate, give the map location of any point located by photo coordinates in the flat surface shown in the picture. These equations are:[1]

$$x_m = \frac{c_1 + c_2 x_p + c_3 y_p}{c_4 x_p + c_5 y_p + 1}$$
and
$$y_m = \frac{c_6 + c_7 x_p + c_8 y_p}{c_4 x_p + c_5 y_p + 1}$$

In these equations are eight calibration constants, C_1, C_2, C_3, C_4, C_5, C_6, C_7, and C_8. For each particular combination of photo and map, values for each of these eight constants must be established. To do this write the two equations for each calibration point. For example, use the coordinates for point B, measured in the example

above. The map coordinates for point B are $x_m = + 63.0$ and $y_m = + 57.3$. These, with the corresponding photo coordinates, x_p and y_p give two calibration equations:

$$63.0 = \frac{c_1 + 106c_2 + 107c_3}{106c_4 + 107c_5 + 1}$$
and
$$57.3 = \frac{c_6 + 106c_7 + 107c_8}{106c_4 + 107c_5 + 1}$$

Doing the same for the other three calibration points gives a total of eight equations with eight unknown constants from C_1 to C_8. These simultaneous equations can be solved to obtain numerical values for the eight constants. How this may be done is explained in algebra textbooks. It is a tedious task beyond the scope of this topic, but there are computer programs for solving the simultaneous equations.[9]

Map locations. With these eight constants for a particular combination of photograph and map, any point on the surface shown in the photo can be translated into map coordinates for that point. The same basic equations are used with measured photo coordinates and the numerical value for each of the calibrating constants. In this way the map location of two or more points on each of the two tire marks visible in the photo are established. So also for the final positions of the vehicles as shown in Exhibit 32.

Practical considerations. Often accident locations, especially in rural areas, provide no sufficiently peculiar characteristics to serve as calibration points. Then this technique is not applicable.

A photograph is usually first examined for possible calibration points. A visit to the site may be necessary to determine whether or not the points still exist. If four photographed points can be identified and measured at the site, the projective relationship can be established and the location of any number of other points or objects shown in the photograph can then be determined.

Appropriate calibration points include any features, markings, or characteristics of the pavement surface or its edges that have not been altered or moved between the time the photograph was taken and the measurements are made. These would include manhole covers, expansion joints, pavement cracks, pavement gouges, pavement patches, drain inlets, traffic detectors, the corner of channelizing islands, pavement legends, and pavement striping.

When photos are taken at the scene to avoid making measurements, results depend on the availability of calibration points. Such points may be established when photos are made by locating four targets in the scene at measured locations. Of course this takes time and trouble which the procedure is supposed to avoid. Indeed the easiest way to be sure of quick and adequate calibration points at the scene would be to use a square perspective grid placed on the road. The corners of this grid then provide premeasured calibration points.

In this way, consequently, any four sided perspective grid would provide a photo which could produce map locations by the mathematical methods described here.

Mathematical methods would not be practical if the calculations had to be made by hand. Computers make a difference. Several computer programs are available for solving simultaneous equations. Computer programs have been developed to perform all of the mathematics involved, thus quickly giving map coordinates corresponding to photo coordinates for any spot.

CALIBRATION	MAP, ft		PHOTO, mm	
SPOTS	x_m	y_m	x_p	y_p
A	+12.3	+42.7	+ 20	+ 97
B	+63.0	+57.3	+106	+107
C	+ 4.0	+10.0	+ 62	+ 4
D	+14.6	+10.0	+136	+ 36

Exhibit 34. *Map and photo coordinates for the four calibration spots shown as an example in Exhibits 32 and 33.*

Equipment has been developed which eliminates measuring coordinates on the photograph. The picture is fastened to a special table. A movable magnifier is adjusted so that cross hairs in its field are centered on the point to be located. Pressing a button then causes the instrument to read the position and compute and print the map coordinates. It may even be arranged to plot the position graphically.

The extent to which such devices can be used in accident investigation depends on their cost effectiveness. As with aerial mapping it is likely that a few agencies will develop capabilities to perform such work for many others, none of which have enough business to warrant maintaining its capabilities.

8. PHOTO RECONSTRUCTION

Application

When circumstances are favorable, natural or portable perspective grids are a satisfactory way to make up for deficient measurements. But the requirements are seldom met in actual accident investigation.

Often the best you can do is to go to the site and try to find positions of things, such as tire marks, which have disappeared but show in photos which you have with you. Then you can locate these positions by measurements in the usual way (Topic 828).

Without Equipment

Relocating things no longer visible at the scene is a common practice. People often take accident scene photos back to the site. They look at the photos, then point to a spot and say, for instance, "That is where the skidmark went off on the shoulder," or, perhaps, "Here is where the body was found." Then they may measure to locate these spots indicated.

Often the only "picture" is in the mind of someone who returns to the scene. He points out, as well as he can, where he remembers things were. Attorneys often have witnesses try to

do this. Again, the spots so indicated may be located by measurements.

Sometimes positions pointed out at the site after the accident are shown on an after-accident situation map. There is nothing wrong with this, *provided* you make it clear how positions were determined so that the degree of precision may be considered by whoever uses the map.

Do not underestimate the usefulness of this primitive, common-sense, inexpensive, approach to "photogrammetry." Every day it clears up matters which might otherwise be misunderstood. It is often the best that can be done under the circumstances.

Equipment for Photo Reconstruction

By using special equipment, the precision, and therefore the usefulness, of determining where things shown in photos were located right after a traffic accident can often be improved.

Experiments have been made with various devices for this purpose, both in the U.S. and abroad, from time to time. Information now available does not indicate that any such equipment can be bought ready made.

The idea is to use a dummy camera. A transparency of the photo is placed in the "dummy." Looking through this transparency, the "camera" is adjusted so that the transparency image coincides exactly with the scene. Then you can see where tire marks or other things were located when the photo was made and direct an assistant to mark these spots on the road. Then you can locate them by measurements in the usual way (Topic 828).

The difficulty in this method is locating and adjusting the dummy camera so that the transparency and the scene viewed through it exactly coincide. Six adjustments are required:

1. Near and far
2. Right and left
3. Up and down
4. Tilt (crosswise axis)

5. Swing (lengthwise axis)
6. Pivot (vertical axis)

When trial and error, which may take hours, has resulted in successful adjustments, lock the device in place usually on a strong tripod.

Location, Aim

A camera, like the one used to take the original photo, has been tried for this purpose. The actual photo negative was used as a transparency in the back of the camera. With the camera back and lens open the scene was viewed through the transparency and camera lens. Two things gave trouble: 1) The image was so small that the trial and error adjustments were tedious and inaccurate; and 2) dark areas in the negative covered light areas in the scene, giving an overall effect of deep shadow in which spots to be located were hard to see.

Enlarged positive transparencies for use in a view camera were considered. The idea was abandoned. That large a camera is cumbersome to adjust. It requires a very heavy tripod for stability. The image is upside down, which is inconvenient. Focusing and lens focal length introduced additional problems.

Then, it was decided to reverse the device, viewing the transparency and the scene through a peep hole to dispense with a lens. A 4- by 5-in. positive transparency in a frame viewed through a peep hole was tried. Enlarged positive transparencies have to be specially made. 4- by 5-in. was still too small and transparency details tend to become confused with scene details making adjustment and use awkward.

Later, a device was constructed which has been used, now and then, for more than 20 years. It has the following features:

1. An ordinary 8-in. by 10-in. enlargement of the photo is made. A clear acetate sheet is put over it. On this outlines of things are traced:
   a. Conspicious landmarks such

as roadway edges, utility poles, roadside signs, roof lines and corners of buildings are traced in black (L's in Exhibit 35).

  b. Items to be located, such as spots at intervals on tire marks, significant gouges, and positions of vehicle wheels, are in red. (Y's in Exhibit 35)

2. The outline transparency is clamped between a pair of aluminum frames as in Exhibit 35.

3. At the center of upper and lower frame edges are brackets. To these are fitted a pair of adjustable horizontal bars connected by an upright member with a peep hole at its midpoint. (Exhibit 36).

4. The horizontal pieces have a device by which it may be attached to a steady tripod.

5. Taken apart, the equipment fits neatly in a box for 11- by 8½-in. typewriter paper.

Method

To adjust the instrument for the

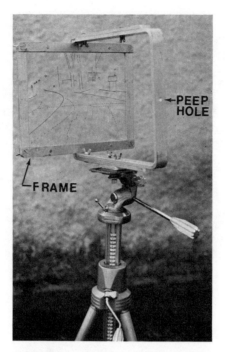

Exhibit 36. Transparency and frame mounted on a tripod for photo reconstruction.

degree of enlargement, measure the distance on the transparency between two clearly identifiable points. Measure the corresponding distance between the same pair of points on the photo negative. Divide the transparency distance by the negative dis-

tance. That gives degree of enlargement. Then multiply the focal length of the lens by degree of enlargement. That gives the proper distance from transparency to peep hole. Adjust the equipment frame accordingly.

Once the equipment is properly adjusted, placed, and aimed so that the outlines of landmarks of the transparency correspond closely with the actual scene, look through the peep hole at one of the points on the transparency to be located. Direct a helper to locate and mark that point, on the road as in Exhibit 37 (which is a different situation than that illustrated in Exhibits 35 and 36).

Finally locate the indicated spots by measuring in the usual way.

The photo reconstruction method has two advantages over the perspective grid procedure:

1. It can be used where no perspective grid, natural or portable, is available.

2. It is not limited to use on a flat surface; it can locate positions shown in photos even if the positions are up on banks or down in ditches.

Example

Exhibit 38 is a photo of a fatal-accident scene. A sport car with three occupants lost control on a left turn, struck a big oak tree, and broke in two. Two occupants died.

An issue in the resulting inquiry was, naturally, speed.

Photographs were made of the scene but no measurements. Three

Exhibit 37. Instructing a helper to mark where a skidmark shown in a photo began.

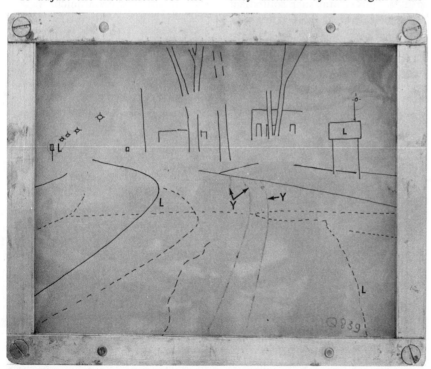

Exhibit 35. Transparent tracing of features of an accident scene mounted in a frame for photo reconstruction of an accident scene.

Exhibit 38. *A fatal accident scene in which the yaw marks were not located by measurements but had to be located months later by photo reconstruction.*

yawmarks (Y in Exhibits 35 and 38) soon faded away at the site of the accident but showed clearly in Exhibit 38). To estimate speed, the curvature of these marks had to be established. To do this, the scene was reconstructed at the site with the dummy camera just described. The transparency tracing of the photo is shown in its frame in Exhibits 35 and 36.

The tire marks so located by this means are shown on an after-accident situation map in Exhibit 39. With this information, the car's speed was estimated to have been 50 miles per hour where the limit was posted as 20 miles per hour.

One only has to experience the trouble in using a gadget for photo reconstruction to be convinced that it is a last resort in data collection and never a substitute for proper at-scene traffic-accident measurements.

9. STEREOSCOPIC PHOTOGRAMMETRY

A single photo establishes only the

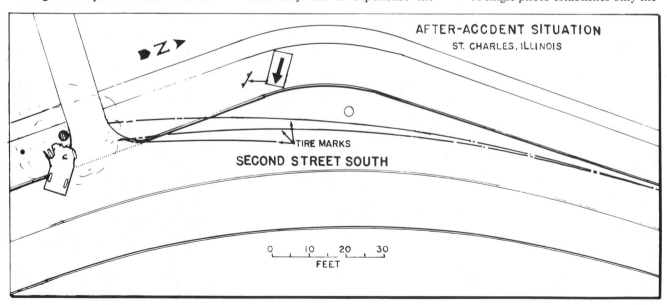

Exhibit 39. *Map of yaw marks shown in Exhibit 38. The marks were located by photo reconstruction.*

angle between the axis of the camera with its lens and the line of sight to a point in the picture. The point in the picture might be a spot of light from a flashlight 25 ft away at night, for instance, or the image of a street light at 1000 ft. The direction of this point can be told by its position in the photograph, but there is no way to judge its distance without something recognizable to compare it with.

However, if this spot is known to be on a surface or a specified distance from other spots, its distance can be judged. This is the principle of all of the photographic mapping described so far.

Stereoscopic Photogrammetry

However, even without a recognizable surface to help in locating on the map, direction and distance can be determined if two pictures are made from somewhat different viewpoints and the relation of these viewpoints to each other is known. This is the function of your two eyes in binocular vision. With cameras, it is called stereoscopic photography, and has been used in one form or another for a century.

You can make stereoscopic photographs in three ways:

1. With two cameras some distance apart picturing the same scene at the same time.[5]
2. With a single camera having two lenses to make two separate pictures at the same time.
3. With one camera making two pictures of the same scene from different angles, one after the other.[2]

If the object to be located is in motion, one of the first two methods is required; it not any of the three will do.

Paired Cameras

For more than 25 years, highly developed optical equipment using a pair of cameras has been available for stereoscopic photogrammetry. This equipment has two precision cameras mounted on a bar an exact

distance apart (Exhibit 40). The axes of the cameras are precisely aligned. The cameras are usually mounted on a tall, strong tripod, and shutters are connected so that exposures are made at the same time.

Elaborate optical and mechanical equipment permits a skilled operator to compare the two photos and so determine a three-dimensional position of points shown in both pictures. This stereo viewer can be connected mechanically to an automatic plotter that locates points on a scale map as the machine is being operated (Exhibit 41).

To cover a desired area, pairs of stereoscopic pictures may have to be taken from several different viewpoint as is sometimes the case with perspective grid photos (Exhibits 22 and 24).

Stereo plotters are very useful in

some engineering and scientific work. They have been experimented with in Europe and, to a less extent, in America for traffic-accident investigation, but have been widely used only in Japan[8] where they are mounted on a vehicle for traffic-accident photography. In Japan, the actual maps are drawn at processing stations located in various parts of the country.

Stereophotography has a number of advantages for traffic-accident investigation:

- Pictures can be made from the roadside so that there is no interference from or with traffic and minimum hazard to photographers.
- Measurements of complex tire mark patterns can be made quickly and accurately.
- Less training in how to make

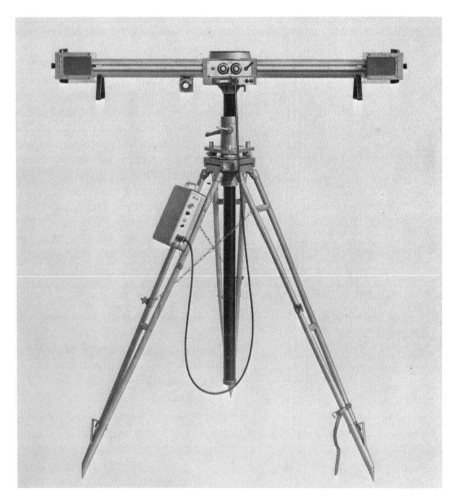

Exhibit 40. Stereoscopic cameras, such as this one, can substitute for measurements under favorable conditions, but are rarely available to traffic-accident investigators.

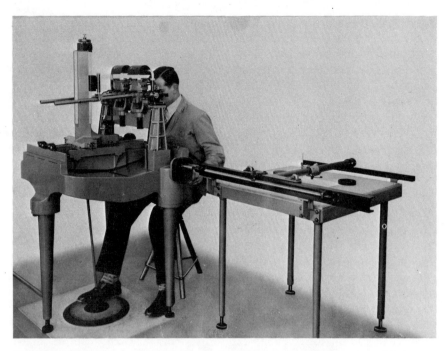

Exhibit 41. Producing a map from stereoscopic photographs requires a special viewer and plotter which require special training and experience to operate properly.

measurements is necessary.
- Measurements in three dimensions are available.

Disadvantages of this method are
- Equipment is very expensive which makes its use uneconomical except where there is much business to keep it busy.
- Very skilled and experienced operators are required to produce good maps from stereophotos.
- Night photos suitable for stereo interpretation are very difficult to make.
- There may be considerable delay between taking the pictures and completing the map.

Paired Pictures with a Single Camera

Recently, another ingenious system for stereophotogrammetry has been developed. It uses a somewhat modified standard 35-mm camera. A tripod is not necessary. To establish dimensions, a three-dimensional perspective grid is included in each picture. This device is assembled from 12 rods fastened together at the ends to form the sides of a rigid cube. These perspective cubes are made in

various sizes; a one meter cube is generally satisfactory for traffic-accident investigation.

In use, the perspective cube is placed in the foreground of the scene to be photographed. Two pictures of the cube and the view from positions some distance apart are made. No measurements are necessary, and precise camera placing is unimportant. Photo coordinates of the corners of the cube in each of the two photos are entered into a computer which generates calibration constants. Then photo coordinates of any point shown in both photos can be entered into the computer which will calculate three-dimensional map coordinates for the point.

Reports of experience with this method in actual traffic-accident investigation are not yet (1985) available.

Comments

Theoretically, all measurements connected with traffic-accident investigation could be made by available photogrammetric techniques. In practice, except, perhaps in Japan, these methods are very rarely used.

Good examples of photos made es-

pecially for measurement purposes (with perspective grids or disks, stereophotos) and resulting maps or other drawings are difficult to find. Those that have come to light usually appear to be experimental.

Reasons for lack of applied photogrammetry in accident investigation readily come to mind:

- Most people, mainly police, entrusted with making measurements and photos in connections with accidents have never heard of photogrammetry. They have certainly not been provided with the equipment and given the necessary training.
- The equipment required for stereo photographic photos and plotting is expensive and and requires special ability to use.
- To be sure that they show well enough in photos made for measurement purposes, tire marks and road scars must be outlined or "enhanced" by chalk or paint, especially at night. (Exhibit 42) This takes time and trouble, offsetting much of the advantage of photographic methods. With wet or snow covered pavements, and on the roadside, enhancement is usually impractical.
- In many situations, there is no advantage in photographic as compared to conventional methods of measuring. Often the only significant measurements required are the lengths of some skidmarks. These can be made with satisfactory accuracy in two minutes with a measuring wheel. Enhancing marks and placing grids for photos would take that much time. The actual measurements are available at once; photo measurements require waiting for processing and interpretation.

The most promising use for photo measurement methods is recording very complex tire mark patterns which might require an hour or more to measure properly with tapes and field sketches.

There is another possibility which has not yet been adequately explored. Current procedures for vehicle examination after traffic accidents call for extensive measurements of crash deformation. These are time consuming and often not well done. Stereophotos of the damaged vehicles might provide a better means of evaluating vehicle damage than present practices.

Exhibit 42. *Photographs made especially for photogrammetric purposes usually require enhancement of tire marks and road scars with chalk, crayon, or spray paint to make sure that they show well in the pictures.*

10. SOURCES

Author

J. Stannard Baker is a traffic engineer specializing in traffic-accident investigation. He was Director of Research and Development at the Northwestern University Traffic Institute from 1946 to 1971.

References

Superscript numbers in the preceeding pages refer to the following publications:

1. Bleyl, Robert L, "Using Photographs to Map Traffic-Accident Scenes: a Mathematical Technique" in *Journal of Safety Research,* June 1976, National Safety Council, Chicago IL. (Pages 59 - 64)

2. *Maco 35/70, 1985,* H. Dell Foster Associates, 2400 Freedom, San Antonio TX 78217

3. Schernhorst, John N., "On Photogrammetry" in *Police,* March-April 1968 (Pages 60 to 71)

4. Imhoff, Ralph K. and Russell C. Doolittle, "Mapping from Oblique Photographs" in *Manual of Photogrammetry*, 1966, American Society of Photogrammetry, Falls Church VA

5. *Photogrammetric Instruments for Taking Photographs for Evidence*, Wild Heerbrugg Ltd. Heerbrugg, Switzerland

6. Hyzer, William G., "Perspective Grid Photography" in *Imaging Technology in Research and Development*, July 1985, Lakewood Publications, New York NY 10016

7. Hyzer, William G., "The Use of Circular Scales in the Perspective Grid Technique of Making Photographic Measurements" in *Imaging Technology in Research and Development* 1985, Lakewood Publications, New York NY 10016

8. Gosh, Sangib K., "Photogrammetry for Police Use: Experience in Japan" in *Photogrammetric Engineering and Remote Sensing*, Mar. 1980 (Pages 329 - 332)

9. Bleyl, R.L. "Traffic Analysis of Time-Lapse Photographs without Employing a Perspective Grid" in *Traffic Engineering*, August 1972.

Notes

The perspective grid technique is not new. As early as 1915, in the *Archiv fur Kriminal-Anthropologie und Kriminalistik*, Dr. Heindl spoke of including in the photograph "a bright square plate, 50 by 50 cm" for measuring purposes.

Crime photography. There is a description of using a "measuring plate" for crime scenes in the following (now out of print):

Oehlinger, S. "Photogrammetric Position Finding" in *Manual of Applied Photography.* Verlag Grossbild-Technik, Munich, 1916. (Page 236)

The author refers to Dr. Heindl's device as "a simple method for this purpose, which unfortunately has remained too little known among police photographers."

Traffic accident investigation uses of the "measuring plate" are briefly described in:

Marquard, Erich. *Wissenschaftliche Grundlagen fur die Arbeit des Verkehrsunfall-Sachverstandigen*, Westdeutscher Verklag, Cologne, 1966 (Page 281).

Part of the data included in this topic was developed for an unpublished study of "Simplified Photogrammetry for Traffic Accident Investigation" prepared in 1964 at The Traffic Institute under contract CPR-11-0879 for the U.S. Bureau of Public Roads.

Exhibits

The following are the sources of photographs, diagrams, charts, tables, and maps used in this topic as exhibits:

Baker, J. Stannard, Glencoe IL
Photos: 13, 14, 22, 24, 26, 35, 36, 37
Maps: 3, 6, 8, 9, 11, 21, 23, 25, 27, 28, 33, 39
Diagrams: 15, 16, 17, 18, 19, 29, 30, 31
Table: 34
Cusker, Thomas L., Villa Park IL
Photos: 4, 5
Morris, Don, Camera House, Joliet IL
Photo: 20
Roller, Robert, Chandler AZ
Photo: 10
Seyfried, Robert, Traffic Institute, Evanston, IL
Photo: 2
Unknown
Photos: 1, 7, 12, 32, 38, 40, 41, 42

MEASURING THE ROAD FOR AFTER-ACCIDENT SITUATION MAPS

Topic 832 of the *Traffic-Accident Investigation Manual*

by
J. Stannard Baker
and
Robert K. Seyfried

NORTHWESTERN UNIVERSITY TRAFFIC INSTITUTE

PUBLICATION HISTORY

1953   *Traffic Accident Investigator's Manual,* Sections 41.614 - 41.685
1954   Revised, Sections 41.614 - 41.685

1957   *Traffic Accident Investigator's Manual for Police,* Sections 41.605 - 41.685
Reprinted 1959
1963   Revised, Sections 41.605 - 41.675
Reprinted 1964, 1965, 1966, 1969, 1970, 1971, 1973

1975   *Traffic Accident Investigation Manual,* First part of Chapter 7
Reprinted 1976, 1979

1985   *Measuring the Road for After-accident Situation Maps*

Copyright 1985 by the Northwestern University Traffic Institute
P.O. Box 1409 Evanston, Illinois 60204

MEASURING THE ROAD FOR
AFTER-ACCIDENT SITUATION MAPS

1. PURPOSE

An attorney or someone else may decide that an accident was serious enough to require investigation beyond that which was done at the scene. Often this calls for some kind of a summary or description of what things were like when the situation at the scene stabilized: where vehicles came to rest, what marks were left on the road, and so on.

By all means the most useful device for such a summary is an after-accident situation map. At a glance, it shows relationships that would be difficult to describe in a thousand words. This *scale* drawing is more precise and detailed than the free hand sketch on an accident report. Such a map may be easier to understand than most photographs because it is limited to essential elements; there are no distracting objects.

In some cases, measurements were made at the scene or are otherwise available to permit a satisfactory map to be drawn without further measuring; but in most cases, the site must be revisited to obtain necessary additional dimensions of the road layout. *The purpose of this topic* is to describe how to get required additional data with the least trouble and cost.

Followup measurements at the site do not need to be made by the same person who made measurements at the scene.

Try to have additional measurements made by the same person who will eventually draw the map. Sometimes it is helpful to have the mapping done by a surveyor who has special equipment and professional training for this purpose.

In any case, whoever measures the road layout at the site should be familiar with the accident and measurements made at the scene. Have this person take with him a copy of measurements previously made and photos showing such results of the accident as final positions of vehicles and significant marks on the road.

2. EQUIPMENT AND ITS USE

Minimum Equipment. Measuring for after-accident situation maps is sometimes done at the accident scene; but usually measurements are made days or even months after the accident. Measuring right at the scene may have to be done with whatever equipment happens to be available, or even without equipment by stepping off distances. Measuring for after-accident situation maps, on the other hand, can be planned and necessary equipment assembled before going to the accident site.

At-scene measuring equipment is suggested in Topic 828, *Measuring at the Scenes of Traffic Accidents.*

Equipment for mapping is much the same with a few additions. The items listed here are all simple, available, and inexpensive, but usually adequate for traffic-accident investigation purposes.

If very precise measuring is needed for some reason, have it done by a professional surveyor who has the special instruments and skills required.

Most of the equipment that you will find useful for such measurements is shown in Exhibit 1. There each item is identified by number as follows:

1. *Cross-section (graph) paper* for field sketches preferably with fine blue lines printed ten-to-the-inch (5 mm apart)

2. *No. 3 pencil* for dimension lines and light lines that can be

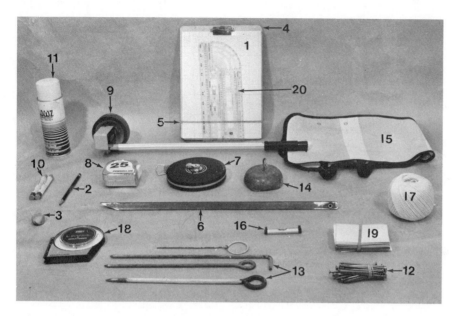

Exhibit 1. *Equipment for use in measuring the road for after-accident situation maps.*

erased, and No. 2 pencil for heavier fill-in lines and for numbers and lettering

3. *Eraser*

4. *Clipboard* of convenient size. It has a hole to permit use of the Traffic Template[1, 2] for measuring grades.

5. *Rubber band* or a pair of small clips to hold the bottom edge of the sheets on the clipboard. It prevents sheets from blowing in the wind.

6. *Straightedge* two feet long

7. *A 100-ft (30 m) tape measure* with large numbers on it. A metal reinforced fabric tape — metallic — is better than a steel tape. Engineer's tapes marked in feet and tenths rather than feet and inches are preferable.

8. *Spring-steel pocket tape rule,* preferably 25 ft (8 m) long. These may be obtained marked in feet and tenths as well as feet and inches.

9. *Measuring wheel.* These can be obtained calibrated to read in feet and tenths or meters.

10. *Yellow lumber crayon* (sometimes called "keel" by surveyors) for writing on or marking pavement

11. *Spray paint* in aerosol can for marking the road

12. *Common nails* 3½ in. (9 cm) long are useful for marking stations off the roadway where crayon marks cannot be used.

13. *Steel pins* to anchor end of tape and to mark its length when making long measurements

14. *A lead weight* with a hook on it to anchor end of a tape when pins cannot be used

15. *A reflective vest,* brightly colored, to be worn whenever you are measuring in or near moving traffic

16. *A line level*

17. *Chalk line*

18. *Small clinometer*

19. *Cards* (3- by 5-in.)

20. *Traffic Template*

Handling Measuring Equipment

Most of the guides for equipment handling at the scene (Topic 828) also apply in measuring for maps. Be careful in measuring on roads, especially with tapes, to protect yourself from traffic and your tape from being run over.

Plan measuring with this in mind. To keep off the road as much as possible, first decide exactly what you want to measure from and to and prepare a place to record your measurements. Thus, you will not have to stop out in the roadway to decide what to do next.

Measurements in heavy traffic may be dangerous and are always tedious. Avoid them if possible. If you can, postpone measurements until traffic is light. If necessary, have traffic warned by flagging.

Whenever you are measuring in or near traffic, wear high-visibility clothing. Lightweight bright orange vests are available for such work. Wear one.

Do not roll up a wet or dirty tape; wipe it off. If it is a steel tape without enamel, wiping with an oily rag helps keep it in good condition.

When you wind up a fabric tape, let the tape feed into the case between two fingers, as shown in Exhibit 2. By this means you can detect kinks and prevent them from winding into the case, which will jam the tape inside.

Distances less than 10 ft (3 m) are best measured with a tape rule. You can use one without help, and often with only one hand, because you do not have to unroll part of a long tape.

Simple measurements from 10 ft. to tape length require a helper. If he is inexperienced, have him hold the end of the tape at the point you show him and do everything else yourself.

Hold tape level in making all ordinary measurements. For example, when measuring from the edge of the roadway to the ditch line, do not measure down the slope of the ditch but hold the tape as level as you can.

Measurements longer than tape length over water, mud, ravines, hills, or buildings cannot be made by usual

Exhibit 2. *When rolling up a fabric tape, let the tape pass between two fingers as it enters the case. That prevents the tape from kinking and jamming inside the case.*

methods. If they must be accurate, get a surveyor. He can measure the distance accurately with special instruments.

Sometimes you can measure an equivalent distance alongside the stretch of mud or water. When this is possible, it will be accurate enough for most investigations.

Avoid making measurements alone. Besides holding one end of the tape in measuring, a helper can keep a look out and, if necessary, direct traffic to slow it down or keep it away; he can also check work as it progresses and thus prevent some mistakes. If necessary, a helper can later bear witness to what you measured.

If you must work alone, provide something to hold one end of the tape. The most useful is a surveyor's pin or an old screwdriver which may be run through the loop at the end of the tape and stuck into the ground or sometimes in a crack in the paving. On paving, pins can rarely be used. Then a weight with a hook in it for the tape ring will help. The weight ought to be at least 5 lbs. Even that is not enough to hold a long tape in a cross wind.

Measuring wheels have many advantages in measurements for after-accident situation maps. They are especially useful

- In heavy traffic, because measurements can be made quickly

- When you have to work alone, because no one is required to hold the other end of a tape

- For long distances, because they measure a thousand feet without stopping

- In strong winds.

A wheel only supplements a tape; it is not a substitute for one. It is useless for measuring across ditches or irregular ground. It is unsatisfactory for any but clean, paved surfaces in fairly good condition. Wet surfaces do not affect a wheel, but snow and ice make a wheel useless. Short distances, like the widths of pavement markings are not well measured by wheels, especially large wheels.

Writing Distance Numbers

Two different divisions of a foot are used on measuring tapes and wheels: inches (twelfths) and tenths of a foot. Inches are used generally by architects and builders; tenths are used by engineers. Examine the equipment you use to know which it is.

Write feet and tenths with a decimal. If your tape is marked in feet and tenths of a foot, record what you read with a decimal point to separate feet and tenths. For example, record six and a half feet as 6.5 ft. (With a metric tape write meters and centimeters as a decimal number.)

Underline inches, if your tape is marked in feet and inches. For example, record 6 ft 5 in. as 6⁵. If your pocket tape reads in inches only, write as inches (underlined) or feet and inches. For example, write 63 inches as 63 or as 5³.

Do not use a prime (') to indicate feet and a double prime (") to indicate inches, as is often done. Primes are sometimes mistaken for 1's. If you want to indicate feet and inches, use their abbreviations, for example, 13 ft 4 in. or 13⁴.

It is rarely necessary to record measurements of less than 1 in. or 0.1 ft.

3. BASIC MEASURING TECHNIQUES

Methods described here are not the only ones that can be used. Some investigators and engineers may have learned or developed other methods. If your way of measuring produces satisfactory after-accident situation maps, including the results of the accident, then there is no reason to abandon or change it. The methods discussed here have produced excellent results with simple equipment and without wasting time, interfering with traffic, or causing unnecessary hazard to the investigator.

Decide on Kind of Map

Before starting to measure for an after-accident situation map, deter-

mine whether the map is for: 1) working purposes; or 2) display, for example, in court. You yourself may know what is wanted or you may have to discuss the matter with whoever plans to use the map.

Working maps have only enough detail to permit studying the accident. But you must know something about the accident to know what this detail is. For example, the accident pictured in Exhibit 3, requires a working map showing only the width of the roadway, width of the east shoulder, and final position of vehicle. This map can be on a small scale, for example, 1 in. = 20 ft (or 1 cm = 2.5 m). An example of a working map for this accident is shown in Exhibit 4.

Display maps are drawn at a greater scale, for example 1 in. = 4 ft, because they may have to be viewed by a group of people, usually a jury. They must also show more detail to be realistic and to correspond better with photos. Shoulders, guardrails, fences, poles, traffic control devices, arcs connecting roadway edges, buildings, hedges, trees, and other objects are put on display maps even though they have no significance in connection with the accident. An example of a display map for the same accident is shown in Exhibit 5.

If you know to begin with that only a working map will be wanted, save time by making only the minium number of essential measurements. Often sufficient measurements have already been made by someone at the scene. You can also make minimum measurements when the site of the accident is near and you could easily return for more complete measurements. But if you are in doubt about what kind of a map will eventually be wanted, and if the site is too far off for easy revisiting, get all the data you think you miqht need while you are at the site.

Measuring The Road

Make basic measurements of roadway dimensions either *longitudinally* (lengthwise—straight along the road-

Exhibit 3. *An example of an after-accident scene for which a scale map is to be drawn for traffic-accident reconstruction purposes.*

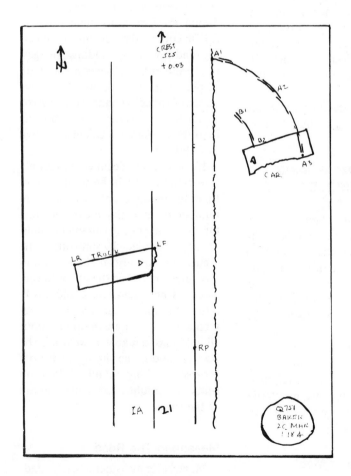

Exhibit 4. *A working map with minimum detail for the after-accident situation pictured.*

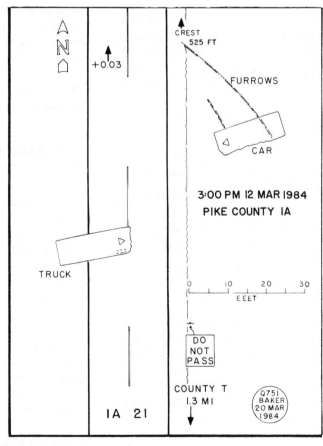

Exhibit 5. *A display map with more detail for the after-accident situation pictured.*

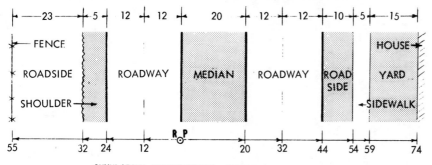

CONSECUTIVE MEASUREMENTS: THIS METHOD INTRODUCES ERRORS

CUMULATIVE MEASUREMENTS: PREFERRED METHOD

Exhibit 6. When you have to measure a series of distances in the same general direction from a given point, measure all the distances from that point. That is better than measuring each distance separately because a mistake in one measurement does not affect subsequent measurements.

way) or *transverse* (crosswise—shortest distance straight across the roadway at right angles to the longitudinal direction).

When you make a series of measurements (such as measuring across a road) measure *cumulatively* rather than *consecutively*. In other words, start at one point and record all measurements as distances from the beginning (reference) point, of the series. This is better than making each measurement separately. Exhibit 6 shows what this means. Here are distances across a highway. You could, as in the upper line, measure each one. But then an error in one measurement might affect the location of several points. It is better, as in the lower line in Exhibit 6, to locate several points from one place, for example, the left edge of the median. It is usually quicker, too, especially if you are working alone. On a field sketch,

show the point measured *from* by a circle (for zero) or a spot. Show each point measured *to* by an arrowhead. Write the distance from the starting point to the arrowhead beside the arrowhead (Exhibit 6).

Show measurements across each street or highway in the manner described above and in Exhibit 6. For a section of highway between junctions, these may be the only measurements needed. Standard nomenclature for the parts of highway cross-sections is shown in Exhibit 7 for an urban street and in Exhibit 8 for a rural road. Other terms may be used in some areas, for example, the shoulder may be called a *berm*; however the terms illustrated are preferable.

Edges to be Located

The edge of roadways to be located may be one of the following:

1. *Painted edge line* or stripe sep-

arating roadway from shoulder (Exhibit 9)
2. *Edge of paving* where there is no painted edge line or stripe. If the paving edge is irregular, measure what seems to be the average edge line (Exhibit 10).
3. *Unmountable curb* (one which you would not ordinarily drive over). The roadway edge is the middle of the most nearly vertical slope of the curb, provided there is no edge line or stripe (Exhibit 11).
4. *Beginning of slope* toward the ditch, limit of maintenance grading, beginning of grass or other vegetation on unpaved dirt or gravel road (Exhibit 12)
5. *Joint* between pavement and mountable curb or gutter unless there is a painted edge line elsewhere (Exhibit 13)

As a rule, measure to the center of lines painted on the paving (Exhibit 9).

Edges of pavements, shoulders, sidewalks and buildings need to be located only if they have significance for the particular accident or might be used on a display map. The same may be said for fences, guardrails, railroad tracks, and property lines.

Measuring Offset Roadway Edges

When measuring a roadway junction, sight to find out whether the roadway edges go straight through (aligned on opposite sides of the junc-

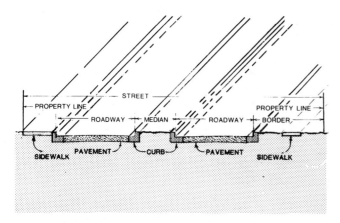

Exhibit 7. Preferred names for parts of an urban street.

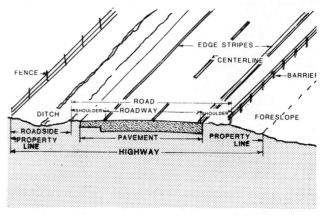

Exhibit 8. Preferred names for parts of a rural highway.

Exhibit 9. *A painted edge line separates the travelled roadway from the shoulder. Where there is such a stripe the edge of the roadway is not the edge of the paving.*

Exhibit 12. *On gravel or dirt roads, locate the edge of the travelled roadway as well as possible by difference in character of the surface. Try to use an average edge line.*

Exhibit 10. *Where there is no painted edge line, use the edge of the paving as the edge of the roadway. If this edge is irregular use what seems to be the average.*

Exhibit 13. *If the road has a gutter or mountable curb, the edge of the roadway is where the curb joins the paving, unless there is also a painted roadway edge line.*

Exhibit 11. *If roadway is edged by a vertical (unmountable) curb measure from the middle of the upright face of the curb unless there is a painted roadway marker stripe.*

tion). At some junctions the roadway may be wider on one side of the junction, or the roadway may jog slightly. This is shown in Exhibit 14. In either case, the roadway edges do not line up on opposite sides even though the roadway continues across; the edges are offset.

To determine which roadway edges go straight through, sight along each roadway edge across the junction to see whether it lines up with an edge on the opposite side. This sighting can best be done at a point about 50 to 75 ft back from the corner. Crouch down to make it easier to sight along the roadway edges, as shown in Exhibit 15.

If the roadway edges are offset, you

can measure the amount of offset by moving over until you are lined up with the edge on the opposite side of the junction. Measure the distance from this point to the edge on the near side of the junction. This method of measuring offsets is illustrated in Exhibit 16.

Measuring Junction Angles

At some junctions, the roadway edges do not line up on oppostie sides because the roadway changes direction. Such a junction is shown in Exhibit 17. You can generally tell well enough by looking at the junction whether the highways intersect at right angles (or near enough to be considered so). When the highways intersect at something other than a right angle, you will have to measure this angle.

An angle is formed when two straight lines meet or cross. Where the two lines, sides of the angle, meet is the *apex* (point) of the angle. Angles are usually measured in *degrees*. A right angle is 90° (90 degrees). Half of a right angle is 45° (Exhibit 18).

If you want to measure directly the angle at which two roadway edges intersect, you will need expensive surveying equipment and expertise in its use. Instead, you can measure the angle indirectly by making three simple distance measurements with a tape.

Think of the angle as being one corner of a triangle (Exhibit 19). Measure the length of each side of the triangle: from the apex, X, to corner A; from the apex to corner B; and from corner A to corner B. These three meas-

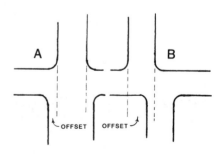

Exhibit 14. *Examples of junctions with offset roadway edges. In A, one leg is wider than the opposite leg. In B, there is a jog in one of the roadways.*

Exhibit 15. *Sighting across a junction to determine whether roadway edges on opposite sides are aligned.*

Exhibit 16. *If roadway edges on opposite sides of a junction are not aligned, while sighting, measure the amount of offset.*

Exhibit 17. *By sighting along a roadway edge, you can tell whether a roadway changes direction at a junction.*

urements establish the triangle. The angle to be recorded (at the apex, X) is one of its three angles. You thus have measurements from which you can reconstruct the angle.

Lengths measured along the two sides XA and XB do not have to be the same, but it is usually more convenient to make them the same. In practice, the angle you want to measure is that between two roadway edges at a junction, and these two edges do not actually meet but are connected by an arc (part of a circle), as shown in Exhibit 20. Find the point in the roadway where the roadway edge lines would intersect if they were extended. Do this by finding the point where, by sighting along each edge, you are aligned with both as illustrated in Exhibit 20. Put a small object, a piece of crayon, for example, on the roadway at this apex intersection to mark it temporarily. Stand back and sight over the object toward one edge of the roadway to make sure it is properly aligned. Do this also for the other edge. Relocate the object on the roadway if necessary. Then, when you are

satisfied, mark the apex intersection clearly with crayon or spray paint.

Lay out sides of angle. Having located the apex of the angle, you are now ready to measure a distance along each side of the angle and mark the roadway edges at those points. If the curve connecting the edges appears to be the arc of a circle, which it often is, make the measurements to where the curve begins (A and B in Exhibit 21). If the curb or roadway edge is a uniform curve, the curve will begin the same distance from the apex on both sides of the angle; that is, A and B in Exhibit 21 will be the same distance from the apex intersection. In practice, roads are not built so perfectly that these distances are exactly the same, and on unpaved roadways, the edges may be irregular or indefinite. So locate, as well as you can, the end of the curve farthest from the apex. Mark that point on the roadway edge, for example, at A in Exhibit 21. Then measure the same distance from the apex along the other side of the angle and mark that point along the roadway edge as at B in Exhibit 21. Final-

ly, measure the distance from A to B.

If equal distances are marked off for the ends of the road-edge arc, no other measurements are needed for the radius of the arc connecting the roadway edges, if the arc is tangent or nearly tangent to the roadway edges.

Non-circular connection. If two roadway edges at an angle to each other appear not to be connected by the arc of a circle, other similar measures can be used to lay out the triangle

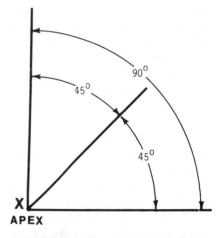

Exhibit 18. *Angles are usually measured in degrees. A 90 degree angle is a right angle.*

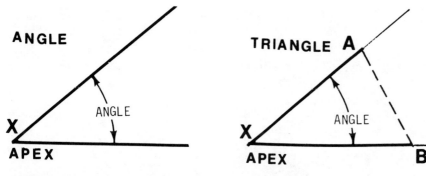

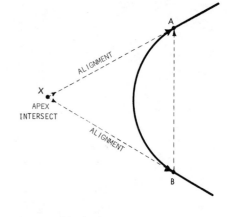

Exhibit 19. *To measure an angle, mark off a point along each side, A and B. Measure the three sides of the triangle thus formed, XA, XB, and the span, AB. This establishes the angle as one angle of a measured triangle.*

Exhibit 21. *By sighting along roadway edges, you can find the apex point of the angle between the edges. Measure an equal distance on each leg of the angle to the beginning of the curve, XA and XB. Then measure the span btween A and B. This establishes not only the angle at X, but also the radius of the curve.*

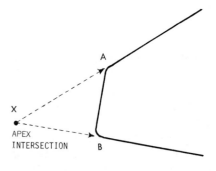

Exhibit 20. *A curve or arc usually connects adjacent roadway edges at a junction. The imaginary intersect of the roadway edges is the apex of the angle between roadway edges.*

Exhibit 22. *Measuring from the angle's apex can also be used to locate the ends of a connector between roadway edges which is not the arc of a circle.*

that establishes the angle. For example, with a straight line connecting the edges of the roadways (Exhibit 22), the best points would be the ends of this line because the distances from the apex that are measured for the angle also fix the line between the two roadway edges. In fact, the same triangle then measures the angles at A and B in Exhibit 22 as well as the main apex angle.

Avoid small triangles to measure angles. If the connecting arc is so small that the distances from its ends to the apex are less than 10 ft (3 m), use these distances to locate the ends

of the arc, but not to measure the angle. For that, use greater distances, preferably 20 ft (6 m) or more. Very small triangles cannot be measured accurately enough to give reliable angle measurements.

One angle is enough for two intersecting roadways if the edges of each roadway are parallel, Exhibit 23. In fact, where two roadways (each with parallel sides) cross, four angles are formed (D1, D2, D3, and D4 in Exhibit 23). They are all equal so only one needs to be measured.

Measure the easiest one of equal angles. Refer to the junction in Ex-

hibit 23. To measure angle D1 would require being right out in an intersection with only alignment lines rather than actual roadway edges to work with. That would be very inconvenient. Angles D3 and D4 would be little better because you would have only one real roadway edge to work with. Angle D2 is the easiest to measure. Furthermore, the same measurement will do for the roadway edge arc between these edges.

Measuring Curves

Two main kinds of curves are in-

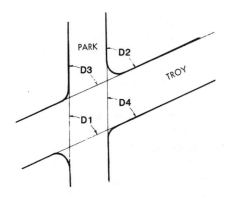

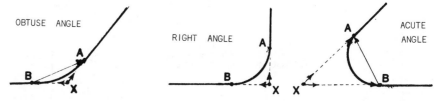

Exhibit 24. *Measurements (XA and XB) from the apex to the ends of an arc which is tangent to both edges of an angle, and a measurement of the span (AB) between the starting point of the arc on each edge, will establish both the arc and the angle. This applies to obtuse, right, and acute angles.*

Exhibit 23. *When one roadway crosses another, two pairs of parallel lines (edges) cross. Then there are are four identical angles, D1, D2, D3, and D4, between roadway edges. These angles are all the same. Therefore, only one needs to be measured.*

volved in preparing after-accident situation maps, both are arcs of circles: 1) curves connecting roadway edges at junctions; and 2) curves in roadways themselves. In both cases, the radius of the curve (distance from the curve to its center) must be found.

Curves (arcs) between roadways edges at junctions have already been mentioned in connection with measuring angles. The easiest way to measure for most of these curves is to do so in connection with measurements for the angle. Simply measure the angle and then find how far from the apex the curve between the roadway edges begins and ends. No other measurements and no calculations are needed. Where roadway edges are at right angles, as most of them are, the angle does not have to be measured, but the ends of the arc must be located. Measurements for curves are shown in Exhibit 24. If it is more than 100 ft (30 m) from the apex to the ends of a roadway edge arc, measure the arc like a curve in the roadway as

described later. At this juncture, we are concerned only with the curve measurements needed. How the curves are drawn on a map from these measurements is explained later in Topic 834.

Curved roadways between junctions are handled differently than arcs at junctions. If you are so situated that you can easily obtain plans from which the road was built, you do not need to measure a curve in the road; you can take it more accurately from the plans. If there are no plans, or if you do not have ready access to them, you will have to make measurements.

Consider a road curve as an arc (part of a circle) for accident-investigation purposes. Most road curves are arcs. A few road curves have arcs with larger radiuses at the beginning and end connected by an arc with a smaller radius. Some unplanned curves do not fit any pattern well. But, unless you know of some special reason for not doing so, handle all curves as arcs; that will serve the purposes of all but a very few accident investigations.

The radius of an arc cannot be measured directly because you cannot easily locate the center of the circle of which the arc is part. Even if you could locate it, you might not be able to measure from it if it were in a building, river, or a forest. But, if part of the arc is measured, the arc's radius can be calculated. To do this, measure a chord of a convenient length (usually 100 ft or 30 m) straight across from one point on the road edge curve to another, as in Exhibit 25 (measure the chord from A to B). From the middle of this chord (at point C), measure the distance to the arc. This is called the middle ordinate (C to D in Exhibit 25). Record these measurements. How to compute radius is in Topic 834.

A modification of this method is to use the width of the road as the middle ordinate. Stand on the outside edge of the curve and sight across the inside edge to a point beyond on the outside edge, from A over C to B in Exhibit 26. Mark the two points, A and B, on the outside edge of the roadway and measure the distance

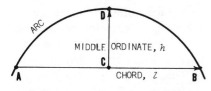

Exhibit 25. *To obtain data from which the radius of an arc may be computed, measure a chord ACB and from the middle of this chord the distance to the arc, CD, which is the middle ordinate.*

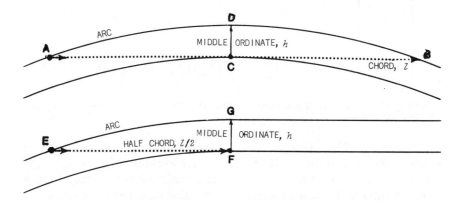

Exhibit 26. *A road curve with a large radius may be measured by sighting across the curve in such a way that the width of the roadway is the middle ordinate of the arc.*

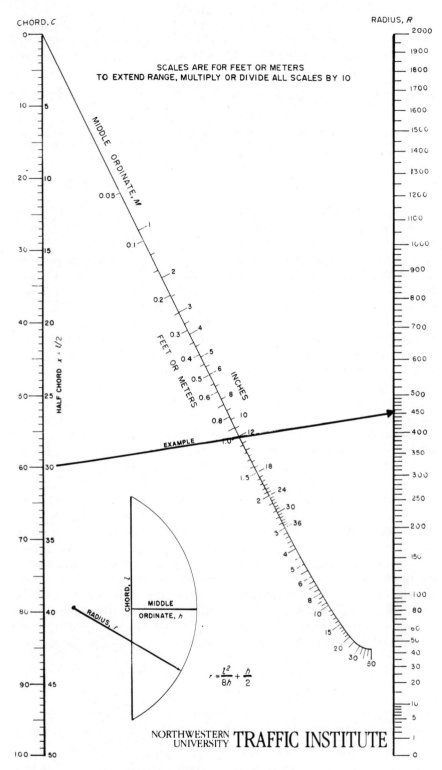

Exhibit 27. *Nomograph for determining the radius of a curve when the chord and middle ordinate are known.*

roadway. Measure from that position to the beginning of the curve. That is half of the chord. Measure the width of the road for the middle ordinate and record the measurements.

Measuring the chord across a long curve may be inconvenient and even dangerous if traffic is heavy. Therefore, measure along the edge of the road, that is, along the arc. Whenever the chord (or arc) is more than 20 times as long as the middle ordinate, it makes no important difference whether you measure along the chord (ACB in Exhibit 26) or along the arc (ADB in the same exhibit). The two distances are nearly the same. In fact, the difference in the two distances will be less than the likely error in locating the points between which to measure. For example, with 2,000-ft radius and a 20-ft roadway width, the difference in measured length is only about 2 feet for the 564-ft chord and the resulting error in radius is 0.7 percent.

The radius can be calculated from chord and middle ordinate by using the following equation, in which l is the length of the chord, h the middle ordinate, and r the radius:

$$r = \frac{l^2}{8h} + \frac{h}{2}$$

For example, if the chord is 60 ft and the middle ordinate measures 2 ft,

$$r = \frac{60(60)}{8(1)} + \frac{1}{1}$$

$$= \frac{3600}{8} + 1$$

$$= 450 + 1 = 451 \text{ ft}$$

A table or chart (nomograph) can be used to determine the radius from a chord and middle ordinate. Exhibit 27 is such a chart. Note that the scale for h, the middle ordinate, is marked for feet and tenths on one side and for inches on the other. For example, the point marked 1.0 ft on the left is marked 12 in. on the right. By drawing a straight line across the chart, you can find the radius of the arc. For instance, use same measurements as in the previous example: chord 60 ft and middle ordinate 1.0 ft. In Exhibit 27, find the chord, 60, on the left scale,

between them. Then measure the width of the road as the middle ordinate and record these two measurements. A still simpler method is possible at the beginning and end of roadway curves where arc joins the

tangent. This is especially useful if you are working alone. Stand on the outside of the curve and move to such a position (E in Exhibit 26) that you can sight along the straight road edge that leads to the inside curve of the

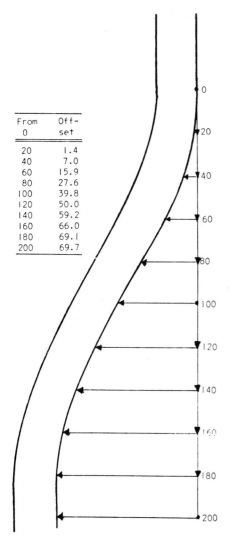

From 0	Off-set
20	1.4
40	7.0
60	15.9
80	27.6
100	39.8
120	50.0
140	59.2
160	66.0
180	69.1
200	69.7

Exhibit 28. *Irregular road curves can be measured as offsets at specified intervals from a straight line; either a stretched cord or a sighted extension of a road edge.*

Exhibit 29. *A stretched cord can be used as a reference line when nothing better is available.*

Z. Find the middle ordinate, 1.0 ft, on the middle scale, *h*. Draw a *straight* line from 60 on scale *c* through 1.0 on scale *h*, to scale *r*. Read the radius on scale *r* at this point. It is 451 ft.

The same equation and calculator can be used to find the radius of a curve by using inches or centimeters instead of feet for all measurements.

Offset method. Sometimes the curve is so irregular or the edges so ill-defined that a chord and middle-ordinate measurement is unlikely to be satisfactory. This can occur in parks, campgrounds, construction sites, loading docks, and such places. Then the easiest way is to establish a base line and measure distances along this line and offsets from it. This is like measuring long curved tiremarks. The base line can be an imaginary extension of a straight edge of the road as in Exhibit 28 where offsets are measured at 20-ft intervals.

Sometimes the easiest solution to a reference-line problem is to stretch a cord across the area (Exhibit 29) and measure offsets from that.

The offset method can also be used to measure very large radius circular arcs where using a chord and middle ordinate might be difficult.

Difficulties of very irregular road-

ways. Junctions in which one or both roadways are curved; junctions that include islands, squares, circles, or plazas; and parts of interchanges are often too irregular to be measured for mapping by the methods described. However, there is a general method which can be used on any area regardless of how irregular. This method is sometimes laborious, but it is not difficult. The roadways are simply divided into triangles and all sides of each triangle are measured.

Exhibit 30 will be used as an illustration. In any irregular area, there will be a number of curves or edges to be located The five steps required to measure this area for mapping are as follows:

1. Designate each curve to be located by a letter (A, B, C, and D in Exhibits 30 and 31).
2. Beginning at one end of an open curve or any point on a closed curve, measure along the curve and mark stations at intervals on the edge of the roadway (Exhibit 31). Make these stations a full number of feet apart; avoid fractions of a foot. Mark the beginning station 0. Mark the following stations with the distance from the 0 station. Thus, on

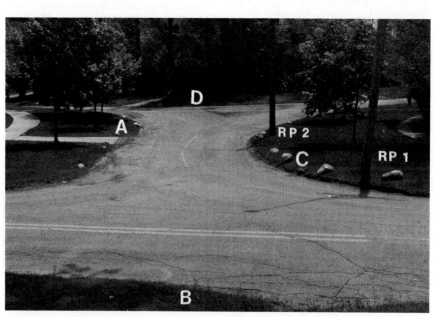

Exhibit 30. *Some junctions have no straight roadway edges suitable for sighting or reference lines. There are only curves. Such areas may be broken up into a series of triangles for measuring.*

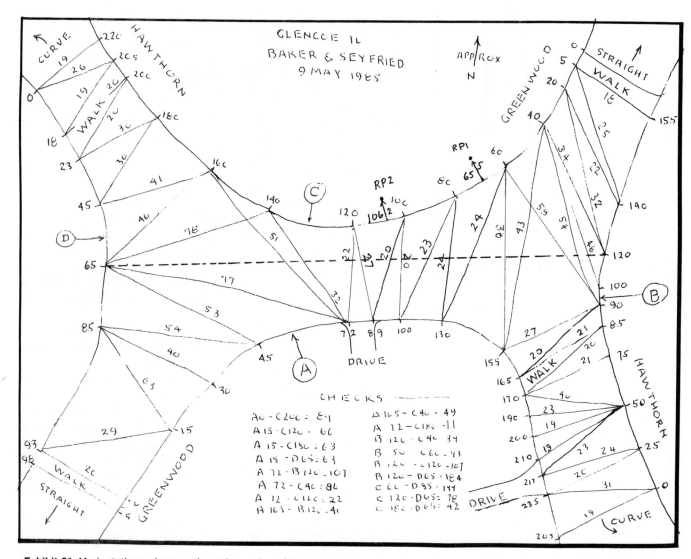

Exhibit 31. *Mark stations along each roadway edge of the irregular junction. Then measure distances between stations on opposite edges. This gives dimensions of a series of triangles which define the roadway configuration. Shown above are field notes for measurements of the roadways pictured in Exhibit 30.*

Curve B in Exhibit 31, the second station is marked 50 because it is 50 ft from the 0 or beginning station. Pull the measuring tape straight from one station to the next. Do not try to measure around a curve. Where a curve is sharp, make the distance between stations short. It is best to locate a station wherever curvature changes. On straight or nearly straight sections, put stations about as far apart as the roadway is wide. At the end of the tape, 100 ft in the case of a tape that long, put a station from which to begin measuring again. How the stations might be located for the area illustrated is shown in Exhibit 31.

3. Make a field sketch and show on it the stations. This sketch does not have to be to scale, but all stations must be shown (Exhibit 31).

4. On this sketch, draw solid straight lines from stations on one side to those on the other side to divide the area into triangles, one side of each triangle being the edge of the roadway between two stations. Thus, the first triangle in the illustration might be from station A0 to station D93 to A15 and along the edge of the roadway 15 ft back to A0. In general, lines across the roadway should be to close points on the opposite side.

5. Measure all the cross distances and record the measurements on the field sketch. If the field sketch is crowded, measurements can be recorded in a table on a separate sheet. If there is traffic in the area, a measuring wheel may be much handier than a tape measure for these measurements, but it will not be as accurate, so it is better to use a tape. Additional connections between stations, for example, B120 to D65 in Exhibit 31, may be drawn as dotted lines on the field sketch. These serve to verify other measurements and are

Exhibit 32. *The grade of slope of a road can be measured with a tape or ruler and an ordinary carpenter's level.*

useful if mistakes have been made. How to draw a map from these measurements is explained in Topic 834.

Measuring Grades

Roadway grades (slopes) are measured by the rise or fall of the surface per foot of horizontal distance, parallel to the center line. For example, if the surface rose 0.01 ft in 1 ft of horizontal distance, the grade would be 0.01. Divide any change in elevation (rise or fall) by the corresponding horizontal distance to get the grade. For example, if the road fell 1.3 ft in 85 ft, the grade would be $1.3/85 = 0.015$. This is change in elevation in feet per foot.

Percent grade is change in elevation in feet per 100 ft. The grade in feet per foot is multiplied by 100 to get the percent grade. Thus, in the example above, the grade would be $0.015 \times 100 = 1.5$ percent.

Measuring grades requires some special equipment. The simplest way

is to use a carpenter's level, the longer the better. Put one end on the surface as in Exhibit 32 and the other end directly down-grade from the end on the road. With the bubble showing level, measure how far the downhill end of the level is from the surface. Then the grade is the distance from road to level in inches and tenths (not eighths or sixteenths) divided by the length of the level in inches.

Grade measuring with the Traffic Template.[1, 2] A clipboard can be adapted for use with the *Traffic Template* to measure grades.

About the middle of the left side, bore a 5/16-in. hole 3/8-in. from the edge. Then draw a line through the center of this hole across the face of the board and at right angles to the right edge as in Exhibit 33.

To measure the grade of a paved roadway (Exhibit 34):

1. Put a pencil through the hole in the clipboard and the pivot hole in the template so that the template covers the line drawn across the board. Put the glossy side of the template next to the board.
2. Place the right edge of the clipboard down on a fairly even spot on the pavement so this edge is on, or parallel to, the center line of the road. Hold the clipboard vertically on edge.
3. See that the template swings freely and comes to rest hanging from the pencil flat against the clipboard.
4. Grasp template and board together tightly so that the tem-

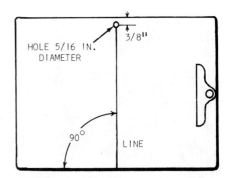

Exhibit 33. *Clipboards are easily adapted for use with the Traffic Template in measuring grades.*

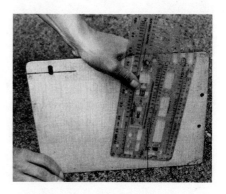

Exhibit 34. *The Traffic Template used with a properly prepared clipboard is useful for measuring grades and super-elevations of roadway surfaces.*

plate does not move from the position where it came to rest and then lift both up so you can look at them.
5. Where the line on the board crosses the scale on the lower end of the template, read the figure for "grade" in feet rise or fall per foot horizontally.

If the pavement is very rough, covered with snow or mud, or if the road

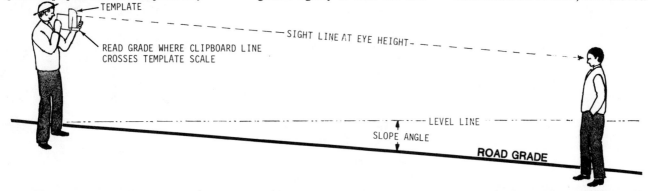

Exhibit 35. *If road surface is too uneven to accommodate clipboard for grade measurements with template, use edge of clipboard for a line of sight parallel to road surface. This is sufficiently accurate for most purposes.*

Exhibit 36. *A small clinometer, used on a straight edge, measures the slope or grade, usually in degrees.*

is unpaved, the traffic template can be used in the follwing way (Exhibit 35):

1. Note where your eye height comes to on a helper when you face him. If he is your height, this point will be his eyes.

2. Then stand 20 to 50 steps away from your helper on the grade.

Degrees	Feet/foot	Percent
1	0.0175	1.75
2	0.0349	3.49
3	0.0524	5.24
4	0.0699	6.99
5	0.0875	8.75
6	0.1051	10.51
7	0.1228	12.28
8	0.1405	14.05
9	0.1584	15.84
10	0.1763	17.63
45	1.0000	100.00

Exhibit 37. *This shows how the angle of a slope in degrees is related to the grade in feet per foot or in percent.*

Each of you should be near the center of the road.

3. Pivot the template on the board with a pencil.

4. Hold the board vertical and sight along the left edge to your eye height on your helper.

5. See that the template swings freely against the board. When it comes to rest, grasp and read.

A grade, as read from the template, is the rise or fall vertically in feet per foot of horizontal distance. For example, +0.10 means a rise of 0.1 ft for a horizontal distance of 1 ft, or a 10-ft rise per 100 ft.

The accuracy of grades carefully measured with this template is within 0.015. This is 0.9° and adequate for most accident-investigation purposes.

Clinometers are instruments for measuring inclines or grades. There are several different types. One kind, which can be had at many hardware

stores, is illustrated in Exhibit 36. Because it is small and road surfaces may be irregular, use it on a carpenter's square or straightedge more than two feet long.

The clinometer may read the grade in either percent or degrees. It is common highway design practice to express the grade in percent.

If your clinometer reads in degrees, you can convert this reading to percent. Mathematically speaking, the grade in feet per foot is the *tangent* of the angle in degress. Exhibit 37 shows the relationship between angle degrees and slopes.

A line level and chalk (snap) line can also be used to measure grades (Exhibit 38). Anchor or have someone hold one end of the line firmly on the road surface. Depending on the grade, pull 10 to 100 ft of line taut. Hang the level on the line. Raise and lower the free end to level it. Then measure the vertical distance from the down-hill end of the line to the ground and the horizontal distance from the anchored end to the down-hill end. Divide the vertical distance by the horizontal distance to get the grade in feet per foot. Multiply by 100 to get the grade in percent.

Vertical curves (Exhibit 39) are parts of the roadway where the grade is changing. For example, at the crest of a hill, the grade gradually changes from an uphill to a downhill grade. If

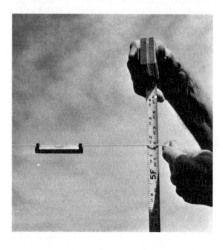

Exhibit 38. *Use a line level to establish horizontal and vertical distances for quickly measuring grades or slopes.*

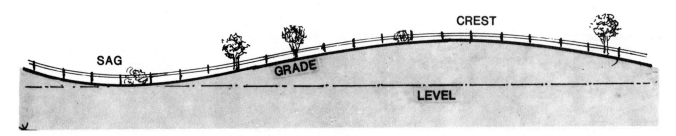

Exhibit 39. *Where the roadway goes up and down hill, the grade may change in a short distance. Measure the grade near the skidmarks or wherever it may be significant.*

you are measuring for an after-accident situation map involving a vertical curve, you can generally use the methods described to approximate the grade for a short length of the road (usually 100-foot or less). If you need to know grades for a greater length of a vertical curve, this measurement will require surveying instruments. Before having an expensive survey made, ask whether the highway engineer has plans for the road which will show this information.

Superelevation (bank) is the grade *across* the roadway at right angles to the center line from the inside to the outside edge on a curve. Measure it at right angles to the center line in the same way grade is measured. Superelevation affects the speed at which a vehicle may safely round a curve. The greater the superelevation, the higher this speed can be. Therefore, measure superelevation at any accident site where a vehicle slid or ran off the highway curve. Measure superelevation where the vehicle went off the road and in the middle of the curve.

Sometimes superelevation is given in inches per foot on engineering drawings. You can change inches per foot to feet per foot by dividing by 12, or change feet per foot to inches per foot by multiplying by 12.

Sometimes superelevation is different on two halves of a road because the pavement has a crown or rise in the middle. In this case, measure the superelevation on the outside half of the road. This may be a minus bank or a slope down to the outside. When you find such a condition in an accident investigation, report it fully. Superelevation is seldom greater than 0.10 or ten percent.

Roadside slopes can be measured using the methods described previously. Roadside slopes are normally measured at right angles to the centerline of the roadway. But if you are investigating a traffic accident you may be more interested in the slope along the path off the road followed by the vehicle. For example, if a vehicle left the roadway and travelled down a roadside embankment, measure the slope in the direction of the path that the vehicle followed (Exhibit 40).

When measuring the roadside slope, be careful to take measurements that are representative of the overall slope. Roadsides are often rough and filled with bumps and dips. As a result, it is difficult to get a representative slope measurement using a device that must be set on the ground surface, such as a clinometer, or carpenter's level. A more representative measurement can usually be made by using the Traffic Template and clipboard as a sighting device as shown in Exhibit 35.

On steep roadsides, measure the distance with a line level and chalk line.

Vertical Measurements

Most vertical measurements are made easily and accurately enough with a tape or a tape rule. These are measurements of the height of scars and scrapes on walls, trees, posts, and other objects; height of hedges, crops, banks, and walls which may be view obstructions; height of curbs, pavement chuck holes, and edge drop-offs which may affect vehicle behavior; height of guardrails, signs, signals, fences, culvert headwalls, which may have some bearing on the accident; and height of vehicle headlamps, and

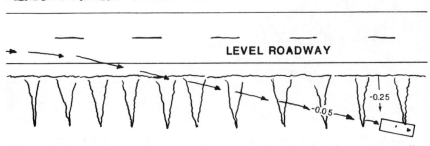

Exhibit 40. *Measure a roadside slope in the direction of a vehicle's path, not necessarily at right angles to the roadway.*

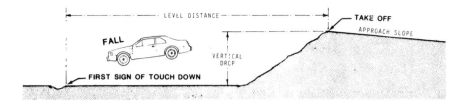

Exhibit 41. *When a vehicle moves unsupported through the air, locate and describe the signs of where it took off and where it landed.*

drivers' eyes. Depth of ditches can be measured well enough for most purposes by measuring from the bottom of the ditch to a sight line across the roadway.

Vertical fall measurements, however, are more complex. Good speed estimates can be made when a vehicle leaves the ground and falls unsupported through the air before landing. For example, a vehicle may go off the edge of a construction excavation and land in the bottom of the excavation or against the opposite side of the hole. To estimate speed, the vertical and horizontal distances travelled in the air by the center of mass must be known.

The horizontal and vertical distances travelled by the center of mass of the vehicle depends in part on the dimensions of the vehicle and on what part of the vehicle touches the ground first. For an after-accident situation map you only need to locate the *signs* of where the vehicle took off and landed, for example, the edge of the

bank and tire marks on landing. This is discussed and illustrated in Topic 828, *Measuring at the Scenes of Traffic Accidents.* Thus, in Exhibit 41 you would locate A, the edge of the take-off surface, and B, the first signs of tiremarks on landing. Whoever makes the speed estimate must allow for the dimensions of the vehicle.

When you cannot readily measure horizontal and vertical distances you may be able to measure the diagonal distance and the angle of the diagonal: You can measure this angle using a clinometer (Exhibit 42). Stand at the take-off point and sight along the clinometer straight edge to the nearest landing mark. Because you measure the angle from your standing eye height, also measure the diagonal distance from this same height. Later, you must subtract your standing eye height from the calculated vertical distance to get the true change in ground elevation between the take-off and landing.

The equations for calculating *h*, the

vertical height and *d*, horizontal distance from take off to landing when you know the diagonal distance, *s*, and angle, *a*, are as follows:

Vertical distance, $h = s \sin a$

Horizontal distance, $d = s \cos a$

Sin (sine) and cos (cosine) are trigonometric functions which may be found on many hand calculators and in published tables.

For example, suppose that the diagonal distance is 70 ft and the angle, a, is 30°. From a table or calculator, sin 30° = 0.50 and cos 30° = 0.87. Then

Vertical distance = 70(0.50) = 35.0 ft

Horizontal distance = 70(0.87) = 60.9 ft.

Subtract your eye height from the vertical distance to get the true height of fall.

Rather than making these computations, you can determine the horizontal and vertical distances from the alignment chart (nomograph) in Exhibit 43.

For example, suppose that the diagonal distance from your standing eye height at the takeoff spot to the beginning of the landing scar was 70 feet and the angle between this diagonal and a level line was 30° Place a mark on the diagonal distance scale of the nomograph (Exhibit 43) at 70 feet. Place a mark on the angle scale for vertical distances at 30° Connect these marks with a straight line that extends to the vertical distance scale. Read the vertical distance as 35 ft. Mark the angle scale for horizontal distances at 30° Connect the 70-foot diagonal distance mark with this 30° mark with a straight line that extends to the horizontal distance scale. Read the horizontal distance as 60 ft. This is illustrated in Exhibit 43. From the vertical height, you must subtract the standing eye height at takeoff to obtain the true difference in elevation.

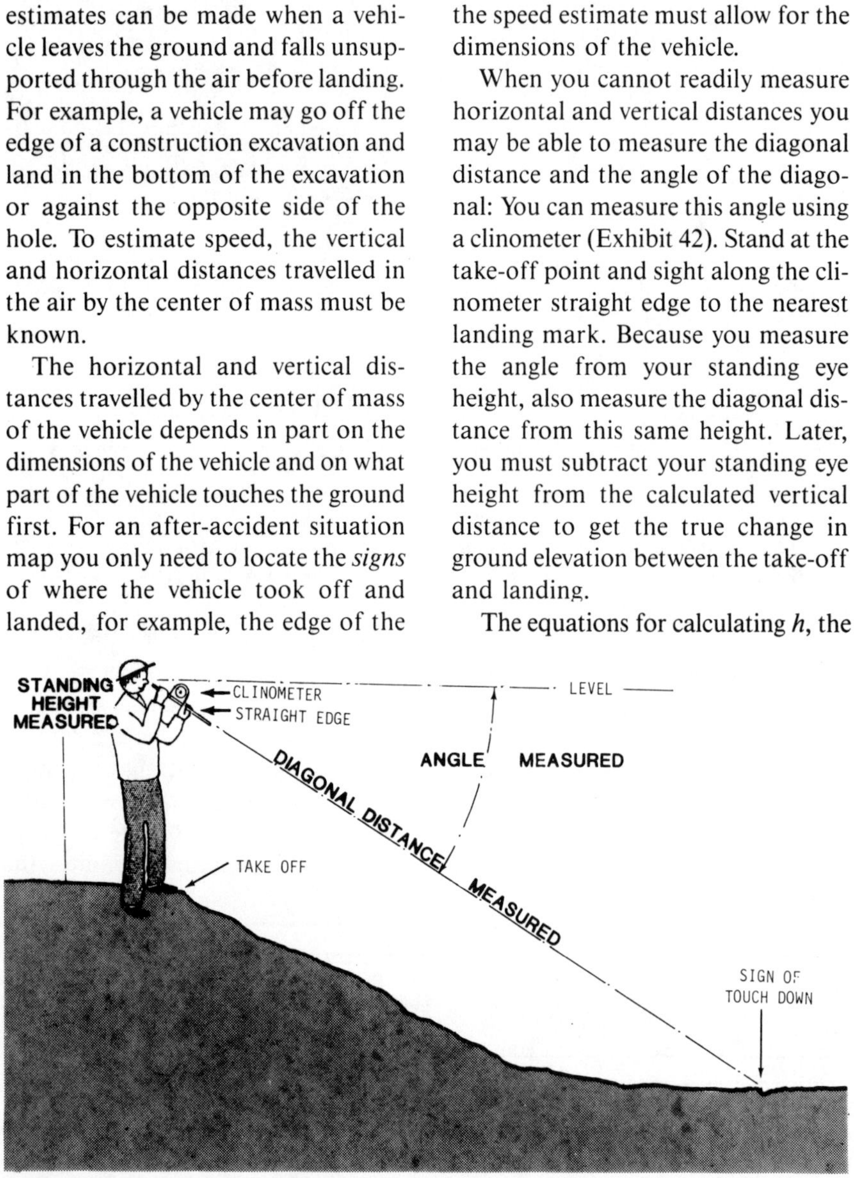

4. AT-SITE MEASURING

Before starting out to make measurements for an after-accident situa-

Exhibit 42. *Knowing the diagonal distance and the angle of the diagonal to horizontal, you can calculate the horizontal and vertical distances.*

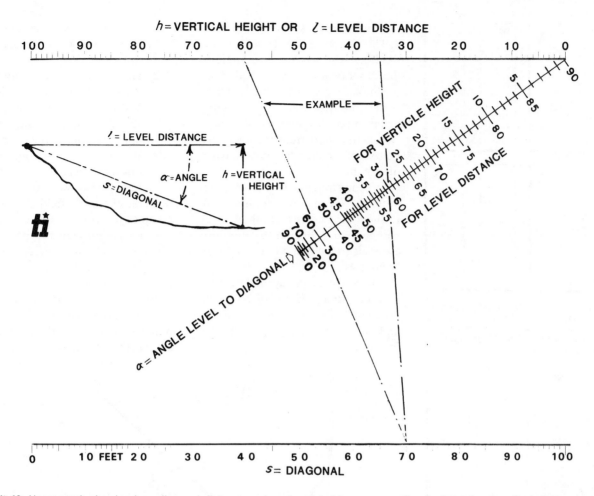

Exhibit 43. *Nomograph showing how diagonal distance and angle related to corresponding horizontal and vertical distances.*

tion map, be sure you know exactly where the accident occurred. Have with you a copy of the accident report, field notes of at-scene measurements, and at-scene photographs to locate the accident site. You might be sent out to get information for a map with directions to the wrong place.

At the accident site, before doing anything else, find the reference lines and points used to locate results of the accidents. You must be able to locate these on your field sketch.

Measurements at the scene must be made quickly and often under unfavorable conditions. But measurements made later at the site can be made more carefully. Take your time and prepare a good field sketch. It will be very worthwhile.

Procedure for making at-site meas-

urements for a map involves five main steps:

1. Make a field sketch of the basic roadways.
2. Add details needed.
3. Plan measurements to be made.
4. Make measurements.
5. Record measurements on your field sketch.

These steps are similar to those for locating results of the accident as described in Topic 828, *Measuring at the Scenes of Traffic Accidents*.

Make Basic Field Sketch

The roadway layout must be visualized and drawn as a sketch on your field notes. This is the point at which many measurements for after accident-situation maps begin to go wrong. Think of the "skeleton" or

"bare bones" roadway to begin with. If no junction or cross road is involved, the matter is a simple one of deciding whether the road is: 1) straight; 2) curved., or 3) a combination where a curve meets a straight road (tangent). If a junction is involved, decide whether it is: 1) a simple T junction; 2) a simple + (crossing) junction; or 3) a complicated junction with offset legs or more than four legs.

Disregard, to begin with, the following details:

- Returns (curves) connecting roadway edges
- Driveways
- Shoulders and ditches
- Traffic control devices
- Structures, such as buildings and bridges

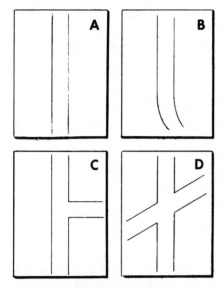

Exhibit 44. *Four skeleton outlines of roadways as beginnings of field notes for recording measurements. A and B are non-junction layouts; C and D are junction layouts for measurements.*

• Parking bays and turning lanes. This leaves a "skeleton" of the roadway which is the first thing to draw as a field sketch for field notes.

Simple layouts are easily represented in a field sketch. Draw lightly a pair of parallel lines, usually about two inches apart from the top to the bottom of the sheet to represent edges of the main roadway. Show them curved or straight, whichever is appropriate (A and B in Exhibit 44). If there is a crossroad, show it by another pair of lines at the appropriate angle to the first pair (C and D in Exhibit 44).

Complex junction layouts take a little more study. Think of what the "skeleton" of roadways is like. As you look at the location, ask yourself these four questions:

1. Can this junction be separated into two or more simple junctions?
2. How many legs (entering roadways) does the junction have?
3. Which roadway edges go straight through (aligned on opposite sides of the junction)?
4. Which legs are at right angles to each other?

Perhaps the best way to explain how to make the basic field sketch of a complex junction is to take an example and go through the procedure. Look at Exhibit 45. At a glance, you can see that this junction is no simple one because it has five legs.

To determine which roadway edges go straight through, sight along each roadway edge across the junction to see whether it lines up with an edge

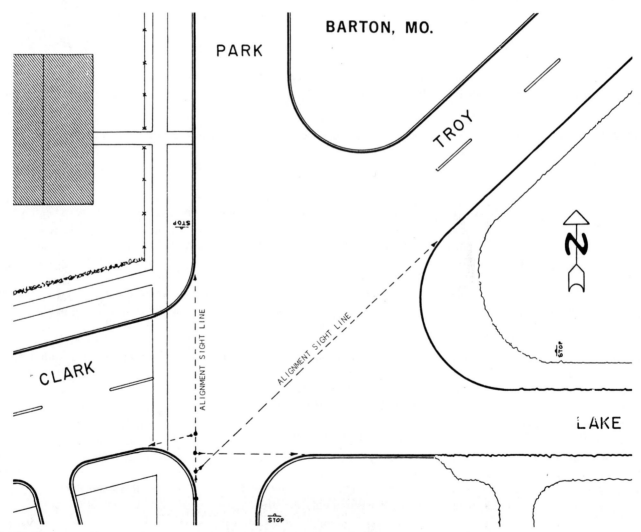

Exhibit 45. *Layout of a junction to be measured and mapped for traffic-accident investigation purposes.*

on the opposite side as in Exhibit 15. In Exhibit 45, sighting north along the west side of Park from south of Clark shows that the west edge of Park is aligned north and south of Clark as shown by the dotted *alignment line*. There are no other roadway edges that are aligned.

You can tell well enough by looking at the angles which are right angles or near enough to be considered so. In the example, only one angle is a right angle: that between the east edge of Park and the south edge of Lake. All of the four questions have now been answered for this example.

Begin the field sketch by drawing the aligned edges clear across the field notes sheet. In this case, there is only one such edge. Draw a line for it across the sheet lightly (A in Exhibit 46). Beginning at this edge line, draw

another light line at right angles to it to represent the south edge of Lake. These form the only right angle at the junction (B in Exhibit 46). Where these lines meet is an *intersect*.

Locate intersects for the other legs. You have already drawn one edge of each of two legs. Where these edges cross is the intersect for Park and Lake. Now imagine you are standing on the west side of Park. Move along the west edge of Park until you are aligned with the south edge of Troy. This point is in the roadway on an extension of the east edge of Park rather than actually on the edge of that roadway. (Exhibit 45). When you find the intersect for the south edge of Troy, mark it on the paving. Note that this intersect is a little south of the intersect for Lake. Therefore, on your field sketch along the west edge line

of Park south of the Lake intersect, mark the Troy intersect, and from there, lightly draw a line northwest to the edge of the sheet to represent the Troy alignment line and south edge of Troy (C in Exhibit 46). This locates a second intersect.

Now, for the next intersect, move along the alignment line for the west edge of Park again until you find the intersect for the south edge of Clark. This will also be in the roadway, not on an edge, and will be a little north of the previous two intersects. Mark it on the paving. Then on your field sketch, mark a point on the line representing the west edge of Park a little north of the Lake intersect to represent the Clark intersect. From there, draw a light line toward the west but at a small angle to the south to represent the south edge of Clark (D

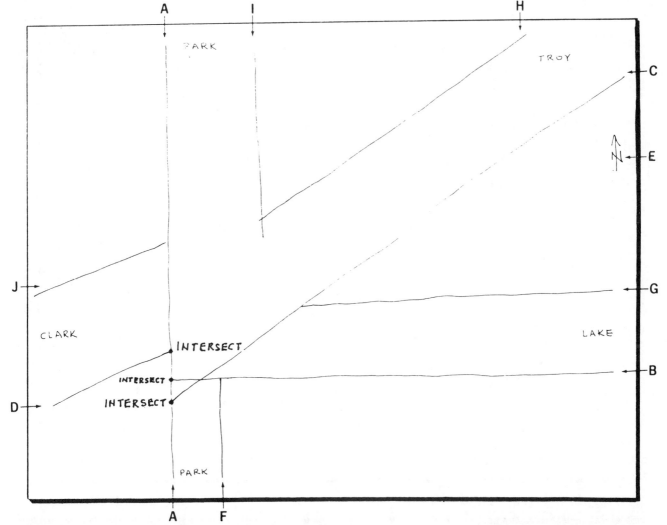

Exhibit 46. *Skeleton for field sketch of junction shown in Exhibit 45. Letters in the margin of the field sketch refer to explanation in the text.*

Either roadway edge can be used to locate an intersect. Thus, in Exhibit 46, alignment with the north edge of Troy, as well as the south edge, could be used for an intersect, but two are unnecessary. The south edge intersect is more convenient because it is not so far out in the roadway where traffic will interfere with measuring.

Mark north on your field sketch if you have not already done so. It will help you to keep your directions in mind (E in Exhibit 46). Place it where it will not be in the way. You now have a "bare bones skeleton" of the junction locating all five legs at their proper angles.

Draw remaining roadway edges on the field sketch which, until now, shows only one edge of each leg.

These other edges are parallel to those already drawn. Show appropriate widths for the roadways. In Exhibit 45, note that Park south of the junction is the narrowest roadway. Park north of the junction, Clark, and Lake are wider; and all are about the same width. So draw the east edge of Park lightly (F in Exhibit 46).

Draw the north edge of Lake, making Lake a little wider than the part of Park already drawn (G in Exhibit 46). Draw the remaining three roadways about the same width (H, I, and J in Exhibit 46). You now have a field sketch of the basic layout of the junction. If you are measuring only to prepare a working map, this may be all the detail you need.

Add returns (curves) between roadway edges. So far, returns between

edges have been disregarded. Now draw them on the field sketch with approximate curvature (A, B, C, D, and E in Exhibit 47). Draw these in strong, not light, and go over the roadway edges from the ends of the curves to the edge of the sheet to strengthen them. Draw strong, smooth lines if the roadway is paved and strong, slightly wavy lines, to suggest small irregularities, if the roadway is not paved (F in Exhibit 47). Do not erase the light lines that are left; they still show intersects. You now have a sketch of the location showing configuration of the roadways and you can begin to put in details.

Add Details Needed

Put in street names if you have not already done so. Put them at the edges

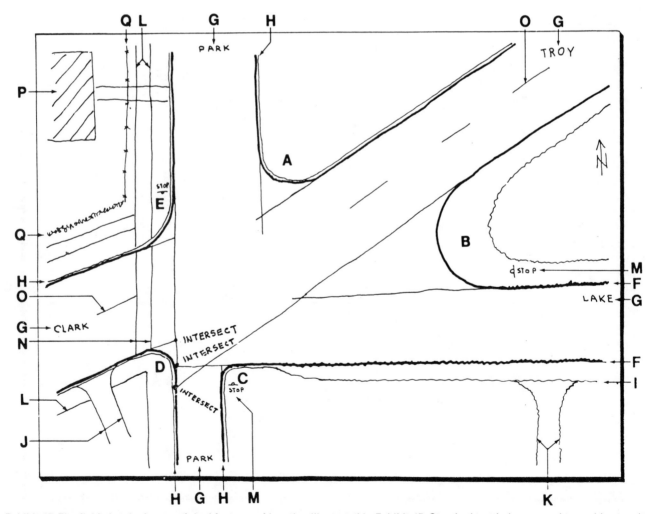

Exhibit 47. *The field sketch shows required features of junction illustrated in Exhibit 45. Standard symbols are used to avoid extensive notes. Field sketch is usually drawn freehand.*

of the field sketch where they will be out of the way (G in Exhibit 47).

Whether the field sketch is very simple or complicated, like Exhibit 47, follow the same scheme for adding details. Use symbols, such as those already mentioned, to distinguish paved from unpaved roadways. You thus avoid many notes on the field sketch.

Reference points and lines used to locate results of the accident must appear on the field sketch of the location. If you know what they are, as you should, see if you can find them on your field sketch. If there are poles or other objects which you have not yet included, add them. Carry a copy of the accident report and at-scene measurements with you to help you identify these reference points.

Show curbs, where they exist, by light, smooth lines outside of the heavier edge lines (H in Exhibit 47).

Show shoulders. If they are unpaved, show them by light, slightly wavy edge lines at approximately the right distance from the roadway to show shoulder width (I in Exhibit 47). If they are paved shoulders, show them with smooth lines like paving edges, but make them light.

Show driveways, like roadways, with smooth edges (J in Exhibit 50) if paved, and with wavy edges if unpaved (K in Exhibit 47).

Show sidewalks if they are necessary, as in some pedestrian accidents or for display maps. Draw edges smooth if sidewalks are paved (L in Exhibit 47), wavy if not.

Show traffic control devices which

may be significant for the particular accident (M in Exhibit 47). Indicate the legend (marking) on any signs and the direction toward which signals face.

Show crosswalks, center lines, and lane lines, if marked on the roadway and relevant to the accident. Do this with light lines (N and O in Exhibit 47).

Show buildings and other structures if relevant to the accident. Cross hatch them to show they are view obstructions (P in exhibit 47).

Show fences, hedges, trees, and poles if relevant to the accident (Q in Exhibit 47).

Other details can be shown if they have meaning, for example, drain inlets, culvert headwalls, bridge railings, railroad tracks, pavement joints or

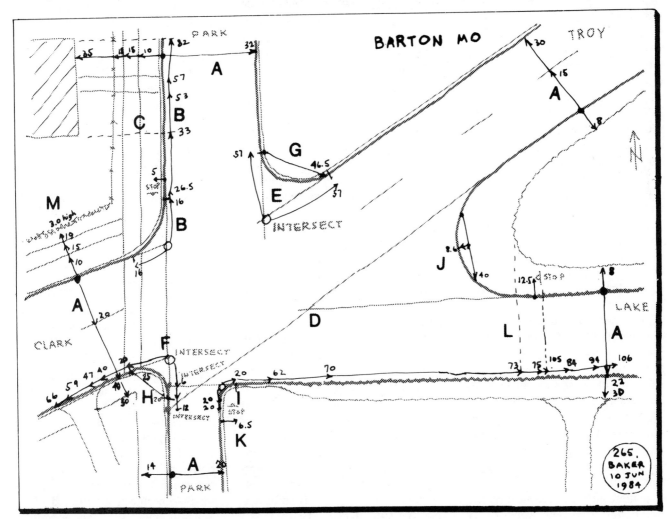

Exhibit 48. *Measurements are added to the field sketch shown in Exhibit 47. This completes field notes for mapping the junction. Final positions of vehicles and other results of the accident are shown on other field notes.*

cracks, ditches, banks, and parking areas. You now have everything on your field sketch that must be located by measurements.

Plan Measurements to be Made

After you complete the field sketch showing what must be measured, show what actual measurements are required.

Show measurements across each roadway as at A in Exhibit 48. As previously described, show the point measured *from* by a circle (for zero) or a spot. Show each point measured *to* by an arrowhead. All such measurements should be made *cumulatively,* as previously discussed (Exhibit 6), not *consecutively.*

Show measurements along each road edge from intercepts (or other reference points) to points to be located. In the example (Exhibit 48), a series of measurements were made along the west edge of Park, starting at the intersect of the north edge of Clark with the west edge of Park (B in Exhibit 48). Continue such measurements along all edges of roadways at the junction. If any point, such as the corner of a building, is more than 10 ft (3 m) beyond the edge of the roadway, carry a straight dotted line from it out to the measuring line (C in Exhibit 48). If sidewalks, buildings, and fences have already been located in across-the-road measurements, as at A in Exhibit 48, they do not need to be included in along-the-edge measuring.

Show angle measurements. In our example (Exhibit 45), two legs of the junction, Troy and Clark, are definitely not square with the other legs or with each other, so their angles must be measured, as explained in Exhibit 19. Although the edges of these streets and those of Park form a number of angles, only one needs to be measured for each leg. Choose the easiest angles to measure.

Remote intersects are inconvenient to measure from. This would be the case of the extension of the north edge of Lake and the south edge of Troy (D

in Exhibit 48). This apex is out in the middle of the intersection. To avoid using this remote intersect as a reference point for measuring, the angle of Troy to the other roadways can be established much more conveniently by measuring from the intersect of the east edge of Park and the north edge of Troy. (E in Exhibit 48). The angle between Park and Clark can be measured conveniently at the southwest corner (F in Exhibit 48). On the field sketch, distances from the apexes to the beginning of the arcs have already been provided for. Now, only the distances across the angles between their sides need to be added (G and H in Exhibit 48).

Show arc measurements. For most junction arcs, simply measure the distances from the intersect (apex) to the ends of the arc (Exhibit 21) as at B, E, F, and I in Exhibit 48. However, large arcs may be difficult to locate from remote apexes. In the example (J in Exhibit 48), the arc connecting the north edge of Lake and the south edge of Troy would require long measurements from a point far out in the intersection. So, use the chord-and-middle-ordinate method to get the radius of the arc (Exhibit 25).

Show other measurements not yet provided for. These may be to locate traffic control devices, trees, poles, street lights, advertising signs, or any other objects. It is usually easiest to use coordinates to locate these objects. Remember that every object must be located by measurement from at least two separate reference lines or points.

Roadway edges are generally handiest to use as reference lines. At most ordinary road junctions, one edge on each roadway provides a natural reference line. You may use intersects with other roadway edges as reference points. Locate spots by measuring a distance along the reference line starting from the intersect and by measuring the shortest distance from the reference line to the object. In the example, the stop sign on the southeast corner (K in Exhibit 48) is located by measuring from the intersect, I, along

the east curb line of Park to a point opposite the stop sign. Then a second measurement, at right angles to the reference line, is made from the reference line to the stop sign (6.5 ft).

Roadway edges are good reference lines because you can measure along them and into the roadway from them without exposure to, or interference with, passing traffic. This is especially important on busy streets and high-speed roads. It is possible to use lines other than roadway edges as reference lines. For example, roadway center lines or lane lines could be used. But generally this is not a good idea. Using such a reference line will increase your exposure to traffic.

Sometimes when areas are irregular, a long cord can be stretched across the location as a reference line as in Exhibit 29. If this is done, at least two recognizable landmark points must be located with reference to this cord so that you can tell exactly where the cord was located. Railroad rails are natural reference lines at railway crossing accidents. In cities, sidewalk edges may be useful as reference lines.

You can sometimes avoid difficulties by careful choice of a reference line. For example, in Exhibit 48, a stop sign and other items must be located north of Lake. Ordinarily, the north edge of Lake would be the logical reference line; but the only available reference point on this line is at D, far out in the intersection. That would be very unhandy. However, because Lake is narrow, the eastward measurements to the stop sign and other things can be included with other measurements from I, with the south side of Lake as the reference line. Then the northward measurements can still be made from the *north* side of Lake as a reference line.

Circumstances are sometimes such that triangulation is more suitable than coordinates for locating roadside objects, for example, when objects are more than 30 feet (10 m) off the roadway, when objects are located where a measurement at a right angle to a reference line would be difficult, or when no good reference line is avail-

Exhibit 49. A reference point for triangulation can be a pole or other object near the roadway. You must be able to identify it.

able.

In triangulation, objects are located by their distance from at least two reference points. In situations in which triangulation is more suitable than coordinates, the reference points are usually specific objects (Exhibit 49) such as

- *Posts, poles*, and sometimes even trees
- *Corners* of bridges, culverts, or buildings
- *Hydrants*, mail boxes
- *Roadway features* such as a point where a sidewalk edge meets a curb or where a curve begins in a roadway edge
- *Point on roadway edge* opposite a landmark.

Measurements are quite simple. The distance of each spot to be located is measured from each of two reference points. The base line connecting the two reference points and the two measurements to the spot to be located form a triangle; that is why this method is called triangulation.

Vertical measurements of certain kinds may also be made, if they are significant, for example,

- Height of traffic signs (measure to the bottom of the sign)
- Depth of ditches
- Height of guard rails

If only a few vertical measurements are necessary, simply note these on the field sketch. The height of the hedge (M in Exhibit 48) is an example of such a notation. Where more detailed vertical measurements are needed, make a second field sketch that shows at least part of the roadway cross-section (Exhibits 7 and 8).

Measure and Record Measurements

Once the field sketch and field notes have been prepared, and intersects and other points marked on the road, actual measuring is the next step.

One measurement for every arrowhead on the field notes must be made.

Record the figures for each measurement near the arrowhead representing that measurement.

Additional measurements for checking can be added. For example, chord and middle ordinate measurements can be made for all curves. Additional measurements can also be made for all angles.

5. PHOTOGRAPHS

Often weeks — sometimes years — may go by after an accident before you are called on to make an after-accident situation map. During that time, important things may have changed; yet the map must represent the situation at the scene.

Commonly snow or crops are different; sometimes the road has been changed or roadside structures modified. If the accident happened while the road was being worked on, it is almost sure to be somewhat different when you take measurements, for example, excavations may be more complete, and barricades may have been removed or rearranged.

Therefore, in addition to field notes of at-scene measurements, try to find and examine photos which were made of the scene. If possible, take these photos with you. Then you can make measurements and a map which represent more truly the exact situation that existed at the time of the accident.

If the results of the accident were not located by measurements at the scene, they may have to be located by some kind of photogrammetry as described in Topic 830. In that case, it may be important to locate, by measurements, things that could be the basis for a natural perspective grid such as beginnings and ends of center line or lane line stripes, pavement joints or cracks, guard-rail posts, and roadside objects which are of no significance with respect to the accident but perhaps useful in helping to locate things shown in photos such as final positions of vehicles.

Taking pictures in connection with site measurements can also be helpful in other ways that make it worthwhile to take a camera with you when you make site measurements for an after-accident situation map.

If signs of the accident are still visible at the site and you have reason to believe that they are not included in available at-scene photos, you may be thanked for your photographic evidence of what took place.

Photos taken in connection with measurements may be advantageous in a number of other ways:

- They may save time in making notes or sketches of such things as arrangement of faces on a traffic signal head, shapes and dimensions of curbs and gutters, character of surface in a median divider, and partial obstructions to view at road junctions and railroad grade crossings.
- They make a record of things which you may have inadvertantly overlooked or misrecorded. Photos may show how you made certain difficult or unusual measurements, such as clearances between vehicles in certain positions, depth of water, and slopes of banks.

You must guard against two things in making photos in connection with measurements:

1. Do not take pictures to avoid making measurements. Photos supplement measurements; they are not a good substitute for them.
2. Be sure to identify each picture either by including in it recognizable permanent landmarks or by written notes referring to photo numbers. It is embarrassing when you look at a picture which you yourself took and

wonder what it is supposed to show or where what it shows was located, for example whether the signal in the picture was at the northwest or southeast corner.

6. ACCURACY

Mistakes

Perhaps mistakes are the greatest source of significant error in measuring at the sites of traffic accidents.

It is easy to measure distances quickly and correctly, but do not let carelessness cause errors. There are six kinds of errors you must guard against:

1. Reading or recording numbers upside down, for example, a 9 for a 6, or backwards, for example a 53 for a 35.
2. Reading wrong footmark, for example, 18.7 as 17.7 or 19.7
3. Losing count of the number of complete tape-lengths measured.
4. Forgetting to reset a measuring wheel before making measurements.
5. Attempting to remember distances rather than recording them immediately.
6. Adding separate measurements mentally (Record each and add them later.)

After you form proper habits, you will automatically make more correct measurements.

If you think it necessary you can guard against your measurements being discredited by having your helper check them when they are made. Here is how:

1. Stretch the tape as usual for a measurement and then let it lie in that position on the ground.
2. Read and record the measurement.
3. Change ends with your helper.
4. Note that the end of the tape is at the beginning point.
5. Have your helper read distance at the other end of tape and record the length.

Now, both you and your helper

"know of your own knowledge" that the reading was correct. A measurement made by two different persons is not easy to discredit. However, such elaborate precautions are seldom necessary.

Precision of Instruments

It is possible that someone may question the accuracy of the tapes or other instruments you use in measuring at the site of a traffic accident. This is usually ridiculous because your equipment is almost sure to be more precise than you need for any measurements you are likely to make.

Do not claim your tape was "accurate." Actually, very few tapes are exactly their graduated length. Temperature makes a tape change length. This change is not much. A 100-ft steel tape will lengthen only about three-quarters of an inch, or this much _____ when temperature goes from 0 to 100 F (− 18 to + 38 C).

Different amounts of pull also cause slight changes in length. A pull of 10 lb too much would stretch a 100-ft steel tape only about a quarter of an inch. A steel tape bought from a reputable manufacturer is usually very nearly accurate — within an inch of its total graduated length in 100 ft.

If you expect the accuracy of your tape to be challenged, compare it with the tape of a licensed surveyor and be able to state how much difference there is. The accuracy of a measuring wheel or roller is more apt to be questioned. Compare it in the same way with a surveyor's tape so that you can say just how much difference there is. The best answer to a question about the accuracy of your measuring instrument is, "I compared the length of the tape I used with that of a tape used by a registered surveyor and it differed only one-half inch in 100 ft," or whatever the amount is. Another reply which is usually satisfactory is, "The department supplied the tape I used. The name on it was that of a well-known manufacturer. I have no reason to question its accuracy."

For greater accuracy in measuring

1. Always hold the tape taut to get correct distances. When using *steel tapes* pull from 7 to 10 lb and a non-metallic *woven* tape from 2 to 3 lb.
2. If possible, have your tape supported over the entire distance measured. When you hold it off the ground it sags and gives you a distance which is slightly long.
3. Hold the tape level when measuring.

Comparative accuracy of measuring devices is shown in Exhibit 50. If you do not make mistakes in reading or counting, your measurement of 100 ft will almost always be within the distance shown in Exhibit 50 for various measuring methods that have been discussed.

Units of Measuring

We describe quantities (for example, dimensions and prices) by the numbers of standard units of measurements equal to those quantities (feet and dollars, for example).

In the U.S.A., dimensions of roads and vehicles are customarily stated in feet. Long distances are measured in multiples of a foot: tens, hundreds, or thousands of feet or in miles. Short distances are measured in fractions of a foot: tenths, inches (1/12 ft), and hundredths of a foot (about 1/8 in.).

The precision with which a measurement is made depends on three things:

1. *The smallest scale interval* of the measuring instrument used. On a 100-ft surveyor's tape (Exhibit 51), the the space between adjacent scale divisions may be no less than a tenth (0.1) of a foot. You can estimate a tenth of this distance. Thus the distance from the zero end of the tape to the point of the arrow in Exhibit 51 indicates 15.22 ft, with the final 2 estimated. With this tape, the closest you could come to measuring the diameter of a dime (Exhibit 51) would be 0.06 ft; and the 6 would be estimated. But with scale graduations at 0.1

Exhibit 50.
ACCURACY OF VARIOUS MEASURING DEVICES

METHOD OF MEASURING	CONDITIONS	SPEED	ERROR Ft per 100 ft
Steel tape, standard	5-lb pull		- 0.005
	10-lb "		0.000
	15-lb "		+ 0.010
Metallic (wire fabric)	5-lb pull		+ 0.065
	10-lb "		+ 0.120
	15-lb "		+ 0.165
Fabric tape, good, new	5-lb pull		- 0.23
	10-lb "		- 0.06
	15-lb "		+ 0.10
Cloth tape, cheap, old	5-lb pull		- 0.31
	10-lb "		+ 0.09
2-ft single wheel	Dry pavement	3 ft per sec	+ 1.3
	"	7 "	+ 3.9
	Dry gravel	3 "	- 4.5
	"	7 "	- 6.2
	Dry grass	3 "	- 4.2
	"	7 "	- 1.3
1-ft single wheel	Dry pavement	3 ft per sec	- 1.0
	"	7 "	- 2.6
	Dry gravel	3 "	- 5.9
	"	7 "	- 5.8
	Dry grass	3 "	- 6.3
	"	7 "	- 6.7
1-ft double wheel	Dry pavement	3 ft per sec	- 0.1
	"	7 "	+ 0.1
	Wet pavement	3 "	- 0.1
	Dry gravel	3 "	- 4.4
	"	7 "	- 7.2
	Wet gravel	3 "	- 2.8
	Dry grass	3 "	- 2.0
	"	7 "	- 1.5
	Wet grass	3 "	- 1.0
Optical range finder			± 5.0
Stepping			± 5.0

The error in feet per 100 ft is the same as the percent error. The errors indicated are the average for several measurements with typical equipment. These error figures should not be used to adjust or correct actual measurements.

in. (Exhibit 52) a dime's diameter can be measured as 0.69 in. with the 9 estimated. An automobile's odometer register reads to a tenth of a mile (528 ft) and you can estimate the next smaller unit. So, in Exhibit 53, the odometer reads 14623.65 miles (*if* the mechanical connections between the odometer and the road have been perfect for all that distance).

2. *The shape or regularity of what is measured.* For example, you might measure the width of a roadway between undamaged curbs as 23.14 ft, with the last digit estimated. Then, 30 ft farther on you measure it again and it comes out 23.85 ft. At another location it may be still another figure. Then, what do you call it? If it is very important, you can measure it at a dozen or more places and average the readings. Otherwise you report what seems to be the width to the nearest foot and call it 24.

But suppose you, have to measure the width of a brook. The edges are difficult to find and they are very irregular. Furthermore, at high water, you cannot reach the far shore with a 12-ft pole; while at low water, you can easily step across. The best you can do is to describe the brook as about 10 feet wide, of course meaning more or less than that figure.

3. *Precision needed* depends on what the measurement is for. If you wanted to know the distance between one intersection and the next one to get some idea of how long it might take a pedestrian to walk that distance, it would be sufficient to call it 700 ft. But if you needed to know how many lengths of fire hose would be required to reach that distance, you could specify the distance to the nearest 10 ft, 660. If an engineer were laying out the road with precision instruments for construction purposes, he would measure from the exact center of one cross street to the exact center of the other to the nearest hundredths of a foot, for example 660.25 ft.

Significant Figures

One person says that the length of a certain city block is 700 ft; another reports that it measured 660.25 ft. You would not hesitate to consider the latter more accurate. Why? Because it is "carried out to more figures." The 700

Exhibit 51. *Accuracy of measuring depends on the scale divisions of the tape or other instrument used. With divisions at 1/10 ft, one can estimate to 1/100 ft, but this is not suitable for short distances such as the diameter of a dime.*

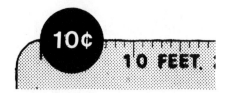

Exhibit 52. *With scale divisions of 1/10 in, one can estimate to 1/100 inch but no closer.*

says that the measurement was made in hundreds of feet, giving seven 100-ft units, only the 7 being the significant count of these 100-ft units. The number 660.25 says that measurement was made in hundredths (0.01) of a foot and that 66025 is the significant count of these small units.

Scientists, engineers, accountants, and others have developed a common sense way of judging and describing the accuracy of a count or measurement. They refer to the *number of significant figures*. The more significant figures, the greater the accuracy. There are rules for counting the number of significant figures.

Do not count zeros at the left (beginning) of a number. Thus 0.0023 has only two significant figures, 23. Zeros alone to the left of a decimal point are only to "protect" the decimal point. They indicate that the decimal point was intentionally and correctly placed where it is. Zeros to the left of a number but to the right of a decimal point help describe the size of the number but they are not significant so far as accuracy goes.

Zeros at the end of a number may or may not be significant figures. An illustration will show how that may be. 200 passengers are reported to be on board a plane. This suggests an estimate in hundreds of passengers.

Exhibit 53. *An odometer registers to 7 significant figures with the last one estimated.*

The 2 is one significant figure, and the two zeros do not count in evaluating the accuracy of the number. But suppose each of the 200 passengers had been counted; there were no more and no fewer than 200 passengers. Then the zeros do count as significant figures, making three significant figure accuracy. You may want to make it clear that the right end zeros are significant in indicating accuracy as well as size.

Perhaps the best way to do this is to specify "*exactly* 200." Another way, often used by statisticians, is to state the number of significant figures. Thus if the number were no more nor fewer than 200, you would say "200 to three significant figures." This has the advantage of specifying the accuracy no matter how many digits there are in the number. A decimal with zeros after a number will also indicate the number of significant figures. This is especially useful in tabulations. Thus 200 would mean one significant figure, but 200. would signify three significant figures and 200.0 four. If there is no other decimal in a number, adding a decimal and zeros after a number can indicate accuracy. For example, a bookkeeper writes $85.00 to mean exactly 85 dollars, no more or no less; that is four significant figures.

Sometimes accuracy is indicated as parts per hundred. You might say that you were measuring to one foot in 100. That would be one part in 100 or one percent or two significant figures. There is a relationship between parts per hundred or thousand and significant figures as follows:

Significant figures	Accurate to one in
1	10
2	100
3	1000
4	10000
5	100000
6	1000000

Calculations

Rounding. Sometimes a number has more significant figures than you want. For example, a six percent sales tax on a 90¢ purchase comes to 0.06 × 0.90 = $0.054. But the smallest coin for change is one cent (0.01). So you "round off" to the nearest cent. If the fraction is less than half, you drop it. In this example $0.054 is rounded to $0.05. If the fraction of a cent is half or more, you add a cent. Thus $0.056 is, rounded to the nearest cent, $0.06.

To add or subtract two or more measurements, round off all to measurement units of the quantity measured with the largest units. (The number of significant figures is not involved). Then add as usual. For example, a roadway is measured as 22 ft, that is in units of one foot. The adjacent sidewalk is measured as 4.7 ft, that is in units of a tenth of a foot. Round the 4.7 to feet, making it 5 feet. The combined width then is 22 + 5 = 27 ft.

To multiply or divide one quantity by another, do the multiplication and division and then round the result to fewest significant figures of any of the numbers involved. For example, to get the slope of a road, the vertical distance, 1.3 ft, is divided by the horizontal distance of 80.1 ft, giving 0.01623096. The 1.3 has the smaller number of significant figures, 2. Round the result to that number of significant figures making it 0.016.

Spurious Accuracy

Many investigators, including some engineers are careless about the number of significant figures in multiplication and division. It is not uncommon to find someone estimating the speed required for a vehicle to slide to a stop using such figures as these: longest tire mark, 45 ft (2 significant figures), drag factor, 0.6 (one significant figure), and a constant of 5.5 (2 significant figures). The resultant speed is quoted as 28.58 miles per hour (4 significant figures), whereas only one significant figure is warranted in the resulting speed estimate, 30 miles per hour.

Testimony in Court

If your equipment is good and you have used the methods described, you will ordinarily have no difficulty testifying to your measurements. However, you can rarely do this from memory. Keep your field sketch and all other original notes to refresh your memory in court. You may be asked to verify from original notes the dimensions on a map drawn by yourself or someone else. Do not tamper or let others tamper with these notes. To do so may cast doubt on testimony you give based on such notes or sketches.

7. SOURCES

Contributors

This topic was developed by *J. Stannard Baker,* a traffic engineer specializing in accident investigation. He was Director of Research and Development at the Northwestern University Traffic Institute from 1946 to 1971 and is a guest lecturer for the Traffic Institute.

Robert K. Seyfried, a traffic engineer specializing in highway design, traffic control, and accident investigation. He is an associate director of the Traffic Engineering Division at the Northwestern University Traffic Institute, Evanston, IL.

References

Superscript numbers in the preceding pages refer to the following:

1. Baker, J. Stannard. *Traffic Template* (SN 1000), 1983, Northwestern University Traffic Institute, Evanston, IL 60204
2. Baker, J. Stannard, *Traffic Template — Metric* (SN 1000M), 1974, Northwestern University Traffic Institute, Evanston, IL 60204

Exhibits

The following are sources of photos, maps, diagrams, charts, and tables appearing in this publication:

Aycock, Thad L. Traffic Institute, Evanston IL
Photo: 38
Baker J. Stannard, Glencoe IL
Photos: 1, 2, 9, 10, 11, 13, 15, 17, 20, 29, 32, 34, 36, 49, 53
Maps: 4, 5, 31, 45, 46, 47, 48
Diagrams: 6, 8, 19, 21, 22, 23, 24, 25, 26, 28, 35, 39, 41, 42, 51, 52
Chart: 27,
Tables: 37, 50
Lawyers Photo Service, St. Louis MO
Photo: 12
Seyfried, Robert K., Traffic Institute, Evanston IL
Photos: 16, 30, 38
Diagrams: 7, 14, 18, 40, 44
Chart: 43
Unknown
Photo: 3
Diagram: 33

DRAWING AFTER-ACCIDENT SITUATION MAPS

Topic 834 of the *Traffic-Accident Investigation Manual*

by
J. Stannard Baker
and
Robert K. Seyfried

NORTHWESTERN UNIVERSITY TRAFFIC INSTITUTE

PUBLICATION HISTORY
Topic 834

1953 *Traffic Accident Investigator's Manual*, Sections 41.705 - 41.910
1954 Revised, Sections 41.705 - 41.910

1957 *Traffic Accident Investigator's Manual for Police*, Sections 41.705 - 41.920
Reprinted 1959

1963 Revised, Sections 41.710 - 41.930
Reprinted 1964, 1965, 1966, 1969, 1970, 1971, 1973

1970 *Manual de Investigacion de Accidentes de Trafico*, Sections 41.710 - 41.930

1975 *Traffic Accident Investigation Manual,* Last Part of Chapter 7
Reprinted 1976, 1979

1985 Drawing After-Accident Situation Maps

DRAWING AFTER-ACCIDENT SITUATION MAPS

The map is a scale drawing of an area at the scene after the traffic-accident situation has stabilized. It shows relevant parts of streets or highways and results of the accident such as tire marks and final positions of vehicles.

An after-accident situation map is the foundation for many accident reconstructions. It organizes and summarizes observations at the scene of the accident.

Do not try to make such a scale map for every accident; that is unnecessary. The need for such follow up work depends on whether law suits or other special circumstances arise. Attorneys or administrators may request after-accident situation maps or they may be part of the accident-reconstruction process.

Keep the map factual; do not try to show on it how you think the accident happened. That can be done better later with an overlay or a copy of the map for that special purpose.

Special Investigators

Often one or two people in an organization are especially good at measuring for and making scale maps. So they may be assigned to make the maps when they are needed. There is no special reason why whoever measured to locate results of an accident at the scene must also measure for and draw the map. In any event the two sets of measurements would require two separate field sketches. However, when at-scene and map measurements are made by different persons, keep one important thing in mind: both must show the same recognizable reference lines and points so that the two sets of measurements can be tied together properly.

Technical help. If you have not had training or experience in drawing maps, and especially if an accurate job must also be done in a short time, it is probably best to get somebody with special experience to make scale maps. Engineers, draftsmen, some commercial artists, manual-arts teachers, and others know about scales and how to use drawing instruments. They can make scale diagrams better and quicker than untrained people. However, investigators can learn to make the drawings. They do have one advantage in making maps of the accidents they themselves investigate: they know what the scene looked like and can understand their own field notes better than anyone else could.

Street and Highway Plans

Plans with accurate road dimensions may be available at the office of the city engineer, county highway engineer, or district headquarters of the state highway department. They usually have plans which were drawn when the highway was built or extensively repaired. Perhaps you can obtain a print of the sheets showing the section of the road where the accident occurred. Highway plans show grades and curves accurately but may not show roadside development and traffic control devices. However, they may save you a trip to the site, and even if they do not, they may make some difficult measurements unnecessary when you get there. If the accident is serious and offical road plans do not provide all that you need, the high-

34-4

Exhibit 1. *(Above) Aerial view of a section of roadway, the site of a traffic accident.*

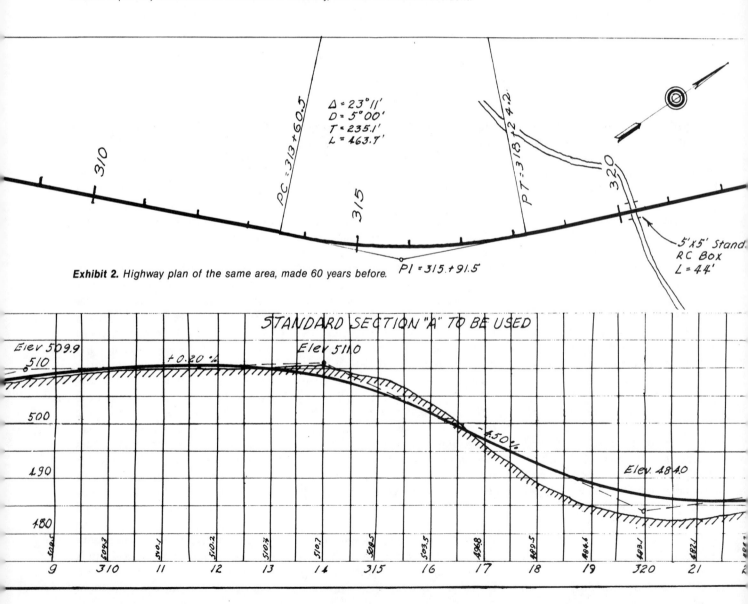

$\Delta = 23°11'$
$D = 5°00'$
$T = 235.1'$
$L = 463.7'$

$PC = 313 + 60.5$

315

$PI = 315 + 91.5$

$PT = 318 + 24.2$

320

310

5'x5' Stand.
RC Box
$L = 44'$

Exhibit 2. *Highway plan of the same area, made 60 years before.*

STANDARD SECTION "A" TO BE USED

Elev 509.9
510
+ 0.20 %
Elev 511.0
-4.50%
Elev. 484.0

500

490

480

9	310	11	12	13	14	315	16	17	18	19	320	21

Exhibit 3. *Highway profile corresponding to the plan in Exhibit 2. The original horizontal scale was 1 in. = 100 ft, and the vertical scale was 1 in. = 10 ft. (This reproduction is not to the same scale).*

way engineer may be willing to have one of his people get what you need. When you use highway plans, verify a few important measurements at the site to be sure that the highway was actually constructed as planned.

1. INFORMATION AVAILABLE

Information needed to draw an after-accident situation map may come from several sources, depending on circumstances.

Measurements to Locate Results of the Accident.

Such measurements are logically part of at-scene investigation (Level 2 of traffic-accident investigation). They must be made before the after-accident situation is disturbed and the signs of what happened have begun to disappear (At-scene measurements are described in Topic 828).

If well made, these measurements easily and quickly locate such things as tire marks and final positions of vehicles on the after-accident situation map; but unfortunately there are often no at-scene measurements or the measurements are so sketchy and inaccurate that they are of little use. Then the map maker must do the best he can with other sources of information.

Measurements of the Road

These can usually wait until the need for a map has been determined. Then measuring for the map and drawing it is part of technical preparation for accident reconstruction, Level 3 of traffic-accident investigation. (Measurements for the map are explained in Topic 832).

In simple cases, sufficient measurements may have been made at the scene, or are otherwise available, so that additional measurements of the road are not needed.

If plans are available, they can greatly reduce the measuring at the accident site. Plans usually include scale drawings that show lane widths, shoulders, curves, bridges, grades,

junctions, and some roadside objects such as barriers, poles, and buildings.

Do not be surprised if plans cannot be found. Generally good records are available for streets and highways built or reconstructed during the last 30 years; older roads may have been built without plans or the plans may have been lost.

Horizontal Alignment. The drawings are essentially bird's-eye views. Compare Exhibit 1, an aerial view, with Exhibit 2, a horizontal alignment plan of the same area.

Distances along the center line of the road are indicated on plans by a system of stations at 100-ft intervals. Sometimes these are marked right on the road when it is built (Exhibit 4). Points are located longitudinally by the station. For example, the notation 12 + 43.7 means 43.7 ft beyond station 12 + 00 or 12 43.7 feet along the center line from a specified reference point.

Curves are customarily described on a horizontal alignment plan by a code near the drawing of the curve. The code ordinarily looks like this:

$$\Delta = 51°37'$$
$$D = 5°0'$$
$$R = 1146.28$$
$$T = 554.44$$
$$L = 1032.50$$
$$E = 127.05$$

It is explained by reference to the geometry of a curve (Exhibit 5) as follows:

    (Delta) *Central angle* between the radiuses at the tangent points PC and PT

D *Degree of curve,* (Described below)

R *Radi⸱ of curve,* distance from cent⸱ to the arc of the curve.

T *Tangent length,* between the PI (point of intersect) and either tangent point, PC or PT

L *Length of arc* along the curve from one tangent point to the

Exhibit 4. Highway design station marked in Portland Cement concrete paving. This mark is 2600 feet from a specified reference point.

other.

E *External distance* from the point of intersect, PI, to the center of the arc.

Some other characteristics of the curve, such as *h*, the middle ordinate, are also shown in Exhibit 5.

Note that the central angle, D, plus the external angle, always equals two right angles, 180 degrees.

Degree of curve, D, is sometimes given in engineering drawings instead of or in addition to the radius, R. It does not show in Exhibit 5. The degree of a curve is the number of degrees of central angle subtended by a chord of 100 ft on the center line of the roadway. It is used by surveyors in laying out roads and so is part of the curve data supplied by the road designer. If you find the degree of the curve on a road design, you can get the radius of the center line of the curve closely enough for accident-investigation purposes by dividing 5730 by D. Thus, if D is 5 degrees, as in the example, the radius is 5730/5 = 1146 ft. This is close enough to the true radius of 1146.28 ft for practical purposes.

Radius in highway plans is almost always that of the center line of the roadway. To find the radius of the outside edge of the curve, add half the roadway width to the center line radius; for the inside edge, subtract half the roadway width.

There are two exceptions to this general rule. Sometimes the roadway is wider on one side of the design "center" line to accomodate turning move-

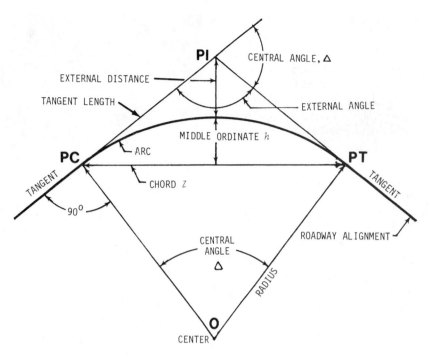

Exhibit 5. *Parts and nomenclature of a highway curve connecting two straight tangents.*

ments. This widening is easy to see. The other exception is not so obvious. On some sharp road curves, the pavement is widened and widened more on one side of the center line than on the other.

Vertical Alignment. Plans show the grades and elevations along the center line of the highway. This is called the profile (Exhibit 3). A profile is also a scale drawing but it is customary to use quite different vertical and horizontal scales. For example, in Exhibit 3, 1 in. = 100 ft is the horizontal scale, whereas 1 in. = 10 ft is the vertical scale. Different scales give an exaggerated view of elevations to accentuate the vertical characteristics of the road.

Keep in mind, when looking at profiles in plans; that grades appear to be much steeper than they really are.

If you have to draw a profile to show to nontechnical people, make the horizontal and vertical scales the same. That will avoid misunderstandings about how steep the hills are.

Cross section plans show the view that you would get if you slice straight down through the roadway and ground at right angles to the center line (Exhibit 6). The cross-section plan shows not only roadway and shoulder widths but also pavement and roadside cross slopes.

Cross slope or superelevation (banking) is generally noted as feet of

rise or fall per foot transversely across the pavement. In Exhibit 6, the cross slope is shown as 0.015 feet per foot (1.5 percent). Sometimes the cross slope is in inches per foot, for example 1 in. per ft. Divide inches per foot by 12 to convert it to feet per foot.

Roadside slopes are customarily shown on plans as the ratio of the crosswise distance outward from the road edge for each foot of rise or fall. In Exhibit 6, the roadside slope is shown as 6 : 1. This means that you must go outward from the road a level distance of six feet for each foot of rise or fall. You can convert this to grade by dividing the second number in the ratio by the first number, for example 6 : 1 is a grade of 1/6 = 0.17 ft/ft or 17 percent.

As in vertical alignment plans, cross section plans may have different horizontal and vertical scales to accentuate vertical dimensions.

If there are important differences between photos and your map layout, be prepared to explain why. For example, a vehicle may have been moved before the pictures were made.

Statements

Witnesses or others who were at the scene or visited the site later may be helpful in locating final positions of vehicles and bodies when better data are lacking.

Try to have witnesses accompany you to the site to point out spots which can then be located by proper measurements. If this is impossible, have the witness mark his recollection of the location on photos or on your

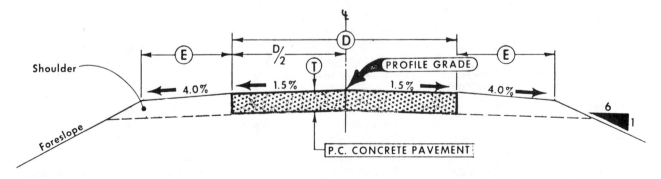

Exhibit 6. *Example of a cross section plan of a highway showing paving and shoulder slopes.*

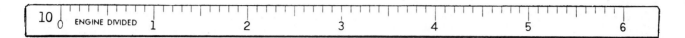

Exhibit 7. Engineer's scale (1 in. = 10 ft) at top and architect's scale (1 in. or ½ in. = 1 ft) below.

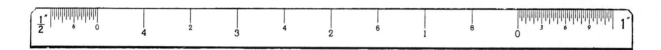

drawing of the location.

To locate final positions, for example, cut out patterns of vehicles to the same scale as the map and have the witness place them as he or she remembers them to have been with respect to features of the location. Model vehicles are best if they are to the right scale. Having the witness place objects on a scale map is much better than having him try to describe distances in feet. If there are photos, let the witness use them if he wishes. If you notice discrepancies between the pictures and the statement, point them out to the witness so that he may have an opportunity to correct what he said or explain the differences. Once you and the witness are satisfied with his placement, mark the map. If there are several witnesses, use a different print of the map for each so that none will be influenced by what another has already indicated. If your final map shows positions located by witnesses, mark the map to show this fact.

Do this soon after the accident so that memory of the witness is as fresh as possible Be careful not to rely too much on what witnesses say about distances; they are likely to be guessing.

Dimensions of Vehicles

It is important to know the sizes of vehicles involved if they are to be shown on the map to the proper scale. These dimensions can be had in one or more of three ways:

1. *Measurement made at the scene* of the accident and included with at-scene field sketch data.

Such measurements are rarely available.

2. *Later measurements* made when the damaged vehicle is examined. The data are usually part of the vehicle examination report.

3. *Dimensions from manufacturer's* or other publications.

Proper at-scene measurements locate at least two spots on each vehicle, ordinarily undamaged corners. The location of these spots and other parts of the vehicle must be consistent with vehicle dimensions. Good figures for overall length, width, and other dimensions are, therefore, useful.

If damage to a vehicle is enough to change its outline, make the outline on the after-accident situation map show that damage.

Photographs

Pictures are the best source of some kinds of information and a useful supplement to many other kinds. They provide a permanent, accurate record of objects specifically observed by an investigator. They also capture the detailed appearance of things, such as marks on the road, which may be difficult to measure accurately or describe fully. But never regard photographs as a substitute for good at-scene measurements. It is true that useful after-accident situation maps can be made from photos; it may be necessary if suitable measurements are lacking. But making maps from photos is difficult and tedious. (See Topic 830, *Photogrammetry*.)

Traffic Template

This device[1] (Exhibit 8) is designed especially to draw traffic-accident maps and other diagrams. It has the two most commonly used scales: 1 in =10 ft (1/120) and 1 in = 20 ft (1/240). It has slots and holes that can be used to draw arcs so that it also serves most of the purposes of a compass. In addition, it has cutouts which permit rapid drawing of outlines of typical cars and trucks. In fact, most accident maps can be easily drawn with only a pencil and the template. An instruction booklet accompanying the template explains in detail its use. The *Traffic Template* is also available in metric units.[2]

2. EQUIPMENT

Draftsmen and other technicians who make maps often have special equipment for the purpose: drawing boards, T squares, triangles, scales, drawing instruments, and so on. But excellent maps can be made with very simple equipment.

Scales. Because maps are drawn to scale, whoever draws one, expert or amateur, must have a scale of some kind by which distances can be measured on a drawing corresponding to those measured with a tape at the location where the accident happened. Any ruler with an edge graduated in inches and eighths or sixteenths can be used to draw maps at a scale of one inch equals 16, 8, or 4 ft, but this is inconvenient because these graduations are not numbered for direct reading. Scales commonly used are of two kinds: 1) *engineers',* in which one

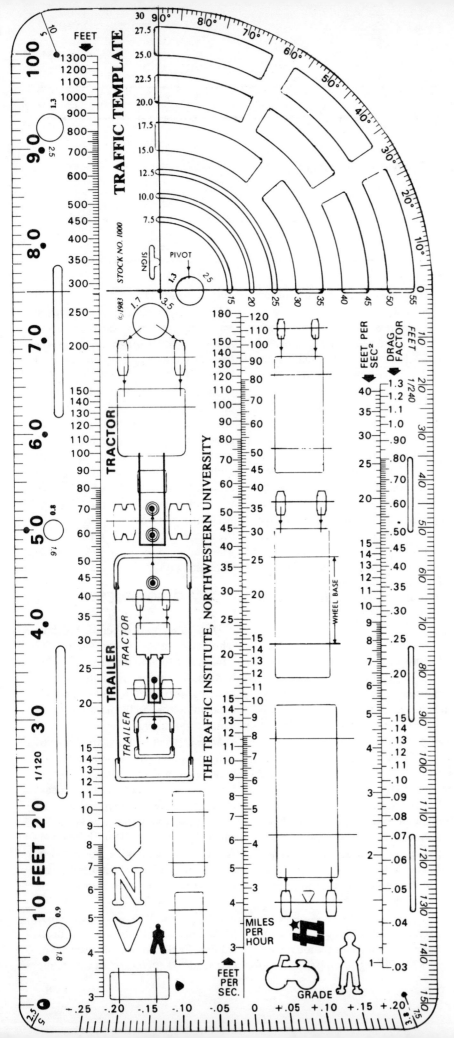

inch equals 10, 20, 30, 50 ft, and so on; 2) architects', in which one foot is represented by one inch, one-half inch, one-quarter inch, and so on (Exhibit 7).

The most commonly used scales for after-accident situation maps in the U.S.A. are 1 in. = 10 ft (1/120 actual size) and 1 in. = 20 ft (1/240 actual size). In the metric system the common scales are 1 cm = 1 m (1/100) and 1 cm = 2.5 m (1/250).

For first drafts and working maps use an ordinary pencil, it makes eraser corrections easy. For a display map, however, pen and ink will make a crisper and more legible drawing. If it is traced from the working map, there is little need for erasing.

A compass is needed to lay out angles and draw arcs. Circle templates are also useful for drawing arcs.

Transparent triangles are useful in some drafting operations as will be explained later.

A drawing board and T square or the equivalent will be helpful, especially if you have to draw after-accident situation maps often.

3. DRAFTING METHODS

To draw even simple maps, you must know how to draw angles, curves, and other geometric elements with whatever equipment that you have.

Parallel Lines

To represent a straight roadway and some other map features, you must draw a line parallel to and a specified distance from a line already in place. There are two ways to do this.

One way is to measure and mark the specified distance from the existing line at two well separated places along that line. Then connect these marks with a straight line.

The other method makes use of a

Exhibit 8. *The Traffic Template provides the two most useful scales for drawing maps of traffic situations. It also provides a simple calculator for some of the computations frequently used in traffic-accident reconstruction.*

drafting triangle and a straight edge, which may be another triangle. First line up the long side of Triangle A with the existing LINE. (Exhibit 9.) Then hold a straight edge or one side of Triangle B against the other side of Triangle A. Next, holding the straight edge firmly in place, slide Triangle A along the straight edge until the edge that was against the LINE is the specified distance from the LINE. The long side of Triangle A is now parallel to the LINE and the proper distance from it. Draw the parallel line along that edge, the second position in Exhibit 9.

Right Angle

To draw a line at a right angle (90°) to a line already in place, you can use the square corner of a drafting triangle, or of a sheet of paper. The long edge of the template and the line across the template can also be used. Put the apex of the right angle at the desired point on the existing LINE, align one leg of the right angle with the existing LINE, and draw the required line along the other leg.

With a drafting triangle and a straight edge, you can also draw a line at a right angle to an existing LINE. Align the long side of the triangle with the existing LINE (Exhibit 10). Place the straight edge against the adjacent side of the triangle. Holding the straight edge in this position, turn the triangle so its third side is against the straight edge, slide the triangle along the straight edge until its long side is at the point on the LINE where the apex of the right angle is to be, and then draw the required line along the long side of the triangle, as in Exhibit 10.

Other Angles

Angles other than right angles are specified either as a number of degrees, or as a particular angle in a triangle of which all three sides have been measured. When a line that forms one side of the angle has been drawn on a map and a point has been marked on this line to represent the apex of the angle, the angle is recon-

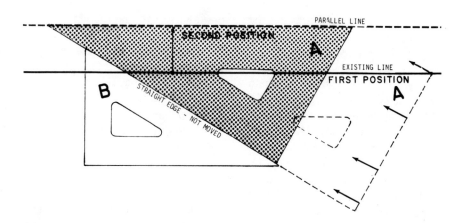

Exhibit 9. A triangle and a straight edge (such as one side of another triangle, may be used to draw a line parallel to an existing line. Place one edge of the triangle against the existing line, and place the straight edge against the other side of the triangle. Then slide the triangle along the straight edge until its farther side is the proper distance from the original line.

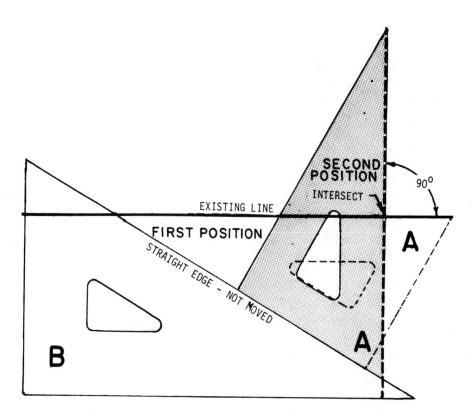

Exhibit 10. A right angle can be drawn by placing a triangle between the existing line and a straight edge. Turning the triangle over to change the side against the straight edge will give a side at 90° to the existing line.

structed on the map by drawing the triangle. As an example, use the angle at the northwest corner of Troy and Park, E in Exhibit 11. The two sides of the angle are both 57 ft and the span across the ends of these sides is 46.5 ft. At apex intersect 0, on existing line P in Exhibit 12, draw this angle. Measure off along line P to scale, one side of the triangle 57 ft from O to point A. In this case, both sides of the angle are the same length, but even if they were different lengths, it would make no difference which one you measured off along the line because the same angle would result. Then, with compass set for the length of the other side, in this example the same 57 ft, put the pin-point leg of the compass at the apex and draw an arc (Q in Exhibit 12). Then with the compass set for the span between the sides, in this

example 46.5 ft, and the pin-point at A, draw another arc (R in Exhibit 12). A straight line through the apex 0 and the point B, where arcs Q and R cross, will form the other side of the angle (S in Exhibit 12).

Transferring angles. In the junction being used as an example, the angle was *measured* between the east edge of Park and the north edge of Troy (E in Exhibit 11). But in making a map, the apex is placed at the intersect of the west edge of Park and the south edge of Troy and the angle is *drawn* here. The angle may be transferred because these two angles are the same. (See Exhibit 13.)

Drawing angle without a compass. If you have a scale but no compass, you can still draw an angle described by three measured sides of a triangle.

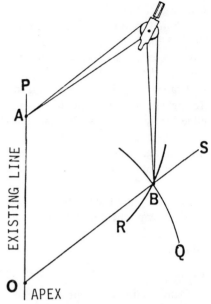

Exhibit 12. *From an angle represented by measurements of a triangle, a compass can be used to reconstruct the angle on a drawing.*

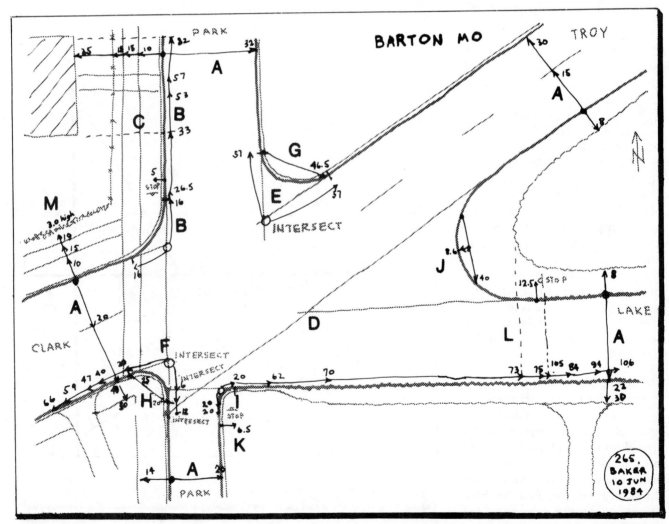

Exhibit 11. *An example of a field sketch of a junction with dimensions used in making an after-accident situation map of that location.*

First, measure one side of the triangle (it makes no difference which) to scale from the apex point along the established side of the angle and mark the distance exactly as described for drawing an angle with a compass. Then mark the length of the span between the sides of the angle to scale on a piece of paper or card. Next, keeping zero on the appropriate scale at the apex and keeping one of the span end marks on the paper or card at the marked distance on the angle side, adjust the paper and scale so that the free end of the span mark is at the other angle side length on the scale as in Exhibit 14. Finally, mark the point determined in this manner and draw the side of the angle from the apex through this point.

Drawing angles measured in degrees. From engineering drawings and surveyor's data, you may have an angle described in degrees instead of the three measured sides of a triangle. Then you will have to use a scale marked in degrees. This is called a protractor. Put the center of the protractor at the apex of the angle and the zero of the protractor scale on the side of the angle already drawn (or that side extended). Then mark the specified number of degrees on the drawing from the protractor scale, remove the protractor, and draw a straight line through the apex and the mark for the number of degrees. It may be more convenient sometimes to put the number of degrees on the line already drawn and mark the place where the zero on the protractor scale comes (Exhibit 15.)

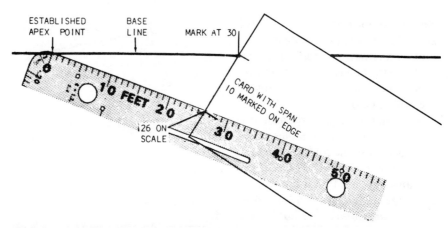

Exhibit 14. *A triangle used to describe one of its angles can be drawn with one side marked along the established line, the other side measured by a template scale, and the span marked on the edge of a card or piece of paper.*

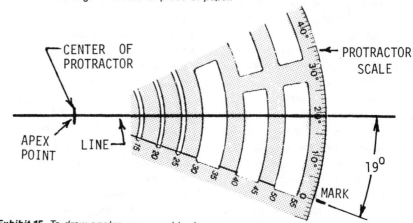

Exhibit 15. *To draw angles measured in degrees, use a protractor, for example the one on the Traffic Template.*

Arcs and Curves of Roads

Curves and angles are related in roadway design. Two straight, intersecting roadway edges (tangents) are almost always joined by a curve (arc). Where the edges of two roadways join at a junction, the radius of the arc joining the tangents may be as little as 10 or 15 feet; but on open highways, the radius of the highway curve is measured in hundreds or thousands of feet (or meters).

If two sides of the external angle

have been measured as in Exhibit 5 to obtain the distances of the tangent points from the apex of the angle, the arc connecting the edges from one tangent point to the other can be drawn directly on the map without actually calculating the radius of the arc. After the straight edges of the road have been drawn to intersect at the proper angle, mark on each leg the tangent points, PC and PT, as measured. If the two are not the same, use the greater for both and make them the same. These points may already

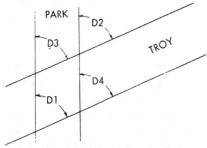

Exhibit 13. *Where two sets of parallel lines cross, for example the edges of two intersecting roadways, eight identical angles are formed. Here D1, D2, D3, and D4 are four of these. Only one of these needs to be measured; it will do for all eight.*

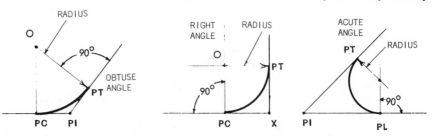

Exhibit 16. *If tangent points of circular arcs connecting sides of an angle are known, the center of the arc can be located. It is where lines at right angles to the sides at the points of tangency intersect.*

have been located in drawing the angle. From the tangent point, P, on each side, draw a line (radius) at right angles to the tangent as in Exhibit 16. Where these lines (radiuses) cross is the center, O, of the arc, O. The distance from the center of the arc to the tangent point, P, is the radius of the desired arc. Put the compass pinpoint at the center, O, set the other leg at the tangent point, P, and draw the arc from one tangent point to the other.

If tangent points were not located by measurements, but the radius of the arc connecting the straight edges is known or can be calculated from chord and middle ordinate measurements, locate the center of the arc by drawing a line parallel to each side of the angle and a distance from it equal to the radius, as in Exhibit 17. Where these parallel lines intersect is the center of the arc, O. Set the compass pin-point there, adjust the other leg to the nearest distance to either edge line, and draw the arc from one tangent point to the other. This construction is only possible, of course, when the arc connecting the road edges is tangent to them.

The Traffic Template can be used to draw arcs quickly at 1 in = 10 ft with radiuses between 0.5 ft and 100 ft. You will find detailed instructions in how to draw arcs with the *Traffic Template* in the manual accompanying the template.

Large arcs cannot be drawn with an ordinary compass. If you have a beam compass available, an arc with a radius of 2 or even 3 ft (50 to 100 cm) can be drawn. But if you must draw an arc larger than can be drawn with

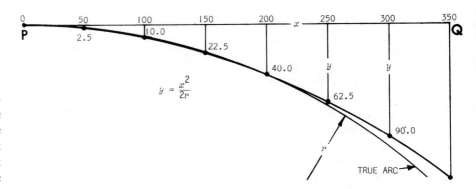

Exhibit 18. Offsets of a curve from a tangent can be calculated and plotted to construct an arc with a large radius. Offsets can be had without calculating from a nomograph, Exhibit 19.

a compass, use the most convenient of two methods: 1) draw an arc with a fine wire as a radius; and 2) plot a series of points on the arc and connecting them with a smooth curve.

Wire for the radius. If you must map a curve on a rural highway, the center of the arc will probably not be on the sheet on which you are drawing. Nearly all rural curves have radiuses greater than 200 ft (60 m) and some will be more than 2,000 ft (600 m), which, at 1 in. = 10 ft, would be a radius of 200 in. or more than 16 ft (5 m). Use a fine wire with a loop in each end of the wire. Make the length of the wire between the ends of the loops equal to the desired radius. Put a thumbtack, brad, or tack in the loop at the arc center and a pencil in the other loop to draw the arc.

Tangent offset method. Another way to draw an arc with a large radius is to plot points along it and connect them with a smooth curve. The points are plotted as offsets from a tangent to the curve. Start with the tangent,

for example, the line PQ in Exhibit 18. Along this line, at convenient intervals, mark points for the offsets. Calculations will be easier if distances from the offset points to the tangent point P are in round numbers. For each point on the tangent, calculate the offset to the corresponding point on the arc. The offset is at right angles to the tangent. If the distance from the tangent point is x and the radius of the arc is r, the offset, y, is given by this equation.

$$y = \frac{x^2}{2r}$$

For example, in Exhibit 18, every 50 ft from P along the tangent has been marked to scale. The radius of the curve is 500 ft. Then 200 ft to scale from the start of the arc, the offset will be,

$$y = \frac{x^2}{2r} = \frac{200(200)}{2(500)}$$

$$= \frac{40,000}{1,000} = 40 \text{ ft.}$$

Compute the offset for each point, plot the points and connect them with a smooth curve.

You may observe that this process is the reverse of the process of measuring an arc by chord and middle ordinate as described in Topic 832. In the tangent-offset method, the distance x, from P along the tangent is half the chord and the offset y, is the

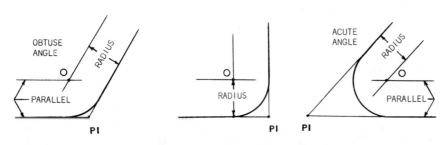

Exhibit 17. If the radius of the arc is known, an arc of that radius can be fitted to connect the two sides of the angle. Draw a line parallel to each side of the angle and the length of the radius away from it. Where these lines cross is the center of the arc.

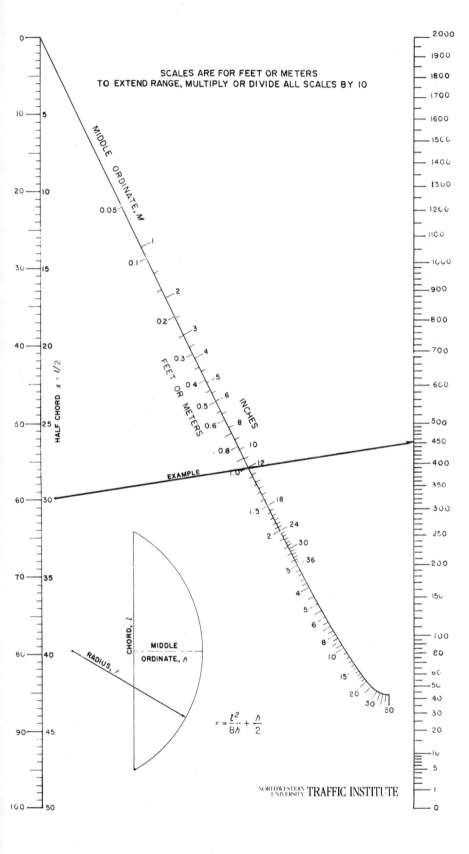

SCALES ARE FOR FEET OR METERS
TO EXTEND RANGE, MULTIPLY OR DIVIDE ALL SCALES BY 10

$$r = \frac{l^2}{8h} + \frac{h}{2}$$

NORTHWESTERN UNIVERSITY TRAFFIC INSTITUTE

Exhibit 19. *The distance, l, along the tangent from the beginning of the arc is the half chord on the left scale. From that point, draw a straight line to the curve radius on the right scale. The offset distance is shown where this line crosses the middle ordinate scale, h.*

middle ordinate. The equation for calculating the offset is derived from that for calculating the radius from the chord and the middle ordinate measurements, except that the $h/2$ is omitted. Thus, the equation given above is only approximate. The equation for the exact offset is more complicated and requires extracting a square root. For arcs that would be plotted by the tangent-offset method, omission of $h/2$ makes little difference. For example, with a chord of 100 ft (½ chord = 50 ft) and a middle ordinate of 2.5 ft, the radius, calculated exactly, is 501.25. Simplifying the equation by omitting $h/2$ gives a calculated approximate radius of 500 ft. The difference could not be detected on a map. In Exhibit 18, in addition to the plotted curve, the true arc is shown. Note that the difference is unimportant so long as the offset is less than a fourth of the distance along the tangent, at which point, the error in the radius would be about 1.5 percent.

For long curves in which no connecting straight road is to be shown, you can save work by putting the tangent point in the middle and working on both sides of it. The same calculated values can then be used on each side.

When a curve has been located by offsets from a tangent, these offsets can be plotted directly on your map to locate the curve there.

The nomograph, (Exhibit 19) described in Topic 832 for computing a radius from measurements of the chord and middle ordinate, can also be used to plot offsets from a tangent to plot a curve. The half chord point on the chord scale at the left is the distance, x, along the tangent from which the offset, y, is plotted. A line from this point on the nomograph to the radius scale crosses the middle ordinate scale at the offset distance. Using this nomograph permits you to plot the arc very quickly.

Irregular Curves
Located by Triangulation

Topic 832 explains a triangulation method of locating curved roadway edges which are too irregular to be located by ordinary tangents and arcs. Exhibit 20 is an example of field notes from such measurements. These notes give dimensions of a whole series of interlocking triangles which define the edges of an irregular four-legged roadway junction.

Drawing the road layout from such field measurements is not difficult. Exhibit 21 is an illustration of how this is done from the field notes given in Exhibit 20.

Start by locating on your drawing any two points shown on the field sketch. Make the distance between them that shown on the field sketch to the scale you have chosen. Let us say you start with points D45 and D23. They are 45 − 23 = 22 ft apart.

This is the base of a triangle of which C180 is the apex on the opposite side of the roadway. With your compass set at 30 ft to scale, (the distance between D23 and C180) and the pin-point at D23, draw an arc. Then with the compass still set at 30, (which is also the distance between D45 and C180) and the pin-point at D45 draw another arc. Where these two arcs cross is point C180. Now you have your first triangle. In Exhibit 20, lines represent its sides. You do not need to draw lines representing the sides of the triangles; they are sufficiently described by the points at the three corners, in this case C180, D23, and D45.

Next, with the compass centered at D45 and set at 41, (the distance between D45 and C160), draw an arc.

Then, with the compass centered at C180 and set at 20 (the distance between C180 and C160), draw a second arc. Point C160 is where these arcs cross. This gives a second triangle, C160, C180, and D45, next to the first one.

Now with line D45 to C160 as a base and 20 and 46 as sides, draw a third triangle. It locates D65.

Add more triangles until all points have been located.

On the field notes are shown a number of check distances, for example B120 to D65, 184 ft. This is shown by a dotted line in Exhibit 20. Scale the check distances on your draft map. If it comes out close to what your triangulation measures, you have done a good job. If not, try other

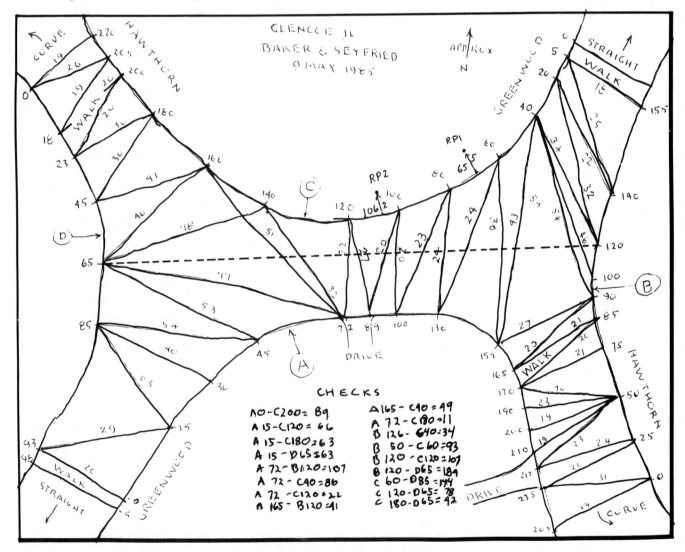

Exhibit 20. *Field sketch of measurements made to locate points along irregular curves of roadway edges in an unusual junction.*

check distances which will help you locate where your mistake is.

Once you have located the points along the roadway edges by triangulation, connect these with a smooth curves to represent roadway edges.

Then be sure to add reference points, as in Exhibit 20, by which results of the accident (not shown) were located.

On the final map, the triangulation points are omitted. They are needed for reference only during construction. The final map shows results of the accident and the usual identifying information.

4. MAP LAYOUT

Planning

Before starting to draw, decide six important things:

1. *How much to include.* You must include all evidence observed, such as skidmarks and final positions of vehicles. If view obstructions or traffic control equipment played a part, they must be shown. Sometimes a long stretch of highway must be mapped to reconstruct the accident, especially where sight distances are involved.

2. *Is it a working or a display map?*

3. *What scale to use.* Use 1 in. = 10 ft (or 1 cm = 1 m) unless the map must represent more than 400 ft (100 m) of road; but do not hesitate to use larger or smaller scales if you think they will help.

4. *The size of the map* is determined by the scale and what is to be included. Try to keep most diagrams on a sheet 8½ by 11 in. (210 by 297 mm). It is a standard size and is very convenient to handle and file. At 1 in. = 10 ft (1 cm = 1 m), this size will include an ordinary city intersection, and at 1 in. = 20 ft (1 cm = 2.5 m),

about 200 ft (60 m) of road. Often 400 or 500 ft (200 to 300 m) must be included. Then larger sheets of paper will be necessary.

5. *What measurements should be shown as numbers?* Numbers representing distances are rarely necessary on a scale map. You will have to show heights and depths, because they will not appear on a map otherwise; but do not show the width of a pavement or the radius of a curve.

6. *Which direction is north?* Make north toward the top of the sheet as usual in maps. However, do not use odd-size sheets just to be able to do this. If the map is to be bound in a report, make north either to the top or to the left of the sheet.

Drawing

Rough draft. It is a good idea to

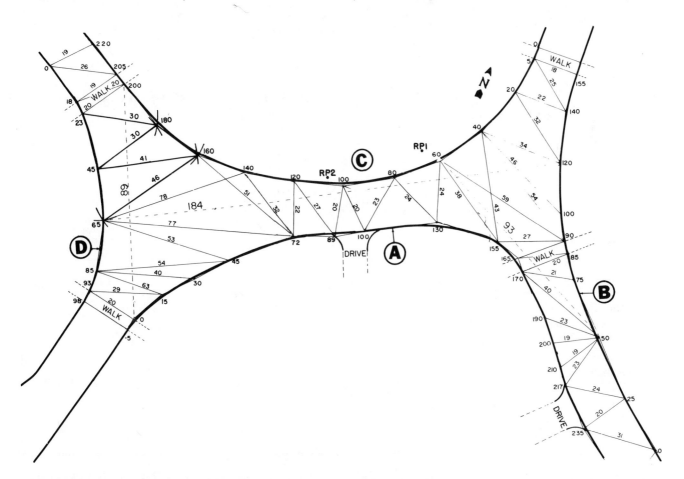

Exhibit 21. *Road layout drawn from measurements shown in Exhibit 20. In a finished map, the triangles would be omitted and final positions of vehicles and other results of the accident added.*

make the first draft a rough one on a sheet larger than needed for the final drawing. This draft, made to the same scale as the final map, can show station numbers and construction lines which would not appear in the final drawing. The rough draft will usually suffice for a working map.

Finished map. After the rough draft is finished, mark off the essential part to be included on a standard-size sheet as the finished map, and then copy it on tracing paper. This is easier and neater than trying to make the original drawing perfect. Tracing eliminates most erasing.

General procedure in drawing a map is much like making a field sketch. Start with a "straight through" line. On this locate an intersect. From that draw a line at the proper angle for another roadway. Then measure off the roadway widths. After the basic roadways are drawn, locate spots representing results of the accident. If it is to be a display map, add detail to make the drawing more realistic.

Exhibit 11 illustrates of how you go about this. There is only one roadway edge that is aligned on both sides of this junction: the west edge of Park. It runs north and south. Draw this lightly across your paper toward the left side. Then parallel to this line and 32 ft to scale from it, draw lightly the east edge of Park north of the junction. Then draw the east edge of Park south of the junction in the same way.

Next you might draw the south side of Troy. Mark its intersect with the west edge of Park at a convenient point. Then, with this as the apex and the west edge of Park as one side, construct the angle between Park and Troy. Remember that this angle is the same as that between the east edge of Park and the north edge of Troy which is measured by a triangle with 57-ft sides and a 46.5-ft span.

Having established this angle, you can draw the south side of Troy. Draw the north side of Troy parallel to the South side and 30 ft to scale away from it.

The angle between Park and Clark is different from that between Park

and Troy. Locate the intersect between the south edge of Clark and the west edge of Park, 12 ft to scale, (Exhibit 11) north of the intersect of the west edge of Park and the south edge of Troy. The angle at that intersect is measured by a triangle with 20-ft sides and a 25-ft span. Draw in the angle and you have the south edge of Clark. The north edge of Clark is parallel and 40 ft away. The edges of Lake are drawn in the same way. You now have a skeleton of the junction.

Depending on how the results of the accident are located, this skeleton may be enough for a working map. Indeed, not all of these streets may be required on a working map.

Adding road detail needed for a display map may take a little time, but is not difficult (Exhibits 24 and 29).

5. ADDING RESULTS OF THE ACCIDENT

Drawing the road layout is usually the easiest part of making an after-accident situation map: the needed dimensions are at hand or may be easily obtained. Locating the final positions of vehicles and other results of the accident is likely to be more complicated.

If after-accident measurements have been properly made and recorded, and if only a few things need to be located, adding them to your road layout drawing is straightforward. Exhibit 22 shows a good set of measurements for results of an accident. The final vehicle positions and furrows have been clearly located by coordi-

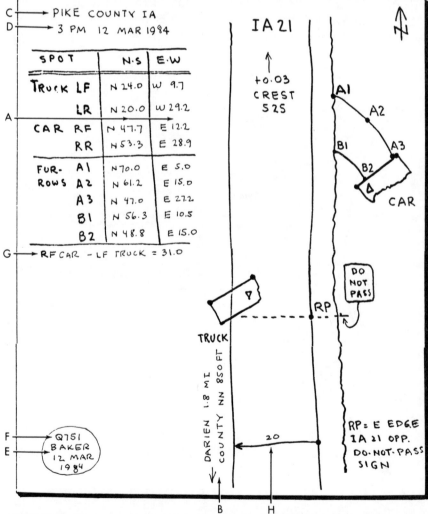

Exhibit 22. *Good at-scene field notes for an opposite-direction collision between a truck and a car. Because the road is very simple, no additional measurements were needed for the map.*

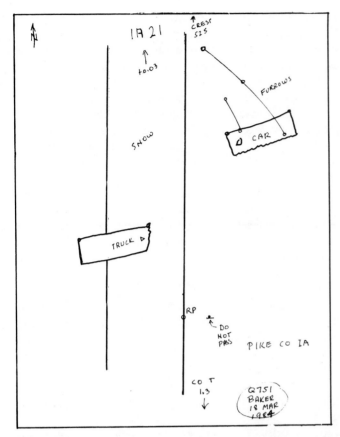

Exhibit 23. A working after-accident situation map prepared from the field notes in Exhibit 22. Essential dimensions are to scale, but refinements and identification have not been added.

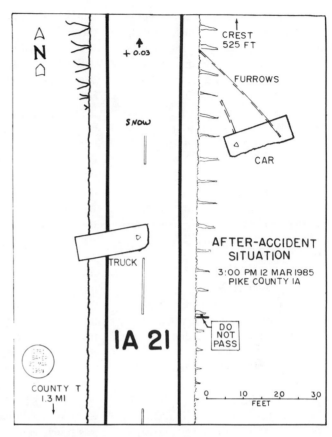

Exhibit 24. Display map corresponding to Exhibits 22 and 23. Unnecessary notations have been removed and full identification added.

nate measurements in which the east edge of the roadway is the reference line and the reference point is opposite an easily recognized traffic sign. Once the map has been drawn showing the roadway and traffic sign, results of the accident can easily be plotted on the map.

Inadequate Data

More often than not, data on positions of results of the accident are disappointing: there are no at-scene measurements at all, or what there are do not position what you need to locate; reference points and lines are not described, or measurements are inconsistent; measurements are made from an indefinite P.O.I., or which vehicle was No. 1 and which No. 2 is not stated.

Making up for such deficiencies in data may challenge your ingenuity. Some help may come from visiting the

site, perhaps when measuring the road layout. Some signs of the accident may be visible long afterward, for example, scars on trees or even oil soaked in on the roadside where a car came

to rest.

Do the Best You Can with What You Have

You may have to patch together in-

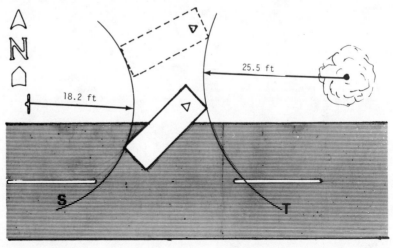

Exhibit 25. To locate a car, its distance from each of two reference points was measured. These measurements are not enough. Using dimensions of the vehicle the car might be located in any number of places, for example as the one shown in dotted outline. Reference to photographs and statemetns of witnesses gave the most probable location: that shown by the solid outline.

formation from a number of sources. Fit together road and vehicle measurements to make sense. Compare these with photos to see whether they look right. Generally cutouts in the *Traffic Template* will helpfully approximate vehicle dimensions. Distances between tire marks must correspond to track width and wheel base of the vehicles which made the marks. An example (Exhibit 25) will illustrate how this is done.

An investigator measured from the right front corner of a vehicle at rest to a tree and from the left rear corner to a traffic sign:

RF to tree 25.5 ft.
LR to sign 18.2 ft.

These measurements do not establish the position of the car. The investigator had not learned that to locate a spot, such as the corner of a car, distances from *two* reference points are needed, in this example, measurements from both corners to *both* the tree and the sign. Now what do you do about this in drawing your after-accident situation map? First, obtain

length and width of the vehicle from measurements or published information. If these dimensions are not easily available, use whichever cut out on the *Traffic Template* fits the vehicle size best. It will be a good approximation until you can get better facts. On a card draw an outline of the vehicle to the same scale as your map.

Cut it out as a pattern. On your map, the sign and tree are located by measurements as reference points (Exhibit 25). Now set a compass at the measured distance of the right front corner of the car from the tree, 25.5 ft, and draw an arc, T, with the tree as the center. Do the same for the distance from the left rear corner to the sign, 18.2 ft, giving arc S. You now have the locus (possible positions) of the right front corner and the same for the left rear corner. Now put your cut out car pattern on the map, right front corner on arc T, and left rear corner on arc S. The car pattern will fit these arcs in hundreds of different positions; one possible position is shown by dotted lines in Exhibit 25.

Now you wish you had some other measurement to determine which of these many possible positions is the proper one. Lacking that, seek other sources: photos which show, perhaps, that the right front corner is about as far north of the roadway edge as the left rear is south, a sketch on the police report that shows the car was headed about northeast where it came to rest, or a witness who says that the vehicle was straddling the north edge of the roadway. Then you can come very close to the correct final position as shown in the solid outline in Exhibit 25.

Photographs

Sometimes when there are no measurements or when measurements are inadequate, there are photographs from which final positions of vehicles or marks on the road can be located. To be able to do this, the photos must include certain permanent features of the site such as lane lines, pavement cracks, fences, poles, and trees. These must be located on the map as refer-

Exhibit 26. *(Below) No measurements were made to locate this important tire mark. Fortunately this photo was taken straight down the road, so the mark's relation to peculiarities in the road was clear enough to permit locating it on a scale map.*

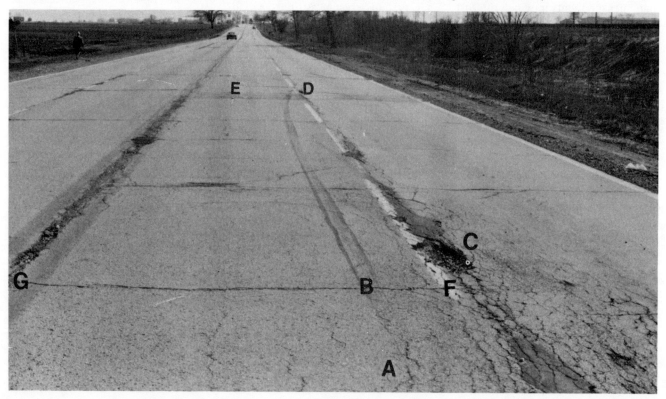

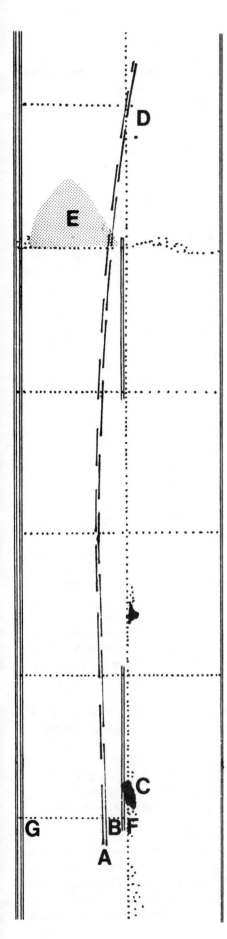

Exhibit 27. (Left). Road peculiarities shown in Exhibit 26 were measured and located on this scale map. Then the tire mark was drawn in from its relation to lane stripes and pavement cracks.

ence points.

It may be necessary to take the photos to the site to know which features appearing in the pictures need to be put on the map to locate short-lived results of the accident. For example, the beginning and end of each stripe in a lane or center line may have to be measured to locate it exactly.

Thus photographs are commonly used to help understand the location of results of an accident. Pictures are especially helpful in showing the relation of vehicles to the roadway as suggested in the discussion of the use of vehicle dimensions. They are also important in indicating the relationship of the final position of one vehicle to that of another.

Note, for example, where a tire mark crosses pavement cracks, lane lines, and roadway edges; what roadside objects it is opposite; and where it lines up with objects in the background. Then locate these spots as well as possible on the map. Sometimes a view straight down a road, as in Exhibit 26, permits quite accurate location of unmeasured tire marks shown in the photo. This is because, if lines straight across a roadway are parallel in the photo as they are on a map, distances along each line in the photo are proportional to distances along the corresponding line on a map. Exhibits 26 and 27 illustrate how a tire mark was located on a map in this way.

Careful measurements of the roadway located pavement cracks and lane stripes, which were shown on a roadway map of the location (Exhibit 27). The tire mark was located on the map by identifying the points where it crossed the pavement cracks and lane stripes in the photo (Exhibit 26). The beginning of the tire mark, (A in the Exhibits) is a few feet before the first pavement joint shown in the photo. The correct joint was identified by its

relation to the pothole and the pavement patch (C and E in the Exhibits). The width of the lane, F to G was measured in the photo as 4.60 in. and on the map as 1.20 in.

Then any distance *along that particular line* is 1.20/4.60 = 0.26 times as long on the map as in the photo. The distance from the center line to the tire mark, F to B, is 0.85 in. in the photo. Hence it must be 0.85 (0.26) = 0.22 in. on the map. Thus the beginning of the tire mark is located on the map. The crosswise distance of the tire mark from the center line is located at the other crosswise cracks in the same way.

The point where the tire mark crosses the lane line, D, in the Exhibits, is located where a pavement crack, visible in the photo, crosses the lane stripe.

From the map so drawn, the length of the tire mark can be scaled on the map as 80 ft, which is accurate enough for practical accident-investigation purposes.

Perspective Grid

Some at-scene investigators and photographers put a 2-ft square perspective grid on the roadway in the foreground of some pictures (Exhibit 28). The purpose of this grid is to put an object of known dimensions in the picture. From it, other points on the surface in the picture can be located by projection. This is especially useful where a complicated collection of marks on the road would require more time to measure than there is available or where the risk from traffic is too great to take measurements.

Limitations. The perspective grid only works for reasonably flat surfaces; but the surface need not be level. The grid is not useful on roads with high crowns or for objects on banks or in ditches. It is not accurate for locating marks more than about 40 ft (12 m) from the camera. Topic 830 explains the use of perspective grids and other aspects of photogrammetry.

Exhibit 28. *If the photo includes a perspective grid, nearby marks on the road can be plotted by photogrammetric methods without measurements.*

6. FINISHING

The working map with minimum detail, Exhibit 23, may be all that is required. File it away with other papers relating to the accident. Now consider some suggestions for a finished map that, by its completeness, leaves few questions about the after-accident situation unanswered, and, by its appearance, inspires confidence.

Scale

In choosing a map scale, consider five things:

1. *Detail required.* Must exact width of tire marks and pavement stripes be shown, or is a single line sufficient to show the roadway width?
2. *Size of drawing.* Less than three inches or more than ten feet are impractical dimensions.
3. *Viewing distance.* Can the map be viewed from a few inches, possibly with a magnifier; or must it be seen on the far wall of a room?
4. *Matching other scales.* Must the map correspond to the scale of other maps such as highway plans or to the scales of available model vehicles which may be used with it.
5. *Is it for U. S. A. measurements* or metric?

For all but a few after-accident situation maps drawn in America, dimensions of vehicles and roadways are to U.S.A. scales; the drawings can be spread out on a desk top and folded easily into a report or file; they will be viewed at normal reading distance (about 1.2 ft); other scales need not be matched; and measurements are in feet and tenths.

Therefore, by far the most common scales used in the U.S.A. are those on the *Traffic Template:* 1 in. = 10 ft (1/120) and 1 in. = 20 ft (1/240).

Odd scales are sometimes preferable. Perhaps the most common reason is to accommodate available scale models of vehicles and to provide for greater viewing distance, for example, in a court room.

If 1 in. = 10 ft is a comfortable viewing scale at tabletop distance (1.2 ft), maps intended for greater viewing distances will require larger scales ap-

proximately as follows:

Viewing distance, feet	Suitable scale 1 in. =	Small map length, inches
1.2	10 ft	11
2.5	5 ft	22
3	4 ft	28
4	3 ft	36
6	2 ft	55
12	1 ft	110

Sometimes a second map showing more area, such as a section of a city or a greater length of roadway, may be useful. Usually this would not show accident results, but rather the general location of the accident.

Put an interval scale on every display map. Do this by drawing a line about 3 in. long in one corner, marking it off in 5-ft or 10-ft intervals to scale, and labeling it (Exhibit 24). This is better than writing "1 in. = 20 ft" because an interval scale remains correct even if the map is enlarged or reduced by photographing.

Size

Working maps are generally made on sheets large enough to permit extensions and possibly associated diagrams, notes, and calculations. The finished map is usually trimmed down to a convenient size for handling, reproducing and filing. You can usually make the map 11 in. high or wide (the length of a sheet of typewriter paper). It may be extended as far as necessary beyond 8½ in. in the other dimension and still fold back and forth to go into a report neatly, handle easily on a desk, and file without crisscross creasing. If necessary, of course, the minimum dimension may be more than 11 in.

The map will be less cluttered if you omit borders. Run the roadway markings to the edge of the sheet.

Details

A north arrow is probably the most important detail. Do not overlook it. Arrange the map and lettering so that north is at the top of the sheet and lettering is upright when the map is

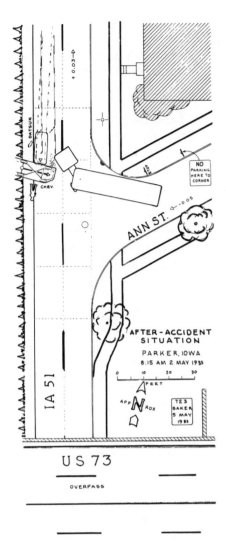

Exhibit 29. *(Left) A completed after-accident situation map illustrates many of the methods explained in this topic. This map was drawn entirely with the Traffic Template.*

Symbols identify certain map details without using words. They reduce clutter. Some of the most common symbols are cut outs in the *Traffic Template*; they may be quickly drawn with that device. The same symbols can be used on field sketches as on scale maps. But if the map is to be examined by people unfamiliar with symbols used, label anything which is not self-explanatory. Exhibit 30 is a system of traffic map symbols which has been widely recognized.

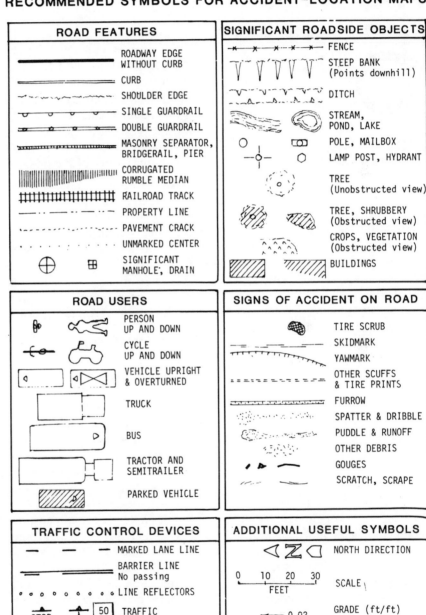

Exhibit 30. *Recommended symbols for use in field sketches, diagrams and maps.*

viewed with north at the top. If the map is much longer north to south than east to west, assume that it can be turned for viewing and put north at the left. Make lettering upright when north is at the top.

The amount of detail depends on how the map is to be used and the complexity of the results of the accident shown on it.

On the finished map do not show numbers for measurements, such as width of roadways. One of the objects of a scale map is to get rid of a clutter of numbers such as appear on the field notes shown in Exhibit 11.

There are exceptions to this rule. Show distances if someone specifically requests you to do so.

Also use numbers to show grades of roads as in Exhibit 24.

1.5 FEET
2.0 FEET
3.5 FEET
4.4 FEET
7.5 FT
15 FT

Exhibit 31. Recommended legible letter size and line width for drawings to be viewed from various distances.

Color sometimes helps make a map more understandable and more interesting. Put permanent features in colors which suggest what they represent: roadway gray; shoulders brown, grass green; water, blue. Outlines of parked vehicles can be shaded to show that they are standing. Do not overdo colors. Use light shades rather than strong colors. Remember that most reproduction processes will not copy colors.

Letters and Lines

Engineering drawings are intended to be looked at close up. Unfortunately they are often used for display purposes and when viewed at a distance of several feet are difficult to read. They are especially unsuitable for photographing as slides for projection. These drawings tend to use the same fine line for all purposes, whereas, heavier lines for roadway edges will make the road configuration much clearer and distinguish roadway edges from lane and center lines.

Engineering drawings also tend to use fine rather than bold lettering with a resultant loss in emphasis.

As a rule, for easy reading, make the capital letter height (in inches) the greatest viewing distance in feet divided by 15. And make the stroke width for significant lettering a tenth or more of the height of capital letters (Exhibit 31).

To judge the suitability of lines and lettering on a map, view it from the maximum expected distance. If significant wording is at all difficult to read, make it bigger and bolder. If roadway edges do not stand out, make them wider.

As a rule, use only capital letters on a display map. Make letters in names of roads and a title for the map about three times as large as the minimum.

Notes, such as sources of information for the map, date the map was drawn and the name of the draftsman can be quite inconspicuous in small letters in one corner of the map.

Make the display map clean and neat. It is best to trace most of it from a working map, leaving off irrelevant matter and adding such things as identification. The final drawing may be in pencil or ink, preferably the latter. If you do not have much drawing experience pencil may be a better choice because it makes erasing easier.

7. IDENTIFICATION

Identify the map completely. It is easy to forget to do this, so here is a check list as a reminder:
- Show a north arrow.
- Put names on every road. If a road has more than one name or a name and a route number, show both, or at least consider this.
- Put on names of railroads, rivers, and any buildings other than residences which appear on the map.
- Indicate what kind of a map it is, for example, "After-accident Situation Map."
- Name the city or county and the state.
- Give the hour and date of the accident.
- Identify vehicles by more than accident-report numbers; label them by type of vehicle, manufacturer's name, driver's name, or owner's name.
- Show legends (lettering etc.) of all signs shown on map.
- Give accident number if known.
- Show name of whoever made the map and the date the drawing was completed.
- If measurements made for the map or made to locate results of the accident were obtained from others, show who they came from. If some things were located from photographs or statements of witnesses, say so on the map.

8. MOUNTING

You may want to mount the after-accident situation map on a stiff backing for ease of handling in court or elsewhere. The backing material must be stiff enough to support the drawing, but light-weight enough so that it is convenient to handle. Poster board, corrugated cardboard, or especially foam-core board are suitable. The drawing can be mounted on the backing using aerosol-spray adhesive or rubber cement.

To make it easier to carry, cut a large mounted display map into a number of rectangles of the same convenient size. Hinge these pieces with adhesive tape alternately on the front and back side. Then you can fold it zig-zag into a handy package as illustrated in Exhibit 32.

9. ACCURACY

We are told that a map is supposed to be a "true representation" of the accident situation. But no representation can be absolutely true or accurate. We must be satisfied if our efforts do not misrepresent things as they were at the accident scene.

As a general rule, three conditions determine the accuracy with which measurements are recorded:

1. *The scale of the map to be produced.* About the smallest distance you can represent on a map on which

Exhibit 32. *A mounted display map too large to be carried easily can be made more manageable by cutting into a number of rectangles of equal size, in this case three. These sections are hinged together with tapes so that they fold into a flat package convenient for transporting and storing. The display shown here had three parallel parts: an after-accident situation map, a diagram of four successive collisions, and a space-speed graph for a three-vehicle fatal accident.*

1 in. = 20 ft is 0.25 ft or 3 in. So there is no point in measuring distances to less than 0.1 ft or 1 in.

2. *The detail necessary.* For example, a good, clean, portland-cement roadway edge can be located to within half an inch but the edge of a gravel road is ragged and usually the best you can do is measure it to within half a foot. The width of a clean tiremark can be measured to within a quarter of an inch but the starting point of a skidmark can usually be located only within a foot and the beginning of a yawmark usually not within 10 ft.

3. *The ultimate use of the measurement.* For example, ordinarily the radius of a curve between road edges at a junction will be satisfactory if it is accurate to within 2 ft. But if the accident involves a bus or truck making a right turn and striking a pedestrian standing on the corner, the measurement may have to be within 2 in. In fact, you may not want to assume that the curve is the arc of a circle; it may be necessary to locate it by measurement of a whole series of points on the curb curve to plot it accurately.

Errors in maps result mainly from deficiencies in field notes. When important measurements are omitted or field notes are not clear as to what point a measurement was taken from or to what spot it was made, whoever draws the map either has to omit something or put it on the map more or less by trial and error. That is why carefully made field notes are so important.

If you have to make assumptions or adjustments in drawing the map, for example locating tire marks from photographs, explain the source of your data in an inconspicuous note on the map. Otherwise it will be assumed that all locations were from actual at-scene or at-site measurements by yourself. Some map makers go so far as to note on the map all of their sources of information.

10. ASSOCIATED DISPLAYS

Toys sometimes help people understand an accident situation more clearly. If you want to use them for this purpose, make your map correspond in scale. Models are most useful on court exhibit diagrams and on accident-reconstruction diagrams (Exhibt 33). Suitable ready made models are not so easy to find as one might think. Some cars are excellent in proportion and detail but most truck and trailer combinations are too wide, low, and short. Hobby shops that stock HO gauge model trains often have excellent trucks, trailers, cars, and even pedestrians to the same scale: 3.5 mm = 1 ft. Special rulers for drawing maps to this scale are available.

Collision Diagrams

The maps discussed so far represent only the situation after the accident. As far as possible, they represent a *factual* situation based on measurements, photographs, and observations. These are acceptable in court as representations of what existed at the scene after the accident. But if positions of vehicles at or before collision are shown on the map, opinions are involved and the map may not be ad-

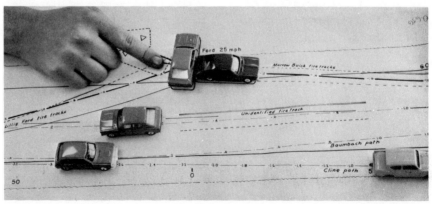

Exhibit 33. *Maps and diagrams made to the scale of model cars can be used to show reconstruction of a traffic accident. This is useful in courtroom presentations.*

missible. Therefore, put whatever represents conclusions on a separate map or collision diagram such as shown in Exhibit 33.

Overlays

On reconstructed accidents, you may want to show successive positions of two vehicles — for example, at the first contact, at maximum engagement, and on approach paths.

Often the best way to do this is to map the location to a scale without showing vehicles involved except in final positions. Then make an overlay showing just the positions of the vehicles for each of several different positions you wish to illustrate. The overlay can be drawn on tracing paper or clear acetate sheets. The after-accident situation map shows facts; the collision diagram shows opinion. Keep them separate.

11. SOURCES

Contributors

This topic was developed by the following:

J. Stannard Baker, a traffic engineer specializing in accident investigation. He was director of Research and Development at The Northwestern University Traffic Institute from 1946 until 1971; since then he has been a consultant at the Traffic Institute.

Robert K. Seyfried, a traffic engineer specializing in highway design, traffic control, and accident investigation. He is Associate Director of the Transporation Engineering Division of Northwestern University Traffic Institute.

References

Superscript numbers in the preceding pages refer to the following publications:

1. Baker, J. Stannard, *Traffic Template* (SN 1000), 1983, The Northwestern University Traffic Institute; Evanston IL 60204

2. Baker, J. Stannard, *Traffic Template — Metric* (SN 1000M), 1974, The Northwestern University Traffic Institute, Evanston IL 60204

Exhibits

The following are the sources of photos, maps, charts, and diagrams used in this publication:

Aycock, Thad, L., Traffic Institute, Evanston IL
  Photos: 26, 32
Baker, J. Stannard, Glencoe IL
  Photos: 3, 28, 33
  Maps: 11, 21, 22, 23, 24, 27, 29
  Diagrams: 4, 7, 8, 13, 14, 15, 16, 17, 18, 21, 22, 23
  Charts: 19, 31
International Association of Chiefs of Police, Gaithersburg MD
  Chart: 30
Keneipp, J. M., Barton-Aschman Associates, Evanston IL
  Diagram: 12
Seyfried, Robert K. Traffic Institute, Evanston IL
  Map: 20
  Diagrams: 5, 6, 9, 10, 25

PHOTOGRAPHY FOR TRAFFIC-ACCIDENT INVESTIGATION

Topic 836 of the *Traffic-Accident Investigation Manual*

by
Lynn B. Fricke
and
J. Stannard Baker

NORTHWESTERN UNIVERSITY TRAFFIC INSTITUTE

PUBLICATION HISTORY
Topic 836

1940 *Accident Investigation Manual* (Chapter 5)
Reprinted 1941, 1942
1946 Revised (Chapter 6)
Reprinted 1947, 1948

1953 *Traffic Accident Investigator's Manual* (Section 44)
1954 Revised (Section 44)

1957 *Traffic Accident Investigator's Manual for Police* (Section 44)
Reprinted 1959
1963 Revised (Section 44)
Reprinted 1964, 1965, 1966, 1969, 1970, 1971, 1973

1970 *Manual de Investigacion de Accidentes de Trafico* (Section 4.5)

1975 *Traffic Accident Investigation Manual* (Chapter 8)
Reprinted 1976, 1979, 1985

1985 *Photography for Traffic-accident Investigation*

PHOTOGRAPHY FOR TRAFFIC-ACCIDENT INVESTIGATION

1. PHOTOS FOR ACCIDENT INFORMATION

Photos record Facts

An important part of accident investigation is recording information so that it can be used later. Photography is an indispensable means of recording certain kinds of accident information and a useful supplement in recording many other kinds.

Photos are employed in two ways to preserve information:

1. As a permanent, accurate, unbiased record of something specifically observed by an investigator.
2. To capture the detailed appearance of something such as a mark on the road or damage to a vehicle, which may later reveal significant details that were not observed at the time the picture was made.

As a record of observations, photos serve 1) to recall later to an investigator's mind details of what he saw; and 2) to explain what the investigator saw to someone else, perhaps in court.

A dozen pages, which could take hours to write, cannot describe details of damage to a vehicle as well as a single picture. The picture of scratches on a vehicle's body, or the pattern of fractures in a windshield defy accurate description in words.

As a reservoir of nondescript information, photos include much unnecessary data and may omit essential facts because the the photographer was unaware of those facts when the photo was made. However, photos made on the chance that they may prove useful do include an immense amount of data that would otherwise be unavailable. Moreover, photos made only to record an investigator's particular observations often also include a wealth of detail not noticed by the investigator at the time he made the photograph.

Use of Photos

Credibility of photos is impressive. People tend to believe that "photos don't lie." Even though a photo may not be a completely "true representation," it is regarded as relatively free from the bias that may influence verbal or written reports. Photos are certainly not subject to the loss of detail and uncertainties that memory is. Hence, photos are very effective in verifying reports of observations.

As a reminder to refresh the memory about something seen in the past, perhaps years ago, photos are unsurpassed.

Writing and sketching are simplified by making photos. Often a photograph makes notes of observations unnecessary. A *spare* print of photograph can be marked with notes giving dimensions, pointing out significant observations, and explaining why the photo was made. Do this as soon as you receive the print of the picture. This makes the photo more effective in reminding you of what you observed. Such a marked photo cannot ordinarily be admitted as evidence in court, but it may be referred to like any other notes you have made. It is useful to mark each photo of an accident scene with a small arrow to show which direction is north, as in Exhibits 1, 2, 3,7, 8, 9, etc.

Copies of documents made photographically by one process or another are frequently used in accident investigation. The most commonly copied document is the official traffic-accident report on a form.

Others besides investigators often use accident photos for a variety of purposes, such as

- Public information, for example, in newspapers and on television
- Supporting damage evaluation by damage appraisers
- Satisfying curiosity, for example, in the case of a photographer with a camera who happens on the accident scene
- Training investigators in accident investigation.

Misused Photos

Investigators can be led astray by the obvious advantages of photography in accident investigation. These investigators are usually "shutter-happy" camera fans, those who think photography an easy way out of arduous observing and measuring, the inept, and the inexperienced.

Observations. An investigator should think of photos only as a means of recording what he has seen that he thinks important; he should avoid taking pictures as a substitute for observations. He should not expect to find in a picture what he failed to note before he made the picture.

Measurements. Anyone who has ever tried to make a map from photographs alone knows why photos are no adequate substitute for measurements. It is true that by photogrammetry, maps can often be made from photos, but this is a tedious and therefore expensive process. (See Topic 830 for a discussion of photogrammetry.) A specially trained engineer may require days to make a scale diagram or map from photographs. The necessary measurements and a useful field sketch at the scene can be made in a matter of minutes.

Photos, therefore, supplement but are not a good substitute for written notes, classification of damage, description of the accident location, measurements, and above all, careful observations.

Photographic prints can also be abused. A spare one may be marked as much as you please, but otherwise mark it only in one of three ways:

1. On the back
2. With a soft "china-marking" crayon which can be cleaned off easily
3. On a transparent or translucent overlay, either tracing paper or acetate.

Photos marked with pens or felt-tipped markers are ruined for some purposes.

Spectacular scenes. Sometimes a badly injured person being extracted from a vehicle or firemen fighting a blaze are of compelling human interest (Exhibit 1). Newspaper photographers avidly seek opportunities to make such "action" pictures. Yet they may be worthless for accident investigation purposes. In fact, such pictures may not be permitted as evidence in court because they tend to bias the jury. Do not let yourself be carried away by such scences, but on the other hand do not hesitate to make such a picture if it really has some purpose in showing how or why the accident happened.

2. HOW THE PHOTOGRAPHS ARE MADE

Who Makes Them

Police traffic-accident investigators make most of the pictures at the scene of accidents. This is natural because information gathering at the scene is considered to be a police function, because police have the communication facilities and transportation to get to the scene promptly, and because their authority to investigate is respected. Police arrange for photos at the scene in four different ways:

1. Investigating officers are provided with the equipment and are trained to take photos by the department employing them. This is usually the situation in county and state highway patrols.
2. Investigating officers call in photographers from the criminal investigation division when pictures at the scene are needed. This is often the situation in city police departments.
3. No official facilities for picture taking are available. When photos at the scene of an accident are required, a professional photographer is called. He may take pictures at the direction of police to be paid for by police, or he may take pictures in the hope of selling them elsewhere with the understanding that police may have or buy copies.
4. No official facilities are available, but investigating officers are permitted or encouraged to carry personal cameras and take pictures. Various arrangements exist by which such pictures can be used by prosecutors or made available to newspapers, attorneys, or others.

Generally, rules which determine when a police investigator shall take pictures are vague. The matter is left largely to the individual investigator's judgment, which means that whether pictures are made depends to a great extent on how convenient it is to make pictures and how interested and skillful the investigator is in making pictures. One reason for classifying accidents for accident-investigation purposes is to guide the investigator in deciding whether to take pictures. In general, he should take pictures in all serious accidents.

Professional photographers on assignment take most of the technical pictures of damaged vehicles and of the accident site. Such pictures are ordered by insurance companies and attorneys. The pictures are generally for exclusive use of whoever commissioned them. Ordinarily they are technically excellent.

Free-lance photographers take pictures, usually at the scene, on the chance that someone may want copies. These are available to whoever wishes to buy prints, but sometimes exclusive rights are sold. Often these photos are offered to newspapers. Sometimes these photographers listen to police radio dispatching for opportunities to make marketable pictures.

Newspaper photograpers and reporters covering an accident often make pictures which may or may not be published but are generally available to whoever wants to buy them for accident investigation purposes. These photos usually emphasize "human interest" which may make them less useful for investigation.

Damage appraisers usually make a few pictures of vehicle damage to support their estimates of repair costs. Often these are Polaroid pictures. They are sometimes useful for other purposes.

Claim adjusters take pictures of the site and damaged vehicles. These are likely to be only moderately useful for accident study purposes.

Amateur photographers who chance to be passing by sometimes get useful and even valuable pictures, but often they are not available simply because the photographer was not identified and cannot be found.

When Photos are Made

The point in the investigation at which to make photos depends on how urgent photography is compared to other procedures. For example, if there are no injuries, but damaged vehicles must be moved promptly to clear the road, photographing the position of the vehicles may be the first thing you should do on arrival at the scene. It may take priority over locating the position of vehicles by measurements because the position can be quickly marked when the pictures are taken and the measurements made later. On the other hand, if no photos are necessary except a general view of the scene, photos may be deferred until just before trial. In this case, photography might be about the last step in the investigation.

Make photographs soon of things that will change. Marks on the road are very important because they may soon be obliterated.

Photograph vehicles on the roadway promptly so that they can be removed to restore traffic movement, but photographs of vehicles off the road can be postponed. You can delay getting views of the general scene, pictures of view obstructions, damage to cars or fixed objects, and positions of signs. Delay in taking pictures may prove to be desirable, because light or weather conditions may be better later. It is good practice to return to the site the day following a serious night accident for better photos than

Exhibit 1. *Human interest photographs make interesting newspaper illustrations, but are not much use in explaining the accident.*

were possible in darkness. Sometimes tire and other marks on the roadway and roadside may be obscured by debris, water, or snow at the time of the accident but become visible later and may be photographed, perhaps even days later. Exhibit 2 is an example of important liquid debris (in this case battery acid) which was covered by snow at the time of the accident but was visible later when the snow was gone and the pavement had dried.

Restrictions on Making Photographs

At the scene anybody may take pictures of anything he can see in connection with a traffic accident. People may object to having pictures taken, but they cannot take legal steps to prevent it or to suppress the use of the pictures for accident investigation purposes.

At the site, after vehicles and other signs of the accident have disappeared, the same rules apply as at the scene while results of the accident are still evident. There may be some difficulty for non-police photographers taking pictures at accident sites on limited access roads where pedestrians are prohibited, but this is a matter of risk and interfering with traffic rather

Exhibit 2. A battery acid stain, snow covered at the scene, was photographed later to show where a collision took place. The little arrow is put in to show which way is north.

than a restraint on photography.

On private property, you can be prevented by the owner from entering the premises to take pictures or for any other reason under the laws governing trespass. You would be trespassing if you went into a man's yard to take a picture of his car after an accident unless he gave you permission to do so. You could, however, stand in the public road and take the picture without trespassing.

Warrants. In some circumstances, peace officers can obtain search warrants to take pictures or locate evidence on private property. Warrants are rarely necessary in accident investigations except in connection with hit-and-run cases.

A peace officer has an advantage in taking pictures. On public streets and highways, anyone attempting to prevent him from making investigation pictures would be interfering with an officer in performance of his duty. He may require people to let him take pictures. Likewise, if someone tries forcibly to prevent him from taking pictures, it may be considered assault.

Ordinarily there is little difficulty in getting pictures of accidents. Almost everybody is cooperative. Diplomacy and courtesy will accomplish more than legal authority in getting cooperation. For example, if you want a picture of a damaged car in a junk yard or garage, just ask the owner or manager for permission. Tell him who you are and why you want the pictures. Usually you will have no difficulty obtaining the information you are after.

Interfering with an investigation or other police activity at the scene of an accident is prohibited. If an aggressive photographer makes a nuisance of himself by ordering you to pose for pictures or delay handling the injured, removal of vehicles, or making measurements so that he can take photos, ask him to desist and, if he refuses, require him to do so. A policeman's first duty is to protect life and property at the scene. Next in importance is getting the required information and restoring traffic movement.

Anything that interferes with orderly performance of these functions is objectionable and may be unlawful.

3. AT-SCENE PHOTOS

The most important — and difficult — traffic-accident pictures are those made at the scene before vehicles have been moved. They are important because they record facts about the situation more accurately, in greater detail, and more quickly than any observer possibly could. They are more difficult because conditions are usually the least favorable for picture taking: there is too little time for thoughtful photography; the light is often bad; other people with more important things to do often get in the way; and the inevitable confusion is distracting.

Special requirements of at-scene pictures will be explained first. Photographing particular things like tire marks and damage to vehicles will be left until later.

Basic At-scene Pictures

The peculiar purpose of at-scene pictures is to show how the situation looked when vehicles came to rest after the accident, how objects were arranged and how things were related to each other. These photos enable any one interested to see quickly how pictures of specific details relate to the whole accident scene.

If you can conveniently do so, have your basic at-scene photos also show details of damage and other abnormalities resulting from the accident, but photographing these details at once is relatively unimportant, especially if they can be pictured as well or better separately or later.

Thus, for the main purpose of at-scene photos, you will need at least one and possibly several general views showing how things were. Therefore plan these pictures to show a combination of two or more of the following:

1. Final positions of vehicles and bodies

2. Signs of the accident on the road
3. Signs of the accident on the roadside
4. Recognizable landmarks such as traffic signs which will identify the location on the road
5. The view that a driver may have had approaching the first contact point or the place where the vehicle left the roadway.

For these pictures treat parts of a vehicle which has broken in two (Exhibit 3), a tractor, and a trailer as separate vehicles.

Also try to arrange each picture so that it will make distances shown in them easy to judge. That means, so far as possible, taking views straight down the road, preferably in the center of a lane in which a vehicle involved had been travelling or straight across the road at right angles to the edge or to the pavement stripe.

Likewise, if you can do it by moving your viewpoint a little this way or that, take the picture squarely toward a side or end of a vehicle as you would do in photographing vehicle damage.

In choosing a viewpoint, consider what camera position will best picture most of the desirable elements.

Exhibit 3. *If a significant part of the vehicle becomes detached, as here, be sure to photograph and locate it. Small pieces of the vehicle are usually considered debris.*

Exhibit 4 shows how a well chosen viewpoint makes a good at-scene picture, in this case a picture of two vehicles, a pair of skidmarks, and some scattered debris resulting from an angle collision.

Position A gives a view straight down the road, includes both cars, some debris, and a landmark stop sign; but the Ford obscures most of the Chevrolet and all of the skidmarks.

Position B is a good view of the damage to the right side of the Ford but it does not show whether the vehicles are actually touching each other and the skidmarks and stop sign are too far off to be clearly visible.

Position C is a good view of damage to the left side of the Chevrolet and it does clearly show that the cars are still engaged but it omits the skidmarks and both landmark stop signs. It does not show position on the road well.

Position D includes everything but is so far off (more than 80 ft) from anything significant to be very useful.

The angles included in these unde-

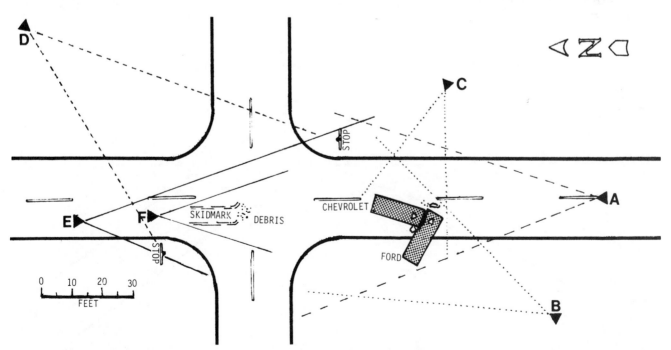

Exhibit 4. *A good photograph taken at position E shows the marks on the road, traffic control devices and the final vehicle positions. View angles shown are for a normal lens.*

sirable views are shown as dotted lines in Exhibit 4.

Position E shows everything that Position D does, but better. It is close enough to show the skidmarks well and also the major debris. Aimed straight down the middle of a lane, it shows well the position of the vehicles on the road and indicates that they are engaged. Thus it is the best overall picture.

Now you can think about additional useful views. A closer view of the skidmarks from Position F shows their beginning well. Then a photo from the direction of B but much closer shows the condition of the whole right side of the Ford. A smiliar picture from the direction of C will do for the left side of the Chevrolet.

A night a flash photo from Position E or F will show the skidmarks, but the cars are to far off to be covered by an ordinary single flash. To show them, you will need a multiple flash or a slave flash from the center of the lane but at a distance to show all of both cars.

A situation on a curve is shown in Exhibit 5. The vehicles came to rest 60 ft apart. This clearly calls for two pictures, one from H and one from G. Both are aimed straight down the road toward the curve. Both show well the angles of the cars to the road and to each other. Each includes a sign as a landmark fixed object; but neither

shows the tire marks and debris well. Consequently, especially with flash pictures, additional views from K and J are needed. Each of these can show the tire marks in the foreground, their relation to a car in the background, and a landmark sign on the roadside.

These cases illustrate how some thoughtful planning can improve the value of the basic at-scene photos.

Once the basic at-scene photos have been made, if time permits and circumstances are favorable, go ahead with detailed pictures of marks on the road and damage to vehicles as explained later.

If vehicles are in contact with each other (still engaged), as in Exhibit 6, take pictures of them first because they may soon be separated for removal.

Next go after the detailed pictures of tire marks which may soon disappear. Detailed vehicle damage pictures can usually wait because damage is likely to remain the same after the vehicle is taken from the scene.

In this connection, try to include photos of vehicles being towed away. That will give an idea of which wheels, if any, were locked by damage and what additional damage may have been done in towing.

Interference and Cooperation

Bystanders and even firemen and

other emergency workers are likely to be a nuisance to photographers at the scene. Do the best you can to keep them out of pictures or at least in the background. You can usually wait for at least some at-scene pictures until the injured have been removed and ambulances are gone. However, further delay may mean that you may not get pictures of things exactly as they were, especially if damaged cars block the roadway and have to be moved as soon as possible.

Usually it is desirable to coordinate picture taking at the scene with measurements. If you do both, that will come naturally. Otherwise whoever does the measuring may suggest pictures which might be helpful, such as difficult to measure collections of irregular marks on the road. If marks on the roadway are identified for measuring by letters made with crayon or spray paint, wait to make these detailed pictures until the letters are in place so that they will show in your pictures. (See Topic 828 for additional suggestions fcr identifying marks on the road.)

If you are assigned or employed to take pictures at the scene of a traffic accident, you must make whatever pictures your supervisor suggests. In addition to those, you may take whatever views you think might be helpful. If you are a press or free lance photographer attending an accident, you may

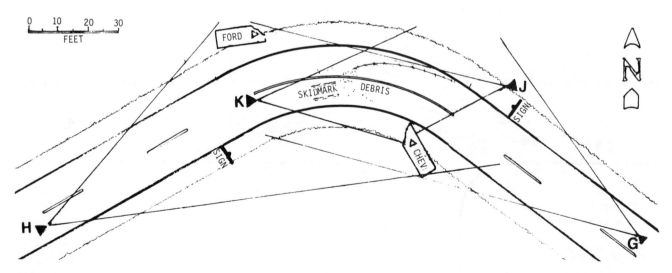

Exhibit 5. *The positions of vehicles and marks on the road are clearly shown relative to the road by this set of camera positions.*

Exhibit 6. *Vehicles stuck together or engaged with an obstacle require special photos.*

take whatever pictures you want, provided you do not interfere in any way with emergency operations or the investigating process.

4. PHOTOGRAPHING WHAT SHOWS ON THE ROAD

Signs on the road of how the accident happened are described in Topic 817. If you are planning to take traffic-accident photographs, you would benefit by a careful study of that topic.

Location Identification
To be able to recognize exactly what they are, tire marks and other signs of what happened must show clear details in photos of them. This generally requires close-ups of the road surface. Too often, however, such pictures fail to give any clue as to where on the road the area pictured was located (Exhibit 7).

To avoid this difficulty, do one or more of three things:

1. Aim the camera to include also some landmark fixed object (Exhibit 8).
2. Especially if the detail picture is straight downward toward the road, (for example to show stria-

tions in a yaw mark), take a second picture which includes with the detail some background object by which the location can be identified.
3. Near the detailed pictured put an identifying mark, a letter or number, which connects the picture with measurements or other location identification. (Exhibit 9).

Long Marks
Tire marks, grooves and scratches that show the path of a vehicle for more than about 10 ft (3m) need to be photographed to supplement rather than subsitute for measurements. If tiremarks are shown adequately in photos of the final positions of the vehicles, no additional photos are required.

For tire or other marks longer than 40 ft (12m), consider taking several photos at intervals along the mark, especially at night with flash. At the beginning of the mark, be sure to show some of the road where the mark does not show. Then questions about how the beginning of the mark looked can be answered by reference to the photo. Compare Exhibits 10 and 11.

If tire or other marks show peculiarities, get good photos of these changes in appearance. For example, tire mark A in Exhibit 12 definitely changes in character at spots 3, 4, and 5. Get photos of these changes; they may be very significant later in accident reconstruction.

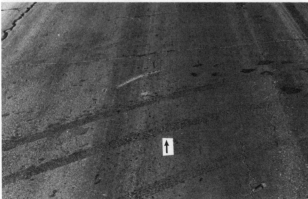

Exhibit 7. *The distance of the gouge from the center of the road can be estimated from this photograph aimed straight down the road. Compare with Exhibit 8.*

Exhibit 8. *A photo crosswise of the road and including a fixed landmark (the signpost) establishes the position of gouges along the road. Make both pictures square with the road.*

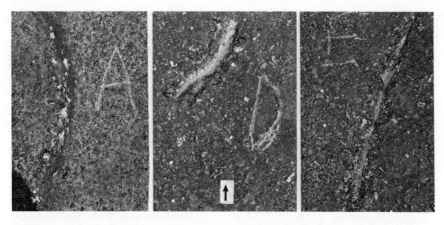

Exhibit 9. *A letter in a close-up picture of a mark on the road ties it in with measurements made to locate that mark.*

Ruts and furrows on the roadside are usually best photographed in the direction of movement of the vehicle that made them. Show the edge of the road where such marks begin (Exhibit 13). If they are more than 40 ft (12 m) long, make a series of two or more pictures.

Smaller marks, especially gouges or groups of gouges, collision scrubs, and irregularities in tiremarks, require close-up photographs to show necessary detail, even if the marks are included in the more general pictures. If there are more than two small marks, be careful to identify each in

some way so as to eliminate possible confusion about which mark shown on the field sketch was the one in the picture. The easiest way to identify a mark is by a crayon letter — A, B, C, etc. — beside it. This can be the same letter used to identify it for measurements or you can make special notes relating to it (Exhibit 9).

Often, close-up pictures of sections of long marks are useful to show exactly what they are like. Such pictures can show pavement texture and striations in a skidmark (Exhibit 14) or in a yawmark (Exhibit 15).

5. PHOTOS OF VEHICLE DAMAGE

Damage

Reasons for photographing damage. Damage is photographed to help reconstruct the accident, to evaluate the probable cost of repairs, or both. In reconstruction, we want to know such things as how one vehicle fitted against another vehicle or fixed object at maximum engagement, from what direction the major force came, whether it was involved in more than one collision during the accident, what areas received contact damage, and what parts of the vehicle were forced into unusual contact with the road. In evaluating cost of repairs for financial responsibility assessments or claims settlements, one wants to know what parts will require replacement. For either accident reconstruction or repair cost evaluation, it is often nearly as important to know what parts of a vehicle were not damaged as to know what parts were affected.

Vehicle damage photos made at the scene are preferable to those made after the vehicle has been moved. Do not show photos damage which may have been done in removing the vehi-

Exhibit 10. *This photograph does not show the beginning of the skidmark. If this is the only photograph of the mark, how do we know what the beginning of the mark looked like?*

Exhibit 11. *This shows the same skidmarks as Exhibit 10. However, it shows where the mark starts which may be useful in studying the accident.*

Exhibit 12. *This tire mark starts at 1. It changes its appearance at 2, 3, and 4. Photograph the mark to show the change in the mark's detail.*

Exhibit 13. *Furrows have been made in the turf as the car left the pavement and moved to its final position in the ditch.*

cle. They also can often show the relation of damage to other vehicles or fixed objects with which damaged vehicles are engaged. Photos of damage can actually often be taken more easily at the scene than elsewhere. For example, during daylight, when the vehicle is in the open, it may be more accessible to the photographer than it will be later in a crowded salvage yard. In Exhibit 6, both vehicles are off the road and in the open; by day, at least, the standard vehicle damage photos could easily be made while the cars are still in place. On the other hand, a vehicle down in a ditch among bushes at night may make good at-scene damage pictures impossible. So you have to make decisions about when and where to make damage photos.

Contact and induced damage usually is recorded better by photographs than in any other way; but do not think that photography makes other records of damage unnecessary. For

Exhibit 14. *Detailed photographs of skids may be useful. Note the rib pattern. Be sure to include the skid also in a general photograph to tell where the close-up was taken.*

Exhibit 15. *Note striations (lines) in the tire mark. Photograph the detail in marks such as this and also include them in a general view.*

36-12

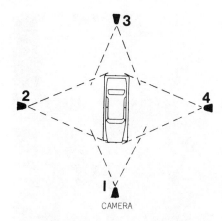

Exhibit 16. *The standard photographic record of vehicle damage consists of four pictures, straight toward front, rear, and both sides. Alignment is with least damage part of the vehicle.*

example, photography is no substitute for measurements to show the crush profile described in Topic 820.

The extent to which detail is photographed depends on the circumstances of the accident and the uses to which pictures are to be put.

Vehicle details. As specialists investigate more complex aspects of an accident, the need for more technical photography of details connected with the vehicle increases. Photographs may be required of lamp filaments, tire damage, brake wear, pedal imprints on shoe soles, bearing failures, exhaust system leaks, door latch failures, seat belt breakages, fingerprints, bloodstains, paint chip comparisons, and numerous other specific details. Most of these require more than ordinary photographic expertise, for example, macrophotography and even microphotography of very small objects. In many instances it is easier and more satisfactory to obtain and preserve the part of the vehicle than it is to try to photograph it. Then it might be appropriate, as a matter of record, to make a photograph of that part as it is being removed from the vehicle. Sometimes the whole vehicle is bought or impounded for future examination. That may save much otherwise necessary photography.

Standard Pictures

For reconstruction purposes, four pictures will often provide the information needed for damage analysis. Exhibit 16 shows what these four are.

Each photo shows completely one side or end of the vehicle. Make one of these pictures on the center line of the vehicle facing directly toward it as in Exhibit 17. Damage to the vehicle often makes it difficult to decide just where the center line is, but, so far as possible, align your camera by undamaged parts of the vehicle. For example, if the front end has been forced to the right, do not take the picture looking directly toward the offset front end, but rather on a line which passes through the centers of the windshield and the rear window if these are in their normal positions. For side views, make the center door posts on the right and left sides coincide so that the one on the near side covers that on the far side (Exhibit 18).

These four pictures make it easy to see how far particular parts have been crushed left or right and forward or backward.

Exhibit 17. *The first standard photo shows right or left deformation of the front end.*

Exhibit 18. *The second of four standard photos is aimed squarely toward the right side and, in this case, shows contact damage along the entire length.*

Exhibit 19. *The third standard photo shows any contact damage to the rear end.*

Exhibit 20. *The fourth and final standard damage photo is straight toward the left side. It shows forward and rearward deformation, if any, in contact damage areas.*

Exhibit 21. *This single photo shows the entire damaged area. It is sufficient to illustrate a damage appraisal.*

If you have a choice, do not use a lens with a short focal length (wide angle). Use either a normal lens (50 mm focal length for 35 mm film) or a longer focal length. A wide angle lens exaggerates the closer parts of the vehicle.

Best single picture. For claim investigation purposes, the minimum number of pictures to illustrate the damage may be all that are required. One may do for this purpose (Exhibit 21) but would certainly be inadequate for accident reconstruction. The best single picture usually shows not only the damaged area but also as much adjacent undamaged area as possible.

Therefore, take the picture to show all of one side and one end as in Exhibit 21. There are exceptions to this rule, of course. For example, the vehicle may be so located that it is impossible to take a picture from the most desirable viewpoint without moving the vehicle or some other object and you cannot or may not move either; or perhaps it is important to show more minute detail of the damage than would be possible from a distance required to include the entire vehicle in the one picture.

Best two pictures. If all the damage cannot be shown in one picture, you should make additional photos. At

least two are required to show satisfactorily which parts are damaged and which are not. Usually, therefore, the best two pictures of a damaged vehicle are those which show opposite corners, each photo showing one side and one end as in Exhibits 22 and 23. Again, these oblique views are not as useful as the basic four for reconstruction purposes. Circumstances may be such that it is impossible to get such pictures, but try to approximate such views as well as possible.

Special requirements. If technical photos are required after vehicles have been removed from the scene, discuss with whoever wants the photos exactly what is needed. Let such requirements guide your picture making.

Details of damage. The general views of the vehicle which have been described are usually adequate for determining contact damage areas and thrust direction, but they will not show many important details of damage such as:

- Imprints of one vehicle on another
- Friction or abrasion marks
- Damage to lamps
- Damage to load
- Sources of injury to pedestrians or occupants
- Detailed damage to tires and wheels.

Exhibit 22. *One of a pair of pictures can show damage, if any, to the front and one side of a vehicle.*

Exhibit 23. *The other photo of the pair shows damage, if any, to the rear and the other side.*

6. STORY TELLING PHOTOS

Important as they are, routine technical photos of the accident scene, signs on the road of what happened, and damage to vehicles are by no means the only traffic-accident pictures wanted. There are others which can illustrate observed circumstances and help to tell a better story of what happened. Most of these result from the imagination of an investigator or the ingenuity of a photographer.

Matching

The study of an accident — reconstruction, if you please — is mainly fitting together bits of information: matching damaged parts of two vehicles to show how they came together in a collision (Exhibit 6), matching scars and other marks on the road with vehicle parts, especially tires, which made them. Photos which illustrate — and prove — such matching may be priceless.

When such areas are discovered, each can be photographed to record the reasons for believing that the areas were in contact with each other. Examples of such matching for which photographs would make appropriate and often compelling records are

- Scored underpart of vehicle and corresponding groove in pavement
- Broken transmission case and corresponding oil spatter

Exhibit 24. *Make photographs to show matching impact areas. In this case a tire imprint on the side of a car.*

- Imprint of tire tread on car and tread of tire that made it (Exhibits 24 and 25)
- Imprint of brake pedal on shoe sole and ribs on pedal that made the imprint (Exhibit 26).
- Marks on the side of a car and guardrail that made them
- Tiremarks on the road and tire that made them.

The foregoing examples should suggest many other possibilities.

Such matching pictures naturally come in pairs.

Close-up photography is sometimes required to illustrate matching surfaces. A technical investigator should be prepared to make such photographs. If his camera cannot be focussed on objects close enough for this purpose, readily available supplementary lenses may be used. These are easy to use with camers that can focused through the lens; with other cameras the photographer must compensate for the fact that the viewfinder is offset from the lens.

Road Situations

General views of the site of the accident, after signs of the accident have disappeared, often serve no useful purpose. As a rule, they can be omitted, at least at the time of the accident, unless they have a direct bearing on the accident, and especially if the conditions at the site of the accident may change. Some of the circum-

Exhibit 25. *The tire itself is on another vehicle. Such pictures are valuable after vehicles are removed and possibly destroyed.*

Exhibit 26. *The imprint of accelerator pedal on shoe indicates heavy pedal pressure. The matching photograph shows clearly that the pressure was on the accelerator, not the brake.*

stances that would make general views advisable are as follows:

- Visibility conditions which may change quickly, for example, fog or smoke
- Positions and conditions of traffic control devices
- Parked vehicles
- Road surface conditions such as snow, water, and significant surface irregularities.

View obstructions should be photographed under two conditions: 1) the driver claims or suggests that his view was obstructed by something near or on the road; and 2) you believe that this may have been the case. Much time and fruitless argument can be avoided in court if photographs are produced which allow others to judge for themselves the nature of the view obstruction (Exhibit 27).

Vertical view obstructions are crests of hills, banks or buildings beside the road, and crops or other vegetation. The object of the photograph is to show how much of a vehicle at one place on a road could be seen by a driver at another place on that road or on a cross road. To do this have a similar vehicle placed at a specific location (position measured and recorded) and take the photo from the viewer's position. It is important to have the object vehicle the same height as the vehicle in the accident, preferably the same vehicle. The picture must be taken from the viewer's

Exhibit 27. *View-obstruction photographs show how little or how much a driver could see of another vehicle on a collision course. Make pictures as nearly as possible under the same conditions as existed at the time of the accident, for example, with respect to vegetation.*

Exhibit 28. *Aerial views taken from airplanes are sometimes useful to show the situation at an accident location, but they are expensive and are not suitable substitutes for maps of the accident site.*

location and at the viewer's eye height. The eye height is important. A short driver in a little car can see much less over a specific view obstruction than a tall driver in a truck cab over engine. This procedure is especially important in railroad grade crossing accidents.

Horizontal view obstructions at curves, at junctions, and a railroad grade crossings would have to be photographed with an extremely wide angle lens to show as much to the side as the human eye can perceive. Such a lens usually gives distorted perspective, so if there is a view obstruction problem, make one approach picture straight ahead down the road and also one at a 45° angle to the side in the direction at which the hazard was located.

Try to make view obstruction pictures under as nearly as possible the same conditions as existed at the time of the accident. For example, if trees and shrubs were bare of leaves at the time of the accident, try to make the picture when they are that way; and if cars were parked at a junction when the accident occurred, make the picture with cars parked in as nearly the same way as possible.

Aerial pictures from planes or helicopters are impressive but are rarely worth what they cost. They can quickly give a jury or someone who has not been to the site of the accident a general idea of the location, but they are not a good substitute for a scale map. They minimize view obstructions, and they cannot show details or marks on the road or traffic control devices. Aerial pictures are generally oblique pictures, made from about 1,000 ft above the ground and are preferable to pictures taken straight down from high altitude (Exhibit 28). Aerial survey photographs do little that a good scale map will not do.

Traffic control devices may be adequately shown by general pictures of the scene at the time of the accident or of the site later. Give special attention to photographing traffic control devices which may have been a factor in the accident. This depends, of course, to a large extent on circumstances of the accident. A few examples will suggest possibilities:

- Signs or signals obscured by snow or foliage
- Disarranged or missing barricades or detour signs at construction sites
- Deteriorated barriers, center lines, lane lines, and edge marking stripes
- Guardrail ends that have damaged vehicles
- Confusing backgrounds for traffic signals.

Series Pictures

Often a planned series of pictures will be much more informative than unrelated individual pictures. A series of pictures is especially helpful in court.

Marks on the road. One series has already been mentioned in connection with suggestions for photographing long marks on the road. For these marks, remember to take pictures of the very beginning, the end, and any pecularities or irregularities in between. Have each part of this distance showing in at least two photos. Take all pictures looking straight down the roadway from the middle of a lane as in Exhibits 29, 30, 31, and 32.

If you are lucky, these pictures can be part of the at-scene photographs. Usually, however, a long series may have to wait until a later when light or other circumstances are more favorable. If the marks are a bit complicated and spread across more than one lane, take another series in the opposite direction in an adjacent lane.

Approach pictures are also likely to form a series. The idea is to show what a driver could have seen as he approached the location of the accident. Often these are a series of view-obstruction pictures. Take the pictures at intervals which will depend on the situation. For a straight road not involving crossings, 200 ft may be close enough; but on curves and where vision is obstructed, the pictures may be as close as 25 ft. If you have a good idea of the path followed, take the pic-

ture along the path looking in the direction the vehicle was moving. Otherwise stick to middle of lane pictures.

If the scene is to include an observed vehicle, it is very important that vehicle be the same height as the vehicle appearing at the scene of the accident, and it is still more important that the camera be at the observer's eye height.

Plan to have the camera located by recorded measurements at each picture position. In that way you can tie the viewing positions in with an accident map.

Extreme close-ups. If you make a close-up photo of a mark on the road or a part of a vehicle, a viewer seeing the picture may not recognize what it is, especially if it is an unfamiliar part, such as something on the underside of a car. He is then puzzled. You can help him visualize what he sees by making a connecting series of pictures, usually three:

1. A general view of the vehicle or area showing objects that the viewer will quickly recognize with the part of special interest indicated by someone pointing to it or by some kind of a marker (Exhibit 33).
2. A medium view containing the part and some surrounding objects which will be recognized from the preceding picture (Exhibit 34).
3. The close-up of the part of special interest which the viewer now understands because of its connection to other things that he recognizes (Exhibit 35).

7. EASY ERRORS

Technically perfect photos may not show what is required; they may even be misleading. In such cases, the photographer succeeds in operating his camera properly but fails in selecting the scene. If this happens he may be accused of misrepresentation.

Some poor choices of viewpoint have already been mentioned. For example, a picture aimed from the left

Exhibit 29. *Marks on the road extending over a considerable distance require a series of pictures for proper representation.*

Exhibit 30. *The first picture showed the beginning of the marks. This second one overlaps the first one to leave no gaps.*

Exhibit 31. *Generally pictures are taken looking straight down the roadway unless the marks leave the road. Additional close-up pictures of details are also desirable.*

Exhibit 32. *Make pictures at intervals of not more than 40 ft (10 m) and take as many as needed for the distance. These are four pictures from a series of 12.*

Exhibit 33. *A series of pictures helps explain close-up pictures of unfamiliar subjects. The first picture shows the general area and includes recognizable objects, such as large areas of a vehicle.*

Exhibit 34. *A second closer picture connects the particular part to be emphasized with the first picture. A pointer or indicator calls attention to the object of interest or its location in the picture.*

Exhibit 35. *The final picture is a close-up showing all necessary detail. From this picture alone, the connection with other parts would not be understood by people who are unfamiliar with the detail.*

front toward a collapsed left front corner can fail to show the direction of collapse properly.

Camera height. The ordinary picture does not show depth or distance away from the viewer as we perceive it with our eyes. All objects appear to be the same distance away — that is, the distance of the picture from the eye. Distance objects seem to be farther away only because they look smaller, or fainter, or higher than the closer ones. To make objects in the picture appear as nearly as possible as they would to a person viewing the scene, hold the camera at eye level. If

you are photographing the approach to an accident scene, for example, hold the camera at the distance the driver's eye was above the road, usually about 42 in. (1.28 m). Otherwise the distance between the objects in the picture appears to be greater or lesser than it really was. To show what an adult male pedestrian or bystander saw, hold your camera about 5 ft 5 in. (1.65 m) above the ground. In photographing view obstructions, this is very important (Exhibits 36 and 37).

Detached parts. Never rearrange parts of the vehicle or move bodies of injured for picture taking purposes at

the scene. If vehicles have been pried open or shifted for rescue purposes, or if bodies have been moved, leave them as you find them when you make pictures. If a wheel is off, for example, leave it off; do not move it back on to the vehicle. Any such rearrangement may be misleading and you may be critized for tampering with evidence. If you know or believe that someone else has moved something before the photos were taken, make notes in your record to that effect. The notes may be helpful later.

The registration plate on a vehicle, if included in the photograph, helps

Exhibit 36. *Camera at 36 in. above the road shows how visibility of a short driver in a sport car is limited. Your photo can illustrate this.*

Exhibit 37. *A tall driver in a recreational vehicle with eyes 80 in. above the road sees much more. Adjust your camera height to the situation.*

Exhibit 38. *Do not let bystanders or others block the view of vehicles when you make at-scene pictures. Ask them to stand aside. They may obscure important details.*

to identify it and authenticate the photograph, but do not move a number plate from one place to another for that purpose. It may give someone the wrong idea of where the plate was after the accident.

Obstructionists. The need for showing in photographs all damage and all marks on the road has already been emphasized. Bystanders at the scene and their vehicles are the greatest obstacle to doing this. When you are ready to take a picture they may block the camera's view of important details (Exhibit 38). Ask people to stand aside for a moment while you make a photo. There is no harm in including people in the picture so long as they do not obstruct something. In fact, useful witnesses are sometimes discovered by identifying people who appear in photographs of the accident.

Position. Sometimes, to show distances between objects, you will have to take pictures from two or three different angles. For example, suppose

your camera is aimed down a highway toward two objects. It will be difficult to tell how much farther away one is than the other. You may have to take another picture of the two objects from directly across the highway to show more clearly the space between them. It is much easier to judge distances from a photograph if objects are across the picture from left to right rather than background (Exhibits 39 and 40).

In general, the closer you can get to objects being photographed, the easier it is to tell which ones are farthest away in the picture.

Sometimes a vehicle leaves the road and comes to rest below on a steep bank or off a bridge. Then, if you stand on the road and aim straight down at the vehicle, the photo may not show how far down the vehicle actually dropped. However, if you move along the road some distance, you may be able to make another photograph aimed parallel to the road, rather than at right angles to it, which

will show much more clearly how far down the bank the vehicle came to rest.

If two vehicles are close together on the roadway after collision, one picture taken across the roadway will show how far apart they are, but another picture taken along the roadway will show how they are placed crosswise of the roadway.

In general, pictures of vehicles on the road are more useful if they are taken with a camera aimed parallel to the road or at right angles to it. Preferably, make one picture in each direction. Photographs made at oblique angles to the road are likely to be difficult to interpret; make them only when you cannot get far enough away to make a right-angle photograph, as on a bridge, or when damage to vehicles, space between vehicles, debris, or marks on the road will show better when the picture is made from an angle.

Tilt. Aiming the camera up or down — tilting it — will sometimes result in misrepresenting perspective. Aiming the camera downward toward the road will sometimes make a road look as though it were going uphill. Pictures taken uphill or downhill will sometimes look as though the road were level if the camera is tilted. You do not have this difficulty in looking at the scene, because your mind automatically takes into consideration whether you are looking up or down, but unfortunately the camera cannot make this correction.

Swing. It is important to be sure

Exhibit 39. *Distances in the direction in which the camera is aimed are difficult to judge in photographs. Select viewpoints with this in mind, it will make better pictures.*

Exhibit 40. *Distances at right angles to camera aim are easy to judge. The car in this picture and in Exhibit 39 are the same distance from the curb, but that shows better in this picture.*

that one side of the camera is not higher than the other. Swinging the camera so that the right and left edges of the picture are not straight up and down makes level roads look like hills, or hills look level, when the picture is taken across the road. It can make a curve in a level road seem to be going up or downhill. The camera swing can usually be detected in the picture, because vertical lines such as trees, poles, and the corners of buildings lean or slope and are not straight up and down. But such clues are not always in a picture (Exhibits 41 and 42).

8. PHOTOGRAPHIC TECHNIQUES

Camera Operation

Operation of a camera will not be explained in detail in this discussion of photography. Of course, knowledge of camera operations is necessary to take pictures; but this topic is discussed fully in many excellent books[2,3], and so need not be repeated here. The manual supplied with the camera you use is probably the best general reference piece.

Practice is as necesary for making good pictures and for maintaining and improving skills as it is in any other specialized effort, for example, shooting a pistol. Especially if you are responsible for at-scene photography, which is not easy, you need practice to avoid the fumbling and guessing that results from unfamiliarity with methods and equipment. Most ac-

cidents serious enough to require pictures occur at night, so practice in taking flash pictures at night outdoors is needed. If possible, this learning should be done under the direction of an instructor; but do not let lack of an instructor prevent you from taking half a dozen rolls of film under simulated accident situations to develop skill. The remainder of a partly exposed roll of film can be used for practice, thereby hastening the processing of the film and avoiding waste of unexposed film. If there is time, additional practice pictures may be made at the scene of an accident. Do not simply take another picture like one you have already made; try a different angle or try making close-up pictures of marks on the road to show greater detail.

Until you have developed skill and experience, it is advisable to avoid experimenting with different films, cameras, and electronic flash equipment. Because there is so little time at the scene of an accident to figure out aperture and shutter speed settings, have an experienced photographer help you work out, for the equipment you have, a table of exposures for various conditions that you can attach to your camera for quick reference (Exhibit 43). Prepare a special table for the flash equipment you use. Take a practice roll of film on which nearly every one of the conditions listed in the table is represented. Many cameras (especially those for 35 mm film) have some type of automatic ex-

posure. If this is the type of camera you are to use, be sure to experiment with it. In some cases the automatic exposure can be improper. Therefore, take the time to become familiar with its operation, even if it is automatic. The manual that comes with the camera explains how to cope with problems you may have with exposure.

Processing film and making prints can be done by a photographic laboratory so that it is not necessary for you to learn how to do that, although learning to do your own laboratory work is good experience and helps you understand more about the photographic process. Processing can compensate for some errors in exposure and can help reduce the extreme contrast between foreground and background in flash pictures; but no processing can help a picture which is out of focus or which shows the blur of camera movement during exposure; those defects must be avoided when the picture is made.

Assistance

The most common form of assistance in making photos at the scene of a traffic accident is a professional photographer who comes to the scene under prearrangement and takes over the whole photographic task. He may be from the detective division of a police department, from the signal corps at a military post, or a freelance photographer who is on call. You must be prepared to specify what

Exhibit 41. *Keep edges of camera frame vertical and horizontal. It gives a better representation of grades and slopes. This picture truly represents the grade. Note that house does not lean.*

Exhibit 42. *If the camera is swung so that one side is lower than the other, the picture may create the wrong impression, as in this illustration. Note that house walls are not vertical.*

FILM SPEED:	ASA 400
BRILLIANT SUN	1/500 @ f/22
BRIGHT SUN	1/250 @ f/22
BRIGHT CLOUDY	1/250 @ f/11
HEAVY OVERCAST	1/125 @ f/11
DUSK	1/30 @ f/4

Exhibit 43. An exposure schedule is helpful for any photographer, but especially for investigators with little photographic experience.

pictures to make, otherwise only general views that are of little value may be made.

Bystanders are usually willing to be of whatever help they can. Sometimes they can be enlisted to help keep onlookers from standing in front of something you want to photograph. They can help at night by holding a flashlight under your direction for focusing purposes. They can also hold a flash slave if you ask them to. If you need to call attention in a picture to some particular detail, a bystander will be glad to stand next to it or to point it out while you make the photo. If someone has been assigned to help with the investigation, strangers will not have to be asked to assist.

Photographers appearing at the scene, professional or amateur, may be able to take pictures when assigned

investigators are not equipped to do so. They will usually welcome a few suggestions on what kind of pictures to take and what pictures will be most likely to sell, if they are interested in that.

If you see a person taking pictures or learn of someone who has them, get the photographer's name and address and write it down in your list of witnesses. Do so whether you think you need the pictures or not. It may be important later.

Before asking anybody to take pictures for you, be sure he will be paid if he expects to be. If you order pictures, especially by a contract in writing, you are personally responsible for paying for them unless you are authorized to order for another person or organization. Any photographer or other person present may take pictures which you suggest on the chance that somebody will buy them later. In such cases, tell him plainly that they may not be needed and will not be paid for if not used. Remember that any person known to have photographs of an accident may be subpoenaed as a witness together with this pictures.

Technical photographers are usual-

ly required when pictures of small parts of vehicles and other special subjects must be made. This work rarely has to be done at the scene and can be arranged for by whoever requires the pictures.

Night Pictures of the Scene

Making good pictures of the scene after dark is, perhaps, the severest test in accident-investigation photography. Choosing a viewpoint (composing the picture), focusing, and exposing are all difficult. Such pictures require flash equipment which must be much more powerful for outdoor night pictures of objects at a considerable distance than for indoor pictures of people only a few feet away. Lighting the scene with photoflash lamps of any kind puts too much light close to the camera and too little at a distance so that the foreground is overexposed (too light) and the distance is underexposed (too dark).

A flashlight is essential for night accident-scene photography. Indeed, two flashlights are useful, a small one carried in the pocket as an aid to reading camera settings and making notes, and a large one to be used to illuminate the scene.

Framing the picture. There is often

Exhibit 44. The camera must be on a tripod or other steady support and you will need an assistant to make the multiple flashes required for a wide area.

insufficent light by which to see in the finder what area will be in the picture. There are three ways to make this easier:

1. Open the lens to its maximum aperture to let in as much light as possible. Most camera lenses do this automatically. Even with very fast lenses, this may not be sufficient.

2. Have an assistant shine a flashlight on objects to be pictured and move it from one place to another to indicate what will be included in the picture. Do this with the camera on a tripod, if you can, because the camera then stays put while the flashlight is moved.

3. Use a wire or sport finder if your camera has one. This is the best way. If you have to do much night photography, consider getting a camera equipped with such a finder.

Focusing at night is also difficult. Focus on bright sharp edges of the object to be photographed, for example, number plates and bright trim. If there are no such edges, for example, with tiremarks, put a flashlight at the point to be in sharp focus and focus on that. Form the habit of verifying a setting obtained visually on a focussing screen (ground glass) by looking at the distance scale on the camera.

Exposure by flash is determined by three factors:

1. Distance from flash to principal object to be pictured
2. Strength of flash source
3. Speed of film.

Exposure is varied mainly by adjusting the lens opening (aperture). Tables relating these values are published for various combinations. Many electronic flash units have a dial on which you set the film speed and then read the correct aperture (exposure) opposite the distance of flash to subject.

Automatic electronic flash units provide considerable flexibility in night photography. One that has a range of at least 40 ft (12 m) is desirable. A less powerful one (or one

that the power can be reduced) is well-suited for close-up details.

Flareback is troublesome in night flash pictures because it produces very bright spots. These are reflections from shiny surfaces such as glass or chrome. Sometimes they cannot be avoided but often a change of camera position will help. Shine a flashlight beam toward the object to be photographed from the flash lamp position and they will show up.

Reflectorized number plates give flareback from a wide range of angles and so usually appear so bright that numbers on them are indistinguishable. Some police investigators put the plastic raincover for their hats over the plate to reduce this flareback.

Avoid falling rain and especially snow when making flash, if you possibly can. Raindrops or snowflakes near the camera show up as blobs of light in the picture. If you can postpone flash pictures until the storm is over, by all means do so. The problem of rain or snow can be minimized by moving the flash away from the lens by at least a foot (30 cm). This would generally require an extension cord.

To minimize foreground overexposure, hold the flash high and do not aim the camera downward. If possible, get up on something to make the flash. If the flash is connected to the camera with a cord, hold the flash as high above the camera as possible. This is easier if two people work together, one operating the camera and one the flash.

For great distances and wide areas, such as tiremarks more than 30 ft (10 m) long or two cars not close together, more than one flash is required. There are three ways to accomplish this:

1. A series of overlapping separate pictures
2. Multiple flashes
3. Slave flashes.

In any of these methods, more than one flash is used. Flashes are so spaced that what would be in the distance, where one flash will not reach, is in the foreground of another flash. How

great this spacing is depends on the combination of film speed, flash strength, and camera settings used because these determine the distance beyond which a flash will not reach.

The series of separate flash pictures is essentially the same as a series of pictures made by daylight except they are made at much more frequent intervals.

Multiple flashes on a single film require a helper and a tripod as follows:

1. Mount the camera on the tripod to hold it still. Place and aim the camera to take the picture you want, and set the aperture for almost maximum flash distance.

2. Hold your hand close in front of the lens to prevent light from entering and open the shutter. The shutter may be at a time (T) or bulb (B) setting to keep it open until all flashes have been made. A cable release will help prevent jiggling the camera.

3. Have a helper use disconnected flash equipment, hold it high, aim it toward the picture, and be prepared to flash when signalled.

4. Start with the helper near the camera. Quickly uncover the lens, tell the helper, "Flash," and cover the lens again.

5. Have the helper move away from the camera nearly as far as the first flash could reach and repeat the process until the desired distance has been covered.

6. Close the shutter.

In this process, be sure to uncover the lens as little as possible. Hold the flash high and forward to prevent the helper's feet from showing too plainly. If wide areas at a distance must be photographed, make multiple flashes as described above but on either side to illuminate the edges of the picture (Exhibit 44). Always be careful to keep light from the flash from reaching the camera lens. Exhibit 45 is a picture made with a single flash and Exhibit 46 is the same view made with four flashes.

"Slave" flash equipment may also

Exhibit 45. *A single flash will light the principal subject quite well but is not enough for surroundings.*

Exhibit 46. *Four flashes were used here. Keep the direct flash light from reaching the lens.*

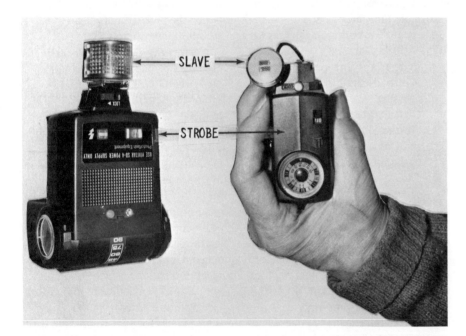

Exhibit 47. *Two forms of electronic slaves to trigger a flash when a master flash is fired some distance away. These permit multiple flashes without using a tripod.*

Exhibit 48. *Accident scene photographed with an assistant holding a slave flash to increase the illumination at a distance from the camera.*

be used to light a larger area than a single flash bulb will cover.

The slave unit flashes at the same time as the unit on the camera. If the master unit is synchronized with the shutter, exposures can be short enough so that no tripod is needed. The slave may be connected to the master with a long electric cord, but usually the slave is a photoelectric control such that when light from the master reaches the slave, the slave device triggers the flash lamp (Exhibit 47). The slave may be mounted on a stand or tripod, but usually a helper holds it as shown in Exhibit 48. The helper needs no special training. The slave flash is placed the same as for multiple flashes, but the number of flashes is limited to the number of flash slaves available.

Night-visibility Pictures

It is sometimes important to have a record to explain what a driver or pedestrian could have seen at night with the light available to him at that time. Photographs can serve this purpose better than written or remembered descriptions of observations. However, photographs do have limitations because photographs can be made that show much more or much less of the scene than the ordinary

Exhibit 49. *Night-visibility picture which shows more than was actually visible at the scene because of overexposure. Made with car headlights.*

Exhibit 50. *Night-visibility picture which closely approximates what could be seen. A visibility target is included in the picture to act as a control.*

Exhibit 51. *Night-visibility picture which shows less than was actually visible because of underexposure. Film processing has an effect on apparent visibility.*

person might see. The object of night-visibility photography is to approximate as closely as the photographer can what the person did actually see.

Many variables are involved in night seeing and additonal variables affect night photography. The seeing variables are difficult to evaluate and the photographic variables are not easy to control. It is also important to remember that people differ considerably in ability to see where there is little light. In general, older people see less than younger people. Morever, everybody sees better after dark adaptation. That means that where there is little light to see by, a person's eyes adjust to the darkness and his perception improves; 15 minutes or more are required for eyes to become well adapted to darkness.

Night-visibility pictures must naturally be taken with the light available at the time. For drivers, this is usually the light supplied by the vehicle's headlights. Adding light by flash equipment would make much more detail visible in the picture than was actually visible at the scene. That is, of course, the purpose of flash photographs.

Night-visibility pictures are rarely made by investigators actually at the scene because they require too much time and their need has not yet been established. They are usually made later, if needed, by technical investigators or photographers.

There are five common subjects for night-visibility photos:
1. Pedestrians and pedalcyclists
2. Railroad cars blocking a grade crossing
3. Obscure roadway configurations
4. Obstacles on or near the road such as construction material, parked vehicles, or stray animals
5. Traffic signs, including barricades.

Such photos are made with the objects arranged as nearly as possible as they were at the time of the accident or with similar objects similarly placed. For example, after a vehicle collides with a pedestrian at night, it may be desirable to determine how well the driver could have seen the pedestrian. So, the situation is simulated with a pedestrian in clothing like that of the pedestrian in the accident and the same or a similar vehicle. The pedestrian stands where the injured pedestrian stood and the vehicle, carrying observers, is driven slowly toward the pedestrian to permit observers in the vehicle to note where the pedestrian can first be seen. To record these observations, three photographs are made in available light; one from a distance at which the pedestrian could not be seen, another from the place where the pedestrian is barely discer-

nible, and a third from a position at which the pedestrian is clearly visible (Exhibits 49, 50 and 51).

Correct exposure and processing is necessary for a good representation of night visibility. Because variations in processing can have a marked effect on what shows in a picture, standardized processing is highly desirable. The best assurance of such processing is using a color film processed in the manufacuturer's laboratory. With such a film and standardized exposures, preferably determined by experiments, reasonably good approximations of night visibility can be produced. One combination which yielded good results was the following:
- Film: Kodachrome 64 (speed rating ISO 64)
- Filter: No. 80 A (light blue with 4-times exposure factor)
- Aperture: f/4
- Exposure: 4 sec.

The film and processing are widely available. The filter, which is for use with a tungsten light source such as motor vehicle headlamps, prevents the transparency from being too yellow. A tripod or some other means of holding the camera still is necessary for so long an exposure. It is well to make at least three exposures at each setup; one at the estimated exposure, one at half that, and one twice as much.

Exhibit 52. *A test target to be included in night-visibility pictures helps to indicate whether the picture represents the scene well. The target is 11 in. wide.*

Standarized viewing is also desirable. A combination which yielded good results was as follows:

- Projector light: 500 watts
- Projector lens: f/3.5
- Width of projected picture on screen; 5 ft (1.5 m) with long dimension horizontal
- Viewing distance: 8 ft (2.4 m)
- Dark adaptation: 15 min or more.

Test target. To make night-visibility pictures more accurate and credible, include a test target in the picture. A test target has a pattern or design that should be equally recognizable in the scene and in the picture. Such a target is shown in Exhibit 52. This is a black card about 11 by 8½ in. (30 by 24 cm) with gray block numbers on each side about 6 in. (15 cm) high. The card is fastened to a block or other base so that it will stand upright. It is moved into a lighted area at the scene by a helper until the number just becomes discernible to the photographer or other observer at the camera. Then, when the picture is viewed, illumination is adjusted so that the target just becomes discernible to the same person.

For prints on paper, especially with black-and-white negatives, print exposure and processing is adjusted so that the target is just discernible when the print is held at the intended viewing distance.

Daylight Fill-flash

Daylight situations requiring ar-

Exhibit 53. *Daylight flash with lens shaded greatly improves parts in shadow. Note the detail under the bumper.*

tificial light are essentially these three:

1. The shaded sides of vehicles in bright sunlight where shadow details would not show
2. Interiors of vehicles, especially when condition of pedals must be shown
3. Undersides of vehicles and details in engine compartments.

All of these can be shown without flash, provided exposures are long enough, but the addition of flash illumination insures better exposures and permits a small lens opening which gives greater depth of focus. Damage to vehicles, even on the sunny side, is usually better recorded with flash fill-in, especially if the damage is extensive because the damage itself leaves areas in shadow.

Exposures for daylight flash pictures generally divide into two classes: 1) medium distances in open areas; and 2) close-up pictures in closed areas. Distant views in which objects to be photographed are more than 30 ft (10 m) away are not suitable subjects for daylight flash because so little

light from the flash carries that far.

For medium distances, such as the exterior of all or most of the vehicle, (Exhibit 53) expose just as you would for daylight without the flash and add the flash to bring more light directly into the shaded areas.

For close-up pictures such as any of the interior of a vehicle or the under side of vehicles, where the subject is near the camera, make the exposure as you would if there were no daylight. If you make an exposure for daylight and then add flash so close, the picture will be overexposed. (See Exhibits 54, 55, and 56).

Automatic flash equipment is not recommended for daylight flash fill-in because daylight has too much effect on the exposure. Simply set the flash on *manual* if the flash is automatic.

Photogrammetry

Good records of size and shape of tiremarks and other results of the accident that show on the road surface are difficult to make, especially if they

Exhibit 54. *The usual attempt to show the inside of the driver's compartment results in a blackout of the area under the dashboard. Details there are obscure.*

Exhibit 55. *If exposures are made for the pedals, everything else is overexposed. A large aperture is required for this exposure for the darkest area.*

Exhibit 56. *A flash exposure for the inside of the car greatly improves the photograph and its usefulness.*

are complicated.

To record dimensions requires complicated sketches and many measurements. Photographs of these marks show shape but not size. Sometimes photographers include a ruler or tape in pictures to show size of objects (Exhibit 57) but this does not help much in showing complicated marks on a map.

A rectangle of known size included in a photo of a flat surface is, however, more useful. With it, marks on the road surface can be transferred to a map. In the picture, the rectangle forms the base of a perspective grid. An ordinary pad of paper will serve this purpose if nothing better is at hand. But if an investigator or photographer plans to take traffic-accident pictures regularly, a perspective grid (Exhibit 58) can be made from a 2-ft (50-cm) square of heavy cardboard for use as illustrated. In taking the photo, keep the near edge of the grid parallel to the lower edge of the picture.

The perspective grid technique is especially useful at the scene of accidents when detailed measurements are difficult or impossible. Then a good dimensional record can be made at the same time photos are made. It takes very little time to include the perspective grid in a photo. Therefore, if the photo is never needed for a map, little time has been wasted.

Methods of mapping from photographs are described in Topic 830.

Technical Problems

Accuracy of photographs. No photograph is an absolutely true representation of the scene. But in most respects, a photograph is more accurate and nearly always more detailed than a diagram or description. All photographs have in them a little *distortion and diffusion* due to technical limitations of the camera, lenses, and film. With a good lens, distortion is usually not visible to the eye. If the focus is sharp, diffusion will not be visible except in enlargements. Color photographs can considerably misrepresent color unless very carefully made.

These limitations of photography are mentioned only so that you will not think of pictures as always being absolutely true. People say that photographs do not lie. What they mean is that, unlike some poeple, they do not *purposefully* misrepresent a situation unless they have been *purposely* tampered with. It is also important, in case you are questioned closely about the reliability of photographs, that you understand some of the technical flaws that may appear in pictures.

A picture does not have to be technically perfect to be useful. Some

Exhibit 57. *A yard stick or tape can help illustrate the size of things on the road surface.*

very poor photographs are good enough to record and prove important facts which would otherwise be overlooked or, perhaps, purposely misrepresented. On the other hand, common photographic errors often make otherwise well-planned pictures practically useless. Technically good pictures inspire confidence. It is important, therefore, to avoid technical flaws in accident photography as much as you can.

Depth of field (desired zone of sharpness) is the range of distance from the nearest object to the farthest object that must be clear in the picture. Suppose that a picture is being made of skidmarks leading to a stopped vehicle. The beginning of the skidmarks is 12 ft (4 m) from the camera and the vehicle is 50 ft (16 m) from the camera. Then the depth of field to be photographed is 12 to 50 ft (4 to 16 m). Anything nearer than 12 ft (4 m) or more distant than 50 ft (16 m) can be out of focus and the picture will still show clearly the detail it is supposed to. The photographer must adjust his camera and lens so as to have as much of this field in sharp focus as possible.

Depth of focus is the range of distances which will be in acceptably sharp focus for any lens setting. This range depends on three things:

1. The focal length of the lens
2. The aperture (f-stop) setting
3. The distance setting of the lens.

For example, a 50-mm lens set at f/5.6 and focussed at 5 m (16 ft) will have an acceptably sharp focus for everything between 3.6 m (12 ft) and 8.0 m (26 ft). The sharpest focus is at the distance setting of the lens; in the foregoing example this is 5 m (16 ft). Depth of focus tables are available for most lenses. Many lens mounts have markings which show depth of focus for any distance setting of the lens. Experienced photographers try to have the depth of focus setting of the camera as great or greater than the depth of field required, although this is not always possible under existing conditions. There are two problems to solve in matching depth of field and

Exhibit 58. *Perspective grid is laid on a flat surface to indicate positions of marks in the vicinity. Grid is useful when detailed dimensions may be wanted later.*

depth of focus: 1) setting the camera for the best distance, and 2) setting the lens opening to give best sharpness at both far and near points. The sharpness of your pictures depends a great deal on how well you solve these two problems.

Distance setting. If you set the camera so that the indicator on the distance scale is at the nearest point that you want to be in focus (Exhibit 59) the farthest point is likely to be out of focus; and if you set the indicator on the farthest point, the nearest point is almost sure to be out of focus (Exhibit 60).

You must, therefore, set the indicator at some point in between, as was done for Exhibit 61. The best point at which to set the camera for distance is one at which the nearest point and the farthest point will be *equally* out of focus. One way to do this is to use the focusing screen (ground glass), if your camera has through-the-lens focusing, and adjust the camera so that the near point and far point seem to be equal in sharpness. At night, or when the near and far points are near the edges of the ground glass, this adjustment is difficult. There is another way to locate

the best point for the depth of field needed. Set the indicator on the distance scale exactly half way between the distance mark for the farthest object and the mark for the nearest object — that is, in the middle of the field to be covered. For example, suppose that the farthest object is a car where it came to rest after a collision. It is 18 ft away. The nearest object is some debris only 7 ft from the camera. In Exhibit 62 the far point is 18 ft on the scale. The near point is at 7 ft. The midpoint on the camera scale, half the distance on the camera scale between 7 ft and 18 ft, is the best focus setting; it is at 10 ft.

Lens opening. When you have set the camera for the best distance, the near and far points will be equally out of focus. How much out of sharpest focus they will be depends on what lens opening or stop you use in making the exposure. You can get a greater depth of focus and, therefore, clearer focus for near and far points if you make the lens opening small, using a large *f* number for the aperture. Of course, you must make up for the decreased lens opening by longer exposure time. How much you have to "stop down" (decrease the lens aper-

Exhibit 59. *Focus is on nearest object that needs to be sharp; farthest object is out of focus.*

Exhibit 60. *Focus is on farthest object that needs to be sharp; nearest object is out of focus.*

Exhibit 61. *Focussed at an intermediate point, both far and near objects are acceptably sharp.*

ture by using a larger *f* number) to get enough depth of focus to cover the depth of field depends on the lens on your camera and some other factors. A good plan, when the near point is less than 25 ft away, is to put the camera on a tripod, use the smallest lens opening, and give the necessary time for that opening. Thus, you will get the greatest depth of focus possible with your equipment. If you have to hold the camera in your hand, use the longest exposure during which you can hold the camera steady, 1/30 sec, and this will give you the smallest stop and, therefore, the greatest depth of focus. If possible, under these circumstances, move back until the nearest point is at least 15 ft away. The picture you get this way will be smaller, of course, but the depth of focus will be more nearly matched to the depth of field, and far and near points will be in sharper focus for whatever lens opening you may have decided to use.

Depth of focus scales. Many cameras have depth of focus scales. Such a scale shows for any lens opening or *f* number the nearest and farthest points from the camera which will be in sharp focus for any distance setting. If your camera has such a scale, learn to use it and use it regularly, because it will help you to get sharp detail into parts of the picture which should be sharp.

Again, suppose that the depth of field to be photographed extends from 12 to 30 ft from the camera. Now, adjust the focusing device of the camera so that the same *f* number is opposite 12 ft on one side of the midpoint and opposite 30 ft on the other, as shown in Exhibit 63. This number is *f*/5.6. Note that the midpoint is at 18 ft. Thus, if the camera is focused at 18 ft, and the aperture is set at *f*/5.6, everything between about 12 ft and about 30 ft will be in sharp focus.

Camera movement spoils about as many pictures as wrong exposures. Most of this is due to hurry. Shoot a picture as you would a gun: take careful aim, hold steady, and squeeze the shutter release without a jerk. Use a shutter speed of 1/125 sec or less, unless poor light requires more time. Never make exposures of less than 1/30 sec without a camera support.

Exposure spoils some accident pictures, but with black-and-white film and color negative film considerable variation in exposure can be corrected in making prints. The main difficulty is under-exposure of dark and shadow areas where damage to car or other detail should show but does not. If in doubt give more, rather than less, exposure. Often accident photographs must be taken toward the sun to show the shady side of a vehicle. In this case, use flash to light up the dark areas as explained before.

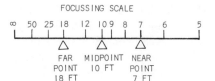

Exhibit 62. *To get best focus on near and far points, set the distance indicator halfway between these points.*

Specular reflection is the reflection of a light source in a shiny surface. Sometimes these can play curious tricks in photography by making black surfaces look white. When a camera faces a source of light, black painted center lines and tar pavement patches with shiny surfaces may look white or may not show at all against a light colored concrete background. The surfaces at *A* in Exhibit 64 show such reflections on a pavement, and Exhibit 65 shows the same surface from a quite different angle without the reflection. Specular reflection can usually be avoided, if it is noticed

Exhibit 63. *Depth-of-focus scale on lens mount helps judge the best setting for the depth of field required.*

when the picture is being made, by changing the position of the camera. It can also generally be suppressed by use of a polarized filter, but these steps are rarely necessary because the effect of specular reflection can generally be explained satisfactorily if any questions are raised concerning it.

Focal Length of Lens

When photographing traffic-accident scenes it is generally best to use the normal lens that comes with the camera. When you look through a normal lens on a camera, objects do not appear nearer or farther than when viewing them without the lens. For a 35mm camera, a 50 mm lens is normal. For a 2¼ by 2¼ inch (6 m by 6 cm) format, the normal lens is 8 mm. The normal lens generally has a focal length equal to the diagonal of the negative.

The proper viewing distance for a photograph (or a transparency shown on a screen) for true perspective depends on the focal length and enlargement. The proper viewing distance for correct perspective with a 35 mm format (24 by 36 mm) with an eight times enlargement to get an 8 by 10 inch photograph is 15 inches. This is the usual, desk-top distance that you would look at an 8 by 10-inch print. The correct viewing distance for an 8 by 8-inch print of a 2¼ by 2¼-inch (6 by 6 cm) format taken with an 80 mm lens is 11 inches. Again this is approximately the distance you would use to inspect an 8 by 8-inch print.

If a lens other than normal is used, the customary 8 by 10 inch enlargement will not have true perspective at normal viewing distance, 15 inches. For example, if a short focal length (wide angle) lens is used, (say a 24 mm lens with a 35 mm camera), objects appear to be farther apart than they actually are if an eight times enlargement is viewed at 15 inches. If a long focal length lens is used (say 200 mm lens with a 35 mm camera), objects appear to be closer together in an eight times enlargement when viewed at the usual 15 inches. To avoid criticism that you are trying to exaggerate

distances, simply use your normal lens. The correct viewing distance for different lenses, formats and enlargements are discussed in more detail in other publications[4].

Filters

Colored filters in photography modify the effect of colored subjects and color of the light source.

In the explanation of night-visibility pictures with color film designed for daylight use, a filter is recommended to reduce the yellow cast of pictures made with motor-vehicle headlamps.

Polarized filters can be used to reduce specular (bright) reflection from shiny spots on the road surface, but that is seldom necessary.

Filters have been suggested to enhance the visibility of tiremarks on roadways in black and white photos. Experiments show that filters have no discernible effect on most paving. A red filter does make a little improvement in pictures of tiremarks on red brick or pink granite block paving.

9. IDENTIFICATION

Too often, when looking at traffic-accident photos, one stops and wonders what a photo is supposed to show, why it was made, what accident it was connected with, who made it, or when. This is especially true of close-up photos of marks on the road, damage to vehicles, and parts of ve-

hicles.

Avoiding such confusion is a matter of identification, always an irksome detail which the photographer puts off or considers unnecessary because what is shown in the picture should identify it sufficiently.

Negatives and Prints

Numbering systems. Professional photographers, who must account for thousands of pictures, nearly all develop some scheme of identifying each negative or slide with a number which distinguishes it from all others in their files and ties each negative to an index card, order form, or other record. The record generally shows at least four things:

1. The event, occasion, object, or person photographed
2. Place where picture was made if not obvious from the above
3. The date the picture was made
4. Who authorized or requested it.

In addition, the record may provide details about the equipment, material, processing, and also the name of the individual photographer if the numbering system covers the work of more than one person.

Every print or transparency ought to be marked with the name and address of whoever was responsible for making the picture. There are three reasons for this:

1. The negatives can be located if additional prints are needed.
2. The photographer can be lo-

Exhibit 64. When the sun is in front, smooth black surfaces, like the tar at A, may look white in the photographs.

Exhibit 65. The same surface as in Exhibit 64 photographed from a different angle shows tar at A as black.

cated to explain the circumstances under which the photo was made, that is, to authenticate it.

3. Credit can be given if the photograph is published.

A rubber stamp is commonly used for this purpose (Exhibit 66).

Additional data is useful on the print but usually unnecessary, provided it can be had if needed. The two most important additional items are 1) the date and possibly time of day when picture was made; and 2) a brief description of what the picture is supposed to show including the direction in which the camera was aimed.

Technical data is sometimes put on the print, but this is very rarely needed. However, the photographer should be able to explain in detail from his records how the picture was made if for no other reason than to enhance his authentication of the photo. The photogrpaher might be asked questions about

- The camera and lens
- Any filters
- The kind of film
- How the film was processed
- Whether the print is an enlargement
- Whether it shows all of the negative or has been cropped (trimmed to leave out irrelevant or unwanted parts)
- Whether the print was dodged (giving some areas of the print in enlarging more exposure than other areas)
- Whether a flash was used
- How high the camera was from the ground
- How far the camera was from the principal object in the picture.

MARDAN CO. POLICE PHOTO

BY _____ J B Durkin _____

DATE _____ Jan 14 1986 _____

No. _____ 41237-3 _____

Exhibit 66. *The photographer should be identified by name and address on the back of each print. This can be done with a rubber stamp. It is also helpful to have the picture identified by a negative number or accident number.*

Describing what the Picture Shows

General pictures of the scene of an accident usually need no special descriptions. Whoever looks at them usually knows enough about the accident to recognize what they represent, especialy if a picture includes recognizable landmarks or road features. The msot useful adjunct to pictures which show some of the road is a small arrow on the negative or print which appears as though it were marked on the road pointing north (Exhibits 3, 7, 8).

This makes it unnecessary to mark each picture with a comment like "view looking east." Small arrows with pressure-sensitive adhesive backing suitable for this purpose are available.

Detail pictures generally do need special description. Notes for these must be made at the time the pictures are made. Identify the notes by whatever negative numbering system is employed. Notes must explain briefly (1 what the picture represents; and 2) where the subject is, what it is connected to or used for. Many professional photographers carry portable tape recorders and immediately after *every* picture record the negative number and what the picture represents. The tape is filed so as to be available if needed.

Do not throw away spoiled negatives. Somebody may remember that you took four pictures at the scene. If you can produce only two, you may be accused of suppressing evidence.

Marking the road with a number or letter beside a gouge, tiremark, or anything important in the picture is useful. The same marks can be used for measurements. Yellow crayon marks must be very strong to show in photographs, especially black-and-white photos. Go over each one several times with the crayon. Spray paint in an aerosol can is more effective.

Vehicle parts such as lamps and tires can also be identified by marks. Usually a label with a pressure-sensitive adhesive is adequate. Keep the

numbers bold so they show up in pictures. Use a number which identifies the accident or object; do not try to put the negative number on the object photographed. Thus, several views of the same object will all show the same number.

Continuity of Custody

Sometimes someone may try to discredit a photo and insinuate that it has been tampered with in processing or that another picture was exchanged for it. Such a challenge is less common in traffic-accident photography than in some other kinds of forensic photography, and today there is less suspicion of photographers than there used to be.

Keep a record of the time, place, and to whom the exposed negatives were given for processing. You must be able to show that they were in competent, authoritative hands, and that there was no chance to tamper with them after you made the exposure. Such a record establishes continuity of custody.

You do not have to be so careful about the prints, because if you can establish continuity of custody of the negative and can produce it, it can be compared with the print to authenticate it.

Some photographers file small notches in the edge of the camera opening in back, through which the film is exposed, to code the particular camera. These notches show on the film so that the negative can easily be identified with the camera in which it was made if occasion arises.

10. EQUIPMENT

The most important thing about photographic equipment is knowing how to use it. Excellent pictures can be made with a very simple camera; yet all the cameras in the catalog will not make pictures by themselves. As a practical matter, selecting equipment is a series of compromises. The decisions involve considerations of policy relating to circumstances under which pictures are to be made, skill of the persons making the pictures, amount of money available, and uses of the pictures to be taken. Accident investigation involves a great variety of photography. Much of it may have to be done by relatively unpracticed people; this suggests the need for simple equipment. But some may be done under quite controlled conditions by professional photographers who can make use of a great variety of equipment. Therefore, suggestions made here concerning equipment must be very general.

Cameras and Lenses

If a camera is supplied as part of your equipment, that is the camera you must ordinarily use. Learn to use it as well as you can.

If you have a camera of your own with which you are familiar, you will probably get better pictures with it than almost any other.

Camera requirements for at-scene traffic-accident photography are quite modest:

- Format 24 by 36 mm (1 by 1.5 in.) or larger (Smaller negatives will not produce the needed size and quality of enlargements. The professional photographer generally uses a camera with a format 2¼ by 2¼ in. or larger.)
- Shutter speeds of 1/500 sec or less suitable for hand holding (In traffic-accident photography, no motion has to be stopped so there is no need for fast shutters.)
- Throught-the-lens or twin-lens focusing and view finding
- Flash synchronization.

Many models of cameras meet these specifications.

The lens needs to be fast, f/2.8 or better, because night pictures with flash outdoors require maximum light.

Focusing to 12 ft (4 m) is close enough for most at-scene photography. For technical photography, focusing by the lens mount or with sup-plementary lenses to 18 in. (50 cm) is needed for close-up pictures of marks on the road and vehicle parts.

Focal length of lens should be normal (equal to the diagonal of the negative) or a little less. This would be a 45- to 50-mm lens for 35-mm film.

A lens shade is worth adding because many pictures will have to be made where the sun might otherwise strike the camera lens. They are also helpful with flash pictures when light from the flash might strike the lens.

Special features can be very helpful, especially built-in exposure meters or automatic exposure controls. These take much of the guesswork out of exposing. Automatic lenses for focusing and finding at a full aperture are also very helpful. Fast film wind and magazine loading are conveniences.

Portability is a secondary consideration because the accident-investigation camera does not have to be carried far from a car, but view cameras are usually too cumbersome.

Flash Equipment

The kind of accidents that require pictures are most likely to occur at night so flash equipment is necessary.

Electronic flash units are preferred to flash bulbs; they are more convenient. A flash for at-scene photos, should have a range of at least 40 ft (12 m). If it can also operate at reduced light output, it will be easier to use for fill-in and close up flash. Models with automatic exposure control greatly assist the photographer by cutting down work in exposure calculating.

Slaves to operate a second or third flash are very useful. But practice with them before you try to depend on them because they are not surefire. Not all slaves will operate all flash units. Some slaves are quite limited in the distance from the camera flash that they will operate. Some photographers prefer an extension cord about 30 ft (10 m) long rather than a slave to fire the second flash, but the cord requires clumsy coiling and uncoiling.

Film

For night pictures, load with fast film such as Tri X or VR 400 with a speed rating of ISO 400. A considerable area often has to be illuminated by flash and a fast film helps get distant detail.

For daylight pictures, film of moderate speed is better (ISO 125). Light is no great problem and the finer grain of lower speed films gives sharper enlargements.

Roll film is generally preferred mainly because less film handling is necessary. Magazine loading film has some advantages, especially for the less experienced photographer.

Polaroid films and cameras have two advantages: 1) they permit the inexperienced photographer to see what he is getting and try again if the result is unsatisfactory; and 2) the picture requires no separate processing. The latter advantage makes Polaroid photos especially useful for damage appraisers who want to include them with a report without waiting for processing. Polaroid pcitures have two disadvantages: 1) they cannot be made in rapid succession and so sometimes opportunities for pictures are lost; and 2) the cost of film tends to discourage picture making, especially in police departments where budgets are limited.

Color film rarely adds much to traffic-accident pictures. It costs more, especially for enlargements, and requires more precise. exposure. But there is no objection to its use. Its principal advantage is in accidents involving collisions of more than two vehicles where a record of paint rub-off may help to establish the sequence of collisions. But do not depend on color pictures to replace close personal observation. In technical accident investigation, color photographs are useful to show signs and signals and pavement markings for display purposes. They are also useful in showing parts of cars that have been burned. As pointed out earlier, highly standardized processing of color film makes it useful for transparencies showing night visibility.

Tripod

A tripod is a nuisance to set up and sometimes you risk your life in traffic if you try to use one. However, a strong tripod is good insurance against technically bad pictures for three reasons:

1. With a tripod, camera movement seldom spoils a picture.
2. You can stop the lens down to f/16 or less to get pictures that are needle sharp from closeup to far off.
3. You can get framing and focusing just the way you want it on the focusing screen (ground glass).

At the scene, there is usually too little time to work with a tripod and so only the most careful investigators and photographers use one. But in technical accident investigation, where there is less urgency, a tripod is quite worthwhile. Photographers who recognize the merits of a tripod but have none available improvise by leaning on a post, resting the camera on a car, bridgerail, or other available supports.

Photographic Paper

When an enlargement is made, photographic paper is exposed to light passing through the negative (or transparency). Many publications explain this process.[2,3] You may never be involved in the actual making of a paper print. However, you may be the one who decides the finish of the paper. For accident investigation purposes, *always* select glossy paper; it gives the most detail. A matte or semi-matte finish reduces sharpness. For black and white prints, the glossy print gives a greater range of grey tones.

11. SOURCES

Contributors

This topic was developed by the following persons:

J. Stannard Baker is a traffic engineer specialzing in accident investigation. He was Director of Research and Development at The Northwestern University Traffic Institute from 1946 to 1971 and is a guest lecturer for The Traffic Institute.

Lynn B. Fricke is a traffic engineer specializing in traffic-accident investigation. He has been with The Traffic Institute since 1975. In 1981, he became the director of the Institute's Accident Investigation Division.

References

Superscript numbers in the preceding pages refer to the following publications:

1. *Advanced Camera Techniques* (Kodak Publication No. AC-56), 1978, Eastman Kodak Company, Rochester NY 14650 (52 pages)
2. Sussman, Aaron, *The Amateur Photographer Handbook,* 1973, Thomas Y. Crowell Company, Inc., New York NY
3. Hedgecoe, John, *The Photographer's Handbook,* 1978, Aflred A. Knopf, New York NY
4. *Viewing a Print in True Perspective,* (Kodak Pamphlet No. M-15), 1977, Eastman Kodak Company, Rochester NY 14650 (4 pages)

Exhibits

The following are the sources of photographs, diagrams, charts, tables, and forms that are used in this topic as exhibits:

Aycock, Thad L., Traffic Institute, Evanston IL
Photos: 17, 18, 19, 20, 21, 22, 23, 27, 33, 34, 35, 41, 42
Baker, J. Stannard, Glencoe IL
Photos: 9, 12, 26, 29, 30, 31, 32, 36, 37, 47, 49, 50, 51, 54, 55, 58, 59, 60, 61, 63
Diagrams: 16, 52, 62
Tables: 43, 66
Borkenstein, Robert, Indiana State Police
Photo: 56
Fricke, Lynn B., Traffic Institute, Evanston IL
Photos: 7, 8, 10, 11, 13, 14, 15, 45, 46, 48, 53
Diagrams: 4, 5
James Photo, West Chicago IL
Photo: 3
Mosel, Brent, Murphysboro IL
Photo: 6
Scheskie, Sheriff's Office, Waukegan IL
Photos: 64, 65
Singleton, D.C., Lancashire Constabulary, United Kingdom
Photo: 44
Tuley, Roy, Chattanooga TN
Photo: 2
Unknown
Photos: 1, 24, 25, 28, 38, 57

INDEX AND GLOSSARY

All topics have two-part page numbers. The parts are separated by a hyphen. The first number identifies the topic, the second one the page in the topic. Topics in this volume are arranged sequentially so that it is easy to locate a particular page from an index reference.

A glossary is combined with the index so that the meanings of important terms can be found without further reference.

Side scuffs - See yawmarks.

Sideslip - See yaw.

Sidewalk, "that portion of a street between the curb lines, or the lateral lines of a roadway, and the adjacent property lines, intended for use by pedestrians."

Significant figures 32-27

Simple reaction, a preplanned reaction to an expected hazard or other stimulus. Time: 0.5 sec, more or less. 18-6

in driving process 15-25

Site, the location of a traffic accident after vehicles and people involved have gone. Compare with scene.

measurements 32-19

Situation hazard, a circumstance that more or less endangers a traffic unit on a trip and which must be avoided to prevent an accident.

Skid
direction of 17-18
tests 18-4

Skidmark, a friction mark on a pavement made by a tire that is sliding without rotation.

after-collision 17-16
broadside 17-13
characteristics 17-7
collision scrubs 17-12
collision skip 17-12
crooks, bends or offsets 17-13
gaps in 17-11
impending 17-17
irregularities 17-10
life of 17-6
measurement of 17-19
measuring length 28-45
photographing 17-19
skip or bounce 17-11
speed estimates 18-3
striations 17-8
studded tire 17-30
swerve 17-13
towing 17-17
unfinished 17-11
varieties of 17-6

Skills
driver 15-30
lack of 15-30

Skip line - See lane line.

Skip skid, a braking skidmark interrupted at frequent intervals; the skidmark made by a bouncing wheel on which brakes keep the wheel from turning. Compare with gap skid. 17-11

collision 17-12

Slave flash, a supplementary photoflash placed at a distance from the master flash to increase the illuminated field in a photograph and fired by a photoelectric device actuated by light from the master flash. 36-22

Sleep
circumstances suggesting 15-22

Slipperiness of road surface 17-50

Slope - See grade.

Smoke
visibility in 17-49

Snow
visibility in 17-49

Soak-in, an area on the shoulder or roadside saturated with liquid debris either at the end of run-off or as a puddle marking the rest position of a vehicle after a collision. 17-31

Soft shoulders 17-51

Spatter, the collection of marks on the road made by liquid from the vehicle or its cargo squirted from containers on the vehicle by force of collision. Spatter areas are irregular in shape and often consist of many spots.

battery acid 17-31
in vehicle placement 17-41
on road 17-31
photos of 36-6

Speed estimates
data for fall 17-42
data for flip 17-43
from skidmarks 18-3
reliability of 18-7

Spin
of vehicle 17-13

Spots
identifying 28-6
marking on road 28-8
order of listing 28-25
to be located 28-5

Spurious accuracy 32-28

Square portable grid 30-11
construction of 30-12
drawing map from 30-12
substitutes for 30-16

Stabilized accident situation, the condition prevailing after motion and other action constituting the events of an accident have ceased and no further harm will ensue unless a new series of events is initiated by some means.

after-accident situation map 36-3

Standards
accident classification 10-11
accident investigation and reporting (18) 10-12
accreditation 10-13
data 12-5
federal government 10-12
law enforcement agencies 12-3
police traffic services (15) 10-13
traffic records (10) 10-12

Statement - See detailed statements and depositions.

Statistical data collection 10-3

Steering wheel damage 20-8

Stepping off distances 28-34

Stereoscopic photogrammetry 30-26

Stopping distances 18-4

Strategy, adjusting speed, position on the road, and direction of motion, giving signals of intent to turn or slow, or any other action in situations involving potential hazards; any maneuvers while on a trip which increase the chance of success in avoiding an actual hazard. 15-25

Street - See highway.

Striations, narrow, light, parallel stripes or streaks usually made by friction or abrasion on the roadway or on vehicle parts.

on field sketch 28-49
photographing 28-51, 36-10
skidmark 17-8
yawmark 17-22

Sun glare 17-50

Superelevation, the degree to which the outside edge of a roadway is higher than the inside edge at a specified point on a curve; the change in elevation per unit distance across the roadway from inside to outside edge; bank.

measuring 32-17

Swerve, a slight deviation from a straight-ahead path. 17-13

while skidding 17-14

Symbols for maps 34-21

T

Tactic, actions taken by a traffic unit to avoid a hazardous situation; steering, braking, accelerating, etc. to avoid a collision or other accident. Often called evasive action. 15-25

Tangent, a line that touches a curve at only one point and is perpendicular to the radius at that point; a term used to describe a straight offset method 34-12

Tape
handling 32-4
measuring 28-32
reading 28-36, 32-26
smallest scale interval 32-26
using 28-34

Tarmac - See bituminous concrete.

Team
multidisciplinary 12-4

Technical follow-up, collection of additional facts from any source and organization and preliminary study of all available data relating to an accident; Level 3 of accident investigation 10-6

photographing 20-10
training 12-12
vehicle examination 20-9

Testimony
of informants 15-16

Tests
chemical 15-19

Y

Yaw, a sidewise movement of a vehicle in turning; movement of a vehicle in another direction than that in which it is headed; sidewise motion produced when centrifugal force exceeds traction force. Often the result of over-reaction or exceeding the critical speed. Sometimes revealed by tire marks on the roadway. 17-20

Yawmark, a scuffmark made while a vehicle is yawing; the mark made on the road by a rotating tire which is slipping in a direction parallel to the axle of the wheel.

Z

NORTHWESTERN UNIVERSITY TRAFFIC INSTITUTE